# THE THREE-DIMENSIONAL NATURE OF RESEARCH APPROACHES

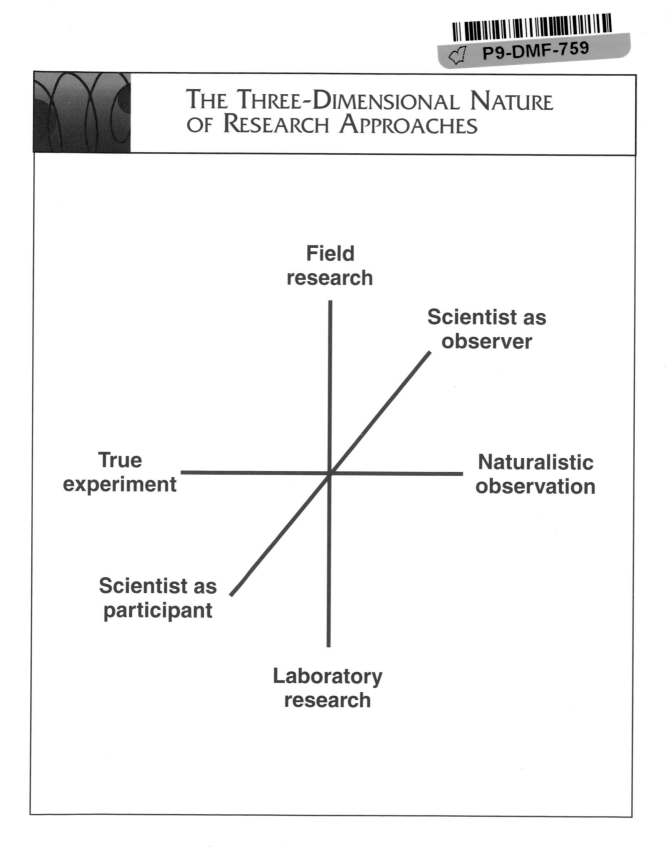

SEVENTH EDITION

# METHODS TOWARD A SCIENCE OF BEHAVIOR AND EXPERIENCE

WILLIAM J. RAY

The Pennsylvania State University

THOMSON

WADSWORTH

Australia • Canada • Mexico • Singapore • Spain
United Kingdom • United States

**THOMSON**™

**WADSWORTH**

Psychology Editor: *Vicki Knight*
Assistant Editor: *Jennifer Wilkinson*
Editorial Assistants: *Monica Sarmiento and Lucy Faridany*
Marketing Manager: *Lori Grebe*
Marketing Assistant: *Laurel Anderson*
Advertising Project Manager: *Shemika Britt*
Project Manager, Editorial Production: *Kirk Bomont*
Print Buyer: *Kris Waller*
Permissions Editor: *Karyn Morrison*

Production Service: *Nancy L. Shammas*
Text Graphic Designer: *Laurie Albrecht*
Copy Editor: *Mary Anne Shahidi*
Cover Designer: *Linda Harper*
Cover Image: *Scott Tysick/Masterfile*
Cover Printer: *Phoenix Color Corp.*
Compositor: *Graphic World, Inc.*
Printer: *Phoenix Color Corp.*

Printed in the United States of America

2 3 4 5 6 7 06 05 04 03

For more information about our products, contact us at:
**Thomson Learning Academic Resource Center**
**1-800-423-0563**

For permission to use material from this text, contact us by: **Phone:** 1-800-730-2214
**Fax:** 1-800-730-2215
**Web:** http://www.thomsonrights.com

Library of Congress Control Number: **2002106174**

ISBN 0-534-53867-3

**Wadsworth/Thomson Learning**
**10 Davis Drive**
**Belmont, CA 94002-3098**
**USA**

**Asia**
Thomson Learning
5 Shenton Way #01-01
UIC Building
Singapore 068808

**Australia**
Nelson Thomson Learning
102 Dodds Street
South Melbourne, Victoria 3205
Australia

**Canada**
Nelson/Thomson Learning
1120 Birchmount Road
Scarborough, Ontario M1K 5G4
Canada

**Europe/Middle East/Africa**
Thomson Learning
High Holborn House
50/51 Bedford Row
London WC1R 4LR
United Kingdom

**Latin America**
Thomson Learning
Seneca, 53
Colonia Polanco
11560 Mexico D.F.
Mexico

**Spain**
Paraninfo Thomson Learning
Calle/Magallanes, 25
28015 Madrid, Spain

*To my parents and teachers.*

One thing I have learned in a long life:
that all our science, measured against reality,
is primitive and childlike—and yet it is the
most precious thing we have.

ALBERT EINSTEIN

# BRIEF CONTENTS

# CONTENTS

## 10 THE ECOLOGY OF THE EXPERIMENT: THE SCIENTIST AND RESEARCH PARTICIPANT IN RELATION TO THEIR ENVIRONMENTS    210

## 11 QUASI-EXPERIMENTAL, CORRELATIONAL, AND NATURALISTIC OBSERVATIONAL DESIGNS    232

# PREFACE

We live in a time when books on science and the nature of ourselves and our world are setting sales records. For many people, science offers an exciting understanding of reality. Society itself is also calling on science for answers to difficult questions. Given problems ranging from AIDS to diminishing energy resources to terrorism to the effect of psychological processes on health and disease, scientists are being asked to present solutions and help shape policy. Despite this great interest in science, the experimental course remains the one that some students dread and put off until the last minute. This seemed strange to us, since many of our colleagues are excited about what they do in psychology and approach research with a real desire to know. This made us think that, in the process of teaching psychological research, we, as faculty, have neglected to include a complete understanding of science, including our own experience in psychology—and especially our reasons for attempting a science of behavior and experience in the first place. Thus, one of our major goals in writing this book was to introduce students to the basics of doing science and to the spirit that motivates many scientists. A second goal was to help students make the transition from viewing themselves as outside observers of science to those who participate in the process of science.

The responses of students and colleagues to the first six editions of this book have been persuasive in suggesting that these initial goals are being accomplished. That is, it is possible to produce a highly readable book that students are able to learn from, and when they are done, they will carry with them a greater understanding of the techniques of science as well as the experience of doing science. As we have moved through the various editions of this book, we have seen psychology change in its approach and subject matter. The current edition reflects many of these changes. This book began with Dick Ravizza as a co-author, and that first edition reflected, as have the later ones, important discussions between the two of us concerning the nature of science, the nature of psychology, and at times, the nature of life. Since that time, these discussions have been continued with colleagues, students, reviewers, and almost anyone else who would listen and discuss these issues. For this reason, the plural "we" has been retained throughout all editions of this book. It is an ever-changing "we," some of whom are acknowledged at the conclusion of this preface, who continue to suggest clarifications, new information, and additional changes that contribute to the overall quality of this book.

## The Seventh Edition

Every chapter in this edition has been revised. In particular, we have added new research examples from the psychological literature. We have also added additional information on effect size and statistical power including the manner in which these measures are reported in a research example. In relation to writing research articles, the American Psychological Association has published a new edition of its *Publication Manual* (the fifth), and these guidelines are reflected throughout this current edition. In this context Appendix A has been expanded to include guidelines for removing a variety of biases in language (e.g., gender, sexual orientation, racial and ethnics identity, disabilities, and age). We also continue to include an increasingly important information resource, the World Wide Web, and to offer links to relevant research sites. For example, links to issues of research integrity from the Public Health Service and American Association for the Advancement of Science as well as National Institutes of Health discussions of placebo research have been included in this edition. Also included with this book is access to InfoTrac® College Edition, which is a wide ranging source of information including encyclopedias, reference books, magazines, and scientific journals accessed through the Web. Although exercises with InfoTrac College Edition are included at the end of each chapter, faculty can also supplement specific topic areas of their own interest through these resources including the use of online research articles. As with every edition of this book, examples and research studies have been updated and clarifications have been added to help students in their learning. Over the past decade, we have seen a shift in the teaching of this course, with a growing number of colleges and universities presenting the methods course in a large lecture format. In response to this, we have followed the suggestions of faculty and students to clarify the presentation of some of the more important or difficult concepts through illustration and extended discussion. Let me briefly describe the goals and directions, which we have continued in this seventh edition.

## Philosophy of Science

One idea we try to convey from the very beginning is the relationship of science and philosophy. We do this not only through the introduction of propositional logic in Chapter 2, but through a discussion of people who have shaped our ideas about science. For example, in the first two chapters, students are introduced to not only Newton's rules of reasoning, but also the views of Karl Popper and Thomas Kuhn on how science works. We show students how some approaches to science, such as the use of strong inference and the development of a research program, have allowed certain fields to move at an accelerated rate. Likewise, we show that science cannot be performed without reference to values. We do this not only in our discussion of the ecology of the experimental situation in Chapter 10 and our discussion of ethics in Chapter 14, but also throughout the text.

However useful, abstractions alone do not teach students about science as it is practiced, much less how to practice science themselves; thus we also emphasize the concrete. We attempt to involve the student earlier in the process of experimentation in this edition. For example, in Chapter 3, we include detailed information on how to use major library reference works such as *PsycINFO, Science Citation Index, Social Science Citation Index,* and the information available from the National Library of Medicine (e.g., *MedLINE*). Since most researchers access this information from the Web, a discussion of Internet resources is also discussed. However, we still need basics. In our discussion of descriptive statistics in Chapter 4, we teach students how to read and plot graphs. In Chapter 15, we not only teach students how to write up an experiment, but we also include a valuable checklist that can be used for writing an article and presenting a research proposal. Numerous examples from published articles also are included. Because of our desire to make science concrete, we have included interviews with active psychologists on how they first obtained the ideas for their studies. These interviews are followed by a discussion of how to turn an idea into a testable hypothesis.

## The Logic of Making Testable Hypotheses

Although most students grasp the idea of asking testable questions, they are often uncertain about what exactly it is they are testing in research. To help clarify this point, we have presented the process of hypothesis testing both conceptually and practically. In Chapter 5, we present a conceptual understanding of inferential statistics and probability. We likewise stress the process of making decisions and the importance of logically ruling out alternative hypotheses. Although this process begins in the first chapter and continues throughout the book, Chapter 2 emphasizes the use of logic and drawing conclusions. This information is important not only for those who seek a career in research but also for anyone who wishes to understand the daily headlines involving scientific research.

## Discussion of Various Designs, Including Correlational Designs

An understanding of the logic of experimental design, including the concept of control as well as the process of making inferences, remains the heart of the present edition. However, we have also expanded our discussion of procedures to employ when the experimental situation does not allow for traditional experimental designs. For example, in the present edition we have expanded our coverage of correlational designs to reflect the ways in which such areas as behavioral medicine and developmental and social psychology rely on such approaches. We have likewise expanded our discussion of single-subject designs in the chapter devoted to this topic. As in the previous edition, information on quasi-experimental approaches and naturalistic observation is also included. An entire chapter (Chapter 13) is devoted to questionnaires, survey research, and sampling, which provides students with a basic understanding of how to construct questionnaires and the logic involved in sampling procedures.

## Clarification of Important Concepts

To help faculty teach this course and students understand the material better, we have made a special effort to define and illustrate what we know to be general problem areas for students. Talks with faculty across the country have led us to pay special attention to certain topics. For example, the concept of interaction effect is not only illustrated with research examples, but numerous possible outcomes are graphically represented. Given that an understanding of interaction effects continues to be a major problem for students, we have added even more actual examples from the literature in this present edition. We also carefully walk students through the interpretation of interaction effects. These discussions are facilitated by our explanation of the concept behind the $F$-ratio.

Beginning in Chapter 6 and continuing throughout the rest of the text, the logic of the *F*-ratio is used in our discussions of experimental control and variation. By emphasizing the factors that influence either the numerator or the denominator of the *F*-ratio, students are able to grasp conceptually what factors will influence their acceptance or rejection of the null hypothesis. We give special attention to two other problem areas for students: the meaning of causation in science and the use of the terms *error* and *chance* in relation to experimentation. Also, we have included material at the end of each chapter that not only summarizes the main points in the chapter but also includes questions to test comprehension and discussion questions and projects for better integration of the material. Included in this section are designs for the students to criticize and conclusions to evaluate.

## New Directions

In using the title *Methods Toward a Science of Behavior and Experience,* we wanted to convey a sense of not only where experimental psychology has been, but where it might be going. We expand on this idea in Chapter 16, in which we discuss the potential for a scientific psychology. We point out that psychology was once almost a battleground for those interested in behavior and those interested in experience. But today, with scientific studies of such topics as attention, emotion, awareness, animal cognition, and especially consciousness, we see a new group of scientists who are interested in both behavior and experience, not only in others but in themselves.

## Acknowledgments

This book grew out of discussions concerning our experience of science and the role it currently plays in psychology. At this time, I would like to acknowledge the many people who joined me in these discussions. For the first edition, Dale Harris spent his time discussing his perspective on the history of the experimental movement in psychology. I appreciate the willingness of Jude Cassidy, Jeff Parker, Nora Newcombe, Carolyn Sherif, and Lance Shotland to discuss how their ideas came about and how they began their important research programs. I appreciate the help of our colleague Mel Mark for his careful reading of and critical suggestions on the chapters related to inferential statistics and survey research. I also appreciate Judith Kroll's willingness to share with me her notes and ideas for helping women to find more of a home in science and Gordon Hall's perspective on multicultural research. Many colleagues at Penn State and other institutions both in this country and in Europe have shared with me knowledge and experiences in doing science. Others told me ways that they use to teach experimental methods as well as the values they wish to impart. For their time and thoughtful consideration, I am extremely appreciative.

There are many colleagues around the country who shared their experience of teaching with us and made this book richer in many ways. I appreciate their careful reading of the earlier editions and their invaluable suggestions based on their experience with the book. In particular I would like to acknowledge the reviewers of the first edition: Robert T. Brown, University of North Carolina, Wilmington; Dennis Cogan, Texas Tech University; Paul Eskildsen, San Francisco State University; Henry Gorman, Austin College; Les Herold, California State University, San Bernardino;

Alan C. Kamil, University of Massachusetts; Nancy Kirkland, Trinity College; Elizabeth Lynn, San Diego State University; Henry Morlock, SUNY, Plattsburgh; Howard B. Orenstein, Western Maryland College; Ronald Rossi, Lyndon State College; Mark S. Sanders, California State University, Northridge; Kathryn Schwarz, Scottsdale Community College; Keith Stanovich, Oakland University; Barbara Tabachnick, California State University, Northridge; W. Scott Terry, University of North Carolina, Charlotte; and Sheila Zipf, San Francisco State University.

I would also like to thank the reviewers of the second edition: Earl Babble, Chapman College; Elizabeth Capaldi, Purdue University; Elvis C. Jones, Frostburg State College; John M. Knight, Central State University; Judith E. Larkin, Canisius College; John J. Meryman, San Jose State University; Thomas O. Nelson, University of Washington; and Mark A. Sabol, Creighton University.

And I express our gratitude to the reviewers of the third edition: Philip G. Benson, New Mexico State University; Alexis Collier, Ohio State University; Eric S. Knowles, University of Arkansas; Mark D. Pagel, Oxford University; Kirk H. Smith, Bowling Green State University; and Marty Wall, University of Toronto.

The comments of reviewers for the fourth edition have resulted in a number of major changes. Reviewers for that edition included Jonathon D. Brown, University of Washington; Clarke A. Burnham, University of Texas at Austin; Henry A. Cross, Colorado State University; Raymond T. Garza, University of California–Riverside; Mary Gauvain, Scripps College; Elizabeth L. Glisky, University of Arizona; Joellen T. Hartley, California State University–Long Beach; Alan C. Kamil, University of Nebraska–Lincoln; Philipp J. Kraemer, University of Kentucky; W. Trammell Neill, Adelphi University; Howard A. Rollins Jr., Emory University; and Barry S. Stein, Tennessee Technological University.

Reviewers for the fifth edition include Deane Aikins, Pennsylvania State University; Steve Buck, University of Washington; Nancy Eldred, San Jose State University; Philip Freedman, University of Illinois; Michael Gaynor, Bloomsburg University; Elizabeth Glisky, University of Arizona; Judith Kroll, Pennsylvania State University; Mark Pitt, Ohio State University; Joseph F. Sturr, Syracuse University; and Jenny Wiley, Virginia Commonwealth University.

I also thank the sixth edition reviewers: Kevin Apple, James Madison University; Jill Booker, University of Indianapolis; Martin Bourgeois, University of Wyoming; Cynthia L. Crown, Xavier University; Lisa Fournier, Washington State University; Elizabeth Yost Hammer, Belmont University; Kurt A. Hoffman, University of California–Davis; Richard F. Martell, Montana State University; Debra L. Valencia-Laver, California Polytechnic University–San Luis Obispo; Heidi A. Wayment, Northern Arizona University; and Doug Wedell, University of South Carolina–Columbia.

Reviewing is somewhat of a lost art and I appreciate the consideration given this present edition by our reviewers who include Carrie Fried, Winona State University; Karen Jordan, University of Illinois at Chicago; William Langston, Middle Tennessee State University; Patricia Loesche, University of Washington; Deidra Schleicher, University of Tulsa; Aurora Torres, University of Alabama in Huntsville; Terri Vescio, Pennsylvania State University; and Jeffrey Walczyk, Louisiana Tech University. I hope the book has not suffered from our inability to implement all of their suggestions.

I found the production staff at Wadsworth and Brooks/Cole to be excellent and wish to thank them for their efforts. It is never an easy task to turn a manuscript into a finished product, and such efforts often go unnoticed. I also appreciate my association with Vicki Knight, psychology editor at Wadsworth, for her consistent concern with quality publishing. Finally, I would like to invite both students and faculty to write me with their comments concerning the book or examples from their courses or the literature that have helped to clarify the material. You can write me at the Department of Psychology, Pennsylvania State University, University Park, PA 16802 or send an e-mail to wjr@psu.edu. I will do my best to include your suggestions in the next edition.

*William J. Ray*

# INTRODUCTION

You are about to begin a voyage of wonder and curiosity, of questionings and doubts. Historically, it is a voyage that human beings began many generations ago and that scientists like yourselves embark on every day. It is a voyage into the nature of ourselves and the world in which we live. It is a voyage with a particular focus: science. For some of you, science offers a new way to view the world. Learning about science, like learning about anything new, offers added perspective, which can in turn lead to a very real expansion of your own consciousness. For those of you already familiar with science, this book offers a deeper exploration of the science of behavior and experience. It is important to emphasize from the outset that learning about science is an expansion of what you already are. It is an option, an alternative that you are free to use or not to use as you explore and interact with your world. You choose how and when to use it. In fact, after taking this course, you may decide it is not a way you wish to view the world at all and you may never use it again.

Some students are hesitant to explore science because they believe it is cold, antihumanistic, and even antireligious. They believe it separates us from our beliefs, our faiths, our feelings, and ourselves. This is a serious and limiting misconception. Many of our colleagues in all fields of science are as open to humanistic and spiritual traditions as they are to science. We believe that science—a science of behavior and experience—will someday assist us in a profound exploration of all our great humanistic and spiritual traditions. This task of helping all of us more fully explore and understand our own potential may be the major function of science in the future evolution of human consciousness.

Our voyage into the science of behavior and experience begins by stressing that there are many childlike qualities that we hope will always remain part of us. Genuine laughter, spontaneous play, intimacy, curiosity, and creativity are some childlike qualities that form the very foundation of mature human experience. In a similar way, the scientific method we are about to explore has firm roots in the simple way children go about exploring their world. With this in mind, we begin our exploration of science by viewing ourselves as children who wish to explore. The world awaiting the child includes not only the outside world, but also the child's own psychological experience. Through this child, who is one aspect of ourselves, we approach the question of how we go about performing a science of behavior and experience. We will watch the child search for knowledge and mature into three distinct roles, which we can define as actors in our drama of psychological inquiry.

The first role is that of the scientist. It is the active role in our drama. The task before you is to learn how the scientist goes about doing science. We will come to see that many activities of present-day, mature scientists are simply extensions of the way we approached the world as children. As you learn about this role, you will learn about the types of questions scientists ask, the types of answers that they accept, and the way in which knowledge is approached and verified.

The second role is that of the research participant. This is the passive role in our drama. The research participant is the particular organism the scientist chooses to study. In fact, it is the various experiences and behaviors of the participant that form the content of psychology. The paradox for scientists interested in the study of human behavior and experience is that although the subject matter is "out there" in the individuals we study, because we are also human it is at the same time "in here" in us. In a very real sense, as we study other people and animals, we also study ourselves.

The third role is that of the witness. This role is not always recognized, yet in many ways it is the most important because it maintains a balance between the scientist and the research participant, the active and passive aspects of this process. The witness, who is also us, stands back and watches the scientist do science and the research participant behave and experience the world. One task of the witness is to teach that both the scientist and the research participant are limited because each sees the world only from his or her own perspective.

As the witness teaches us that there is a broader perspective from which we can appreciate both viewpoints simultaneously, we begin to mature and realize the richness of the scientific process and the wonder of approaching knowledge of reality. In this vein, it is the role of the witness to remind us that the experience and understanding of life require more than just a description of miles of blood vessels, reinforcement schedules, and chemicals interacting with each other. It is the witness who asks whether the science of the scientist is relevant, ethical, and generally worth doing. But most important, it is the witness who brings together the procedures of the scientist and the experience of the research participant and allows them to have a relationship in the first place.

Once we have developed these aspects of ourselves—the scientist, the research participant, and the witness—we will be in a better position to understand the strengths and weaknesses of using science to study ourselves. Until that time, we would like to suggest that you neither accept nor reject the scientific approach but rather that you allow that it may have something to offer you. That is, you can allow yourself to become actively involved in trying to solve problems and answer questions using this method while remaining free to remember the problems and limitations of the scientific approach. As in anything else, it is only through active involvement that you will come to understand fully what the method has to offer. Let us now begin the drama of science with a problem—how did we as children come to know the world?—and from this develop methods for a science of behavior and experience.

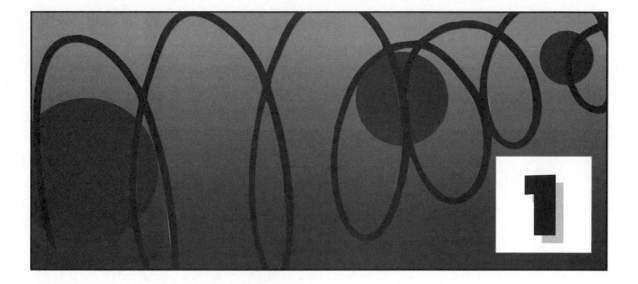

# WHAT IS SCIENCE?

Science is above all a human activity. One obvious meaning of this is that science is performed by people. Another equally accurate meaning is that all people perform science in some form. After all, the methods of science are simple extensions of the ways all people learn about their world. Science in many ways is similar to the way we have been learning about the world since we were infants. We learn through interacting with our world. Consequently, each of you knows this aspect of science well because you have been using it in one form or another since you first began toddling about and discovering the world. You probably know much more about the scientific method than you think you do.

Watch a young child. When something catches his or her eye, the child must examine it, study it, observe it, have fun with it. Next, the child wants to interact with it, touch it, feel it. From passive observations and active interactions, the child slowly learns about the world. Some interactions are fun: "If I tip the glass, I get to see the milk form pretty pictures on the floor." Others are not so much fun: "If I touch the red circles on the stove, my fingers hurt!" From each interaction, the child learns a little more about the world.

Like the child, scientists are exploring the unknown—and sometimes the known—features of the world. All basic research strategies are based on one simple notion: *To discover what the world is like, we must experience it.* To have an idea about the nature of the world is not enough. Instead, like the child, scientists experience the world to determine whether their ideas accurately reflect reality. Direct experience is an essential tool because it alone allows us to bridge the gap between our ideas and reality.

However, there is another aspect to science that many people do not think about. This is the aspect of *doubt.* One way in which we doubt is to question the common wisdom—whether it holds that the world is flat or that all our behavior is learned—and to seek different models of the world. Another way we use doubt is to question our research and ask whether other factors might have contributed to the results. As we will discuss throughout this book, science is more than just watching; it is rare that data actually speak for themselves.

In general, there is no single scientific method, any more than there is one art or one education or one religion, yet there is a general process called *science.* This process consists of experiencing the world and then drawing general conclusions (called *facts*) from observations. Sometimes these conclusions or facts are descriptive and can be represented by numbers. For example, we say that the moon is 238,000 miles from the earth or that the average human heart rate is 72 beats per minute. Other times these facts are more general and can describe a relationship or a process. For example, we say that it is more difficult to learn a second language after puberty than before or that as we age we hear fewer high-frequency sounds. Whatever the topic, the known facts about a particular subject are called *scientific knowledge.*

Much of our scientific knowledge is based on a history of research in a particular area. How we perform research is what this book is all about. Many conceptions of scientific research picture a man or a woman in a white lab coat, laboriously writing down numbers and later milling about in a cluttered office trying to make theoretical sense out of these findings. This conception may be partly accurate, but it is not a total picture of science.

In this book, we stress another aspect of science, which becomes apparent when the available facts are viewed in light of human value. It is this aspect of value that allows us to see one set of numbers as more relevant or potentially more useful than another. This combining of fact and value results in a humanistic approach to scientific understanding. Scientific understanding helps us to see the *how* and *why* of the world and thereby to understand nature in a fuller perspective. In many cases, this understanding raises new questions, which in turn can be answered by using science to examine the world. In other cases, these new facts can be applied in real-life settings (technology) and make life easier for everyone. Thus, at its best, science begins and ends in human experience.

In the introduction to this book, we described three actors in the drama of science: the research participant, the scientist, and the witness. In our study of behavior and experience, it is the scientist who experiences the world and then formulates general facts or conclusions that describe it. The participant is the one who is studied in an experiment. In some cases, these roles are simple; in others, such as the study of human consciousness, the situation is more complex because we use our own consciousness to study consciousness. Finally, the witness provides the perspective, the concerns for value, and the relationship of science and its facts to other aspects of human life.

 ## SCIENCE AS A WAY OF KNOWING

All of us at times fall into the trap of viewing science as the best way, or even the only way, to study behavior and experience. If you find this happening to you, beware! Although our culture emphasizes science as an important way of knowing, it is not the only way, and like all ways of knowing, it has certain limitations in its methods. To emphasize this, we offer science as merely one way of examining human nature. There are others; art, philosophy, religion, and literature are all fruitful ways or channels through which we can gain new ideas about human behavior and experience. Psychology has drawn on many of these traditions and will surely continue to do so.

Having a fruitful source of ideas, whether it is our literary, spiritual, scientific, or artistic traditions, is an important part of understanding behavior and experience. However, a second and perhaps even more important aspect of learning about psychology is the process of determining whether a new idea is accurate. In contrast to other ways of knowing, science offers not only a fertile source of new ideas but also a powerful method for evaluating the ideas we have about reality.

For example, suppose someone tells you to buy a new exercise machine, or a well-known spiritual leader says that if you meditate twice a day you will be happier, or someone tells you that if you eat only a low-fat diet you will be healthier and live longer. These are instances in which you are confronted with new ideas that may have an important impact on your life. Because some time and effort are involved in these examples, and given the track record of some exercise specialists, spiritual teachers, and fad diets, you may be hesitant to change your habits unless you know it will be worthwhile. So you are faced with the task of evaluating the suggestions and deciding whether these ideas are right for you. How do you decide? In the remainder of this section, we examine several ways people decide whether to accept new ideas about the world. For a more detailed discussion of these ways of accepting belief, see the work of American philosopher Charles Peirce (Cohen & Nagel, 1934; Kerlinger, 1973, 1986). We are obviously biased and believe that the best way to respond to new ideas, especially for society at large, is to use science to evaluate these new ideas and then use the results of this research to help make a decision.

## ■ Tenacity

Peirce uses the term *tenacity* to refer to the acceptance of a belief based on the idea that "we have always known it to be this way." People at various times have said, "Women make bad soldiers," "You can't teach an old dog new tricks," or "Science is always beneficial." These statements are presented over and over again and accepted as true, yet they are rarely examined and evaluated. This is an all-too-common method of accepting information. Television advertising and political campaigns use this technique when they present a single phrase or slogan repeatedly. Even an empty phrase repeated often enough becomes accepted as true. As has been said, if you tell people something often enough, they will believe it.

As a way of learning about the world, there are two problems with this method. First, the statement may be just an empty phrase, and its accuracy may never have been evaluated. The statement may gain wide acceptance through its familiarity alone. Second, tenacity offers no means for correcting erroneous ideas. That is, once a belief is widely accepted solely on the basis of tenacity, it is difficult to change. Social psychologists have shown that once a person accepts a belief without data to support it, the person often will make up a reason for accepting the belief as true; the person may even refuse to accept new information that contradicts this belief. In the case of the diet example, a decision to begin a certain diet simply because it is said to be beneficial would be acceptance based on tenacity. Accepting ideas about experience and behavior simply because they are familiar to us or widely believed by others is an extension of the childish behavior of the 3-year-old who copies the words and behaviors of others. For the child this is an efficient beginning for learning about the world, but for the rest of us it is limiting.

## ■ Authority

A second way we may accept a new idea is when an authority figure tells us it is so. Acceptance based on authority is simple because we only have to repeat and live by what we are told. In many cases, referring to an authority, especially in areas about which we know nothing, is useful and beneficial. When we were young, our parents often used the method of authority for directing our behavior. In the past, health care and education were based almost exclusively on authority. If a famous physician or educator said something was true, almost everyone believed it to be true. Even today, we often rely on the judgment of an authority when we consult physicians, psychologists, scientists, or stockbrokers. Likewise, religious training often relies on the authority of religious leaders and elders for establishing correct religious procedures.

Although authority brings with it a stability that allows for consistency, it is not without problems. The major problem of accepting authority as having sole access to truth is that authority can be incorrect and thus send people in the wrong directions. For example, as long as everyone accepted the view that the earth was the center of the universe, no one thought to study the orbit of the earth. Consequently, it is important to examine the basis of the authority's claims. Are these claims based on opinion, tradition, revelation, or direct experience? How valid are the sources of this information? In the meditation example, if you decided to meditate simply because a well-known spiritual leader advised it, you would be basing your decision solely on the authority of this person. Box 1.1 discusses the transition from authority to experimentation in the beginning of modern science.

## Box 1.1

## Galileo: The Transition from Authority to Empiricism

For many scientists Galileo is a symbol of change in the rules of evidence. Of course, many people influenced the beginning of scientific thought during the Renaissance, beginning with Copernicus, Kepler, and the philosopher Bacon. However, Galileo and Newton (see Box 1.2) often are called the greatest founders of modern science (cf. Holton, 1952; Russell, 1984). Before their time, intellectual questions were answered by referring to authority, usually the authority of the church. The church of this period in turn looked to the Greek philosopher Aristotle for answers to "material" questions—what today we call natural science.

Suppose a person wanted to know which of two balls would hit the ground first if they were dropped from a tall building. Until the time of Galileo, the method of answering this question would be to refer to Aristotle's theory, which stated that the world is made up of four elements: earth, air, water, and fire. According to Aristotle, each element acts according to its own nature. To answer the question of which of two bodies would hit the ground first, one would reason that the two objects, composed of the element earth, would seek to return to earth and thus fall down. If one object weighed more than the other, it would be reasoned that this heavier object contained more of the element earth than the lighter one and would naturally fall faster. Thus, it would be concluded that the heavier

body would hit the ground before the lighter one. No one would have thought to actually drop two objects from a tower and observe which hit the ground first. Answers were always given in terms of authority.

Galileo successfully replaced the method of authority with that of experimentation. This movement toward experimentation was greatly aided by Galileo's own inventions, such as the telescope, the thermometer, an improved microscope, and a pendulum-type timing device. Each of these instruments allowed people to experiment and answer for themselves the questions of nature. After establishing that balls rolling down an inclined plane act similarly to falling objects, Galileo successfully challenged the authority of Aristotle concerning two falling weights. With Galileo's work, a new science based on observation and experimentation was beginning. Galileo was part of a revolution that was to challenge authority. In fact, Einstein, in a later preface to Galileo's *Dialogues,* said that Galileo's main theme in his work was the "passionate fight against any kind of dogma based on authority." Although initially Galileo was well received in some quarters and even given life tenure in his professorship at the University of Padua, he later found himself at odds with the Church in Rome and spent the last 9 years of his life under house arrest near Florence.

### ■ Reason

Reason and logic are the basic methods of philosophy. Reason often takes the form of a logical syllogism, such as "All men can't count; Dick is a man; therefore, Dick can't count." We all use reason every day as we try to solve problems and understand relationships. As useful as it is to be reasonable, however, reason alone will not always produce the appropriate answer. Why? One potential problem in the reasoned approach is that our original assumption must be correct. If the original assumption is incorrect or at odds with the world in which we live, then logic cannot help us. For example, the syllogism that concluded that Dick can't count is logically valid even though it is based on the absurd premise that all men can't count. The weakness of using reason alone is that we have no way to determine the accuracy of our assumptions. Thus, we can have situations in which our logic is impeccable, but because our original assumption is inaccurate, the conclusion is silly.

## ■ Common Sense

Common sense offers an improvement over acceptance based on tenacity, authority, or reason because it appeals to direct experience. Common sense is based on our own past experiences and our perceptions of the world. However, our experiences and perceptions of the world may be quite limited. The optical illusions that you probably studied in introductory psychology gave you a clear example of how our perceptions can lead us to incorrect conclusions. There can also be a bias in the way we think.

Piattelli-Palmarini (1994) suggests that just as there are optical illusions, there are also cognitive illusions that lead us to be certain but wrong in our answers. Furthermore, research in social psychology has shown that we make different psychological attributions depending on whether we observe or participate in a given situation. If we are asked to explain why someone made a bad grade, we tend to make internal attributions, such as "She didn't study" or "He isn't smart." However, if we received a bad grade on a test, we would tend to make external attributions, such as "I had three tests that day" or "The test was unfair."

Whereas common sense may help us deal with the routine aspects of daily life, it may also form a wall and prevent us from understanding new areas. This can be a problem, particularly when we enter realms outside our everyday experience. For example, people considered Albert Einstein's suggestion that time was relative and could be different for different people to be contrary to common sense.

Likewise, it was considered contrary to common sense when Sigmund Freud suggested that we did not always know our own motivations or when B. F. Skinner suggested that the concept of free will was inapplicable to the behavior of most individuals. We might also assume that the stable process is the more healthy one. However, research using nonlinear (chaos) analysis has suggested, for example, that the patterns of a healthy heart are erratic and those of a pathological heart can be regular (Goldberger & Rigney, 1991).

## ■ Science

We end our discussion of the ways people accept new ideas by discussing science. Philosopher of science Alfred North Whitehead (1925) suggested that there are two methods for what he called the "purification of ideas" and that these methods are combined in the scientific method. An idea is evaluated or corrected through (1) dispassionately observing by means of our bodily senses (for example, vision, hearing, and touch) and (2) using reason to compare various theoretical conceptualizations based on experience.

The first method is a direct extension of the common-sense approach just described. Unlike a given person's common sense, however, science is open to *anyone's* direct experience. Presumably, any observation made by one scientist could be verified by any other person with normal sensory capacities. To aid people in repeating the observations of others, some scientists (see Bridgman, 1927) have emphasized the importance of *operational definitions* in research. As you will see in Chapter 2, operational definitions direct *how* observations are to be made and what is to be observed and measured.

The second method is a direct application of the principles of logic. In this case, however, logic is combined with experience to rule out any assumptions that do not accurately reflect the scientific experiment. This blend of direct sensory experience and reason gives science a self-corrective nature that is not found in other ways of accepting ideas about the world. One important technique is replication, in which a procedure is repeated under similar conditions. For example, if an experiment is found to give similar results in different labs and even in different parts of the world, this lends support to the conclusions. This means that scientific conclusions are never taken as final but are always open to reinterpretation as new evidence becomes available. In other words, the method of science includes a feedback component by which conclusions about the world can be refined over time. It is the refining of ideas through both experimentation and reason that allows science to be a fruitful method for knowing about the world.

Historically, the methods of modern science can be traced to the 17th century. The work of Sir Isaac Newton generally is credited as representing the beginning of modern science. Box 1.2 describes Newton's rules of reasoning in science. These rules form the basis of the modern scientific approach: the law of parsimony, the assumption that there exists a unity to the physical universe in which we live, the possibility of generalizing from experiments, and the acceptance of empirical data over opinion. In many ways these rules are as applicable today as they were when they were written more than 300 years ago.

# THE SCIENTIFIC APPROACH

In this chapter we examine the scientific approach through various informal illustrations, examples, and stories. In Chapter 2 we discuss more formally the methods of natural observation and experimentation. Among other things, we emphasize that a major characteristic of science is a reliance on information that is *verifiable through experience.* That is, it must be possible for different people in different places and at different times using a similar method to produce the same results.

Once you know the methods of science and have used them in a variety of situations, you will be in a position to evaluate science as a method of knowing about the world that includes the behavior and experience of yourself and others. More important, you will be in a position to decide whether science is the way you choose to understand the world. First, however, let us begin to understand what science is by looking at three early efforts to understand the world. Although these efforts attempted to be systematic, today we would call them preexperimental or quasiexperimental. That is, in none of these procedures was an actual experiment conducted. Our purpose is to focus on the manner in which the problem was solved—particularly the efforts to be systematic—and what errors were made. You might also recall instances from your own life when you attempted to solve problems in similar ways.

## Newton's Rules of Reasoning

Born the year after Galileo's death, Newton produced a body of work that represents the beginning of modern science as we know it. Whereas Galileo fought with philosophers of his day and was persecuted by the Church for his beliefs, Newton lived in a new age in which science through experimentation and reason began to bear fruit.

In the 1680s, Newton's classic work *Principia* was published (Newton, 1969 reprint). Designated by science historian Gerald Holton (1952) as "probably the greatest single book in the history of science," this work describes Newton's theories of time, space, and motion as well as his rules of reasoning for science. Science, called *natural philosophy* by Newton, is based on four rules of reasoning.

### Rule 1

*We are to admit no more causes of natural things than such as are both true and sufficient to explain their appearances.*

*To this purpose the philosophers say that Nature does nothing in vain, and more is in vain when less will serve; for Nature is pleased with simplicity, and affects not the pomp of superfluous causes.*

Today we call this rule the law of parsimony. The rule simply states that natural events should be explained in the simplest way possible.

### Rule 2

*Therefore to the same natural effects we must, as far as possible, assign the same causes.*

*As to respiration in a man and in a beast, the descent of stones in Europe and in America; the light of our culinary fire and of the sun; the reflection of light in the earth, and in the planets.*

This rule reflects Newton's belief in a natural order, which requires that the same gravity causes stones to fall in Europe and in America.

### Rule 3

*The qualities of bodies, which admit neither intensification nor remission of degrees, and which are found to belong to all bodies within*

## EARLY APPROACHES

The first example concerns extrasensory perception (ESP). According to the historian Herodotus (1942 trans.), Croesus, who was king of Lydia from 560 to 546 B.C., became concerned with the increasing power of the Persian army because Lydia was located between Persia and Greece. King Croesus knew the Persian armies to be strong and therefore did not want to attack them unless it was certain he would win. He needed someone who could foretell the future. As an enlightened consumer, Croesus wanted to know that the information he received was true. To determine this, he constructed a test of the oracles who

*the reach of our experiments, are to be esteemed the universal qualities of all bodies whatsoever.*

*For since the qualities of bodies are only known to us by experiments, we are to hold for universal all such as universally agree with experiments; and such as are not liable to diminution can never be quite taken away. We are certainly not to relinquish the evidence of experiments for the sake of dreams and vain fictions of our own devising; nor are we to recede from the analogy of Nature, which is wont to be simple, and always consonant to itself. We in no other way know the extension of bodies than by our senses, nor do these reach it in all bodies; but because we perceive extension in all that are sensible, therefore we ascribe it universally to all others also.*

Newton continues with a long discussion of this principle. Briefly, it states that what we learn from our experiments can be applied to similar structures outside the reach of our experiments. For example, the properties of gravity and inertia should apply to the moon and other planets as they apply to stones and other objects with which we experiment.

## Rule 4

*In experimental philosophy we are to look upon propositions inferred by general induction from phenomena as accurately or very nearly true, notwithstanding any contrary hypotheses that may be imagined, till such time as other phenomena occur, by which they may either be made more accurate, or liable to exceptions.*

*This rule we must follow, that the argument of induction may not be evaded by hypotheses.*

This rule simply states that theories obtained from experiments should be considered true or approximately true until new experimental evidence shows the old to be incorrect. Ideas developed from experiments should not be changed just because we like another hypothesis better.

These four simple rules have directed the physical sciences for the past 300 years. In this century they have been applied to the social and behavioral sciences as well.

were said to foretell the future best. Croesus's assistants were to go out into Greece and Libya where famous oracles lived. The assistants were to visit each oracle on a specific day and at a specific time and ask, "What is the king doing at this moment?" Because the king told no one what he was actually doing at that moment, he reasoned that only a true oracle, one capable of extrasensory perception, could answer correctly. The assistants all returned to the king and reported their answers. Only one oracle, the oracle at Delphi, gave the correct answer. In fact, according to Herodotus, this oracle answered the question before it was even asked. (The king had been making lamb stew.)

Although the king had the beginnings of a scientific approach to experience, he had not learned the role of chance in science or the nature of the language of science. Trusting his research, the king honored the oracle and asked the important political question of whether he should go to battle against the Persian armies. The oracle replied that in such a contest a mighty empire would be destroyed. This was all the king needed to assemble his armies and attack. When the battle was over, a mighty empire had been destroyed as the oracle had predicted; the problem for the king was that the empire destroyed was his own, and he was taken prisoner.

The king, like many others after him, failed to realize that a single correct answer may not be sufficient to allow us to draw valid conclusions. Likewise, the king did not realize that the language of prediction must be precise in directing our attention toward possible outcomes. Let us look at another attempt to understand the world, this one dating back almost 2000 years.

In the 2nd century A.D., Galen, a well-known physician, described a woman who complained of insomnia (Mesulam & Perry, 1972). The problem was to determine the factors that led to the insomnia. Galen first decided that the problem was not mainly physical. Following this determination, he began to notice the woman's condition during his examinations. It happened that during one examination, a person returning from the theater mentioned the name of a certain dancer, Pylades. At this point Galen observed an increase in the woman's pulse rate, along with a change in her facial color and expression. What did Galen do next? To answer his questions about what was affecting the woman, he began to experiment. In his own words,

> The next day, I told one of my following that when I went to visit the woman he was to arrive a little later and mention that Morphus was dancing that day. When this was done the patient's pulse was in no way changed. And likewise, on the following day, while I was attending her, the name of the third dancer was mentioned, and in like fashion the pulse was hardly affected at all. I investigated the matter for a fourth time in the evening. Studying the pulse and seeing that it was excited and irregular when mention was made that Pylades was dancing, I concluded that the lady was in love with Pylades, and in the days following, this conclusion was confirmed exactly. (Galen, 1827 trans.)

Galen went past observation and began to ask, "I wonder what will happen if I do this?" He performed what we now would call a *single-case experiment* (see Chapter 12). Notice that Galen checked to determine that it was not the name of just any dancer that produced a change in pulse rate or even just a man's name. He sought to discover what factors brought on an irregular pulse by examining a number of alternatives. From this investigation, he concluded that only the name of one particular man, repeated on different occasions, produced the effect.

Consider a story that took place in Europe about 150 years ago. A physician named Ignaz Semmelweis faced a serious problem when he noticed that previously healthy women who had just given birth to healthy children were dying. The women died of a condition that included fever, chills, and seizures. Although numerous theories were offered—which attributed the deaths to such causes as bad diet, unhealthy water, and even the smell of certain flowers—Semmelweis knew that other women in the same hospital who ate the same food, drank the same water, and smelled the same flowers did not die. Consequently, he reasoned, it was not the food, water, or flowers that caused the deaths. Yet the fact remained that women who had just given birth died of the mysterious condition.

Semmelweis became aware of a crucial clue when he learned that an assistant who had accidentally cut his hand during an autopsy later died after displaying the same symptoms as the mothers. What was the connection between the death of the assistant and the deaths of the mothers? Was there any connection at all? Semmelweis reasoned that the autopsy laboratory where the assistant had worked might be the cause of the mysterious deaths. To evaluate this notion, he traveled to other hospitals and recorded what physicians did just before delivering babies. From these observations, he learned that when the physicians who delivered the babies came directly from a pathology lecture in which diseased tissues were handled or from performing an autopsy, the death rate was highest. Semmelweis suggested that it was the physicians who were transferring the diseases from the pathological tissue to the healthy mothers, just as the assistant had accidentally infected himself with the knife cut.

The physicians of the day were outraged at the suggestion that they were the cause of the women's deaths. But Semmelweis found further evidence by demonstrating that in hospitals where some births were assisted by midwives rather than physicians, the mothers assisted by midwives survived at a much higher rate. In a rather striking, though not totally controlled, experiment, Semmelweis is said to have placed himself at the door to the delivery ward and forced all physicians who entered to wash their hands first. The number of deaths decreased dramatically. Although not everyone accepted Semmelweis's findings, the data spoke for themselves, and modern medical practice has been shaped by this event (Glasser, 1976).

These three stories—of Croesus, Galen, and Semmelweis—show the beginnings of a scientific approach to human problems. Croesus faced the problem of how to evaluate information offered by various oracles. To do this, he devised a test: an evaluation of the sources to decide which one he would use to direct his behavior. But we do not consult oracles today, you might argue. True, but we do develop far-reaching social programs and treatments. For example, is *Sesame Street* a useful means for teaching disadvantaged children? In psychotherapy, would you gain more by just talking with your favorite professor than by going to a clinical psychologist? If you want to avoid heart attacks, should you change your diet, run 4 miles a day, meditate, or just do nothing? To answer these questions, we, like Croesus, need to perform evaluation research, and the methods of science offer us one approach.

Croesus's experience also reminds us of two potential pitfalls to knowing about the world. These are the roles of chance in the events we observe and the need for unambiguous statements. Croesus's single question to the oracle might have been answered correctly by a lucky guess. To decrease the chance of a lucky guess, Croesus might have asked the oracles several questions. In essence, such a safeguard would have constituted a replication (repeating a procedure under similar conditions) of his experiment. Today, simple replication of a new finding is a powerful way to decrease the likelihood that it is a fluke. Croesus also surely recognized, in retrospect, that he had misinterpreted the oracle's ambiguous answer about the battle. To minimize the chances of ambiguities, scientists carefully and systematically define their words as precisely as possible.

Galen wanted to learn why a particular woman did not sleep. To do this, he first observed the woman; that is, he just spent some time with her and noticed what happened. Once he realized that the woman's heart reacted to a dancer's name, he began to test his observations. At this point, Galen moved to a more sophisticated process than Croesus's simple consultation with the oracle. Galen sought evidence of a causal relationship by examining the woman directly. In doing this, he anticipated a major shift in how we seek to know about the world.

Croesus, by contrast, sought his answers from authority. The authorities of his time were the gods, who spoke through the oracles. A more empirical approach would have been for Croesus to develop a system of spies and scouts to provide information about the Persians' strength based on direct experience. Galen went beyond the ungrounded opinions or guesses of available authorities and relied on his direct experience. Galen's appeal to direct experience reflects an alternative approach to knowing and in a real way reflects an alternative level of consciousness, toward which modern science continues to evolve. Indeed, for several generations now science has been rebuilding our knowledge and understanding of the world on the basis of direct experience.

The choice of basing our actions on evidence from experience or on unfounded opinion probably has been with us in some form for thousands of years and currently confronts each of us countless times every day. Yet basing one's actions on direct experience of the world sometimes appears time consuming and more difficult than simply consulting some expert or acting on a hunch. In the long run, because our actions invariably take place in the world, the wiser alternative is to base actions on experiential knowledge of the real situation. Mere opinions of others provide a convenient answer, but in the long run, as Croesus found out, reality prevails.

In the third story, Semmelweis had a different problem to solve. To determine why some previously healthy women were dying after giving birth, he examined a number of factors. *He observed the patients with a definite purpose in mind.* He asked, "How are these women being treated that is different from the way other patients are treated?" That is, he sought to determine what was unique to these patients. Was it diet? Flowers? Doctors? Then an unexpected event occurred; an autopsy assistant died of the same symptoms. This gave him the clue that led to the solution of the problem. This example shows that science is not only a method that scientists engage in to solve problems and learn about the world, but also a procedure that allows for unexpected events to play a part, whether in the form of accident or human error. One of the rich aspects of science includes unpredictability, serendipity, and what is often called luck. However, luck can work either way, as Croesus found out.

Notice how Semmelweis used logic and simple common sense to design his tests so that his observations would lead to a better understanding of the problem. Semmelweis was trying to understand what was related to the mothers' deaths. For example, because the laboratory assistant died with similar symptoms, Semmelweis reasoned that perhaps he died from the same cause. Semmelweis's observation that more deaths occurred when doctors delivered babies after handling diseased tissue led him to reason that perhaps the cause was somehow related to the diseased tissue. In other cases he tried to rule out *factors that were not responsible* for the deaths. For instance, because patients who did not die ate the same food and drank the same water as those who died, Semmelweis reasoned that the food and water were not possible causes and could be eliminated from further consideration.

There was nothing particularly extraordinary about any of these conclusions. In fact, they reflect the simple common sense we all possess. What was exceptional was that Semmelweis saw relationships that others overlooked. When simple common sense and reason are combined with direct sensory experience, a desire to understand reality, and the courage to accept new facts, science emerges as a powerful means of asking and answering questions about reality.

Our final comment on Semmelweis's work is that his desire to know and understand led to the development of a series of investigations that approached the problem from several directions. Once he had gained the clue from the death of the assistant, he set out to answer his question through a series of observations. First, he observed that the new mothers in his hospital were not treated differently from other women; that is, he observed that they were not given different food or flowers or treated by different doctors. Second, he allowed himself to consider a possible connection between the death of an assistant and the deaths of the mothers. Third, he went to other hospitals to determine whether his ideas or hypotheses were limited to his hospital or whether they were true for other hospitals as well. Fourth, he concluded that the problem was that the physicians handled diseased tissue and then delivered babies without washing their hands, even though this conclusion was unpopular. Fifth, he performed an indirect test of his theory by comparing the difference in death rates of women assisted by physicians who had handled diseased tissue and those assisted by midwives who had not. Sixth, he began a direct test of his theory by insisting that physicians wash their hands as they came into the delivery ward. The power of Semmelweis's procedure was not in any one test of his ideas, because it is almost impossible for any single procedure to answer all questions. Semmelweis was successful because he began with a problem and followed it through to the end by means of a series of observations.

Before you think that what Semmelweis did was an historical event and has nothing to do with our time, you might want to read an article published in *The New England Journal of Medicine* in 1998. The story began in an intensive care ward in New England in which newborn babies were getting sick from an unusual form of yeast infection. When experts were called in to investigate, they began to suspect that the yeast infection came from dogs. Of course, there are no dogs in a newborn intensive care unit, so how did the yeast infection get to the unit and, once there, how did it spread from child to child? The experts' best guess was that it got to the unit from one or more pet owners. Now how do you think it spread? You got it! It was spread by the nurses and doctors on the unit when they did not wash their hands thoroughly. There is one additional piece of information you may want to know, especially if you are planning to do research in this type of situation. When asked, two-thirds of the professionals said they scrubbed between patients 100 percent of the time. However, when the experts watched the staff at work, they discovered that these professionals washed their hands between handling newborns only about one-third of the time. As we will see later in this book, verbal reports and observed behaviors may not always go together. Thus, scientific approaches often use multiple measures for gaining more complete information concerning a topic.

## OVERVIEW

Let us pause for a moment and review what we have covered so far. In the preceding sections we described the scientific approach to problem solving. We began with children learning about the world by interacting with it. In particular, we suggested that such interaction leads to a notion of science as a way of knowing through experience. We characterized science as a process for drawing conclusions that describe the world. We discussed science not as a sacred entity to be worshipped but as a simple extension of the way all of us—not just children—learn about the world.

We then gave an overview of science by relating the stories of Croesus, Galen, and Semmelweis. We pointed out the manner in which aspects of these stories anticipated important issues in present-day science. These correspondences included the need for unambiguous statements, the need for discovering what does not affect the behavior as well as what does affect the behavior, and the importance of a series of tests or research studies for developing a solution to the problem. Science combines experience, reason, and the desire to answer questions about our conceptions of reality. To accomplish this goal, scientists create theories to help explain their experiences. As we shall see later, evaluating ideas and theories is also a large part of what science is all about. Furthermore, the approach to solving problems that we call science is not new but represents a way of solving problems that we *all* use to some extent every day.

---

 CONCEPT CHECK 1.2    "The major reason why Semmelweis's approach was superior to that of Croesus is that we know ESP not to be real—no one can foretell the future." Do you agree?

---

## STUDYING BEHAVIOR AND EXPERIENCE

In the preceding discussion we emphasized that scientists view themselves as using sensory experience to evaluate their ideas concerning the world. This appeal to experience and experimentation as opposed to authority is crucial for two reasons. First, it represents a genuine attempt to pause and observe the external world. Second, reliance on sensory experience means that not only scientists but *any other person* with normal sensory capacities and training can observe the particular behavior under study. The ability of anyone to use his or her own senses to verify the raw data of any scientist provides a strong and essential safeguard that our observations of the world remain as free as possible of the unintended or intended biases of any particular scientist. The process of relying on sensory experience to verify our ideas about reality is called **empiricism**. Empiricism has been an important approach in the history of psychology. Of course, pure empiricism can lead us to erroneous conclusions, but combined with the scientific method it has been a productive approach for psychology.

It also should be pointed out that in our study of behavior and experience, we study our topics on a variety of levels. At times, we discuss at a cognitive level, as when we consider how people think or solve certain problems. At other times, we may move to the physiological level and consider how a particular neurotransmitter is involved in memory, emotion, or schizophrenia. At still other times, we may examine behavior from an extremely broad perspective as we ask how a group of people behaves and experiences a particular event, such as an earthquake or a nuclear reactor accident. As we point out throughout the book, answering a particular research question may lead to one type of research approach rather than another. It is part of your job to ask which type of research approach will give you the most useful information for the question you are asking. Helping you understand how to choose an appropriate research approach is part of the goal of this book.

Throughout the book, we also want to help you understand what science will *not* do for you. For example, it will not give you the final answers to all questions of importance to humans. Science will give you a method for understanding the reality in which we live. It is also important to understand that the answers we receive from science depend on the perspective from which they are asked; there exist various levels of analyses. Although we assume and have assumed for at least the past 100 years that the fundamental processes on each level—cognitive, emotional, physiological, molecular—can be explained scientifically, it is a mistake to assume that information from one level can explain completely the worlds of behavior and experience on another level.

As the title of this book implies, we are dealing with two worlds in our study of behavior and experience. One is the objective, physical world in which anyone can observe appearance and *behavior.* The other is the subjective world of personal psychological *experience,* which is completely private. Science, whether it be biology, physics, chemistry, psychology, sociology, or zoology, focuses on the objective world of appearances and behavior. In the behavior of people, molecules, internal organs, or electrons, what scientists observe and measure are observable objects in the real world. Psychology has continued this tradition, and many studies you perform and read about consist of the observation and measurement of behavior. However, because the subject matter of psychology focuses in part on humans, psychology is faced with a greater challenge. Not only can we observe humans behaving, but we also can ask them about their inner experiences: their thoughts, feelings, and sensations. Furthermore, because we share the same array of psychological processes, we also can observe our own behavior and experiences.

This diversity offers us a challenge. The challenge is to explore and understand scientifically the behaviors as well as the experiences of ourselves and others. E. F. Schumacher (1977) emphasized this diversity when he pointed out that using experience and behavior to study psychological processes in ourselves and others leads to four possible fields of knowledge. For our purposes, we consider these as four possible ways of studying psychological processes. They are summarized in Table 1.1.

In Table 1.1, the first cell (1) represents that with which we are all immediately acquainted. This is our private experience of being who we are and living in our world. It is a largely unshared, subjective experience open to no one but ourselves. However, as we suggest later, it may be possible to explore this space scientifically and systematically. For example, Irwin and Whitehead (1991) asked whether the methods of psychophysics could be applied to the experience of pain to give us a more objective measurement of an individual's subjective experience.

The second cell (2) represents the inner world of all beings other than ourselves. Of course, we have no direct experience of the subjective world of others. But we can ask such

Table 1.1

| Four Ways of Studying Psychological Processes | | | |
|---|---|---|---|
| | | *Process Under Study* | |
| | | Inner Experience | Outer Appearance (Behavior) |
| *Focus of Study* | "I" (self) | 1 | 3 |
| | "You" (others) | 2 | 4 |

intriguing yet unanswerable questions as, "What does it feel like to be you?" "Do my cats experience the world as I do?" "Do you and I both see a red apple as the same color?" Some researchers in psychology try to understand how other people perceive the world and how those people might represent their perceptions internally (cf. Shepard, 1983; Simon, 1978). Such a researcher is interested in the experience of other people as they deal with their world cognitively.

For example, Simon and others have sought to describe how expert and novice chess players decide on making a particular move. They found that a chess expert does not plan ahead any further than a novice does. This is only one of the many observations cognitive scientists have made as they try to understand how we experience and process the world around us. In seeking to understand how someone experiences the world, clinical and personality researchers have studied the types of associations that one has to different categories of knowledge, as well as the manner in which certain groups (e.g., schizophrenics) experience the world. Physiological psychologists also consider questions from the second cell when they ask whether the nervous system of a cat produces a view of reality different from that produced by the nervous system of a human.

The third cell (3) represents our outward behavior: "How do I appear in the eyes of others?" Some aspects of psychology, such as psychotherapy, may focus on helping people learn about how others perceive them. We could also ask, "How am I represented in the sensory system of nonhuman organisms?"

The fourth cell (4) represents the behaviors of other people or animals that anyone can directly observe, measure, or objectify. Included are physiological responses, such as heart rate or electroencephalogram (EEG) measures, as well as self-report responses, as in a memory experiment. This cell has been the traditional domain of psychological research in this century.

We can use the four ways of studying psychological processes presented in Table 1.1 to ask how we might conduct a science of behavior and experience. In cell 1 we ask, "How do I study my own inner experience?" In cell 2 we ask, "How do I study your inner experi-

"ALTHOUGH HUMANS MAKE SOUNDS WITH THEIR MOUTHS AND OCCASIONALLY LOOK AT EACH OTHER, THERE IS NO SOLID EVIDENCE THAT THEY ACTUALLY COMMUNICATE WITH EACH OTHER."

ence?" In cell 3 we ask, "How do I study my own behavior in terms of how others see me?" In cell 4, the one we focus on most in this book, we ask, "How do I study your behavior?"

But what about the subjective experience of participants in psychological experiments? We cannot study these subjective experiences directly using the methods we know today. However, we can use a research participant's behavior, which includes self-report, as a means of learning about his or her internal world. That we use behavior to study subjective experience indirectly is an important idea. Consequently, it will be helpful to step back and discuss the idea in some depth.

## BEHAVIOR: A ROAD INTO THE SUBJECTIVE EXPERIENCE OF RESEARCH PARTICIPANTS

Sometimes we want to ask questions that are difficult for participants in scientific experiments to answer directly. For example, we cannot just ask an animal (other than humans) directly whether it is color-blind or what particular color it sees. However, we can create situations in which an animal would display different behavior in the presence or absence of a particular color. We discuss this and other approaches later in this section. There are also cognitive, emotional, and out-of-awareness processes that are difficult to identify even in humans. For example, how can you explain an image you have in your head? How do we know when someone is dreaming?

At times, we are able to answer such questions through the use of **marker variables.** A marker variable is an event that occurs along with the process we are studying. For example, Aserinsky and Kleitman (1953) discovered that dreaming was accompanied by rapid movements of the eyes; hence, the state in which dreaming occurs is called rapid eye movement (REM) sleep. In neuropsychology research, we may want to know whether people can perceive certain forms or patterns after damage to a particular part of the brain that leaves them without personal awareness of what they have seen. For example, such people may be able to recognize that they have seen a face but not that the face was of a person they had known. It is possible to use psychophysiological markers in such cases, particularly electrodermal activity, to demonstrate that a person with brain damage is physiologically able in the absence of conscious recognition to differentiate between faces from his or her past and unknown faces.

There is even a phenomenon called *blindsight,* in which people who are normally blind and say they see nothing can correctly identify the locations of particular patterns in experimental situations. Surprising as it may seem, Kolb and Braum (1995) used a similar blindsight procedure with normal-sighted people to suggest that information can guide behavior without entering subjective awareness.

What if we want to study what appear to be nontraditional claims? For example, Cytowic (1989) was interested in studying the process of synesthesia: perceiving with a different sense than would usually be the case. He studied people who said they saw colors when music was played or perceived weight when tasting an intense flavor. How you go about researching difficult processes may be different in each case, but it will still rely on inference, or drawing conclusions based on theoretical and experimental situations.

Assume you want to know whether an animal sees colors. You cannot directly experience what the animal experiences in the presence of color; you must find a method for asking the animal. You must accept that you can never scientifically answer the question directly, but you can answer it indirectly. That is, you begin by reasoning how the animal's behavior would be different in the presence and in the absence of color. You can create a situation in which being able to experience color is necessary for the animal to solve a certain problem.

One way this problem has been approached is through the use of a conditioning paradigm using a Skinner box or similar apparatus. The Skinner box was designed for use with small animals such as rats or pigeons. It contains a lever on one wall near a food dish. Most Skinner boxes are electronically automated so that a single press or a certain number of presses on the lever causes food to be dropped into the dish. For example, you could program the food delivery system in such a manner that the animal would receive food each time the lever was pressed when a light of a particular color (e.g., green) was on. When either a light of another color (e.g., blue) or no light was on, the animal would not receive food for pressing the lever. How do you think the animal would respond if it could see colors? How would it respond if it could not see colors?

Imagine yourself as this animal, and you will see how we could use the animal's behavior to tell us whether it can distinguish green from blue. If, as an animal, you could see colors, then you would soon learn to press the lever only when the green light was on and not to press the lever when either the blue light or no light was on. What if you could not see colors? When would you press the lever? You would probably learn quickly not to press the lever when no light was on. But what about when there was a green or blue light on? If you could not see colors, you would never distinguish between the blue and the green light. Thus you would probably guess whenever either light was on.

If we made systematic recordings of your lever pressing over a period of time, we would be able to infer whether you could distinguish a blue light from a green one. We might then set up other discrimination problems (red versus blue, yellow versus green, and so forth). From this information, we could infer whether you could see colors. In our approach to solving this problem, we used two techniques for inferring the experience of our research participants.

The first is to create a situation in which different experiences give rise to different behaviors. The second is to imagine yourself as the research participant and role-play the responses to gain an experimental perspective. Of course, this second technique is difficult to use when the organism (e.g., a bat or a dolphin) has a nervous system sensitive to entirely different stimuli. Also, we must avoid the mistake of assuming that other organisms (or even other humans) think, feel, and act in the same manner as we do.

The scientific study of experience rests on the assumption that a person's behavior is a manifestation of what he or she is experiencing. This assumption is made whether we are studying how animals see colors or how a baby distinguishes his or her parents from other adults. (How might you conduct this experiment?) If we are studying human emotions, we may assume that aggressive, attacking behaviors are related in some way to an experience of anger in our research participants.

In a similar way, if we are studying factors that facilitate the experience of joy in preschool children, we might take increased laughter as evidence that joyful experiences have taken place. In these cases we use the behavior of our research participants (aggressive attacks and laughter) to study their subjective experiences (anger and joy). Seen in this light, *behavior and experience are two sides of the same coin.* In the case of anger, for example, the research participant's feeling of anger is the internal and unseen experiential aspect, and the research participant's aggressive attacks are the external and observable behavioral aspects. In a preceding section, we saw how Galen inferred his patient's love for Pylades when he observed her behavioral—in this case, physiological—reactions to hearing Pylades's name.

The use of objective behavior to study subjective experience is by no means new. We are all good at reading the psychological states of people from their behavior. If your professor walks into class with a scowl, you immediately assume he or she is experiencing some sort of negative emotion. In science, however, we would go a step further and test our assumption.

For example, MacLeod, Mathews, and Tata (1986) were interested in whether anxious people tended to pick out either socially or physically threatening words (such as *failure* or *cancer*) when presented with both threatening and nonthreatening words. In more technical terms, was there a processing bias for encoding emotionally threatening information?

In an intriguing study, these researchers asked research participants to watch a computer screen on which both threat and nonthreat words were presented quickly. During the study, a dot would appear on the screen, and the research participants were instructed to press a button as fast as possible when they saw the dot. At times, the dot appeared at the location just occupied by a threat word and, at other times, in the location occupied by a nonthreat word. It was reasoned that if the research participants' reaction times were shorter in the case of the threat words than the nonthreat words, then it could be inferred that the research participants were directing their gaze to the threat words. That is, by measuring the reaction time from the appearance of the dot to the time the individual pressed the button, these researchers were able to infer the manner in which emotionally threatening words are processed. From the results of the study, the authors concluded that in comparison to nonanxious people, anxious people shift their attention toward emotionally threatening words.

It should be stressed that the use of objective behavior and appearances to study phenomena that cannot be observed directly, such as subjective experience, is not unique to psychology; it is a common feature of all sciences. For example, in physics we discuss the construct *gravity,* yet we never see gravity. Instead, we observe the movement of objects toward the earth and make inferences about gravity. Nor do we study magnetism directly, but we do observe the movements of iron filings, iron bars, charged particles, and various types of gauges, and we make inferences about magnetism.

In the same way, Semmelweis never saw a physician carrying germs into the delivery room; indeed, at that time germs could not even be seen. Yet using indirect evidence, Semmelweis was able to pinpoint the unobservable but very real cause of the mothers' deaths. A construct is a concept used in a particular theoretical manner that ties together a number of observations. In a nutshell, many major constructs of science—such as gravity, time, evolution, electricity, genetic transmission, learning, and even life itself—are discussed and examined indirectly through their manifestations in the physical world. Thus, in science we use the observation of physical events to make inferences about not only the physical world but also the unseen processes that underlie it.

---

☑ **CONCEPT CHECK 1.3**    You read in a newspaper that dogs can hear tones that humans cannot hear. How might you design an experiment to test this?

## THE PEOPLE WHO PERFORM SCIENCE

As we said at the beginning of the chapter, science is a human activity; it is performed only by people, and it is performed by all people in one form or another. It is important to remember that all people means *all* people. This reality is not portrayed accurately in the movies and on television. Typically a white man in a white lab coat is shown, and often not a very interesting one at that. However, this is only part of the truth. Men and women of all races are scientists. Not only is it true today, but it has always been the case.

Every great culture has an important history of scientific achievements, whether it be in mathematics, physics, chemistry, or the social sciences. It is clear that all the people of the world are represented in the history of science. However, some people are more visible than others and sometimes we do not even see the people who are there. For example, you may have heard of the Ladd-Franklin theory of color vision and assumed it to be the work of Mr. Ladd and Mr. Franklin when in fact it was the work of Ms. Christine Ladd-Franklin in the early 1900s (Furumoto, 1992; Scarborough & Furumoto, 1987).

It is important to remember that women have been an integral part of psychology since its beginning as a science more than 100 years ago. In fact, even from the beginning, psychology has had a larger percentage of women than any other scientific discipline (Furumoto & Scarborough, 1986). Although we say this, we know that some students in our classes still do not believe that they can become scientists because of their race or gender. We hope that those who believe this way will reconsider this assumption or at least gather data to test their hypothesis. To this end, there are Web sites directed at sharing information for minority students interested in a career in science (e.g., http://hyper1.hunter.cuny.edu/jgh/).

Another meaning of the statement that science is a human activity is that we perform science with the support of, and in communication with, other scientists. Because a group of people shares our search and values, it is possible for scientists to work together as a larger body of searchers after truth. Sometimes scientists communicate with each other harmoniously, and new discoveries and formulations are the result of the work of many different people. At other times, the opposite is the case. As if in a race, the individual scientist, hoping to be the first to make a discovery, competes against other scientists and even against scientists as a group.

Remember, performing science is just one role or activity of scientists. Scientists are people, and as people they do what people everywhere do. They love and hate. They have good ideas and they have bad ideas. They have thoughts and feelings. Some may want attention and fame, and others may want to be left alone. Scientists feel lonely and sad as well as happy and gregarious. Science is not a means for avoiding what is human within us, although some scientists try to use science in this way. Science is merely a systematic way of using experience to test our ideas about the world.

At times in our history, we have forgotten that scientists are human. We have thought of scientists as *objective*, without feeling, and oblivious to the human condition in general and to what is going on around them in particular. To be sure, there have been such instances, but in these cases it is the failure of the witness and not of the scientist or the research participant that is the basis of the problem. In Chapter 10 we develop this idea further.

In the final analysis, the human sensitivity of scientists adds life and spirit to the scientific enterprise. Thus, what is unique about science is not the people who are scientists but their methods and the relationships between the people who practice science with these methods.

# KEY TERMS AND CONCEPTS

1. **Nature of science**
   A. Roles of scientist, research participant, and witness
2. **Ways of accepting knowledge**
   A. Tenacity
   B. Authority
   C. Reason
   D. Common sense
   E. Science
3. **The scientific approach**
   A. Verifiable through experience
   B. Newton's rules of reasoning
4. **Examples of early approaches to science**
   A. Croesus and the establishment of criteria for evaluation

   B. Galen and the examination of alternative factors
   C. Semmelweis and the development of a series of studies
5. **Studying behavior and experience**
   A. Empiricism
   B. Studying experience through behavior
   C. Use of constructs
6. **The nature of scientists**
   A. Science is performed by people.
   B. All people perform some type of science.
   C. Science requires the support of and communication with others.

# SUMMARY

1. The purpose of this chapter is to introduce you to science as an approach to learning about ourselves and our world. As a problem-solving approach, science offers an important means of evaluating ideas.
2. People have used a variety of ways of accepting or rejecting ideas throughout history. Basing our approach on the work of Charles Peirce, we discussed the strengths and weaknesses of five of these (tenacity, authority, reason, common sense, and science).
3. Science is useful for evaluating ideas because it is self-corrective; that is, results from experiments offer a feedback mechanism to help clarify ideas.
4. For thousands of years, people have tried to understand their world better. We looked at three historical events to help clarify the scientific approach. The stories of Croesus, Galen, and Semmelweis pointed to the need for unambiguous statements, the need for testing factors that do and do not affect behavior, and the

importance of a carefully designed series of observations. In sum, science combines experience, reason, and a desire to answer questions about reality.
5. Psychology is interested in the study of outer appearances (behavior) as well as inner experiences. Using a schema presented by Schumacher, we asked how we might study the behavior and experience of ourselves and others.
6. There are times when researchers want to know about the internal processing of an organism but either cannot or, as we discuss in later chapters, do not want to ask directly. Because we can assume that an organism's behavior is related to its experience, we can ask such questions as, "Does a cat see colors?" or "Can babies tell the difference between their parents and other adults?" In this manner, we use behavior to make inferences concerning the inner worlds of various organisms.

# REVIEW QUESTIONS

1. What are the ways of accepting or rejecting ideas, as suggested by Peirce?
2. Discuss the changes in science before and after the time of Galileo.
3. How is science self-corrective?
4. In simple language, what are Newton's four rules of reasoning?
5. What was progressive about Croesus's approach to the oracles?
6. How was Galen's approach scientific?
7. How did Semmelweis approach the problem of mothers dying soon after childbirth?
8. Give some examples of what would be included in a discussion of behavior and experience and how modern psychology approaches these areas.
9. Describe an experiment that would show whether an animal is color-blind.

# DISCUSSION QUESTIONS AND PROJECTS

Questions in this section are based on ideas presented in the text and require you to use what you have learned or to draw from your own experience. Some of the questions are designed to stimulate discussion; they have no single right answer.

1. While watching television, pick out five commercials and notice the way in which they try to convince you that their products are good. Which of Peirce's ways of knowing do they suggest? (*Hint:* Some of the suggestions may be nonverbal; for instance, the use of a famous person suggests knowledge through authority.)

2. Discuss the statement "Science is above all a human activity."

3. Discuss how the roles of scientist, research participant, and witness are exemplified and portrayed in our society. What different disciplines in a college or university are devoted to each of these roles?

4. It was suggested that science is a self-corrective process. What are the advantages and disadvantages of a self-corrective system?

5. Develop an experiment that would determine whether someone who was unable to speak could experience emotions.

6. Name some constructs that cannot be seen but are important in our everyday lives.

7. Discuss how you might study your own behavior. For example, how would you determine whether you practiced your guitar better in the morning or at night? How could you determine the effects of extra sleep on your school work and on your feelings in general? What could you do to get your professor to tell better jokes?

8. A researcher was looking for the reasons people fail in college. To help answer this question, the researcher took a group of students who flunked out of college and a group of students who got good grades. Both groups were given a test of self-esteem. It was found that the group that flunked out had lower self-esteem than the group that did not. From this the researcher concluded that low self-esteem is one of the causes of failure in college. Comment on this conclusion.

## Exercises with InfoTrac College Edition

Throughout this book, we will give you sources of information that are found on the Internet. We begin this most intensively in Chapter 3. However, for now we want to acquaint you with a source of information available with this book, InfoTrac College Edition. This is a wide-ranging source of information including encyclopedias, reference books, magazines, and scientific journals. To learn about InfoTrac, you should go to its Web site http://www.infotrac-college.com/wadsworth/ and enter the site and then the password included with this book. Once into the system, enter the name Semmelweis, whom you learned about in this chapter, and read about his life in one of the reference books available. You can also enter particular terms, such as *empiricism*, and learn more about this approach. Throughout the book, if you encounter a specific scientific phenomenon in a chapter, such as REM sleep or blindsight, that you wish to know about, you can also enter those terms. As an exercise, use InfoTrac College Edition to find an article entitled "The gestural origins of language," by Michael C. Corballis. (*Hint:* Enter the author's name and you also see other articles this author has written.) It was published in the March–April 1999 issue of *American Scientist.* In reading this article, think about how scientists use logic and reason to understand processes that are difficult to study in a laboratory. In this case it is the role that gestures played in the evolution of human language. You may also be interested in an article on career development in women, which can be found by entering "Women and career development," written by Susan Phillips and Anne Imhoff. This article was published in the 1997 volume of the *Annual Review of Psychology.*

## Answers to Concept Checks

1.1 Although it is possible that cancer could be cured in the next year, the basis of your acceptance was authority, not science. Accepting what a famous person says, whether he or she is a scientist, the president, or a 6-year-old child, is a reliance on authority, not science. Science requires that the information be evaluated through observation and reason according to an established procedure. As you will see, we could accept the statement that a particular type of cancer would be affected by a particular treatment as a hypothesis to be tested. After the test, we could make a scientific statement about the hypothesis.

1.2 One major reason Semmelweis's approach was superior was that he sought to determine not only what *did* influence an event but also what *did not*. That is, he sought to determine which factors were not related to the deaths of the mothers as well as the one that was. Another important reason was that he used a series of observations to test his question. Whether ESP is real is in no way related to why Semmelweis's approach was more productive than that of Croesus.

1.3 An easy way to test this hypothesis is to observe the dog's reaction to the tones. If you wanted to determine which tones the dog could or could not hear, then you could pair each tone with a cue for receiving food. You would need to make sure that the dog did not use any of its other senses to obtain the food. For example, you would not want the dog to be able to see you producing the tones.

# INTRODUCTION TO THE METHODS OF SCIENCE

Most of us remember how different our first few weeks of college were from anything we had known before. Remember how you expected your roommate or your professor to act, and how you reacted when they did not act that way? If you stop and think about your first reactions to college, you can see that there were three aspects of these experiences. First, there was an idea or expectation concerning what was about to happen in college. Second, there was the actual experience of what did happen during those first few weeks—and it was probably quite different, at least in some respects, from what you had expected. Third, there was the resulting reorganization of your ideas about college and the potential impact of this experience on your life.

The methods of science closely parallel these three aspects of your experience. First, scientists begin with an idea or expectation. As we will discuss, a formally stated expectation is called an *hypothesis.* The scientist says, "I expect this to happen under these conditions," and thus states the hypothesis. Second, scientists look to experience to evaluate the accuracy of their ideas or expectations about the world. That is, they try to find or create the situation that will allow them to observe what they are interested in studying. Through observation and experimentation, scientists can begin to evaluate their ideas and expectations about the world. As mentioned in Chapter 1, learning about the world through observation and experimentation is an example of *empiricism,* which means nothing more than the acceptance of sensory information as valid. Third, on the basis of their observations and experiments, scientists seek to draw conclusions or inferences about their ideas and expectations. They reorganize their ideas and consider the impact of the new information on their theoretical conceptualizations.

As mentioned earlier, science is a way of determining what we can infer about the world. In its simplest form, the scientific method consists of asking a question about the world and then experiencing the world to determine the answer. When we begin an inquiry, what we already know about our topic leaves us in one of a number of positions. In some cases, we know little about our topic or our topic may be very complex. Consequently, our ideas and questions are general. For example, how does our memory work? What causes mental illness? What factors make a fruitful marriage? How can we model the brain?

If little is known about a particular phenomenon, it often is useful simply to watch the phenomenon occur naturally and get a general idea of what is involved in the process. Initially, this is accomplished by observing and describing what occurs. This scientific technique is called **naturalistic observation.**

A classic example of this approach is Charles Darwin's observation of animals in the Galápagos Islands, which formed the basis of his theory of evolution. More recently, the study of animals in the wild has led to new insights into animal cognition and social systems. Scientists have continued to return to the Galápagos Islands with more advanced methods (such as observing molecular DNA changes) and still continue to update and confirm Darwin's original ideas. (See Weiner, 1994, for a review of this work.)

Another example of this method has come from observing female dwarf mongooses in Tanzania's Serengeti National Park over several years (Morell, 1996). Before this research was conducted, it was assumed that the dominant female in a pack of animals would be under the least stress and the subordinate females under the most. However, by examining some 14 packs of animals, scientists have found that dominant female mongooses show the highest level of cortisol, a stress hormone, when compared with all other females in the pack. Other researchers (e.g., de Waal, 2000) seek to understand how animals and humans use peacemaking to resolve aggressive episodes. Did you know that chimpanzees, like humans, often kiss their partner on the mouth after a fight?

At other times, we may want to understand certain aspects of a complex system with the goal of better describing how one aspect of the system may be associated with another aspect. For example, we may want to know whether people who have friends have fewer health-related problems than people who do not, or whether eating certain foods is associated with not having cancer. How would you go about answering such questions? One way is to examine and note the relationship between a person's health and the number of friends that person has. But how are you to understand these data? Look at an example of a similar question of the relationship between smoking tobacco and having lung cancer. The first step is to ask whether two events go together. In this example, researchers sought to determine whether, when one event occurred (a person smoked tobacco), the other event also occurred (the person had cancer). Such a scientific approach is called by various names, including the **correlational approach.**

As we will see later in this book, just finding that a relationship exists between two events does not allow us to determine exactly what that relationship is, much less to determine that one event actually caused the other event to happen. If we want to state that one event produced another event, we need to develop a much stronger case for our position. For example, we could see how some single event over which we have control affects the phenomenon we are studying. To do this, we begin to interact with the phenomenon. We structure our question in this form: "If I do this, what will happen?" Numerous questions can be asked in this way, such as, "Will you learn words better if each word is of the same class (e.g., food words) than if they are from different classes (e.g., foods, cars, and toys)?"

As our knowledge grows, we may even get to the point of formulating specific predictions. In this case, our questions are structured in the form, "If I do this, I expect this will happen." Sometimes our predictions are more global, and we predict that one factor will be stronger than another. We might predict that more people are likely to help a stranger if they perceive the environment to be safe than if they think it is dangerous. Sometimes, however, we may know enough about an area to make a more precise prediction, or *point prediction*. For example, we might predict that 3 months of exercise will lead to a 10-mm Hg decrease in blood pressure. These approaches, in which we interact directly with the phenomenon we are studying, are examples of the **experimental method.**

During the 1980s, a different type of scientific approach was developed within psychology, especially in response to cognitive questions. The approach was based less on observation or direct manipulation than on attempting to establish a model (either conceptual or mathematical) capable of performing operations similar to the topic being studied. This approach is called **modeling.** For example, Freeman and his colleagues asked whether they could develop a model based on calculus that would mimic the brain's electrical patterns of an animal sensing odors (Freeman, 1991, 1999).

A broad program of modeling was instituted by Rumelhart and McClelland (1986) in which they sought to model human cognitive processes by assuming that the architecture of the brain is that of a massive parallel processing machine. Testing such models requires that one compare the output of the model with that obtained in actual experimentation. For example, Cohen, Dunbar, and McClelland (1990) compared simulated data based on their model and actual data from an experiment in the performance of a Stroop color-word task. Although these techniques are beyond the scope of this text, we wanted you to know about their existence.

Before we continue, we want to emphasize that there is no set number of methods for practicing science. Methods are developed in response to specific questions. Often our area of study determines which methods we use. For example, in sciences such as astronomy and zoology, scientists often use **retrospective** or **post hoc** (after the fact) **methods;** like Darwin, a zoologist might ask how a certain species developed. Clinical psychologists use similar methods when they speculate on the development of personality or the origin of mental illness. Other areas of psychology may rely on *single-case approaches* when the problem they are studying is rare, such as a specific brain disorder.

For example, Antoine Bechara and his colleagues studied three patients with particular lesions or injuries to areas deep within their brains (Bechara et al., 1995). The first patient had damage to the hippocampus, the second had damage to the amygdala, and the third had damage to both areas. Using a classic conditioning procedure in which a loud sound (unconditioned stimulus) is paired with a color or sound (conditioned stimulus), these researchers were able to show different effects depending on the type of damage to the brain. In particular, damage to the amygdala resulted in a lack of conditioning, but the person was able to describe the color or tone paired with the unconditioned stimulus of a loud sound. However, damage to the hippocampus resulted in the opposite effect: The person did show conditioning but was unable to describe the conditioned stimuli. The person with damage to both areas of the brain neither knew about the stimuli nor showed the effects of conditioning. We discuss single-case experiments as well as case study and other approaches to research later in this book.

We also want you to know about another approach, called **qualitative methods** (Leong & Austin, 1996; Taylor & Bogdan, 1998). Qualitative methods emphasize the subjective state of the person under study and are particularly useful when we wish to describe the experience of a particular person or group. For example, there are times when it is important to understand how clients experience various forms of psychotherapy, or what the experience of depression is for a particular person, or even how parents experience their children or their parenting roles.

In one study, Deutsch and Saxon (1998) interviewed mothers and fathers concerning how much praise or criticism each participant received from others concerning the amount of time spent in parenting and at work. One aspect of the qualitative tradition is a reliance on the phenomenological or subjective aspect of experience. There can be a real richness and depth in the description of subjective experiences. This approach has a long history in philosophy and sociology and has recently gained recognition in psychology. For example, qualitative approaches reveal that some parents of young children with conduct disorders often feel that they are being held hostage by the situation and lose contact with their partners. This work by Webster-Stratton & Spitzer (1996) describes the progression from coping efforts, to intense feelings of inadequacy, to feeling of helplessness in such parents. Such insight into the subjective feelings of parents of oppositional and aggressive children may help therapists to develop better approaches for both the parents and the children in such a situation.

For an overview in relation to clinical psychology, the interested reader should consult Kazdin (1998). As with any approach, the question arises as how to view the trustworthiness of the information presented, which is a current topic of debate within qualitative methods (Leong & Austin, 1996).

In contrast to qualitative methods, the methods we emphasize in this book often are called **quantitative methods.** Using quantitative methods, there is generally an emphasis on behavior as opposed to experience as well as an attempt to describe constructs in terms of numbers and find laws or patterns that describe behavioral processes. In the present chapter, we focus on three main approaches: *naturalistic observation, correlational approaches,* and *experimental manipulation.*

Let us consider the relationship between the scientist and the research participant in each of these methods. With the naturalistic method, it is the job of the scientist to be passive and observe carefully the activity of the research participant. In this method, the scientist does not try to change the environment of the research participant. The research participant simply goes about normal activity and the scientist watches, preferably without influencing the participant's behavior. In this way, the scientist is able to make a detailed description of some aspect of the research participant's natural behavior.

In contrast, when using the experimental method, the scientist is more active, and the research participant's activities are restricted. The scientist intentionally structures the situation so that he or she can study the effect of a particular factor on the research participant's behavior. In between these two approaches are correlational methods, which may range from simple observation and correlation of factors to a more active manipulation, although without the same degree of manipulation and control characteristic of the experimental method.

As an analogy, we can view each of these methods as an extension of the way a child explores his or her world, although the scientist and the child have very different goals in mind. A common way children and scientists begin to explore a new phenomenon is simply to watch it occur naturally. In the process of watching, the child and the scientist may describe what they see. However, the scientist usually goes further and uses mathematical terms to specify what is being seen. As a further step, both children and scientists extend their observations by means of limited interaction with the phenomenon.

Once we as scientists begin to see the relationship involved in a particular phenomenon, we can study it more precisely with more controlled manipulations. From this understanding, we may even move from science to technology and use our understanding profitably in our everyday lives. This general approach works for a child, and it works for scientists, too, although on a more complex level.

To provide you with a more accurate conception of how the scientific method is an extension of our everyday activities, we examine the three fundamental scientific strategies mentioned previously: the naturalistic observation technique, which is akin to a child observing a phenomenon; the experimental method, which is akin to a child interacting with the phenomenon to learn more about it; and the correlational approach, which, depending on the situation, may be more or less like either of the other two methods. Let us now turn to a more detailed discussion of each method.

 # NATURALISTIC OBSERVATION

Imagine that it is 20,000 years in the future and you have been sent to a strange part of the galaxy to study members of a particular species that have been described by astronauts as "cultural apes." Assume you could arrive at the appointed place and remain undetected.

Because you know virtually nothing about these cultural apes, the method of naturalistic observation would be an efficient way to get a general idea of these beings.

Like many scientists who have studied animals in the wild on 19th- and 20th-century Earth, you might set up a blind so that you would not be detected and observe the behavior of these apes. Often with animals in the wild, scientists try to find a place where the animals come together, such as a watering hole, and set up an observation post near this place. After some preliminary observations, you find that these cultural apes come together every morning in large structures. Consequently, you set up your observation post within one of these structures. Assuming you remain undetected, what would you do next?

The answer is deceptively simple yet difficult to accomplish. *You just watch.* "Just watching" might be compared to seeing a movie in a foreign language that you do not understand. It is easy to see that there are interactions between the actors in the movie, yet you can only guess what they mean. In the beginning, the most difficult part of just watching is not to guess. Until you have observed a given interaction repeatedly, you can easily distort what you are seeing by your expectation that it occurs in a certain way. After much observation, you may begin to notice certain patterns of behavior by the apes. For example, they may say "Hello" each time they meet and "Goodbye" each time they leave each other. One hallmark of naturalistic observation is the discovery of patterns in the behaviors of different organisms.

An important part of the naturalistic technique is to record what you observe. At one time, the only method of recording was to reduce the observations to written notes or drawn pictures, much as Darwin did when he went to the Galápagos Islands. Today, however, we can record the observed behavior on audiotape or videotape. Of course, scientists are still an important part of the process because they select what will be recorded and thus determine the observations for later analysis. So once we have observed many instances of the typical behavior of this species, we can withdraw from our observation post and begin to analyze our recorded observations. We now can begin to make summary statements about the natural ongoing behavior of these species.

Coming down to earth, let us consider the work of one scientist who has used the naturalistic method. Nikolaas Tinbergen (who received the Nobel Prize for his research) became interested in autistic children. Because little was known about the overall behavior of autistic children, Tinbergen began his work by using the naturalistic observation method and simply observed autistic children (Tinbergen & Tinbergen, 1972). Autistic children do not communicate with others. Often they just walk around making sounds to themselves or hitting their heads against a wall. As Tinbergen watched these children, he observed that there was a pattern to their abnormal behavior in that this behavior appeared most often when they were in an unfamiliar social situation. Even a smile from a stranger might be followed by an attempt by the autistic child to withdraw from the situation.

Tinbergen also was interested in how autistic children were different from "normal" children. To understand these differences, Tinbergen observed normal children and also children with varying degrees of autism. He found that some facial expressions displayed by the autistic children differed from those of the normal children. Thus, the naturalistic method offered a starting point for describing differences between autistic and normal children.

Another scientist who used the naturalistic method of observation is Konrad Lorenz. (Lorenz also received the Nobel Prize for his behavior research.) Lorenz (1952) described the behavioral interactions in a colony of jackdaws:

> A jackdaw sits feeding at the communal dish, a second bird approaches ponderously, in an attitude of self-display, with head proudly erected, whereupon the first visitor moves slightly to

one side, but otherwise does not allow himself to be disturbed. Now comes a third bird, in a much more modest attitude which, surprisingly enough, puts the first bird to flight; the second, on the other hand, assumes a threatening pose, with his back feathers ruffled, attacks the latest comer and drives him from the spot. (p. 149)

At times, field observations may bring to light unknown patterns of behavior that in turn lead to new theories concerning these behaviors. For example, Nelson, Badura, and Goldman (1990) reviewed field studies showing a seasonal shift in the activity patterns of rodents. These animals tend to show the greatest amount of activity at night during the summer; in the winter, they show more activity during the daylight hours. Once a scientist knows an animal's patterns in the wild, ideas can be developed concerning the function such patterns serve as well as the mechanism that controls these patterns.

Rowsemitt (1986), for example, suggested that the winter/summer pattern of activity level in the rodents allows for better use of energy because being active during the winter day allows the animals to avoid extreme cold, and being active during the summer night allows them to avoid the extreme heat of day. To understand the mechanism that mediates the seasonal shift in activity patterns, a scientist may want to use the experimental method, which we discuss later in this chapter. Rowsemitt thought the change in the activity level of the rodent to be controlled by one particular hormone, testosterone, and centered his research in this area. However, one could also study a variety of other factors.

In summary, there are four characteristics of the naturalistic observation method. First, noninterference is of prime importance. Scientists using this method must not disrupt the process or flow of events. In this way we can see things as they really are, without influencing the ongoing phenomenon. Second, this method emphasizes the invariants or patterns that exist in the world. For example, if you could observe yourself in a noninterfering manner, you might conclude that your moods vary with the time of day or with particular weather patterns or even with particular thoughts. Third, this method is most useful when we know little about the subject of our investigation. It is most useful for understanding the big picture by observing a series of events rather than isolated happenings. Fourth, the naturalistic method may not shed light on the factors that directly influence the behavior observed. The method provides a description of a phenomenon; it does not answer the question of why it happened.

To better understand how one variable is related to another, we use the correlational method. This method emphasizes scientists' ability to describe whether and to what degree two variables are associated with each other. Through this approach, scientists are better able to understand and describe our world.

# THE CORRELATIONAL APPROACH

At times you may want to know whether a relationship exists between two events that cannot be manipulated easily. For example, you may want to know whether playing sports or drinking alcohol in high school is more associated with developing heart problems later in life. Barefoot, Dahlstrom, and Williams (1983) sought to determine whether one's emotionality (especially hostility) during medical school was associated with coronary heart disease later in life. In many studies of this type, it would be unethical or impractical to manipulate the events actively (e.g., drinking alcohol in high school or provoking emotionality in graduate school). What you can do instead is to collect information on the particular events under study without attempting to manipulate these events. Formally, we ask whether the frequency or magnitude of one event is related to the frequency or magnitude of the other event, but we do not attempt to establish how one event influences the other. This type of research is called correlational research or natural association research (Ray, 1989).

Correlation is a measure of association that we present statistically in Chapter 4. For now, we can introduce some of the basic ideas. In correlational studies, the researcher is interested in asking whether there is an association between two variables, but he or she does not attempt to establish how one variable influences the other. Establishing that such an association exists may be the first step in dealing with a complex problem.

For example, a physiological psychologist might ask whether a person's pulse rate is related to the age of the person. To answer this question, she could simply measure various people's heart rates and correlate these measures with their ages. What would this tell us? First, it would tell us how heart rate and age are related. If they were to increase together—that is, if low heart rates were associated with young ages, medium heart rates with middle ages, and high heart rates with older ages—then this relationship would be called a *positive correlation*. However, if low heart rates were associated with older ages and high heart rates with younger ages, then this relationship would be called a *negative correlation*. Of course, as you will see in Chapter 4, few relationships are perfectly related to one another. Thus, the correlation statistic offers a means of describing the *degree* of an association between two variables.

What we cannot know from correlational research is whether either variable influences the other. That is, if two variables are related, what might the reason be for the relationship? As you begin to suggest factors that might have produced a high degree of relationship, you realize that a third, unspecified variable actually may have influenced the two variables in the correlational study. Thus, the nature of a correlational study is to suggest relationships but not to suggest which variable influences which other variable.

It is often said that correlation does not imply causality. For example, a researcher might want to know whether a relationship exists between the type of food one eats and the likelihood of one having a heart attack. An approach would be to examine the diets of people who have had heart attacks and of those who have not. What if there were a high association between eating steak, for example, and heart attacks? You could conclude little other than that there was an association or correlation between the two variables. The association of two factors does not in itself imply that one influences the other. However, if there is a *low* correlation between the events, you can infer that one event does *not* cause the other. A high degree of association is necessary for establishing that one variable influences another; a correlational study is often the first step for providing the needed support for later experimental research, especially in complex areas.

---

✓ **CONCEPT CHECK 2.1**    A physician reports data from a study that compares the amount of television a person watches with his or her health. The point is made that people who watch more television are sicker; therefore, watching TV is bad for your health. Someone in the audience says, "No! That is not the case. Sick people have nothing to do, so they watch TV." Whom do you believe?

# THE EXPERIMENTAL METHOD

As we suggested, you already know a great deal about the experimental method. Indeed, all of us have used it in one form or another to explore our world since we were small children. Like the child, the scientist begins to interact with the phenomenon he or she is studying and asks the question "If I do this, what will happen?" From these interactions, the scientist gains increased understanding of the phenomenon under study. To test this understanding further, the scientist asks, "Was what happened really a result of what I did?"

To give you a more accurate understanding of how scientists learn from interacting with the environment, let us consider the following line of fictitious research. Before we actually describe the study, we want to suggest that you, both as a scientist and as an informed consumer, consider many of the "scientific" claims you hear on television or read in magazines and look for alternative explanations to the claims being made. Thinking scientifically is not something you do only when you design experiments; rather, it is a way of approaching all information.

Assume that the makers of a brand of children's cereal, Roasty-Toasties, claim that their breakfast cereal helps children to grow. In their enthusiasm to demonstrate the claim and add "scientific evidence" to their television commercials, the company designed the following experiment. A group of children were given daily a bowl of Roasty-Toasties with cream, bananas, and sugar. After several months, each child was weighed. It was found that they gained an average of 8 pounds each. The company concluded that the weight increase was due to the nourishing breakfast, and consequently the company recommended this breakfast for all children. When a thoughtful scientist heard the results, he admitted to their appeal but added that he was bothered by several things. One thing was that the children also ate lunch and dinner. Consequently, the weight gain might be due to the food eaten at these other meals.

Dismayed that they had not thought of that, the company designed a new experiment. This time it used two groups of children. The average age and average weight were the same for each group. For breakfast, one group received the recommended cereal with cream, bananas, and sugar; the other was given scrambled eggs. The two groups ate approximately the same foods for lunch and dinner. After several months, each child was weighed. It was found that there was an average gain of 5 pounds in the group that received the recommended breakfast cereal and an average gain of only 1 pound in the group that was given eggs for breakfast.

Needless to say, the company was excited and assailed our thoughtful scientist with the new findings, which seemed to confirm the earlier results. The scientist pointed out that he was even more impressed than before. However, he grew silent again, looked up, and asked, "Could the weight gain be caused by the cream, sugar, and bananas and not by the cereal?" Although the company was confident that the results were due to the cereal, logically the scientist was right. The entire effect could have been due to the cream, sugar, and bananas, not the cereal.

Crushed by the scientist's keen insight, the company's researchers returned to the laboratory. After much debate, they decided to do the following experiment. As before, one group received the cereal with cream, sugar, and bananas for breakfast, but now another group received equal amounts of cream, sugar, and bananas (but no cereal) each morning. Once again, lunch and dinner were approximately the same for both groups, and the children's weights at the onset of the study were about the same. The company researchers were confident of replicating the earlier findings. After several months, they weighed each child. Much to their dismay, they found that children in both groups gained an average of 5 pounds. The group that received cereal did not gain more weight than the other group.

## ■ Definitions in the Experimental Method

The goal of the fictitious study just described was to determine whether eating cereal affected the growth of a child. The **hypothesis** or idea being tested was that eating the new cereal influenced growth. To test its hypothesis, in the final study the company gave its cereal to one group of children and not to a second group. The group that received the cereal is called the **experimental group.** The group that did not receive the cereal is called the **control group.** A control group is a group that is treated exactly like the experimental group except for the factor being studied. In this case, the factor being studied was the breakfast cereal. The control group was subject to the effects of all the same factors as the first group except for the cereal. The study is characterized in Table 2.1.

In any experiment we must define the terms in the hypothesis so that the hypothesis can be tested. To minimize possible confusion, the crucial terms in the hypothesis are defined clearly in reference to concrete operations. This definition is called an **operational definition,** and it forms a crucial link between our ideas and the world. Kerlinger (1973, 1986) suggests that there are two types of operational definitions: *measured* and *experimental*. The first type relates to measurement and may specify both *how* observations are to be made and *what* is to be observed and measured. For example, in a study that measures anxiety during certain types of tasks, it would be necessary to define operationally how anxiety was measured. That is, were the anxiety scores derived from self-report measures, physiological measures such as heart rate, or observation of a specific behavior? The second type of operational definition refers to experimentation. This type of operational definition describes how experimental procedures are to be followed.

For example, in a study that examines the effects of praise on improvement in psychotherapy, it would be necessary to define operationally both what praise is and under what conditions it is to be given and withheld. In one sense, operational definitions function like a recipe for a cook. In the same way that it would be difficult to follow a recipe that said only

Table 2.1

| Design of the Final Roasty-Toasties Study | | | |
|---|---|---|---|
| | Pretreatment Weight | Treatment | Posttreatment Weight |
| Group 1 (experimental) | 50 lb. | Cereal with cream, bananas, and sugar | 55 lb. |
| Group 2 (control) | 50 lb. | Cream, bananas, and sugar without cereal | 55 lb. |

"Heat eggs, milk, and flour" (without specifying the amounts of the ingredients, the temperature at which the mixture is to be heated, and so on), it would be impossible to test an hypothesis that said only "Anxiety hurts performance." For a complete understanding, it would be necessary to specify (that is, operationally define) how anxiety is to be measured and how performance is to be assessed. Thus, one of the first tasks in developing a research study is to specify the operational definitions related to measurement and experimentation.

It should be pointed out that we are using the term *operational definition* in the more popular and less technical sense. We are not speaking of the total definition of a construct, a point we discuss in more detail in Chapter 3. (For a more complete discussion of operational definitions and the related concept *reduction sentences,* see Suppe, 1977.)

In the imaginary cereal experiment, the researchers had to define operationally both what was meant by the construct *growth* and how the eating of the cereal was to be manipulated experimentally. The variable that an experimenter manipulates in an experiment is called an **independent variable.** A variable is said to be independent when its levels are established by the experimenter before the experiment begins and are thus independent of anything that happens during the experiment. In this manner the independent variable precedes and potentially influences the measurements that we take in an experiment.

The aspect of the world that the experimenter expects will be affected by the independent variable is the **dependent variable.** The dependent variable is so called because if a relationship does exist, its value *depends* on the independent variable. Our experience suggests that some people confuse the concept of independent and dependent variables. Thus, it is important to remember that it is the independent variable you as experimenter control and that it is the dependent variable that you as experimenter measure. Because the independent variable is the variable you manipulate, some people remember this by saying "**I** manipulate the Independent variable."

In the cereal experiment, the researchers hoped that growth would be enhanced through ingestion of the new cereal. However, because there are many aspects of growth (physical maturation, height, weight, intellectual ability, emotional maturation), the task of deciding which aspect to measure is difficult. Notice that their final decision to define growth operationally in terms of weight is quite arbitrary and ignores other aspects of growth that might be evaluated.

The difference in the magnitude of the dependent variable for the control and experimental groups is called the **treatment effect.** Ideally, the only difference between the experimental and control groups should be the independent variable. If we are certain that this is the case, then we can infer that any difference in the magnitude of the dependent variable is due to the independent variable. If there were more than one difference between the two groups, then we would not know which of these differences was responsible for any treatment effects we might observe. (Note, however, that there are more complex experimental designs, called *factorial designs,* that allow us to investigate the effects of two or more independent variables in the same experiment. This class of designs is discussed in Chapter 8.)

If we suspect that some unintended factor may also be operating, then the truth or validity of the experiment is seriously threatened and the entire experiment must be questioned. In the second cereal experiment, the fact that the control group did not receive cream, bananas, and sugar constitutes an alternative explanation for that group's lower weight gain. Whenever two or more independent variables are operating, the unintended independent variables (those not chosen by the experimenter) are called **confounding**

**variables.** In the second experiment, the cream, sugar, and bananas represent this type of confounding variable.

Other confounding variables may covary with the independent variable and be more difficult to notice. For example, assume a researcher compared a new medication against a problem-solving approach for the treatment of anxiety. If she found the problem-solving approach to show a greater reduction in anxiety, could she conclude that problem solving produced the reduction? Although that is one possibility, it also may have been the case that the reduction in anxiety was produced by spending time with a professional. That is, because giving medications requires less time with a patient than discussing problem-solving techniques, the results found may not have been due to the independent variable as planned in the study but by a confounding variable: time with the patient. We discuss confounds and their influence in more detail in Chapter 6.

---

✓ **CONCEPT CHECK 2.2**     A study was conducted to determine whether using videotapes rather than audiotapes to learn German during the semester influenced the grade received on a final exam in German. Name the independent and the dependent variables in this study.

---

## ■ Causation

Before we continue, we would like to clear up some confusion experienced by a number of people when the word *caused* is used. In psychology, when we speak about an independent variable causing a change in a dependent variable, we mean that these two variables reflect a consistent association. That is, with every change in the independent variable, there comes a related and predictable change in the dependent variable. The idea of causality in science is generally a conclusion concerning the relationship between the independent and dependent variables. If research shows that each time we change one aspect of a situation, then a predictable change follows in another aspect, we usually say that the first aspect caused a change in the second. As we repeat an experiment in varying situations and under different conditions, if the same relationship between the independent variable and the dependent variable continues to hold true, then we have more confidence in our conclusion. Many philosophers of science see causation as something we ascribe to the situation, and they remind us that what we are really doing is making inferences about the world (i.e., epistemology) rather than making statements about what really exists (i.e., ontology). As we discuss later in this chapter, modern physics is now regarded as the study of *observations of reality* rather than the study of *reality* itself.

Another way to discuss causation is to consider what conditions are required for an event to occur. In particular, we discuss *necessary* and *sufficient* conditions (cf. Copi, 1986). A necessary condition is the condition that *must* exist in order for the particular event to occur. For example, it is necessary for a human being to be a woman in order to become pregnant. Although it is a necessary condition, just being a woman in itself will not make you pregnant. For this to occur, there must also exist a sufficient condition. A sufficient condition for the occurrence of an event is a situation that, when it happens, produces the event. For example, we say that fertilization through intercourse is a sufficient condition for producing an embryo.

To consider another example, we can say that the presence of oxygen alone is a necessary but not a sufficient condition for combustion to occur. However, the presence of oxygen at a certain critical range of temperatures is a sufficient condition for combustion. Likewise, we would not say that feeding milk to a child is a necessary condition for producing growth, because a variety of substances fed to a child will produce growth. In the scientific literature, the word *cause* sometimes has been used in the sense of a necessary condition and at other times in the sense of a sufficient condition. This has led many researchers to suggest that we avoid the word altogether. Although we find it difficult to avoid the word completely, we have sympathy with the search for exact definitions. In this book, when we do use the word *cause,* we do not mean the one and only cause but rather the case in which two events (the independent variable and the dependent variable) are systematically connected in a variety of situations.

## ■ Exploratory Research

Psychologists often use the experimental method either more or less rigidly, depending on how much they already know about the phenomena they are studying and the types of questions they want to ask. In some cases, following an extensive library search for relevant information, a scientist may realize that almost nothing is known about a particular phenomenon and simply wonder what effect a given treatment will have on a person's experience. Given this situation, the scientist can use the experimental method in either of two ways.

First, when we have no idea what the effect of the independent variables will be, we are sometimes content to give the experimental treatment to a single group of research participants and then informally observe the research participants to get some idea of what aspects of behavior are affected by the independent variable. This initial exploratory use of the experimental method often is used in the initial stages of various experiments, including psychotherapy research and drug evaluation studies. Strictly speaking, this way of gaining information is not an experiment because it does not involve a control group or test specific hypotheses. It is no more than a simple demonstration that may provide either clues to fruitful independent variables for more refined analysis or potential attributes of behavior that should be reflected in the future selection of dependent variables.

The second way we use the experimental method as an exploratory tool occurs when we have some idea about which aspects of behavior will be affected by the independent variable and, consequently, have a reasonable idea of what types of dependent variables and control groups we should use, yet we do not understand the phenomenon well enough to make a specific prediction. In this way, our understanding of the phenomenon is refined progressively by a more detailed search for influential factors (independent variables that produce treatment effects) and by a more accurate estimate of their influence (measured by the dependent variables) on the phenomenon under study.

At other times, when we know a great deal about a particular topic, we can move beyond the exploratory uses of the experimental method. In these cases we are able to formulate specific predictions that reflect a more detailed theoretical understanding of the phenomenon. Because we have a clearer understanding, we are able to refine our independent and dependent variables and our use of control groups so that we can isolate more precisely the important relationships involved in the phenomenon being studied.

Whether we use the method of naturalistic observation, the correlational approach, or the experimental method, the task before us is to make inferences about the research participants' experience from the behaviors we observe. These inferences generally are related to our hypothesis or some larger theory we want to evaluate. Thus, after we look at the world through these methods, we are faced with the task of deciding how to evaluate new information we receive in light of both the methods used and our theoretical perspective. To accomplish this task, we use reason and logic. In particular, we ask whether the results of our methods as well as our conclusions are valid. To aid you in evaluating your own research and that of others, we focus on the question of validity and differentiate among some common types of validity in the next section. We also take a brief look at propositional logic.

# LOGIC AND INFERENCE: THE DETECTIVE WORK OF SCIENCE

Perhaps you have heard the story of our friend from Boston who got up every morning, went outside his house, walked around in a circle three times, and yelled at the top of his voice. His neighbor, being somewhat curious after days of this ritual, asked for the purpose behind his strange behavior. The man answered that the purpose was to keep away tigers. "But," the neighbor replied, "there are no tigers within thousands of miles of here." To which our friend replied, "Works quite well, doesn't it?"

How could we demonstrate to our friend that his yelling is not causally related to the absence of tigers? One strategy might be to point out that the absence of tigers might have come about for other reasons, including the fact that there are no tigers roaming in the greater Boston area. In technical terms, we would say that yelling could be a *necessary* condition but not a *sufficient* condition for the absence of tigers. Our friend's reasoning was incorrect because it overlooked many other plausible explanations for the obvious absence of tigers. Although our friend sought to infer a relationship between his yelling and the absence of tigers, his inference was weak.

Logic is particularly important in science as an aid to answering the question "What question should my experimental study answer to test my ideas about the world?" That is, logic can help us to answer questions of *inference*. Inference is the process by which we look at the evidence available to us and then use our powers of reasoning to reach a conclusion. Like Sherlock Holmes engaged in solving a mystery, we attempt to solve a problem based on the available evidence. Did the butler do it? No, the butler could not have done it because there was blond hair on the knife and the butler had black hair. But perhaps the butler left the blond hair there to fool us. Like a detective, scientists try to determine other factors that may be responsible for the outcome of their experiments or to piece together available information and draw general conclusions about the world. Also like the detective, the scientist is constantly asking, "Given these clues, what inference can I make, and is the inference valid?" Logic is one method for answering these questions.

## ■ Validity

Logical procedures are also important for helping us to understand the accuracy or validity of our ideas and research. *Valid* means true and capable of being supported. In psychological research we are particularly interested in two general types of validity (Campbell & Stanley,

1963). The first is **internal validity.** The word *internal* refers to the experiment itself. Internal validity asks the question, "Is there another reason that might explain the outcome of our experimental procedures?" Students are particularly sensitive to questions of internal validity, for example, when it is time for final exams; they are able to make a number of alternative suggestions as to what the exam actually measures and why it does not measure their knowledge of a particular subject. Like students, scientists look for reasons (threats to internal validity) that a particular piece of research may not measure what it claims to measure. In the case of our friend from Boston, the absence of tigers near his house could have reflected a long-standing absence of tigers in his part of the world rather than the effectiveness of his yelling. We discuss specific threats to internal validity in Chapter 6.

The second type of validity is **external validity.** The word *external* refers to the world outside the setting in which the experiment was performed. External validity often is called **generalizability.** Remember the story of Semmelweis from Chapter 1. His finding that the deaths of the mothers who had just given birth were the result of physicians touching them after handling diseased tissue was true not only for his hospital but for all other hospitals as well. Thus, in addressing the question of external validity of Semmelweis's work, we would infer that his answers could be generalized to other hospitals with other women and not just to his own original setting. Now consider the story of Galen. We would not fault his research concerning why the woman did not sleep, but we would say that it lacked external validity or generalizability. Although the insomnia of one particular woman was attributed to her love of a particular dancer, it is not true that all women who suffer from insomnia are in love with dancers. In summary, internal validity refers to the internal consistency or logic of the experiment that allows the results to be meaningful. External validity, however, refers to the possibility of applying the results from an internally valid experiment to other situations and other research participants.

We logically design our research to rule out as many alternative interpretations of our findings as possible and to have any new facts be applicable to as wide a variety of other situations as possible. In many real-life situations in which external validity is high, however, it is impossible to rule out alternative interpretations of our findings. In a similar way, in laboratory settings in which internal validity is high, the setting is often artificial and in many cases our findings cannot be generalized beyond the laboratory. Consequently, designing and conducting research is always a trade-off between internal and external validity. Which one we emphasize depends on the particular research questions being asked.

In the next section we examine propositional logic. However, before you begin that section, we suggest that you try to solve the problem presented in Box 2.1. (*Hint:* In problem solving, as well as in science, it is often more important to show what is not true rather than just focus on what is true. The solution to the problem relies on one type of logical argument, called *modus tollens,* that you will learn about in the next section.)

---

✓ **CONCEPT CHECK 2.3**    A tabloid newspaper recently described a diet in which sleep caused a person to lose weight. All the person needed to do was to exercise directly before going to bed and not eat for 6 hours before this time. The diet worked not only with the original group of research participants but also with a variety of other groups. Discuss the internal and external validity of this study.

## Box 2.1

## "Think" Squares

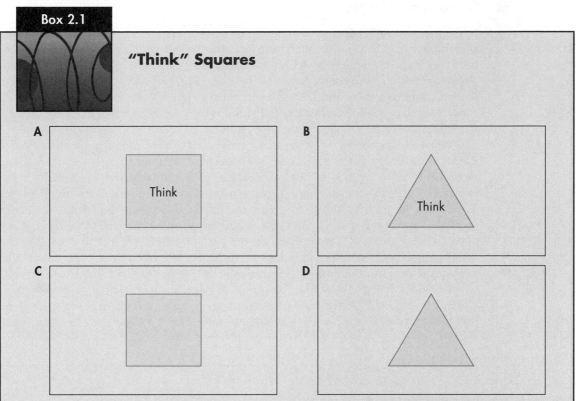

A    Think

B    Think

C

D

The illustration in this box represents four cards: A, B, C, and D. Assume that each card has a square with or without the word "Think" on one side, and a triangle with or without "Think" on the other side. Which of the cards would you have to turn over to determine whether every card that has a "Think" square on one side has a triangle without "Think" on the other?

We will make a prediction, based on previous experience, that you chose cards A and D. You may be in good company—many people choose these cards—but you were wrong. However, you were right when you chose card A. As you correctly reasoned, card A must have a triangle without "Think" on the other side for the statement to be true. However, if you turned over card D, which we did when we first tried the problem, you missed the point of the statement. The statement talks about what is opposite a "Think" square and says nothing about what is opposite a triangle. The other card that we need to turn over to solve the problem is card B. We need to

demonstrate that the negative of the statement is not true; that is, we need to demonstrate that there is no card that has a "Think" square on one side and a "Think" triangle on the other side.

We begin with the hypothesis that all cards with a "Think" square on one side have an empty triangle on the other side, which we want to test. We then move to the real situation in which there are four cards. One of these four cards, A, has a "Think" square, and we can test the truth of the statement just by turning over card A. Now comes the problem. We have tested all the visible "Think" squares (card A), so what do we do next? If it is true that all "Think" squares have empty triangles on the other side, then it must also be true that no card with a "Think" triangle has a "Think" square on the other side. Once we realize this, we know that we must look at card B to test this assumption. Thus the correct answer is cards A and B.

*Source:* After Wason (1977).

## ■ Propositional Logic

In the previous subsection, we introduced the terms *internal validity* and *external validity* and emphasized the scientist's attempt to rule out alternative explanations. In this subsection, we emphasize the way in which a scientist relies on the rules of formal logic to both *deduce* and *induce* valid conclusions. As a starting point, keep in mind that **deduction** (to deduce) is the process by which one moves from a general theory to particular statements concerning data, whereas **induction** (to induce) is the process by which one moves from a particular set of data to a general theory or concept.

When one begins with a statement and arrives at its logical consequences, this is called *deductive* reasoning. For example, one uses deductive reasoning when saying, "If it is true that schizophrenia is genetically determined, then we should find greater similarity in the presence or absence of the disorder between twins than between strangers." On the other hand, when one begins with an observation and figures out a general rule that covers it, this is called *inductive* reasoning. For example, inductive reasoning might be of the form, "I just saw a monkey use sign language to ask me for food; therefore, it is true that monkeys can communicate with humans." In summary, deductive reasoning goes from theory (the premise) to data (the conclusion), whereas inductive reasoning goes from data to theory.

Suppose a friend said to you, "You know, all experimental textbooks are really dull." You might respond, "That's not true; I am reading one right now that is really interesting." (Well, what did you expect we would have you say?) This is a logical way to disprove the

**Table 2.2**    **Forms of Propositional Logic**

| | | |
|---|---|---|
| | *Modus Ponens (confirmatory)*<br>If *p*, then *q*.<br>*p*.<br>Therefore, *q*. | *Modus Tollens (disconfirmatory)*<br>If *p*, then *q*.<br>Not *q*.<br>Therefore, not *p*. |
| Valid Arguments | If anxiety is increased, then heart rate will be increased. | If anxiety is increased, then heart rate will be increased. |
| | Anxiety is increased. Therefore, heart rate will be increased. | Heart rate is not increased. Therefore, anxiety is not increased. |
| | *Affirming the Consequent*<br>If *p*, then *q*.<br>*q*.<br>Therefore, *p*. | *Denying the Antecedent*<br>If *p*, then *q*.<br>Not *p*.<br>Therefore, not *q*. |
| Invalid Arguments | If anxiety is increased, then heart rate will be increased. | If anxiety is increased, then heart rate will be increased. |
| | Heart rate is increased. Therefore, anxiety is increased. | Anxiety is not increased. Therefore, heart rate will not be increased. |

statement "All experimental textbooks are really dull." By finding an exception to a statement, you can show it to be false.

To begin an introduction to deductive logic, let us consider this procedure in a formal way. You begin with the statement "If this is an experimental textbook, then it will be really dull." This statement is presented in a certain "If . . . then" form. Each part has a particular name. The first part, "If this is an experimental textbook," is called the **antecedent.** The second part of the statement, "then it will be really dull," is called the **consequent.** The antecedent is referred to by the letter $p$ and the consequent by the letter $q$. We now will discuss four types of propositions of the form "If $p$, then $q$." These four types are presented in Table 2.2. We should point out that other forms besides "If $p$, then $q$" are studied in propositional logic (cf. Copi, 1986; Kourany, 1987).

Let us return to our original statement. Several logical consequences may follow from that statement. Suppose that this is indeed an experimental textbook; then it follows that it will be really dull. In propositional logic, the reasoning is written out as follows:

> If this is an experimental textbook, then it will be really dull.
> It is an experimental textbook.
> Therefore, it will be really dull.

Technically, this is an argument of the form "If $p$, then $q$; given $p$ (it is an experimental textbook), then we can conclude $q$ (it will be really dull)." This form of argument is called confirmatory reasoning or **modus ponens.** Confirmatory reasoning is logically valid. We use it often both in our everyday lives and in science.

However, not all forms of argument are logically valid. Suppose we have an instance in which $q$ is true; what does this say about $p$? That is, if I can find a book that is dull, does that demonstrate that it is an experimental textbook? Of course not. There may be other kinds of books that are dull. Yet people make the following type of argument:

> If anxiety is increased, then heart rate will be increased.
> Heart rate is increased.
> Therefore, anxiety is increased.

In such a situation, we can think of many reasons why heart rate could be increased (e.g., running up the stairs, doing mental arithmetic) without anxiety being increased. This form of argument is called **affirming the consequent.** Although it is a logically invalid form of argument, one sees it used almost daily. The cartoon on the previous page offers one example of this form of reasoning. Technically, the argument could be stated as follows:

> If I were a cat, I would have four legs.
> I do have four legs.
> Therefore, I am a cat.

Let us now take the situation in which $p$ is shown not to be true. What can we logically conclude? Again, we begin with a statement of the form "If $p$, then $q$."

> If I were a cat, I would have four legs.
> I am not a cat.
> Therefore, I do not have four legs.

Of course, this is not a valid argument. We know that other animals besides cats have four legs. The dog in the cartoon is not a cat but has four legs. Thus, if $p$ is not true, it does not follow that $q$ is also not true. This invalid form of argument is called **denying the antecedent.** Consider the following:

> If Freud's theories are correct, then his therapy will be effective.
> Freud's theories are not correct.
> Therefore, his therapy will not be effective.

This is logically invalid. However, we still hear people using this form of invalid reasoning by suggesting that because Sigmund Freud's (or Fritz Perls's or B. F. Skinner's or Carl Rogers's) theories have been shown to be incorrect, his therapy cannot be effective. The effectiveness of a particular therapy is determined empirically; such a determination has little to do with theoretical formulations.

This brings us to the fourth situation. If the consequent is not true, then what does this tell us about the antecedent? (If $q$ is not true, then $p$ is . . . ?) If $q$ is not true, then $p$ is also not true. Returning to a previous example and modifying it appropriately, we have the following argument:

> If I were a cat, I would have four legs.
> I do not have four legs.
> Therefore, I am not a cat.

This is a valid form of reasoning. It is called *disconfirmatory reasoning* or **modus tollens.** In the Freud example, we could make the following valid argument using modus tollens:

If Freud's theories are valid, then his therapy will be effective.
His therapy is not effective.
Therefore, Freud's theories are not valid.

Karl Popper (see Box 2.2) suggests that *modus tollens* arguments are at the heart of the scientific testing of theories. He points out that our theories should lead to some prediction. If the prediction is found to be untrue, then we conclude that our theory is incorrect. This is valid reasoning. However, the opposite is not the case. Finding that a prediction is true does not logically lead one to conclude that the theory is true, any more than having four legs made the dog in the cartoon into a cat. Research results may fail to refute a theory, but they cannot prove the theory to be correct. Thus, Popper suggests that our efforts in science should be concentrated on attempting to disprove hypotheses; he calls this procedure *falsification*.

---

**Box 2.2**

## Philosophy of Science: Sir Karl Popper (Falsification Approach)

Sir Karl Popper has devoted much of his career to answering the questions "What is science?" and "How is science performed?" Although these questions may at first seem easy to you, consider such areas as astrology and Marxism. Could these approaches be considered scientific? Why not?

*Falsificationism* is the name given to Popper's description of how science is performed. Falsificationism suggests that science should be concerned with disproving or falsifying theories through logic based on observation. How is this accomplished? First, a scientist must create a consistent falsifiable hypothesis. A falsifiable hypothesis is one that can be shown to be false. For example, the hypothesis "It will rain in Tuscaloosa, Alabama, on Tuesday, December 23, 2007" is falsifiable: If it does not rain on that day, the hypothesis will be shown to be false. Likewise, the hypothesis "All objects regardless of weight will fall to earth at approximately the same speed" is falsifiable; it can be tested by experiment. However, a hypothesis such as "ESP (extrasensory perception) exists" is not falsifiable. Even the hypothesis "Gravity exists" is untestable. It may be true that both ESP and gravity exist, yet until the hypothesis is stated in a form that can be falsified, the hypothesis is not testable. Second, once a scientist has a falsifiable hypothesis, the task is to develop a test of the hypothesis. Third, the hypothesis is tested. Fourth, if the hypothesis is shown to be false, a new hypothesis is developed.

Using this model, Popper emphasizes science as a process for the elimination of false theories. If you accept the suggestion that all psychological research is inductive in nature, you must then conclude with Popper that the major role of science is the falsification of incorrect theories. This line of reasoning also leads one to conclude that science, particularly psychology, never *proves* a hypothesis. Science, according to Popper, only shows that the hypothesis has not been proved false.

*Note:* Although Popper usually is discussed in terms of the falsification position, his recent writings emphasize research programs rather than single theories.

We want to emphasize that deductive logic is one of many tools of the scientist. Like the experimental method, logic is an approach to knowledge designed to help us evaluate and direct our research questions. Because of the complexity of the world in which we live and the limits of our own minds in perceiving this complexity precisely, we find ourselves as scientists using a combination of both inductive and deductive approaches to knowledge in our science as well as in our lives. We often use deductive and inductive approaches as a means of gaining information, which becomes a clue as we attempt to interact with and understand the world in which we live. Logic offers us a means of evaluating the inferences we draw from these clues. Logic helps us to understand the limits on our claims to certitude. Quite often logic helps us to see that we do not know enough to make any claim at all. In this manner, logic tends to make the scientific process conservative in its claims. However, it does not follow that our research topics, our ideas, or our theories also must be conservative.

# SCIENTIFIC OBSERVATION: THE RAW DATA OF SCIENCE

Have you ever heard the question "If a tree fell in the middle of the forest without anyone around, would there be any sound?" This question reflects a philosophical problem in science that was solved in physics at the beginning of this century. Until that time, the notion of physicists was that they study *events* in the world. In this earlier worldview, the job of the scientist was to be a passive observer and accurately watch events that take place either in the real world or in experiments. There was no thought that the process of observing might influence the perception of the very events being observed. From the earlier perspective, it was meaningful to ask whether the sound existed. However, this has changed.

According to modern physics, scientists do not record events. Instead, scientists record their *observations of events.* They record their experience of the world and base their science on these perceptions. This development amounts to a simple acceptance of the fact that in science we can get no closer to the world than our observations of it.

Let us return for a moment to the child who is discovering the world for the first time. Imagine that you are a small child who is still crawling and cannot yet stand. As you move around your world, what do you see? What do you know about events that take place and objects that are more than 3 feet above the ground? Some events you may know by their sound, such as a passing car or your father's electric razor. Other events you may recognize only by smell, such as the cooking of bacon or bleach being added to the wash. Other events you could know only from the sensation involved, such as your father or mother picking you up and throwing you in the air and catching you. Suppose someone could talk with you at this age and ask you to describe what the world was like. What would you say? How would the adult you were talking to react to your description? Would he or she say it was a true, accurate, and acceptable view of the world?

As you begin to answer these questions, you see that your description as a child was from your own perspective. You also may realize that it is difficult to say whether this description was true or false. From your viewpoint as an adult, it was incomplete. In the same way that the view of a child's world is relative to where and when the child lives and observes the world, the view of the scientist and, consequently, the *facts of science* are *relative* to the current notions of working scientists and the instruments they use to make observations.

The current notion concerning science and accepted methods, which encompasses a philosophical way of seeing the world, is called a **paradigm.** Philosopher of science Thomas Kuhn has elaborated a particular view of how science progresses, based on the concept of paradigm (see Box 2.3). Although there is much debate about the exact meaning of the word *paradigm,* most scientists understand it to mean shared beliefs, which include topics to be studied and the types of answers that will be given. For example, the current scientific paradigm in psychology emphasizes the importance of quantitative measurement. Thus scientific psychology, as you will learn it, directs you toward topics that can be measured quantitatively.

Not only are the results and conclusions of our research relative to our current notions of science, but they also may relate to our own psychology. Consider the role of the experimenter in the psychological experiment. Do you think your own state (hungry, sad, tired, excited, and so on) could influence the data of an experiment? That is just one of the

---

**Box 2.3**

## Philosophy of Science: Thomas Kuhn

When Newton said, "I stand on the shoulders of giants," he was referring to the people who came before him and on whose work he was able to build his scientific system. Many of us have similar ideas when it comes to the progression of science. We think that each new discovery is simply added to old discoveries, with the results being a gradual accumulation of knowledge.

Thomas Kuhn (1970) suggests that this view is wrong. Kuhn proposes that science actually goes through a series of revolutions. Following each revolution, a new system or method for performing science is instituted. The new system or worldview is called a paradigm, or set of assumptions, which guides scientific activity until a new revolution and paradigm shift take place. The stable period between revolutions is called normal science. Normal science is the process of problem solving, which most of us think of when someone uses the term *science.* Normal science for Kuhn is always science performed in relation to a particular paradigm.

As an example of the role of paradigms, assume that you were a mapmaker before the time of Columbus. You would draw your maps as if the world were flat because that was the accepted belief. As a mapmaker, you would never think to question this belief; it was a given in your task of drawing maps. Then there came a mapmaker's version of a scientific revolution. The paradigm shifted to that of a world that was round. As a mapmaker, you would now draw the world as if it were round and you would continue with this system until a new revolution came along. This, of course, was the replacing of the earth as the center of the solar system with the sun as the center. In the same way that mapmakers work in relation to present-day assumptions and beliefs about the world, Kuhn suggests that scientists also work in relation to a set of beliefs or paradigms until these are replaced by a revolution.

factors we consider later in this book. The important point now is to realize that the state of the experimenter is important. Because the scientist is not *passive* but is *actively* searching for answers, he or she can actually influence the event being recorded by the very manner in which the observation is being made. The scientist can change the world and our understanding of it. Thus, the scientist is more than a passive observer; he or she is a real actor in the drama of science.

## EVALUATING SCIENTIFIC RESEARCH

Regardless of the amount of work involved in scientific research, an extremely important aspect of *any* research endeavor is whether the final product is worthy of being reported to the scientific community. We must ask whether our conclusions are *accurate,* capable of being *replicated,* and *relevant* to others. In this book we emphasize four ways to ensure the high quality of our research.

The first is through impartial, systematic observation using logically sound experimental design. The experimental method based on random sampling and assignment (as we describe later) is the most powerful class of research design currently available. We emphasize this technique in the initial chapters of this book and later discuss some other scientific approaches.

The second way to ensure meaningful research is through statistical description and inference. We show how statistics can help us decide whether our results are due to some causal agent or merely to chance.

The third method of quality control is through reason and logic. In discussing logic, we emphasize types of validity as well as types of propositional logic and how they help us evaluate research.

The fourth and final way is by emphasizing perspective and context. In particular, we suggest that conclusions be viewed from the perspectives of the scientist, the research participant, and the witness.

Although this book emphasizes the perspective of the scientist, it is important to remember the experiences of the research participant and the perspective of the witness if our conclusions are to have meaning. We believe that through these four ways of evaluating research a person can use science and maintain the high level of excellence that a science of behavior and experience requires.

## COMMUNICATION IN SCIENCE

Unlike the child who is busy learning about the world, scientists must share what they learn about the world with other people, especially other scientists. More than 2000 years ago, Aristotle emphasized this when he taught that science had two parts: inquiry and argument. In modern terms, inquiry is represented by the research that answers our questions about the world, and argument refers in part to the scientist's responsibility to inform others of the findings. Consequently, we design our research, record our observations, and summarize our findings in a manner that others can understand. For scientists to answer a question in terms that only he or she can understand would not be complete science because it is not shared knowledge. The final product of mature science is a communication that summarizes a conclusion about the world and is directed to both scientists and non-scientists.

Learning to communicate in science may be compared to learning a foreign language. One of your first tasks is to learn the vocabulary of science. You need to understand what a scientist means by certain words. You initially may say that is easy, because many scientists speak English anyway. That may be true, but it can also be a problem because English words can have slightly different or even totally different meanings when used in the context of a scientific statement.

For example, suppose you were reading a newspaper article concerning a new discovery in subatomic physics. The article is about particles with "color and charm." If you were to talk to a physicist, you would find that in this context *color* and *charm* have nothing to do with colors or with the particles being appealing. These words have special meaning for the physicist.

Likewise in psychology, common words may be used in a special or technical way. For example, B. F. Skinner discussed *negative reinforcements* as applied to people, yet *negative reinforcements* have nothing to do with punishment, as many people think. Likewise, Carl Jung used the words *extravert* and *introvert,* which have a technical meaning different from their uses in newspapers and magazines. Even as common a word as *sex* was given a scientific meaning (by Freud) as distinctive as the physicists' terms *color* and *charm.*

At first, the language of science may seem strange. Yet, as with any language, once you learn some words and phrases, you can begin to understand what is going on. This understanding will be useful not only to those of you who pursue careers as scientists, but also to all of us in our daily interactions with the world as we try to understand what we read about science and strive to become more educated consumers. You have a twofold task. First, you must seek to understand how words are used in research in a technical way. You cannot just assume that because you have heard a word you already know its meaning. Second, in writing your own reports you must seek to define your words and ideas as precisely as possible so that others can understand and follow what you are saying.

# KEY TERMS AND CONCEPTS

1. **Overview of science**
   A. Hypothesis
   B. Observation, correlation, and experimentation
   C. Inference and conclusion
   D. Modeling
   E. Qualitative methods
   F. Quantitative methods
2. **Types of questions**
   A. "If I do this, what will happen?"
   B. "If I do this, I expect this will happen."

3. **Role of scientist**
   A. In naturalistic observation
   B. In experimental method
4. **Naturalistic observation**
   A. Four characteristics
      ▪ Noninterference
      ▪ Determining patterns
      ▪ Useful for "big picture"
      ▪ Descriptive
5. **Correlational approach**

*(continued)*

## KEY TERMS AND CONCEPTS *(continued)*

**A.** Positive and negative correlations
**B.** Association versus causality
**6. Experimental method**
  **A.** Key question
  - "Was what happened really a result of what I did?"
  **B.** Definitions
  - Hypothesis
  - Experimental group
  - Control group
  - Operational definition, two types
  - Independent variable (also called *treatment variable)*
  - Dependent variable
  - Treatment effect
  - Confounding variables
**7. Causation in science**
  **A.** Necessary conditions

**B.** Sufficient conditions
**C.** Correlation
**8. Validity**
  **A.** Internal validity
  **B.** External validity and generalizability
**9. Forms of propositional logic**
  **A.** Deduction and induction
  **B.** Correct reasoning
  - Confirmatory (modus ponens)
  - Disconfirmatory (modus tollens)
  **C.** Incorrect reasoning
  - Denying the antecedent
  - Affirming the consequent
**10. Falsificationism**
  **A.** Karl Popper
**11. Paradigm**
  **A.** Thomas Kuhn
**12. The language of science**

## SUMMARY

1. Science is one way of learning about the world that involves articulating an idea or hypothesis, using experience developed in research to evaluate the idea, and drawing conclusions or inferences from experimentation and observation about the idea or hypothesis.

2. Observation is an important part of science. The naturalistic observation procedure emphasizes observation and has four characteristics: (1) noninterference, (2) observations of patterns and invariants, (3) development of the "big picture" or learning about an unknown process, and (4) provision of descriptions rather than pinpointing specific factors that influence one another.

3. Experimentation offers a means of creating control and determining the manner in which one factor influences another. This determination is aided by the use of a control group, which allows you to evaluate the effects of the independent variable on the dependent variable.

4. The purpose of correlational study is to determine the association between two variables but not the manner in which one variable affects another.

5. Scientists use logic and inference to draw conclusions and rule out alternative hypotheses. The study of propositional logic points to both the logical and the illogical conclusions that may be drawn from general statements.

6. A researcher must question the validity of conclusions drawn from research. Two major types of validity are discussed. Internal validity refers to the experiment itself and asks whether there are alternative explanations (such as confounding variables) that would invalidate the reported relationship between the independent and dependent variables. External validity poses the question of generalizability and asks to what other groups or situations a particular set of findings might be applicable.

7. Science reflects a history of observations of events. As a recorder of observations, it is important for you to be sensitive to factors that can influence the record you make and to understand that any record is always presented from a certain perspective, recently called a *paradigm*. It is likewise important that communications in science be clear and be stated in such a manner that they can be evaluated.

# REVIEW QUESTIONS

1. What is one difference between qualitative and quantitative methods?
2. What are four characteristics of naturalistic observation?
3. What is an experimental group, and what is a control group?
4. What is an operational definition, and is there more than one type?
5. In the final cereal experiment, identify the independent variable and the dependent variable.
6. Distinguish between a sufficient and a necessary cause.
7. What is meant by the terms *internal validity* and *external validity*?
8. What does the term *falsificationism* mean in science?
9. How would modern physics answer the question "If a tree fell in the forest without anyone to hear it, would there be any sound?"
10. What are the two invalid forms of propositional logic discussed in this chapter? Give an example of each.
11. What are the two valid forms of propositional logic discussed in this chapter? Give an example of each.

# DISCUSSION QUESTIONS AND PROJECTS

1. Use the library as the site for a naturalistic observation study. Go to the library, find a place from which you can observe, and record what you see. One focus might be the pattern of interactions among people in the library. If you were an outsider looking at these data, what might you conclude about the function of the library for students?
2. Give the "Think" squares problem in Box 2.1 to some of your friends. Using naturalistic observation, record what they do as they go about solving the problem. You might time them, record what they say (if anything), notice facial expressions, and so on.
3. Have another group verbalize what they are thinking as they try to solve the "Think" squares problem. You might decide whether there are similarities in the verbalizations of the different people. If you record the verbalizations, it will make the task easier. How do you go about deciding whether the verbalizations of two different people are similar? What categories do you look for?
4. Put people who are knowledgeable about a particular sport in one group and people who know little about it in another group. A knowledgeable person should describe in detail some particular play or move from the sport; you then ask both groups to recall what was said. Notice whether there is any difference between the two groups in the amount of re-

call. What other differences are there between the two groups?
5. Discuss how you might turn the observations in Questions 3 and 4 into experiments. What would be the independent and the dependent variables?
6. Assume that you followed the directions in Question 4 and found that people who knew about the sport remembered more. Discuss the following conclusion: "This experiment demonstrates that playing sports helps to increase your ability to remember, so sports should be required in all schools."
7. Discuss the statement "Scientists do not record events but only their observations of events."
8. An experimenter was interested in creativity. In particular, she wanted to know whether a person is more creative at one time of day than another. At the time, she was teaching two sections of an introductory psychology course. One class met from 8:00 to 9:00 A.M. and the other from 4:30 to 5:30 P.M. She used a well-known creativity test and gave the test to each of her classes. When she scored the test she found that those who took the test in the morning did better than those who took it in the afternoon. The experimenter concluded that, in general, college students are more creative in the morning than in the afternoon. Discuss this conclusion. Are there other ways in which these data might be interpreted?

## InfoTrac College Edition: Exercises

Using InfoTrac College Edition, you can learn more about two philosophers of science who were introduced in this chapter, Sir Karl Popper and Thomas Kuhn, by entering their names.

Another topic introduced in this chapter was logic. Using InfoTrac College Edition, look up the article called "Deductive reasoning," by Johnson-Laird, which was published in the 1999 *Annual Review of Psychology.* (*Hint:* You can either enter *Johnson-Laird* or the term *deductive reasoning.*) As you read this article, think about how we may use logic differently in everyday life as compared with science. You may also think about how our tendencies to think in a certain way in everyday life (e.g., to always look for proof and not refutation) may bias our scientific world.

You can also look at the article on "thinking" by Arthur B. Markman and Debre Gentner in the 2001 *Annual Review of Psychology.* This article also discusses deductive reasoning.

If you entered the term *deductive reasoning* in InfoTrac College Edition, you will note a research article entitled "Neuroanatomical correlates of human reason," published in *The Journal of Cognitive Neuroscience* in 1998. As you read this research article using brain imaging techniques, you will learn that deductive reasoning is associated with left hemispheric brain activation but not right hemispheric activation. What does that tell us about deductive reasoning?

## ✓ Answers to Concept Checks

**2.1** Neither, we hope. Although either or both could be correct, a correlation will not give you that information. A correlation will only describe a relationship but not the direction of the relationship. That is, you cannot state whether one variable influenced another or even whether there was a third variable that influenced both.

**2.2** The independent variable is the variable that the experimenter manipulates. The type of tape, video versus audio, is the independent variable. The dependent variable is the score or measurement influenced by the independent variable. In this case, the final exam grade is the dependent variable.

**2.3** Because the results were obtained in a variety of settings, we may assume there are few problems with the external validity of the study. However, there may be a problem with the internal validity because the experiment does not actually show that sleep is a necessary condition for weight loss to take place. It may be that the exercise and not eating for 6 hours will result in a weight loss even without sleep.

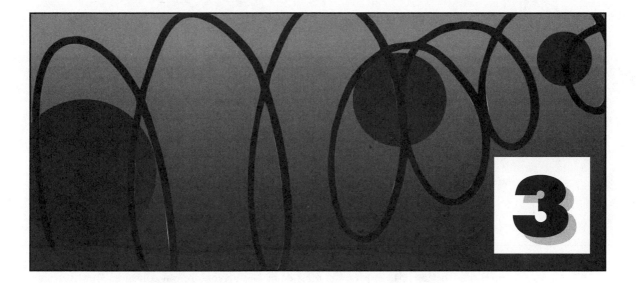

# DEVELOPING THE HYPOTHESIS

Imagine that your instructor in this course has just announced that you are to begin an *experiment* of your own and that you are to start right now. What do you do? Where do you begin? This chapter answers these questions and helps you to begin your first experiment. As Lewis Carroll once said, the best place to begin is at the beginning.

As with any other human activity, excellence and enjoyment in research begin with genuine interest in the topic. When confronted with their first experiments, students may overlook the fact that research begins with interest. Consequently, your first task is simply to sit back and let your interests emerge. Some of you have already done this and are aware of your interests in various areas of psychology. For most of you, however, strong interests have not yet begun to emerge. One way of discovering your interests is to begin exploring various areas of psychology and observing your reactions to each area.

For example, you might look through your introductory psychology book and see which areas engage you. Once you realize what areas interest you, you might go to the library and look through some textbooks or other books specifically devoted to these areas. You might also talk with psychologists who live in your community and learn more about what they do and what types of questions they ask in their daily work. As your interests unfold, keep in mind that the interests of even the most dedicated person are not constant. They fluctuate from day to day; sometimes they are strong and sometimes they are forgotten. Over a period of years, a scientist may change interests many times. Regardless of the constancy of interests, they can be valuable guides that enable us to enjoy our interactions with the world.

When researchers are interested in a given topic, they learn all they can about it. They go to the library and read about the topic. They go to conferences and talk to other researchers about it. They actively think about the topic. After a time, many researchers find their topic spontaneously arising in their thoughts as they take showers, as they fall asleep, as they eat breakfast. Like a child playing with a new toy, scientists consider their topics from ever-changing perspectives. Some researchers even amuse themselves by trying to describe their topics as if all their ideas about it were backward. The main idea is that they *play* with their thoughts to gain new perspectives.

## MAKING OUR HYPOTHESES CONCRETE

The essence of a scientific experiment is to see whether our ideas about the world are accurate. In its simplest form it is an interface, a meeting point, between our ideas and reality, between our psychological world and the physical world. This distinction is one aspect of the differentiation we made in Chapter 1 between experience (psychological world) and behavior (physical world). To bridge this gap successfully, we first must realize that our intellectual ideas or hypotheses about the world, like our emotions or sensory experiences, are personal experiences. They cannot be shared directly with other people, no matter how hard we try. They are private knowledge. Yet science is objective in that its conclusions can be seen and checked by anyone.

This points to a dilemma: How can we scientifically evaluate our completely private ideas about the world? One answer is to define or represent our private ideas in terms of specific behaviors or concrete activities that anyone can witness or repeat. These representations of psychological events in the physical world are called *operational definitions*. An operational definition defines events in terms of the operations required to measure them and thus gives our idea a concrete meaning. For example, the idea that watching violence on television increases aggression is certainly a reasonable and potentially important notion. Yet before we can test it, we must define exactly what is meant by violence on television. Is a program with an unseen murder more violent than an exciting boxing match? Should violence be rated by how many minutes it appears on the screen, by the particular type of act, by how much blood is shown, or by a combination of all three? Likewise, to perform this research we need to devise some measure of aggression. Let us take another example. Suppose we wanted to test the idea that psychotherapy is effective. Before we could do that, we have to define what psychotherapy is and what can be considered a measure of effectiveness. We would have to adopt operational definitions.

An operational definition takes a general concept, such as aggression or effectiveness, and places it within a given context; that is, *it redefines the concept in terms of clearly observable operations that anyone can see and repeat.* For example, we might define aggression as the number of times a child hits a toy after watching a violent television show. Likewise, we might define effectiveness in psychotherapy as measured by a score on a personality test or how well a person functions in personal relationships or at work. We could also use the number of days that a person stays out of a mental hospital as an operational definition of the effectiveness of therapy.

In each of these cases we have redefined an idea in terms of specified operations. We define an idea (psychological world) in terms of operations (physical world) that are required to produce the phenomenon (physical world) that the idea (psychological world) represents. The cyclic nature represents what science is all about: movement back and forth between our ideas and physical reality. Operational definitions make it possible to tie our ideas and hypotheses to objects and operations in physical reality.

One problem we face with operational definitions is that a given concept may be defined in several ways. Conversely, a given operational definition defines only a limited aspect of the original concept. Although we all realize that the grade you receive on a multiple-choice final exam is a narrow facet of all you may have learned in a college course, it is, strictly speaking, an adequate operational definition of your performance.

Suppose we were interested in studying the effectiveness of a new form of psychotherapy on severely depressed people. Regardless of the research design we use, one task we would face is operationally defining the dependent variable: depression. We know that depression can manifest itself in a variety of ways (see Figure 3.1). Each of these ways can become the focus of an operational definition of depression. For example, we know that the biochemistry of depressed patients undergoes certain changes, so these characteristics would constitute an adequate operational definition of depression. We also know that therapists generally agree on which patients are depressed, so we might operationally define the degree of depression in our research participants by the estimates of various therapists. However, the question of which operational definition is best is tricky. Ideally, it is safest to use several operational definitions. In this case, we might define depression as a certain score on some depression test plus a "depressed" rating by a therapist and the participant's subjective report of feeling depressed. If this battery of operational definitions is not possible, then at least we should select one that is known to be correlated with others. In selecting operational definitions, remember that they are arbitrary but are often guided by previous research in the area.

When we specify the operational definition, we are helping others to understand the manner in which our measurements took place. As Cronbach and Meehl (1955) point out,

Figure 3.1

From any one global construct, there are several possible operational definitions, depending on the questions asked and the type of population studied.

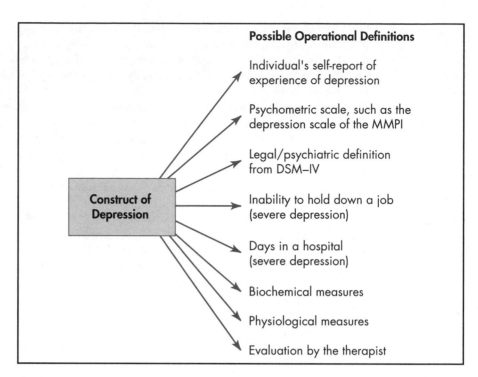

**Possible Operational Definitions**

Construct of Depression

Individual's self-report of experience of depression

Psychometric scale, such as the depression scale of the MMPI

Legal/psychiatric definition from DSM–IV

Inability to hold down a job (severe depression)

Days in a hospital (severe depression)

Biochemical measures

Physiological measures

Evaluation by the therapist

however, it is rare for a researcher to accept an operational definition as the sole definition of the construct being studied. Although we may define *hunger* operationally in an animal experiment as "amount of time since last feeding," Cronbach and Meehl suggest that we also have other ideas in mind when we use the construct *hunger*. For example, the construct of hunger might also be related to the amount of energy an animal would expend to seek food. This multiplicity of meaning represents such an important point that Cronbach and Meehl suggest that we need to be concerned about a particular type of validity they call *construct validity*.

Construct validity asks whether the procedure we are using is actually an adequate definition of the construct we are measuring. This is an important concept. If we have a test for intelligence, we would want to know what factors or constructs determine the score of this particular test. In terms of an experiment, we want to know how valid is our inference about the construct we are measuring, based on the specific manipulations and measurements used. Thus, one must ask whether dropping an apple gives us an adequate basis for making inferences about the construct of gravity. Likewise, in our depression example, one must ask whether a particular measure of depression allows us to make valid inferences about the construct of depression.

---

✓ CONCEPT CHECK 3.1    Which of the following is an operational definition of verbal ability: (a) the ability to read a book, (b) the ability to watch television, (c) the score on the verbal part of the SAT, or (d) the ability to have a conversation?

# MAKING OUR HYPOTHESES LOGICAL

As mentioned in Chapter 2, when we begin our experiment we are in either of two positions concerning what we already know about a research area. In some cases we already know a great deal and can use the experimental method to test specific predictions and hypotheses. Hypotheses of this type take the form "I expect this will happen if. . . . " In other cases we know little and use the experimental method as an exploratory tool. Hypotheses of this type take the form "I wonder what will happen if. . . . " As it turns out, the types of logic underlying these two types of hypotheses are fundamentally different.

## ■ The "I Wonder What Will Happen If" Hypothesis and Inductive Reasoning

If we are working in a new area (e.g., the early days of AIDS research) and know little about the phenomenon we are studying, we have no clear ideas from which to make specific predictions. In this case we use naturalistic observation, correlational studies, and the experimental method to generate new data from which we can begin to formulate a preliminary idea about how the phenomenon is organized. This process of generalizing from a specific instance or even several new facts to a more general idea is called *inductive reasoning* (see Figure 3.2). We use inductive reasoning to increase our knowledge by generalizing new facts to a new understanding.

For example, we use inductive reasoning when, observing a chimpanzee using sign language with a person, we conclude that chimpanzees can communicate with humans. We are generalizing from a specific event to a general idea about how the world is. The danger with this form of logic is overlooking unobserved factors that may be responsible for the effects we observe. For example, you may know someone who is 106 years old and eats yogurt. From this observation, you may conclude that yogurt makes people live longer. This is an invalid use of inductive reasoning because any number of other factors may contribute to this person's longevity. As mentioned in Chapter 2, the internal validity supporting this conclusion is questionable.

## ■ The "I Expect This Would Happen If" Hypothesis and Deductive Reasoning

If we already knew a great deal about a particular phenomenon and had formulated a clear-cut idea or theory, then we might deduce a specific hypothesis to predict how unexamined but related phenomena operate. In its simplest form, deductive reasoning takes the form of an if-then statement: If my idea about the world is correct, then this cause should produce the following effect. For example, we use deductive reasoning when we say: "If it is true that schizophrenia is determined genetically (general idea about world), then we should find a greater incidence of the disorder between twins than between strangers (specific consequence of heredity)." The terms of the hypothesis could be defined operationally, an experiment conducted, and a decision made about the accuracy of this particular hypothesis. If the hypothesis is supported, then this new fact strengthens the confidence we have that schizophrenia is genetically determined. If it is not supported, then we have reason to

**Figure 3.2**

Inductive and
deductive
relationships
between
observation
and theory

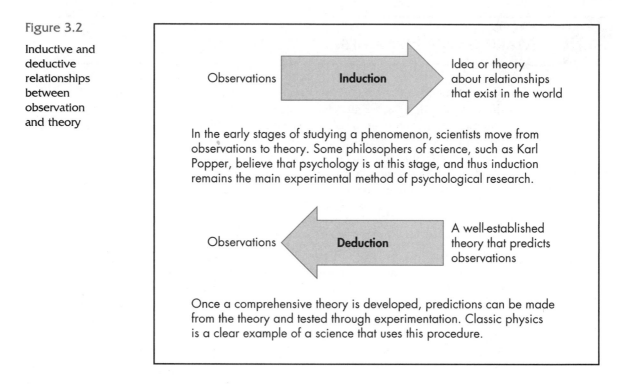

Observations → **Induction** → Idea or theory about relationships that exist in the world

In the early stages of studying a phenomenon, scientists move from observations to theory. Some philosophers of science, such as Karl Popper, believe that psychology is at this stage, and thus induction remains the main experimental method of psychological research.

Observations ← **Deduction** ← A well-established theory that predicts observations

Once a comprehensive theory is developed, predictions can be made from the theory and tested through experimentation. Classic physics is a clear example of a science that uses this procedure.

question our idea that schizophrenia is determined genetically. Thus, the outcome of the experiment helps us to infer logically the relationship between events. As we observe throughout the book, the stronger our research design, the better we are able to infer a given relationship between events.

## ■ Strong Inference

An important procedure for examining hypotheses is that of *strong inference* (Platt, 1964). Platt proposes that certain fields of science have progressed quickly because of the adoption of the method of strong inference. Strong inference is characterized by the following four steps:

1. Devise alternative hypotheses.
2. Devise a crucial experiment (or several experiments) with alternative possible outcomes, each of which would exclude one or more of the hypotheses.
3. Carry out the experiment to get clear results.
4. Return to step 1 with further refinements of the supported hypothesis.

Let us see how we could apply this technique. Assume you lived during the time of Galileo and wanted to apply this procedure to the study of falling weights. Aristotle assumed that if you dropped two weights, the heavier would land first, whereas Galileo suggested that both weights would hit the earth at the same time. Applying the method of strong inference, we could drop two weights and hypothesize that if the heavier weight hit first, then Aristotle's hypothesis would be supported, whereas if they hit at the same time,

Galileo's hypothesis would be supported. Once it was determined that Galileo's hypothesis was supported, then a scientist could begin further refinements of the theory.

Platt likens the procedure of strong inference to climbing a tree: Each choice is dependent on the previous one taken. Platt sees strong inference not only as a method for rapid progress in science but also as a procedure at the heart of every scientist's thinking:

> Obviously it should be applied as much to one's own thinking as to others'. It consists of asking in your own mind, on hearing any scientific explanation or theory put forward, "But sir, what experiment could disprove your hypothesis?"; or on hearing a scientific experiment described, "But sir, what hypothesis does your experiment disprove?" (Platt, 1964, p. 352)

This quote includes an extremely important point. We need to consider not only what results would support our hypothesis but also what results would disprove our hypothesis. In this manner, Platt's procedure of strong inference emphasizes the problem-solving aspects of science and the search for adequate theoretical conceptualizations, as well as serving as a heuristic to help you determine whether your ideas about the world are stated in the form of a testable hypothesis.

# CREATING TESTABLE RESEARCH HYPOTHESES AND THE PROBLEM OF MEASUREMENT

Making the transition from a general idea to a testable research hypothesis is not always a simple task. Most students present their ideas in the form of a general statement and tend to ask global questions. It is not that their questions are unimportant or uninteresting; it is just that they are untestable in the form in which they are presented. It is only with considerable work and practice that an interesting idea can be rephrased into a testable hypothesis that clearly spells out a specific relationship among variables.

Many areas of psychology are rarely researched because of the difficulty in making the transition to adequate research hypotheses. Areas such as romantic love, creativity, extrasensory perception, sanity, and mental illness are some examples. Because of the nature of the questions, some areas may even be outside the realm of testability, as illustrated by the cartoon. Even for the experienced scientist, the transition from a general idea to a specific research hypothesis requires careful thought and consideration. Often, as Cohen (1990) suggests in his discussion of methodology, "less is more." By this he means that in designing a study it is important to keep it simple and not to study too many different aspects of a particular phenomenon at one time. It is not always easy to ask a question that can be answered scientifically.

One aspect of the transition to a testable research hypothesis is **measurement**. Measurement considerations help determine the way we develop our operational definitions. We want to make certain that our variables are measured accurately and consistently. In technical terms, we speak of **reliability** and **validity**. For a method of measurement to pass the test of reliability, the measurements must be consistent.

For example, a bathroom scale is reliable if it gives you the same weight no matter how many times you stand on it (assuming your weight does not change between weighings).

"IT MAY VERY WELL BRING ABOUT IMMORTALITY, BUT IT WILL TAKE FOREVER TO TEST IT."

Most of our measures such as intelligence or treatment effectiveness show more variation than a physical measure such as weight. For this reason when researchers are first designing a measure for a particular construct (e.g., depression), it is common for the researchers to give the same measure over a number of occasions under similar conditions. They then examine the consistency of the research participants' responses to determine **test-retest reliability,** which is the correlation between the scores on each of the testing occasions.

In any study you want to use instruments that show a high positive correlation between these occasions. In addition, we also need the people who make the observations in a research study to be reliable in their ratings of particular behaviors. Like test-retest reliability, we can correlate the ratings of different observers when examining the same behavioral pattern. This is referred to as inter-rater reliability and will be discussed in greater detail in Chapter 10.

For a method of measurement to pass the test of validity, it must be accurate. In the example of the bathroom scale, the reading must accurately reflect your weight in some unit of measurement such as pounds. Now suppose that a well-meaning friend wanted you to lose weight, so he or she set your scale at 5 pounds overweight. At 5 pounds overweight, your scale would still be reliable; that is, it would continue to give you a *consistent* weight each time you weighed yourself. However, at 5 pounds overweight, the measurement would not be *valid;* that is, the scale would not reflect your *true* weight.

To be valid, a measurement must reflect the *true* score within certain limits. These limits are determined by what we know scientifically about a given construct. Unlike a physical measure such as temperature, which is based on the kinetic theory of heat, most of our measures—such as anxiety or intelligence or reaction time—are based on less well articulated theory. For this reason, questions of reliability and validity must be considered in some detail and we will address them throughout this book. Our goal is to use methods of measurement that as much as possible are both accurate (valid) and consistent (reliable) in our experiments.

To return to your psychological experiment, it is your task to choose methods of measurement that are both accurate (valid) and consistent (reliable) in relation to the question you are asking. Yet how do you select methods of measurement that are both reliable and valid for your purposes? You can either begin from scratch and demonstrate that your methods of measurement are indeed reliable and valid, or review the literature to determine which methods of measurement have been used by others and adopt those methods.

Because the first option for many areas of study often is a difficult and lengthy process requiring highly technical expertise, we recommend that you choose the second option and pattern your measurement devices on those that have been established in the literature. We do not recommend that you do this blindly, however, but that you continue to remember the problems of reliability and validity. Even if you are merely having a person press a button that measures reaction time, you still must determine what construct this device validly measures. In other words, if you were interested in the construct of information processing, you would first ask what would be a good measure of information processing. You would look for a measure with numerous empirical studies to support it, and you might conclude that reaction time was one such measure. In the final analysis, the task of choosing good measures is yours, although you may be greatly aided by previously published studies, as well as by your own experience in experimentation.

---

☑ CONCEPT
CHECK 3.2    The clock in the animal behavior lab is always 5 minutes fast. Would it be a reliable instrument to use to time 30 minutes of free play for animals?

---

# OVERVIEW

It may seem as if you have many decisions to make—and in a sense you do—but you also must remember that much of the process of performing science is learned through experience. Although there are guidelines for how to perform experiments and answer questions through science, many of the procedures that must be devised are learned through performing experiments. As you become more familiar with the process of experimentation, you will come to see which considerations of good experimental design are most appropriate in which situations. For now, you must rely mainly on understanding the logic of experimentation.

As we discuss in the next section, all experiments begin with an idea or consideration of the world in which we live. This consideration or idea is then formulated in terms of a general statement or question. For example, you may think that schizophrenia is related to diet or that

Figure 3.3

Steps required before experimentation

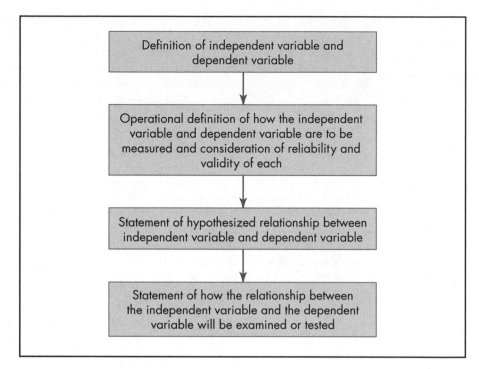

anxiety is related to too much homework, or you might be interested in the factors that produce helping behavior. Whatever your idea, you must then translate it into a scientific research question or hypothesis; that is, you must develop a testable statement that points out what specific variables are to be examined and the hypothesized relationship between them.

At this point you rely on operational definitions, as we discussed previously. If you have clearly stated (1) your independent and dependent variables; (2) how each is measured, taking into account reliability and validity; (3) the hypothesized relationship between the independent and dependent variables; and (4) how this hypothesized relationship is to be tested, then you have passed one of the major hurdles of performing a scientific experiment (see Figure 3.3).

Once you have overcome this hurdle, you are ready to move on and consider the process of experimentation itself, which we return to in Chapter 6. As you consider this process we also want you to think about how your research participants may be influenced by your procedures (which we describe in great detail in Chapter 14 when we discuss ethical considerations). Before that, we want to supply you with some tools that can help you with your research. Let us first look at how some psychologists came up with ideas for research.

## IDEAS COME FROM EVERYWHERE

Every experiment begins with an idea. These ideas can come from anywhere. As we shall see, we may get our ideas from other people, newspapers, television, other scientists, students, our own experiences, or just out of thin air. One of our colleagues, Jude Cassidy, is a developmental psychologist who began her career as a dancer. Although most of us do not make a connection between dance and psychological research, she was able to use her previous experience to inform her award-winning research in the area of mother-infant attachment. Here, she describes her work in her own words:

I never had a psychology course in college. I was an English major, and after college I went to New York and I was a dancer. At that time I had some friends who were doing infancy research, looking at mother–child interactions. Because it was New York, there were lots of conventions and meetings and conferences in the city. When various friends would go to one of these mother-baby conferences, sometimes I went along as a friend. At these conferences they would show a lot of videotapes of mother-infant interaction, and I found these tapes aesthetically pleasing—beautiful to watch—very, very powerful. Babies obviously don't talk in that first year, yet this is really an incredibly rich relationship and a lot happens in that first year between the mother and her infant.

By the time the baby is a year old it is not hard at all to see which babies are really depressed. I spent a lot of time looking at videotapes and looking at movements; it was like a dance. When I watched these videotapes I felt that I was watching a dance between this mother and this baby. As a dancer I was very tuned in to the power of the nonverbal communication—the power of physical movements to communicate meaning. So when I would see mothers and babies doing things together, it was very clear to me and very easy for me to believe and understand that these were powerful ways of communicating with each other. These physical movements had messages and meanings for the babies in relation to the babies' developing a sense of their relationship with their mother and their own self-worth. I really liked watching them.

I hurt myself dancing and after a while realized that I might have to stop dancing. During that same time, I decided to take a graduate course in New York about parent-child interaction. I took this course just for fun while I was still dancing. I read lots of all the basic mother-infant interaction literature and found it interesting, and liked it. I quickly discovered that the best way to learn what I wanted to know was to study developmental psychology. I just kept reading and reading, one book led to another, and I quickly found out about Mary Ainsworth and went to study with her.

My first research project actually grew out of being a dancer. Ainsworth's main procedure for looking at attachment quality in infants is called the "strange situation." It is a 20-minute laboratory procedure with the mother and baby in which the mother leaves the room and then returns. I was learning how to code videotapes of this situation—how to qualify the infant-mother attachment. Basically, the main thing that you look at is the baby's responses to the mother on her return. But you also see a lot of other things happening during that 20 minutes of time which previously had not been coded. The session takes place in a toy-filled playroom. So you see the baby playing. There are also a couple of chairs in the room where the mother sits. I was coding 18-month-olds—toddlers—who can walk, but a lot of them are still uneasy on their feet and still sort of precarious sometimes. Here is this room full of toys and very quickly the toys get spread out all over the floor, and the mother leaves and returns. Most babies would be interested in getting to her, or getting to the door to look for her. So they would have to negotiate around these toys.

When I was watching the tapes, because I had been a dancer, I was really tuned in to movement and people's use of their body. There is a wide variation in the way babies use their bodies in this space. Some babies would plough through the toys instead of carefully stepping over them. They would pick up a toy and misjudge its weight. They'd get tangled in things. They would trip, fall, bang their heads. They'd walk into the wall. They would try to get on a chair and keep falling off.

Even though naturally all babies would fall and look like Charlie Chaplin in some way, some babies seem to be more careful of their own body boundaries and to have a beginning sense of negotiating the environment with their bodies. There seemed to be a wide range in this. Both Ainsworth's research and Bowlby's attachment theory suggest that secure babies, because they are secure in their mother's availability if needed, can attend better to the environment. Secure babies can explore and can attend to the rest of the environment whereas insecure babies are less free to explore the environment. So, here was something that I noticed by watching. We label this "the ability to negotiate the environment." We made a very simple checklist and we watched and coded the first 6 minutes in the laboratory playroom before the mother leaves. In this study we found individual differences associated with attachment categories, as the theory predicted. (Used with permission of Jude Cassidy)

Because of her experience with dance, Dr. Cassidy started noticing the patterns of behavior between mothers and their infants. She then asked whether a relationship existed between the patterns of these interactions and some psychological factors such as activity level or depression. This, in turn, brought her into contact with the literature in the field and sent her to graduate school. In graduate school she learned to research mother-child interactions, and she began a series of correlational studies to find out whether the types of mother-child interactions described by attachment theory were related to developmental processes, such as the ability of young children to move about in their world. As we think about this research, we realize that questions such as the ones Dr. Cassidy asked can be approached using a variety of designs, including naturalistic observation, correlational studies, and more experimental lab situations, such as the "strange situation."

Another of our colleagues, Lance Shotland, is a social psychologist who was discussing bystander behavior with his class. Their discussion turned to the factors that influence whether one person will help another in times of trouble. This discussion raised questions that led him to conduct a series of studies. Here is how his idea developed:

While teaching social psychology I got interested in why people don't seem to act when men attack women. For a long time I gave the standard explanation of why people don't help. What happened was that students in the class began to give me other explanations to account for why people don't help. The questions from students gave me the idea that the standard explanation may not be the total answer. What I did was go back to an actual situation in which a woman named Kitty Genovese was killed in front of over 30 people in the streets of New York without anyone calling the police or giving aid.

The story is that at 3 A.M. a woman named Kitty Genovese arrived home and parked her car in a parking lot across from her home. She walked across the street from the parking lot and started to walk toward her home. She became uneasy as she was walking since someone was walking toward her and she didn't like the way he looked. She became extremely uneasy and turned around and started to walk toward a police telephone. She never reached the police call box. He overtook her and stabbed her. She screamed, "OH MY GOD, I HAVE BEEN STABBED!" With that scream, windows were opened, people's heads came out, and lights came on. The people shouted. With that, the man got scared and ran off. He then jumped into his car and drove away. A bus then came by and people got out of the bus. People in the houses then closed their windows and went back to sleep. She apparently was not helped by anybody. She managed to crawl to another building and the man came back and overtook her and stabbed again. Again she screamed. Again, windows opened and lights came on. Again the people shouted and the man again ran off. The third time, he came back again, and this time he killed her. The entire event took over a half an hour.

This is a true event that happened in New York City in 1964. No one who looked out of the apartment windows had done anything that was effective except to scare him off. To have been really effective, the people would have to have helped her, but no one bothered to do that. At that time, the New York papers said "What's going on in New York?" and talked about apathy. A couple of psychologists named Latané and Darley decided to research the question of bystander intervention. In their research, Latané and Darley concluded that numbers in themselves may not be important and in fact people in large crowds may leave it to others. These psychologists called this "diffusion of responsibility." Also, the fact that other people are not intervening gives others the feeling that they are not really seeing the situation correctly.

Well, this is what I always told my class, and my class felt there were other things going on. So I returned to a book that was composed of interviews with the people who watched the Kitty Genovese murder. In this book, *Thirty-Eight Witnesses,* I read the bystanders' own accounts of what was going on. One of the things they said was that they were scared. I really don't know why, because they were safe in their homes. But also what they seemed to say was that they thought it was a lovers' quarrel. I became interested in that, and what I did was to go to *The New York Times* and started to search through several years, looking for cases where men were attacking women, and what I found is that it does occur with fair frequency since *The New York Times* generally does not report crime news.

Another case happened in the middle 1970s. There was a situation where a man raped a woman in full view of some 30 people. They watched the whole thing. They didn't do anything, and it was only a half block away from a police station. Again, what you find from interviews was that the people thought it was her boyfriend. I began to wonder if this was the controlling factor in the behavior of bystanders. What I did was to test this. I also went further and wondered what bystanders assume if they don't know the relationship between people. The first thing I wanted to test was: If bystanders perceive a relationship between a woman and her attacker, will they intervene less frequently than if it is a situation where a strange man is attacking a strange woman? (Used with permission of Lance Shotland)

At this point, Dr. Shotland had an idea, an educated guess, that stemmed partly from his students' dissatisfaction with the standard explanation and partly from his reading of first-person accounts of crimes. His idea was that one of the important factors that determines whether a woman would be helped is whether the man and woman are perceived to have a relationship. As a social scientist, Dr. Shotland wanted to test his idea in an experiment. Before he could design the experiment, however, he had to restate the idea in a statement or hypothesis that could be tested in a scientific manner. The steps that Dr. Shotland needed to go through before he could begin an experiment are outlined in Figure 3.4.

We have already discussed the first two steps: (1) being interested in a topic and having an idea and (2) considering and thinking about the topic from different perspectives. The third step is formulating the initial question: whether a bystander's perception of the relationship was important for a woman to be helped. The fourth step is reformulating the question into a research hypothesis.

The specific research hypothesis Dr. Shotland sought to test was this: If bystanders perceive a relationship between a woman and her attacker, they will be less likely to intervene than if the victim and the attacker are perceived to be strangers. To test this hypothesis, Dr. Shotland designed an experiment in which a fight was staged between a man and a woman. Suppose you were a research participant in the experiment. What would you do if you walked out of a classroom and saw a man and a woman fighting and yelling at each other? Do you think you would be more likely to intervene if the woman yelled, "I don't know why I ever married you," or if she yelled, "I don't know you"?

To determine the dependent and independent variables, let us reexamine the structure of a research hypothesis. When a researcher sets up an hypothesis, it is of the general form "If I do this (independent variable), then this will happen (dependent variable)." In his study, Dr. Shotland manipulated the bystanders' perceptions of the relationship between the man and the woman. In one condition the man and woman were portrayed as married ("I don't know why I ever married you") and in the other as strangers ("I don't know you"). Thus, the independent variable (the variable under Dr. Shotland's control) was the relationship between the man and the woman. The dependent variable—that is, what was measured—was whether the research participants, who were genuine bystanders in the experiment, intervened.

A good question at this point is, "What do you mean by *intervene*?" Dr. Shotland operationally defined *intervening* as any one of four activities: (1) calling the police on a nearby phone, (2) asking a person working nearby to help, (3) shouting at the man attacking the woman, or (4) trying to stop the fight. Now that you know what was measured, an extremely important question arises: How was the dependent variable measured? In this study, Dr. Shotland used a simple procedure; he just counted the number of people who did or did not intervene in the staged fight.

**Figure 3.4**

Steps involved in forming a research hypothesis

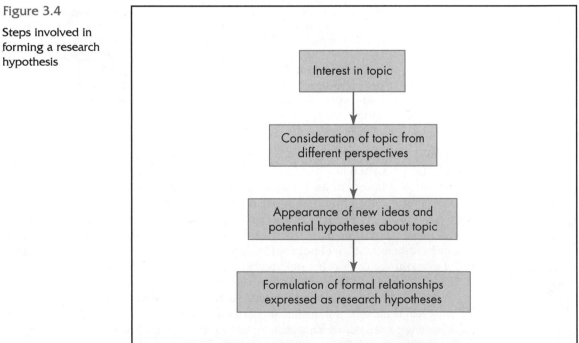

The results were consistent with Dr. Shotland's hypothesis. Under the condition in which there was an apparent marriage relationship, 20% of the bystanders intervened, whereas in the stranger condition, 80% of the bystanders intervened. Dr. Shotland did not stop at this point but performed additional studies that controlled for alternative explanations of the data (Shotland & Straw, 1976). The article describing the study illustrates well how scientists perform research, control for alternative explanations, and modify their studies as new information comes to light.

Following these studies, the research was extended to examine what type of cry for help brought the most help (Shotland & Stebbins, 1980), as well as what behaviors and attributions would be necessary in a perceived dating situation for bystanders to decide that rape was involved (Shotland & Goodstein, 1983). Further research has examined which social norms and behaviors lead to compliant sexual behavior, to "token" resistance to sexual advances, and to various forms of rape (Shotland, 1992).

Let us now turn to another researcher and see how she obtained her ideas. The researcher is a developmental psychologist, Nora Newcombe.

> It all began in graduate school when I shared an office with another woman. One day she asked me what I thought about studying how children go about saying what they want. That is, how they express imperative intent (for example, saying, "Bring me some orange juice"). I thought that was a very interesting idea. It is interesting to me because there is a theoretical position presented by Robin Lakoff that adult men and women differ in how they express imperatives. She stated that women are more tentative and unsure. According to Lakoff, women say things like "Would you please open the door" rather than "Open the door," or even hint by saying "It's hot in here" rather than "Open the window."
>
> Assuming Lakoff was right, I thought it would be interesting to see if children already showed this type of sex-role differentiation. But first I wanted to test Lakoff's theory with adults. You see, Lakoff is a linguist and had presented her ideas in the form of a theory but had never tested them in a scientific manner. That is, she never collected data from men and women to see if their speech styles indeed did differ.
>
> Another woman, Diane Arnkoff, and I began our research at this point. We did what seemed most straightforward, which was to bring people in and ask them to talk with each other. We brought people in two at a time—either two men, or two women, or a man and a woman. We did this because we thought it was probably important to determine not only if men and women differed in their speech styles but also whether they differed according to whether they were talking to a member of the same sex or opposite sex. In our first study the people didn't know each other. We gave them a set of topics to talk about, but also told them they could talk about anything else they liked. We then turned a tape recorder on and left them for 15 minutes. (Used with permission of Nora Newcombe)

In performing this study, Dr. Newcombe sought to test the general idea that men speak differently from women, especially when asking for something or giving commands. If we look at the general pattern of "If I do this, what will happen?" we can see that Dr. Newcombe paired men with men, women with women, and men with women and then observed the outcomes. The next question we ask is, "What was measured?" The dependent variable was speech style, which was operationally defined in relation to Lakoff's theory. Specifically, the number of qualifiers (such as "you know," "kinda," "I guess," and "maybe") and the number of indirect statements (such as "It is really cold in here, isn't it?") were noticed. The next question is, "How were these measured?" Dr. Newcombe used two measures. The first was to count the number of qualifiers and indirect statements each person uttered during the 15 minutes of recording. Then she measured the total amount of time each person spoke. (If one person in the pair spoke almost all the time and the other one said little, then it would be difficult to draw conclusions from the frequency numbers alone.) Thus, Dr. Newcombe used a second measure, which was the number of qualifiers each person used, divided by the total time that person spoke. Likewise, she calculated the number of indirect statements divided by the time the person spoke. She found that there were no differences between the speech styles of men and women as operationally defined.

Let us conclude this section with an interview with Jeffrey Parker, who is a developmental psychologist. Dr. Parker studies the nature of children's friendships. You will notice that he became interested in the nature of children's friendship based on his own personal experience. However, he needed to go beyond his own experience and examine some of the universals in children's relationships. For those of you interested in research careers, he offers an excellent model of finding research opportunities at your university as well as finding a graduate school that offers the type of research to which you are attracted. As you read his description of his work, notice the manner in which he attempts to develop a rich understanding of the phenomena under study through interviews with children and how he in turn uses this information to design experimental studies to better define the variables at play. Finally, he defines friendship scientifically in terms of five critical dimensions, which are used for future research.

> I study kids' friendships and I study them as basic relationships. I didn't set out to be a psychologist. In college, I set out to be a journalist. I liked doing journalism. But in retrospect, I realized that it wasn't the events that I was attracted to. What I really liked about journalism was meeting the people and interviewing the people. It was the interesting people that I liked talking to. I was really drawn to that. However, I took a child psychology course outside my major and really loved it. I realized I was mostly interested in the social dynamics, especially in children. Some of that came from my own history. We moved several times and they were at critical ages. I found those moves very tough. It was tough to relocate and to make new friends. However, my best friends had also been my real source of support during those moves. In looking at developmental psychology, I thought that friendships had been underrated resources in people's lives. Thus, I wanted to study friendships from a scientific standpoint—to ask the question what are these friendships that kids have? How do they work?

> As an undergraduate I volunteered in a research lab which was looking at social support. The goal of the lab was to quantify the amount of social support that kids had and see what difference social support made. My task was to go interview kids. Actually, what I did was to walk through a kid's neighborhood and to let them tell me about all the kids they knew in the neighborhood and all the adults and all the sources of support they had. By walking with them, they would remember when they got to the park where they played and they would tell me all these very rich stories about their lives and their friends. I remember one girl who lived in a very upscale neighborhood who could have everything she wanted. But there were no kids in the neighborhood. We sat on the steps and it was very touching that she had lots of people in her life who loved her but no kids nearby to play with. It became clear how important it is for kids to have people close by who are your peers. So in undergraduate school I learned how to interview kids and read everything I could about friendship. When it was time to go to graduate

school, I knew this was what I wanted to study. Fortunately for me I found a graduate school that had a number of faculty who studied children and their interaction patterns. One of the people I worked with taught me how to carefully observe interactions which we coded from videotapes. I spent endless hours as a graduate student watching two best friends talk to each other. This really taught me to notice how kids manage their interactions. The other faculty member taught me how to do survey research and to constantly ask, "what does it all mean?" And "how can we help kids who have problems with relationships?"

Since graduate school my students and I have been doing a lot of work on children's friendships beginning with naturalistic observation and following that up with more experimental methods. We've been looking at the variety and evolution of friendships. Sometimes, we will do a naturalistic observation study and see how kids interact when adults are not around. We think a lot about interpersonal processes such as self-disclosure and gossip and how individuals show intimacy. We then think about how to quantify that and relate it to kids' lives. For example, our work has shown that popularity and friendship are different processes. Even if you are not popular, just having a best friend makes a big difference in quality of life for kids.

Another type of study we did was to go to a summer camp and live there. We had a cabin of our own and the kids knew we were researchers from the university. It was basically a naturalistic observation study. We were able to ask kids about their relationships every week or so. We could actually follow the relationships over time so we could see how their friendships begin to develop. We got to see the friendships forming and breaking up and reforming again. In the literature no one had looked at the evolution of friendships over time. One of the things we discovered was that there were differences between the friendships of boys and girls. With boys, for example, if two boys and their friends came to summer camp and if these two boys became friends at summer camp, then their friends also tended to become friends. With girls we found that although two girls might become friends at camp their friends would not necessarily become friends. When I mentioned this study to someone they suggested that perhaps girls were more jealous and therefore did not encourage their friends to become friends with each other. In this way they were able to manage their relationships. This made us ask the question of how the kids manage their relationships in a broader social context and also got us interested in the question of jealousy.

We went to the literature concerning jealousy and essentially nothing was known concerning kids. We did find information on jealousy in adults. However, that research was basically about romantic relationships. Thus, in terms of kids and jealousy we found ourselves in completely new territory. However, we were able to adopt some of the core concepts from the adults' jealousy literature to that of kids. The students in the lab and I had a lot of discussions about what it meant to be jealous and what jealousy is. We especially discussed how to measure it. We knew that jealousy was something that could not just be observed so we had to think what could we do to get into the minds of these kids. We set out then to think about all the standard ways of doing this. What we decided to do was to create realistic scenarios that would describe specific interactions. In order to do this we asked everyone we knew to tell us stories about kids and jealousy. Some of our friends told us about times they had been jealous when they were kids. We also talked with our neighbors' kids and we asked them to tell us about being jealous. From this huge collection of events we were able to create scenarios. For example, one scenario might talk about you and your friend planning on going to a new CD store when it opened. You read in the paper that the store has opened. You call your friend only to learn that your friend has already gone with someone else. How would you feel?

It turns out that some kids would feel jealous at their friend going with someone else and other kids would not. Anyway, we were able to put together about 40 or so of these stories. We first gave these stories to some pilot kids to make sure there was a range of reactions to the stories, that is, not everyone reacted the same way. We were also able to remove the stories that were confusing and difficult to understand. At this point we had about 25 stories of which some 15 related to jealousy which we could have kids react to.

Overall, in studying the critical aspects of friendship, we came up with five critical dimensions which helped us to measure friendship. First, there is the amount of time and enjoyment that two kids derive from each other. Second, there is intimacy and the disclosure of personal secrets. Third, there is the dimension of advice in terms of do you go to this person for information about living life. Fourth, there is the dimension of validation. Simply stated, this dimension just asks if the other person makes you feel good about yourself. And finally on the negative side, there is the dimension of conflict. Using these dimensions we were able to develop and validate a questionnaire that measured friendship. Using this measure, we are examining in our research what aspects predict which kids have high quality friendships and which don't. (Used with the permission of Jeffrey Parker)

The focus of this chapter is on obtaining ideas. We hope that the four interviews in this chapter have increased your understanding of several important ideas related to the science of behavior and experience. One of these ideas is that scientists are people, and as people they differ in the manner in which they discover and develop ideas. Some people learn from their previous experience, some from their classes, some from talking to other people, some from reading the work (scientific or not) of others, and for some the ideas just seem to come out of thin air.

 # INTUITION AND REVELATION

Depending on the particular era in which people have lived, ideas that seem to pop into one's mind have been considered the voice of God, meaningless chatter, an activation of the right hemisphere of the brain, nonscientific, mystical as well as meaningful, or an example of psychological intuition. We really do not know much about the workings of our brains, especially when it comes to our own thought processes. At this point in our understanding of the process of science and how we obtain our ideas, we are much like the baby in Chapter 1, who watches and tries to see the world. Although we do not know where spontaneous ideas come from, we can examine some cases in which spontaneous or intuitive ideas have influenced the course of science and the work of individual scientists.

One of the most famous examples of a scientist whose ideas just popped into his consciousness is Albert Einstein. When asked how he came upon ideas and solved problems, Einstein replied,

> The words or the language, as they are written or spoken, do not seem to play any role in my mechanism of thought. . . . The above mentioned elements are, in any case, of visual and some of muscular type. Conventional words or other signs have to be sought for laboriously only in a secondary stage. (Koestler, 1964, p. 171)

In other places, Einstein speaks of having a bodily sensation concerning the answer to a problem or says that ideas just came to him while sailing. However, he goes on to state that often the translation from the body state to scientific notation required years. Einstein's image of a man riding on a beam of light proved to be one intuitive vision that changed science. Although this vision came in a single instant, Einstein spent considerable time working out his theory of relativity and communicating it to other scientists.

Another interesting example of ideas coming from unexpected places is the case of the German chemist Friedrich Kekulé. In 1865, Kekulé was sitting in a chair watching the fire when he fell asleep. He later reported the following dream:

> Again the atoms were gamboling before my eyes. This time the small groups kept modestly in the background. My mental eye, rendered more acute by repeated visions of this kind, could now distinguish larger structures, of manifold conformation; long rows, sometimes more closely fitted together; all twining and twisting in a snakelike motion. But look! What was that? One of the snakes had seized hold of its own tail, and the form whirled mockingly before my eyes. As if by a flash of lightning I awoke. (Koestler, 1964, p. 118)

This simple dream of a snake biting its own tail led to the idea of a ring of carbon atoms, which led to research that changed the field of organic chemistry. Through this dream, Kekulé came to suggest the idea that the molecules of certain chemical compounds are best described as consisting of closed rings.

Despite the spontaneity of these insights, they were preceded by years of intensive work by these scientists in their respective areas of interest. Furthermore, their insights had to be translated into the language and workings of science, which requires not only effort on the part of the scientist but also adequate preparation for understanding the insight in the first place.

# THE SCIENTIST'S GUIDE TO HAVING AN IDEA

In the 1920s, Graham Wallas became interested in how scientists solve problems. Because little was known about this process, Wallas began by reading the works of famous scientists, particularly Hermann von Helmholtz and Henri Poincaré. Wallas (1926) concluded that the scientific process could be described in four stages.

The first stage is *preparation*. This is the stage in which a person becomes interested in a problem, learns all he or she can about it, and examines it from various perspectives. Although we do not know why we become interested in the topics that we do, at some point one topic or idea becomes more interesting to us than others. It was at this stage that Dr. Shotland became interested in the alternative reasons his class gave for people's failure to help a woman who is being attacked. This initial stage begins with the scientist's interest and then involves assembling available information on the topic. Assembling information to get an accurate picture of a research area may take many trips to the library and may involve reading and rereading many crucial articles. Dr. Shotland not only talked with his class but also read all he could about bystander behavior, finally examining eyewitness accounts of an event that concerned his topic.

The second stage described by Wallas is called *incubation.* This is the stage in which Einstein goes sailing or Kekulé takes a nap. This stage is close to meditating on a topic but not thinking about it. One common report is that these new ideas often appear spontaneously and catch us by surprise while we are thinking about something else. Keep in mind also that the incubation stage may take years, as it did with Einstein.

The third stage of the process described by Wallas is called *illumination.* At this point, the idea or solution begins to emerge into consciousness. The emerging idea could take the form of the dream of Kekulé or the bodily sensations of Einstein, or it could be simply an idea that comes out of nowhere. In this stage, one sees an answer that was not seen before or even a totally new method of viewing the world.

For a scientist, seeing the picture is not enough, and this brings us to the fourth stage: *verification.* This occurs when you test your idea or hypothesis to see whether it fits the real world. The verification stage is what the remainder of this book is all about.

Yet it is important to realize that there are some human aspects to performing science, which involve learning everything you can about a topic that interests you, then mulling over this information, and finally permitting yourself to find your answers in strange places. In trying to understand how scientists obtain the ideas for their experiments, keep in mind that they are already familiar with much of the published work in their areas of interest. Consequently, an essential first step is to spend time in the library becoming familiar with various content areas in which you might be interested. To assist you in this process, the next section of this chapter describes several resource tools that psychologists commonly use to explore new areas of interest.

---

✓ CONCEPT CHECK 3.3    Professor Fraud said that all research ideas should come from your dreams. His archrival, Professor Limited, said no idea that comes from a dream has a place in science. How would you react to their statements?

---

# TOOLS FOR LIBRARY RESEARCH

Sometimes people are interested in a general area and would like to learn more about it before they attempt to perform an experiment. For example, beginning psychology students may say they want to study memory or health and emotion or why people help others in emergency situations or what the important factors in understanding date rape are or what makes one person a leader. Where can they go for more information? Of course, they can go directly to experience and attempt to learn more about the topic from the world itself. Yet this may not be an efficient method because it ignores previous attempts to describe and understand the process under study. Most people begin by reading what others have written on the topic.

For most of us, the library is the best source of materials concerning our topic. With the advent of the World Wide Web, the library and its resource materials may no longer be totally in one physical location, but stored virtually around the world. Although this information is available from almost any location, you may still need the expertise of such people as the reference librarian to aid in your search. Your librarian is particularly helpful in determining what is available to you because there are a variety of methods for storing information, including books, journals, CDs, and DVDs. In this section, we discuss both the traditional sources of information, such as books and journals, and their electronic versions. We end with a discussion of the Internet as a source of information, although reference to specific Web pages is presented throughout the following sections.

## ■  Books

Books can be found in the library catalog or in *Books in Print,* which lists all books currently in print. *Psychological Abstracts* and its Web-based companion, PsycINFO, describe current books and chapters in psychology as well as journal articles. The entry for a given book or chapter includes publishing information (title, authors, publisher, etc.) as well as a summary and a table of contents, if it is a book. Indexes for author, subject, publisher, and title aid in finding desired information.

## ■  Journals

Journals are the major outlet in which scientists describe their research. A scientific journal is a collection of experimental reports and other articles written by scientists. There are journals both for broad areas, such as the journals *Science* and *Nature,* and for more specific areas, such as the journal *The Behavioral and Brain Sciences.* The  latter is different from others in that it includes commentaries from other scientists at the conclusion of each article. Psychologists publish their research in such journals as the *Journal of Experimental Psychology, Journal of Abnormal Psychology, Developmental Psychology, Journal of Personality and Social Psychology, Psychological Science, Psychophysiology, Health Psychology, Journal of Applied Psychology,* and *Psychosomatic Medicine.* Your reference librarian can tell you which journals your library carries.

When you examine a particular journal, you will notice that the articles cover various topics within the given area. However, you probably want to examine articles on a particular topic. One way is to use one of the large computer databases available at many libraries, which we discuss later in this chapter. Another way to conduct your search for journal articles is to look in one of the major indexes for the specific topic in which you are interested. The major indexes that cover psychological research are *Psychological Abstracts, Science Citation Index, Social Science Citation Index,* and *Index Medicus* (which ceased publication in 1998 in favor of its electronic counterpart, MEDLINE).

*Psychological Abstracts*  *Psychological Abstracts* is published each month, and cumulative indexes that cover the preceding 5 years are also published. *Psychological Abstracts* indexes English-language journal articles, book chapters, and books in psychology and the behavioral sciences. It reflects research in psychology, biology, management, sociology, education, and other areas. Each article entry includes bibliographic information and a summary that gives a clear idea of what the item contains. Book entries also list the table of contents. The summary provides a description of what the article, chapter, or book contains so that the reader can decide whether it would be appropriate for his or her research project. The citation also supplies the information necessary to find the item in the library.

The following example illustrates one possible use of *Psychological Abstracts*. Suppose you and a friend are arguing about the nature of emotions. How might you find information concerning the nature of emotions—that is, the role emotions play in cognitive abilities, personality, or psychopathology, and what mechanisms produce emotions? Using the most recent index issue of *Psychological Abstracts*, look up "Emotions." Where you begin depends on what type of question you are asking. If you want only general scientific information, a good place to begin is with a review article. (*Psychological Abstracts* notes when the article is a literature review.) For example, if you were to look at the 1999 edition of *Psychological Abstracts* you will notice that in the 1999 edition (Volume 50) of the *Annual Review of Psychology*, John Cacioppo and Wendi Gardner have a review article on emotion. However, because the topic of emotions is broad, we might want to be more specific in our search. We might limit ourselves to investigating emotional regulation or the underlying brain mechanisms that are related to emotions, or to some particular emotion such as joy or fear.

## ■ Computer Databases

With the development of computers and media such as CD-ROM to store and access large sets of data, it has become possible to search a large database and retrieve bibliographic information in a few seconds. A number of libraries offer computerized searches, and you should check with your reference librarian to see what is available to you. One of the major databases for psychology is PsycINFO, which is similar to the online version of Psychological Abstracts. MEDLINE performs the same service for the medical literature and also includes a number of psychological journals.

The basic principle behind computer searches is no different from what we described previously for using any of the major reference materials. However, the computer is able to speed up the process and to aid in a variety of sort procedures. For example, if we were to search articles published during the past 10 years and ask which of them discussed the topic of psychotherapy, we would see on the computer screen that there are more than 10,000 such articles. If we now requested the psychotherapy articles that were descriptions of research in psychotherapy, we would find the number of articles available to be fewer than 200. If we asked for only those that studied patient-therapist matching ("Is psychotherapy more effective if patients and therapists are matched on particular characteristics such as age, sex, race, and therapeutic orientation?"), we would find that there are only a few articles. At this point we could ask the computer to print out the titles and the journals in which these articles were published. Some databases also contain a summary of each piece of research, which also can be printed. Computer databases are particularly useful for their ability to search for categories of research that normally might not be indexed. Many databases allow you to search for a particular word within the title or summary of the article.

PsycINFO    Because completing a large or broad search using *Psychological Abstracts* can be tedious, it is recommended that the computerized searching system PsycINFO be used for most searches. This system contains basically the same information as *Psychological Abstracts* does. Because most university libraries subscribe to such computer systems, students generally can perform these searches for no cost. PsycINFO is maintained by the American  Psychological Association and you can find recent information on this database including how to use it by going to their home page (http://www.apa.org/). By using the electronic version, you can have the computer do the searching and sorting for you.

How would you do such a search? You first need to determine whether the database is available only on CDs in your library or whether you can access it from the Web. Once you have access to PsycINFO, you will be asked to choose which years you want to search and to enter a keyword for which the computer will search. If you were to search for research on emotions in PsycINFO, you might discover that more than 10,000 different articles and books were published on the topic. Thus, you would need to limit your search. One way to do this is to consider what aspect of the topic you are interested in studying.

For example, you may be interested in emotional regulation. You could then enter the term *emotional regulation* and see that your search has yielded few articles. At this point you could begin to examine the entries of interest to you. You might discover that even the topic *emotional regulation* is not specific enough. If you were interested in emotional regulation in children, you would need to specify this also. But how would you do that? You could enter the phrase "emotional regulation in children." You could also combine two searches and look for all the research articles that included both *emotional regulation* and *children* in the text. An example of this search is shown in Box 3.1.

National Library of Medicine: MEDLINE, PubMed, and Grateful Med    Whereas PsycINFO covers published material of interest to psychologists, MEDLINE performs the same function for medical journals. Most topics of interest to psychological researchers, such as Dr. Shotland's research on bystander intervention, are not found in MEDLINE. However, at times there are overlaps; some research could be published in either a psychological journal or a medical one, as would be the case with social support and its relation to cancer or how one measures quality of life. At these times, MEDLINE is a source for research literature that may not be listed in PsycINFO.

MEDLINE is published by the U.S. National Library of Medicine (http://igm.nlm.nih.gov), which is part of the National Institutes of Health (http://www.nih.gov/) in Washington, D.C. MEDLINE can be accessed through a variety of sources, including PubMed (http://www.ncbi.nlm.nih.gov/PubMed/) and Grateful Med (http://igm.nlm.nih.gov/). Both PubMed and Grateful Med are rich sources of information related to medicine and health, including U.S. government databases. Fortunately, these sources of information are free and can be accessed through any Internet connection. Both systems have extensive sets of instructions for use, including how to perform MEDLINE searches. MEDLINE's search function is similar to that of PsycINFO. A sample search (on psychoneuroimmunology) is shown in Box 3.2.

*Science Citation Index* and *Social Science Citation Index*    The *Science Citation Index* (SCI) and the *Social Science Citation Index* (SSCI) list articles published in either the sciences (such as physics, chemistry, and biology) or the social sciences (such as sociology and economics). Areas of psychology are referenced in either or both, depending on the area of study. As you can see from the example in Box 3.3, SSCI lists articles by topic and author. This is most useful for finding a specific type of research within a general area of study. For example, when we look under *memory*, we see specific areas such as picture memory, recognition memory, and rat memory. Next to the topic is the author's name. We then look up the author's name and find a listing that tells the journal in which the article was published.

One advantage of the SSCI over other indexes is that it includes in a separate volume a list of all studies that cited a particular study (hence the name *Social Science Citation Index*).

**Box 3.1**

# PsycInfo Search Results

**found 7 documents, (7 returned).**
**for Your Query :** *((emotional regulation) AND (children)) AND (2001<=Year<=2002)*

---

1. **Parental drinking problems and children's adjustment: Vagal regulation and emotional reactivity as pathways and moderators of risk.**
   By El-Sheikh, Mona
   Journal of Abnormal Psychology. 2001 Nov Vol 110(4) 499-515
   View Full Text | View Abstract | View Full PsycINFO Record score 707

2. **Mother's emotional expressivity and children's behavior problems and social competence: Mediation through children's regulation.**
   By Eisenberg, Nancy; Gershoff, Elizabeth Thompson; Fabes, Richard A.; Shepard, Stephanie A.; Cumberland, Amanda J.; Losoya, Sandra H.; Guthrie, Ivanna K.; Murphy, Bridget C.
   Developmental Psychology. 2001 Jul Vol 37(4) 475-490
   View Full Text | View Abstract | View Full PsycINFO Record score 665

3. **Parental socialization of children's dysregulated expression of emotion and externalizing problems. .**
   By Eisenberg, Nancy; Losoya, Sandra; Fabes, Richard A.; Guthrie, Ivanna K.; Reiser, Mark; Murphy, Bridget; Shepard, Stephanie A.; Poulin, Rick; Padgett, Sarah J.
   Journal of Family Psychology. 2001 Jun Vol 15(2) 183-205
   View Full Text | View Abstract | View Full PsycINFO Record score 646

4. **Instruction begins in the home: Relations between parental instruction and children's self-regulation in the classroom. .**
   By Stright, Anne Dopkins; Neitzel, Carin; Sears, Kathy Garza; Hoke-Sinex, Linda
   Journal of Educational Psychology. 2001 Sep Vol 93(3) 456-466
   View Full Text | View Abstract | View Full PsycINFO Record score 642

5. **The relations of parental emotional expressivity with quality of Indonesian children's social functioning.**
   By Eisenberg, Nancy; Liew, Jeffrey; Pidada, Sri Untari
   Emotion. 2001 Jun Vol 1(2) 116-136
   View Full Text | View Abstract | View Full PsycINFO Record score 637

6. **School readiness: Integrating cognition and emotion in a neurobiological conceptualization of children's functioning at school entry.**
   By Blair, Clancy
   American Psychologist. 2002 Feb Vol 57(2) 111-127
   View Full Text | View Abstract | View Full PsycINFO Record score 603

7. **Narrative representations of caregivers and emotion dysregulation as predictors of maltreated children's rejection by peers.**
   By Shields, Ann; Ryan, Richard M.; Cicchetti, Dante
   Developmental Psychology. 2001 May Vol 37(3) 321-337
   View Full Text | View Abstract | View Full PsycINFO Record score 599

**Box 3.2**

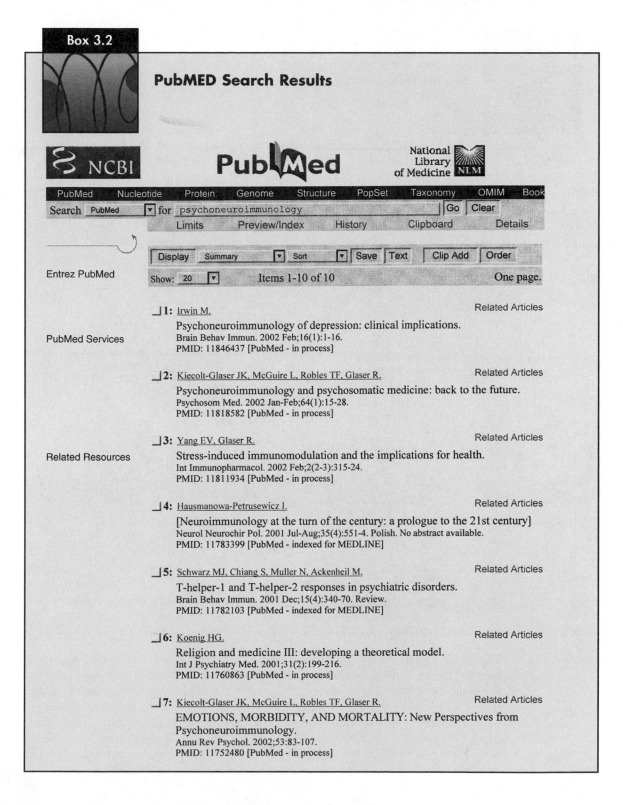

## PubMED Search Results

NCBI    Pub**M**ed    National Library of Medicine NLM

| PubMed | Nucleotide | Protein | Genome | Structure | PopSet | Taxonomy | OMIM | Book |

Search  PubMed  ▼ for  psychoneuroimmunology    Go  Clear

Limits    Preview/Index    History    Clipboard    Details

Entrez PubMed

Display  Summary  ▼  Sort  ▼  Save  Text    Clip Add    Order

Show:  20  ▼    Items 1-10 of 10    One page.

PubMed Services

**1:** Irwin M.    Related Articles
Psychoneuroimmunology of depression: clinical implications.
Brain Behav Immun. 2002 Feb;16(1):1-16.
PMID: 11846437 [PubMed - in process]

**2:** Kiecolt-Glaser JK, McGuire L, Robles TF, Glaser R.    Related Articles
Psychoneuroimmunology and psychosomatic medicine: back to the future.
Psychosom Med. 2002 Jan-Feb;64(1):15-28.
PMID: 11818582 [PubMed - in process]

Related Resources

**3:** Yang EV, Glaser R.    Related Articles
Stress-induced immunomodulation and the implications for health.
Int Immunopharmacol. 2002 Feb;2(2-3):315-24.
PMID: 11811934 [PubMed - in process]

**4:** Hausmanowa-Petrusewicz I.    Related Articles
[Neuroimmunology at the turn of the century: a prologue to the 21st century]
Neurol Neurochir Pol. 2001 Jul-Aug;35(4):551-4. Polish. No abstract available.
PMID: 11783399 [PubMed - indexed for MEDLINE]

**5:** Schwarz MJ, Chiang S, Muller N, Ackenheil M.    Related Articles
T-helper-1 and T-helper-2 responses in psychiatric disorders.
Brain Behav Immun. 2001 Dec;15(4):340-70. Review.
PMID: 11782103 [PubMed - indexed for MEDLINE]

**6:** Koenig HG.    Related Articles
Religion and medicine III: developing a theoretical model.
Int J Psychiatry Med. 2001;31(2):199-216.
PMID: 11760863 [PubMed - in process]

**7:** Kiecolt-Glaser JK, McGuire L, Robles TF, Glaser R.    Related Articles
EMOTIONS, MORBIDITY, AND MORTALITY: New Perspectives from
Psychoneuroimmunology.
Annu Rev Psychol. 2002;53:83-107.
PMID: 11752480 [PubMed - in process]

## Box 3.3

# Social Science Citation Index

*Social Science Citation Index* is published by the Institute for Scientific Information in Philadelphia. The SSCI is actually composed of three separate indexes. The first is the subject index, which lists articles related to a specific topic. The second is the source index, which lists authors and the articles or books they published during the period covered. The third is the citation index, which lists articles published during a certain period that cite as a reference a particular article. By using this third index, one can determine what work has followed up a specific research article. Presented here is a portion of a page from the subject index of the SSCI.

### MEMORY

```
MEMORY (CONT)          MEMORY (CONT)           MEMORY (CONT)           MEMORY (CONT)
ASSOCIATIO. - ▶CLARK SE    DISORDERS-- MCCARTHY AM   GENETIC --- JOHANSSO.B    LIGHT-FLAS.- ▶ROBERTS WA
ATTENTION. - ▶DISTEFAN.G   DISSOCIATE - CHAO LL      GERIATRIC -- HARVEY PD    LIST------ KORSNES MS
         - ▶MCCARTHY AM    DISSOCIATI. - BUCHNER A   GERMAN --- MARTENFI.S     LISTS----- PARKER PY
         - ▶ROBINSON P          - ▶GLISKY EL         GESTURES -- THOMPSON LA   LOCALIZATI. - PARSONS M
         - ▶SUTKER PB           - ▶ISINGRIN.M        GHOST ---- ▶TWIGGS DG+    LOCATION-- HATWELL Y
ATYPICAL-- ▶FORGAS JP      DISSOCIATI. - ▶NILSSON LG GILLES-DE-.. STEBBINS GT       - MEANS LW
AUDIT---- ▶TAN HT          DISTRACTION ▶ERBLICH J    GOOD ----- PSY PSY MED■   LONG ----- BOOTH GG
AUDITORY-- ▶CHAO LL        DISTURBANCE JOUVENOT C    GRAFTS---- LI YJ               - HIEMSTRA C
         - ▶KELLER TA                MCNALLY RJ      GROUPS---- LORENZIC.F     LONG-TERM - ▶ANDREASE.NC
         - ▶RECORDS NL     DISTURBANC. ▶SCHMIDTK.K   GUIDE---- RAITT D         LONGITUDIN.- KNOPF M
AUSCHWITZ -▶SCHROEDE.RL+   DOMAIN-SPE. LUSZCZ M      GULF-WAR-- BEAMISH TD     LOSS------ BEACH ME
AUTOBIOGRA. ▶MCNALLY RJ    DOUBLE---- GLISKY EL      HANDBOOK-- MATTHEWS G+         - ▶HODGES JR
         ▶WRIGHT J         DOWN-SYNDR. ▶RAST M            - SERGEANT JA+            - MOSS HE
AUTONOETIC ▶PERNER J       DRAWING--- ▶BUTLER S      HAPTICS --- HATWELL Y          - UMEDA K
AVIATORS - ▶WILLIAMS LJ    DRINKERS -- ▶FOX AM       HAUNGS,PET. ▶JESSE E      LOTS----- MEANS LW
AWARENESS- TAN HT          EAR ------ PARKER PY      HEALTHY--- EUSTACHE F     LOW------ PARFITT G
BASED ---- ▶SEAMON JG      EARLY ---- CHAO LL        HEART-RATE- OSATO E       LTP------ BEACH ME
BATTERY -- TOMBAUGH TN          - DIAMOND A          HIGH ----- GUYNN MJ       MALLEABILI.-▶LOFTUS EF
BEHAVIOR-- DIAMOND A            - FORSTL H                - PARFITT G          MANAGERS-- RAITT D
         - ▶HIGHHOUS.S           - HODGES JR         HIPPOCAMPAL BEACH ME      MARCH ---- BIRELEY SJR+
BELIEFS -- LUSZCZ M              - ▶MYSLIVEC.J@            - GAFFAN D+          MARKETS--- BOOTH GG
BIAS ----- ▶GOODMAN GS          - NEWCOMBE N@        HIPPOCAMPUS BROCKWAY JP   MATCHED--- LANGE KW
         ▶PINCUS T          EASTERN--- KOIVISTO K         - HOPKINS RO         MATTERS--- ▶YONEYAMA L
BIRTH----- LESPERAN.M      EDITION --- QUANTE M+          - RIDLEY RM          MAY------ STOCK WA
BLOCKING --▶HOUGH MS       EDUCATION-- ZAPPALA G     HISTORY --- ▶JACOB MC+    MEANING--- FISCHER AH+
BLOOD-GLUC. ▶PARKER PY     EFFECT---- BUTLER S            - ▶TAPPAN MB+        MEASURE -- MCDONOUG.L
BRAIN ---- GUILMETT.TJ          - CASSIDY DJ         HOMOGENEITY LORENZIC.F    MEASUREMEN. BUCHNER A
BRIEF---- ▶FRANZEN MD            - CLARK SE          HONEST---- FREEMAN NH     MEASURES-- GUILMETT.TJ
         - ▶LOVELACE CT          - HALMIOVA O        HUMAN---- GRADY CL        MECHANISMS MYSLIVEC.J
BRITISH-IS. - ▶WRIGHT K          - HOUGH MS          HUMANS--- ▶GUILLEM F      MEDICAL-CA. EUGENIO M
BURSTS---- ▶BROCKWAY P           - ▶PERSINGE.MA      HUNTINGTON. LANGE KW      MEDICATION- SPIERS MV
CAMKII --- ▶BEACH ME             - ▶PEZDEK K         HYPNOSIS -- MCCONKEY KM   MENTAL --- DUTKE S
CAMPUS --- ▶NAKA M               - RUSS MO           HYPOTHESES BREDENKA.J     MERE----- SEAMON JG
CANDIDATES- WALLACE WP           - SEAMON JG         HYPOTHESIS- MOSCOVIT.M    METHOD --- ▶XANTHAKO.M
CARBON-MON. HOPKINS RO           - UMEDA K                - ROBINSON P         MICE----- BEACH ME
CARD----- ▶RAGLAND JD      EFFECTS --- BOLLER K      IDENTITIES- MARTENFI.S         - GIESE KP
CATEGORY-- ▶PALMERI TJ           - FORGAS JP         IMAGINED -- CONSTANS JI   MIDDLE---- BROCKWAY JP
CAI ------ ▶RIDLEY RM            - GOODMAN GS        IMITATION -- MCDONOUG.L   MIGRATION- CARSTEN J
CENTRAL -- ▶BOLLER K             - ▶NELSON DL        IMMEDIATE - OSATO E       MILD----- GUILMETT.TJ
CEREBRAL-- EUSTACHE F            - NILSSON LG        IMPACT---- GIESE KP       MINIREVIEW- MYSLIVEC.J
CHECKERS-- ▶CONSTANS JI          - PARFITT G         IMPAIR---- ERBLICH J      MIS)INFORM.- HIGHHOUS.S
CHILDREN-- ▶COLILLA JL           - SAFANDA J         IMPAIRED -- GRADY CL      MISINFORMA. MARCHE TA
         - ▶KILLAM RB            - SPIES K                - HODGES JR          MISTAKE--- FREEMAN NH
         - ▶HALMIOVA O           - TAN HT            IMPAIRMENT BEACH ME       MODELED--- MCKDON G
         - LESPERAN.M       EGG------ BROCKWAY P           - FORSTL H          MODELING-- CLARK SE
         - MCCARTHY AM      ELABORATION NILSSON LG         - GILLAM RB         MODELS---- DUTKE S
CHILDRENS ▶CASSIDY DJ      ELDERLY--- ▶BISIACCH.PS        - KOIVISTO K              - MCCLELLA.JL
         GOODMAN GS              - SPIERS MV              - LARRABEE GJ             - MOSCOVIT.M
         ▶HATWELL Y         ELDERS---- ▶MCDOUGAL.GJ       - MIYOSHI K          MODULARITY- MISERACH.DC
         ▶LIWAG MD          ELECTRODES- BROCKWAY P    IMPAIRMENTS RECORDS NL   MODULATION- REARDON R
         ▶NEWCOMBE N        ELECTRODES- BROCKWAY P         - HOPKINS RO        MONTHS---- BAHRICK LE
CHOLINERGIC ▶LI YJ         ELECTRONIC - RAITT D           - FORGAS JP         MOOD ----- FORGAS JP
CHORDS---- ▶BROWNE SH+     ELICITED -- GUILLEM F          - RIDLEY RM              - ▶MAYER JD
CHRONIC -- ▶SCHNURR RF     EMOTION -- ▶ELLIS HC@          - STEBBINS GT        MOOD-CONGR.    "
         - WRIGHT J              - ▶MATTHEWS G+     IMPLICATIO. - GUILLEM F    MOOD-DEPEN. BECK RC
```

**LEGEND**

▶  UNIQUE ARTICLE INDICATOR
@  AUTHOR OF MORE THAN ONE ARTICLE WITH SAME PRIMARY AND CO-TERM
■  SEE ANONYMOUS SOURCE SECTION
+  REVIEW

```
MEMORY (CONT)              MEMORY (CONT)
POTENTIALS - GUILLEM F     SOUTHWESTE. BRISON KJ+
POW------ SUTKER PB        SPACED---- LOVELACE CT
PRACTICAL-- QUANTE M+      SPATIAL --- ALAN AJ
PRAISE --- PSY PSY MED■         - BEACH ME
PREMATURE - LESPERAN.M          - DUTKE S
PRESCHOOL- GATHERCO.SE          - LI YJ
PRESCHOOLE. MARCHE TA           - UMEDA K
PRESENT--- HOGGART R+      SPATIAL-LE.- UMEDA K
PRESENTATI.- LOVELACE CT   SPECIFIC--- RECORDS NL
PRESENTED - BIRCH S        SPECIFICITY- GUILMETT.TJ
         - PARKER PY       SPEECH---- THOMPSON LA
PREVALENCE KOIVISTO K      SPINDLE--- BROCKWAY P
PREVIOUSLY- BAEZ AT        SPOKEN---- WALLACE WP
PRIOR----- ELLIS HC        STATE----- CARSTEN J
         - TAN HT          STATUS---- GOODMAN GS
PRIORITY--- GUYNN MJ       STIMULI--- PINCUS T
PROBABLE -- DEWEER B            - RAGLAND JD
PROBLEMS-- MCCARTHY AM     STORIES--- ELLIS HC
         BERGMAN MM        STORING--- MOHR G
PROCEDURAL ALLAIN H        STRANGE--- TWIGGS DG+
PROCESS --- BUCHNER A      STRATEGIES - COCHRAN JC
PROCESSES -                     - HASSELHO.M
         - CHAO LL         STRATEGY-- MCDOUGAL.GJ
         - DUJARDIN K      STRENGTH-- AYLWARD GP
         - LESPERAN.M      STRUCTURE- FRANZEN MD
PROCESSING- BIRELEY SJR+   STUDIES--- GUILLEM F
         - WALLACE WP           - ZELIZER B
PRODUCED -                STUDY---- GIESE KP
PROGRESSIVE VANDERHU.PR    SUBJECTS-- MILDERS MV
PROPERTIES- HATWELL Y           - HOPKINS RO
PROSPECTIVE BISIACCH.PS    SUBSTANCE- FRANZEN MD
         ▶TOMBAUGH TN      SUBSYSTEMS EUSTACHE F
PROTOTYPIC.- FORGAS JP     SUCCESSES- MCCLELLA.JL
PSYCHOLOGY- BREDENKA.J     SUCCESSFUL- MCDOUGAL.GJ
         - LIEURY A+       SUGGESTIBI.- ACKIL JK
PUBLIC---- BROWNE SH+           - PEZDEK K
QUANTITATI.- HOPKINS RO         - SIEGAL M
QUESTIONING CASSIDY DJ     SUPERIORITY METCALFE J
RANDOMLY-- KOIVISTO K      SUPRANUCLE. VANDERHU.PR
RANGE---- BEACH ME         SURFACE--- BIRCH S
RAPID----- BERGMAN MM      SURVEY --- WRIGHT M
                          SURVEYS--- RIANDEY K
```

This would be particularly useful to a researcher such as Dr. Newcombe. As she was beginning to plan her study examining the relationship between sex and speech types according to the theory of Robin Lakoff, she would want to know whether anyone else had tested this theory. As you will see later, in their articles scientists refer to the research and theories of others, so it would be possible to find all the studies that refer to Dr. Lakoff's work. To do this, Dr. Newcombe would look up "R. T. Lakoff" and note all the articles that cited her work. Dr. Newcombe then could check these articles to see whether any other scientists had asked the specific question in which she was interested. Both SCI and SSCI are available in an electronic form.

## ■ The Internet

You can access a great variety of information via the Internet from professional organizations such as the American Psychological Society (http://www.psychologicalscience.org/), the American Psychological Association (http://www.apa.org), and the Canadian Psychological Association (http://www.cpa.ca/). Government agencies, such as the National Institutes of Health (http://www.nih.gov/), the National Institute of Mental Health (http://www.nimh.nih.gov/), the National Science Foundation (http://www.nsf.gov/), and the National Academy of Sciences (http://www.nas.edu/), also have Web sites.

Most colleges and universities have home pages that describe their programs and give you resources for psychology. For example, both Hanover College (http://psych.hanover.edu/) and Skidmore (http://www.skidmore.edu/~hfoley/resources.htm) have pages that describe a variety of resources on the Web. The Hanover site has links to tutorials and demonstrations, journals on the web, psychological software and other links to similar materials. The Skidmore resources page lists a variety of sites related to general psychology, biological psychology, clinical psychology, sensation and perception, and statistics. At these sites you can view tutorials in psychology or demonstrations of visual illusions, for example. Also, many journals can be accessed through their Web pages. There are even separate books describing psychological resources on the Web (Kardas, 1999).

Various home pages are limited to a specific area of interest. For example, there are a variety of neuroscience Web sites. These home pages include both general reference pages, such as ones addressed to neurosciences (http://www.neuroguide.com/), as well as specific pictures of brain images. The neuroscience general home pages can also send you to other sets of information related to the neurosciences, neurology, psychiatry, psychology, cognitive science, and artificial intelligence. If you click on the area related to academic centers, you will find a list of home pages from universities and researchers around the world.

Because the Internet makes it possible for any computer to be connected to any other computer, and because anyone can set up a home page, there is no guarantee that the information you receive is always correct or unbiased. However, when you go to sites maintained by major institutions, you are more likely to find accurate information.

# CONCLUSION

We have discussed developing an hypothesis, the use of operational definitions, how various scientists have arrived at their ideas for research, and some library resources that you will use as you begin to explore your own ideas. At this point, you should be able to begin developing research studies of your own.

All experiments begin with an idea about the world in which we live. This consideration or idea is first formulated as a general statement or question. Whatever your idea, you
must translate it into a specific research question or hypothesis; that is, you must develop
a testable statement that points out what specific variables are to be examined and what the
hypothesized relationship is between them, relying on operational definitions. At this point
you should have stated clearly (1) your independent and dependent variables; (2) how each
is measured, taking into account reliability and validity; (3) the hypothesized relationship
between the independent and dependent variables; and (4) how this hypothesized relationship is to be tested. Before we turn to the question of experimental design, we want to
review the major points of descriptive and inferential statistics in the next chapters.

# KEY TERMS AND CONCEPTS

1. Making hypotheses concrete
   A. Operational definition
   B. Construct validity
2. Types of reasoning
   A. Inductive
   B. Deductive
3. Measurement
   A. Reliability
   B. Validity
4. Developing ideas
   A. Jude Cassidy
   B. Lance Shotland
   C. Nora Newcombe
   D. Jeffrey Parker
5. Strong inference
   A. Four steps according to Platt
      ▪ Develop alternative hypotheses

   ▪ Perform the crucial experiment
   ▪ Obtain clear-cut results
   ▪ Repeat with supported hypothesis
6. Wallas's four stages
   A. Preparation
   B. Incubation
   C. Illumination
   D. Verification
7. Library tools
   A. *Psychological Abstracts* and PsycINFO
   B. *Index Medicus* and MEDLINE
   C. *Science Citation Index*
   D. *Social Science Citation Index*
   E. Computer databases
   F. Internet
   G. World Wide Web

# SUMMARY

1. Unlike Humpty Dumpty, who said to Alice in *Through the Looking-Glass,* "When I use a word it means just what I choose it to mean—neither more nor less," a re-searcher needs to present ideas in a form that others can understand. Creating an operational definition is one way researchers clarify their ideas and make their hypotheses more concrete. An operational definition presents an hypothesis in terms of observable opera-tions that others can see and repeat.

2. Construct validity is the degree to which the procedure we are using is an adequate definition of the construct we are measuring. For example, a person could define *intelligence* operationally as the time required to re-spond to a stimulus. The question of construct validity

would then arise, asking whether response time was a valid measure of the construct of intelligence.

3. Inductive reasoning is the process of generalizing from a specific event to a general idea. Deductive rea-soning is the process of reasoning from the general to the particular.

4. Measurement is the means by which we test an hy-pothesis. *Reliability* is the consistency of a measuring instrument. *Validity* is its accuracy.

5. Scientists obtain ideas for research from a variety of sources. Dr. Shotland explained how reading the news-paper and listening to his class helped him to develop a productive line of research. Dr. Newcombe explained how talking to a friend led to her thinking about the

manner in which men and women ask for what they want. Dr. Parker drew from his own history. Passages from Einstein and Kekulé suggest that ideas and solutions may also come in terms of vague bodily sensations or even dreams.

6. Graham Wallas was interested in how scientists solve problems. He suggested four stages: preparation, incubation, illumination, and verification.

7. Because science represents a history of observation and theory development, it is important to know what others have observed and said about a particular topic. Reference libraries contain important tools for helping us find articles related to our interests. Library tools that are important in psychological research are *Psychological Abstracts, Science Citation Index, Social Science Citation Index,* and computer databases such as PsycINFO and MEDLINE. Also, information is available on the Internet and the World Wide Web.

8. In performing research, you begin with an idea or theory. Through operational definitions, this idea must be turned into a testable hypothesis. This can be seen as a four-part process: (1) the definition of the independent and dependent variables, (2) a statement of how the independent and dependent variables are to be measured, considering issues of reliability and validity, (3) a statement of the hypothesized relationship between the independent and dependent variables, and (4) a statement of how this relationship is to be examined or tested.

# REVIEW QUESTIONS

1. Discuss what operational definitions are and give some examples.
2. What is construct validity?
3. Describe Dr. Shotland's study in terms of the independent variable, the dependent variable, and operational definitions.
4. How do intuition and revelation play a role in research?
5. What is meant by the term *strong inference*?
6. Name the reference work in which you would find a summary of most psychological articles.
7. Using a bathroom scale as an example, describe the difference between reliability and validity.

# DISCUSSION QUESTIONS AND PROJECTS

1. Give some examples of inductive and deductive reasoning from newspapers, magazines, or television.
2. Discuss the topics you are most interested in researching and describe how you might construct an experiment to study these areas.
3. Discuss some important and interesting topics that may be difficult or impossible to research experimentally.
4. Find the reference section of your library and list five studies performed in the past 10 years that look at the relationship between watching television and aggression.
5. Design a study to determine whether people who take vitamins get better grades. What are the steps necessary to design such a study? What control groups would you need? What might some rival hypotheses be in such a study?
6. How might you design a study that would still be useful even if your hypothesis were refuted?
7. Assume that there exists a construct related to achievement called *motive to achieve*. Describe a way to measure this construct that would be reliable but would have no validity whatsoever.

## InfoTrac College Edition: Exercises

William McGuire in a 1997 *Annual Review of Psychology* article suggests that most students are taught more about hypothesis testing than hypothesis generation. Look up his article "Creative hypothesis generating in psychology: some useful heuristics" in InfoTrac College Edition and use one of his 49 heuristics to develop an hypothesis.

In terms of having an idea, Albert Rothenberg wondered about Kekulé's consciousness when he came upon this discovery. You can find this Fall 1995 *American Journal of Psychology* article "Creative cognitive processes in Kekulé's discovery of the structure of the benzene molecule" in InfoTrac College Edition. As you read it, think about how you would determine the nature of Kekulé's experience.

## ✓ Answers to Concept Checks

**3.1** Only the score on the verbal part of the SAT can be considered an operational definition. The other alternatives do not tell us how to measure verbal ability. However, just because we have an operational definition does not mean that it provides a good measure of the construct; it only specifies clearly how to make the measurement.

**3.2** The lab clock would be a reliable instrument to use if you only wanted to time 30 minutes of free play.

**3.3** Change professors, we hope. Both have an incorrect view of science. Research has to do with taking an idea, restating it as a testable hypothesis, and then designing an experiment or series of experiments to test the hypothesis. The origin of the initial idea is not important in terms of this process.

**3.4** The *Social Science Citation Index* would be a good start. It would list others who referenced Bower's work, including those who replicated it.

# DESCRIPTION OF BEHAVIOR THROUGH NUMERICAL REPRESENTATION

Behavior can be described in many ways. In naturalistic observation studies, descriptions may consist of simple lists of behaviors or behavior sequences. For example, an ethologist might describe the detailed movements in the feeding behavior of some common fish. A developmental or clinical psychologist might describe the manner in which a family interacts. In experimental studies, behaviors usually are expressed in more quantitative terms. Some examples of quantitative measurements are the number of millimeters by which an observer overestimates the length of a line in a visual illusion experiment, the number of words recalled in a memory experiment, the change in a person's heart rate as a result of watching an emotionally charged film, and the results of an IQ test taken under different conditions.

As we pointed out in Chapter 3, there are a variety of ways to measure a particular process. If you were interested in emotional responding, for example, you could videotape facial expression; measure psychophysiological activity, such as EMG (electromyography) facial muscle activity, electroencephalographic (EEG) brain activity, or heart rate; obtain self-reports of internal states; and so on. Even when you decide which measure or measures to obtain, you still must decide whether to record the frequency of response, the intensity of response, the duration of response, the reaction time to the first response, or some combination of measures most appropriate to the question being asked. But how do we determine the appropriateness of a measure? One answer to this question is related to the conceptual question being asked. We discussed this aspect in Chapter 3, in relation to operational definitions and hypotheses.

Another answer comes from understanding basic statistical properties and operations. An introduction and review of descriptive statistics are the focus of this chapter. First, numbers are used in science to represent something beyond themselves, so we start the chapter with the concept of measurement. Second, it is important to know how to view data in terms of their underlying distribution, so we introduce simple pictorial methods of describing data and simple graphing. Third, it is important to be able to create the major statistical descriptors that describe a set of data; we therefore introduce the ideas of central tendency and variability. Fourth, we discuss the manner in which data may be transformed; in this context we present the idea of a standard score. Fifth, we discuss a simple way of describing the relationships within a set of data, using measures of association and particular correlational procedures. It should be noted that even in today's environment, when computer programs are readily available for describing, graphically representing, and analyzing data, it is still important that one have a fundamental understanding of how these processes work and their advantages and disadvantages.

## MEASUREMENT

How we measure things is part of the field of study called measurement theory (Krantz, Luce, Suppes, & Tversky, 1971; Luce & Narens, 1987). Two of the first questions we are faced with in doing research are "What can we measure?" and "What do the measurements mean?" A number may be used in a variety of ways. Sometimes numbers are used to identify particular objects or events, as when a friend tells you she lives at 56 Walnut Spring

Lane. Sometimes numbers are used to mean "more than," as when a child says that a bike must cost $1 million more than a candy bar. As adults, we do the same thing when we tell someone that we woke up in the middle of the night and stayed awake for hours. Numbers can also be used to indicate an exact relationship. We know that the difference between 700 and 900 is the same as the difference between 300 and 500. Finally, numbers can be used to specify a unit of measure, such as 25¢.

We have just discussed four different ways in which numbers may be used in terms of four specific properties: identity, magnitude, equal intervals, and absolute zero. We can use these properties to help us define levels of measurement, or **scales of measurement** as they are sometimes called.

# SCALES OF MEASUREMENT

We commonly discuss four basic levels or scales of measurement. These are nominal, ordinal, interval, and ratio. They are summarized in Table 4.1 and discussed in this section. Our discussion will be somewhat brief; for more technical presentations see Coombs, Raiffa, and Thrall (1954), Roberts (1979), and Stevens (1946, 1951, 1957).

## ■ Nominal Measurement

*Nominal* (sometimes called *categorical*) *measurement* occurs when people are simply placed into different categories. This form of measurement is a classifying or naming activity (hence the term *nominal*). For example, you can classify your research participants as men or women, as right-handed or left-handed, as Catholic or Protestant. The differences between categories are of kind (qualitative) and not of degree (quantitative). In many research problems, it is sufficient to determine simply whether the number of individuals in a given category varies as a function of some treatment in which you are interested. For example, you might want to determine whether the percentage of people willing to try a new product is altered by a particular type of advertising. Your behavioral measure would then be whether an individual is willing to try a new product. Numbers themselves sometimes can be used as nominal categories. For example, the numbers on baseball jerseys, telephone numbers, and ZIP codes illustrate nominal uses of numbers, as do coding data (e.g., male = 1, female = 2).

## ■ Ordinal Measurement

In the case of *ordinal measurement* there usually is a single continuum that underlies a particular classification system. College football standings, pop music charts, and class standings are examples of ordinal measurements. In a psychological experiment, you might divide up your research participants on the basis of creativity and end up with three categories: noncreative, creative, and highly creative, which can be given the values 1, 2, and 3, respectively. These scores reflect an underlying continuum: the *relative amount* or *magnitude* of creativity. An ordinal scale represents some degree of quantitative difference, whereas a nominal scale does not.

Table 4.1

| Scales of Measurement | | |
|---|---|---|
| | Properties | Examples |
| Nominal | Identity | Telephone numbers, numbers on uniforms, results of races, brands of soup, employment statuses, diagnostic categories (schizophrenic, paranoid, neurotic, etc.) |
| Ordinal | Identity, magnitude | Class standing, weekly college football polls |
| Interval | Identity, magnitude, equal intervals | Temperature (Fahrenheit or Celsius), scores on intelligence tests, scores on personality adjustment inventories |
| Ratio | Identity, magnitude, equal intervals, absolute zero point | Length, weight, time, reaction time, number of responses made by an individual |

Ordinal scales can be obtained whenever you rank research participants or events along a single dimension. With ordinal measures, you are making statements only about order; the differences between consecutive values are not necessarily equal. Notice that numbers used in ordinal measurement have no mathematical properties other than providing categories and rank. Nothing is implied about the magnitude of the intervals between the categories. For example, in the case of the top 20 football teams, there is no assumption that the difference in excellence between the number 1 team and the number 4 team is the same as that between the number 6 team and the number 9 team. Furthermore, it does not make sense to say that the number 1 and 4 teams together equal the number 2 and 3 teams.

What we are really doing is transforming information expressed in one form to that expressed in another. For example, think of the food you ate for supper last night. One way of presenting this information is to name the foods: pizza, soft drink, salad, green stuff (no one really knows what green stuff is, but every college cafeteria has a large supply of it). We can take this list of food and transform it into numerical representations. One simple method uses the property of identity. We can assign numbers to our food items to identify or distinguish single foods or groups. For example, we might let "1" represent all food that we feel better after eating and "0" stand for all food that we feel worse after eating. Pizza, soft drink, and salad would get a "1," and green stuff would get a "0." We have mapped the aspects of one set onto another set. All this means is that we have found another way (other than just listing) to represent our data.

This is not the only way that we can represent our data, however. We could also assign numbers to refer to how much we like the food. We could assign pizza a "1," salad a "2," soft drink a "3," and green stuff a "4." We have now presented the data in terms of the characteristic of magnitude. From this you know that pizza is ranked higher than a soft drink but, as with a list of finishers in a race, you do not know anything about how much distance exists between them.

## Interval Measurement

In *interval measurement,* the scale values are related by a single underlying quantitative dimension (like ordinal data) and there are also equal intervals between consecutive scale values. *Equal intervals* means that there are equal amounts of the quantity being measured between every two successive numbers on the scale. Thus, on an interval scale, the interval between 1 and 4 equals the interval between 6 and 9. The household thermometer is an example of an interval scale. The degree lines are equal distances apart and reflect equal volumes of mercury; the difference between 20° and 40° is equivalent to the difference between 50° and 70°. When we say it is 0° outside, we do not mean that there is no temperature; we mean only that 0° is assigned a certain place on the scale.

## Ratio Measurement

In *ratio measurement,* scores are related by a single quantitative dimension (as with interval or ordinal measurement). Also, they are separated by equal intervals (as with interval measurement), *and* there is an absolute zero. The most common ratio scales are found in the measurement of the physical attributes of objects, such as weight or length. There is no length shorter than 0 inches, no weight lighter than 0 pounds.

For example, if we were to represent our list of foods according to calorie content, we would know that the relationship between the 300-calorie salad and the 150-calorie soft drink was the same as that between the 300-calorie salad and the 450-calorie pizza; there is a 150-calorie difference between each pair.

We could also describe the food in terms of nutritional value, such as its ability to support life or its vitamin content. As you begin to make this mapping, you realize the need to have an absolute zero point. There is no way that green stuff could ever support life, much less contain vitamins. Thus, we could use numbers to represent the amount of a particular vitamin in the food. Pizza might have 33 units, the soft drink 12 units, salad 52 units, and of course, green stuff would have 0 units. Zero in this case means that the vitamin is not present at all; 0 represents an actual quantity.

## Identifying Scales of Measurement

Frequently, the scale of measurement depends on the device (scale, questionnaire, etc.) used for measuring the particular concept being studied. Even clear examples from the physical sciences (e.g., temperature or length) that are normally viewed as being an interval or ratio measure could not be so called if the measuring instrument itself were not well constructed. In turn, the design of the measuring instrument depends on a theoretical understanding of the underlying concept. For example, until the development of the kinetic theory of heat, the measurement of temperature was inconsistent. There were many devices, each giving different results that could not be converted from one scale to another as they can now (e.g., Celsius to Fahrenheit). Once a theoretical description of heat was developed, the problems of measurement were reduced. This may also be the case in psychology, with our many concepts lacking well-developed theory (e.g., anxiety or intelligence).

Scales of measurement are related to how a particular concept is being measured and the questions being asked. For example, if we were to record the order of finish in a marathon, we would have an ordinal scale, whereas if we were to record times for the race, we would have a ratio scale. Measuring devices should be both reliable and valid; these concepts were discussed in Chapter 3, and we refer to them throughout this book.

---

 **CONCEPT CHECK 4.1**    Which scale of measurement best describes the following: telephone numbers; distances from Budapest to cities in the United States; temperatures throughout the year in Tuscaloosa, Alabama; and the ranking of basketball teams in the Big Ten?

---

## MEASUREMENT AND STATISTICS

Mitchell (1986) tried to place the question of measurement scales and statistics in an historical and a philosophical context. He suggested that there are different theories or paradigms of measurement. For example, when we were in college taking methods courses, it was commonly taught that a direct relationship existed between the particular scale of measurement (nominal, ordinal, interval, or ratio) that we were using and a statistic (e.g., *t*-test or sign test) that was appropriate to use with it. This idea, along with the idea of scales of measurement, was introduced by S. S. Stevens in the 1940s (Stevens, 1946). The basic idea as traditionally taught is that the statistics used must be appropriate to the scale of measurement used.

Statisticians, as well as present-day experimentalists, no longer hold this view, and they continually point out that where a number comes from does not determine the appropriate statistical test. Gaito (1980) has presented a brief but clearly stated review of this issue. If you are interested in pursuing this further, you should consult Gaito's *Psychological Bulletin* article (1980) as well as Mitchell's *Psychological Bulletin* article (1986).

The main point is that no statistical reason exists for limiting a particular scale of measurement to a particular statistical procedure. The numbers do not care what you do to them. Lord (1953) illustrated this in a humorous manner with football numbers on the backs of players' jerseys. One could find the mean of all the players' numbers on a football team but keep in mind that, as Lord pointed out, "the numbers do not remember where they came from." Like a computer, a statistical technique does not care what numbers it uses or where the numbers come from. Numbers are numbers as far as a computer or statistic is concerned. However, if you want to make reasonable conceptual decisions based on your numbers, then you must be concerned about where your numbers came from, and this is an issue of measurement, not statistics.

To this end, some researchers make a pragmatic distinction between qualitative measures and quantitative measures. Using measurement theory, we try to assign numbers in a manner in which we can make sense out of what we are doing. But to restate, your statistics do not know and do not care where your numbers come from. It does not matter to a statistic whether your numbers mean what you claim they do, much less whether your experiment was performed well or poorly. However, as a researcher you should care greatly about your inferences and logic. But, as we discuss in this chapter, statistics *do* tell us about numbers.

# PICTORIAL DESCRIPTION OF FREQUENCY INFORMATION

A useful way to begin analyzing the results of any experiment is to convert your numerical data to pictorial form, and then simply look at them. One way to depict the results of an experiment is to draw a **frequency distribution.** In a frequency distribution you simply plot how frequently each score appears in your data. Suppose you were interested in dreaming. One initial baseline measurement might be to ask 20 people to write down their dreams for a week. To get an idea of how often people dream, you might begin your analysis by seeing how many dreams each person recalls.

Table 4.2 demonstrates such an experiment and shows the number of dreams each person remembered dreaming. To create a pictorial representation, a first step would be to find the smallest number of dreams recalled (0 in our case) and the largest number of dreams recalled (7). You could then list all the numbers between 1 and 7. Going through all the responses recorded in Table 4.2, you could make a mark by the number of dreams recalled for each person in your study. Now you have two variables (number of dreams recalled and number of people who recalled a certain number of dreams). This information can be plotted on a graph. Figure 4.1 shows such a graph, which represents a frequency distribution for these data. The vertical or *y*-axis (**ordinate**), labeled "frequency," is the number of people who fall into each category, and the horizontal or *x*-axis (**abscissa**) is the number of dreams recalled. This type of presentation is called a *bar graph.*

Table 4.2

| Hypothetical Dream Study | | | |
|---|---|---|---|
| Participant | Number of Dreams Recalled | Participant | Number of Dreams Recalled |
| 1 | 1 | 11 | 7 |
| 2 | 4 | 12 | 1 |
| 3 | 5 | 13 | 2 |
| 4 | 2 | 14 | 5 |
| 5 | 0 | 15 | 6 |
| 6 | 2 | 16 | 5 |
| 7 | 0 | 17 | 2 |
| 8 | 6 | 18 | 6 |
| 9 | 1 | 19 | 7 |
| 10 | 3 | 20 | 5 |

In Figure 4.1, the two blocks above a 0 score mean that two people reported no dreams during the week. Counting the other blocks, we learn that three people reported only one dream, four people reported two dreams, and so forth. Because the measurements along the *x*-axis may be treated as interval data, we could also present them in the form of a *frequency polygon*. A frequency polygon of the dream data is presented in Figure 4.2.

On closer inspection, it appears that measurements for most people tend to be clustered either to the left or to the right on the *x*-axis. This means that, for these 20 people, dreams were recalled either infrequently (one or two dreams) or frequently (five, six, or

**Figure 4.1**

Bar graph of
dream data

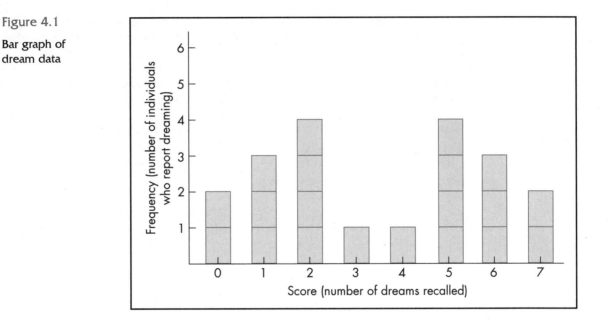

**Figure 4.2**

Frequency polygon
of dream data

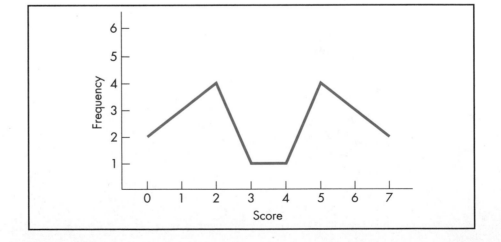

seven dreams). This particular type of distribution, in which the people tend to fall into two groups, is called a **bimodal distribution.** Some common types of distributions you might encounter are illustrated in Figure 4.3.

For our purpose, we call a distribution *normal* if it approximates a *bell-shaped* distribution (see Figure 4.3a). We will present a more exact definition later, but for now we will say that a distribution is normal if most of the scores are concentrated in the center of the abscissa, with few at the extremes. Intelligence test scores for 1000 randomly selected people approximate a normal distribution. In a bimodal distribution, the scores tend to be concentrated at two points along the abscissa (see Figures 4.2 and 4.3b). The distribution of heights for an equal number of men and women tends to be bimodal.

A *skewed distribution* occurs when more scores occur at either end of the abscissa (see Figures 4.3c and 4.3d). For example, a distribution of verbal Scholastic Aptitude Test (SAT) scores among honors English majors would be skewed because few people with low verbal SAT scores would be included in this group. A skewed distribution can be skewed in either a positive or a negative direction. The slopes of the curves indicate whether the distribution is positively or negatively skewed. Simply said, if we begin at the point of our graph where the *x*- and *y*-axes meet (the left side of the graph), we can ask whether the values represented in the graph increase faster than they decrease. If this is the case, then we would say there is a steeper slope on the ascending curve that indicates that the distribution is positively skewed. A steeper slope on the descending curve indicates that the distribution is negatively skewed. Of course, in a normal distribution, the slopes of the ascending and descending curves are equal.

Figure 4.3

Four types of frequency distributions: (a) normal, (b) bimodal, (c) positively skewed, and (d) negatively skewed

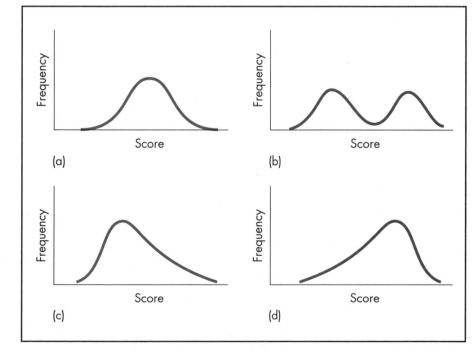

# DESCRIPTIVE STATISTICS

## ■ Measures of Central Tendency

There are three measures of central tendency that we discuss in this section. These are the mean, the median, and the mode. If you listen carefully to the television news, you will notice that these measures often are used to describe the way we "typically" live. You will hear one report discussing the median income of college professors; another report may discuss the mean price of a new house in different cities in America. Modal (mode) descriptions are used less often.

Mean  Of the three measures of central tendency, the mean is used most often. The **mean** of a set of scores is the arithmetic average of those scores. It is obtained by adding the scores and dividing the total by the number of scores. In our dream data, a total of 70 dreams recalled was reported by 20 people.

$$\text{mean} = \frac{\text{sum of scores}}{\text{number of scores}} = \frac{\text{number of dreams recalled}}{\text{number of individuals}} = \frac{70}{20} = 3.5$$

In this particular example, 70 divided by 20 equals exactly 3.5. However, other times the answer may give us a recurring decimal, which must be rounded off to a given number of decimal places. For example, if the total score for 7 participants were 100, the mean would equal 14.285714285714. . . . The simple rule used by most researchers is to round up if the number is greater than or equal to 5 and to round down if it is less than 5. In this case, if we were to round to four decimal places the mean would be 14.2857, whereas if we were to round to two decimal places the mean would be 14.29. We follow this rounding rule for any calculation performed in this book.

Median  The **median** of a set of scores is the middle score, that is, the score that has an equal number of scores both above and below it. To calculate the median of a set of scores, list all the scores in order of magnitude (from largest to smallest or vice versa); the median is the middle score or, in the case of an even number of scores, the score halfway between the two middle scores. In our dream data, the two middle scores are 3 and 4. Consequently, the median is 3.5.

A slight problem in calculating the median arises when the median interval contains a large number of scores. In this case, we must interpolate so that an equal number of scores are above and below the median. This procedure is not required in this book. It is discussed in various statistics books, such as McCall (1980, pp. 64–66).

Mode  The **mode** is the most frequently occurring score. The only mathematical calculation required to compute the mode of a distribution of scores is to count the frequency of each score. The score that occurs most frequently is the mode. If there are two scores with the same frequency, we report two modes. For example, the dream data presented earlier had two modes: one at two dreams and one at five dreams recalled.

Choice of Measures  Given these three measures, you may be wondering which provides the best estimate of central tendency. There is no clear-cut answer. The appropriate choice varies with the particular frequency distribution and the intent of the researcher. For example, in a normal distribution the mode, median, and mean all have the same value

**Figure 4.4**

**Figure 4.4**

Mean, median, and mode of (a) a normal distribution and (b) a skewed distribution

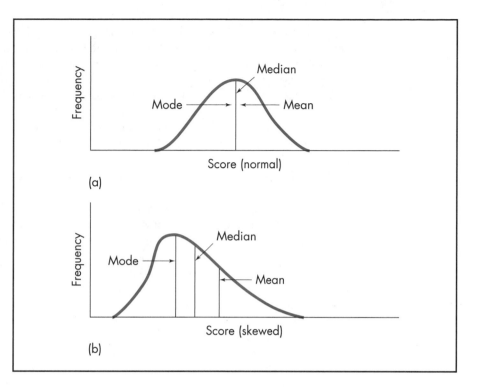

(a)

(b)

(Figure 4.4a). This is not the case in a skewed distribution (Figure 4.4b). In a skewed distribution, the mean is affected by extreme scores.

For example, before you take a job in a company where the mean salary is $100,000 a year, you might want to find out the median salary; a mean of $100,000 could be produced by 10 people making $10,000 each and 1 person making $1,000,000 (1,100,000/11 = 100,000). If you were a stock market analyst concerned with how much a company pays out in salaries, however, the mean would be the appropriate measure. In other words, if you are interested in the scores of a whole group, then the mean is the most appropriate measure.

However, if you are more interested in a representative individual score, then the median is more appropriate. In psychological research, we tend to use the mean most often both for historical reasons and because it fits into already developed statistical theory. In summary, the measure of central tendency you use depends on the question you are asking. In the final analysis, you must use your judgment to determine which measure of central tendency to use.

---

✓ CONCEPT CHECK 4.2    You have just graduated from college and you are applying for a job at three companies. Widget, Inc., tells you that its mean salary is $50,000. Fast Food, Inc., tells you that its median salary is $50,000. And Deals-Are-Us, Inc., tells you that the modal salary of its workers is $50,000. If salary were your only concern in taking a job, which company would you be most interested in, and what additional information might you want to know?

## ■ Measures of Variability

You probably have completed a science course assignment requiring you to make measurements of some physical dimension, such as the length of a line. The exact readings among students probably differed. Thinking about this, we can gain some intuitive understanding concerning an important concept: **variability.** If we were to plot each measurement, we would see that the measurements varied around a particular point. We could also imagine that contained within these measurements was the actual length of the line or the true score. Thus, we can imagine any measurement to be composed of a true measurement plus the variability associated with that measurement. From this understanding, we can move to a more general notion that processes themselves may vary. For example, your weight may change from day to day while still remaining constant when viewed over a series of measurements. Thus, to describe a set of measurements more accurately, we need the concept of variability.

As we have seen, a measure of central tendency gives us some information concerning a set of scores; however, it does not give any information about how the scores are distributed. To obtain a more complete description of a set of data, we use a second measure in addition to the measure of central tendency. This is a measure of *variability*. Measures of variability are merely attempts to indicate how spread out the scores are. We can also call this variability *dispersion*. One common measure of dispersion is the **range,** which reflects the difference between the largest and smallest scores in a set of data. The actual computational formula given for the range in most introductory statistics books is the largest score minus the smallest score. (In the dream data presented earlier, the range is 7; that is, $7 - 0 = 7$.) This is technically called the *exclusive range* (Keppel & Saufley, 1980). Although computing the range is easy, the range tells us only about the two extreme scores; it provides no information about the dispersion of the remaining scores if we know nothing about the underlying distribution.

Let us now demonstrate this graphically. Consider the following two sets of data for Group A and Group B.

| Group A | Group B |
|---------|---------|
| 2 | 2 |
| 3 | 5 |
| 4 | 5 |
| 5 | 6 |
| 6 | 6 |
| 7 | 6 |
| 8 | 7 |
| 9 | 7 |
| 10 | 10 |

In these two distributions, the ranges are the same (8) and the means are the same (6), yet the actual shapes of the distributions are very different (Figure 4.5). The scores in Group B appear more concentrated in the center of the distribution, yet our estimate of range does not reflect this. To provide a more sensitive description of the dispersion of *all* the scores, we use a second measure of the variability of data. This measure is called the *variance.*

Simply stated, the variance is a description of how much each score varies from the mean. One way to describe the dispersion of *all* the scores would be to subtract each score from the mean and then add these deviations and divide the total by the number of scores. Unfortunately, for both technical and practical reasons, this approach does not give us the type of information we need. Because the sum of the positive deviations is always equal to the sum of the negative deviations from the mean, adding these deviations gives a sum of 0. Instead, we

**Figure 4.5**

Two different distributions with the same range and mean but different dispersions of scores

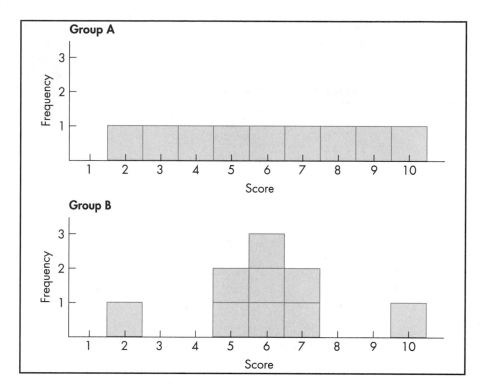

square each deviation, add the squares, and then divide the total by the number of deviations. This gives us a description of how much each score varies from the mean. From this we arrive at the definition of *variance:* the average of the squared deviations from the mean.

To determine variance, we must first calculate what is called the **sum of the squares;** that is, we add the numbers squared. The sum of the squares is often abbreviated as *SS*. The first formula for *SS* that we will describe is called the deviation method: The sum of the squares is equal to the sum of the squared deviation scores. Thus,

$$SS = \sum (X - \bar{X})^2$$

where $\sum$ = sum of, $X$ = the individual score, and $\bar{X}$ = the mean of scores.

The deviation method is a useful teaching device because it requires that you compute the actual deviations for each score. The method is cumbersome, however. Once you master the concept, you might want to consider a second way to calculate the sum of squares. This is called the *computational formula* and sometimes is used simply because it requires less work, particularly on hand-held calculators:

$$SS = \sum X^2 - \frac{\left(\sum X\right)^2}{N}$$

where $X$ = individual score and $N$ = number of observations.

In Table 4.3, the sum of squares, *SS*, of a set of data is calculated by the deviation method. In Table 4.4, the sum of squares for the same set of data is calculated by the computational method. The difference in *SS* for the two methods reflects the rounding of the data to two decimal places during computation. As you remember the definition of variance—the average of the squared deviations from the mean—you will realize that we must now determine the average of the sum of squares. However, in determining the variance, we divide by $N$ for a description of a single population. Remember we are discussing descriptive statistics at this point. As you will learn in the next chapter, $N - 1$ will be used with inferential statistics since this has been shown to be more accurate.

$$\text{variance} = \frac{\sum \text{of squares}}{\text{number of scores}} = \frac{SS}{N}$$

Using the example in Table 4.4, in which the sum of squares equals 93.75, we determine variance by dividing this sum by the number of scores (20). Thus,

$$\text{variance} = \frac{SS}{N} = \frac{93.75}{20} = 4.69$$

This calculation formula for variance now appears as follows:

$$\text{variance} = \frac{\sum X^2 - \dfrac{(\sum X)^2}{N}}{N}$$

At this point, let us return to the two sets of data used in Figure 4.5. We saw that even though these distributions look quite different, the range for each distribution is the same.

Table 4.3

| Deviation Method | | |
| --- | --- | --- |
| Individual Score ($X$) | Deviation ($X - \overline{X}$) | ($X - \overline{X}$)² |
| 1 | −2.75 | 7.56 |
| 4 | 0.25 | 0.06 |
| 5 | 1.25 | 1.56 |
| 2 | −1.75 | 3.06 |
| 0 | −3.75 | 14.06 |
| 2 | −1.75 | 3.06 |
| 5 | 1.25 | 1.56 |
| 6 | 2.25 | 5.06 |
| 1 | −2.75 | 7.56 |
| 3 | −0.75 | 0.56 |
| 7 | 3.25 | 10.56 |
| 1 | −2.75 | 7.56 |
| 2 | −1.75 | 3.06 |
| 5 | 1.25 | 1.56 |
| 6 | 2.25 | 5.06 |
| 5 | 1.25 | 1.56 |
| 2 | −1.75 | 3.06 |
| 6 | 2.25 | 5.06 |
| 7 | 3.25 | 10.56 |
| 5 | 1.25 | 1.56 |
| Sum ($\sum$) =0 | Sum ($\sum$) =93.70 | |

$\overline{X} = 3.75$

$SS = \sum(X - \overline{X})^2$

$= 93.70$

Granting for the moment that variance is a more sensitive measure of dispersion, let us see whether it provides a more useful tool than range for describing the dispersion about the mean of a group of scores. Table 4.5 shows the calculation of the variance for Group A using the deviation method; Table 4.6 shows the calculation for Group B.

We see that Group B has a lower variance (4) than Group A (6.67). This supports our earlier subjective analysis, which indicated less variability, or dispersion, in Group B than in Group A. Because variance uses squared scores, however, the variance does not describe the amount of variability in the same units of measurement as the original scores; that is, a variance of 6.67 exceeds the greatest absolute deviation in either sample. Consequently, many researchers prefer to use the square root of the variance as their estimate of variability. The square root of the variance is called the **standard deviation** (*SD*):

$$SD = \sqrt{\text{variance}}$$

For Group A (variance = 6.67),

$$SD = \sqrt{6.67} = 2.58$$

For Group B (variance = 4),

$$SD = \sqrt{4} = 2$$

By making this transformation, we return to the original units of measurement and can therefore make meaningful comparative statements.

Table 4.4

| Computational Method | |
|---|---|
| Individual Score (X) | $X^2$ |
| 1 | 1 |
| 4 | 16 |
| 5 | 25 |
| 2 | 4 |
| 0 | 0 |
| 2 | 4 |
| 5 | 25 |
| 6 | 36 |
| 1 | 1 |
| 3 | 9 |
| 7 | 49 |
| 1 | 1 |
| 2 | 4 |
| 5 | 25 |
| 6 | 36 |
| 5 | 25 |
| 2 | 4 |
| 6 | 36 |
| 7 | 49 |
| 5 | 25 |
| Sum $\left(\sum\right) = 75$ | Sum $\left(\sum\right) = 375$ |

$$SS = \sum X^2 - \frac{\left(\sum X\right)^2}{N}$$

$$= 375 - \frac{(75)^2}{20}$$

$$= 375 - \frac{5625}{20}$$

$$= 375 - 281.25$$

$$= 93.75$$

Table 4.5

## Group A Variance

| Individual Score ($X$) | Deviation ($X - \overline{X}$) | $(X - \overline{X})^2$ |
|:---:|:---:|:---:|
| 2 | −4 | 16 |
| 3 | −3 | 9 |
| 4 | −2 | 4 |
| 5 | −1 | 1 |
| 6 | 0 | 0 |
| 7 | +1 | 1 |
| 8 | +2 | 4 |
| 9 | +3 | 9 |
| 10 | +4 | 16 |
| | $\sum = 0$ | $\sum = 60$ |

$$\text{Variance} = \frac{\sum (X - \overline{X})^2}{N} = \frac{60}{9} = 6.67$$

Table 4.6

## Group B Variance

| Individual Score ($X$) | Deviation ($X - \overline{X}$) | $(X - \overline{X})^2$ |
|:---:|:---:|:---:|
| 2 | −4 | 16 |
| 5 | −1 | 1 |
| 5 | −1 | 1 |
| 6 | 0 | 0 |
| 6 | 0 | 0 |
| 6 | 0 | 0 |
| 7 | +1 | 1 |
| 7 | +1 | 1 |
| 10 | +4 | 16 |
| | $\sum = 0$ | $\sum = 36$ |

$$\text{Variance} = \frac{\sum (X - \overline{X})^2}{N} = \frac{36}{9} = 4$$

 **CONCEPT CHECK 4.3**    Given the numbers 6, 5, 7, 9, 4, and 5, what are the mean, the variance, and the standard deviation?

# PICTORIAL PRESENTATIONS OF NUMERICAL DATA

In addition to using numerical descriptions of data—such as frequency counts, measures of central tendency, and variance—it usually is helpful to use graphs to present our results pictorially.

In psychology we have borrowed graphing procedures from other fields, such as mathematics, and we use many of their conventions. For example, the independent variable is placed on the *x*-axis and the dependent variable on the *y*-axis. Two main types of graphs are used: line graphs and bar graphs.

A *line graph* is used when the values of the independent variable correspond to points along a continuum. For example, you could graph the data from a study of the effects of room temperature on response rates in rats, as shown in Figure 4.6.

A *bar graph* is used to depict information that is categorical. For example, the results of a study that examined the effects of different forms of therapy could be illustrated, as shown in Figure 4.7. It would not be appropriate in this case to construct a line graph

**Figure 4.6**

Effects of room temperature on response rates in rats

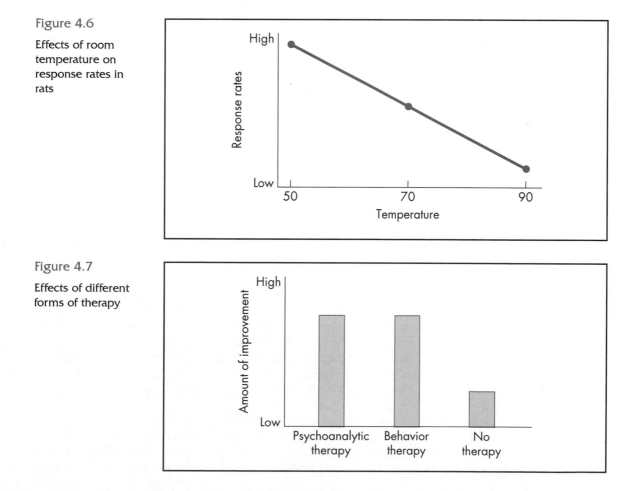

**Figure 4.7**

Effects of different forms of therapy

because these types of therapy do not lie along a continuum. (However, a line graph would be appropriate if the independent variable was the amount of a particular drug given because dosage levels of the *same* drug would form a continuum.)

## TRANSFORMING DATA

After collecting the data, a researcher may discover that the numbers are too large or too small to work with comfortably. At this point the question arises, "How can I change these data to make them easier to work with?" The procedure is to transform the data. There are a variety of techniques for accomplishing this goal, depending on the type of data and the desired outcome of the transformation. In this section, we introduce the topic briefly.

If you were to travel to Canada, Mexico, or Europe, you might be surprised to look at the temperature listed and see that it was only 30° when you were sweating. The explanation, of course, is that these countries use the Celsius scale, whereas the United States uses the Fahrenheit scale. Water freezes at 0° on the Celsius scale and boils at 100°. To convert to Fahrenheit, you multiply the Celsius reading by 9/5 and add 32. Thus, our reading of 30° would equal 86°.

When we converted the temperature from Celsius to Fahrenheit, we performed what is called a *linear transformation*. This means that if we were to draw a graph of the relationship between temperatures expressed in Fahrenheit and in Celsius, the resulting figure would be a straight line. You might try this for yourself by looking in a newspaper and recording the temperatures from around the world, then converting these into Celsius and plotting the relationship between Celsius and Fahrenheit. Using the example of temperature, we can see that there is a general formula that describes a linear transformation. Using three values that remain constant ($A$, $B$, and $C$), the formula is as follows:

$$\text{new number} = \frac{A}{B}\,(\text{old number}) + C$$

Because the values A, B, and C may be either positive or negative, we can add, subtract, multiply, or divide the values or perform a combination of these operations in a linear transformation.

Transformations are important for several reasons. The first is simply that researchers can use transformations to compare data collected using one scale with those collected using another. For example, in a biofeedback study designed to determine how well participants can raise their hand temperature, some researchers might report their data using Fahrenheit and others Celsius. Transforming the reported data makes it possible to compare the results.

Another reason for the importance of data transformation relates to statistical assumptions that are suggested for performing inferential statistical comparisons. If the researcher violates one of the assumptions, the results sometimes are difficult to interpret; one can sometimes avoid this problem by transforming the data so that the assumption is not violated. (This topic is discussed in some advanced statistical textbooks.)

We can now introduce a concept that Roberts (1979) calls *meaningfulness*. He holds that a statement is meaningful if the truth or falsity of the statement remains unchanged when one scale is replaced by another. To understand this better, let us look at an example. Imagine that you have performed a study in which you measured people's weights after a certain amount of exercise. One group received more exercise than the other. If we were to transform our data from weight in pounds to weight in kilograms, we still would be able to make meaningful statements concerning the relationship between the two groups. However, in other cases this might not be true. For example, one measure (and underlying theory) of anxiety might reflect a scale construction different from that of another and thus prevent meaningful comparative statements because the scores from one anxiety scale could not be transformed to the other.

# STANDARD SCORES

We are often interested in understanding a score in terms of its relationship to other scores. For example, just knowing that a friend scored a 76 on a chemistry test and a 62 on a physics test does not tell the complete story. When one examines the distribution, it might turn out that the 62 would actually be the higher grade if these tests were graded on a curve. That is, if the mean of the chemistry test were 85 with a standard deviation of 5 and the mean of the physics test were 50 with a standard deviation of 10, then our friend would be above the mean on the physics test but below the mean on the chemistry test. We could not compare the scores of the two tests unless we could present each of them in terms of its relative position on a particular distribution.

By asking the relative position of a particular score in terms of its mean and standard deviation, we create what is called a standard score. We also could transform all the scores of a particular set (e.g., the chemistry test) into standard scores. The most common transformation of this kind is the z score transformation. In more formal language, a z score for one particular measurement is a deviation score that is calculated by subtracting the mean of the distribution from that score and then dividing the difference by the standard deviation (which is the same as the square root of the variance). The formula is written as follows:

$$z = \frac{\text{score} - \text{mean}}{SD} = \frac{\text{score} - \text{mean}}{\sqrt{\text{variance}}}$$

It is possible for a z score to be either positive or negative, depending on whether it is greater or less than the mean. There are two important characteristics of the z score. First, if we were to transform a set of data to z scores, we would find that the mean of these scores would equal 0. Second, the standard deviation of this set of z scores would equal 1. Being able to make this transformation has a number of advantages, which we discuss more fully later. For example, once we transformed our friend's chemistry and physics test scores, we could make a statement comparing how well he was doing relatively in each class.

For ease of presentation, z scores sometimes are transformed. For example, negative z scores can be transformed so that the negative numbers are removed. The SAT exams that are required for admission to some colleges can be viewed as transformed z scores based on a mean of 500 and a standard deviation of 100 for each portion of the test. For your information, the actual formula of the SAT score is 100 times the z score plus 500. A similar

"THIS IS THE PART I ALWAYS HATE."

transformation of the *z* score that also allows all the numbers to be positive is the *T* score. In this case the formula is 10 times the *z* score plus 50. *T*-score information is commonly seen in psychometric presentations such as intelligence tests.

## MEASURE OF ASSOCIATION

Psychologists have long been interested in the question of whether our behavior and our self-reports go together—that is, whether we actually do what we say we will. To understand this question better, we could develop a questionnaire that asked people how often they would help people in need of assistance. We could also set up a situation in which there were many opportunities to help another person. If we had conducted this study, we could plot our data as shown in Figure 4.8. In this graph, called a *scatter diagram* or scatterplot, the score on the helpfulness questionnaire is on the *x*-axis and the number of times the person actually helped someone is on the *y*-axis. Each point on the scatter diagram represents one person and two scores: the score on the questionnaire and the number of times that the person helped someone in the experiment.

Note that those who score high on one measure also score high on the other measure. Likewise, those who score low on one also score low on the other. A useful statistic to apply to this type of analysis is the *correlation*. A correlation helps us to understand the relationship or degree of association between two measures. When we perform a correlation, we derive a correlation coefficient, which ranges between +1 and −1. A positive correlation represents a linear relationship between two factors, such that large values of one measure are associated with large values of the other.

**Figure 4.8**

Scatter diagram
showing positive
relationship
between two
measures

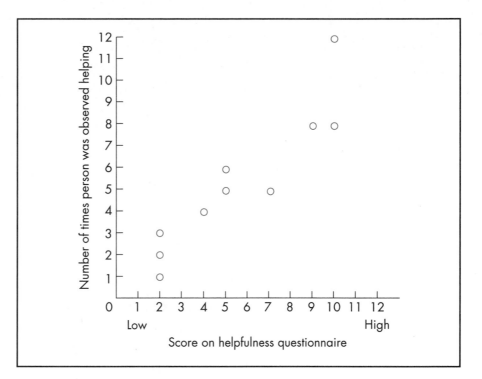

In our example, a positive correlation would show a positive association between reporting that one would help in a situation and actually helping in a situation (see Figure 4.8). A zero correlation would show no relationship; that is, how a participant filled out the questionnaire would not be related in any way to how he or she actually behaved. A negative correlation would be found for people who either said they would help but did not or said they would not help but did. An illustration of a negative association is shown in Figure 4.9. Figure 4.10 illustrates various relationships between two variables.

One of the most common correlation coefficients is the Pearson Product Moment Correlation Coefficient, or *r*. A *moment* measure is the distance between the mean and a score. In determining the correlation, we standardize the scores as *z* scores, which would include determining the moments (i.e., the differences between the scores and the mean) and use these to calculate correlation. The advantage of this procedure is that the two measures that you are correlating do not have to be in the same units of measurement because each is standardized. The exact formula is

$$r_{xy} = \frac{\sum z_x z_y}{N}$$

We begin by showing you this formula to help you gain an intuitive understanding of the correlation coefficient. However, this is not the formula you will see most commonly because rarely has the *z* score of your measures been calculated previously. Using the most common formula that begins with raw (non-*z*) scores, we will create a set of data to illustrate how you would determine the Pearson *r* using hypothetical measures of helping behavior (see Box 4.1). In your own class you might measure everyone's height and weight, and then compute a similar correlation coefficient.

Figure 4.9

Scatter diagram
showing negative
relationship
between two
measures

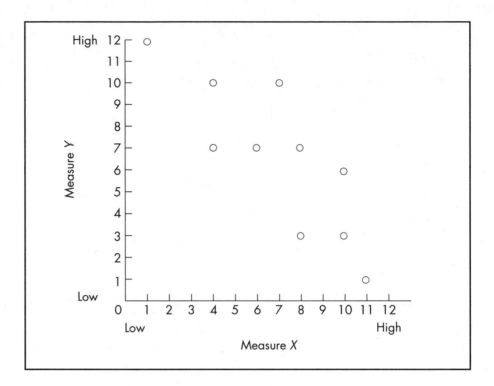

An important question now arises: What can you say about the underlying causal relationship between the two measures under study (e.g., height and weight, or self-report and observed measures of helping)? Nothing! Correlations have to do with associations between two measures; they tell us nothing about the causal relationship between the two variables. We do not know whether either variable caused the other, or even whether both variables were influenced by a third, extraneous variable.

For example, we could tell you our latest theory, stating that the size of your feet determines how fast you read. We could then show you data, collected from thousands of children, showing that as foot size increases, so does reading speed. Great theory, right? Although it may be a great theory, a positive correlation coefficient will do nothing to support it. Correlations do not help us to understand causality because there are numerous factors that are not in any way considered. In our example, the size of the feet and the reading speed were both related to development and had nothing to do with each other.

---

✓ CONCEPT
  CHECK 4.4

It was found that as the temperature increases, the sales of fur coats decrease. Would such a relationship result in a positive, negative, or zero correlation? If you were to draw such a scatter diagram, making up your own numbers, how would the graph look?

---

Additional information can be derived from the correlation coefficient. When you square the correlation coefficient (referred to as $r^2$) and multiply this number by 100, you

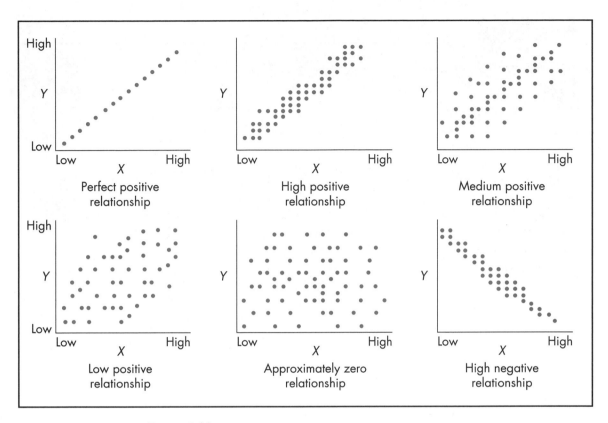

Figure 4.10

Scatter diagrams showing various relationships that differ in degree and direction

have the amount of the variance in one measure due to the other measure. For example, in a study relating EEG functioning and spatial ability performance, Ray, Newcombe, Semon, and Cole (1981) found a −.71 correlation between hemispheric activity and spatial performance for males with high spatial abilities and a .20 correlation for a similar group of females. From this, one could calculate $r^2$ [$(−.71)^2$ = approximately .50; $.20^2$ = .04] and multiply by 100. We can then say that for males, 50% of the variability of the spatial performance is due to EEG activity; for females, 4%. Where we used the phrase "due to," others will say "explained" or "accounted for" or "predicted," but not "caused." Because correlations may go in either direction, you could also say that for males, 50% of the EEG activity is accounted for by spatial performance.

We can discuss not only the amount of variability accounted for but also the amount not accounted for. For example, if EEG activity explains 4% of the variability on spatial performance for high–spatial-ability females, then 96% of the variability is not explained by EEG activity and must be related to other factors. Although it is beyond our present discussion, it should also be noted that you could determine the amount of variance explained by multiplying the total variance by 4% in this example. The same procedure (e.g., 96% times total variance) could be used for determining the amount of variance

## Box 4.1

## Pearson Correlation Coefficient

Using hypothetical scores from the helping experiment, we will compute a Pearson correlation coefficient. In this example there are 10 people with two scores each. We will call the score on the helpfulness questionnaire $X$ and the score derived from the observation of the person $Y$. More information concerning this and other types of correlation coefficients can be obtained in most statistical textbooks. There are also statistical "cookbooks" that show you how to perform these calculations step by step (Bruning & Kintz, 1968; Linton & Gallo, 1975). Some books also include Fortran, C, and BASIC computer programs for finding correlation coefficients (Cohen & Holliday, 1982; Press et al., 1992).

| Participant | Questionnaire | | Observation | | |
| | Score ($X$) | $X^2$ | Score ($Y$) | $Y^2$ | $XY$ |
| --- | --- | --- | --- | --- | --- |
| 1 | 2 | 4 | 3 | 9 | 6 |
| 2 | 10 | 100 | 12 | 144 | 120 |
| 3 | 9 | 81 | 8 | 64 | 72 |
| 4 | 4 | 16 | 4 | 16 | 16 |
| 5 | 7 | 49 | 5 | 25 | 35 |
| 6 | 10 | 100 | 8 | 64 | 80 |
| 7 | 1 | 1 | 2 | 4 | 2 |
| 8 | 5 | 25 | 6 | 36 | 30 |
| 9 | 2 | 4 | 1 | 1 | 2 |
| 10 | 5 | 25 | 5 | 25 | 25 |
| $N = 10$ | $\sum X = 55$ | $\sum X^2 = 405$ | $\sum Y = 54$ | $\sum Y^2 = 388$ | $\sum XY = 388$ |
| | $(\sum X)^2 = 3025$ | | | $(\sum Y)^2 = 2916$ | |

$$r = \frac{N\sum XY - (\sum X)(\sum Y)}{\sqrt{N[\sum X^2 - (\sum X)^2][N\sum Y^2 - (\sum Y)^2]}}$$

$$= \frac{(10)(388) - (55)(54)}{\sqrt{[(10)(405) - (3025)][(10)(388) - (2916)]}}$$

$$= \frac{3880 - 2970}{\sqrt{(4050 - 3025)(3880 - 2916)}}$$

$$= \frac{910}{994.03} = .915$$

not explained. In doing this, we would say we have *partitioned* the total variance into that explained and that not explained. Although we are getting ahead of ourselves, what you should remember is that the statistical technique *analysis of variance*, which we discuss later in the book, and that of *regression*, which we discuss in the next few paragraphs, are both mathematically and conceptually related to the degree of association between two variables in terms of the amount of variance accounted for.

As a digression, we should point out that a low $r^2$ in itself does not mean that the finding is not important. For example, Rosenthal (1990) pointed out that although some studies show that psychotherapy accounts for only 10 percent of the variance, this is still higher than what has been called "the dramatic effects of AZT" in the treatment of AIDS, which accounts for approximately 5% of the variance. As we discuss later in this book, the value of a finding goes beyond a simple descriptive statement of the numbers. But we always need to consider how the numbers were derived.

However, at times we may want to go beyond just knowing the degree of association between two variables and actually predict how one variable influences the other. Of course, we need a good theoretical reason for doing so, but we will talk about that later. Suppose we wanted to predict someone's grade on a research methods exam based on how many hours he or she studied. One statistical technique to accomplish this goal is called *regression*. Conceptually, regression begins with a scatterplot and, like correlation, seeks to draw the best straight line through all the data points. It then asks for every corresponding change in $X$ (hours studied) what would be the change in $Y$ (grade). In this example, $X$ is the independent variable and $Y$ is the dependent variable. If the correlation between studying and grades is high (close to 1) then for every change in study time there should be an equal change in grade received, although on a different scale. If there is no correlation between studying and grades, then a change in studying would have no effect on the grade.

Regression is a mathematical way to use our data to estimate how well we can predict that a change in one variable (studying) will lead to a change in another variable (grades). Although beyond this current discussion, the formula for predicting our dependent variable (grade) from our independent variable (study time) is composed of two terms. The first term is called a *regression coefficient* or *slope* because it estimates the change in grades (dependent variable) for each additional hour studied (independent variable). The term is nothing more than the standard deviation of the dependent variable divided by the standard deviation of the independent variable, which is then multiplied by the correlation of our independent and dependent variables. The second term is a *constant* that simply asks what would be our grade (dependent variable) if we did not study at all (independent variable). That is, we might expect that we would get some points on the test from going to class or reading the textbook even though we did not study for the test, and this amount must be added when taking into account the effects of studying. Thus, the actual regression equation states that our estimation of the dependent variable is equal to the dependent variable times the regression coefficient plus the regression constant.

Based on these ideas, additional important statistical techniques (such as path analysis and causal modeling) also focus on making statements concerning causal connections. For example, Plomin, Corley, DeFries, and Fulker (1990) sought to determine the role of genetics and environment on television viewing in young children. By examining the correlations between the viewing habits of children and those of their biological siblings and parents, and the same correlations for adopted children, the researchers concluded that individual differences in television viewing are influenced by both genetic and environmental factors.

Let us return again to the underlying distribution, as can be illustrated by a scatterplot (see Figures 4.8–4.10). Sometimes just a single value that lies outside the normal pattern (often called an *outlier*) can change the magnitude of a correlation drastically. Furthermore, if the relationship of the two variables we are studying is not linear, then the correlation that we obtain will not adequately reveal the underlying relationship between them. In this case, a graphic representation would be an important first step to supply us with valuable information and help us to determine immediately whether there are outliers or whether the underlying distribution is not linear.

For example, if we were to plot age in months against the number of words that a very young child speaks, we would see that there is a sudden and dramatic shift at a certain age, which of course would produce a nonlinear relationship. Another example of a nonlinear relationship would be the *U*-shaped curve that is said to relate motivation and performance. In this example, one would perform poorly under conditions of high motivation or low motivation. The best performance would occur when there is a moderate amount of motivation. A correlation would not represent this *curvilinear* relationship accurately. Thus, for a correlation to give us the information we desire, the underlying relationship between the variables must be a linear one. Visually inspecting a scatterplot is an important first step in determining the nature of the relationship between two variables.

In closing, it should be noted that there are other correlation coefficients in addition to the Pearson *r*. These are designed for use when data are based on rank orders (e.g., Spearman *D*) or dichotomous data (e.g., point-biserial). These and other types of correlation coefficients are included in many textbooks and handbooks on statistics.

# KEY TERMS AND CONCEPTS

1. **Measurement**
   A. Scales of measurement
      ▪ Nominal
      ▪ Ordinal
      ▪ Interval
      ▪ Ratio
   B. Measurement and statistics
   C. Meaningfulness
2. **Pictorial description of frequency distribution**
   A. Bar graph
   B. Frequency polygon
   C. Bimodal distribution
   D. Positive skew
   E. Negative skew
   F. Normal distribution
3. **Measures of central tendency**
   A. Mean
   B. Median
   C. Mode

4. **Measures of variability**
   A. Range
   B. Variance
   C. Sum of the squares
   D. Standard deviation
5. **Graphs**
   A. Line graphs
   B. Bar graphs
6. **Transforming data**
   A. Transformations
   B. $z$ scores
   C. SAT scores
   D. $T$ scores
7. **Measure of association**
   A. Scatter diagram
   B. Positive correlation
   C. Negative correlation
   D. Amount of variance accounted for ($r^2$)
   E. Regression

# SUMMARY

1. An important question in research is what we measure and what these measurements mean. One aspect of this question is the realization that a number does not always mean the same thing. When we use a nominal scale of measurement, differences between categories are qualitative but not quantitative. Ordinal data reflect amount or magnitude along a continuum. Interval data reflect magnitude in terms of equal intervals between successive scale values. For ratio data, scores are related by a single continuum (like interval and ordinal data), have equal intervals (like interval data), and have an absolute zero.

2. A pictorial or graphic presentation of data is an important first step. The vertical axis of a graph is called the *y*-axis, or *ordinate*. The horizontal axis is called the *x*-axis, or *abscissa*. There are several kinds of graphs; one of the more commonly used is called a *bar graph*.

3. Common distributions have special names. Those presented in this chapter were normal, bimodal, positively skewed, and negatively skewed.

4. Three important measures of central tendency are the mean (determined by adding the scores and then dividing by the number of scores), the median (the middle score), and the mode (the most frequently occurring score).

5. Some scores may be transformed from one scale to another, as when a temperature on the Fahrenheit scale is transformed to a temperature on the Celsius scale. If such a transformation can be made, statements made about the original data also apply to the transformed data. This is called *meaningfulness*.

6. Measures of variability are important in psychological research. Variability, or dispersion, is related to how spread out a set of scores is. The most common measures of variability are range, variance, and standard deviation.

7. Special statistical techniques have been developed to determine how two sets of data are associated with each other. One such technique is correlation. A correlation aids us in understanding how two sets of scores are related, but it does not tell us whether one score influences the other or whether both scores were influenced by a third, unmeasured factor. Certain distributions, such as curvilinear ones, are not reflected accurately in a correlation coefficient.

# REVIEW QUESTIONS

1. What is measurement?
2. What are the four scales of measurement? Give an example of each.
3. Describe the bar graph presented in Figure 4.1 and name the type of distribution shown (e.g., normal curve or bimodal).
4. What is the formula for a mean?
5. What is a median?
6. What is a mode?
7. What is the simple definition of variance?
8. What is meant by the term *SS*, and how is it calculated?
9. What is the relationship between standard deviation and variance?
10. Describe the different types of data you would use with a line graph and with a bar graph.
11. What is a *z* score?
12. What does $r^2$ mean?

# DISCUSSION QUESTIONS AND PROJECTS

1. Find out the number of dreams the people in your class remember having had this week. Using these data, construct a frequency distribution and present it graphically.
2. Determine the mean, median, and mode as well as variance and standard deviation for the maximum daily temperatures in your area for April.
3. Construct a set of numbers in which the mean, median, and mode are the same, and another set in which they are different.
4. Why do some people say you can lie with statistics?
5. What are the differences between measurements and statistics?
6. Why do some people say that, in science, if you cannot measure it, it does not exist? What do you think?

*(continued)*

# DISCUSSION QUESTIONS AND PROJECTS *(continued)*

7. Ask the people in your class to write two things on a piece of paper: the populations of their high schools and a rating of how well they enjoyed their first weeks at college. How might you do this in such a way that you can obtain a measure of association between the two? Would this prove (or disprove) that coming from a small high school makes one enjoy college more in the first weeks? What are the problems with making such a statement?

8. For 2 weeks, record two numbers from a newspaper each day. For example, you might pick out the daily Dow Jones Industrial Average and the daily temperature in Redwood City, California. Determine the correlation between these two variables and discuss what conclusions you can draw.

9. A study reports that smoking is associated with cancer, with a correlation coefficient of .86. Discuss the amount of variability in cancer rates that is accounted for by smoking. Discuss what can be concluded from the study.

## InfoTrac College Edition: Exercises

Researchers use graphs for showing patterns and exploring relationships. In the 2001 *Annual Review of Psychology* article entitled "Statistical graphics," Howard Wainer and Paul Velleman describe the use of graphical presentations throughout the history of science and some new ideas for psychology's future use of graphics. Look up this article and other recent *Annual Review* articles in InfoTrac College Edition. (*Hint:* You can click on the PowerTrac button and then "journal" and "Annual Review of Psychology" to see which articles are available).

As you look at some of these articles, note each graph in the article (you may need to click on the graph to make it larger). What type of graph is it (e.g., line graph, bar graph, etc.)? What is the graph telling you? As you read the article, note when statistics are used to make a particular point.

Another article you can read is by Holly Wilcox and her colleagues in the journal *Adolescence* entitled "Correlations between BDI and CES-D in a sample of adolescent mothers." In it, you can see how the mean and standard deviation are used to present data. You could graph the data presented in Table 1 of the article to help you learn about graphs. As you read the article, you can see how correlations are used in scientific research. In this case, correlations are used to determine the relationship between measures of depression.

## Answers to Concept Checks

4.1 Telephone numbers represent nominal measurements, distances from Budapest represent a ratio scale, temperatures throughout the year represent an interval scale, and a team ranking represents an ordinal scale.

4.2 Of course, the best additional information to know would be what your salary would be. Barring that information, the shape of the distribution of salaries of the company would also give you important information to evaluate the meaning of the particular mean, median, and mode of salaries. If the distribution were normally distributed, then you would know that the salary distribution of each company was the same. If this were not the case, then the mean, median, and mode would have different meanings for each company. For example, many fast-food companies have

most of their employees making the least amount of money. In this situation, you might want to know the mode. Given the information presented in the question, we would go with Fast Food, Inc.

4.3 The mean is the sum divided by the number of entries. In this case the sum is 36 divided by 6, which equals 6. The variance equals the sum of squares, which is 16 divided by 6, which is 2.67. The standard variation is the square root of the variance, which equals 1.63. The relationship is a negative correlation. Such a graph is found in the lower right-hand corner of Figure 4.10.

4.4 The relationship between temperature and sales of fur coats would result in a negative correlation. The graph should look similar to Figure 4.9 or the bottom right figure (high negative relationship) in Figure 4.10.

# INFERENTIAL STATISTICS: MAKING STATISTICAL DECISIONS

PROBABILITY

THE NORMAL DISTRIBUTION

HYPOTHESIS TESTING

EXAMPLE OF INFERENTIAL STATISTICS:
THE *t*-TEST

Most of us are able to learn from experience. Like the child who touches a hot stove, we make decisions concerning future events based on past experiences. And like the child, we create for ourselves subjective probabilities about what the future will bring and what will happen if we touch the same hot stove again. We can do the same in regard to research. As we will see, one way to view research statistically is to ask what results we could expect if we ran the same experiment over and over again. The answer most of us would give is that we would expect the results to be similar. This answer reflects a long heritage of science, best exemplified by the Newtonian approach to physics. When we use such a classic approach, it does not matter where or when we conduct an experiment, as long as certain conditions are met. As Newton suggested in his second law, force is always related in the same manner to mass and acceleration. Thus, to infer that the results of one experiment will be similar to those of similar experiments poses no major problem.

Likewise, in simple chemical studies, it does not matter which actual sample of a pure element one uses. There is little question that the results found with one piece of pure gold would generalize to all pieces of pure gold. In such situations, there is little reason to invoke an inferential statistical procedure; to do so would be like trying to predict what card would be drawn from a deck of all aces.

However, there are situations in which we have reason to believe that the particular sample we are working with may *not* be like every other possible sample and that it may contain more or less of some measure. Most of the measures we study in psychology may be described in this way. Because the variables we study can be influenced by a wide variety of factors, there is generally variability in our measures across samples. In such situations we attempt to understand the properties of all possible samples (called the *population*) by looking at the particular sample with which we are working. This process requires **inferential statistics.**

In more technical language, inferential statistics is used to infer, from a given sample of scores on some measure, the parameters for the set of all possible scores (i.e., the population) from which that sample was drawn. Implicit in this statement is the assumption that the sample we are discussing is the result of random sampling or some systematic form of sampling. That is, each element (e.g., each person in the population of all people) is equally likely to be included in the sample, with some known probability. We will have more to say about random sampling later. For now, the important thing to remember is that inferential statistics constitutes a set of tools for inferring from a particular sample to larger populations. One way of viewing this conceptually is to ask how the statistics of our sample (that is, the mean and the standard deviation) match the parameters (the actual mean and standard deviation) of the entire population (the population values). The purpose of inferential statistics is to estimate these population characteristics.

Another way of viewing the inferential process conceptually is to assume that the same experiment was run an infinite number of times, each time with a different sample of individuals chosen from the entire population. If we were to plot the statistics from each experiment, the population of estimates would then represent all the possible outcomes of the experiment. For our purposes, it does not matter which conceptual approach you use; they are equally valid for understanding the logic of inferential statistics. To understand the logic of inferential statistics, we must introduce the related topic of probability.

## PROBABILITY

We want to get ahead of ourselves for a moment and discuss how probability is used in the experimental report. We all have a sense of probabilities. For example, we do not plan to picnic in midwinter or to go snow skiing in midsummer.

A weather forecast may say that there is a 9 out of 10 chance it will rain tomorrow. This means that 9 out of 10 times the weather in the past has been the same as that predicted for tomorrow: It has rained. Mathematically speaking, this can be described as a 9/10 chance, a .9 chance, or a 90% chance. They are all the same, but the traditional way is to see probability running on a continuum from 0 (0% chance) to 1 (100% chance) and to use the decimal notation, as you will see in psychological articles.

Whether in science or in life, we accept that we live in an uncertain world and that even the best predictions can be influenced by accidents. There are risks in all that we do. We know that there is a possibility that the results of a study could have come out differently if we had performed the same study several times. But how do we assess this possibility? In empirical research, we usually do this by assuming that the study was run many times and try to guess how the results would have come out each time. This helps us understand the results of a particular study. As you will see in published articles, the results of a study usually contain a probability statement. For example, in a study on how children inhibit negative facial expression, Cole (1986) reported that preschool girls aged 3 to 4 displayed more negative facial expressions when the experimenter was not present than when the experimenter was present.

Included in Cole's report were the means and standard deviations for the frequencies of various types of facial expressions, as well as statistical statements that compared one

type of expression with another (e.g., positive versus negative emotions) in various conditions (e.g., with and without the experimenter present). Included in these statistical statements were probability estimates of the form $p < .001$. The statement $p < .001$ means that if a large number of similar experiments were conducted, we would expect to replicate these results *by chance alone* (i.e., to obtain the same results without the experimental manipulation) less than 1 time in 1000. In making such a statement, we create a degree of certainty on which to rest our conclusions concerning particular experimental results. Because an understanding of probability is at the heart of this endeavor, it is important to have some understanding of its origins and theoretical basis.

Questions of probability date back thousands of years. Roman author Cicero (106–43 B.C.) tried to understand how one should interpret the event in which four dice were thrown and all came up the same. Was this an act of the gods or a rare event of chance? You might read *De Divinatione* for his answer. You might also want to look into the modern-day roots of probability theory: gambling. In fact, much of what we know about probability came about because some people wanted to make games of chance less chancy for themselves. It may also interest you to know that making better beer was one of the practical problems that led to the development of one popular statistical technique, Student's *t*. Actually it was William Gosset who wrote under the name Student. He worked for the Guinness Brewery in Dublin and asked what could be inferred about an entire batch of beer from sampling a small portion of it (Student, 1908). In other words, what is the probability that this particular sample is similar to the entire batch?

A traditional illustration of probability is tossing a coin. Let us assume that you watch me toss a coin and record whether it lands heads or tails. On the first throw, it lands heads. Which way will the coin land the next time? It may be heads, or it may be tails. The coin has no memory. It does not remember how it just landed; thus, every toss is like starting all over again. If you think coins remember, you are committing what is called the *gambler's fallacy*. You are failing to realize that coins have no memory; neither do games of chance. Every time the coin is tossed, it is starting over, and thus is equally likely to come down heads or tails. In more technical terms, we say that each outcome is *independent*; that is, the outcome of one toss is not influenced by that of any previous toss.

Suppose that on the second throw the coin lands tails. Now we have described two events. The first is that the coin lands heads, and the second is that the coin lands tails. We could call the first event A and the second B. For any given throw, what would be the probability of event A (the coin landing heads)? It is 1 out of 2, or .5. What is the probability that A will not happen? Formally, we can determine the probability of "not A" by subtracting the probability of A from 1. The answer is .5. If A represented rain tomorrow and the probability were .9, then the probability of its not raining ("not A") would be .1 ($1 - .9 = .1$), or 1 out of 10. In sum, to discover the probability that an event will not occur, you subtract the probability of that event occurring from 1.

What if we want to know the probability of two events rather than just one? For example, we might ask the probability of tossing heads on the first throw and tails on the second. To answer this question, we must first ask the relationship of these two events; that is, does one event influence the other? In this case, the answer is no; these events are independent. The rule for determining the probability of two independent events is to multiply the probability of the first by that of the second. In our example of a heads throw followed by a tails throw, we would multiply the probability of the first event (.5) by that of the second (also .5): $.5 \times .5 = .25$. Thus, there is a .25, or 25 out of 100, chance of having two coin tosses land as heads followed by tails. The rule is stated as

$$\text{probability (A and B)} = \text{probability (A)} \times \text{probability (B)}$$

if A and B are independent.

Another method is to list all the possible results and see how many ways each result could be reached. The following list shows all the possibilities for two coins (or two consecutive tosses of one coin).

| Coin 1 | Coin 2 |
|--------|--------|
| heads  | heads  |
| heads  | tails  |
| tails  | heads  |
| tails  | tails  |

There are four outcomes: heads-heads, heads-tails, tails-heads, and tails-tails. Each outcome has a one in four chance of occurring on any trial. Once again, the probability of heads followed by tails is 1/4, or .25.

What if the order is not important to us, and we want only to know the probability of one heads and one tails in any order? In other words, the outcome could be either heads followed by tails or tails followed by heads. We use what is called the additive rule:

$$\text{probability (A or B)} = \text{probability (A)} + \text{probability (B)}$$

In our example, event A is the result heads-tails (with a probability of 1/4) and event B is tails-heads (also with a probability of 1/4). Thus, probability A + probability B = $1/4 + 1/4 = 1/2$. Figure 5.1 shows in graph form the probabilities of the various combinations that result from tossing two coins.

Let us make the story more complicated by using three coins. Assume that the outcome of throwing three coins is one heads and two tails. What is the probability of throwing three coins and having them land heads-tails-tails? The probability of obtaining heads on the first toss is 1 out of 2, or .5, as is the probability of obtaining tails on the second toss, as is the probability of obtaining tails on the third toss. Multiplying the three probabilities, $.5 \times .5 \times .5 = .125$, or $1/2 \times 1/2 \times 1/2 = 1/8$.

**Figure 5.1**

Probability distribution for combinations resulting from tossing two coins

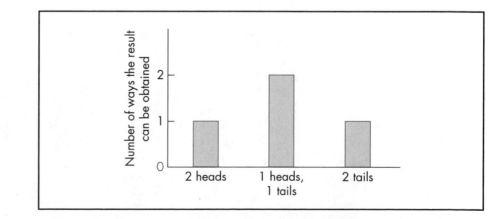

As before, we can list all the possible results:

| Coin 1 | Coin 2 | Coin 3 |
|--------|--------|--------|
| heads  | heads  | heads  |
| heads  | tails  | heads  |
| tails  | heads  | heads  |
| tails  | tails  | heads  |
| heads  | heads  | tails  |
| heads  | tails  | tails  |
| tails  | heads  | tails  |
| tails  | tails  | tails  |

Looking at this list, we see that there is only 1 out of 8 possible results that will give the sequence heads-tails-tails. Therefore, the probability of this result is 1/8.

If we do not care about the order and just want to know how many results have one heads and two tails, we see that the answer is three: tails-tails-heads, heads-tails-tails, and tails-heads-tails. The probabilities are shown in Figure 5.2. We also could have obtained the answer mathematically by the additive law of probability. The probability of tails-tails-heads is 1/8, as is the probability of heads-tails-tails and that of tails-heads-tails. The probability of two tails and one heads in any order is thus 1/8 + 1/8 + 1/8 = 3/8.

However, there is more to the additive formula. What we have told you thus far works only as long as it is impossible for the events to occur at the same time. For example, it is impossible to throw three coins and obtain on one toss both the sequence heads-tails-tails and the sequence tails-tails-heads. If it is possible for the events to occur together, then the additive formula must be modified. For example, suppose you counted the number of people in your class and specified how many are male and how many are female and specified how many are 20 years of age or older and how many are under 20. Let us assume that the numbers came out as shown in Table 5.1. If you were to put everybody's name in a hat and draw one name, what would be the probability of picking a male? If, out of 40 students, 20 are male, then the probability of picking a male would be 20/40, which equals 1/2, or .5. What would be the probability of picking someone under 20 years old? There are 28 people out of the class of 40 who are under 20 years of age, so the probability would be 28/40, which equals 7/10, or .7.

**Figure 5.2**

Probability distribution for combinations resulting from tossing three coins

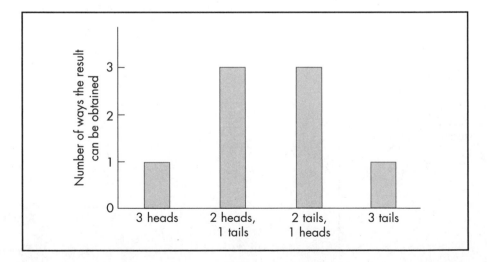

Table 5.1

| Number of Students in Class, Grouped by Age and Sex | | | |
|---|---|---|---|
| | Male | Female | Total |
| Age 20 or older | 5 | 7 | 12 |
| Under 20 years of age | 15 | 13 | 28 |
| Total | 20 | 20 | 40 |

What about the probability of picking someone who is either under 20 years old or male? Notice that unlike the coin-tossing experiment, these two results can both occur at the same time: Someone can be both under 20 and male. Technically, we say these events are not mutually exclusive; that is, one event does not exclude the other. We must take this into account to determine the probabilities. When we want to find the probability of drawing the name of someone who is either male or under 20, we add the probabilities of each event occurring alone and then subtract from that the probability of both events occurring together. In our example, the probability of drawing the name of someone male or under 20 equals the probability of drawing someone male ($p = 20/40$, or .5) plus the probability of drawing someone under 20 years of age ($p = 28/40$, or .7) minus the probability of drawing a male under 20 years of age ($p = 15/40$, or .375). Thus, the probability of drawing a male or someone under 20 is $.5 + .7 - .375 = .825$.

---

☑ CONCEPT CHECK 5.1    If you were to toss a coin 50 times, and, in the last 30 of these, you received heads each time, what would be the probability of having the next coin toss be tails?

---

☑ CONCEPT CHECK 5.2    In the example of having a coin land on heads for the previous 30 times, what would be the probability of having the next 3 coin tosses each be heads?

---

# THE NORMAL DISTRIBUTION

Let us imagine you toss a coin a large number of times. What would you expect the results to be? Of course, we would expect to have an approximately equal number of heads and tails over a large number of throws. If, rather than one coin, you had two or three coins, what would you expect? In Figures 5.1 and 5.2, we saw a graphic representation of the number of possible ways each combination could be obtained. In fact, the two graphs are distributions of probability. If we were to extend our study to include 10 coins, we would find that there are 1024 possible combinations. A probability distribution of the combinations resulting from tossing 10 coins is shown in Figure 5.3. If we were to continue this process and develop probability distributions for even larger numbers of coins, we would eventually arrive at a distribution like the one shown in Figure 5.4. This distribution is similar to a normal probability curve, or normal distribution.

The normal distribution has a number of interesting practical and mathematical properties. For example, some characteristics of humans, such as height, intelligence, and even shoe size, tend to occur in this distribution. In other words, the majority of people wear similarly sized shoes, with only a few wearing very large or very small sizes. To obtain a graph of this distribution, we would plot shoe size along the *x*-axis (horizontal axis) and the number of people who wear that size along the *y*-axis (vertical axis). If we were to identify the places where the curve changes direction (the points of inflection) and draw lines from these points perpendicular to the *x*-axis, we would find that these lines divide the *x*-axis into segments, each equal to one standard deviation from the mean. If we let the area under the curve equal 100 percent, or the whole population, then we can describe how much of the population is found in each standard deviation (Figure 5.5). You can approximate this information by plotting a probability distribution for tossing a coin a large number of times and then counting the numbers that fall under these areas.

Let us assume that shoe size distribution constitutes a normal curve. You would then know that 68.26% of all people wear a shoe size that falls within one standard deviation in each direction from the mean. We could also say that for any person (randomly chosen)

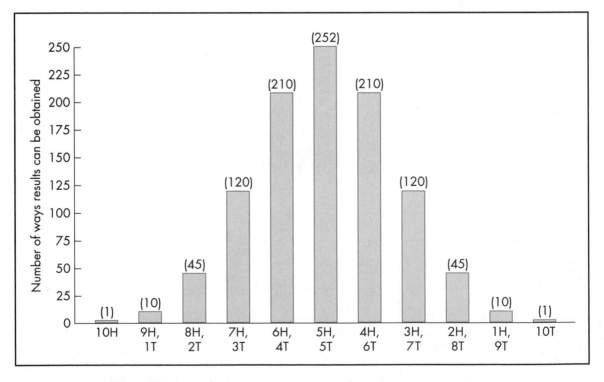

Figure 5.3

Probability distribution for combinations resulting from tossing 10 coins

there is a 68.26% chance that he or she would wear a shoe size within one standard deviation of the mean size. More than 95% of all people fall within two standard deviations of the mean (in both directions); that is, choosing any person at random, you would have more than a 95% chance of finding that that person's shoe size falls within two standard deviations of the mean.

Unless you run a shoe company, however, you probably do not care very much about shoe sizes. But we can use this normal distribution for making inferences from our research. We could generate a graph of what the possible outcomes would be if we performed the same study over and over again (similar to assuming a normal distribution for people

**Figure 5.4**

Probability distribution for combinations resulting from an extremely large number of coin tosses

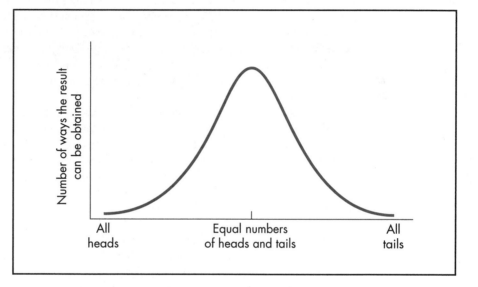

**Figure 5.5**

Normal distribution showing standard deviations

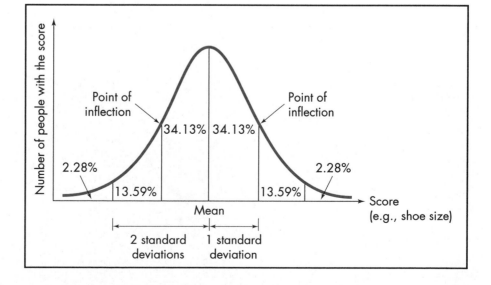

who wear different size shoes). For example, most of you took some type of college admission test, such as the Scholastic Aptitude Test (SAT). Let us assume that we have access to all the verbal scores on this test from students across the country. Then we could have a computer randomly select a sample of names and determine the mean and standard deviation of this sample. A given sample could appear as in Figure 5.6. The x-axis represents the scores available on the test, and the y-axis represents the number of people who received a particular score on the test for a given sample.

Because computers do not care what they do, or how often, we might have the computer repeat this procedure a large number of times. We could then draw a plot of the distribution of the means found in all the samples. It would look much like the normal curve presented in Figures 5.4 and 5.5. This finding is based on what is technically called the *Central Limit Theorem* and lies at the heart of inferential statistics. It simply states that if a number of samples are drawn from a population at random, then the means of the samples tend to be normally distributed. As you can imagine, the larger the number of people in each sample, the less variability there will be in the means. Using the SAT example, we would expect to see means varying only slightly from 500 if the sample sizes were large, but more variability if the sample sizes were small.

If this were represented graphically, the bell-shaped curve would be skinny if the sample sizes were large but broad at the bottom if the sample sizes were small (Figure 5.7). Ask yourself why this is so. As you do, you will realize that, if you had only a few people in each of your many, many samples, an extreme score from any person would have more influence on the mean. Thus, when you plot your means, you would expect more variability in the scores than if you had many people in each of your many, many samples. This is an important idea that lies at the heart of determining the probability levels of such statistics as the *t*-test, which we illustrate at the end of this chapter. Said simply, if you reran the same experiment a large number of times with only 5 people, you would expect the mean of the 5 participants found each time the experiment was run to vary more than if you reran the experiment with 100 people each time. In fact, when you look at probability levels, which we discuss later, you are examining such a hypothetical situation.

**Figure 5.6**

**Distribution derived from giving a standardized test to a number of students**

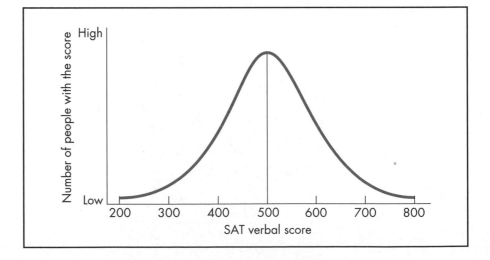

To return to the Central Limit Theorem, it should be noted that it is not a requirement of this theorem that the individual samples be randomly distributed. Even samples of numbers from a table of random numbers (in which every number from 1 to 100 appears equally often) would give a normal distribution of means, although the graphic illustration of any one sample would look more like a rectangle (no one number would be picked any more often than any other number). Thus, it is the sample of samples (also called the sampling distribution) that we are discussing. Furthermore, we can find the mean of all our means and the standard deviation of all our means. The standard deviation of all our means has a special name: *the standard error of the mean.*

If we had just one sample of students who took the SAT, what would be the best guess regarding the mean of all students who took the test? Of course, our best guess would be the mean of our sample. It is fortunate that we do not have to stop at this point; we can also estimate how far off we might be from where the population mean would be. To do this, we estimate the standard error of the mean using the data from our sample. The formula is as follows:

$$\text{standard error} = \frac{\text{standard deviation}}{\text{square root of the number of scores}}$$

For example, if our sample of scores had a mean of 505 and a standard deviation of 100 and we had given the test to 900 people, then the standard error would be 100 divided by 30 ($\sqrt{900}$), or 3.33. Because the Central Limit Theorem says that the sampling distribution is normally distributed, we can now make the same type of statements about our research that we made previously about shoe size. Thus, we can say that 68.26% (percentage of cases within one standard deviation of the population mean; see Figure 5.5) of all means will be within one standard error (3.33 in our example), or 95.44% of all sample means will be within two standard errors (6.66). Or we can say, in probability terms, that we are more than 95% confident that the population mean is between 498.34 (mean of 505 − 6.66) and 511.66 (mean of 505 + 6.66). This is the idea of *confidence intervals,* or the area in which

**Figure 5.7**

Hypothetical distribution of means derived from giving a standardized test to either a large or a small number of students a large number of times

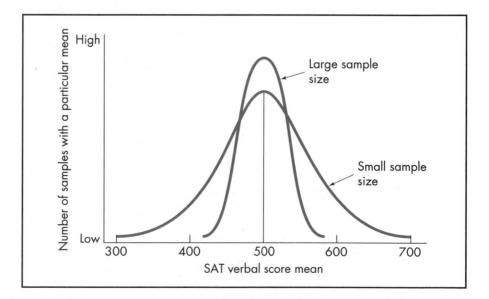

you expect a certain mean to be found. What if someone asked you whether it is more probable that, in your next sample of SAT scores, the mean would be about 500 or about 750? If you said "750," you should put your money in a bank and never place a bet. It would be more probable for the mean to be about 500. This is the basic logic of inferential statistics in general and hypothesis testing in particular.

# HYPOTHESIS TESTING

Hypothesis testing is one of the main branches of inferential statistics. Underlying hypothesis testing are the ideas we have just discussed in talking about the normal distribution. We assumed that if we tossed many coins we would expect to find heads on half of the tosses and tails on the other half. Thus, we begin with the idea that the probability of heads is the same as that of tails. Thus, said in other words, we assume that there are no differences between the number of times heads would come up and the number of times we would see tails. The idea of no differences is going to form the basis of the null hypothesis. The null hypothesis was developed by Sir Ronald Fisher (1935) who sought to determine whether a set of results differed from what would be expected. What would be expected, you might ask? In the example of the coin toss we would expect an equal number of heads and tails.

To draw upon another of our previous examples, what would be expected if we measured the shoe size of a number of individuals? We would expect the average size to be the mean shoe size of all individuals. To remind you of what we said at the beginning of this chapter, when we talk about all possible individuals or all possible samples, we are referring to the statistical term population. Let's look at another example of SAT scores. Suppose you claim that the students in your class scored higher on the SAT than students around the country. You are essentially claiming that the students in your class come from a population (the population of high-scoring students) that is different from the population of all students taking the SAT. We can use what we have learned so far to test this assumption. The mean of your sample should be similar to the population mean of all students taking the SAT. This particular hypothesis, that the population mean is the same as the sample mean, is called the **null hypothesis**. If the null hypothesis cannot be rejected, then we cannot claim that your class comes from a different population.

On the other hand, what if we can reject the null hypothesis? If the null hypothesis can be rejected, then we make a statistical statement concerning the null hypothesis. Assume that the mean of your class was 750 on the verbal SAT while the mean of all people taking the verbal SAT is 500. The probability of finding a mean of 750 in a random sample drawn from the population of all people taking the test would be low, but it would be possible. In the same way that we could determine the probability of tossing 10 coins and having them all be heads, we can make a statement of probability that a sample mean is associated with a certain population mean some percentage of the time. We might say that a sample mean of 750 could have been drawn from a population with a mean of 500 less than 1 time in 1000. Thus, if we found a sample mean of 750, we would reject the null hypothesis and make this rejection with a conditional statement about the probability that this could have happened by chance.

In the psychological literature, the null hypothesis has taken on a broader meaning, resulting from the common practice of using two or more groups to test a particular treatment. For example, in the cereal experiment described in Chapter 2, we wanted to know whether the cereal affected one group more than the other. In such a situation, the null hypothesis as commonly used states that no differences exist between the two groups. Most students then assume that we are testing to see whether a difference exists between the means of the two groups (that is, does the mean of Group 1 equal the mean of Group 2?). This may appeal to our common sense, but statistically we are asking whether these two groups came from the same population. *Inferential statistics always refer to a population.* Although we discussed only the mean, a number of other parameters, such as the population variance (which we discussed in Chapter 4) and the size of the sample, are also important considerations and play a role in statistical hypothesis testing.

Let us use the logic we have just developed on probability, distributions, and the null hypothesis to discuss some particular statistical techniques. One statistical technique, the *t*-test which we describe in the next section, uses the null hypothesis that two samples were drawn at random from identical populations. Let us imagine that someone was interested in comparing the effects of coffee and tea on memory. Such a researcher might give coffee to one group and tea to another group and then have both groups learn particular words. We would have one score—the number of words remembered—for each person. If we were to find the mean number of words remembered for each group, what would we expect? We begin as R. A. Fisher suggests with the idea that coffee and tea did not influence the number of words recalled, thus the null hypothesis. However, if the null hypothesis were not true, then we would expect that the number of words remembered in one group would be higher than those in another. For example, if coffee were associated with remembering more words, then the coffee group would show a higher score. Statistically, the *t*-test examines the difference between the scores of the two groups and helps us to determine whether to accept or reject the null hypothesis.

# EXAMPLE OF INFERENTIAL STATISTICS: THE *t*-TEST

Theoretically, there are a variety of ways to view the *t*-test. One way to view it is related to the correlation procedures we discussed previously and say that the size of the *t*-statistic is related to the size of the association between two variables and the number of people studied. Conceptually, we could say

$$t = \frac{\text{association}}{\text{lack of association}} \times \text{sample size}$$

Because we know that $r^2$ equals the variance accounted for, we could be more precise and say

$$t = \frac{\sqrt{\text{variance accounted for}}}{\sqrt{\text{variance } not \text{ accounted for}}} \times \sqrt{\text{size}}$$

Or, in numerical terms,

$$t = \frac{r}{\sqrt{1 - r^2}} \times \sqrt{df}$$

The term *df* stands for *degrees of freedom,* which we discuss a bit later.

From your statistics course you may be more familiar with considering the *t*-test as the standardized difference between group means, which is the same as determining the difference between sample means divided by the standard error. Conceptually, we might consider how knowing the standard error of each of your groups would help you decide whether your two groups were different. As we move to the computational formula, recall the meaning of some basic terms. Throughout this chapter, we have discussed a population and a sample from that population. In Chapter 4, we discussed the mean, variance, and standard deviation. We use different symbols to refer to the mean, variance, and standard deviation of the population as opposed to those characteristics of the sample. We speak of *population parameters* and use the following Greek letters:

| | |
|---|---|
| population mean | $\mu$ |
| population variance | $\sigma^2$ |
| population standard deviation | $\sigma$ |

In discussion of the sample, we say *sample statistics* or *characteristics* and use italic letters as follows:

| | |
|---|---|
| sample mean | $M$ or $X$ |
| sample variance | $S^2$ |
| sample standard deviation | $S$ |

When we find the variance of the sample, we use a slightly different formula from that used for population variance, which was presented in Chapter 4 in our discussion of descriptive statistics. Rather than divide the sum of the squares by the number of scores $(N)$, we divide by $N-1$. Statistical theory tells us that with repeated sampling using $N-1$ gives us more accurate inferences. Thus, the formula becomes

sample variance = sum of squares / number of scores $-1$

Since the denominator is technically called the *degrees of freedom* the formula can also be written

$$S^2 = SS / df$$

Although a formal discussion of degrees of freedom is beyond the scope of this presentation, the basic idea is simple. *Degrees of freedom* refers to the number of scores that are free to vary. To illustrate this, imagine that you and two friends are eating out and you are waiting for your order. One of you has ordered chicken salad on rye, another has ordered a yogurt and fruit cup, and the third has ordered pastrami on white bread with mayonnaise. The waiter comes with the food, but he has forgotten who ordered what. From his standpoint, he has a number of degrees of freedom in that he can place the dishes in any of several different combinations. However, if you were to remind him that you ordered chicken salad and the friend on your right the yogurt and fruit cup, this would limit his *degrees of freedom.* Once you had fixed the order in two of the three selections, the third was determined and not free to vary.

The same is true with numbers. What if someone asked you to pick three numbers that added up to 20? You could pick any number you wanted for the first number. Say you pick the number 7. You could also pick any number you wished for the second. Perhaps you picked 8. However, once you picked the first two numbers, the third number could only be one number. In this example, the number must be 5. Thus, the general idea behind the term *degrees of freedom* reflects how many scores are free to vary.

Let us assume that we had run the cereal experiment discussed in Chapter 2 and obtained the results presented in Table 5.2. We could then perform a *t*-test on the posttreatment scores for the experimental and control groups. From Table 5.2, we can see that there are seven people in each group; the mean weight gain in Group 1 was 7.857 pounds, and in Group 2 it was 3.00 pounds. (These numbers are rounded.) We can use the computation formula for determining the sum of the squares (see Chapter 4):

$$SS = \sum X^2 - \frac{\left(\sum X\right)^2}{N}$$

Substituting the values from Table 5.2,

$$SS_1 = 455 - \frac{55^2}{7} = 22.857$$

$$SS_2 = 103 - \frac{21^2}{7} = 40$$

The particular formula we use for *t* is as follows:

$$t = \frac{\overline{X}_1 - \overline{X}_2}{\sqrt{\frac{SS_1 + SS_2}{(N_1 - 1) + (N_2 - 1)}\left(\frac{1}{N_1} + \frac{1}{N_2}\right)}}$$

Table 5.2

| Cereal Experiment Results: Weight Gain | | | | | |
|---|---|---|---|---|---|
| **Group 1 (Experimental Group)** | | | **Group 2 (Control Group)** | | |
| | Weight Gain | | | Weight Gain | |
| Person | $X_1$ | $(X_1)^2$ | Person | $X_2$ | $(X_2)^2$ |
| 1 | 10 | 100 | 1 | 0 | 0 |
| 2 | 10 | 100 | 2 | 3 | 9 |
| 3 | 7 | 49 | 3 | 2 | 4 |
| 4 | 6 | 36 | 4 | 1 | 1 |
| 5 | 5 | 25 | 5 | 7 | 49 |
| 6 | 8 | 64 | 6 | 6 | 36 |
| 7 | 9 | 81 | 7 | 2 | 4 |
| | $\sum X_1 = 55$ | $\sum (X_1)^2 = 455$ | | $\sum X_2 = 21$ | $\sum (X_2)^2 = 103$ |
| | $\overline{X}_1 = 7.857$ | | | $\overline{X}_2 = 3$ | |

Substituting our numbers from Table 5.2 into this formula, we have

$$t = \frac{7.857 - 3}{\sqrt{\dfrac{22.857 + 40}{(7 - 1) + (7 - 1)}\left(\dfrac{1}{7} + \dfrac{1}{7}\right)}} = \frac{4.857}{\sqrt{1.497}} = 3.97$$

What does the value of *t* mean? The next step is to look up this value of *t* in a *t*-table. (See Table D.2 in Appendix D.) The degrees of freedom are listed down the side of this table; across the top, the various probability (*p*) levels for one- and two-tailed tests. *One-tailed* refers to a unidirectional prediction (e.g., "The experimental group is larger than the control group"); *two-tailed* refers to a bidirectional prediction (e.g., "The experimental group is either larger than or smaller than the control group"). Using the list for two-tailed tests and looking up the value 3.98 with 12 degrees of freedom, we see that it is significant at the .01 level. In more formal notation this would be written as $t(12) = 3.98, p < .01$. This means that if the cereal experiment were conducted a large number of times, we would expect the results to occur by chance fewer than 1 in 100 times. Because most researchers use standard computerized statistical packages (e.g., SAS, BMDP, Minitab), it is now easier to report the exact statistical probability associated with our value of *t*.

Table 5.3 shows the cereal experiment results as analyzed by BMDP statistical software. From this table, we can see that with a *t*-value of 3.97 and 12 degrees of freedom ($7 - 1$ plus $7 - 1$), the exact *p*-value is .0019. Thus, we would have expected these results to have occurred by chance fewer than 19 times in 10,000. In the common language of research, we would say that the difference between the two groups in the experiment is statistically significant. As you may have guessed, *S.E.M.* in Table 5.3 stands for *standard error of the mean*. Often, graphs of results include the standard error plotted, as shown in Figure 5.8. If you think about the meaning of the standard error, you also may discover how looking at the graph can give you a visual estimate of the differences between the groups in the experiment and help you to understand intuitively the statistical differences present.

For completeness, we should point out that the *t*-test we have just discussed is formally called the *t*-test for independent groups; it assumes that the participants were assigned ran-

**Figure 5.8**

Graphic illustration of cereal experiment

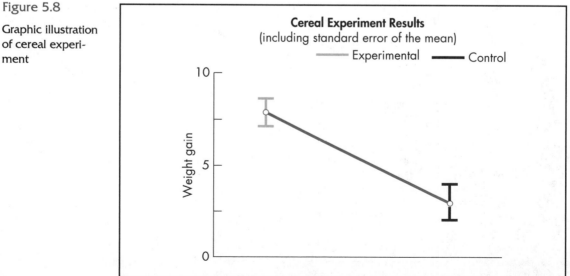

Table 5.3

| *t*-Test for Cereal Experiment | | | | | | |
|---|---|---|---|---|---|---|
| Group | Exp. | Control | Test | Statistics | *p*-Value | *df* |
| Mean | 7.857 | 3.000 | | | | |
| Standard deviation | 1.9518 | 2.5820 | | | | |
| S.E.M. | 0.7377 | 0.9759 | *t* | 3.97 | .0019 | 12 |

domly to groups. (We discuss random assignment to groups in Chapter 7.) However, when the groups were matched according to some characteristic or composed of the same participants (e.g., tested before and after a particular treatment), then a *t*-test for matched scores would be used.

As we show in Chapter 6, there is more to research than just the statistical decision related to the null hypothesis. We hope you are beginning to understand why random sampling is an important aspect of the experimental method. We discuss this idea in more detail in the next few chapters. We also consider the ways in which we decide what can be inferred from our data on a number of levels.

 **CONCEPT CHECK 5.3**   What is the difference between the variance formula for descriptive statistics and that for inferential statistics?

# KEY TERMS AND CONCEPTS

1. **Inferential statistics**
   A. Sample
   B. Population
2. **Probability**
   A. Independent events
   B. Mutually exclusive events
   C. Additive law of probability
   D. Multiplicative law of probability
3. **Normal distribution**
   A. Distribution of probability
   B. Distribution of scores
4. **Hypothesis testing**
   A. Null hypothesis
5. ***t*-test**

# SUMMARY

1. Using inferential statistics, we attempt to understand the characteristics of a population (all possible samples) from looking at a particular sample.
2. We discussed the multiplicative and additive laws of probability mathematically.
3. In the same way that we can create a distribution of scores, we can also create a distribution of probability.

For example, if we were to flip coins repeatedly a large number of times and plot the results, we would create a distribution curve that looks similar to that of a normal distribution.

4. The fundamentals of probability can be used to aid researchers in testing statistical hypotheses. The major statistical hypothesis tested is the null

*(continued)*

# SUMMARY *(continued)*

hypothesis, which states that no difference exists between the population mean and a particular sample mean.

5. Using the example of verbal SAT scores, the question was asked whether a sample with a mean of 750

could be drawn from a population with a mean of 500. The answer was that it is possible but rare.

6. One of the more common statistical tests used in psychological research is the *t*-test, the procedure for which was illustrated in the chapter.

# REVIEW QUESTIONS

1. What is inferential statistics?
2. What is the gambler's fallacy?
3. Describe events that are independent of each other.
4. In what situations would you use the additive law of probability?
5. What is the multiplicative law of probability?
6. What does it mean for events to be mutually exclusive?

7. Describe the normal distribution.
8. In the SAT score example, which would be more likely: to draw a sample with a mean of 400 or one with a mean of 502?
9. Describe hypothesis testing.
10. Discuss the null hypothesis.

# DISCUSSION QUESTIONS AND PROJECTS

1. Name some common uses of inferential statistics in everyday life.
2. Discuss some ways in which you see others using the gambler's fallacy in their everyday lives.
3. If you put all the names of the people in your class in a hat, what would be the probability of your name being drawn? What would be the probability of drawing the name of someone who has heard of your professor's favorite musical group? What would be the probability

of drawing the name of someone who has one brother but no sister? Of someone who has one brother and one sister? Of someone who has either one brother or one sister?
4. Plot the number of hours of sleep the people in your class reported having last night. Draw one graph for males and one for females. Determine how you would test statistically the hypothesis that there is a sex-determined difference in the amount of sleep people report.

## InfoTrac College Edition: Exercises

In this chapter, we discuss probability and statistical tests. Using InfoTrac College Edition, you can learn more information about the concepts we discussed in the chapter. For example, if you enter the term *normal distribution* in the InfoTrac College Edition search system, you can examine how statistical principles are being applied using professional sports scores. In the May 2000 issue of *The American Statistician*, Paramjit Gill discusses how to think

about later game reversals by first assuming that basketball and football scores are normally distributed. (You can find this article by either looking up *normal distribution* or the author Paramjit Gill.) You can also read a study asking "Are babies normal?" In this case Traci Clemons and Marcello Pagano wanted to know if the birth weight of babies formed a normal distribution (*The American Statistician*, Nov. 1999).

## ✓ Answers to Concept Checks

5.1 The probability of having the coin land on tails the 51st time would be .5, or 50 percent. Because each coin toss is an independent event, it does not matter how the coin has landed in the past.

5.2 The question is, what is the probability of having three coins in a row all land on heads? It is the

probability of first heads, or .5, times the other probabilities, or $1/2 \times 1/2 \times 1/2$, which equals 1/8.

5.3 In descriptive statistics, variance is found by dividing the sum of the squares by the number of scores. In inferential statistics, the sum of the squares is divided by the number of scores minus 1.

# TESTING THE HYPOTHESIS: A CONCEPTUAL INTRODUCTION

Once you have developed your research hypothesis, what do you do next? Most students answer, "I perform an experiment to prove that my hypothesis is correct." It is true that the hypothesis must be evaluated in the light of an actual experiment. However, contrary to the manner in which science is sometimes portrayed, the evaluation of an hypothesis is a complex process that takes place on a number of levels. In fact, you need to ask three basic questions in order to evaluate your original research hypothesis. The first question is related to statistics and asks whether the numbers found in an experiment could be due to chance alone. The second question is related to alternative explanations for the research findings and asks whether the results of the study could be due to factors other than the independent variable as hypothesized; that is, are there threats to the internal validity of the study? The third question concerns the research hypothesis and asks what support exists for assuming that the independent variable is directly related to the results.

Thus, we are like detectives who sort through one set of clues and then another, hoping to determine how a particular situation occurred. What caused this event? Who did it? Although the detective might start by suspecting the butler, in research we begin with the possibility that *no one did it;* that is, we ask whether the experimental results, as we found them, happened not because of a crucial factor (the independent variable) but because of chance. Once we determine that chance alone did not produce the results, we are ready to look for other factors. "If it was not chance, then it was the independent variable," Watson might suggest to Sherlock Holmes. "Not yet," the sage of experience admonishes. "Let us first look to unknown factors that might be responsible for our experimental outcome." "But how can we know the unknown?" Watson might ponder. "Through logic, common sense, and knowledge of the literature" is the answer.

Interpreting the results of an experiment is a three-stage decision process. The first stage does not directly involve our research hypothesis at all. Instead, it involves the possibility that chance fluctuations between the performances of our groups might be solely responsible for any differences. The possibility that there are no differences between the groups makes us consider the null hypothesis. Because chance is always involved in our sampling and observations of the world, the null hypothesis is *always* one possible interpretation of even the most striking differences between our groups that must be evaluated. Regardless of how great the differences are between our groups, according to whatever dependent measure we are using, it is always possible that the results are due to chance fluctuations. Thus, when we make a statement about cause and effect in a psychological experiment, we never state that the independent variable *certainly* caused the effect on the dependent variable. Rather, we make the probabilistic statement that we can be relatively certain that our results were not due to chance alone.

It was a realization of the probabilistic nature of experimental outcomes that led to the development of statistical procedures at the beginning of the twentieth century. Because of the central importance of chance in modern science, we will have much to say about chance, the null hypothesis, and the importance of statistics (see also Chapter 5). In the meantime, an essential idea to keep in mind is that the initial phase of interpreting the outcome of any experiment is a statistical decision process. Thus, when confronted with differences between our groups, we first use statistics to determine the probability that these differences are due to chance (the null hypothesis).

Once we have satisfied ourselves that our results are unlikely to be due to chance, we must turn to the second stage and examine another possibility: that our results are due to some systematic but unplanned factor, which we call a **confound.** If our results are indeed due to some factor other than our independent variable, then the internal validity of the experiment is threatened (see Chapter 2). In the fictitious series of breakfast cereal experiments described in Chapter 2, we saw that the weight gain that occurred in the experimental group was not due to the new cereal, as the manufacturers had hoped, but to the cream, bananas, and sugar the participants ate along with the cereal. In confounded experiments like this one, the treatment effect is due not to the independent variable but to one or more overlooked factors. Thus, *we seek to eliminate sources of uncontrolled variance that operate in a systematic manner*. It is not necessary to control every possible factor that could influence our study, but to control the factors that we know influence our results in a systematic way. Otherwise, we would be paralyzed and would never be able to perform even a simple experiment.

One way in which we learn which factors may influence our research systematically is through reading the published literature and examining our own research. Because it is always possible that the internal validity of an experiment is weakened by some unknown factor causing the observed differences, we routinely scrutinize both the published experiments of others and our own work for the possibility that confounds are present. However, it is in the nature of science that even with careful scrutiny we can never be certain that some unknown factor (other than the independent variable) is not responsible for the experimental results.

Once we have rejected the null hypothesis and considered various confounds as influencing our results, we can turn to the third consideration. We then can assume that our results reflect an action on the part of the independent variable; that is, there is now a greater probability that our research hypothesis is accurate. At this point we are ready to interpret our data in relation to the research hypothesis. Many people who are not familiar with the process of science tend to view it as consisting of only this third consideration. However, most scientists do not speak so much about "proving a hypothesis" as they do about "drawing inferences" and "controlling and seeking alternative explanations." In fact, many research scientists argue that the heart of experimentation lies in ruling out alternative explanations. In this chapter, we emphasize the process of minimizing the likelihood of alternative explanations through a discussion of the null and confound hypotheses. In Chapter 7, we emphasize experimental control through a discussion of techniques for controlling, reducing, and eliminating various potential confounds.

Before we continue, let us emphasize that throughout this and the next chapter, we discuss experimental design and the interpretation of experimental results from the standpoint of the *scientist*. We present the experimental method in its ideal form. However, although internal validity and eventual statistical analysis are important determiners of experimental design, they are by no means the only factors to consider when conducting research. Some of the other factors such as ethical considerations or cultural factors will be discussed in greater detail in later chapters.

In the present chapter, we wish to emphasize design and the types of interpretations we can make. As discussed by well-known statistician John Tukey (1962), we are more concerned with data analysis than with statistical analysis. That is, we are like detectives using critical thinking to guide our understanding of the relationship between our variables rather than just paying attention to the statistical tests themselves, as important as they are. Now let us turn to an actual experiment and observe how we evaluate the three possible interpretations of experimental results.

Name the three considerations that must be made in evaluating the results of an experiment.

# THE CONTEXT OF EXPERIMENTATION: AN EXAMPLE

Bransford and Johnson (1972) performed an experiment to explore some of the factors that influence how we remember and encode what we hear. In particular, they were interested in the role of context in the comprehension and recall of information. Imagine you are a participant in that experiment and you are asked to listen to and later recall the following passage:

> If the balloons popped, the sound wouldn't be able to carry since everything would be too far away from the correct floor. A closed window would also prevent the sound from carrying, since most buildings tend to be well insulated. Since the whole operation depends on a steady flow of electricity, a break in the middle of the wire would also cause problems. Of course, the fellow could shout, but the human voice is not loud enough to carry that far. An additional problem is that a string could break on the instrument. Then there could be no accompaniment to the message. It is clear that the best situation would involve less distance. Then there would be fewer potential problems. With face-to-face contact, the least number of things could go wrong.

After the passage was read, the participants in the experiment were asked to rate it for comprehensibility; that is, they were asked to rate how well they understood the passage, with a rating of 7 meaning it was highly comprehensible. You might try this yourself. If you are like the participants in the experiment, you would rate the material as incomprehensible. Their actual average rating was 2.3 on the 7-point scale. The next task for the participants was to recall what they had read. Here they were instructed to write the main ideas that they remembered from the passage. How many ideas did you remember? The research participants in the experiment recalled, on the average, 3.6 ideas out of a possible 14.

A second group of participants was shown Figure 6.1 before they heard the passage. As with the group that did not see a picture, their task was to recall as many ideas from the story as possible. If we were to discuss these two groups in terms of levels of the independent variable (the picture), we would say that one group received the complete treatment and the other group received a zero level. One could also present other levels between the total picture and no picture. Bransford and Johnson actually did this in their complete experiment, but that is beyond the scope of this discussion.

After you have seen the picture, go back and read the passage. How would you rate its comprehensibility now? The participants in the group that saw the picture rated comprehensibility more than twice as high as those in the group that did not see the picture; they gave it a mean rating of 6.1 (versus 2.3 for the first group) on the 7-point scale. The second group also recalled many more ideas than the first group (8 versus 3.6 ideas). Although the Bransford and Johnson experiment was much more complex than we have presented it thus far, we draw on this simplified version to illustrate the task of evaluating the null, confound, and research hypotheses. We begin with a discussion of types of variation.

# TYPES OF VARIATION

For centuries, philosophers have told us that everything varies, and in psychology we know this all too well. Some things vary a little; some things vary a lot. Some factors vary systematically; some factors vary by chance. In the process of experimentation we have set the goal of understanding what part of our results may be attributed to **systematic variation** (for example, the influence of the independent variable on the dependent variable) and what part is due to nonsystematic or **chance variation.**

## ■ Chance Variation

Chance variation may also be called error variation. In this context, the words *chance* and *error* have a similar technical meaning. *Chance or error variation* refers to factors that influence the performance of the research participants in a nonsystematic manner. This means that *within the frame of reference of the experiment,* chance variation cannot be ascribed to any particular factors. This is not to say that we cannot find an explanation for the observed performance of the individual research participants. It does say, however, that the explanation given for any one individual cannot be ascribed to the group as a whole.

Consider a memory experiment like the one conducted by Bransford and Johnson. One person in the experiment might have performed poorly because he did not sleep well

Figure 6.1

**Complete context picture**

*SOURCE:* Bransford & Johnson (1972).

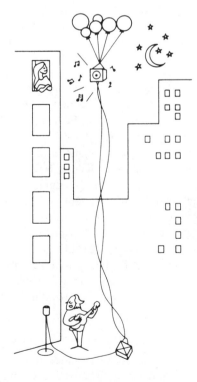

the night before. Another person might have done well because she had just received some good news from home. Another might have had too much coffee, whereas another could have been anxious because of a test the next period. Each of these factors would be considered as a chance factor or error factor *from the standpoint of the group* of participants who took part in the experiment.

## ■ Systematic Variation Due to the Independent Variable

Let us continue with the Bransford and Johnson example, in which one group of participants heard the description without seeing the picture and another group heard the description after being shown the picture. Once we have collected the results, we are faced with the task of interpreting them in relation to three possibilities: (1) there are no differences between our groups (the null hypothesis), (2) the results were produced by some systematic influence other than the independent variable (a confound), and (3) the results were produced in a systematic fashion by the independent variable.

Ignoring the question of confounds for the moment, let us discuss our results in terms of the effects of the independent variable and of chance or error. In evaluating the Bransford and Johnson study, we are trying to determine how much influence seeing the picture had on remembering the passage. To answer this question, we begin with what some students feel is a backward approach. We ask the questions, "What if seeing the picture had no effect on memory? What would the results look like then?" We already know the answer theoretically. The results from the two groups would look alike. Because the groups presumably were chosen to be similar, they would continue to be similar if the independent variable (and confounds) did not influence them.

We can present this point in a more technical way. First, let us use a more statistically oriented language, that of the **F-ratio.** The $F$ stands for (Sir Ronald) Fisher, the man who developed the statistical technique of analysis of variance. The logic of the $F$-ratio applies exactly to the $t$-test presented in Chapter 5 because mathematically there exists an exact relationship between the $t$ and $F$ distributions such that $F = t^2$ when one compares the two groups. The particular terms we use in discussing the $F$-ratio are *within-groups variance* and *between-groups variance.* Within-groups variance reflects the factors of chance or error variance.

For example, in the Bransford and Johnson study, factors such as mental alertness, physical health, and emotional state are expected to have a random or chance effect on the groups as a whole. They do not contribute to any systematic differences between the two groups, which were selected *randomly.* (Random selection is discussed in detail in Chapter 7.) Factors that systematically influence a group of research participants, such as showing one group the picture before the memory task, are reflected in the between-groups variance. In other words, between-groups variance reflects the difference between the experimental group and the control group (that is, the effect of the treatment). Chance factors also contribute to the total between-groups variance (although when the latter term is used conceptually, we are referring mainly to the effect of systematic variations). Thus, between-groups variance equals the effect of treatment plus error variance, whereas within-groups variance is a result of chance or error variance alone. Thus, the $F$-ratio is

$$\frac{\text{between-groups variance}}{\text{within-groups variance}} = \frac{\text{treatment effect} + \text{chance variance}}{\text{chance variance}}$$

Consider the relationship of between-groups variance and within-groups variance if the independent variable has no effect in a study. That is, if showing one group the picture had no effect on the participants remembering the passage, what is the relationship of between-groups variance and within-groups variance? They are the same. If there are no treatment effects, then

$$\frac{\text{between-groups variance}}{\text{within-groups variance}} = \frac{0 + \text{chance variance}}{\text{chance variance}}$$

Still ignoring confounds, if the independent variable has no effect on the dependent variable, the $F$-ratio is roughly equal to 1. Thus, if the independent variable and confounds do not systematically influence the results, then

$$\frac{\text{between-groups variance}}{\text{within-groups variance}} = \text{approximately } 1$$

## ■ Systematic Variation Due to Confounds

Another aspect of the total variance in any experiment is related to confounds. Kerlinger (1973) called this *secondary variance* or *uncontrolled systematic variance* because it results from secondary variables (that is, variables other than the independent variable) that can affect the experiment in a variety of ways. Confounds may occur along with the independent variable and thus differentially affect the performance of the two groups. This chapter focuses on some of these confounds.

What is a confound? Almost anything can be a confound. A confound is something that systematically biases the results of our research. It may be the fact that the day before we ran the experimental group in a social psychology experiment on conformity, there was a television special on how we always do what other people tell us. Or a confound may be introduced into a weight-reduction experiment if one group is asked to lose weight at a time of the year when people eat less and their gastrointestinal systems work faster (summer), whereas another group was started at a time when people eat more (winter). A confound may be introduced when one group is made up of more men than women.

In one behavioral medicine study, the control group was instructed by young, inexperienced technicians, whereas the experimental group was instructed by an older, more experienced physician. This difference may have produced a confound in the results. As you consider these and other possible confounds, you will quickly realize that some confounds can be prevented or controlled. In the next chapter we emphasize techniques for controlling systematic bias. However, other factors can never be controlled. You cannot control world events, but you can ask whether there is any reason to believe that a particular event that took place inside or outside of the laboratory could have influenced one group more than another and thus introduced a confound.

In addition to confounds that influence our groups differently, you also should consider the possibility that extraneous variables may occur independently of the independent variable. In this book we differentiate confounds from extraneous variables by referring to confounds as factors that influence the groups in an experiment differently whereas extraneous variables tend to have a similar impact on the performance of all research participants.

Another way of saying this is that confounds vary systematically with the independent variable. Thus, confounds are a special case of extraneous variables. For example, if all participants in a memory experiment were run during a period when the building next door was being renovated, then we would expect the noise of the renovation to influence everyone in a similar fashion. We would call this an extraneous variable since it could influence everyone's memory score, but not a confound since it would not influence our groups differentially. Some examples of such extraneous variables include the season of the year, consistent sounds from an adjacent room (e.g., an air conditioner), the color of the room, or the temperature in the experimental setting. These are variables that could have been controlled by the experimenter but were not (a point on which we elaborate in Chapter 7). Sometimes they are unknown; sometimes we realize their existence but decide they are not worth eliminating.

Because these extraneous variables affect both groups, they do not influence the internal validity of our experiments. Hence, they often are ignored. However, as we shall see, they do contribute to the overall individual variability (i.e., nonsystematic variation) and thereby affect the acceptance or rejection of the null hypothesis.

Thus, on a conceptual level, the variability in an experiment can be divided into three parts: (1) systematic variation due to the independent variable (treatment effect), (2) systematic variation due to confounds, and (3) variation due to chance, error, or nonsystematic variation. All sources of variation can be described in terms of these sources, although many terms are used to refer to these same concepts (e.g., Kerlinger, 1973).

# STATISTICAL HYPOTHESIS TESTING

Let us consider how the null hypothesis is related to the ratio of between-groups variance to within-groups variance. If the ratio is close to 1, then we will not be able to reject the null hypothesis. If the ratio is a large number, however, then we can reject the null hypothesis and explore the possibility that there are real differences between our groups. The meaning of the ratio must also be understood in relation to the sample size. Given the same sample size, as a general rule, the larger the ratio, the more certain we can be that there are real differences between our groups that are not caused by chance alone. The smaller the ratio, the less certain we can be that the results are not due to chance.

Actually, we are never fully certain that our results are or are not due to chance. Instead, we use statistics to help us make a best guess by assigning a probability to the statement that our results are not due to chance alone. That is, we may say that results from our study could have happened by chance only 1 time out of every 100. In the published literature, you will see this written as $p < .01$. You will see the $F$-ratio in published papers as $F$ equals some number (for example, $F = 5.8$). In the "Results" section of an article quoted in Chapter 15, you will see "$F = 21.54, p < .001$." In that example, we would expect that the particular differences between the groups would occur by chance less than 1 time in 1000.

The current convention in the published literature is to use a probability level of less than .05, which is a chance of less than 5 times in 100, as the accepted level of statistical significance. The use of the .05 level of acceptance has been traced to Sir Ronald Fisher and its history has been reviewed by Cowles and Davis (1982). As with any bet based on probability, we can be wrong, and we do make mistakes. Rejecting and failing to reject the null hypothesis are given special names. We call them Type I and Type II errors (see Box 6.1).

Box 6.1

## Type I and Type II Errors

Suppose we reject the null hypothesis and as-sume that our results are not simply due to chance. Our decision may reflect the world ac-curately (correct rejection of the null hypothesis) or it may not (incorrect rejection of the null hy-pothesis). An incorrect rejection of the null hy-pothesis is called a Type I error.

A Type I error occurs whenever we incorrectly re-ject the null hypothesis and the true state is that chance fluctuations are solely responsible for the differences between our groups. Suppose that

we accept the null hypothesis and bet that our re-sults are merely due to chance. Our decision may reflect the world accurately (correct accep-tance of the null hypothesis) or it may not (incor-rect acceptance of the null hypothesis). An in-correct acceptance of the null hypothesis is called a Type II error.

A Type II error occurs when factors other than chance (e.g., the independent variable) are re-sponsible for the differences between our groups, and we conclude that they are not.

### True state of affairs

| | | Chance is responsible | Chance is not responsible |
|---|---|---|---|
| **Null hypothesis decision** | Fail to reject | Correct acceptance | Type II error (incorrect acceptance) |
| | Reject | Type I error (incorrect rejection) | Correct rejection |

---

CONCEPT CHECK 6.2    Name some factors that might increase chance or error variation in an exper-iment in which students learn nonsense syllables.

---

CONCEPT CHECK 6.3    Describe the *F*-ratio in terms of variance.

---

A **Type I error** occurs when we reject the null hypothesis as being false when it is actu-ally true. In other words, if we think that there are differences between our groups because of our experimental manipulation (and thus we reject the null hypothesis that no differ-ences exist) when in fact the differences were the result of chance and not our independent variable, then we would have made a Type I error. We all have had problems with the luck of the draw. What is the actual chance of making this mistake? It is the probability or *p*-level (e.g., $p < .01$), also called the **alpha level,** symbolized by $\alpha$. Thus, when we see in a research article that $F = 5.89, p < .01$, we know that the chance of making a Type I error is less than 1 in 100. In general, the larger the $F$-ratio, the lower the chance of making a Type I error.

A **Type II error** occurs when we fail to reject the null hypothesis when it is actually false. In other words, if we think there are no differences between our groups but in fact our independent variable did have an influence, then we have committed a Type II error. In such a situation, chance has influenced our results such that the influence of the experimental manipulation is not apparent statistically. The probability of making a Type II error is called the **beta level**, symbolized by $\beta$. The real importance of $\beta$ is that its inverse $(1 - \beta)$ equals the probability that a researcher will correctly reject the null hypothesis when it is false. This probability, $1 - \beta$, is called the **power** of a statistical test.

The concept of power has gained importance in the past decade and is becoming a common word in the research vocabulary. Consider the situation in which you have a great research idea for a class project. What do you want to happen? Of course, you want to be able to demonstrate that your independent variable influenced the data you collected. You want to be able to reject the null hypothesis that, for example, your two groups were drawn from the same population and thus were not different from one another. A strong effect— one in which the between-groups variance is much larger than the within-groups variance and thus the $F$-ratio is large—will help you reject the null hypothesis. From a personal standpoint, you particularly do not want to commit a Type II error. That is, you do not want to conclude that your two groups were not different when in fact they were.

Why might you make such a mistake? One reason might be that your *within-groups variance* (i.e., chance variance) was large in comparison to the *between-groups variance,* which includes the influence of your independent variable. Another way of saying this is that you did not run the study very well. Another way you might make a Type II error would be if you used too few research participants to show the effect you wanted to demonstrate.

Thus, you need to be concerned about *power.* In essence, power calculations help us to understand how many research participants we need, depending on the magnitude of change—called the **effect size**—that our independent variable has on our dependent variable. The goal is to reduce the chance of Type II errors. If we are studying a phenomenon that is strong and our manipulation has a definite effect, we will need fewer participants to avoid Type II errors than if the phenomenon we are studying is weak.

One common measure of effect size is that of Cohen's *d,* which is basically the difference in the mean score in two groups divided by standard deviation of the measure from both groups. Alternatively, you can consider effect size in terms of the $F$-ratio and discuss the amount of variance associated with a particular treatment effect which is referred to as eta squared or $\eta^2$ (see Murphy & Myors, 1998 for an extended discussion of power in relation to the $F$-test). As you read the scientific literature, you will note that articles may include both a statement of probability and a measure of effect size. Thus, three factors (1) effect size; (2) the alpha level (e.g., $p < .05$); and (3) the number of participants in a research study defines power which is the probability that a study will correctly reject the null hypothesis when it is false.

In summary, on a statistical level we must decide whether our groups are equal (null hypothesis). Many kinds of inferential statistics can be used in a variety of situations. In the final analysis, these statistical manipulations boil down to a consideration of the size of our treatment effect and the amount of individual variation in our experiment. This comparison takes the form of the $F$-ratio. As discussed previously, the numerator of this ratio reflects the difference between the scores of the experimental and control groups on the dependent variable. This difference, also called the *treatment effect,* is assumed to result in part from the independent variable. The difference between the experimental and control groups on the dependent measure is reflected in the statistical measure of *between-groups variance.*

The denominator of the $F$-ratio reflects the amount of variability on our dependent measure among the research participants in this experiment. Because the individual variability is calculated by determining the amount of variation of our research participants within each group, it is sometimes called the *within-groups variance.* If there is a lot of individual variability on the dependent measure within our experimental and control groups, we would say that the within-groups variance is high; as a matter of common sense, we would insist that the treatment effects be quite large before assuming that any treatment effects were due to any cause other than chance.

In contrast, if there were only small individual differences on the dependent measure among the research participants in each group (low within-groups variance), it would be reasonable to assume that smaller differences between the experimental and control groups were not caused by chance. Thus, our confidence that the treatment effect is not due to chance fluctuations in the performance of the participants in our two groups is directly related to the size of the treatment effect and inversely related to the variability of scores within our groups.

On a concrete level, you can draw some important practical conclusions related to the $F$-ratio that should help you design your experiments. It is important to understand that a large $F$-ratio can be produced mathematically by *increasing the between-groups variance,* by *reducing the within-groups variance*, or by some variation of both. The practical implication of this fact is that positive experimental results can be obtained both by having a strong independent variable (i.e., maximizing treatment variance) and by *controlling* the error variance (i.e., minimizing error variance). The presentation of the independent variable may be made stronger by using extreme levels of the independent variable; for example, a zero level of a drug might be given to one group and a high dosage level given to another. Likewise, controlling error variance, which we discuss in the next chapter, offers another way of influencing the size of the $F$-ratio and our rejection of the null hypothesis.

In accepting or rejecting the null hypothesis, we can make mistakes. These mistakes are called *Type I* and *Type II* errors, and the probabilities associated with these are symbolized by $\alpha$ and $\beta$, respectively. Power is the probability $(1 - \beta)$ of avoiding a Type II error and is related to effect size, the alpha level (e.g., $p < .05$) and the number of participants in a research study. From a logical standpoint, even when the null hypothesis is not rejected, we cannot conclude, however tempting it may be, that we now have proof that there are no effects of the treatment. As we pointed out in Chapter 2, we would have confirmatory evidence but not proof.

The question now arises regarding how to interpret our results. If we have not rejected the null hypothesis, which states that our groups are equal after treatment, we interpret our data theoretically to mean that the independent variable did not affect the dependent variable. If we reject the null hypothesis, then we must decide what did produce the results of our experiment. Because the $F$-ratio cannot tell us whether the systematic variation reflects the independent variable or a confound, we must logically and conceptually deduce the source of the systematic influence. To do this, we turn first to the question of confounds and then to our independent variable. At each stage of this process, we are attempting to become more and more certain of whether the independent variable affected the dependent variable.

CONCEPT
CHECK 6.4     In an experiment with no confounds, the treatment had no effect on the dependent variable. What would be the *F*-ratio in such a case?

 CONCEPT
CHECK 6.5     Imagine a study in which the independent variable was drinking coffee (2 cups versus 0 cups) and the dependent variable was emotional mood. If you were to run five participants (in each group) in such an experiment, should you be more concerned about a Type I or a Type II error?

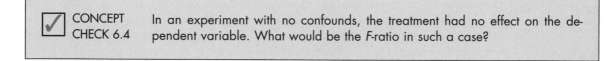

# THREATS TO INTERNAL VALIDITY

In determining internal validity, we ask what contributes to the treatment effects we see. Is it our independent variable or perhaps one or more confound variables? To help researchers answer this question, Campbell and Stanley (1963) and Cook and Campbell (1979) presented a list of possible threats to internal validity that must be considered. We discuss this list for two reasons. First, we want to introduce you to some of the possible confounds that can influence the groups in our experiments differently. However, the list does not include every possible confound because many confounds are related to the specific type of research being performed and cannot be listed in a general manner. Second, we want you to begin thinking about ways in which you might control the effects of these confounds. You already know one way: the use of appropriate control groups. This discussion should help to set up your thinking in preparation for an introduction to experimental design. Let us now turn to several examples of threats to internal validity.

## ■ History

*History* refers to events that take place between measurements in an experiment and are not related to the independent variable. In general, the longer the time between two measurements—a pretest and a posttest, for example—the greater the possibility that outside events will influence the situation. In the cereal experiment described in Chapter 2, the availability of other foods made it impossible to know whether the experimental cereal caused the weight gain. Some confounds are subtle and difficult to detect. For example, in a long-term treatment study with psychiatric patients, such factors as new staff or a change of diet can influence the outcome. Cunningham (1979) has shown that the amount of sunshine present during a helping behavior experiment can influence the degree to which participants aid an interviewer.

Even more subtle confounds may be introduced simply by a person taking part in research. For example, in clinical research studies in which participants come in for the treatment of some specific disorder, such as alcoholism or anxiety, it has been noted that once a person is defined as a patient under treatment, that person's family and friends begin to

"OF COURSE I'VE BECOME MORE MATURE SINCE YOU STARTED TREATING ME. YOU'VE BEEN AT IT SINCE I WAS FOURTEEN YEARS OLD."

act differently toward him or her. Thus, it is impossible to know whether any change came about because of the treatment or because of relationships outside the treatment setting.

## Maturation

*Maturation* refers to problems of interpretation resulting from the research participants' growing older, wiser, stronger, and healthier, as well as more tired, more bored, and so forth. The cartoon illustrates this problem. If a scientist is conducting a study that lasts for a period of time, it is imperative that maturational factors be controlled. This is accomplished by the use of a control group. Confounds of this type plague many inexperienced researchers because they often have their research participants perform too many tasks over too long a time. The research participants become bored and frustrated, and then the results can be attributed to boredom and not to the independent variable in the study.

## Testing

*Testing* refers to the problems that result from repeated measurement of the same person. For example, if a participant is given the same math test repeatedly, then both the practice of taking the test and the memory of certain items could influence the results. Another example is when blood pressure is taken once a minute for 30 minutes. With the standard cuff method of measuring blood pressure, each inflation and deflation of the cuff results in temporary changes in the tissue of the arm itself. Thus, just taking repeated measurements during a short time results in a change in blood pressure readings. Another example of testing as a confound occurs when participants are monitored for certain behaviors and after repeated observations they become aware of what behaviors the experimenter is recording.

## ■ Instrumentation

The problem of *instrumentation* is related to changes that occur in the measuring device, be it a person or a machine, during the course of an experiment. For example, if you are measuring aggressive behavior in children, you would become more accurate at making ratings as the study continues, and this could influence your results. To avoid this problem, Newcombe and Arnkoff (1979), in the study of speech styles discussed in Chapter 3, had more than one rater of the same material and compared the ratings for consistency. If possible, the ratings for each group should be made concurrently so that any improvement in ratings does not systematically influence the groups in the study.

Another possible source of confounds is the use of machines. Many believe that machines are more reliable than people, but this does not mean that machines are always perfect. For example, some computer screens leave a slight afterimage once the screen is cleared. Thus, a stimulus that the experimenter believed to be presented for 250 milliseconds actually may have remained visible to the participant for a longer period. This would become a critical problem if a number of different computers were used for the experiment, each with a slightly different screen type.

## ■ Statistical Regression

A simple example of *statistical regression* occurs when participants are selected because of some score or measurement that turns out to be extreme. On the next testing, the score may return to normal. If this had happened during an experimental treatment, we might conclude that the change in the score was the result of the treatment, when in fact it represented only a regression to the mean or average score. Statistical regression thus occurs when extreme scores (very high or very low) change over time (low scores become higher and high scores become lower) without any treatment. A related problem is found in medical, psychotherapy, biofeedback, and drug studies that focus on people who come to a professional's office. Most people go to see a professional when a given disorder, such as a cold, is at its worst. With such disorders, some improvement can be seen over time without any treatment, and we may conclude incorrectly that the improvement is related to the treatment alone.

## ■ Selection

*Selection* confounds occur when the participants in one group differ initially from those in another group. Suppose you were testing a new speed-reading technique. For the experimental group, you used people who came to the reading clinic; these people received the treatment. For the control group, you used students in a psychology course. There are at least three possible problems with this design. First, there could be a difference (in IQ, reading level, achievement, and other factors) in the types of people who come to a reading clinic and those in a psychology class. Second, those who come to the clinic might have a lower reading score initially and be able to improve more than the students, who may already be reading at their optimal level. Third, the people who come to the clinic probably would be more motivated and work harder at learning to read faster, no matter what technique was used. This third type of problem must be guarded against in any treatment study (e.g., a study of the effects of a drug, relaxation training, or meditation) when the group receiving the treatment seeks the treatment and the control group does not.

In each of these cases, some characteristics of the participants might initially constitute important differences in the groups even before the independent variable is introduced. Thus, it is best to have both the experimental and the control groups consist of people seeking treatment. In this way, the groups are more likely to be similar at the beginning of the experiment.

## ■ Mortality

The problem of *mortality* occurs when participants drop out or refuse to take part in an experiment. The problem is greatest when participants differentially drop out of one group. For example, suppose you want to measure whether children are more creative after playing with dull toys than after playing with fun toys. You first classify the toys as dull or fun and then establish your measure of creativity. As you run the experiment, some of the children who are given dull toys to play with might leave the experiment or not return for other sessions. Thus, after a period of weeks, the fun-toy group might be composed of all the children who began the experiment, whereas the dull-toy group is composed of only half of the original children from that group. If you try to analyze these results, you are faced with the possibility that only a certain type of child remained in the dull-toy group. The dull-toy group would then consist of a different population from the fun-toy group, thus making your conclusions invalid.

## ■ Selection–Maturation Interaction

*Selection–maturation interaction* refers to the situation in which one group of participants changes along a given dimension faster than another group. For example, children whose families have lower-than-average incomes tend to develop cognitive abilities at different rates from children whose families have average incomes. If this difference is not taken into account, the experimenter could ascribe the difference to a specific treatment. Likewise, girls tend to develop verbal abilities before boys; when working with preschool children, this differential development must be taken into account.

Another possibility in this broad category is selection-testing interaction. For example, Fry and Greenfield (1980) examined job-related attitudes in a Midwestern city. They collected data from 529 policemen and 21 policewomen. Assume that this represented the total police force of the city and that other researchers were also collecting various data from these people. It could occur that every policewoman would be called on in each study, whereas only some of the 529 policemen would be called on in every study. This could cause each policewoman to become sophisticated and experienced at being a participant in an experiment, whereas it would remain a new experience for any given policeman. Thus, experimental results that compared policemen and policewomen in this city could be biased because of the policewomen's greater participation in psychological research. Cook and Campbell (1979) expand this category to include selection-history and selection-instrumentation interactions.

## ■ Diffusion or Imitation of Treatments

Participants in an experiment may communicate with each other, and by this communication they may reduce the differences between the groups. This phenomenon is called *diffusion*.

If the difference between the experimental and control groups is that one group has information that the other does not have, then if the participants communicate with each other it is possible that this difference may be reduced or even removed completely.

Consider what would happen if a participant in the picture condition of the Bransford and Johnson study mentioned to a friend that he was in a psychology experiment and described the experiment and the picture he saw. If the friend were later in the experiment and assigned to the no-picture group, her results would be influenced greatly by her previous knowledge. The sharing of information among participants is a problem, particularly when they are drawn from a group that has daily contact. In his simulated attack study, outlined in Chapter 3, Dr. Shotland avoided this problem by helping the participants to understand the importance of his research and the necessity that they tell no one of the experiment until the study was completed. This may take place in the debriefing process, which we discuss in Chapter 14.

---

✓ **CONCEPT CHECK 6.6**    Consider a school district that gives its students a particular achievement test each month to see how well they are learning. Describe one of the major threats to internal validity in such a situation.

---

# CONCLUSION

After ruling out the null hypothesis and the confound hypothesis, we can assume that the results reflect the action of the independent variable. We then go back and reexamine our numerical results in light of the assumption that our independent variable is the crucial agent. We begin to generalize from our set of data and consider both the implications of our results for other groups of people and the theoretical implications of the data. Sometimes we are led to new ideas, which in turn generate new research hypotheses, which can be interpreted with additional experiments.

Figure 6.2 presents a simplified outline of this procedure, which reflects the evolutionary nature of science. The steps include (1) the development of the hypothesis, (2) the translation of this hypothesis into a research design, (3) the running of the experiment, and (4) the interpretation of the results. You will notice that there is also an arrow from Step 4 back to Step 1. Researchers take the results and interpretations of their studies and create new research studies that refine the previous hypotheses.

Although Figure 6.2 shows a circular process, it would be represented better by a spiral in which each rotation adds additional information. This is the idea of the self-correcting nature of science, discussed in Chapter 1. The goal of the process is to help us understand more about what we are studying and to lead us in new directions that we could not have discovered by reasoning alone. That is, experimentation gives us an interaction with reality that is not available solely through reason.

Figure 6.2

Schematic represen-
tation of the four
major steps in the
experimentation
process

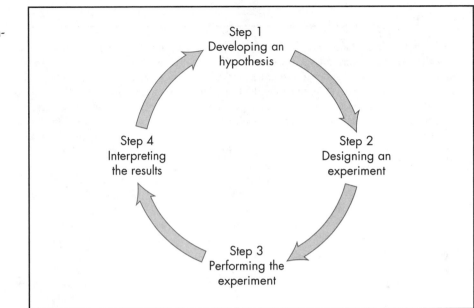

## KEY TERMS AND CONCEPTS

1. **Types of hypotheses**
   A. Statistical (null hypothesis)
   B. Confound hypothesis
   C. Research hypothesis
2. **Variation**
   A. Chance or error variation
   B. Variation due to confound
   C. Variation due to independent variable
3. **Variance**
   A. Within-groups
   B. Between-groups
   C. Ratio of between-groups and within-groups variance
   D. *F*-ratio
   E. Factors that influence ratio of between- and within-groups variance

4. **Type I and Type II errors**
   A. Effect size
   B. Power
5. **Threats to internal validity**
   A. History
   B. Maturation
   C. Testing
   D. Instrumentation
   E. Statistical regression
   F. Selection
   G. Mortality
   H. Selection–maturation interaction
   I. Diffusion or imitation of treatments

## SUMMARY

1. Interpreting the results of an experiment may be seen as a three-part process, each part consisting of a separate hypothesis. The first consideration relates to the null hypothesis and is concerned with a statistical decision process, such as the one we discussed in Chapters 3 and 5. The second consideration relates to the possibility of rival hypotheses, such as confounds, that influenced the results in our research. The third consideration relates to the manner in which the independent variable influenced the dependent variable.

# SUMMARY

2. Variation is an important concept in research. We hope that systematic variations between groups in an experiment are planned and result from the influence of the independent variable on the dependent variable. Variations in an experiment may also be nonsystematic and result from chance; these are also called error variations.

3. The *F*-ratio is a common inferential statistic in research. This ratio reflects the effect of the independent variable plus chance, divided by the effects of chance variation alone. In more technical language, this is called between-groups variance divided by within-groups variance. If there were no treatment effects, this ratio would be equal to 1.

4. An *F*-ratio equal to 1 would not allow us to reject the null hypothesis. To be able to reject the null hypothesis, we would need an *F*-ratio larger than 1; how large depends on a number of factors, such as the number of participants in each group. Conceptually, a researcher could increase the size of the *F*-ratio in two ways. The first way would be to decrease the amount of chance or error variance. This may be accomplished

through careful control. The second way would be to increase the size of the treatment effect.

5. Even if the null hypothesis is rejected, it is still necessary to consider factors other than the independent variable that might have influenced the results. These other factors—confounds—have been called threats to internal validity by Campbell and Stanley. These threats include such possibilities as history, maturation, testing, instrumentation, statistical regression, selection, mortality, selection-maturation interactions, and diffusion of treatments.

6. The conclusion that the independent variable influences the dependent variable is considered only after the null hypothesis and the confound hypothesis have been ruled out.

7. The process of experimentation may be considered as a spiral that consists of four major steps, continually repeated. These include (1) the development of the hypothesis, (2) the translation of the hypothesis into a research design, (3) the running of the experiment, and (4) the interpretation of the results, which leads back to Step 1, the development of a better hypothesis.

# REVIEW QUESTIONS

1. How are a scientist and a detective alike?
2. Describe the hypotheses that a researcher must consider in performing research.
3. Describe the Bransford and Johnson study in terms of the independent variable, the dependent variable, and the hypotheses.
4. What is the meaning of *error* when discussing error or chance variations?
5. What factors influence within-groups variance?
6. What factors influence between-groups variance?

7. If no systematic variation affected the results of a study, what would the following ratio equal?

$$\frac{\text{between-groups variance}}{\text{within-groups variance}} = ?$$

8. What is the difference between a Type I error and a Type II error?
9. What is meant by the term *power*?
10. List Campbell and Stanley's threats to internal validity.

# DISCUSSION QUESTIONS AND PROJECTS

1. Discuss the meaning of *chance* in science. In an experiment, how is chance related to the individual? To the group?
2. Use the Bransford and Johnson study as an example for the following questions: (1) How could between-groups variance be increased? Decreased? (2) How could within-groups variance be increased? Decreased?

3. A company gives its employees money if they lose weight. Records of weight loss are kept over a 6-month period. A control group also tries to lose weight but is not given money. The results will determine whether it will become part of company policy to reward employees for weight loss in the future. What would a Type I error mean in this study? A Type II error?

4. The president announces on television that he has just completed a study in which he applied his economic program to the economy and found positive results. He presents a graph showing that the economy is improving, starting from the time he introduced his eco-nomic policy. Discuss the president's presentation in terms of possible confounds.

5. Discuss the Bransford and Johnson study in terms of threats to internal validity.

## InfoTrac College Edition: Exercises

In this chapter, we discussed three different hypotheses: the null hypothesis, or the possibility that the results are due to chance; the confound hypothesis, or the possibility that the results are not due to the independent variable; and the research hypothesis, which suggests that the results are due to the independent variable. Using InfoTrac College Edition, find the article by Robert Sternberg and his colleagues entitled "If you changed your name and appearance to those of Elvis Presley, who would you be?" published in the Fall 1998 issue of the *American Journal of Psychology*. In the pilot study and the four experiments these researchers describe, what is the research hypothesis and what is the null hypothesis? Can you think of any alternative hypotheses or confounds that could influence each experiment? (You could also consider the threats to internal validity discussed in the chapter.)

## ✓ Answers to Concept Checks

6.1 The three broad considerations that must be evaluated include the null hypothesis, the confound hypothesis, and the research hypothesis.

6.2 Many different factors could influence the results in a nonsystematic manner. Some of these could include how particular participants felt that day, whether they had arguments with their boyfriends or girlfriends, a grade they may have received that day, or the amount of sleep they had the night before.

6.3 The $F$-ratio equals the between-groups variance divided by the within-groups variance.

6.4 The $F$-ratio would be equal to 1.

6.5 If we expected that coffee would have a positive but small effect on mood, there would be a greater chance of a Type I error with five participants. That is, with a few participants and a small effect we would be more likely to reject the null hypothesis when it is actually true.

6.6 There are many problems in such a study, but one of the major threats is that of testing. Because the students see the same test each month, the improvement in results may be a consequence of simply recognizing the questions on the test and learning their answers, rather than of a general improvement in ability.

# CONTROL: THE KEYSTONE OF THE EXPERIMENTAL METHOD

CONTROL ACHIEVED THROUGH
PARTICIPANT ASSIGNMENT AND
SELECTION

RANDOMIZATION
Random Sampling
Random Assignment

CONTROL ACHIEVED THROUGH
EXPERIMENTAL DESIGN

CONTROL AS RELATED TO THE
LOGIC OF EXPERIMENTATION

In the preceding chapters, we have followed the transformation of an idea into a research hypothesis. We have also begun the process of interpreting experimental results in terms of three separate hypotheses: (1) the chance hypothesis (the results are influenced by chance) and its inverse, the null hypothesis (each group is drawn from the same population, and thus the effects of the conditions are not different one from another); (2) the confound hypothesis (the systematic results are influenced by a factor other than the independent variable); and (3) the research hypothesis (the results are related to the independent variable). We also developed the conceptual thinking underlying the *F*-ratio and pointed out how this ratio is related to differences between groups in an experiment (between-groups variance) and error or chance variation (within-groups variance). Our ultimate goal, both conceptually and practically, is to understand what influence, if any, the independent variable has on the dependent variable. In our experiments, we want to be reasonably certain that once we reject the null hypothesis, the observed difference between our groups is indeed a result of the independent variable and not of other factors such as confounds.

In psychological research, we have some powerful techniques to help us achieve this goal. Unlike the detective, who must always reconstruct events after the fact, the researcher has the advantage of being able to create a new situation in which to test ideas. This is comparable to a homicide detective's being able to bring a dead man back to life and place him in the presence of each suspect until the murder is reenacted. Such a reenactment might lack suspense and not make it in prime time, but it would increase the certainty of knowing who committed the murder. Increased certainty is a large part of the experimental process. Scientists increase certainty by creating an artificial situation—the experiment—in which important factors can be controlled and manipulated. Through **control** and manipulation, participant variables may be examined in detail, and the influence of one variable on another may be determined with certainty.

However, the experiment is an artificial environment created to answer a small number of specific questions, and it may not mirror the real world. When it does not, we are faced with a problem of generalizability and a threat to the external validity of our research. We approach these questions in Chapter 10. For now, however, we assume that our research does reflect the real world. In this discussion, we present research in its more ideal form from the standpoint of the scientist, with an emphasis on techniques for reducing threats to the internal validity of an experiment. We emphasize the theme of control in three ways: (1) control as related to participant assignment, (2) control as related to experimental design and the assurance of internal validity, and (3) control as related to the logic of experimentation.

## CONTROL ACHIEVED THROUGH PARTICIPANT ASSIGNMENT AND SELECTION

To illustrate some techniques available for participant assignment, let us begin with the simple illustration of a class designing an experiment. This particular class began with the idea that people can be taught to estimate time more accurately if they are given feedback about their performance. From this idea came a formal research hypothesis followed by a discussion of how to conduct the experiment. We pick up the discussion as someone suggests that the experiment should use two groups. One group of participants would receive verbal feedback on the accuracy of their estimates of a given time interval, and the other group would not be given feedback. Thus, we would have two levels of the independent variable: a zero level and a high level.

The first question asked is, "How do we go about assigning participants to the groups in this experiment?" It is suggested that someone could contact an equal number of male and female participants. They could then place the male participants in one group and the female participants in the other. After thinking about this for a moment, the rest of the class disagrees. They argue that there might be a difference between men and women in their ability to estimate time. This inherent difference might create unequal groups before the experiment even begins. Indeed, one student points out that in her recent readings in psychological literature on time estimation, she found a study indicating that there are sex differences in people's ability to estimate time. More specifically, she found that men are more accurate in estimating intervals of time than women.

As it turns out, this student had seen only one part of a larger and somewhat confusing story. Some of the published literature reports that there are sex differences in time estimation, and some reports that there are not (see Roechelein, 1972; Rammsayer & Rammstedt, 2000 for some examples and a discussion of this literature). Faced with this ambiguity, the students need to decide how to control for possible sex differences. Note that the objection stemmed from common sense—namely, that men and women *might* differ in their ability to estimate time. The fact that one student was familiar with experimental evidence supporting this common-sense idea greatly strengthened the objection to dividing the participants into groups according to sex.

In view of this objection and the evidence supporting it, the class decides not to have all the women in one group and all the men in another group. If they did this, they could not be sure whether any difference between the two groups was a result of feedback or of a difference in men's and women's abilities to estimate time. The experiment would be confounded because they would not know which of the variables—that is, feedback or sex differences between the groups—caused any treatment effects they might observe. Although they might be able to obtain a treatment effect, they could not be sure what the causal factor was.

"Wait a minute!" someone in class yells out. "All of you are getting ahead of yourselves. Even before assigning participants to groups, we have to establish who our participants are and how many we should use, and only then how we are going to select them." The question of who our participants are is, of course, related to the topic we are studying. If we are interested in time estimation in college students, then college students are the appropriate population. If we decide to use our own college, then we have to ask whether it is in any way different from colleges across the nation. Although this consideration does *not* affect the internal validity of our results, it does influence the generalizability or external validity of our results. The question of how many participants to use depends in part on the question being asked. We suggest that the literature is the best guide for this consideration. Although using a number of participants similar to those used in other experiments is not infallible (they can be wrong), it is a good guide. The class decides on 20 participants, 10 men and 10 women.

"We could select our participants by just calling them on the phone," one student suggests. "That's true," someone says, "but you may just call your friends, and they may not be a representative sample of all college students. Also, you would probably start calling and just keep on calling until you found 10 men and 10 women. The set of people you find in their dorm rooms at a given hour might be different from the set of college students in general. Thus, you could select a biased group of participants: those who spend a lot of time near their phones." Our technique for avoiding this last criticism is to use a procedure known as random selection or random sampling (discussed in detail in the next section). With random selection, every person in the potential participant pool is equally likely to be selected for the study.

There are a number of ways random sampling can be accomplished. Box 7.1 illustrates the most common technique: the use of a **random number table,** which is available on many computers today. Random selection helps to control systematic confounds that could be introduced unknowingly into the participant selection process, and it helps ensure that the participants reflect the population of the people we are studying. After the 20 participants have been selected randomly, the next question is how to assign them to groups.

The class wants to avoid the potential confound created by sex differences. Someone points out that one way to eliminate this potential confound would be to limit the participants to one sex. Then, quite correctly, he points out that if they used this *elimination procedure* to remove the potential confound due to sex differences, they would be limiting the generality of the finding tremendously because any new facts they uncover would pertain to only one sex. (This person's concern about the generality of the results is very important; we return to a more extended discussion of its importance in Chapter 10.)

Someone else suggests that they could assign participants so that an equal number of men and women are in each group. We describe this process as an *equating procedure* and save the term *matching* for use in its more traditional sense, in which participants are matched in terms of a pretest (discussed later in this chapter and in Chapter 11). In this particular experiment, equating for sex differences consists of placing the same number of men and women in each group; alternatively, sex difference could be controlled by proportional assignment. Because we know there may be sex differences in the ability to estimate time, equating provides an important control. We do not want to mistake a difference in men's and women's abilities to estimate time for a difference caused by our independent variable: verbal feedback.

Before proceeding, it is important to understand exactly how equating controls for a possible confound due to sex differences. This procedure *does not eliminate sex differences,* as does the elimination procedure, which would limit the experiment to only men or only women. Instead, we *control for any sex differences.* By placing an equal number of men and women in each group, we ensure that any sex differences in time estimation affect both groups equally—that they do not differentially affect our experimental and control groups. Thus, equating for sex differences eliminates a potential confound from this experiment. The original experimental design and the revised design are contrasted in Figure 7.1.

One member of the class then suggests that they could ask all 20 participants to report to the laboratory at 2 P.M. As the participants arrive, they could simply assign the first five men and the first five women to the experimental group and the second five men and the second five women to the control group. After a moment's hesitation, someone points out that one group would then be made up of the participants who arrived on time and the other of participants who arrived somewhat later.

If a relationship exists between one's ability to get to an experiment on time and the ability to estimate time, another confound would be introduced. Although no one had

## Box 7.1

## Random Number Table

A random number table is a table of numbers ordered in such a manner that their occurrence cannot be predicted from a mathematical formula. There are entire books of such numbers that researchers can use for selecting subjects randomly. An example of a random number table is given here.

Because there is no order to random number tables, it does not matter whether you read up the page, down the page, across the page, in either direction, or even diagonally. All that matters is that you state beforehand how you will use the table. A simple example would be to use the table to pick out 10 subjects from a possible 63 for use in the study. First, you might decide that you will use only the last two digits in each number. Second, you might decide you will read the numbers from the bottom to the top of the page. Third, you might decide you will ignore any number greater than 63.

Assume you turned to the page shown here. You would begin by closing your eyes and placing your finger on some part of the page, or any other method you wish to use. Once you have your first number (91511), you read up the page, using only the last two digits. The first 10 numbers are as follows: 11, 95, 24, 45, 25, 75, 50, 18, 06, and 71. Because you cannot use numbers larger than 63, you ignore 95, 75, and 71 and keep reading upward until you find three numbers smaller than 64. These are 54, 33, and 25. Because 25 occurred twice, you need to pick one final number, which is 05. At this time you could take your list of 63 possible participants and pick participants who are listed in positions 11, 24, 45, 25, 50, 18, 06, 54, 33, and 05. You now have a group of randomly selected subjects.

A larger random number table is reproduced in Appendix D.

| | | | | | | |
|---|---|---|---|---|---|---|
| 69298 | 82732 | 38480 | 73817 | 32523 | 41961 | 44437 |
| 54224 | 35083 | 19687 | 11052 | 91491 | 60383 | 19746 |
| 35552 | 35970 | 19124 | 63318 | 29686 | 03387 | 59846 |
| 75366 | 76554 | 31601 | 12614 | 33072 | 60332 | 92325 |
| 20801 | 72152 | 39339 | 34806 | 08930 | 85001 | 87820 |
| | | | | | | Last number |
| 39908 | 05607 | 91284 | 68833 | 25570 | 38818 | 46920 |
| 73823 | 73144 | 88662 | 88970 | 74492 | 51805 | 99378 |
| 88815 | 16553 | 51125 | 79375 | 97596 | 16296 | 66092 |
| 31355 | 86064 | 29472 | 47689 | 05974 | 52468 | 16834 |
| 56302 | 00033 | 67107 | 77510 | 70625 | 28725 | 34191 |

encountered any published evidence of a relationship between one's ability to get to an experiment on time and ultimate accuracy in estimating time, it is reasonable to suspect that there might be a correlation. If there were, we would not know whether any observed treatment effect is due to the feedback or to the fact that there are punctual people in one group and tardy people in the other group. Consequently, it is agreed to control for a possible confound due to the participants' arrival time as well as controlling for sex differences.

| | | | | | | |
|---|---|---|---|---|---|---|
| 34537 | 33310 | 06116 | 95240 | 15957 | 16572 | 06004 |
| 42080 | 97403 | 48626 | 68995 | 43805 | 33386 | 21597 |
| 60397 | 16489 | 03264 | 88525 | 42786 | 05269 | 92532 |
| 93454 | 68876 | 25471 | 93911 | 25650 | 12682 | 73572 |
| 15263 | 80644 | 43942 | 89203 | 71795 | 99533 | 50501 |
| | | | | | | |
| 14486 | 29891 | 68607 | 41867 | 14951 | 91696 | 85065 |
| 06878 | 91903 | 18749 | 34405 | 56087 | 82790 | 70925 |
| 48542 | 42627 | 45233 | 57202 | 94617 | 23772 | 07896 |
| 73923 | 36152 | 05184 | 94142 | 25299 | 84387 | 34925 |
| 49071 | 39782 | 17095 | 02330 | 74301 | 00275 | 48280 |
| | | | | | | |
| 05422 | 13442 | 78675 | 84081 | 66938 | 93654 | 59894 |
| 95348 | 78662 | 11163 | 81651 | 50245 | 34971 | 52924 |
| 17869 | 45349 | 61796 | 66345 | 81073 | 49106 | 79860 |
| 86482 | 05174 | 07901 | 54339 | 58861 | 74818 | 46942 |
| 42865 | 92520 | 83531 | 80377 | 35909 | 81250 | 54238 |
| | | | | | | |
| 64816 | 51202 | 88124 | 41870 | 52689 | 51275 | 83556 |
| 62570 | 26123 | 05155 | 59194 | 52799 | 28225 | 85762 |
| 29789 | 85205 | 41001 | 12535 | 12133 | 14645 | 23541 |
| 54990 | 71899 | 15475 | 95434 | 98227 | 21824 | 19585 |
| 18611 | 47348 | 20203 | 18534 | 03862 | 78095 | 50136 |
| | | | | | | First number |
| 86367 | 21216 | 98442 | 08303 | 56613 | (91511) | 75928 |
| 25651 | 83325 | 88428 | 85076 | 72811 | 22717 | 50585 |
| 26113 | 99447 | 68645 | 34327 | 15152 | 55230 | 93448 |
| 74014 | 64708 | 00533 | 35398 | 58408 | 13261 | 47908 |
| 09013 | 07832 | 41574 | 17639 | 82163 | 60859 | 75567 |

SOURCE: From the *Handbook of Tables for Probability and Statistics*, 2/E, by William Beyer (Ed.). © 1968 Chemical Rubber Company (CRC Press, Inc.). Reprinted with permission.

As to exactly how the class might do this, one student suggests that, as the participants arrive, they should be assigned to either the experimental group (E) or the control group (C). With this alternating assignment procedure, participants would be assigned in the pattern "ECECECEC. . . ." Another student disagrees, saying that because E always precedes C, this would create a small but possibly relevant bias. He suggests assigning participants the way he and his friends used to choose players for baseball teams in fifth grade: The first choice goes to one team, the second and third choices go to the other team, the fourth and fifth choices go to the first team, and so on, until all players are chosen. Although he did not realize it at the time, he and his fifth-grade teammates had reinvented a commonly used *counterbalancing* procedure. With this procedure, participants would be assigned in the pattern "ECCEECCE. . . ." Like simple alternation, this ensures that each condition (early versus late arrival) appears equally often, and it has the additional advantage that each

Figure 7.1

Experiment to discover the effect of verbal feedback on subjects' estimation of time: (a) original experimental design and (b) revised experimental design

---

(a) *Original design*

| Experimental (feedback) all men | Control (no feedback) all women |
|---|---|
| ○○○○○○○○○○ | △△△△△△△△△△ |

*Note:* With this design we would not know whether any observed treatment effects are due to the independent variable (verbal feedback) or to sex differences.

(b) *Revised design (equating for sex differences)*

| Experimental (feedback) half men, half women | Control (no feedback) half men, half women |
|---|---|
| ○○○○○ △△△△△ | ○○○○○ △△△△△ |

*Note:* Any sex differences in time estimation are distributed evenly across both groups. Thus, we are closer to assuming that any treatment differences are due to the independent variable (verbal feedback).

---

condition precedes and follows the other condition an equal number of times. In Figure 7.2, this design is contrasted with the previous design, which controlled for sex differences but ignored the potentially confounding influence of arrival time.

By using these equating and counterbalancing procedures, our students arrive at the final experimental design depicted in Figure 7.2b. This design is superior to the original plan because it adequately rules out two potential confounds: that time estimation performance may be different for men and women, and that time estimation may be related to a participant's ability to get to an experiment on time. By using equating and counterbalancing, the students feel confident that they have a confound-free design and decide to go ahead with their experiment.

Pause for a moment and think about their final design. Can you think of any other factors that might constitute potential confounds in an experiment designed to determine the effect of verbal feedback on time estimation? If you suspect that some factor may constitute a potential confound, you will strengthen your argument greatly if you can find some evidence supporting your concern (as the student did when she cited evidence that men and women differ in their ability to estimate time). In the absence of direct evidence, however, common sense can be a useful tool. For example, it makes sense to suppose that participants who get to an experiment on time might be better time estimators, so it is reasonable to control for this factor. However, our common sense tells us that factors such as where the participant was born are probably not related to the ability to estimate time; consequently, we would not bother to control for the place of birth of our participants.

As you become increasingly familiar with conducting experiments and with a particular research area, you will gain a better idea of what factors are reasonable to control for and what factors can be ignored safely. As we pointed out in Chapter 1, although common sense can be a useful tool, it can sometimes mislead even seasoned researchers. For example, in reaction time experiments, very few researchers bother to control for eye color or recent coffee drink-

Figure 7.2

Effect of feedback on estimation of time: (a) revised experimental design and (b) final experimental design using equating and counterbalancing procedures

**(a)** *Revised design (equating for sex differences but ignoring arrival time)*

| Experimental (feedback) half men, half women | Control (no feedback) half men, half women |
|---|---|
| ○○○○○  △△△△△ | ○○○○○  △△△△△ |
| 1 2 3 4 5  1 2 3 4 5 | 6 7 8 9 10  6 7 8 9 10 |

The numbers represent the arrival order of each man and woman.
*Note:* With this design, although we have controlled for sex differences, we do not know whether any eventual treatment differences are a result of the independent variable or of some relationship between the ability to get to an experiment on time and the ability to estimate time.

**(b)** *Final design (equating for sex and counterbalancing for arrival time)*

| Experimental (feedback) half men, half women | Control (no feedback) half men, half women |
|---|---|
| ○○○○○  △△△△△ | ○○○○○  △△△△△ |
| 1 4 5 8 9  2 3 6 7 10 | 2 3 6 7 10  1 4 5 8 9 |

The numbers represent the arrival order of each man and woman.
*Note:* Both sex differences and arrival time differences are now evenly distributed across our two groups. Because this design balances for both sex and arrival time differences, any experimental effect can be assumed with greater probability to be a result of the independent variable.

ing. Yet studies indicates that people with dark eyes tend to have slightly faster reaction times than people with light eyes (Landers, Obermier, & Patterson, 1976) and that certain levels of coffee drinking may influence sex differences in time estimation (Botella, Bosch, Romero, & Parra, 2001). Because of such possible confounds, random assignment of participants to groups is generally the best procedure to follow, as we see in the next section.

# RANDOMIZATION

In the preceding discussion, when considering sex differences or arrival time differences, the students proposed using equating and counterbalancing procedures. These procedures would ensure that either sex differences or arrival time differences between the two groups would be controlled. Otherwise, we would not know whether any observed difference between our experimental and control groups was a result of verbal feedback (the independent variable) or of sex or arrival time differences (confounds) in the groups. Thus, if either of these variables were permitted to affect the groups differentially, a serious confound would result. To control the impact of these potentially confounding variables, we typically use such procedures as equating groups and the counterbalancing of participant selection. However, as we shall see, randomization is our most powerful tool to distribute potential confounds between our two groups.

The most powerful technique we have for eliminating unintended participant assignment confounds from the design of experiments is *randomization*. Randomization is the compilation of participant assignments solely on the basis of chance. For example, a simple way to assign participants randomly to either of two groups is to flip a coin. If the outcome is heads, we assign the participant to one group; if it is tails, we assign the participant to the other group. We would continue this process until one group is completely filled, and then place the remaining participants in the other group. Another common method of making random assignments is to use a random number table (see Box 7.1).

Let us take a moment to differentiate between two terms that are sometimes confused. These are **random sampling** and **random assignment.** Random sampling is the selection of participants from a larger population to participate in a piece of research. Random assignment is the assignment of selected participants to groups—for example, an experimental group and a control group—in an experiment. Let us now discuss these in more detail.

## ■ Random Sampling

Random sampling is the selection of the entire group of participants who will participate in an experiment. As we emphasize later in our discussion of external and ecological validity, when we conduct an experiment we want our conclusions to have relevance for more people than just those who took part in the experiment. One way we ensure this relevance is to have our participants constitute a representative sample of the entire population in which we are interested. By *representative,* we mean that our sample is similar, in all major aspects, to the overall population from which it is taken.

For example, if I am interested in the time estimation ability of adult men, I must randomly sample my participants from the entire adult male population in such a way that all men in the population have an equally likely chance of being selected. I would want to be sure that the local lawyer has just as much chance of being selected as the local sanitation worker. In a similar way, I would want to be sure that a given 21-year-old man is just as likely to be selected as the town's only World War I veteran.

In our psychological experiments, the random sampling of a large population of participants to obtain the sample we work with is crucial if we want to generalize from the data we obtain in the laboratory to the entire population. For example, as many of you know, most research conducted in experimental psychology has used college sophomores as participants. In a sense, our psychology is a psychology of college sophomores and may not generalize to the entire adult population. We return to this consideration later in this book.

## ■ Random Assignment

After we have randomly selected our participants from the larger population we are studying, we can randomly assign them to our experimental and control groups as a way of equating the groups before the experimental treatment. Randomly assigning participants has an important advantage over other procedures for equating groups: *Randomization controls for both known and unknown potentially confounding variables.* Unlike the equating and counterbalancing procedures, which attempt to equate our two groups directly on known relevant dimensions, randomization leaves solely to chance the assignment of our participants to a group. In this way, not only will any *suspected* participant selection biases between our two groups (such as sex or arrival time or eye color differences) be nullified, but any other differences, even unknown or unsuspected differences, will also be nullified by being randomly distributed between our two groups. Indeed, it is not an overstatement to say that *randomization randomizes everything.*

As with equating and counterbalancing, it is important to realize that randomization does not remove the differences among the people in our experiment. The differences are still there. However, these differences are no longer differentially affecting either group. They affect both groups equally. Randomization thus provides a powerful tool for control because the impact of both known and unknown potentially confounding assignment biases can be distributed evenly between our experimental and control groups.

CONCEPT CHECK 7.1    A newspaper article suggested that people who eat breakfast are healthier than those who do not. When this research was criticized, the researchers replied, "What's the problem? All of our participants were randomly selected." How might you respond to these researchers?

## CONTROL ACHIEVED THROUGH EXPERIMENTAL DESIGN

As we emphasize throughout this book, science is a way of asking questions about the world. The quality of the answers we receive is influenced by several factors, one of the most important being the structure we use to reach our answers. In research, this structure is determined by our experimental design. Somewhat like a blueprint, the experimental design directs our procedures and gives form to the experiment. In essence, an experimental design is a plan for how a study is to be structured. In an outline form, a design tells us what will be done to whom and when. To be evaluated favorably, a design must perform two related functions. First, it must provide a logical structure that enables us to pinpoint the effects of the independent variable on the dependent variable and thus answer our research questions. Second, it must help us to rule out confounds as an alternative explanation for our findings. In this section we discuss experimental designs and introduce you to three specific designs that meet these criteria. In later chapters we discuss experimental design in greater detail.

A sound design must allow us to determine logically the effect of the independent variable on the dependent variable and to rule out alternative explanations. We informally introduced you to this idea in Chapter 2 with the cereal experiment. As you remember, the cereal company first tried to demonstrate the value of the cereal by giving it daily to a group of children and weighing them after several months to determine their weight gain. If we were to diagram the design of this study, it would be

Select the group      Give them cereal      Measure their weight gain

We could diagram the design in a more generalized manner as

Group A            Treatment            Measurement

Such a design would not be much help in pinpointing the effect of the independent variable on the dependent variable, nor would it rule out confounds. As was pointed out in Chapter 2, a stronger design would use a control group. This design would appear as

Experimental group      Cereal      Measurement

Control group            No cereal      Measurement

Again, we could diagram this in a more generalized manner, using *T* as an abbreviation for *treatment* and *M* for *measurement:*

Group A      T                  M

Group B      T (zero level)      M

This new design helps us to determine the effects of the independent variable. However, it does not help us to rule out some of the threats to internal validity presented in Chapter 6. In particular, we could not rule out the possibility of biased participant selection unless we had randomly assigned participants to the two groups. To denote random assignment of participants, we place an *R* before each group in the diagram. Campbell and Stanley (1963) call this design a *posttest-only control group design.* The design is diagrammed as

R      Group A      T                  M

R      Group B      T (zero level)      M

Let us now consider a modification of this design that is similar to the final cereal experiment discussed in Chapter 2. This new design adds a measurement before the treatment. Such a measurement before the treatment is called a **pretest**, whereas a measurement after the treatment is called a **posttest**. In the terminology of Campbell and Stanley (1963), this design is called a *pretest-posttest control group design.* It is diagrammed as

R      Group A      M      T                  M

R      Group B      M      T (zero level)      M

This design would allow us to determine the effects of the independent variable on the dependent variable, as well as to control for the threats to internal validity discussed in Chapter 6. Let us briefly review the threats to internal validity presented by Campbell and Stanley (1963) in relation to the pretest-posttest control group design. History is controlled by including a control group; any effects of history on one group would apply equally to the other group. Maturation is similarly controlled in that any changes during the course of experimentation would affect both groups equally. Likewise, testing would affect both groups similarly. Notice that when we use the word *controlled*, we use it in the sense of being constant and not just in the sense that we can manipulate some factor. Controlling a factor in experimentation is the same as holding the effect of that factor constant for all groups throughout a research study. Such threats as participant selection and statistical regression would be controlled because the groups were randomly assigned in the first place. Mortality, or the dropping out of participants, would likewise not be expected to occur more often in one group than the other because the participants were randomly assigned. Random assignment would also control for the participant-maturation interaction. As you can see, this same design without random assignment would be much weaker.

Although Campbell and Stanley (1963) recommend the designs presented in this section as being useful for controlling threats to internal validity, the designs are not perfect. Confounds such as history can be introduced easily if participants are not treated consistently throughout a study. Common sense would say that if you are nice to one group of participants and nasty to another group, a confound will be introduced that could affect the results. In a rating study, if you rate the entire control group before the experimental group, an instrumentation confound may be introduced if your rating ability improves over time. The point is that designs serve their function only if used correctly.

A design such as the pretest-posttest control group design has been used by social psychologists in studying the persuasive effects of movies and lectures on participants' attitudes. Using this design, the researchers randomly assign participants to one of two groups. The participants are given a questionnaire concerning their attitudes toward a certain topic (being politically conservative, for example). The experimental group may be shown a movie supporting an extremely conservative position, whereas the control group sees no movie. The participants in each group then receive a questionnaire concerning their attitudes toward conservatism. Using this design, it is possible to measure the amount of attitude change brought about by the movie by comparing the mean change in the experimental group's scores (on the pretest and posttest questionnaires) with the mean change in the control group's scores.

As researchers used this type of design, it became apparent that the administration of a pretest alone could influence the persuasiveness of a movie or lecture; that is, if someone were asked his or her views on being conservative and were then shown a movie encouraging agreement with an extreme conservative position, the questionnaire itself could influence the attitude change produced by the movie. To control for this problem, Solomon (1949) suggested the use of a four-group design. Although we see this design used less often today, it does help us to consider the logic of experimentation, and we include it for this reason. In this design, Groups 1 and 2 would be the experimental and control groups described previously. Groups 3 and 4 would be like the experimental and control groups, except that neither Group 3 nor Group 4 would receive the pretreatment questionnaire. The design could be outlined as

| R | Group 1 | Pretest | Treatment | Posttest |
|---|---------|---------|-----------|----------|
| R | Group 2 | Pretest |           | Posttest |
| R | Group 3 |         | Treatment | Posttest |
| R | Group 4 |         |           | Posttest |

By using the *Solomon four-group design,* researchers are able to determine not only the effects of the treatment but also the interaction of the treatment with the presence or absence of a pretest. One can also use this design to determine the effects of maturation and history by comparing the posttest results of Group 4 with the pretest results of Groups 1 and 2.

The three designs presented in this section (posttest only, pretest-posttest, and Solomon four-group) are considered by Campbell and Stanley (1963) to be examples of experimental designs that lead to a *true experiment*. According to Campbell and Stanley, a true experiment includes at least three characteristics, and sometimes a fourth.

The first characteristic is that participants are assigned randomly to groups, such that a given participant is equally likely to be assigned to any of the groups. As we already mentioned, there are a number of procedures for accomplishing this goal, including the use of a random number table. In certain cases, you may want to equate the participants before they are randomly assigned to groups. A simple procedure after the equating has been done is to flip a coin and allow the heads or tails to determine in which group the first participant of the pair is placed.

The second characteristic of a true experiment is that there are at least two levels of the independent variable. One level can be zero, as in the Bransford and Johnson study cited in Chapter 6; that is, not presenting one group with the picture is the same as presenting a zero level of the independent variable.

The third characteristic of a true experiment is that it controls for the major threats to internal validity (discussed in Chapter 6), such as history and selection.

Sometimes a fourth, theoretical characteristic is included. Although it is not agreed on by all researchers, this characteristic requires that a true experiment compare two alternative theoretical positions. We introduced you to this idea in Chapter 3, with Platt's discussion of strong inference. We used the example of falling weights lending support to either Galileo's theory or Aristotle's theory. This example illustrates the fourth criterion.

In this section we presented the most ideal cases of experimental design. Specifically, we presented three designs that can lead to true experiments and reduce the threats to internal validity. However, a general point must be made, which we continue to develop throughout this book: Research designs are created in response to the needs of researchers as they attempt to answer specific questions and rule out alternative explanations. This being the case, designs are not sacred in themselves but are valuable only insofar as they allow us to make accurate interpretations of experimental results. Thus, an experimental design is never a replacement for an understanding of your research area. With such an understanding, it is important to create useful experimental designs that actually control for the factors involved. Although true experimental designs aid greatly in our search for understanding, they can never replace logic, common sense, and a thorough knowledge of our research area.

☑ CONCEPT CHECK 7.2    Name one advantage of the pretest-posttest design over the posttest-only design.

# CONTROL AS RELATED TO THE LOGIC OF EXPERIMENTATION

In this section we want to pull together some of the themes related to the logic of experimentation. Figure 7.3 is a summary of the four conceptual steps in experimentation.

Imagine an experiment in which participants are selected and then randomly assigned to one of two groups (Steps 1 and 2 of Figure 7.3). The experiment is diagrammed as

R     Group A     T     M

R     Group B           M

To help us logically determine the effect of the independent variable on the dependent variable, we must first ask whether Group A is equal to Group B before any treatment (independent variable) is introduced. We can assume this to be the case if we have randomly assigned participants to these two groups. The *F*-ratio conceptually would equal approximately 1 at this point (assuming we have a measure of the dependent variable in each group). If the two groups are chosen to be equal, then we can assume that there are no systematic effects on one group compared with the other *before* the independent variable is introduced. There should only be variations due to chance. As you remember, between-groups variance is influenced by differences between the groups as well as by chance variation; within-groups variance is influenced mainly by chance variation. The *F*-ratio is

$$F = \frac{\text{between-groups variance}}{\text{within-groups variance}} = \text{approximately } 1 = \frac{\text{treatment effect} + \text{error}}{\text{error}}$$

If, for some reason, the two groups were unequal at the beginning of the experiment, then the *F*-ratio would be greater than 1 *before* the independent variable is ever introduced.

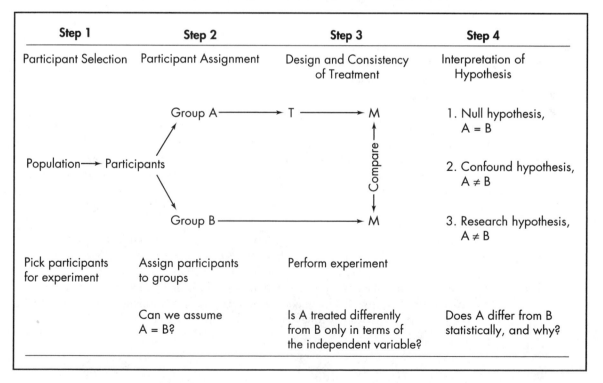

| Step 1 | Step 2 | Step 3 | Step 4 |
|---|---|---|---|
| Participant Selection | Participant Assignment | Design and Consistency of Treatment | Interpretation of Hypothesis |

Figure 7.3

The four conceptual steps in experimentation

In this situation we might find ourselves rejecting the null hypothesis (Group A = Group B) and drawing an inappropriate conclusion. Thus, for the logic of experimentation to be valid, it is imperative that we control the participant assignment to the groups. The best method for ensuring that the participant groups are equal is through the random assignment of participants to groups. This is especially true when our design lacks a pretest measure from which our assumption of equal groups can be verified.

Having selected the participants and assigned them to groups, we proceed to Step 3 of Figure 7.3: introducing the independent variable. In relation to the logic of experimentation, the main question that we ask here is, "Are the different levels of the independent variable the *only* way in which Group A is treated differently from Group B?" If the answer is no, then we face a possible confound, which makes interpretation of the data difficult, if not impossible. Thus, we must be able to control the experimental situation at Step 3, or the logic of our experimental design falls apart. Statistics cannot help us at this point because any systematic change in Group A as compared with Group B because of either the independent variable or a confound will increase the between-groups variance, and it may cause us to erroneously reject the null hypothesis.

If an extraneous variable affects *both* Group A and Group B, then the within-groups variance is increased, thus making it more difficult to reject the null hypothesis and to see the effect of the independent variable on the dependent variable. For example, if a study with an independent variable that provoked anxiety was performed at the same time that college students (both men and women) were being called into the army on short notice, some students (those who could be drafted) might show higher anxiety scores, which would lead to greater variability than normal, making it more difficult to see changes related to the independent variable. As pointed out earlier, the more variability in an experiment, the greater the within-groups variance. However, if we treat all our participants the same and every participant is exposed to exactly the same experimental situation, then the within-groups variance is minimized. The simple rule is that the more consistently participants are treated in every way, the less the within-groups variance will be.

A simple rule for internal validity is to achieve as much control as possible over the experimental situation and to use this control to make the experiment as similar as possible for all participants. The first type of control that we exercise at Step 3 is the control gained by a good experimental design. A design with sound structure helps us to rule out possible confounds or threats to internal validity. The second type of control we exercise at this point is consistent treatment of our participants. Consistency of treatment helps us to reduce needless variation.

Step 4 in Figure 7.3 represents the interpretation of our experimental results. We discussed this in detail in Chapter 6. If we have achieved control in Steps 1, 2, and 3 of our experiment, then interpretation of the experimental results becomes an easy task. That is, once we have controlled group differences by randomly assigning participants and have controlled confounds by designing good experiments and minimizing needless variability among participants, we can assume that our results are due to the independent variable.

✓ CONCEPT CHECK 7.3    Using Figure 7.3, describe the main consideration at each of the four stages of experimentation.

# KEY TERMS AND CONCEPTS

1. **Participant assignment**
   A. Equating
   B. Counterbalancing
   C. Random assignment
2. **Participant selection**
3. **Random number table**
4. **Difference between random sampling and random assignment**
5. **Experimental designs**

   A. Posttest only
   B. Pretest-posttest
   C. Solomon four-group
6. **True experiments**
   A. Participants randomly assigned
   B. At least two levels of independent variables
   C. Controls for major threats to internal validity
7. **Control as related to the logic of experimentation and the *F*-ratio**

# SUMMARY

1. Controlling the experimental situation is an important way that the researcher can make more accurate inferences about how the independent variable influences the dependent variable.
2. There are a variety of methods for equating groups to ensure that differences in an experiment are not a result of biased participant assignment. Three of these are equating, counterbalancing, and randomization.
3. Two terms sometimes confused are *random sampling* and *random assignment*. Random sampling is the selection of participants from a larger population. Random assignment is the assignment of selected participants to a particular group in an experiment.
4. Strong experimental designs help to rule out alternative factors that may account for the results in an experiment. Although no design is perfect, the posttest-only design, the pretest-posttest design, and

the Solomon four-group design help to rule out a number of potential threats to internal validity. Because of this ability they are called true experimental designs by Campbell and Stanley (1963). Three characteristics (and sometimes a fourth) are seen as representative of a true experiment: (1) participants are randomly assigned to groups, (2) there are at least two levels of the independent variable, (3) the design can control for the major threats to internal validity, and (4) the experiment compares two alternative theoretical positions. (The fourth characteristic is not required by some researchers.) Figure 7.3 presents in a schematic fashion the major steps in experimentation once the hypothesis has been developed. These are participant selection, participant assignment, experimental design, and the interpretation of the hypothesis.

# REVIEW QUESTIONS

1. Describe a random number table and explain how it is used.
2. What are the disadvantages of using equating as an assignment procedure?
3. What is the difference between random assignment and random sampling?
4. What is the purpose of random assignment of participants to groups?
5. Diagram a posttest-only control group design.
6. What threats to internal validity does a Solomon four-group design control for?
7. Name three characteristics of a true experiment.
8. In terms of the null hypothesis, why is it important that all groups be equal at the beginning of the experiment?

# DISCUSSION QUESTIONS AND PROJECTS

1. A university sets up a computer lab that students can use as they wish. At the end of the year the administration decides to determine whether using the lab helps

to increase a student's grade point average. To answer this question, the administration divides the students into two groups: those who have used the computer lab

*(continued)*

# DISCUSSION QUESTIONS AND PROJECTS *(continued)*

and those who have not. They determine the mean grade point averages of the two groups and conclude that using the computer results in a student's making better grades. Discuss this conclusion.

2. Assume another university was about to install a computer lab and asked you to help them design a study for determining its effect on grades. How might you design such a study?

3. If you could either randomly select participants or randomly assign participants to groups in an experiment, which would be the better procedure? What would be some of the problems in the interpretation of the data in each case?

4. How might one determine on what factors participants need to be equated? Give an example of a situation in which equating might offer an advantage over randomization. What would be some of the problems in making inferences from such a study?

5. A large corporation wants to develop a long-term project to test a series of leadership training courses it is designing. These training courses are to be offered after work for low-level employees. The courses are to be run on a volunteer basis, and the workers will not be paid for staying late to attend. To evaluate the effectiveness of the courses at the conclusion of 5 and 10 years, the corporation decides that the measure of effectiveness will be how many of the employees who took the course had assumed levels of leadership in comparison to those who did not take the course. Discuss this design. Assume that, after 10 years, it is found that those who took the leadership course were in higher positions of leadership than those who did not. The corporation concludes that the leadership course produced leaders. Comment on this conclusion.

## InfoTrac College Edition: Exercises

This chapter discusses control as an important aspect of the experimental method in order to prevent biased results. Using InfoTrac College Edition, you can read research articles to determine how control is achieved. You can discover how David Johnson and his colleagues used a pretest-posttest control group design in a study entitled "The effects of conflict resolution training on middle school students," published in February 1997. By using

the advanced search feature of Infotrac, you search for the text word "pretest posttest control group design" to see how other researchers have used this design. You could also search for the Solomon four-group design. For example, John Spence and Chris Blanchard in a 2001 study on "Effect of pretesting on feeling states and self-efficacy in acute exercise" used the Solomon four-group design to control for pretest effects.

## ☑ Answers to Concept Checks

7.1 You might respond by saying that although it is important to select participants randomly, it is also important to assign them randomly to groups. In the breakfast study, there may have been preexisting reasons why people did not eat breakfast, such as feeling sick in the morning, which would have differentially influenced the results. That is, people who did not eat breakfast may have been sicker before the experiment began.

7.2 One of the major advantages is that it is possible to accurately measure the changes (from pretest to posttest) that the treatment had. It is also possible to see whether there were changes (between pretest and posttest) in the no-treatment condition that

can further help to evaluate the changes in the treatment condition.

7.3 At Step 1, we want to select participants randomly in such a way that our population under study is well represented. At Step 2, we want to assign participants randomly to Groups A and B in such a way that we can assume Group A equals Group B before the experiment begins. At Step 3, we want to perform the experiment in such a way that the only difference between Groups A and B is that Group A receives the experimental treatment. Finally, at Step 4, we ask whether the two groups differ statistically (null hypothesis) and, if they do, whether this difference results from our research hypothesis or from some confound.

# Applying the Logic of Experimentation: Between-Subjects Designs

In Chapter 7, we emphasized the importance of control in experimentation and presented concepts underlying the design of experiments. We also introduced the idea of the true experiment and its advantages in helping us to infer causation. Specifically, we presented the blueprints for three designs that give a large degree of control over the experimental situation. In this manner, potential confounds are reduced, thus limiting the threats to the internal validity of experiments. We want to build on that discussion in this chapter. We show how the potential usefulness of experimental designs can be increased by using more than two levels of the independent variable. We also introduce designs that examine the effects of more than one independent variable on the dependent variable; these are called **factorial designs.**

From the onset of this discussion, it is important to remember that no design is perfect. Each design has its own strengths and weaknesses in relation to the specific scientific questions being asked. Part of your task as a scientist is to learn which designs are best suited to which types of questions and how existing designs may be modified to answer future questions. Whenever possible, we will make specific suggestions about the appropriateness of designs and point out potential problems with certain designs. However, without an exploration of the specific context in which a given design is to be used, it is impossible to evaluate fully its appropriateness.

# BETWEEN-SUBJECTS DESIGN TERMINOLOGY

**Between-subjects designs** are a general class of designs in which different research participants are used in each group. To be more precise, these designs involve comparisons *between* different groups of participants. In the illustrations of research presented thus far in this book, we have emphasized between-subjects designs. For example, the cereal experiment presented in Chapter 2 compared the weight gained by a group of children who ate cereal with that gained by a group that did not. The true experimental designs presented in Chapter 7 are also between-subjects designs. One characteristic of the between-subjects design is that any given participant receives only one level of the independent variable. Another characteristic is that only one score for each participant is used in the analysis of the results. Although the children in the cereal experiment were weighed more than once (before and after the treatment), the comparison between groups was based on the differences between these two measurements; a single score reflected the amount of weight gained.

The alternative to between-subjects designs is within-subjects designs. These present different levels of the independent variable to the same group of participants. For example, we could use a within-subjects design to determine the value of feedback in shooting baskets by having participants shoot baskets blindfolded (no feedback or zero level of feedback) and then without the blindfold (high level of feedback). In this case, each participant would receive both levels of the independent variable and would have more than one measure of the dependent variable. We examine these designs in much greater detail in Chapter 9.

## COMPLETELY RANDOMIZED DESIGN

One of the simplest between-subjects designs is the **completely randomized design,** which is also called the *simple randomized design* or the *simple random-subject design.* In this type of design, the assignment of participants is completely randomized between groups. In its simplest form, it is composed of two levels of the independent variable. In Chapter 7, we used the following type of diagram:

| R | Group A | T (high level) | M |
|---|---------|----------------|---|
| R | Group B | T (zero level) | M |

As you remember from that chapter, Group A received a high level of the independent variable and Group B received a zero level. Let us quickly go through the procedure for using this design. Assume that we have already chosen 50 participants for our experiment, for two groups of 25 each. The next task is to assign randomly 25 participants to Group A and 25 to Group B. As mentioned earlier, this may be accomplished in several ways (for example, with a random number table), with the outcome being that every participant is as equally likely to be placed in Group A as in Group B. This process of randomization initially equates our two groups, and it enables us ultimately to infer that the independent variable influenced the dependent variable. The next task prescribed by the design is for Group A to receive a high level of the independent variable and Group B to receive a zero level. The task then is the measurement of the dependent variable for each group. Finally, the dependent variable is compared between the two groups; this comparison gives us our treatment effect.

## MULTILEVEL COMPLETELY RANDOMIZED DESIGNS

The completely randomized design can contain more than two levels of the independent variable. Such a design is called a *multilevel completely randomized design* and can be diagrammed as

| R | Group A | Level 1 T | M |
|---|---------|-----------|---|
| R | Group B | Level 2 T | M |
| R | Group C | Level 3 T | M |
| R | Group D | Level 4 T | M |

As an example of a completely randomized design with four levels of the independent variable, consider a study of the effects of drinking coffee on the performance of airplane pilots. Participants in four groups would be given a prescribed number of cups of coffee and then tested in a laboratory equipped with a flight simulator. The number of errors made by the participants in each group would be the dependent variable. In this hypothetical example, Level 4 could equal six cups of coffee, Level 3 could equal four cups, Level 2 could equal two cups, and Level 1 could equal zero cups. Of course, if you actually were to run this study, you would need to consider a number of possible confounds (e.g., the amount of liquid consumed is not equal in the four groups), so you might design the actual study differently.

In Chapter 6, we presented the Bransford and Johnson (1972) study in a simple two-group form, with one group seeing the entire picture before hearing the passage and the other group seeing no picture. That was an incomplete description of the study. In the actual study, there were five groups; the study thus was based on a multilevel completely randomized design. In addition to the two groups described previously, Bransford and Johnson included three other groups. As you remember, the independent variable was the amount of context (prior knowledge), with the appropriate picture representing total context. Group 1 saw this picture before hearing the passage. Group 2 also saw a picture before hearing the passage, but the picture presented to Group 2 represented only a partial context for the passage, although the individual components were the same as those presented to Group 1 (Figure 8.1). The third group was presented with a zero level of the independent variable and saw no picture before hearing the passage. There were also fourth and fifth groups that served as controls. Group 4 saw the picture representing the total context but not until after the passage had been heard. Group 5 heard the passage twice but did not see the picture.

Another illustration of a between-subjects design comes from clinical research. Strupp and Hadley (1979) asked how important technical skills are for the therapist in the process of psychotherapy; that is, does a professional psychotherapist learn certain skills or techniques that are required for a successful outcome in psychotherapy? To answer this question, these researchers compared the psychological improvement of clients seeing experienced psychotherapists with that of clients seeing college professors chosen for their ability to form good human relationships. Notice how Strupp and Hadley were attempting to control for the relationship factor in their study. In essence they were asking whether something more than a good relationship is needed for successful psychotherapy to take place.

For research participants in the study, they used college students who requested therapy and who scored high on certain scales of a traditional psychological test (the Minnesota Multiphasic Personality Inventory). On the basis of traditional diagnostic systems, the research participants were classified as having neurotic depression or an anxiety reaction. The design of the study called for students to be assigned randomly to one of three groups. Group 1 was treated by experienced psychotherapists, Group 2 talked with college professors chosen for their ability to form good relationships, and Group 3, called a *minimal treatment* group, was told that treatment would be delayed. Group 3 thus served as a no-treatment control during the time the first two groups received therapy. The design of the study was

| R | Group 1 | M | T (experienced therapist: therapy skills plus good relationship) | M |
| R | Group 2 | M | T (college professor: good relationship) | M |
| R | Group 3 | M | T (waiting list: no treatment) | M |

As you can see, this is a multilevel completely randomized design with pretest-posttest measures. In the actual study, a number of dependent variables were measured.

These included changes in psychological tests and ratings of change by the therapists, students, and outside clinicians. Strupp and Hadley thus were able to assess changes over time. This study is a good example of how to perform clinical research, and it illustrates some factors that must be controlled to achieve a scientific understanding of such clinical processes as psychotherapy.

Let us turn to the logic of hypothesis testing as it is related to multilevel between-subjects designs. As with the simple two-level completely randomized experiments presented earlier in the book, we still must answer three questions. First, are the results due to chance? Second, are the results due to a confound? And third, are the results due to the independent variable? The first question is approached through a statistical test of the null hypothesis, which states that no differences exist between the groups. Thus, the null hypothesis for a three-level design states that Group 1 = Group 2 = Group 3. Again, we evaluate this through the $F$-ratio. If the $F$-ratio is statistically significant, then we know there is a difference between the groups; however, we do not know which group or groups caused this difference.

To determine whether there is a statistically significant difference between any combinations of groups, we must use a post hoc test that compares each group to another in a pairwise manner. This is similar to performing a $t$-test between Group 1 and Group 2; and then a $t$-test between Group 2 and Group 3; and then a $t$-test between Group 1 and Group 3. As you read advanced statistics books describing these tests (e.g., Ramsey & Schafer, 2002; Winer, 1971), you will see that the number of tests that you do influences the probability of significant results and must be included in your analysis. That is to say, if you perform a large number of post hoc tests you would expect more of them to be significant by chance than if you performed only a few tests and this needs to be taken into account when you perform the statistics.

The alternative to using post hoc tests is to plan particular comparisons *before* the study is performed. Planned comparisons do not take advantage of chance in the same way as post hoc comparisons. Planned comparisons are called **a priori tests.** This is the statistical approach Bransford and Johnson took. They compared the "context before" condition (Group 1 in Figure 8.1) with each of the four other conditions. (For this comparison, they used something called *Dunnett's test,* which is beyond the scope of this book.)

The most common way to analyze a completely randomized design is to use a single-factor **analysis of variance** (ANOVA). In this case, the null hypothesis would state that each research participant group was drawn from the same population and thus the effects of the conditions would not be different from one another. If we did reject the null hypothesis and found that one or more groups differed significantly, we would then need to apply post hoc tests and compare the differences between the groups taken as pairs. In the hypothetical study of the effects of drinking coffee on airplane pilots, we would want to know not only whether the groups as a whole statistically differ from one another but also which particular groups differ from which other groups. After doing such a post hoc analysis, we might find that six cups of coffee cause different results from no cups of coffee but do not cause any statistical differences compared with two or four cups of coffee.

After you have rejected the null hypothesis, you turn to the question concerning confounds and use the logic presented in Chapter 6 to track down factors that might have played a role in the results. As you can see, if we were not able to assume that our groups were equal before we began the treatment, it would be impossible to conclude what effect,

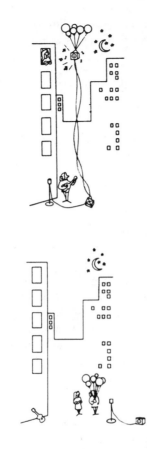

**Group 1**
(seeing complete-
context picture
before hearing
passage)

If the balloons popped, the sound wouldn't be able to carry since everything would be too far away from the correct floor. A closed window would also prevent the sound from carrying, since most buildings tend to be well insulated. Since the whole operation depends on a steady flow of electricity, a break in the middle of the wire would also cause problems. Of course, the fellow could shout, but the human voice is not loud enough to carry that far. An additional problem is that a string could break on the instrument. Then there could be no accompaniment to the message. It is clear that the best situation would involve less distance. Then there would be fewer potential problems. With face-to-face contact, the least number of things could go wrong.

Recall
measure

**Group 2**
(seeing partial-
context picture
before hearing
passage)

If the balloons popped, the sound wouldn't be able to carry since everything would be too far away from the correct floor. A closed window would also prevent the sound from carrying, since most buildings tend to be well insulated. Since the whole operation depends on a steady flow of electricity, a break in the middle of the wire would also cause problems. Of course, the fellow could shout, but the human voice is not loud enough to carry that far. An additional problem is that a string could break on the instrument. Then there could be no accompaniment to the message. It is clear that the best situation would involve less distance. Then there would be fewer potential problems. With face-to-face contact, the least number of things could go wrong.

Recall
measure

**Group 3**
(hearing passage
without
seeing picture)

If the balloons popped, the sound wouldn't be able to carry since everything would be too far away from the correct floor. A closed window would also prevent the sound from carrying, since most buildings tend to be well insulated. Since the whole operation depends on a steady flow of electricity, a break in the middle of the wire would also cause problems. Of course, the fellow could shout, but the human voice is not loud enough to carry that far. An additional problem is that a string could break on the instrument. Then there could be no accompaniment to the message. It is clear that the best situation would involve less distance. Then there would be fewer potential problems. With face-to-face contact, the least number of things could go wrong.

Recall
measure

**Figure 8.1**

**Pictorial representation of the Bransford and Johnson (1972) study**

Group 4
(seeing complete-context picture after hearing passage)

If the balloons popped, the sound wouldn't be able to carry since everything would be too far away from the correct floor. A closed window would also prevent the sound from carrying, since most buildings tend to be well insulated. Since the whole operation depends on a steady flow of electricity, a break in the middle of the wire would also cause problems. Of course, the fellow could shout, but the human voice is not loud enough to carry that far. An additional problem is that a string could break on the instrument. Then there could be no accompaniment to the message. It is clear that the best situation would involve less distance. Then there would be fewer potential problems. With face-to-face contact, the least number of things could go wrong.

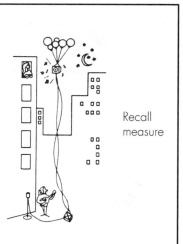

Recall measure

Group 5
(hearing passage twice)

If the balloons popped, the sound wouldn't be able to carry since everything would be too far away from the correct floor. A closed window would also prevent the sound from carrying, since most buildings tend to be well insulated. Since the whole operation depends on a steady flow of electricity, a break in the middle of the wire would also cause problems. Of course, the fellow could shout, but the human voice is not loud enough to carry that far. An additional problem is that a string could break on the instrument. Then there could be no accompaniment to the message. It is clear that the best situation would involve less distance. Then there would be fewer potential problems. With face-to-face contact, the least number of things could go wrong.

If the balloons popped, the sound wouldn't be able to carry since everything would be too far away from the correct floor. A closed window would also prevent the sound from carrying, since most buildings tend to be well insulated. Since the whole operation depends on a steady flow of electricity, a break in the middle of the wire would also cause problems. Of course, the fellow could shout, but the human voice is not loud enough to carry that far. An additional problem is that a string could break on the instrument. Then there could be no accompaniment to the message. It is clear that the best situation would involve less distance. Then there would be fewer potential problems. With face-to-face contact, the least number of things could go wrong.

Recall measure

if any, the independent variable had on the dependent variable. Even if you do not read the random number table every night before you go to bed, we hope you have come to understand the extreme importance of the random assignment of research participants to your groups in an experiment. When we are reasonably sure that no significant confounds are present in our study, we can consider the third question concerning the independent variable. If we reject the null hypothesis and rule out confounds, then we may conclude that the independent variable influenced our results, and we may interpret this relationship theoretically.

> **☑ CONCEPT CHECK 8.1**     Students told a professor that they learned foreign language words best in the morning after drinking coffee. To test this possibility, one morning in class, the professor gave students foreign words to learn and tested them on these words. The professor then asked the students whether they had drunk coffee that morning. At this point, the professor compared the scores of words learned by the two groups (drank coffee versus did not drink coffee). Can you think of a better way to perform this study?

# FACTORIAL DESIGN

An early survey of published psychological research reported that most research using inferential statistics relied on more complex designs, such as factorial designs (Edgington, 1974) and this remains true today. The popularity of factorial designs seems related to our acceptance of the fact that there are few, if any, isolated cause-and-effect relationships in psychological processing. Rather, most psychological processes have several causes that interact with each other in various ways and cannot be determined from simple experimental designs such as those we have discussed thus far. The advantage of factorial designs is that they allow us to examine scientifically the effects of more than one independent variable, both individually and collectively, on the dependent variable.

An easy way to conceptualize factorial designs is to view them as a composite of several simple completely randomized designs, such as those we have discussed previously. Let us illustrate this point. Consider a completely randomized design to determine the effect of money on memory in psychological experiments. A simple design would be to randomly assign research participants to two groups. Each group would hear the same passage. The participants in one group would receive 1¢ for every idea remembered and those in the other group would receive $1 for every idea remembered. This would be diagrammed as

| R | Group 1 | T (1¢) | M (recall task) |
| R | Group 2 | T ($1) | M (recall task) |

Now consider a second completely randomized design such as the two-treatment version of Bransford and Johnson's study presented in Chapter 6. We described this study as consisting of a zero level of the independent variable (no picture) and a high level of the independent variable (complete-context picture). This single-factor experiment can be diagrammed as

| R | Group 1 | T (picture: high context) | M (recall task) |
| R | Group 2 | T (no picture: zero context) | M (recall task) |

We could perform these two studies separately; however, then we could not determine the collective effect of both independent variables (money and context) on the dependent variable. Let us see how we might go about combining these two separate studies into one experiment.

An alternative to performing these studies separately would be to combine them into a factorial design. For ease of representation, let us diagram the first experiment in a horizontal fashion as

*Money*

| Level 1 (1¢) | Level 2 ($1) |
| :---: | :---: |
| Group 1 | Group 2 |

Likewise, we can diagram the second experiment in a vertical fashion:

| | |
| :---: | :---: |
| Level 1 (no picture) | Group 1 |
| *Prior knowledge* | |
| Level 2 (picture) | Group 2 |

Now, if we simply combine our graphic representations of these two studies, the diagram appears as

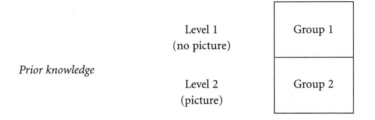

*Money factor*

| Prior knowledge factor | | Level 1 (1¢) | Level 2 ($1) |
| :---: | :---: | :---: | :---: |
| | Level 1 (no picture) | Group A | Group C |
| | Level 2 (picture) | Group B | Group D |

Notice that with this design we have four separate groups, with each participant receiving a specified level of *each* independent variable. Group A will receive 1¢ for each correct idea recalled and will be given the minimum context: no prior knowledge (that is, no picture). Group B will be given 1¢ for each correct idea recalled and will be given the maximum context or prior knowledge (the picture). Group C will receive $1 for each idea recalled and minimum context (no picture). Group D will receive $1 for each idea recalled and maximum context (the picture).

This type of design is called a 2 × 2 (read "two by two") factorial design. In this notation, *2 × 2* refers to the two levels of one independent variable and two levels of another. The independent variables are also called *factors*. If we had a design involving six levels of Factor A and two levels of Factor B, then it would be called a 6 × 2 factorial design. Similarly, a design that consisted of two levels of Factor A, three levels of Factor B, and four levels of Factor C would be called a 2 × 3 × 4 factorial design.

The treatment differences (between levels of a given factor) in a factorial design are called **main effects.** It is possible to determine the main effect for each factor. In our previous example, this would be equivalent to performing two single-factor experiments; one would compare the amounts of money given for recall and one would compare the levels of pictorial context. However, in factorial designs the independent variables may combine in various ways in their effects on the dependent variable. Such a combined effect is called an **interaction effect.** Interaction effects cannot be determined by performing separate single-factor studies and thus are unique to factorial designs.

An interaction effect is the result of two independent variables combining to produce a result different from that produced by either variable alone. An interaction effect occurs when the effect of one independent variable depends on the level of another independent variable. For example, an interaction would be present if the two independent variables had a greater influence in combination than would be expected from adding the main effects of each variable together.

To illustrate, imagine a study measuring physiological reactivity (such as an increase in blood pressure) with one independent variable being that of social role (whether or not one were required to be a leader) and the other independent variable being stability of situation (whether the social environment was stable or always changing). In this study, an interaction might appear such that social role had a greater influence when there was an unstable environmental situation.

To create a more extreme example, on a biological level we might find that two drugs in combination (for example, alcohol and a barbiturate) would create a greater effect (illness or even death) than would be expected from statistically adding the main effect of alcohol and the main effect of the barbiturate. Thus, it is only in combination that the interaction effect is produced.

This is only one type of interaction. We present other possible interaction effects later in this chapter. We should note that there has been some debate concerning how interaction effects should be presented (e.g., Petty, Fabrigar, Wegener & Priester, 1996; Rosnow & Rosenthal, 1995, 1996). Rosnow and Rosenthal (1995, 1996) note that statistically the interaction represents the residuals remaining after the influence of the main effects have been removed and suggest that interactions be presented in this manner. However, most research journals present interactions in terms of cell means, which include both the influence of the main effect and the interactions, and we follow this convention.

Before we leave the question of terminology, let us look at schematic diagrams of three different factorial designs (Figure 8.2). The blocks in the diagram are called cells. Notice that the individual cells are labeled according to the level of each independent variable that affects the cell. For example, the group of research participants that receive Level 1 of Factor A and Level 2 of Factor B is labeled $A_1B_2$. Remember that in between-subjects designs, which we are discussing here, each cell represents a different group of research participants that has been randomly assigned to that cell.

**Figure 8.2**

Schematic representation of $2 \times 2$, $3 \times 3$, and $2 \times 3 \times 2$ factorial designs. Note that the total number of treatment conditions in each design can be obtained by multiplying the number of levels of each factor.

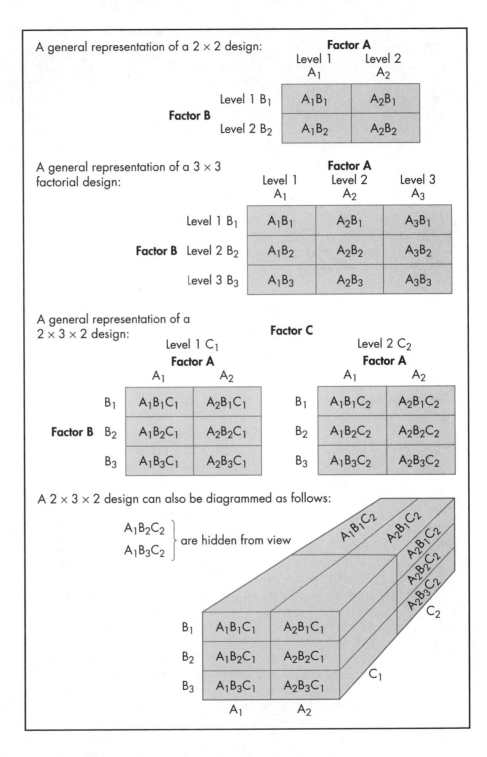

**CONCEPT CHECK 8.2**    Recall the previous example, in which students told a professor that they learned foreign language words best in the morning after drinking coffee. Having thought more about the study, the professor randomly assigned students to one of four groups. These groups included (1) learn words in the morning and drink two cups of coffee, (2) learn words in the afternoon and drink two cups of coffee, (3) learn words in the morning and drink no coffee, and (4) learn words in the afternoon and drink no coffee. Diagram and describe this study as a factorial design, noting the independent and dependent variables.

## FACTORIAL DESIGNS: THE LOGIC OF EXPERIMENTATION AND THE INTERACTION EFFECT

The logic of experimentation for factorial designs is similar to that already described for single-factor experiments. As with these other experiments, in factorial designs we must be able to assume that the groups are equal before any of the treatments are presented. Once we can make this assumption, we may turn to an evaluation of our hypotheses. As with other designs, we seek the role of chance, confounds, and the independent variable in the results of our experiment. Because a factorial design involves the simultaneous evaluation of two or more factors and their interactions, the evaluation process is more involved than in a single-factor design.

For example, in a factorial design there are many null hypotheses, one for each factor of our design. As in a simple design, these null hypotheses state that the effects of the treatment at a given level are equal to those at every other level. In our $2 \times 2$ example, one null hypothesis would concern the main effect of Factor A. It would state that the effect of the treatment of Level 1 of Factor A is the same as that of Level 2 of Factor A. A second null hypothesis would concern the main effect of Factor B. It would state that the effect of the treatment of Level 1 of Factor B would equal that of Level 2 of Factor B. A third null hypothesis is also required. This null hypothesis would state that there are no interaction effects.

It is theoretically possible for any combination of these three null hypotheses in a $2 \times 2$ design to be accepted or rejected. Once we have made this determination, we can then continue to look for confounds, and eventually we can conclude what effects, if any, the independent variables have on the dependent variable. With more than one independent variable, the logic of searching for confounds is similar to that of the single-factor study, although the complexity is greater.

Let us continue to illustrate factorial designs and their evaluation with a hypothetical experiment. In this experiment we want to study two factors and their effects on the learning ability of old mice (see Warren, Zerweck, & Anthony, 1982, for an actual study in this area). The dependent variable will be the number of errors in running a maze. One factor is whether the mice live in an enriched environment, with other mice and many playthings, or live alone in a standard laboratory cage. The second factor is the feeding schedule of these old mice. More specifically, we want to determine whether unlimited access to food and water (called an *ad libitum* or *ad lib* schedule) affects these mice differently from a feeding of enough food once a day to maintain normal body weight. In our tentative design we have designated the living environment as Factor A (with $A_1$ = enriched housing, $A_2$ = standard housing) and the feeding schedule as Factor B (with $B_1$ = ad lib, $B_2$ = once a day). Consequently, in this design there are four possible combinations of the two independent variables: $A_1B_1$, $A_2B_1$, $A_1B_2$, and $A_2B_2$. This particular design is represented by the matrix in Figure 8.3. Each cell of the matrix contains one of the four possible combinations of our two independent variables.

In executing such a factorial design, we would follow the procedure shown in Figure 8.4. We would first obtain, say, 40 mice to participate in our experiment. Our research subjects would then be randomly assigned to any one of these four possible combinations of independent variables until there was an equal number of participants in each cell of the matrix. Next, the subjects in the upper left-hand cell would receive the first level of both independent variables, A and B ($A_1B_1$ = enriched housing/ad lib feeding). Consequently, their performance on our dependent measure (the number of errors in running a maze) would reflect a combined effect of enriched housing and ad lib feeding. The participants in the upper right-hand cell of the matrix would receive the second level of independent variable A and the first level of independent variable B ($A_2B_1$ = standard housing/ad lib feeding). Their performance would reflect the influence of standard housing and ad lib feeding. The participants in the two lower cells would receive, respectively, the combinations $A_1B_2$ (enriched housing/fed once a day) and $A_2B_2$ (standard housing/fed once a day).

In analyzing the outcome of any factorial design, we are interested in two major questions. First, does either of our independent variables produce a statistically significant treatment effect? As mentioned earlier, in a factorial design we call the treatment effect of each independent variable the *main effect* of that variable. In the preceding experiment we have two independent variables: (1) type of housing and (2) type of feeding schedule. To determine the extent of the main effect of each independent variable, we compare the different

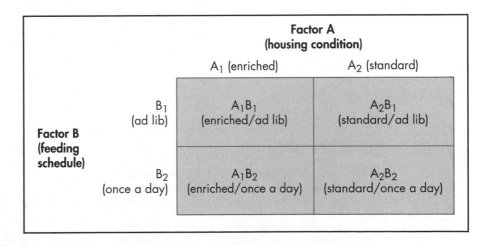

Figure 8.3

Matrix showing the four possible combinations of each of the two levels of a 2 × 2 factorial random-subject design. Notice that each cell contains one of the four possible combinations of our two independent variables (housing condition and feeding schedule).

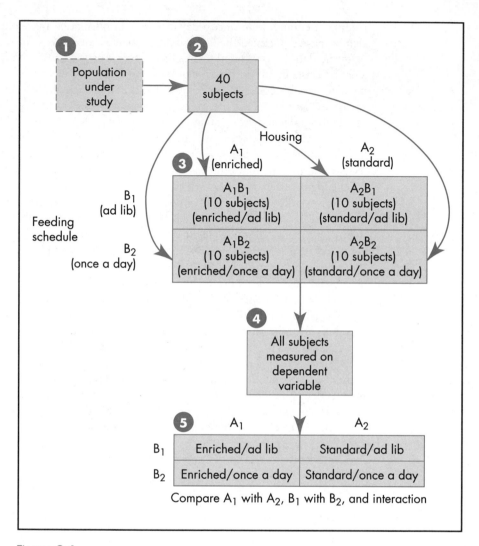

Figure 8.4

Schematic representation of the five steps involved in a factorial random-subject design involving two levels of each of two independent variables. (1) The entire group of 40 mice is obtained from a commercial animal supplier. (2) These 40 mice are randomly assigned to four groups of 10 each. (3) Each group is exposed to the appropriate level of each factor. (4) All subjects are measured on our dependent variable. (5) We determine whether the interaction effect and the main effects are statistically significant.

performances at the two levels of each of our two independent variables. We calculate the performance on our dependent measure for each row and column of our matrix.

For example, Table 8.1 presents hypothetical data from 40 old mice tested on our dependent variable following a 6-month period of living under our two experimental conditions. To determine the main effect of the type of housing, we compare the mean score for all animals housed in the enriched condition with the mean score for all animals housed in standard cages

| Table 8.1 | Hypothetical Results of Maze-Running Experiment with 40 Old Mice | | |
|---|---|---|---|

| | Type of Housing | | |
| | Enriched | Standard | Row Mean |
|---|---|---|---|
| Ad lib feeding | 6 | 21 | |
| | 4 | 23 | |
| | 8 | 22 | |
| | 5 | 22 | |
| | 7 | 24 | |
| | 7 $\bar{x} = 6$ | 20 $\bar{x} = 22$ | 14 |
| | 5 | 20 | |
| | 6 | 24 | |
| | 4 | 22 | |
| | 8 | 22 | |
| Once-a-day feeding | 13 | 14 | |
| | 15 | 14 | |
| | 15 | 13 | |
| | 13 | 15 | |
| | 18 | 12 | |
| | 16 $\bar{x} = 14$ | 16 $\bar{x} = 14$ | 14 |
| | 10 | 14 | |
| | 12 | 14 | |
| | 14 | 15 | |
| | 14 | 13 | |
| Column mean | 10 | 18 | 28 |

(10 versus 18 errors; see Table 8.1). To determine the main effect of the type of feeding schedule, we compare the mean score for all animals who were fed ad lib with the mean score for all animals who were fed once a day (14 versus 14 errors; see Table 8.1). Just from glancing at these data, it appears that the type of housing had a definite effect on the final performance of the old mice on our dependent variable, whereas the type of feeding schedule apparently did not result in differences in performance. These data must be subjected to appropriate statistical tests before any final conclusions can be drawn regarding the null hypotheses.

With a factorial design, the second question we want to ask is, "As our two independent variables occur together, do they influence each other or do they remain independent of one another?" The extent to which the impact of one independent variable varies as a function of the level of the other independent variable in the experiment is called the *interaction effect*. To assess the interaction effects, we determine whether the difference between the means of the results pertaining to the two levels of one independent variable changes with the level of the other independent variable.

Consider the hypothetical data shown in Table 8.1 for the 40 mice tested on the learning task. As we pointed out, animals housed in the enriched environment learned the maze with fewer errors than animals housed in standard cages (10 versus 18 errors). In contrast, the type of feeding schedule *did not* have an effect on overall maze performance (14 versus 14 errors).

Although there was no overall difference in the mean number of errors for the mice on ad lib versus once-a-day feeding schedules, the performance of these mice was quite different depending on whether they lived in enriched or standard cages. More specifically, the animals fed once a day all performed about average regardless of housing (14 versus 14 errors). In contrast, the mean performance of the ad lib animals ranged from very good (only 6 errors) for the mice that lived in enriched housing to very poor (22 errors) for the mice that lived alone in standard cages. Thus, performance on the learning task showed a strong interaction effect. In this particular case, the ad lib animals were affected differentially by the type of housing, whereas animals fed once a day were affected uniformly by their living conditions.

Let us now turn to an example of an interaction from the research literature. This interaction occurred in an experiment dealing with intimacy, summarized by Rubin (1974). In this experiment, the researchers wanted to know what effect the amount of perceived freedom or spontaneity has on both high or low levels of intimate behavior. To answer this question, they conducted a laboratory experiment involving written exchanges of self-disclosure statements between dating couples. The study relates to how you would respond if your boyfriend or girlfriend sent you a message (either very intimate or not very intimate) when you believed that the experimenter told him or her to write the message versus how you would respond when you believed that your boyfriend or girlfriend sent the message spontaneously. As you might predict, the return message (the message back from the boyfriend or girlfriend) was related both to the level of intimacy of the first message and to whether the person believed that the boyfriend or girlfriend had produced the message spontaneously or under the direction of the experimenter. See whether you can draw a graph to illustrate this interaction, making up your own numbers.

When you interpret the results of a factorial experiment, *you always interpret the interaction effects first.* If there is an interaction effect, then the main effects cannot be discussed without a qualifier. If you consider the example of barbiturates and alcohol, you can see that an interaction effect makes it impossible to discuss the effects of either drug alone without qualifying the statement to include the interaction. That is, you can say that moderate drinking does not immediately lead to illness, but you should include the qualifier that this is true only when barbiturates are not taken simultaneously. To give another example, if you look at the data in Table 8.1, you can see that it would be inaccurate to conclude that type of housing is an important independent variable without qualifying the statement to say that this is true only if the feeding schedule is ad lib. Thus, the interaction effect must be interpreted before the main effects so that any necessary qualifiers can be added to a statement of the main effects.

Let us examine a table summarizing an analysis of variance, such as we might see when reading a report of an experiment using a factorial design (see Table 8.2). For our present purposes, we are concerned only that you know how to read such a table; it is not necessary that you understand the calculative procedures. In the first column we see listed the sources of the variance. In a simple experiment, such as the cereal experiment described in Chapter 2, there would be two sources listed in this column. The first would be the treatment variance as a result of eating cereal (between-groups variance) and the second would be the error variance (within-groups variance). In a factorial experiment, this column would list the treatment variance as a result of each independent variable and the interactions. The second column would list the degrees of freedom (*df*), discussed in Chapter 5. The third column would list

Table 8.2

| Analysis of Variance F-Table for the Mouse Study | | | | | |
|---|---|---|---|---|---|
| Source of Variance | df | SS | MS | F | p |
| Housing (Factor A) | 1 | 640 | 640 | 245.21 | .001 |
| Feeding (Factor B) | 1 | 0 | 0 | 0 | ns |
| A × B (interaction) | 1 | 640 | 640 | 245.21 | .001 |
| Error (within groups variance) | 36 | 94 | 2.61 | — | — |

the sum of the squares (*SS*). The fourth column would list the mean square (*MS*). *Mean square* is what we call a variance when it comes from the statistical analysis of variance. The fifth column would depict the *F*-ratio, which, as we discussed, is the between-groups variance divided by the within-groups variance (error variance). In a factorial design, you must evaluate the treatment effect for each independent variable and for the interactions involved. Thus, you will have an *F*-ratio for each main effect and interaction. The error term (within-groups variance) remains the same for each *F*-ratio. Often there is an additional column listing the probability (*p*); "ns" indicates that it is nonsignificant. It is on the basis of this probability that we either accept or reject the null hypothesis (see Table 8.2).

Table 8.2 is the analysis of variance *F*-table for the mouse study presented earlier in this chapter. On the basis of this table, we would reject the null hypothesis for Factor A (housing) and for the A × B interaction (the interaction of housing and feeding schedule). We would not reject the null hypothesis for Factor B (feeding schedule). It is rare in actual practice that we obtain an *F*-ratio of less than 1, although it is possible in actual calculations, as was the case for Factor B (feeding schedule). After the null hypotheses have been evaluated for the interaction of A × B, the main effect of Factor A, and the main effect of Factor B, then conceptually one turns to the role of confounds and the independent variable in causing the results. By the way, there is a possible confound in the mouse study we just presented; see whether you can find it.

Because factorial designs are used frequently in published reports, it is helpful to have some idea of how the main effects and interaction effects are manifested in data. With this goal in mind, the next section describes a hypothetical series of eight factorial experimental outcomes. In each case the outcome is depicted in two ways: numerically and graphically. Allow yourself several careful readings to get an understanding for the main effects and interaction effects.

✓ CONCEPT CHECK 8.3

Recall the example concerning learning foreign words, in which a professor randomly assigned students to one of four groups as follows: (1) learn words in the morning and drink two cups of coffee, (2) learn words in the afternoon and drink two cups of coffee, (3) learn words in the morning and drink no coffee, and (4) learn words in the afternoon and drink no coffee. What are main effects and interaction effects in this design, and what questions do we want to ask in order to evaluate these effects?

# EIGHT POSSIBLE OUTCOMES OF 2 × 2 FACTORIAL EXPERIMENTS

The purpose of this section is to clarify the ideas of main effects and interactions in factorial designs. To achieve this goal, we will work directly with specific and hypothetical examples (Figures 8.5–8.12). First, we describe some actual examples of main effects and interactions from the research literature and then present the eight possible outcomes of a 2 × 2 factorial experiment using hypothetical data. We also plot the cell means. Let us begin with actual examples.

The first example involves eyewitness identification of suspects in videos of a mock crime. Stewart and McAllister (2001) examined the manner in which mug shots were presented to eyewitnesses and used the number of false positives (incorrectly identified the person) as the dependent variable. In one experimental condition, mug shots were presented one to a page whereas in the other condition, pictures were presented 12 to a page. These two conditions made up the first factor. The second factor was picture arrangement in that the mug books were either arranged by as to how similar the person in the picture looked to the perpetrator or the pictures were randomly arranged in the book. Thus, the first factor was grouping (1 vs. 12 to a page) and the second was picture arrangement (similar vs random). If you were to look up this article in the *Journal of Applied Psychology*, you would see their first graph similar to that of Figure 8.12 (page 187) ($A_1$ = random presentation, $A_2$ = grouped by similarity; $B_1$ = 12 to a page; $B_2$ = 1 to a page). They found that when the pictures were arranged by similarity more false positives were present when the pictures were presented one at a time as compared to 12 on a page. There was no difference in false positives when the pictures were randomly arranged.

The next example involves a series of experiments reported in the *Journal of Experimental Psychology: Learning, Memory and Cognition,* in which Fendrich, Healy, and Bourne (1991) studied long-term repetition effects. As part of the research, participants were asked on a number of days to enter a list of three-digit numbers using a computer keypad. On a separate day, participants were asked to rate whether the list they were entering was a new list or one they had seen previously. Participants were also asked to rate how certain they were of their rating. In terms of speed of entry into the computer, a significant 2 × 2 interaction was found for list type (old, new) by recognition rating (correctly identifying the list, incorrectly identifying the list). That is to say, old lists were entered faster than new lists when the old lists were recognized correctly, but more slowly when they were identified incorrectly. This relationship corresponds to Figure 8.8 ($A_1$ = correct recognition, $A_2$ = incorrect recognition, $B_1$ = new list, $B_2$ = old list).

When the authors measured time to the first keystroke (which they assumed to be equal to encoding time), they found an interaction similar to that described in Figure 8.10 (page 186). In this case, the average latency to the first keystroke for the old list was faster than for the new lists if the old lists were recognized correctly. Old lists were entered only somewhat more slowly than new lists if the lists were identified incorrectly.

If the time to the second keystroke is measured, then neither an interaction nor a main effect is present (as illustrated in Figure 8.5). In the actual article, this figure was presented in the form of a bar graph. You may want to redraw the results in this way to see how an interaction is represented in the form of a bar graph. Box 8.1 presents additional examples of interactions from the literature.

In each of the following examples (Figures 8.5–8.12), a different hypothetical outcome is described, in which either the main effects or the interaction effects may be assumed to be statistically significant. The first outcome is presented in Figure 8.5, in which the same results are shown in two different ways: first numerically and then pictorially. In the left-hand portion of this figure is a matrix. The numbers inside the box represent the outcomes for each of the four groups in a hypothetical experiment.

For example, the group that received treatment combination $A_1B_1$ is represented in the upper left-hand cell of the matrix, the group that received condition $A_1B_2$ is in the lower left-hand cell, the group that received $A_2B_1$ is in the upper right-hand cell, and the group that received $A_2B_2$ is in the lower right-hand cell of the matrix. The numbers to the right of the box represent the means for conditions $B_1$ and $B_2$, respectively, and the numbers below the box represent the means for conditions $A_1$ and $A_2$, respectively. In the right-hand portion of the figure, the outcome is represented in graph form with the cell means plotted. The $x$-axis of this graph (the horizontal axis) indicates groups $A_1$ and $A_2$. The $y$-axis (the vertical axis) gives the values 10, 20, 30, and so on.

In this first example, the outcomes for the four groups are 20, 20, 20, and 20. Obviously, there was no main effect and no interaction effect. This same outcome is represented pictorially to the right of Figure 8.5. Participants who received treatment combination $A_1B_1$ responded with a dependent variable measure of 20, and this outcome is represented by the triangle above $A_1$ on the $x$-axis. In a similar way, the outcome of group $A_2B_1$ is represented by a triangle above $A_2$ on the $x$-axis. The line connecting these points is intended to highlight the total effect of the first level of condition B. The outcomes from groups $A_1B_2$ and $A_2B_2$ are represented by squares above $A_1$ and $A_2$ on the $x$-axis and are joined by lines to show the total effect of the second level of condition B. In this example, the results are the same for all groups. Neither the main effects nor the interaction effects are statistically significant. In the graph, this is indicated by the lines representing conditions $B_1$ and $B_2$ falling directly on top of one another. This shows that there is no difference between the main effects of $B_1$ and $B_2$. The fact that $A_1$ and $A_2$ are both equal to 20 is shown by the corresponding points falling at 20 on the $y$-axis, so in this case nothing is significant.

## Figure 8.5

The main effects and interaction effect of treatments A and B are all nonsignificant.

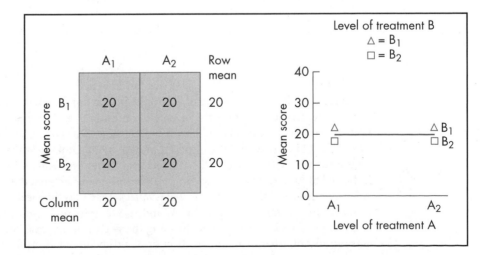

## Box 8.1

# Research Examples of Interaction Effects

Bower (1981) summarized a series of studies on mood and memory. The following graphs are from this 1981 paper.

An experiment by Bower, Monteiro, and Gilligan (1978) produced an interaction similar to that portrayed in Figure 8.8. In this study, college students were hypnotized and put in a happy or sad mood. Once the mood induction had been completed, the students memorized a list of 16 words. After the list was memorized,

the opposite mood was induced. The students then learned a second list. At a later time (either 10 minutes or one day later), the original mood was again induced and the students recalled the first list. The results are shown in the following graph. (Figure based on Bower et al., 1978.)

Does the graph show that participants could learn more or fewer items when they were in the same mood as when they first learned the list?

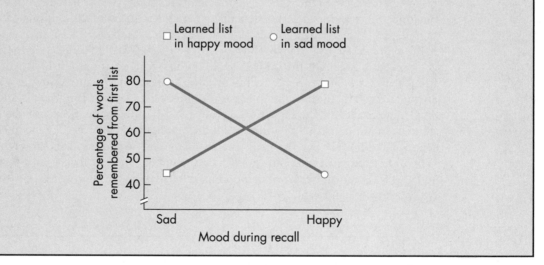

Figure 8.6 shows a hypothetical condition in which the main effect of A is statistically significant, while the main effect of B and the interaction between A and B are nonsignificant. In the left-hand portion, the mean for condition $B_1$ and the mean for condition $B_2$ are both 30; that is, there is no difference between these two levels of factor B. In contrast, the mean effect of $A_1$ is 20 and the mean effect of $A_2$ is 40. Looking at the figure at the right in Figure 8.6, we see this graphically. The fact that there is no difference between $B_1$ and $B_2$ is indicated by the two lines overlapping. Furthermore, the fact that the midpoint of each line corresponds to a value of 30 on the $y$-axis reflects that 30 is the mean for both levels of condition B. In contrast, the values for $A_1$ and $A_2$ are quite different, which accounts for the slope in the lines between 20 and 40 along the $y$-axis. In this case, then, the main effect of A is significant, whereas the main effect of B and the interaction effect are nonsignificant.

A later study by Bower and Gilligan (1979) resulted in an interaction similar to that portrayed in Figure 8.9. In this study, participants were asked to remember personal experiences in either a positive or a negative mood. In the description of the remembered event, participants were asked to rate the event as pleasant or unpleasant. These data are presented graphically here. (Figure based on Bower and Gilligan, 1979.) In what type of mood would unpleasant events be most completely remembered?

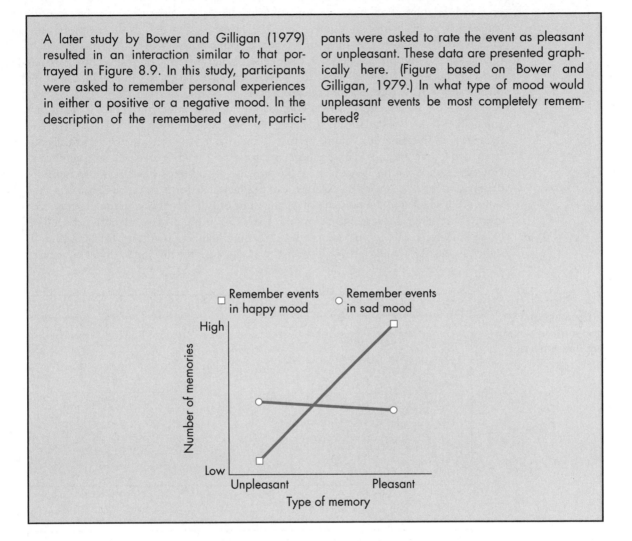

Figure 8.6

Treatment A is significant; treatment B and the interaction are nonsignificant.

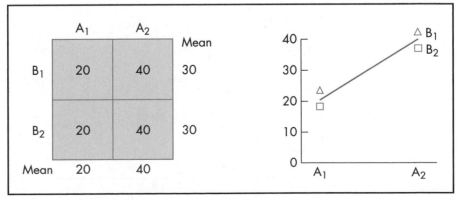

Figure 8.7 shows a case in which the main effect of B is significant and the main effect of A and the interaction effect are nonsignificant. There is a large difference between the values of $B_1$ and $B_2$ across conditions $A_1$ and $A_2$. The mean value of $B_1$ is 40. The mean value of $B_2$ is 20. The mean values of $A_1$ and $A_2$ across both conditions of B are the same: 30. In the right-hand portion of Figure 8.7, these same results are depicted graphically. Two parallel lines occur at 20 and 40 along the $y$-axis. Note also that there is no difference in the mean value of A. The average of both levels is 30.

Figure 8.8 shows a hypothetical example in which the interaction effect is significant and neither A nor B is statistically significant. In this case, the means of levels $A_1$, $A_2$, $B_1$, and $B_2$ are exactly the same: 30. This means that $A_1$ and $A_2$ and $B_1$ and $B_2$ are not statistically different from one another. Thus, the main effects of A and B are both nonsignificant. However, notice that the effect of $B_1$ in the presence of $A_1$ is 40, whereas the effect of $B_1$ in the presence of $A_2$ is 20. For $B_2$, exactly the opposite occurs; for $B_2$ in the presence of $A_1$, the value is 20, whereas in the presence of $A_2$, the value of $B_2$ is 40. Although the mean of each group is the same, the actual value of both levels of B is highly dependent on which level of A is involved. This is what we mean by a strong interaction effect. The same thing is shown in the right-hand portion of the figure. In this case, the line for $B_1$ slopes downward

**Figure 8.7**

B is significant; A and the interaction are nonsignificant.

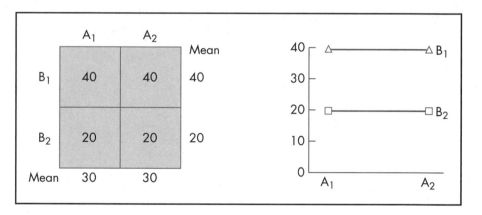

**Figure 8.8**

The interaction is significant; A and B are nonsignificant.

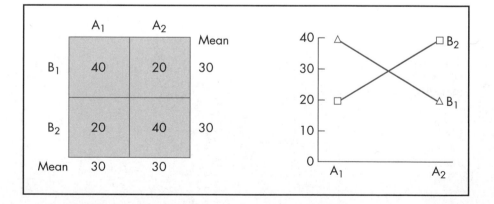

as you move from $A_1$ to $A_2$. In contrast, the line for $B_2$ slopes upward from $A_1$ to $A_2$, illustrating that $B_2$ is larger in the presence of $A_2$, so that the effect of $B_1$ and $B_2$ varies depending on whether it occurs in the presence of $A_1$ or $A_2$. Again, this is exactly what we mean by a significant interaction.

Hamann (1996) reports such an interaction in an implicit memory study in which blind people listened to or read in Braille a list of words (study phase). The participants then listened to or read in Braille the beginning of a word and were asked to complete the word (test phase). Although there were no main effects for percentage correct in terms of how the word was initially presented during the study phase (auditory or Braille) or how the word was presented during the test phase, there was an interaction.

Before proceeding, note that in Figures 8.5, 8.6, and 8.7, the lines representing $B_1$ and $B_2$ are parallel. In Figure 8.5, they are parallel and superimposed in the horizontal direction. In Figure 8.6, they are parallel and superimposed in an inclined direction. In Figure 8.7, they are not superimposed but are parallel in the horizontal direction. In each case, the interaction is nonsignificant. In Figure 8.8, however, when the interaction is statistically significant, the lines are not parallel. Indeed, a useful guideline is that whenever the outcome of a factorial experiment involves nonparallel lines, you may have a significant interaction effect, although there are exceptions. This same sort of result can be seen in several of the following examples.

In the next case (Figure 8.9), an example is shown in which the main effect of A and the interaction effect are statistically significant, but the main effect of B is nonsignificant. The means for the two levels of A are 30 and 10, and the means for the two levels of B are 20 and 20. There is also an interaction effect illustrated by the fact that $B_1$ in the presence of $A_1$ and $A_2$ is markedly different from $B_2$ in the presence of $A_1$ and $A_2$. In one case there is no decrease, and in the other case there is a decrease. The same outcome is depicted in the right-hand portion of the figure. Note that $B_2$ is the same whether in the presence of $A_1$ or $A_2$, whereas the effect of $B_1$ varies considerably depending on whether it is occurring in the presence of $A_1$ or $A_2$. Note also that the lines are not parallel, which, as mentioned previously, is a clue that perhaps we are dealing with a significant interaction effect. Remember, interaction simply means that the various levels of the independent variable are not affecting one another in the same way.

**Figure 8.9**

A and the interaction are significant; B is nonsignificant.

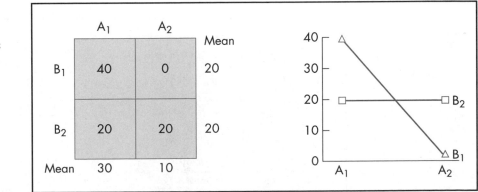

Figure 8.10

B and the interac-
tion are significant;
A is nonsignificant.

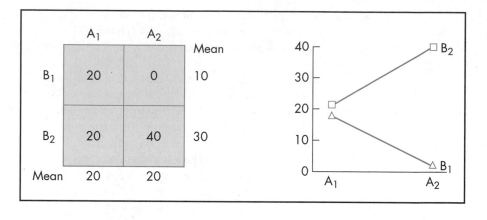

Figure 8.10 shows a case in which B and the interaction effect are significant and A is not. The means for $B_1$ and $B_2$ are 10 and 30; the means for $A_1$ and $A_2$ are 20 and 20. In the right-hand portion of the figure, the data are represented by two lines divergent from one another. Note that once again the two lines are not parallel, suggesting a possible interaction effect.

In Figure 8.11, the main effects of A and B are statistically significant and the interaction effect is not significant. The mean differences between levels $B_1$ and $B_2$ are 10 and 30, and the means for levels $A_1$ and $A_2$ are also 10 and 30. In the right-hand portion of this figure, this outcome is depicted as two parallel lines rising from left to right. The fact that the lines are parallel demonstrates the lack of an interaction effect.

In Figure 8.12, an outcome is shown in which all main effects and the interaction effects are significant. The means for $B_1$ and $B_2$ are 20 and 30, respectively. The means for $A_1$ and $A_2$ are also 20 and 30, respectively. In the right-hand portion of the figure, we see two nonparallel lines; $B_1$ is the horizontal line representing the scores 20 and 20, and $B_2$ is a rising line from 20 to 40. The fact that at $A_2$ the effect of $B_1$ and $B_2$ is quite different from the effect of $B_1$ and $B_2$ at $A_1$ is consistent with the idea that we are working with a statistically significant interaction.

Figure 8.11

A and B are signifi-
cant; the interaction
is nonsignificant.

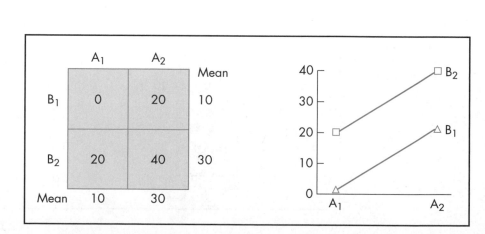

Figure 8.12

A, B, and the inter-
action are
all significant.

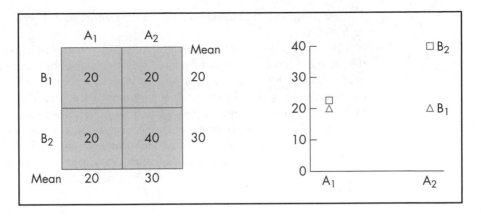

## INTERPRETATION OF SUBJECT VARIABLES WITH FACTORIAL DESIGNS

In this section we offer a warning based on the type of research in which some students try to use factorial designs, although this warning is equally true for single-factor or multifactor designs. For the logic of experimentation to work best, you must be able to randomly assign participants to groups in such a way that any participant may be placed in any cell of the factorial design. This is not possible if one of the factors in the design is what has traditionally been called a **subject variable.** A subject variable is a characteristic or condition that a participant is seen to possess in a relatively permanent manner (that is, relative to the time frame of the experiment).

In the broadest sense, any physical or mental characteristic of a participant that can be measured is a subject variable. Some common examples of subject variables used in research are sex of the participant, eye color, being shy or outgoing, having cancer, being schizophrenic, and being intelligent. We could perform a study and choose our participants according to any of these characteristics. For example, we might ask whether feedback concerning accuracy improves basketball scores differently for men and women. Such a factorial study could be diagrammed as

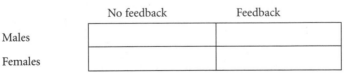

Such a design could examine the effect of feedback on making basketball shots. Because the participants could be assigned randomly to either the feedback or the non-feedback condition, it would be logical to conclude that feedback did (or did not) affect performance. However, we could not assign participants randomly to either the male or female condition because sex is a subject characteristic. Thus, if we found a difference between the performance of men and women, it would not be logical to conclude that the difference was due to sex. For example, the men and the women might have had different amounts of practice in basketball before the study. As an exercise, you might note other possible confounds that could account for differential results between men and women in such a study.

When we cannot randomly assign participants to groups, it is difficult to control for the past experiences of the participants. Thus, the logic of our conclusions becomes weakened and causality is impossible to specify. With this word of caution, we must also point out that the study of subject variables is an important part of psychology. For example, many studies in psychology are devoted to the differences between schizophrenic and non-schizophrenic participants, or males and females, or high-anxiety and low-anxiety participants, or even children and adults. In such comparisons, the logic of experimentation is considerably weakened, and additional control measures are required for a meaningful interpretation of the results. We return to this point in Chapter 9.

# ADVANTAGES OF FACTORIAL DESIGNS

Before concluding this discussion of factorial designs, it will be useful to point out several strengths of such designs. One major strength we have already seen is that we can examine simultaneously more than one hypothesis or factor. This is important because human behavior often is influenced by more than one factor. A second advantage is that because factorial experiments simultaneously evaluate each factor, they are much more economical in the number of participants and the total experimenter effort than studying each factor separately.

For example, suppose we wanted to investigate two independent variables, each of which has two factors (Figure 8.13). Furthermore, suppose we wanted 20 participants to experience each condition. If we used two separate, completely randomized designs, a total of 80 participants would be required (Figure 8.13a). If we used a single $2 \times 2$ factorial design, only 40 participants would be required (Figure 8.13b). The third, and perhaps the most important, advantage of factorial designs is that by examining the extent of interactions between the different levels of the factors, we can see how the various causal factors influence performance.

(a) *Two completely randomized design experiments*

|  | **Experiment 1 (money)** | | **Experiment 2 (prior knowledge)** | |
|---|---|---|---|---|
|  | Level 1 (1¢)<br>20 participants | Level 2 ($1)<br>20 participants | Level 1 (no picture)<br>20 participants | Level 2 (picture)<br>20 participants |
| Total number of participants for each experiment | 40 | | 40 | |
| Overall total | | | 80 | |

(b) *One 2 × 2 factorial design experiment*

|  | **Money** | | Total participants across factor A |
|---|---|---|---|
|  | Level 1 (1¢) | Level 2 ($1) | |
| Level 1 (no picture) | 10 | 10 | 20 |
| Level 2 (picture) | 10 | 10 | 20 |
| Total participants across factor B | 20 | 20 | |
| Overall total | | 40 | |

**Prior knowledge** (row label for factor B)

Figure 8.13

Participant requirements for (a) two completely randomized experiments and (b) a single 2 × 2 factorial design experiment. Note that the factorial design experiment requires half as many participants.

# KEY TERMS AND CONCEPTS

1. **Between-subjects design**
2. **Completely randomized design**
   A. Bransford and Johnson (1972)
   B. Strupp and Hadley (1979)
3. **Factorial designs**
   A. 2 × 2
   B. Main effects

C. Interaction effect
D. Cells
4. **Interpretation of**
   A. Interaction effects
   B. Main effects
5. **Advantages of factorial designs**

# SUMMARY

1. Between-subjects designs are those that involve comparisons between different groups of participants.
2. One of the simplest between-subjects designs is the completely randomized design, also called the simple randomized design. When such a design contains more than two levels of the independent variable, it is called the multilevel completely randomized design. The Bransford and Johnson memory study is one illustration of this design.
3. A factorial design allows for the simultaneous assessment of more than one independent variable on the dependent variable. It is one of the most popular designs in psychology.
4. An important aspect of factorial designs is that they allow for the assessment of the combined influence of two or more independent variables on the dependent variable. This is called an interaction effect. An interaction effect reflects the extent to which one

independent variable varies as a function of the level of the other independent variable.
5. Table 8.2 presents an analysis of variance table illustrating the null hypotheses for each independent variable and the interaction between the independent variables.
6. In a factorial design with two independent variables there are three separate null hypotheses: one for each independent variable and one for the interaction effect. A statistically significant interaction may result from a variety of numerical relationships. These are presented graphically in Figures 8.5–8.12.
7. Three advantages of factorial designs are (1) the simultaneous examination of more than one independent variable, (2) economy in the number of participants and total experimental effort, and (3) the determination of interactions between different levels of the factors.

# REVIEW QUESTIONS

1. What is a between-subjects design, and how is it different from a within-subjects design?
2. What are post hoc tests?
3. What is a factorial design, and what is a 2 × 2 design?
4. Describe a 2 × 2 design, and explain the terms *main effects* and *interaction effects*.
5. In what order should main effects and interaction effects be interpreted? Why?
6. Describe the different aspects of the analysis of variance table presented in this chapter (Table 8.2).
7. Draw a graph that would reflect a significant interaction effect.
8. What are subject variables, and how should they be interpreted in relation to changes in the dependent variable?

# DISCUSSION QUESTIONS AND PROJECTS

1. Look up the Strupp and Hadley (1979) or Bower (1981) research in your library, and note how these researchers controlled for possible confounds.
2. Develop rules for determining from a graph whether an interaction effect might be present.
3. Develop an experiment in which participants learn a series of sentences. Before presenting the sentences, give one group something pleasant to drink (e.g., orange juice) and the other group nothing. Graphically present the results, and discuss how these data would support the hypothesis that a pleasant experience before a memory task helps recall. What are some alternative ways of interpreting the data that point out potential confounds?
4. Take the design you constructed for the recall experiment in Question 3 and add the variable of the sentences being either simple or complex in meaning. Diagram this study and discuss potential outcomes. Would there be any advantage of performing two separate studies, one looking at the effects of pleasant experiences on recall and one looking at the level of complexity and its effect on recall? Would there be any disadvantage?
5. Construct a study examining factors related to helping behavior. For example, you might ask whether the physical appearance of the person in need of help influences how many people offer help, and then ask whether physical appearance influences men and women differently. How would this study be designed, and what conclusion could you draw from the data? What other factors might you need to consider?

## 🎧 InfoTrac College Edition: Exercises

In this chapter we discussed factorial between-subjects designs. As you read the published literature, you will see this design used often. For example, Rachel Herz, in an *American Journal of Psychology* article published in 1997, examined whether the presence of odors influenced people's ability to remember words. Using InfoTrac College Edition, search for her article entitled "Emotion experienced during encoding enhances odor retrieval cue effectiveness." Looking at the "Design and procedures" section of experiment 1 and experiment 2, notice the factors included in the 2 × 2 between-subjects factorial design. Looking at the section that describes the number of words recalled for experiment 2, notice the manner in which the results from the ANOVA are presented. Using the description of these results, construct a graph similar to the ones presented at the end of this chapter that shows the interaction that was found.

## ☑ Answers to Concept Checks

**8.1** The major problem with the study is that participants were not assigned randomly to groups, and thus it is impossible to know whether the two groups were equal before the study began. A better study would be a completely randomized design in which students were assigned randomly to either a coffee-drinking or a non–coffee-drinking group, and then tested for learning foreign language words.

**8.2** There are two independent variables in this study. The first independent variable is the amount of coffee drunk (zero cups versus two cups). The second independent variable is the time of day at which the experiment was conducted (morning versus afternoon). The dependent variable is the number of words learned. The study can be diagrammed as

**8.3** One main effect would be the coffee factor (zero versus two cups). One could ask whether there was any difference between students who drank two cups and those who drank none, regardless of the time of day. The other main effect would be time of day (morning versus afternoon). Likewise, one could ask whether there was any difference between when the students learned the material (morning versus afternoon), regardless of the amount of coffee drunk. However, the two main effects could combine in a variety of ways. For example, students might perform best with two cups of coffee in the morning or no cups in the afternoon. The graph in Figure 8.8 shows such a relationship, with A being coffee ($A_1$ = 0 cups and $A_2$ = 2 cups) and B being time of day ($B_1$ = afternoon; $B_2$ = morning). This would be one example of an interaction effect.

|  |  | *Time of day factor* | |
|---|---|---|---|
|  |  | Morning | Afternoon |
| Coffee factor | Level 1 (zero cups) | Group A | Group C |
|  | Level 2 (two cups) | Group B | Group D |

# Extending the Logic of Experimentation: Within-Subjects and Matched-Subjects Approaches

From the beginning of our discussion of experimental design in Chapter 6, we have stressed two themes. First, we stressed the logical necessity of beginning our experiments with groups that can be assumed to be equal. Second, we stressed the statistical importance of reducing variation, especially the within-groups variation (error variance) component of the $F$-ratio. In relation to the need for beginning an experiment with equal groups, we suggested that the random assignment of participants is one of the best techniques for ensuring that no systematic differences are present at the onset of our experiment. In Chapters 7 and 8, we discussed a number of experimental designs, the logic of which was based on the random assignment of participants to groups. However, as we shall see in this chapter, there are times when random assignment alone may not be the most appropriate approach.

In this chapter, we discuss two approaches to experimental design that do not use random assignment alone. In the first section of this chapter, we discuss **within-subjects designs,** in which the same participant is exposed to different experimental conditions. Later in the chapter, we discuss what are called **matched-subjects designs.** We discuss how matching can be used both as a control procedure and as an experimental procedure for analyzing differences between groups. As in the previous chapters, we stress the need for beginning our experiment with equal groups and the importance of reducing the within-groups variance component of the $F$-ratio. Although the overall logic of experimentation presented in this chapter is similar to that discussed previously, the specific techniques for achieving these goals are slightly different.

# WITHIN-SUBJECTS DESIGNS

In previous chapters, we discussed designs that compare the performance of one group of participants with the performance of a different group of participants. These designs were called between-subjects designs. In within-subjects designs, the participant's own performance is the basis of comparison; that is, every participant serves in every group and receives all levels of the independent variable. In these designs, we compare the performances of the same set of participants on the dependent variable following different treatments.

Let us look at an experiment performed first as a between-subjects experiment and then as a within-subjects experiment. In a simple between-subjects experiment, the experimenter wants to determine the role of immediate feedback in shooting basketballs. One group is instructed to shoot baskets while wearing a blindfold (zero level of feedback) and another group is told to shoot without a blindfold (high level of feedback). This design is diagrammed as

| | | | |
|---|---|---|---|
| R | Group 1 | T (feedback) | M (number of shots successful) |
| R | Group 2 | T (zero level of feedback) | M (number of shots successful) |

If we identify the individual participants, the design is

|  |  |  |  | M (number successful) |
|---|---|---|---|---|
| R | Group 1 | Participant 1 | T (feedback) | 24 |
|  |  | Participant 2 |  | 15 |
|  |  | Participant 3 |  | 17 |
|  |  | Participant 4 |  | 26 |
|  |  | Participant 5 |  | 15 |
| R | Group 2 | Participant 6 | T (zero level of feedback) | 20 |
|  |  | Participant 7 |  | 12 |
|  |  | Participant 8 |  | 13 |
|  |  | Participant 9 |  | 14 |
|  |  | Participant 10 |  | 12 |

We can perform this same study as a within-subjects design in which each participant is exposed to both levels of the independent variable; that is, every participant in the study shoots baskets both with and without a blindfold. We can diagram such a study in a fashion similar to the previous two-group study except that Group 2 contains the same five participants as Group 1. Thus, the total experiment is composed of only five participants.

| Group 1 | Participant 1 | T (feedback) | M (number |
|---|---|---|---|
|  | Participant 2 |  | successful) |
|  | Participant 3 |  |  |
|  | Participant 4 |  |  |
|  | Participant 5 |  |  |
| Group 2 | Participant 1 | T (zero level of | M (number |
|  | Participant 2 | feedback) | successful) |
|  | Participant 3 |  |  |
|  | Participant 4 |  |  |
|  | Participant 5 |  |  |

For simplicity, we usually list the participants only once in a within-subjects design:

Factor A

|  | Level 1 (zero feedback) | Level 2 (feedback) |
|---|---|---|
| Participant 1 | 20 | 24 |
| Participant 2 | 12 | 16 |
| Participant 3 | 13 | 17 |
| Participant 4 | 14 | 26 |
| Participant 5 | 12 | 15 |

Within-subjects designs accomplish both of our goals: equating groups before the presentation of the independent variable and reducing error variance. Because the same participants are used in each group, we can be certain that before any treatment has begun, the groups are exactly the same. A within-subjects design also increases the sensitivity of a study by decreasing the chance or error variance because it removes the variance that results from individual variability. Like other authors (e.g., Kerlinger, 1973, 1986), in this book we call error variance within-groups variance. To be technically correct, however, we need to point out that a within-subjects design will not reduce the variability of scores in each condition. Thus, when we speak of a reduced within-groups variance, we are referring to the reduction of error variance. The logic behind the reduction of error variance with a within-subjects design is that we would expect the behavior of the *same* participant in a series of different conditions to be more similar than the behavior of *different* participants in different conditions.

The error variance term of the *F*-ratio for a within-subjects design is statistically smaller than that of a comparable between-subjects design. This means that smaller treatment differences are adequate for rejecting the null hypothesis. In Table 9.1, we show you the analysis of variance (ANOVA) tables associated with the basketball experiment performed both as a within-subjects and as a between-subjects design. As you can see, the *F*-ratio is 3.99 for a between-subjects design and in a within-subjects design the *F*-ratio is 10.57. In this particular case, we would reject the null hypothesis with the within-subjects design but not with the between-subjects design using the $p < .05$ level.

Some of you probably have noticed a potential problem in our basketball study: The results from the no-feedback condition might have a potential carryover effect on the feedback condition. The act of shooting a basketball, even without feedback, might lead one to perform better in the next condition. Thus, practice could confound this design. One way to control for this potential problem would be to use a counterbalancing procedure, as described in Chapter 7. All participants would first shoot the basketball in the no-feedback condition, then in the feedback condition, then in the feedback condition again, followed by the no-feedback condition. This would generate an ABBA order and thus help to control for the effects that are carried over from one trial set to another. One could also use a BAAB order to accomplish the same effect. Regardless of the order, we call this type of counterbalancing procedure **intrasubject counterbalancing** to contrast it with *intragroup counterbalancing*, which we discuss later in the chapter. Let us now illustrate a within-subjects design with an actual experiment.

## ■ An Illustration of Within-Subjects Research

The Boeing 727 airplane was introduced in the fall of 1965. Although pilots liked the airplane and the early test flights were good, within a year there were four accidents involving the plane (Kraft, 1978). The first accident involved a 727 flying into Chicago from the northeast. This plane began an approach from 22,000 feet and continued to descend until it flew into Lake Michigan, some 19 miles from the shore. The second accident occurred as a 727 flew into the Cincinnati area from the east. To make the landing, the plane had to fly over the river at night and land on a built-up runway. Unfortunately, the plane attempted to land some 12 feet below the level of the runway. The third accident happened as a 727 approached Salt Lake City from the south. From the airplane, the lights of Salt Lake City could be seen past the runway and to the right. In front of the runway it was dark. This airplane attempted to land short of the runway. The fourth accident occurred as a 727 attempted to land in Tokyo. It was a clear night, so the pilot decided to use the flight rules for visual landings (VFR) rather than for instrument landings (IFR). The pilot began the descent over Tokyo Bay with the lights of the city visible. The descent was halted abruptly when the plane hit the water, 6 miles east of the runway.

What happened? Assume that you are a psychologist called in to help determine what caused the accidents. How would you go about this? First, you need to rule out mechanical problems with the airplanes, especially the altimeters (instruments that indicate altitude). Assuming that various experts eliminate mechanical problems as a cause, you might look to the manner in which the planes were being flown by the pilots. You also might look for any pattern of events present at each of the accidents. The initial clues that you find are that (1) all accidents happened at night, (2) the pilots were all operating under visual rather than instrument flight rules, (3) the instruments did not appear to be malfunctioning, and (4) each approach required pilots to fly over dark areas with lights in the distance.

Conrad Kraft, a researcher for the Boeing Company, reported that from this information it was hypothesized that the problem was a miscalculation of space perception on the part of the pilots. This hypothesis suggested that the pilots saw the equivalent of a vi-

Table 9.1

## Analysis of Variance F-Table for the Basketball Study as a Between-Subjects Design and as a Within-Subjects Design

If we were to use the data in the basketball example, we would find that the mean number of shots that went through the basket was 14.2 for the condition with the blindfold and 19.6 for the condition without.

As a between-subjects design in which we used a different group of participants in the blindfold versus feedback condition, the summary table would appear as

| Source of Variance | df | SS | MS | F | p |
|---|---|---|---|---|---|
| Between-groups variance | 1 | 72.9 | 72.9 | 3.99 | .081 |
| Within-groups variance (error) | 8 | 146 | 18.25 | — | — |

As a within-subjects design in which we use the same participants in both conditions, the summary table would appear as

| Source of Variance | df | SS | MS | F | p |
|---|---|---|---|---|---|
| Treatment variance | 1 | 72.9 | 72.9 | 10.57 | .031 |
| Error | 4 | 27.6 | 6.9 | — | — |

From this, you can see that the error variance is reduced in the within-subjects design, resulting in a larger F-ratio than in the between-subjects design. The reason for this is that variability as related to subjects is included with the between-subjects error term and thus influences the F-ratio, but it is partitioned separately in the within-subjects design and does not influence the F-ratio. For more discussion of this issue, you can consult almost any statistical textbook (e.g., Jaccard & Becker, 1990).

sual illusion, which resulted in their misjudging the location of the ground. An analysis of the accidents also suggested that for various reasons—for example, looking for another airplane—the pilots had been distracted from their instruments. In the factorial language presented in Chapter 8, we would guess that the plane crashes were the result of an interaction effect: That is, they were caused by a visual illusion but only when the pilots were distracted from the instruments. To determine whether this was the case, we could perform a simple $2 \times 2$ design. One level of factor A would be the necessary conditions for the visual illusion (a clear night, no lights before the runway, and lights in the distance), and a second level would be a zero level of these conditions. The first level of factor B would be pilot distraction from the instruments, and the second level would be a zero level of distraction. We could represent this factorial design schematically:

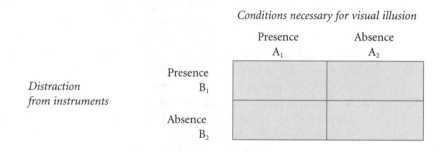

The dependent variable in such a factorial design would be the amount of landing error. Because flying can be simulated on flight simulators, this entire study could be performed in the laboratory, which would not only save money but would also control for environmental factors, such as wind speed and pressure level. Using a between-subjects design, we would randomly assign pilots to one of the four possible conditions ($A_1B_1$, $A_1B_2$, $A_2B_1$, $A_2B_2$). We could then conduct the study and determine any main effects or interaction effects.

Let us think about the realities of this situation and see whether a between-subjects design is really the best alternative. One factor we must consider is the research participant population. In this example, we are interested in a rather special population: pilots who fly 727 airplanes. Thus, it seems somewhat wasteful, in terms of both time and money, to bring a large number of research participants to the laboratory just to make one landing in the simulator. We probably would want to collect as much data as possible from each pilot. Another consideration is to make the experimental and control groups as similar as possible. Are there any factors that we want to vary systematically between our groups? Experience with night flying in general, or with the 727 aircraft in particular, might be such a factor.

One solution to both considerations would be to use a within-subjects design. This would answer our first consideration by having each pilot serve in every condition. It would address our second consideration by allowing each pilot to serve as his or her own control. Allowing each pilot to serve as a research participant in each of the groups would automatically equate the groups for such factors as total flying time and knowledge of the 727 airplane. We can represent such a within-subjects design schematically exactly as we would a between-subjects design, except that each cell is composed of the same participants.

## ■ Advantages and Disadvantages of Within-Subjects Designs

Several advantages to within-subjects designs have been mentioned previously. Because the same participants serve in each group, this experimental procedure ensures that all groups are equal on every factor at the beginning of the experiment. An additional benefit derived from using a within-subjects design is that the total number of research participants can be reduced dramatically. For example, in the simulator study just described, suppose we wanted to have 12 research participants per cell. In a between-subjects design, 4 cells $\times$ 12 research participants = 48 total research participants. By using a within-subjects design, we would need only 12 research participants in the entire experiment. The advantage with regard to the number of research participants becomes even greater as the complexity of the design increases. (For example, a $2 \times 3 \times 2$ between-subjects design would have 12 cells and would require 12 times as many research participants as the equivalent within-subjects design.)

Another advantage to within-subjects designs is that they are statistically more sensitive to changes in the treatment effect. Why is this so? Most of the error variance in psychological studies results from differences among participants in the study. Within-subjects studies reduce this source of variance by using the same research participants in every condition. Because of this, in the $F$-ratio there is a smaller within-subjects variance term. The within-subjects variance term is derived by taking the within-subjects variance as it would be found in a between-subjects design and subtracting an estimate of how consistent research participants are over the different treatment conditions. This means that the $F$-ratio for within-subjects designs is more *sensitive* to changes in the treatments; that is, given the same treatment difference, we would be more likely to reject the null hypothesis with a within-subjects design than with a between-subjects design.

Before you throw out Chapter 8 and build your research career around within-subjects designs, let us consider some of the disadvantages. Remember, experimental designs are plans for helping us to answer research questions, and some questions cannot be answered appropriately by a within-subjects design. For example, if a treatment has any lasting effect on the research participants, then a within-subjects design is inappropriate. To illustrate this point, consider the Bransford and Johnson (1972) study (discussed in Chapter 6) as a within-subjects design. Each research participant would both be shown the picture and not be shown the picture. Clearly, seeing the picture would have a carryover or residual effect when research participants were asked to remember the passage in the no-picture condition.

Clinical treatment studies, such as the Strupp and Hadley (1979) psychotherapy study (discussed in Chapter 8) or a drug treatment study, would be difficult to interpret with a within-subjects design. If the same participant in the Strupp and Hadley study received counseling from both an experienced therapist and a college professor, it would be difficult to determine which changes in the participant should be attributed to which counselor. Thus, the within-subjects design is not appropriate when the treatment has a lasting effect or when the purpose of the study is to test for a lasting effect.

Another disadvantage of within-subjects designs is that they are extremely sensitive to time-related effects. To illustrate, consider a simple learning study in which the independent variable is the complexity of the material learned. The participants could be given progressively harder sets of materials to learn. If the material is presented in this order, can you see any confound that would make interpretation difficult? One possible confound might be fatigue; that is, by the time the participants reach the difficult material, they may be tired. The results would then be a result not only of the complexity of the material (the independent variable) but also of participant fatigue (a confound).

Another confound that could give us a misleading result is practice; each time the participants perform the experimental tasks, they may become better through practice. The effects brought about through continued repetition of the tasks, whether they are increases or decreases, are generically called **order effects.** At times, the terms *fatigue effects* (to note a decline in performance) and *practice effects* (to note an improvement in performance) are used.

## ■ Counterbalancing

In many cases, order and time can be controlled (but not eliminated) through such procedures as counterbalancing. For *complete counterbalancing,* certain conditions must be met. First, each condition must occur equally often; second, each condition must precede and follow all other conditions an equal number of times. Counterbalancing ensures that every possible sequence appears at each presentation of the treatment. We will call this procedure *intragroup counterbalancing* to contrast it with the *intrasubject counterbalancing* procedure discussed previously.

In the learning study mentioned earlier, assume that there are three levels of difficulty. We could counterbalance the easy, medium, and hard levels so that in the first presentation of the independent variable the first participant would receive the easy level, the second participant the medium level, and the third participant the hard level. In the second presentation the first participant would receive the medium level, the second participant the hard level, and the third participant the easy level. The third presentation would have the first participant receive the hard level, the second the easy, and the third the medium, and so forth. This is diagrammed as

| Participant 1 | easy | medium | hard |
| Participant 2 | medium | hard | easy |
| Participant 3 | hard | easy | medium |
| Participant 4 | easy | hard | medium |
| Participant 5 | hard | medium | easy |
| Participant 6 | medium | easy | hard |

This type of design would control for such time-related effects as an improvement in performance through practice or a deterioration in performance through fatigue or boredom.

Note that there are only six possible orders when one has three conditions (e.g., easy, medium, hard). However, as the number of conditions increases (e.g., learning a variety of paragraphs or geometric shapes), a greater number of participants is required for a complete design. For example, 120 participants would be required if there were five conditions. Most researchers at this point use an *incomplete counterbalancing* procedure. For example, rather than easy, medium, and hard, suppose we had six conditions that we will call a, b, c, d, e, and f. One such incomplete counterbalancing procedure is

| Individual 1 | a | b | c | d | e | f |
| Individual 2 | b | c | d | e | f | a |
| Individual 3 | c | d | e | f | a | b |
| Individual 4 | d | e | f | a | b | c |
| Individual 5 | e | f | a | b | c | d |
| Individual 6 | f | a | b | c | d | e |

In this example, you will note that each condition occurs equally often, but it is unbalanced in that each condition does not precede and follow all other conditions (e.g., condition a never follows b). With a large number of conditions, an incomplete design is the most appropriate. A special case of incomplete counterbalancing is the *Latin square design*. To form a Latin square we must have the number of rows equal to the number of columns, which equals the number of conditions. The selection of the conditions traditionally has been performed randomly in a Latin square design (cf. Edwards, 1962; Fisher & Yates, 1948). That is, in a $6 \times 6$ matrix a random six-digit number (including only the numbers from 1 to 6) would be chosen and the rows rearranged in that order. If the random number was 514632, Row 5 would be placed at the top of the matrix, then Row 1, then Row 4, then Row 6, then Row 3, then Row 2. This procedure would then be repeated for the columns and the columns rearranged according to that particular random number.

One common use of the Latin square design is with psychopharmacological research. For example, Rush, Higgins, Hughes, and Bickel (1994) used a Latin square design to study the effects of caffeine and triazolam on learning and performance. By using nine participants, these researchers were able to give all possible combinations of the two drugs (three levels of each). They found that caffeine administered alone did not significantly affect learning or performance but that caffeine did attenuate the triazolam-induced decrements in learning and performance.

Counterbalancing will not control for a *differential order effect*. For example, presenting the picture condition before the no-picture condition in the Bransford and Johnson study would produce a different effect from presenting the no-picture condition first. Counterbalancing would not control for this confound. Such a possibility can be tested for through an examination of the *treatment-by-order interaction*. With such an interaction, the effects of the treatments would depend on the order of presentation. This type of confound would also be inevitable in drug or clinical treatment studies such as the Strupp and Hadley psychotherapy study.

## ■ Repeated Measures

One common application of within-subjects designs uses repeated measures as one factor in a factorial design. This design is useful in studying psychological processes that occur over time and widely used in studying human and animal learning processes. We might present the same subjects with different levels of problem difficulty (e.g., easy versus difficult problems), which would be one factor, and the other factor might be the number of trials (the repeated-measure factor). The dependent variable in such a study could be the number of problems solved correctly. This design would tell us whether there are differences in the number of problems solved over repeated trials—that is, whether the two levels of difficulty are mastered at different rates. In this case, we use repeated measures to study the process of learning or practice effects directly. At other times, we use a repeated-measures design as a control technique to ensure that learning or practice effects are not present in our study. If, as in the previous example, we had presented the easy problems to one set of participants and the difficult ones to another, we would have what is called a mixed design.

---

**CONCEPT CHECK 9.1**    Recall the example presented in Chapter 8 in which a professor randomly assigned students to one of four groups: (1) learn words in the morning and drink two cups of coffee, (2) learn words in the afternoon and drink two cups of coffee, (3) learn words in the morning and drink no coffee, and (4) learn words in the afternoon and drink no coffee. Describe this study as a within-subjects design. What effects would you have to consider with such a design?

# MIXED DESIGNS

Probably the most common design used in psychological research combines a between-subjects design with a within-subjects design. Designs that include both "within" and "between" components are called **mixed designs.** For example, assume we want to perform a biofeedback experiment to determine the effect of feedback on our ability to control heart rate. One factor is the amount of feedback (either total or partial feedback). Should we use a between-subjects or a within-subjects design? If one can learn the ability to control one's heart rate, there could be a carryover effect or a transfer of training from one condition to the other, especially if a research participant learned to control heart rate with total feedback first. This suggests that it would be better to use a between-subjects design and to assign research participants randomly to two groups: one that receives total feedback and one that receives partial feedback. We also might want to look at the effects of this training over a period of days. Thus, our second factor would be a repeated-measures component consisting of the number of days. Such an experiment is diagrammed as

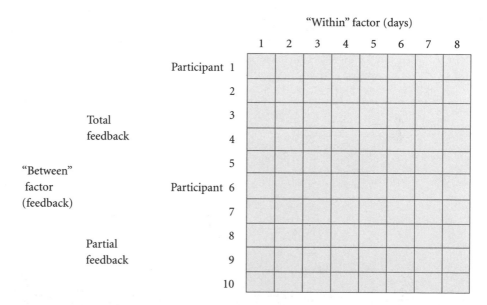

As with between-subjects designs discussed in Chapter 8, in mixed designs we are also interested in the main effects of each independent variable (e.g., level of feedback and days) and the interactions among them. In terms of an interaction effect in the biofeedback study, we can ask whether one type of feedback produces a different learning rate than another. That is, we would ask whether the effects of feedback would depend on the time involved, or conversely, whether the effect of time would depend on the type of feedback presented.

The statistical analysis of mixed designs is complicated because they use different error terms in the $F$-ratio. The error variance for the "between" comparison (level of feedback in our example) is computed differently from that of the "within" comparison (days in our example). Although a discussion of these statistical procedures is beyond the scope of this presentation, the logic of the *F*-ratio remains the same, and you still must interpret the role of the independent variable and rule out the role of chance and confounds in the results.

Beilock and Carr (2001) in a *Journal of Experimental Psychology* article used a mixed design to determine the theoretical underpinning of choking under pressure. In one of their series of experiments, they examined the role of distraction (required to pay attention to additional stimuli) and self-consciousness (being videotaped) on putting errors (distance from target) in a golf game. Participants in the study were randomly divided into either the distraction group or the self-consciousness group and then given a series of 36 putts to perform, which were averaged into the first 18 and the second 18. In this 2 (distraction, self-consciousness) × 2 (errors in first series of putts vs. errors in second series of putts) design, these authors found a main effect of practice but not of group. There was also no statistically significant interaction effect.

Since these authors were interested in choking under pressure, they created low- and high-pressure posttests. In the high-stress situation participants were told that they could win money if their scores improved by 20% and that their score would influence the chance of a randomly assigned team member also winning money. The low-pressure posttest was just putting as normal. In this 2 (distraction, self-consciousness) × 2 (low-pressure posttest, high-pressure posttest) ANOVA, Beilock and Carr found a statistically significant interaction. Basically, there were no differences in errors between the distraction and self-consciousness condition in the low-pressure condition. However, in the high-pressure condition there were more errors in the distraction condition as compared with the self-consciousness condition. The graph of this interaction would appear as follows:

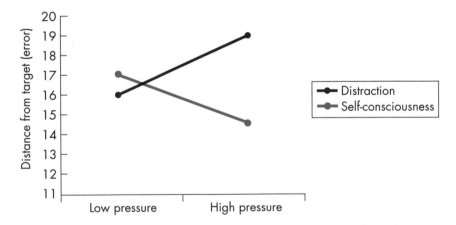

Although one of the more common "within" factors in a mixed design is a temporal one, such as days or trials, there are other alternatives. For example, in social or industrial psychology, the dependent variable could be ratings along certain characteristics (e.g., attractiveness, perceived ability, perceived motivation). Participants in the study would rate different groups of individuals (e.g., white vs. black vs. Asian or males vs. females) which would be the "within" factor. Before the rating, participants in the study could be shown videos that would portray these groups in positive or negative ways (the "between" factor).

| ✓ | CONCEPT CHECK 9.2 | A university administrator seeking to save money suggested that if math skills were taught by faculty in all departments, then there would be no need to have a math department. To prove this point, the administrator designed a within-subjects design in which students received math training from professional mathematicians and from other college faculty. The administrator reported that students showed improvement in math after training with college faculty as well as with professional mathematicians, and thus the math department was to be closed down. Comment on this finding. |

| ✓ | CONCEPT CHECK 9.3 | The same experiment was performed as a between-subjects design and as a within-subjects design, with the same results. We know that the F-ratio would be larger in the within-subjects design. What is the reason for this difference? |

## MATCHED-SUBJECTS PROCEDURES

In this section, we examine matching as a procedure for accomplishing the goals of equating groups in an experiment and reducing the within-groups variance (error variance). To help us in this discussion, we build on the logic of the within-subjects design. As you remember, within-subjects experiments equate groups by using the same participant in every treatment condition. Likewise, by using the same participants in each group, the within-groups variance is reduced because a participant will perform more consistently in different situations than different participants will perform in different situations. What if, rather than using the same participants in different groups, we use participants who are very similar? By using this procedure, we could reap some of the advantages of within-subjects designs and simultaneously take advantage of the random assignment of participants that is possible with a between-subjects design.

Our first task would be to find participants who are very much alike. We might use identical twins, for example, whom we would expect to perform more similarly on a variety of tasks than strangers because they are more alike physiologically. If we randomly assign one twin to the experimental group and the other twin to the control group, we should be able to equate our groups at the beginning of the experiment and reduce within-groups variance (error variance). However, because we cannot use identical twins in every study we perform, an alternative is to match participants. If we pair participants along some factor and then randomly assign the members of each pair to two separate groups, we can assume that our groups are equal at the beginning of the experiment and we can reduce within-groups variance (error variance). In terms of error variance, by this method we create a type of design that is a hybrid of within-subjects designs and between-subjects designs. We would not have as much error variance as in a between-subjects design or as little error variance as in a within-subjects design.

The characteristics we use to match our groups of participants obviously are of central importance to this design. In the broadest sense, any physical or mental characteristic of a participant that can be measured may be used for matching. Characteristics such as height, weight, intelligence, anxiety level, achievement motivation, hair color, and emotional sensitivity are all individual characteristics that can be measured. Consequently, they are all potential individual variables on which matching can be based. For a matching procedure to work, there must be a high correlation between the variable used for matching and the dependent variable. If the participants are matched on a factor that does not correlate with the dependent variable, then the within-groups variance will be no smaller than the variance obtained by random selection alone, and the amount of effort required for matching will have been wasted.

Matching can be used in either of two ways. First, it can be used as a control procedure. For example, if we were studying spatial ability, we might want to control for general intelligence. That is, we would want to make certain that each participant in one group would be matched with one in the other group who had the same IQ, but we would not analyze the intelligence factor itself. Second, if we were to analyze the intelligence factor, we would be using matching in the second way: as an experimental procedure. We discuss this use in more detail later in this chapter. Although it would be technically correct to refer to this second use of matching only as an experimental design, as contrasted with a control procedure, few researchers follow this procedure.

## ■ Matching as a Control Procedure

When we know that a particular individual variable or characteristic has a high correlation with the dependent variable, equal groups may be obtained by matching along this characteristic. The task of forming matched groups of participants consists of two steps. First, pairs of participants are matched on some measure that is correlated with performance on the dependent variable. Second, one member of each pair is assigned randomly to either the experimental or the control group; the other member is then assigned to the other group. Such a design can be represented schematically as

| MR | Group 1 | T | M |
| MR | Group 2 | T (zero level) | M |

Notice that we placed an M before the R to denote that the participants were matched before they were assigned randomly to groups. In essence, we have a completely randomized design.

Let us look at another example of matching as a control procedure. Suppose we are interested in neurochemical changes that result from prolonged periods of sensory deprivation. For a number of reasons, we decide to use monkeys as subjects. Because monkeys are difficult to obtain, we decide to use as few as possible. To control for potential bias in the groups, we might decide to match along a dimension that is highly correlated with our dependent variable: a certain amino acid in the brain, for example. The overall procedure is presented in Figure 9.1. We begin by performing a blood chemistry analysis of our monkeys and then rank order them on the basis of this analysis. After we complete the initial rank ordering, we pair the animals (for a two-group study) according to the rankings. We begin with the two animals that have the highest rankings, then go to the next two, and so on. We randomly assign one member of each pair to one group and the other to the other group, and then proceed with the experiment.

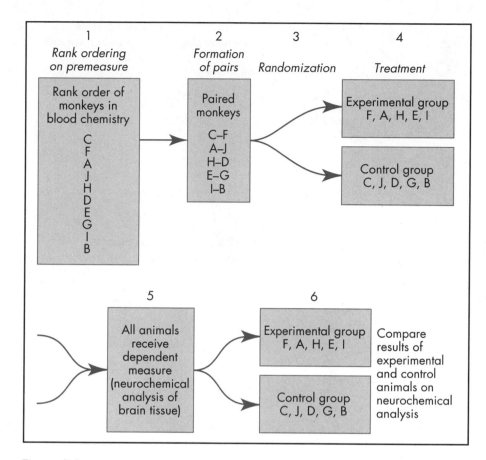

Figure 9.1

The six major steps in a matched-subjects design used to study changes in brain chemistry resulting from prolonged sensory deprivation. (1) Rank order all subjects on the aspect of blood chemistry that is known to be correlated with brain neurochemistry. (2) Form pairs of subjects on the basis of this rank order. (3) Randomly assign one member of each pair to the experimental group and one member to the control group. (4) Conduct the experimental treatments. (5) Conduct neurochemical analyses. (6) Compare the results for the experimental and control animals. Note that, except for our ranking and matching procedures, the design is similar to the completely randomized designs discussed previously.

## ■ Matching as an Experimental Procedure

In the previous examples of matching as a control procedure, participants are matched according to some factor (individual variable), but the factor itself is not analyzed. It is possible to analyze the matching factor, however. When the matching factor is analyzed, the resulting procedure is traditionally called a *randomized block design*. The term *block* in this case refers to the development of the design by Sir Ronald Fisher when he studied agricultural procedures on different blocks of land.

Let us now discuss how the matching factor can be described and used experimentally. To begin, let us again schematically represent a randomized design in which matching is used as a control factor. Take the time estimation study, for example, in which an equal number of men and women are placed in each group. We might diagram such a design as

| MR | Group 1 (males and females) | T | M |
|----|-----------------------------|---|---|
| MR | Group 2 (males and females) | T (zero level) | M |

We could further break down this design as

| Group 1 | Males | T | M |
|---------|-------|---|---|
| Group 1 | Females | T | M |
| Group 2 | Males | T (zero level) | M |
| Group 2 | Females | T (zero level) | M |

At this point it is possible to convert this experiment into a two-factor factorial design and analyze the factor of sex. Such a factorial design is diagrammed as

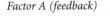

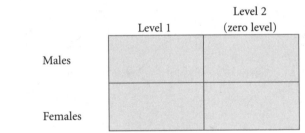

We can now analyze for the main effect of Factor A, the main effect of Factor B, and the interaction of A and B. It must be remembered that the factor according to which the participants are classified is not a factor on which the participants are randomly selected, and it must be interpreted with caution. If there is a significant main effect for this factor, we may be able to conclude that there is a relationship between this factor and the dependent variable, but we cannot conclude that the relationship is a causal one. However, this does not mean that we want to ignore the classification factor. If there is an interaction between the classification variable and the treatment variable, there is much information to be gained. Such an interaction will tell us to which groups and under which conditions the findings of a particular study may be generalized.

For example, in a study of the effects of feedback on performance, Ray, Katahn, and Snyder (1971) divided participants into high- and low-anxiety groups and then randomly assigned them to either a high-feedback condition (feedback on the number of correct responses after each study trial) or a low-feedback condition (feedback only after a series of study trials). It was found in this study that there was no difference between the high- and low-anxiety groups when feedback was given at the end of a series of trials, but there was a difference when feedback was given at the end of each trial. With feedback after each trial, the low-anxiety group increased the number of items learned more than the high-anxiety group did. Such an interaction may be valuable in generalizing from this particular study to other studies concerning the role of feedback in learning.

In addition to the knowledge gained from the interaction effect, we have discussed two other advantages resulting from the prior matching of participants to groups. The first is that such matching ensures that the groups in a study are equal (on the measure by which they were matched) before the treatment is introduced. Equating groups in this way is especially valuable for situations in which we have a limited number of participants but cannot use a within-subjects design. The second advantage is that matching participants reduces the within-groups variance (error variance) and thus makes our design more sensitive to treatments than a comparable between-subjects design. However, this is possible only when the matching factor has a high correlation with the dependent variable.

### ■ Terminology

Before we leave this discussion of matching, let us briefly introduce a more sophisticated terminology concerning what traditionally has been called the randomized block design. Glass and Stanley (1970) suggest that we reserve the term **blocking** for cases in which the matching takes place on a nominal-scale factor such as sex. They also suggest that the use of twins likewise be considered matching on a nominal-scale factor. When the matching uses ordinal measurements such as ranking, they further suggest that the term *stratifying* be used.

Ranking participants into high, medium, and low socioeconomic divisions is one example of using a stratifying variable. When interval or ratio scales are used, Glass and Stanley suggest that the term *leveling* be used. Some common examples are dividing participants according to intelligence levels (e.g., IQs of 120+, 100–120, 80–100, < 80), anxiety levels, or depression levels. It must be remembered that although the groups are developed in terms of individual variables—the members of each of the blocks, strata, or levels—it is still necessary to assign participants randomly to treatment conditions.

## KEY TERMS AND CONCEPTS

1. **Within-subjects designs**
2. **Order effects**
3. **Counterbalancing**
4. **Repeated-measures designs**
5. **Mixed designs**
6. **Matched-subjects procedures**
   A. As a control procedure
   B. As an experimental procedure
7. **Randomized block design**
8. **Individual factors**
9. **Terminology of randomized block design**
   A. Blocking
   B. Stratifying
   C. Leveling

## SUMMARY

1. Within-subjects designs are those in which every participant serves in every group and receives all levels of the independent variable. Performance on the dependent variable is compared following different treatments on the same set of participants.

2. Within-subjects designs have a number of advantages: (1) Because each participant serves in every group, all groups are equated at the beginning of the experiment, (2) fewer participants are needed than would be the case in a similar between-subjects design, and (3)

*(continued)*

## SUMMARY *(continued)*

within-subjects designs are statistically more sensitive to changes in the treatment effect.

3. There are two problems with within-subjects designs: (1) They are sensitive to time-related factors and (2) they cannot be used when a treatment has a lasting effect on the participant.

4. A mixed design is one that combines both "within" and "between" designs, as illustrated by a study that

compared differences between two different groups of participants over a number of days.

5. A matched-subjects procedure may be used either as a control procedure or as an experimental procedure, in which case the matching factor is analyzed statistically. Matching used as an experimental procedure traditionally has been called a *randomized block design*.

## REVIEW QUESTIONS

1. Name some advantages of within-subjects designs.
2. In what situations would you *not* use a within-subjects design?
3. What is a practice effect, and why is it important?
4. For which effects will counterbalancing control? For which will it not control?

5. Give an example of the use of repeated measures.
6. What is a mixed design? Give an example.
7. Discuss matching as a control and as an experimental procedure.
8. Discuss random assignment to groups and the results from not assigning participants in this manner.

## DISCUSSION QUESTIONS AND PROJECTS

1. Discuss the situations in which within-subjects designs are particularly useful.
2. Using an overhead projector and colored pens, it is easy to construct a transparency that demonstrates the Stroop effect. Construct an experiment to determine whether it is easier for students to read the names of the colors while they are tapping their right index fingers or their left index fingers. Discuss how you might design this experiment to look for sex differences.
3. What would be the advantages of performing the experiment in Question 2 as a within-subjects experiment?
4. Why is error variance reduced in a within-subjects experiment?
5. Discuss research areas in which within-subjects designs would be difficult to use and explain why.

6. Assume that a company is interested in finding which of three visual illusions airline pilots are most sensitive to and hires you to help construct such a study. How would you go about it? Would you want to counterbalance? Outline your study and then describe potential confounds and how you would control for them.
7. A company introduces a new beer. In three identical cups labeled *A*, *B*, and *C*, respectively, the new beer and two other brands are placed before the participant. The participant is instructed to taste each beer and state a preference. What would be the problems with using this procedure, and how could these be corrected?

## InfoTrac College Edition: Exercises

Researchers have been interested in how humans make inferences about the mental states of people other than themselves. A study examining this question by Valerie Stone and her colleagues was published in the *Journal of Cognitive Neuroscience* (Sept. 1998) entitled "Frontal lobe contribution to theory of mind." This study examined the ability of individuals with particular types of brain damage to use social reasoning. As you read this study in InfoTrac College Edition, notice how the authors use counterbalanc-

ing. What was its purpose? What makes this study able to be described as one using a within-subjects design?

Another example of the use of counterbalancing is seen in an article by Anthony Wagner published in *Journal of Cognitive Neuroscience* (Nov. 2000). The study, using a brain imaging technique, examined the question of why some experiences are remembered better than others. Note how counterbalancing was used in this study.

✓ Answers to Concept Checks

**9.1** As a within-subjects design, each participant would take part in every condition. Because of possible practice effects, you would want to counterbalance the order.

**9.2** There is a good chance that students would show improvement, but it would be difficult to determine with a within-subjects design the source of the change. That is, if the students saw the math profes-sors first, the students may have learned skills that they used when learning math from the other faculty. Thus, a within-subjects design is not appropriate when the possibility exists to carry over knowledge or skills from one condition to another.

**9.3** The error term of the $F$-ratio would be smaller in a within-subjects design, resulting in a larger $F$-ratio.

# THE ECOLOGY OF THE EXPERIMENT: THE SCIENTIST AND RESEARCH PARTICIPANT IN RELATION TO THEIR ENVIRONMENTS

In this chapter, we want to move beyond our consideration of specific designs to a discussion of the context in which psychological research takes place. By *context* we mean not only the particular laboratory or setting in which the research is conducted but also the world in which scientists and research participants live outside the experiment. It is especially important to realize that the world in which we grew up may differ in significant ways from that of people of other cultures. It is this cultural context that we stress in this chapter.

Rogoff (1990), among others, argues that much of what we learn as children is really an apprenticeship to learning the thinking and doing of the culture in which we live. Thus, we cannot assume that our values or even our views of constructs such as intelligence, sanity, and competency are universally shared. This does not mean that these constructs can never be researched, but it does suggest the importance of agreed-on operational definitions and a willingness to examine the manner in which our previous cultural experiences shape our current views of psychological processes. Initial discussions in this book related to various perspectives of performing a science of behavior and experience. We suggested that science can be viewed from three separate perspectives: that of the scientist, that of the research participant, and that of the witness. In this chapter, we extend that discussion to suggest the importance of the cultural context.

In the previous chapters, we emphasized the role of the scientist and the manner in which he or she interacts with the subject matter of psychology through research. The scientist plays an active role in science through the types of questions he or she asks, the methods by which he or she answers these questions, and the types of answers that are ultimately acceptable. We were particularly interested in one's ability to infer valid connections between variables using experimental procedures. In doing this, we were speaking from the perspective of the scientist.

We are equally interested in one's ability to make valid statements from a broader perspective. Not only will we discuss methods for performing more valid experiments as seen from the perspective of the scientist, but we will also give you a clearer picture of how the humanity of both the scientist and the participant influences the actual conduct of the experiment. If these factors are not considered, the internal and external validity of an experiment may be threatened. To facilitate conveying these issues, we now shift our perspective to include that of the *witness,* who observes the interplay between the scientist and the research participant.

We realize that for some people, the perspective of the witness may be frustrating because it reminds us of aspects of science that are beyond our control and contradicts the picture of science as completely objective. It also shows us that our own culture may shape the manner in which we see the world and especially how we see people from cultures different from our own. However, as a careful reading of history will show, science has never been—and probably never will be—completely objective. As we have shown throughout this book, science is a means of helping us to explore, passionately at times, the world in which we live and to come to some understanding of this world. In our better moments, science may offer us a means of transcending some of our limitations as human beings. Yet, most often, science faithfully reflects our humanness and thus our limitations. The viewpoint of the witness, through an observation of the interactions of the scientist and the participant, helps us to understand the value and relevance, as well as the limitations, of any new information our research produces.

In this chapter, we look at how some of these limitations affect science from the perspective of the witness. As scientists we can control for some limitations; others we can only accept. In this vein, we consider the psychological worlds of the scientist and the participant and how these might influence, either collectively or separately, the outcome of psychological research.

The consideration of participant–scientist interactions is so important that some researchers believe all human experimentation is really a social event that should be viewed from a broad perspective (Petrinovich, 1979). As with any social event, each person may have a variety of reasons for participating. In an experiment, certain social roles may be adopted; these roles, along with their historical origins, are discussed by Danziger (1985). In particular, Danziger suggests that psychological research in this country has been influenced by two historical models dating from the 19th century: the Leipzig model and the Paris model. The Leipzig model, typified by the research of Wilhelm Wundt and others about normal cognitive processes, makes little differentiation between the participant and the experimenter in terms of expected roles or social status. In fact, in the Leipzig model, the same person might serve in both capacities at different times. Psychophysics, in its study of the relationship between physical properties of a stimulus and our sensory experience of it, is one example of the Leipzig model in its methods.

The Paris model, typified by research about hypnosis and abnormal psychology, makes a clear distinction between the roles of the scientist and the research participant. In this model, scientists and participants are different, and one would never play the role of the other. Danziger concludes his discussion by suggesting that American psychological experimentation has been influenced greatly by the Paris model and that this influence has

"You can't build a hut, you don't know how to find edible roots and you know nothing about predicting the weather. In other words, you do terribly on our I.Q. test."

shaped the type of information derived from the experimental context. He further suggests the importance of understanding the relationship between the social structure of knowledge-generating situations—experiments, for example—and the nature of their products.

Several themes involved in understanding the participant-scientist interaction are discussed in greater detail throughout this chapter. One theme is that all parties enter into an experimental situation with expectations that are in part directed by their cultures; thus, a complete understanding of the situation requires an exploration of these expectations and the cultures from which they arise. Another theme, perhaps the most important for our purposes, is that there exists a mediating relationship between the social structure of an experimental situation and the type of information generated in this situation. Thus, experimental results are never just facts, but require a broader understanding for their interpretation and the evaluation of inferential considerations. This focus is important both for the broad perspective it gives us of psychological research and as a means of understanding and perhaps eliminating or reducing the potential biases that enter into the process of research, with or without the knowledge of the scientist. To study the relationships among the scientist, the participant, and the experimental environment, we refer by analogy to the science of ecology.

# ECOLOGY

The term *ecology* was coined more than 100 years ago. Ecology is the scientific study of the relationship of living organisms with each other and their environment (Miller, 1988). Most people are familiar with the word *ecology* as it is applied to the relationship between humans and their environment. For example, by following the food chain we may find that if certain chemicals are used to kill weeds on a farmer's field, the same chemicals might later appear in the breast milk mothers feed their babies. In the 1970s, it was shown that when an atomic explosion took place in China, the fallout could be found in the cow's milk consumed by people in Philadelphia. Most recently, relationships have been reported between dust storms in Africa and certain medical problems (e.g., asthma) in North America. We have also seen that decreases in the population of one type of animal—the lion, for example—have led to increases in that of another animal, such as deer. The general lesson we have learned from the study of ecology is that all parts of nature are closely interconnected and that it is impossible to make environmental changes without affecting the entire system, at least to some extent.

In the same way that we can discuss the ecology of nature by looking at the interrelationships between humans or animals and their environment, we can discuss the ecology of the psychological experiment by examining the relationships among the scientist, the research participant, and the experimental situation. By using the word *ecology,* we emphasize that there are ongoing dynamic interactions—among the scientist, the research participant, and the context—that must be considered before a complete understanding of experimental psychology is possible.

Bronfenbrenner (1979) has written extensively about the importance of including the ecological perspective in human development research. In particular, he stresses the importance of looking beyond the immediate observational or experimental situation. As an example, Bronfenbrenner suggests that to understand classroom development, one may need to study not only the types of teaching methods used but also the home environment, or even the employment situations of the parents, and how these impact on the child's development.

The context of the experiment is also important; numerous studies in the past 50 years have shown that *where* the observation takes place plays an important role. For example, mothers play with their children differently in a laboratory setting than they do in a home setting. Also, it has been shown that blood pressure readings from the same person are higher when measured in a doctor's office than at the person's house. It follows that without an understanding of the ecological aspects of the scientific context, our conclusions and theoretical ideas may be invalid. From this perspective, we can introduce the concept of *ecological validity.*

Ecological validity seeks to determine whether the impact of the important relationships among the scientist, the participant, and the context have been considered fully in evaluating a given piece of research. As we see in this chapter, this evaluation includes examining the relationship of the scientist and the research participant to each other, to the particular research being conducted, and to the greater context of the society in which each lives and works. We discuss some of the possible threats to the ecological validity of research. We present these in a broad perspective but do not attempt an exact definition of the construct because it has been used in a variety of ways in the past. Probably the best-known historical usage of the term is that of Brunswik (1947), which we discuss later in this chapter. Our discussion is more from the perspective of the witness—a metaperspective of the experimental situation.

The witness's motivation is somewhat like that of a consumer protection agency. It is not to suggest that no scientific study can ever be acceptable but rather to offer considerations and at times outright warnings concerning the ecological validity of science. Just as no consumer product or service has been developed that gives perfect results each time, there will never be the perfect scientific experiment. Remember, our goal in science is not to perform a perfect experiment but *to use science to ask questions and to increase our understanding of a given phenomenon.* When used in an appropriate manner, science is one of the most powerful tools we have. When it is used out of context or in a haphazard manner, it is important that caveats and even warning labels be attached. Let us now turn to some of the considerations to keep in mind when assessing ecological validity.

# EXPERIMENTER FACTORS

One initial warning in the acceptance and generalizability of research is the possibility of scientist or **experimenter effects.** To examine experimenter effects is to ask what portion of the results of an experiment can be said to be affected by the attitudes or behavior of the experimenter. In this section, we discuss two types of experimenter effects: those due to biased data collection by the experimenter and those stemming from the experimenter's biasing the participant's performance.

## ■ Biased Data Collection

One potential source of experimenter **bias** in collecting data stems from our individuality: Two experimenters actually may see the world differently. In his history of psychology, Boring (1950) tells of an incident in the late 1700s and early 1800s that points up the importance of experimenter variability in scientific research. The story concerns an astronomer, Maskelyne, and his assistant, Kinnebrook. The method of noting star movement in those days was to look at a clock and then, listening to its ticking, count the ticks until a star crossed a wire in the telescope. Maskelyne dismissed his assistant when he discovered that the assistant timed the passing of stars almost a second later than Maskelyne did. Some 20 years later, after reading of this event, another astronomer named Bessel began to compare his own observations with those of others. Bessel found that different observers using the same method differed by a constant amount. However, Bessel did not fire his assistants. Rather, he became one of the first researchers to point out the effect that inherent differences in experimenters can have on the data they record.

The constant error in the observations of different scientists is what we call the **personal equation** in psychology. The personal equation suggests that because of one's physiological and psychological makeup, there are differences—albeit consistent differences—in the way we, as experimenters, observe the world. And these unique experimenter differences form a real source of experimenter bias. For this reason, it is a common procedure in an observational or rating experiment for two or more independent observers to be used.

The use of a number of observers is particularly important in areas that might be culturally influenced. For example, what might be perceived as anxiety in one culture could be seen as shame or guilt in another. Thus, it is important that a piece of research begin with a clearly stated operational definition and that the observers be trained to code similar information in a similar manner. Fortunately, there is a way to check for inconsistent observations. The method computes a correlation of observations between two observers, using the correlational procedures we described in Chapter 4.

Another common statistic for computing this correlation, called *Cohen's kappa,* is described in a variety of sources (e.g., Bakeman & Gottman, 1989). Whatever the actual statistical procedure, the logic for establishing agreement between the results recorded by different observers or raters is similar. The correlation between two raters is called **interrater reliability.** The higher the correlation between the ratings of two independent observers, the less the ratings represent inconsistent subjective factors of the raters. However, a high correlation may also result from different but consistent ratings from raters; Cohen's kappa attempts to correct for this difference. A low correlation suggests that better operational definitions are required or that additional training of the raters is needed. This is an important area; you should consult Bakeman and Gottman (1989) if you are interested in an extended discussion of interrater reliability and its measurement.

In addition to the inherent differences between experimenters in the way they perceive and respond to the world, personality may create a source of experimenter bias. Scientists are human, and at times the desire to see their hypotheses supported outweighs their honest viewing of the world as it is. In most cases, this temporary reversal of priorities asserts itself in an unconscious or unintentional manner. For example, psychologists have studied carefully other scientists conducting research and have learned that if an experimenter makes an error recording a single piece of data, that error is most likely to be in support of the research hypothesis (Rosenthal, 1979).

In addition, there are more subtle ways a scientist can influence the outcome of an experiment. For example, any unintended variations from the experimental plan tend to favor the hypothesis, the decision about whether to accept or discard a participant's data tends to be influenced by whether the performance supports the hypothesis, and the use of inappropriate statistical techniques, such as unplanned ad hoc analyses, may be misleading. As it turns out, this confusion of priorities is by no means limited to modern researchers. In fact, Barber (1976) suggests that some of our more famous scientists, including Isaac Newton, John Dalton, and Gregor Mendel, may have presented their data as being more precise than was possible during the time in which they lived. Some of these scientists' assistants, like college students performing an experiment when they know what the results ought to be, may have helped the data to fit the predicted theory to please the person for whom they worked.

In the first half of the 19th century, a new and exciting field was emerging that sought to do what intelligence testing does today: The field was called *craniometry*. Proponents of craniometry believed that there was a relationship between brain size (calculated from measurements of the skull) and intelligence. Today we know that there is little relationship between brain size and intelligence in humans, but at that time it was part of the accepted beliefs. Millions of people are said to have had their heads measured in hopes of learning about their abilities.

One of the leading figures in this field in America was Samuel George Morton, a well-known physician and scientist. Morton expanded the work by studying the skulls of people from various races and countries. He measured the quantity of BB pellets that the skull would hold and used this as a measure of intelligence. Before you decide that he was crazy, you should realize that when he died, the *New York Daily Tribune* proclaimed that "probably no scientific man in America enjoyed a higher reputation among scholars throughout the world than Dr. Morton" (Gould, 1978).

Much of his reputation was based on his use of objective scientific measurements, in the spirit of modern-day empiricism. However, one of his major conclusions was that there is a difference in intelligence between the races of the world as well as within races. For example, Morton concluded that English and German people were more intelligent than Jewish people and that Jewish people were more intelligent than Hindu people. In terms of races, white people were seen as being at the top of the intelligence ladder, with Indian people in the middle and black people on the bottom. Gould, a scholar interested in the history of science, reexamined Morton's data and the methods by which he came to his conclusions (Gould, 1978). Gould found that Morton "unconsciously" had selected his samples in such a way that the mean head sizes of the Indians were smaller than those of the whites. Morton also made two errors in his mathematical computations; both favored the view of white supremacy, which was in vogue at that time.

There are other cases in which scientists did more than unconsciously or consciously push the data in the direction of their hypotheses; there are cases of outright fraud. Of course, these are problems of ethics but we discuss them at this point. Two representative examples are the studies of Sir Cyril Burt and Walter Levy.

Burt was interested in demonstrating that intelligence is the result of genetic factors. One method of testing an idea such as this is to examine the intelligence of monozygotic twins (twins in which both individuals develop from the same egg and thus are genetically identical). Burt maintained that if twins who are genetically identical but have had different environmental influences have similar IQs, then it can be concluded that heredity has more effect on IQ than environment does. (These same types of studies are used for determining the genetic component of disorders such as schizophrenia.) However, when Burt's data were reexamined, the results of his studies were seen to present an almost impossible occurrence. The correlation between the IQs of monozygotic twins reared apart was .771 in the first sample of sets of twins, .771 in the second sample, and .771 in the third sample. As Burt found more and more twins who could be used in his study, he performed other correlations to measure how closely the IQs of the twins were similar, and whether the correlation was done using 21, 30, or 51 pairs of twins, the result was always .771. It is extremely unlikely that the correlations in all three studies would be exactly the same; most scientists familiar with Burt's work assume that his data were misreported to support his theory (for a discussion of this case, see Hearnshaw, 1979).

The second case is that of Walter Levy, who performed research in parapsychology. It came to light that Levy had altered data to support his previous research. He subsequently resigned and admitted that he had fudged the data. Barber (1976) not only discusses these cases but also points out that in a number of studies, college students who have been asked to run laboratory experiments have been shown to change data or alter the instructions or procedure of the experiment. Whether these students wanted to get a good grade or were in a hurry to finish their midterm exams is not known.

The journal *Science* reports a case that resulted in the resignation of two scientists from two major medical centers and the retraction of 11 research reports from the scientific literature (Broad, 1980). The story began when a researcher submitted her paper to a scientific journal for publication. In the journal review process (which we discuss in Chapter 15), another scientist saw the paper and made a copy of it. During the next month, the second scientist wrote a paper that included passages from the first scientist's paper without reference to her. By chance, in the review process for this second paper, the first scientist saw the paper and realized that it included passages from her own work. She then wrote to the journal and to the dean of the medical school where the other scientist worked and accused the other scientist of plagiarism. According to the *Science* article, the dean at first felt that the scientist at the medical school had acted improperly in copying from the work of another, but that because the copying was not related to the actual data collection, it did not call into question the research itself. However, further investigation revealed that the original research had never been performed completely and that the results had been fabricated. In the process of the investigation, another scientist was implicated, and the results from 11 published papers were called into question.

During the 1990s, renewed attention has been directed to the question of scientific conduct. For example, a Commission on Research Integrity was established by the National Institutes of Health and held its first meeting in June 1994. Some purposes of this commission have been to help define scientific misconduct and to gather experiences of scientists and others in terms of research fraud and misconduct. There is now a permanent Office of Research Integrity within the U.S. Government Department of Health and Human Services, which has a Web site (http://ori.dhhs.gov/).

International journals such as *Science* and *Nature* also address these issues. For example, the journal *Science* devoted a section of its June 23, 1995, issue to the question of conduct in science. With increased competition for funds and the human need for recognition, this report emphasizes the importance of helping students to understand early in their careers the overall ecology of the scientific research enterprise, as we are doing in this chapter. Noting that little research has been directed at understanding research integrity issues,

the U.S. Department of Health and Human Services funded a series of new projects beginning in 2002. Additional information about the freedom and responsibilities of scientists in relation to society and how they apply to beginning scientists like you can be found in the online publication *Professional Ethics Report* (PER) at the American Association for the Advancement of Science Web site (http://www.aaas.org/spp/dspp/SFRL/SFRL.htm).

*Experimenter bias* not only can affect the data the experimenter records, but also can exert a strong influence on the theoretical interpretation of the findings. Like any other human beings, scientists may consciously or unconsciously choose to view their own and other scientists' results from a biased position that supports their earlier viewpoints. Although few people would consider this type of behavior fraudulent, it is important to be aware of its possibility when evaluating published theories, reviewing papers, or even just reading the discussion sections of published papers.

## ■ Biased Interactions with Research Participants

To understand one way an experimenter might unintentionally bias the interactions with research participants, consider yourself a participant in an experiment in which the scientist is testing the hypothesis that more college men than women dream about violating social taboos. Imagine what type of person (male or female, attractive or unattractive, old or young) you would be most willing to tell your uncommon dreams to. Imagine what type of person you would be least likely to tell your dreams to. As you realize that you react differently to different people in your life, you can also see how research participants in a psychological experiment might react differently to different experimenters. With some experimenters, participants would be reticent, and with others they would talk freely. Such experimenter characteristics as gender, attractiveness, dress, race, and age are known to influence many types of psychological experimentation and should be considered in evaluating a set of studies.

Once the experimenter begins to interact with participants in the actual experiment, additional factors are likely to influence the research. If you have performed research, remember your first experiment. Otherwise, imagine what it would be like to ask people to serve as participants in an experiment. In the real or imagined experiment, did you feel anxious? Did you feel that you were imposing on these people? Did you want one group to respond differently from another? Most experimenters do want their experimental groups to be different from their control groups. It is only natural, but it is also a source of bias if the experimenter communicates to the participants that they are expected to respond in a certain manner or if the experimenter treats one group differently from another. Let us now consider two examples of biased interactions with participants.

Animals can be bred for certain characteristics, such as color, temperament, and predisposition for specific diseases. In the first study, students were given rats to train in running a maze. Half the students were told that they had received rats specially bred for being maze-bright and the other half were told that they were given maze-dull animals. In reality, all the animals were bred the same and were randomly assigned to the two groups of student experimenters. At the end of the study, the authors reported that the rats trained and tested by experimenters expecting bright behavior showed statistically significant superior learning over that of the rats run by the experimenters expecting dull behavior (Rosenthal & Fode, 1963).

A second study using a Skinner box showed the same findings with other experimenters and animals (Rosenthal & Lawson, 1964). Rosenthal and Rubin (1978) have reviewed 345 studies of interpersonal expectancy, and it is now apparent that scientists, like people everywhere, have expectations and that these expectations may influence the outcomes of their studies. They may even influence the type of interaction a research participant is required to complete. For example, a persuasion study examining sex differences might report inaccurate results if the male experimenter selected topics on which he could perform well and ignored those that he did not understand but were part of the working knowledge of women.

This same type of bias may appear as we attempt to study the behavior and experience of people from cultures other than our own. For example, researchers are only beginning to understand the factors that influence how ethnic minority college students experience emotional distress (cf. Okazaki, 1997) or factors that determine how Asian Americans, African Americans, Mexican Americans, and white clients use and respond to mental health services (Sue, Fujino, Hu, Takeuchi & Zane, 1991).

As we begin to study other species with which we cannot communicate directly, an even more difficult situation occurs. Often, we attempt to modify the methods we have used with humans and apply them to animal populations. This is especially problematic when we assume that animals are exactly like humans and ignore important differences in nervous systems or, conversely, when we say that animals are totally different from humans and ignore the great similarities. As we move toward more cognitive and experiential types of research with animals (e.g., Ristau, 1991; Budiansky, 1998), we also move toward a greater potential for biased attributions regarding animal cognition, be it language, emotion, or mental imagery. The problem of this bias is that it may divert the discussion from the real breakthroughs in our understanding of animal cognition toward an argument concerning a few overinterpreted issues such as *animal language* or *animal consciousness.*

Although we all like to think of ourselves as objective in our research, it is important to realize that our passionate commitment to our own hypotheses may lead us to give special attention to the outcomes we expect from our research. In this way, we create self-fulfilling prophecies; that is, we expect something to happen and look for confirmation of our expectations. Even researchers who study self-fulfilling prophecies may have self-fulfilling prophecies, as suggested by some who have tried to replicate Rosenthal's research.

In this section, we have discussed two major sources of experimenter bias: biased data collection by the scientist and biases conveyed by interactions between the experimenter and the research participant. Although research has described various possible sources of experimenter bias, this issue is complex and our understanding of these sources of bias is far from complete. Consequently, it is difficult to say exactly how various situations bring forth bias. Thus, it becomes the task of the scientist when designing a new study—and of the witness when evaluating research—to ask whether experimenter bias might influence either the treatment of participants or the collection of the data. Perhaps the best way we can minimize the effects of this problem is to remind ourselves that the only way we will ever understand human behavior and experience is to examine it in its complexity, which includes the manner in which scientists and participants interact.

## ■ Some Ways to Avoid Experimenter Bias

A number of possible procedures can help to reduce experimenter bias. As suggested, one of the most common is to use several different experimenters, and even to include this as a factor in the study. Maher (1978a) suggests that it may be necessary, especially in clinical psychology research, to expose the participants to a number of different experimenters and experimental situations. This suggestion is based on Brunswik's notion that we should sample not only from research participant populations but also from a number of stimuli situations (Brunswik, 1947). By this, Brunswik meant that the psychological phenomenon under study should be presented not only to a representative sample of research participants, but also in a representative sample of situations.

Another way to reduce experimenter bias is to keep the person who is interacting with the participants blind to the hypothesis and to the particular groups with which he or she is working. For example, blind studies often are used in drug research in which behavioral ratings are made after a certain drug is administered. In this type of study, the raters are not told which participants received which drugs or even whether they received a drug at all. In this way, the experimenter's expectation cannot be conveyed to the participants, nor can it affect the manner in which the data are recorded. For more recommendations for improving research, see Box 10.1. (We discuss double-blind studies in more detail later in the chapter.)

The most useful way to begin eliminating experimenter bias from your own experiments is to try consciously to see the experiment from varying perspectives. We are in a stronger position if we accept that we all are human and make mistakes. The important point for science is not that we were wrong but that we are willing to change.

## Box 10.1

## Recommendations for Research

In an attempt to improve psychological research, Theodore X. Barber (1976) suggests 13 changes that must be made in the way research is performed. This is a summary of these changes.

- In light of Kuhn's analysis of the importance of paradigms, researchers need to be aware of their underlying assumptions and state them explicitly when possible.

- There will be less bias if the person who plans the study (the investigator) is not the same person who analyzes the data.

- There will be less bias if the person who plans the study (the investigator) is not the same person who actually performs the study (the experimenter.)

- Researchers should be pilot participants in their own experiments, to understand the actual experience of experimentation as encountered by the research participants.

- Investigators (those who plan studies) should specify *exactly* what the experimenters (those who run the studies) should and should not do and when.

- Pilot studies carried out by experimenters should be run and supervised carefully by investigators to ensure correct and rehearsed procedures before the actual experimental phase begins.

- Researchers should be trained in the complexity of data analysis and the manner in which different types of analyses may lead to different conclusions.

- Students should be taught more the value of good research methods in answering questions and less the importance of finding significant results.

- Teachers in beginning experimental courses should emphasize the importance of following research procedures to the letter and recording the data honestly.

- When investigators use experimenters to run the experiment, the investigators should monitor carefully to see that the procedures are being followed.

- Investigators should use multiple experimenters, who vary in personal attributes, to collect the data.

- Whenever possible, experiments should be performed blind; if possible, the experimenter giving the treatment should be different from the experimenter recording the results.

- One should not rely on any one study for the answer but seek replications performed by different experimenters in different locations. For the student, a replication of a previous experiment should be encouraged and rewarded as a worthwhile activity.

---

☑ CONCEPT CHECK 10.1    Four developmental psychologists each watched and rated the same set of videotapes of children expressing aggression while playing. From these tapes, the psychologists concluded that boys are more aggressive than girls when they play. What additional information would you want before you accepted this conclusion?

# SUBJECT FACTORS

Another potential source of misinterpretation traditionally has been called **subject factors.** *Subject factors* are present when the research participants are not behaving *in the way we expect them to behave.* Some of these factors occur because we have not considered how a particular participant might experience our study. Subject factors boil down to the realization that research participants are human. In some cases, participants are highly motivated to please the experimenter. In other cases, they may try to figure out the experiment and behave in a way that will support or sabotage the experiment.

In many psychology departments, introductory students serve as participants in experiments to earn extra points on their final grades. Scientists working in these settings will be quick to tell you that near the end of the term, when students are working under increased pressure, participant bias can become a real problem. At exam time, the available participants may be harassed, anxious, tired, and generally negative toward participating in research. From a broader ecological perspective, it is clear that such a participant has little motivation to be part of a psychological experiment. Thus, it is the task of the scientist to consider how the participant experiences the experiment and to look for personal and social factors that might bias the results of the experiment.

One classic example of an initially overlooked subject factor occurred in an experiment conducted in the 1930s. The experiment took place at the Hawthorne plant of Western Electric and was designed to determine how factors such as lighting and working hours affect productivity. The participants were a group of women who worked at the plant; they were asked to work under varying conditions. The productivity of these women was compared with general productivity. When the data were analyzed, a strange finding emerged. In many cases, the productivity of these women increased. It even increased under a condition in which the lighting in the experimental condition was not as good as that in the actual plant. From an experimental design standpoint, it was difficult to understand the data, until the experimenters examined how they had treated these women. The answer they came up with was that the women in the experiment had been given special attention just by being in an experiment. This attention caused the women to consider themselves *special,* and this feeling was reflected in the work they performed.

Today the **Hawthorne effect** remains a warning to experimenters that being given attention and considering oneself special may produce, either directly or indirectly, results much stronger than those of the experimental independent variables. This is not to suggest that you treat the research participants of your experiments in a cold, impersonal manner, but you should take into account the way in which the research participants experience your experiment. In some cases, you may need a control group that is treated just as "special" as the experimental group. The easiest way to evaluate participants' perceptions of their treatment is simply to ask a few people to be participants in your study and then ask them how they felt and how they reacted to your study.

Another example of participant bias took place during the Depression and involved a group of dental students who were paid to be research participants. The study had been designed to examine a new type of toothpaste and its effects on bacterial concentration and tooth decay. Participants with high bacterial concentrations were sought. To qualify for the study and earn some needed money, the students ate candy bars to increase their bacterial concentrations. Once the study was over and the participants were paid, they quit eating candy, and the bacterial counts decreased. The experimenters did not realize that the participants had been eating candy bars, and in their analysis of follow-up reports they stated that the decrease in bacterial concentration was due to the new experimental toothpaste (Simon, 1978). This story demonstrates that in research we are dealing with human beings, whose behavior may be motivated by any number of factors, many of which we do not even suspect. The dental study illustrates that the participants were reacting not only to the demands of the experimental environment by using the new toothpaste but also to the demands of a larger environment, in this case an economic one.

In psychological experiments, the witness reminds us that it is not enough to watch the behavior of human beings as one would watch inanimate objects. Although people may *just* react to the experiment as designed, their reactions may also reflect many factors of which we are not aware. It is our delightful human complexity that makes psychological research both difficult and exciting. Psychological scientists have had to learn that participants are not passive robots; they are active, creative people with definite motives. It is impossible for any experimenter to know exactly which aspects of the study the participants are responding to and what their motives are. For example, when a participant takes part in a psychological experiment, it is impossible to predict (regardless of the design of the study) whether the participant will react to the experimenter as someone to make contact with, as someone to talk to, as a neutral person just doing a job, or as a person who is keeping the participant away from some important work such as studying for an exam.

Because the participant in an experiment is an active, creative, complex human being, he or she may decide not to follow the instructions of the experiment and second-guess the experimenter by acting in a certain manner. Consider an experiment in which the participants are shown erotic films and then a physiological measure such as pulse rate is taken. In reality, the participants might find the films boring, but because they like the experimenter and want to help him or her, they might decide to think about someone who does make them feel erotic and thus give the experimenter more interesting results. Unfortunately, the results have nothing to do with the research as it was designed.

Let us now examine three possible ways the participants might respond in such an experiment. If the experimenter asks participants to watch an erotic film, they might (1) just watch the film and react naturally; (2) react, out of humanness, more to the experimenter than to the film; or (3) consciously construct what they think the experiment is about and respond to the thought rather than to the film. Restated in broad terms, participants may react to the experimental situation, to the experimenter, or to themselves. What makes the interpretation of scientific research even more difficult is that these three possibilities may be brought forth systematically and thus bias the results in a number of complex ways. In the erotic film example, we might find a gender and experimenter interaction in which men and women react differently to a female experimenter.

As we shall see, participants may react differently not only to the experimenter but also to the experimental situation itself. In this section we consider two important phenomena: the placebo effect and demand characteristics. These two phenomena remind us of the importance of having a broad ecological understanding of the relationships among the scientist, the research participant, and the experimental situation.

✓ CONCEPT
CHECK 10.2

A famous psychologist comes to campus. As part of her visit she selects a small group of research participants and conducts a demonstration of a new cognitive self-help technique with the group. When asked about the new procedure at a meeting of the psychology club, the students all gave testimonials as to how the new technique changed their lives. What different factors might have led to such testimonials?

## ■ Placebo Factors

One potential problem in an experiment is the influence of *placebo* effects. Imagine you have just picked up your newspaper and there is a story that says, "Scientists have found a new cure for headaches." As you continue to read the story, you are told of a technique called biofeedback, in which information about physiological changes from a person's body is fed back to the person; it is through the use of this feedback that headaches are being cured. As a consumer of scientific research, how would you go about evaluating this story? First, you might use common sense and note that it seems reasonable that as one learns to relax there should be a decrease in muscle tension and that the number of headaches that are thought to be related to tension should also decrease. Second, you might check the experimental design to see whether the study included a baseline condition in which the number of headaches per person was recorded before biofeedback was administered. If you have headaches yourself, you might be ready to run out to the local biofeedback practitioner and sign up. But even if the biofeedback treatment worked for you as it did for the people in the study, it still would not have been demonstrated scientifically that biofeedback was the ingredient that caused your headaches to decrease. Both the consumer and the scientist would need to consider the placebo factor.

The term *placebo* comes from the Latin verb *placere*, "to please." It refers to the phenomenon that some people show physiological changes just from the suggestion that a change will take place. For example, in a number of studies that have attempted to treat tension headaches with a variety of procedures, it has been shown that 60% of the people report signs of improvement when given only placebo treatments, such as a pill containing nothing but sugar or other inert ingredients (Hass, Fink, & Hartfelder, 1963). In recent years, research has suggested that endorphins (naturally occurring chemical compounds with analgesic properties) may be released internally on the expectation of change. This finding may contribute to our understanding of the placebo effect.

The placebo phenomenon is so strong with some people that a placebo operation (opening up the chest but not performing a heart operation) has been shown to result in recovery rates for patients with angina pectoris (pains in the chest) similar to those following an actual coronary bypass operation (Cobb et al., 1959). To control for the placebo effect in research, various procedures have been used. One is to use a control group that receives either no treatment or a treatment previously shown to be ineffective for the particular disorder under study.

A more powerful control is to use a **double-blind** experiment, in which the experimental group is divided into two groups. One group is given the actual treatment and the other is given a treatment exactly like the experimental treatment but without the active ingredient. For example, in a study of medication, the placebo group would receive a medicine that looks and tastes like the experimental one but does not contain the sub-

"IT WAS MORE OF A 'TRIPLE-BLIND' TEST. THE PATIENTS DIDN'T KNOW WHICH ONES WERE GETTING THE REAL DRUG, THE DOCTORS DIDN'T KNOW, AND, I'M AFRAID, NOBODY KNEW."

stance being tested. Neither the placebo group nor the experimental group would know which medication they were receiving, and in this way these research participants are said to be *blind*. The term *double blind* indicates that the physicians or nurses giving the medication also do not know which medication is experimental and which is placebo. A more sophisticated version of this design would allow for the placebo and experimental research participants to be switched systematically during the study; thus, the same participant would receive at times the active treatment and at times the placebo treatment (see Shapiro, 1997; White, Tursky, & Schwartz, 1985, for an overview). Placebo research continues to be an important topic as evidenced by a National Institutes of Health conference on the Science of Placebo devoted to the topic. The conference was held in 2000 with a book published in 2002 (for information see http://placebo.nih.gov/).

## ■ Demand Characteristics

A phenomenon similar to the placebo effect is that of **demand characteristics** in psychological research. Demand characteristics occur when a participant's response is influenced more by the research setting than by the independent variable. For example, in a test on the effect of marijuana on behavior or on the effects of hypnosis, most participants have some idea of how they will be expected to act, and they may respond in this manner. The response may include actual faking on the part of the participant. If demand characteristics play an important role in the experiment, then they pose a significant threat to internal validity and offer an alternative explanation for understanding the influence of the independent variable.

Orne and Scheibe (1964) sought to understand the role of demand characteristics in a sensory deprivation experiment. Sensory deprivation research has focused on the effects of reducing the amount of stimulation a person receives from the environment. In such an experiment, participants are asked to lie in a room with pads on their arms and legs and goggles over their eyes, which blocks out stimulation. Early descriptions of this research reported in the popular press suggested that without sensory stimulation, research participants would hallucinate, feel disoriented, and have a difficult time working on any type of task.

Orne and Scheibe set up a sensory deprivation experiment without any sensory deprivation. They divided participants into two groups. Participants in the first group received a physical exam and gave a short medical history. Although they were told that the experiment was safe, they were allowed to see a tray labeled "Emergency Tray" that had drugs and medical instruments on it. This group was asked to report any problems that they might have in concentrating, as well as any unusual visual imagery, fantasies, or feelings (including disorientation) that they might have. The participants were told that during the experiment they were to work on an arithmetic task. They were then placed in a special room with food, water, and the materials needed for the arithmetic task. Inside the room was a button marked "Emergency Alarm" that they could press if they wanted to get out of the room.

The control group was not given a physical exam or shown the "Emergency Tray." The people in the control group were told only that they were to perform the arithmetic task and that if they needed to get out of the room, they should knock on the window. In actuality, neither group received any type of sensory deprivation. However, the results reported by the experimental group were similar to those reported in the previous sensory deprivation experiments. This study suggests that the previous results may have been related to the expectations of the research participants—expectations based on either their own knowledge or an experimenter's leading questions—rather than sensory deprivation alone. Thus, in any type of research that asks for a participant's reaction (such as studies using alcohol, drugs, or hypnosis), it is important to consider the possible influence of demand characteristics. If possible, a demand-characteristics condition should be built into the experiment.

One study of hypnosis that attempted to control for demand characteristics was reported by Orne (1969; Orne & Evans, 1966). The purpose of the study was to find out what would happen if a hypnotist left the room after deep hypnosis had been induced. This particular experiment had theoretical importance because one theory of hypnosis suggested that the research participants would return to their normal state of awareness rapidly, whereas another predicted that it would take some time. The study was designed to see which of the two theories more accurately reflected reality. In the study, a group of hypnotic participants was compared with a control group in which research participants were asked to simulate hypnosis and act as if they were hypnotized. Orne and Evans called their control group a *quasi-control group* because the control group was being used more to check out the experimental conditions than to compare directly with the experimental group.

The experimenters wanted to design a study in which the hypnotist left the room in an apparently accidental manner, in order to avoid breaking the implicit agreement that the hypnotist would remain with and take care of the hypnotized research participant. To accomplish this end, the experimenters staged a power failure. During the second of two sessions, after the experimental participants had been hypnotized and were tapping their feet to imagined music, a tape recorder in the room stopped and a desk light went off. The experimenter said that a fuse had blown, and left the room.

The findings of the study were apparently clear. The quasi-control group continued to act as if hypnotized until the experimenter returned some 30 minutes later. However, the experimental participants brought themselves out from the hypnotic trance. This required varying amounts of time, and, once out from under the trance, they appeared somewhat confused.

During the postexperimental interviews it was learned that the quasi-control research participants believed that the power failure was not real. The experimental group did not seem to suspect the deception. Because the quasi-control research participants were aware of the deception, it was difficult to conclude anything directly from the study. The experimenters then considered ways to make the power failure seem more real. They reexamined the experimental situation and realized that although the tape recorder and the desk lamp had gone off, the room lights and a small polygraph continued to be on. Also, the room had a one-way mirror, and this suggested to the research participants that they were being observed, which they were.

A new study was designed. This study also used an experimental and a quasi-control group, but the room was changed. There was no one-way mirror, and when the pretended power failure occurred, all the equipment and the lights in the room went off. The experimenter was blind as to which was the real hypnotic group and which was the simulated one. Under the new conditions, the results for the experimental group were the same. However, the quasi-control group showed quite different results. As soon as the experimenter left the room, the great majority of these participants stopped simulating and acted as if they were not being observed.

Orne and Evans concluded from the second study that the power failure was considered real by both groups and that their experimental manipulation was therefore meaningful.

"WHAT IT COMES DOWN TO IS YOU HAVE TO FIND OUT WHAT REACTION THEY'RE LOOKING FOR, AND YOU GIVE THEM THAT REACTION."

Without a control for demand characteristics, an experimenter might have concluded that the theories were correct when in fact the results might have been due to the research participants' acting as they believed they should.

When evaluating research, it is important to consider the role of placebo factors and demand characteristics. It is also important for the researcher to check through such techniques as the quasi-control group and the credibility of the experimental manipulations. *It is not enough to assume that the participants in an experiment believe what is being said and accept rationales as true; this must be verified, especially in any study that uses deception.*

**CONCEPT CHECK 10.3**    A researcher interested in the manner in which vitamins help a person feel better devised a study in which she gave vitamins along with orange juice to one group of research participants and orange juice alone to another group. How might you design this study to reduce placebo and other similar effects?

## CULTURAL AND SOCIAL BIAS

You may think it strange to suggest that the society and environment in which you live could cause significant bias in scientific research. Yet science is not immune to a shared cultural view, whether it be that a certain racial group is inferior or that one type of science is better than another. Sometimes a scientist may perform a research study and not realize that his or her data are biased.

For example, a number of studies have shown that people who go to an outpatient psychiatric facility for intervention often receive treatment based not on their disorders but on other factors such as their ethnic backgrounds. In general, in these studies African Americans tended to receive psychopharmacological interventions and Caucasians tended to receive verbal psychotherapy. If a researcher were to conduct a study using past medical records, there would be an unintended confound of race because the two types of treatment used different populations. It is also the case that health psychology and other medical studies previously relied heavily on male participants, which could bias the results.

In order to combat such bias, a policy was implemented in 1994 by the U.S. National Institutes of Health to require all federally funded research involving human participants to include women and members of minority groups. In response to this requirement, *The Journal of Consulting and Clinical Psychology* devoted a special issue (October 1996) to the recruitment and retention of minorities in clinical research. Not only do we see an emphasis to perform research that more adequately reflects the characteristics of our own society but we are also beginning to see a greater emphasis of understanding worldwide processes in terms of cross-cultural research methods (Lyons & Chryssochoou, 2000).

One common way in which scientific research may be influenced is through a shared paradigm (Kuhn, 1970). A paradigm is an accepted worldview; it may include ideas about the value of what one is doing as well as specific assumptions about how the world is. Because a paradigm shapes the way in which you see the world, when it changes, everything seems to change. A number of paradigm changes in science have altered the manner in which scientists see the world. One of the first was the change from seeing the earth as the center of the universe to seeing it as just another planet. Once the earth was seen as just another planet, a new scientific cosmology became possible, as did a new idea about the place of humans in the universe.

In psychology, we have seen changes in scientific viewpoints that have allowed research never considered possible. For example, at one time it was considered impossible to have a scientific study of consciousness. However, consciousness has now become an important focus for the neurosciences with research journals devoted to this topic. Today there are a number of research projects in which chimpanzees are being taught to communicate either through a computer or through sign language, thus opening an entirely new field of research that a few years ago was considered impossible. Likewise, we are gaining a new view of both young people and old people that suggests they are capable of far greater potential than we had assumed previously. Whereas the previous paradigm emphasized the negative and pathological, today's view is currently being expanded to include a positive psychology. We now are beginning to realize that children can interact with their external environment— for example, by recognizing faces—immediately after birth. Not only our children, but we ourselves are beginning to be seen in a new light.

We are also beginning to realize that the body and its physiology are influenced directly by emotional and cognitive factors previously thought to have little influence. For example, we now know that brain connections can be modified, which was previously thought impossible. We need to keep in mind that by limiting ideas, important questions are not asked and productive relationships are left unexplored. We introduce a bias into our scientific research by letting the believed limitations of our time restrict the scope of our vision. Consequently, we never consider certain aspects of behavior that lie beyond our limited view. Every scientist and every society holds limited views of the world. That is not the point; rather, the point is to *realize* that this is the case.

# KEY TERMS AND CONCEPTS

1. **The role of the witness in science**
2. **Ecology**
3. **Experimenter factors**
   A. Personal equation
   B. Interrater reliability
   C. Experimenter bias

4. **Subject factors**
   A. Hawthorne effect
5. **Placebo factors**
6. **Demand characteristics**
7. **Double-blind experiment**
8. **Cultural and social bias**

# SUMMARY

1. All research takes place in a specific context, which extends beyond the laboratory. This context includes the scientist-research participant interactions during an experiment, the world of the scientist when he or she is not performing science, and the world of the research participant when he or she is not being part of an experiment.

2. Ecology as a science interested in the relationship of living organisms and their environment offers a model for studying the overall contextual relationships between the scientist and the research participant. *Ecological validity* depends on whether the relationships among the scientist, the research participant, and the context have been fully considered in evaluating a piece of research.

*(continued)*

## SUMMARY *(continued)*

3. *Experimenter effects* are changes in the dependent variable produced by the attitude or behavior of the experimenter and not related to the independent variable. These effects may be a result of biased data collection by the experimenter or by experimenter influence on the research participant's performance.

4. The threat of experimenter bias can be reduced by using multiple experimenters and having the experimenter not know (be blind to) a research participant's group.

5. Research participants may also bias an experiment. They live in their own psychological worlds, and this factor must be considered, as illustrated by the Hawthorne experiment. In that experiment, the research participants felt themselves to be special and responded accordingly. Some research participants may want to help an experimenter and in so doing give the data that they think the experimenter wants. Other research participants may try to sabotage an experiment.

6. The word *placebo* comes from the Latin word for "to please." The placebo effect is the phenomenon (especially likely in drug or psychotherapy studies) in which a suggestion of change actually produces a change. Recent research suggests there may be a biochemical basis to the placebo response.

7. The term *demand characteristics* refers to the research participants' being more influenced by the experimental setting than by the independent variable. An example of this would be the case in which research participants who have been told to consume a large quantity of alcohol produce behaviors that they believe someone who is drunk would produce.

## REVIEW QUESTIONS

1. How can the concept of ecology be applied to the experimental situation?
2. Give some examples of experimenter bias. How would you attempt to reduce this bias?
3. What are placebo effects?
4. How might a drug company control for placebo effects?
5. Discuss demand characteristics.
6. What potential experimental biases might result from the interaction between the research participant and the experimenter?

## DISCUSSION QUESTIONS AND PROJECTS

1. Discuss how research results depend on the context in which they are derived. How do they transcend the context?
2. It is said that experimenter bias does not affect the internal validity of an experiment. What does this mean? In what cases is this statement true and in what cases false?
3. How could the Hawthorne effect play a role in the experiments you perform in class?
4. When does a research participant in an experiment know what the independent variable is?
5. Design your own double-blind study. What information would you give to the research participants and what information would you give to the experimenters?
6. A researcher is interested in the effects of alpha-wave feedback on feelings of well-being. The researcher develops an experiment in which the experimental group receives alpha biofeedback and fills out a "feeling of well-being" questionnaire before and after the experimental session and again the next day. The control group is shown a cartoon book and also fills out the questionnaire before and after the session and on the next day. Both the control and experimental groups showed similar positive scores after the session, but only the alpha-feedback group reported more positive well-being on the next-day questionnaire. The researcher concludes that alpha biofeedback has lasting effects on a person's well-being. Discuss this conclusion.

## InfoTrac College Edition: Exercises

When researchers code videotapes or rate participants' responses, using more than one coder helps to control for bias. It is important to determine how similar two coders are in their classification of events or responses. One method is to determine the correlation between two judges' responses. Mary Ann Foley and her colleagues had two judges rate imagery responses in terms of self-references. You can read about this study using InfoTrac College Edition by looking up either the author or the study ("Self-referencing: How incessant the stream?") that was published in the *American Journal of Psychology* (Spring 1999).

In terms of biased data, we discussed the work of Sir Cyril Burt. You can read more about the papers of Burt in an article ("Some further observations concerning Sir Cyril Burt") by Brian Butler and Jennifer Petrulis, which was published in the *British Journal of Psychology* (February 1999).

We also discussed how research participants may give biased results as illustrated by the Hawthorne effect. Using InfoTrac College Edition, you can see how current human factor researchers control for the Hawthorne effect in a study ("Workplace changes associated with a reduction in musculoskeletal symptoms in office workers") by Nancy Nelson and Barbara Silverstein, published in the journal *Human Factors*.

## Answers to Concept Checks

**10.1** One important piece of information would be the interrater reliability, using the specific operational definition of aggression. If this correlation were low, you might conclude that the operational definition of aggression was not a good one. You might also want to know the sex of each rater and whether there were any systematic errors in the manner in which the ratings were made.

**10.2** A variety of factors might have influenced the students' testimonials. First, the cognitive self-help technique might actually have changed their lives. However, before you would want to accept this conclusion, you should rule out a number of other factors. Some of these include being associated with a famous psychologist, the changes that result from being selected to be part of a small elite group, and the desire to please.

**10.3** One obvious problem with the initial study is that the results could be influenced by the manner in which the experimenter gave participants the vitamins. That is, she could convey additional encouragement or expectancy that would bias the results. A simple improvement would be to run the study as a double-blind placebo study, such that one group received a vitamin and the other group a placebo pill that was similar in appearance to the vitamin tablet. In addition, neither the research participants nor the experimenter would know which were the actual vitamin pills and which were the placebos.

# QUASI-EXPERIMENTAL, CORRELATIONAL, AND NATURALISTIC OBSERVATIONAL DESIGNS

CLOSED AND OPEN SYSTEMS

QUASI-EXPERIMENTAL DESIGNS
Time Series Design
Interrupted Time Series Design
Multiple Time Series Design
Nonequivalent Before-After Design
Retrospective and Ex Post Facto Designs

CORRELATIONAL PROCEDURES

NATURALISTIC OBSERVATIONS
Concerns While Making Naturalistic Observations
To Conceal or Not to Conceal; To Participate or Not
  to Participate
Strengths and Weaknesses of Naturalistic
  Observation

In the previous chapters, we presented a more idealized approach to experimentation, one in which the experimenter has a high degree of control over the experimental manipulation. Such experiments play an important role in making inferences because few variables are uncontrolled by the experimenter. However, one cannot always construct an experimental situation with a great deal of control—for example, when we study the psychological reaction to natural disasters such as earthquakes. There are other times when the researcher is faced with a situation in which uncontrollable or unpredictable factors influence the experimental outcomes. Even a well-designed study may be compromised by problems such as unequal attrition rates, in which randomization can no longer be assumed. For example, a researcher may discover that a data collection device did not function properly on a particular day or that an unequal number of participants in one condition did not complete the experiment.

The design task for all of these situations is still to help support inferences of the greatest strength possible. Although the logic remains the same, the methods for accomplishing this task may vary somewhat, hence the designation **quasi-experimental design.** Quasi-experimental designs are one focus of this chapter. A second approach we examine is that of *correlational procedures*. We conclude with a discussion of *naturalistic observation*. Because these three procedures often are used in research conducted outside the laboratory, we illustrate their use in such a context. However, moving a study to the field does not preclude the use of tight experimental control or the use of designs centered on the manipulation of variables. Many of the designs we have discussed previously may be applied in the field, depending on the questions asked.

Throughout the chapter, we discuss the more philosophical issue of when one would want to give up rigorous experimental controls in order to better study real-world processes and thus collect data more relevant to our everyday lives. Such a debate in relation to memory was presented in *American Psychologist* in January 1991. In considering the more general issue of tight design as opposed to more real-world research, we discuss the relationship between internal and external validity as we seek to design research that is both sound and relevant.

# CLOSED AND OPEN SYSTEMS

Throughout the history of science, experimental control of the research situation has been a prime objective. You can see this desire for control in classic studies in the physical sciences as well as in psychological research. Scientists try to create a research environment in which they can control the important factors that influence the topic under study. That is, they try to create a *closed system*. For our purposes, a closed system is one in which the important factors that influence the environment are controlled by the experimenter. For example, the technique of studying falling objects such as feathers and weights in the closed system of a vacuum chamber illustrates the great degree of control achieved in classical physics. Likewise, B. F. Skinner's use of the Skinner box and the precise caring for and feeding of animals offers the experimenter a high degree of control over the environment to which an organism is exposed and makes possible detailed studies of animal learning.

When we have a high degree of control over the environment, the types of designs we discussed in Chapters 8 and 9 are extremely important. With these experimental designs we have the greatest confidence that our dependent variable truly reflects the effect of our independent variable. In particular, these designs help us to rule out alternative explanations and rival hypotheses, and in this manner they ensure a greater degree of internal validity.

Sound experimental control and the resulting high degree of internal validity are extremely desirable features in any experiment. Yet whatever the importance of internal validity, it is equally important that our designs reflect other issues as well. For example, our research findings should be generalizable. Can the results of an experiment be generalized beyond our particular research setting to ongoing life situations? For example, would waiters perform the same on a laboratory memory task—in which they have little personal investment—as they would when they take your order in a restaurant? Such questions are important as we seek to generalize our results beyond one specific setting to a broader context. The generalizability of an experimental outcome is called its *external validity*. When Campbell and Stanley (1963) first used the term *external validity*, they were asking to what other groups, settings, treatment variables, and measurement variables an experimental outcome could be generalized.

Today, many scientists and nonscientists are insisting that research findings should have direct relevance to everyday psychological issues that affect us all. This growing concern for the applicability of our research findings to the real-life situations we all face influences our research efforts in two ways. First, the theoretical questions and hypotheses we generate increasingly deal with complex, relevant psychological issues and processes. Second, our research participants and settings increasingly reflect real-life situations.

One method for increasing the generality and relevance of our research is to move the research from the laboratory to the setting in which the phenomenon we are studying occurs naturally. For example, in a laboratory you could not study the psychological effect of experiencing some unplanned event such as an inner-city riot, the bombing of the Federal Building in Oklahoma, the nuclear reactor accident at Three Mile Island, the destruction of the World Trade Center in New York City, or a natural disaster such as an earthquake. Neither can you study in the laboratory the impact of some large-scale intervention policy such as the Head Start Program. If we are studying the effect of anxiety on final examination performance, a possible natural setting would be the actual final examination session of a college course. If our theoretical issue deals with interpersonal relationships between strangers in a large city, then the natural setting is the streets of that city.

Although moving research into the field does not preclude rigorous experimental designs, it is often the case that as we move outside the laboratory and its highly controlled environment, we find ourselves able to control fewer of the factors that influence the behavior of our participants and thus less able to rule out alternative hypotheses. Whereas we often consider the laboratory a closed system, the world outside the laboratory is an open system in which the participants are influenced by a number of factors over which experimenters have little control.

In some cases, we cannot manipulate the levels of the independent variable; in others, we cannot adequately eliminate potentially confounding variables; and in most we have little real control in terms of participant selection and assignment. Outside the laboratory, we have little influence over what humans do, feel, or think as they move about in the everyday world. In these situations we cannot achieve the same degree of control that we accomplish in a closed system. Thus, we need research designs that are appropriate to situations in which we have greater difficulty ruling out alternative explanations and that give us less certainty that the changes in the dependent variable were really the result of changes in the independent variable. In these situations (which also may include some laboratory situations), we may find ourselves relying more on reasoning and logic than on direct control of the experimental situation.

In fact, in some cases the time required for developing control of the experimental situation brings about unforeseen consequences. Let us consider one striking anecdote told by developmental psychologist Dale Harris. When Professor Harris was teaching at the University of Minnesota, one student decided to perform an experiment that enlisted the participation of elderly people in retirement homes around Minneapolis. To sample participants randomly, the student collected the names of all the residents of the retirement homes and began random selection in such a way that each resident had an equal chance of being selected for the study. However, the time required to complete this sampling process correlated with an event that was unforeseen by the student. During the time in which this random sampling was taking place, 12% of the residents in the retirement homes died! This points up the importance of reducing tight experimental controls when the phenomenon under study occurs in a changing environment. Additional examples of such studies are those performed in a changing work environment or clinical studies performed in hospitals and clinics, where both patients and staff change frequently. These changes make tight experimental controls impractical.

It is possible to perform useful research in the field even with lowered control. For example, one applied study asked whether rear-end collisions could be reduced by adding a warning device to the backs of cars (Voevodsky, 1974). The independent variable was an amber light that indicated the rate of deceleration and was affixed to the rear ends of taxicabs. A group of cabs that did not have the device served as a control group. At the end of the experimental period, the group of cabs with the device had a rear-end collision rate lower than that of the control group.

What types of questions might you ask in evaluating this study? One question would relate to the Hawthorne effect, which we discussed in Chapter 10. Might the drivers in the experimental group have seen themselves as part of an experiment and been more careful in their driving? The author of the research suggested that if there were such an effect, then we would expect to see an overall reduction in accident rates for the cabs. That is, one might expect that both the control and experimental groups would have had lower accident rates during the experimental period than during similar periods in previous years. The rate for front-end accidents, in which the taxi runs into another car, was the same for both the experimental taxis and the control taxis. Also, there was no reduction in front-end accidents. The only reduction in accidents was for those caused by other cars running into the taxis from behind, and that reduction occurred only in the experimental group. Thus, it could be assumed that driving a cab with the device did not influence how carefully the driver of the cab drove, but that it did influence the driving of those who were following the cabs.

This taxi study offers an example of a valid and useful study performed with less control than found in the laboratory. In this study, reasoning and logic were used to arrive at the conclusions drawn from the research results. Such research may have a direct influence on our lives because all new cars sold in this country come equipped with a third rear brake light, mounted at eye level (generally above the trunk).

Sometimes significant events that change our lives cannot be predicted and make designing research more difficult. However, as we will see there are procedures for helping us to answer research questions. The critical issue in such situations is formulating the research question and logically ruling out alternative explanations. The attacks on the World Trade Center on September 11, 2001, came as a surprise. Yet, even such a tragic event can offer us insights into human behavior as well as appropriate methods for treating those who experience such tragedies. As you look into the psychological literature, you will see a variety of tragedies and natural phenomena that have been researched.

For example, suppose we were interested in studying the psychological effects of a disaster such as the World Trade Center in 2001, the nuclear accident at Three Mile Island in 1979, or the Loma Prieta earthquake in 1989. There is no way we could control the onset or even the site of such an occurrence, nor could we randomly assign some people to a *potential meltdown* or *earthquake group* and others to a *no-meltdown* or *nonearthquake group*.

In the case of the World Trade Center, it would be difficult to find someone who was not affected in some manner including fear of flying or desire to learn more about certain areas of the world or religious movements. Furthermore, when dealing with the people affected, it would be difficult to eliminate other factors that may have coincided with the disaster itself. Some of these influences may have been positive, such as the concern expressed by friends, relatives, and strangers all over the country. Others were probably more negative, such as fear of future terrorist attacks and concern over local and national security.

Let us assume you are interested in some of the effects of the 1989 Loma Prieta earthquake. It occurred at the time when much of the country was watching a World Series game being broadcast from San Francisco and thus the earthquake was witnessed by a large part of the population. Let us examine briefly a few different approaches, which we can discuss in more detail later. One approach would be to ask *retrospective* questions and simply look for changes in such factors as psychological well-being, physical health status, or accident rates before and after the event. In a retrospective study, as the name implies, we simply look back at an event. For example, Berkowitz (1970) reported an increase in violent crime following the assassination of President John F. Kennedy in 1963.

Social psychologist James Pennebaker wanted to find out whether the 1989 Loma Prieta earthquake had an effect on conflict levels in the population in general. He collected data from the San Francisco police department on reported assaults occurring before and after the earthquake. We refer to such research as **archival research** because it uses existing records collected before the time of the study and not for the purpose of the study. Figure 11.1 shows the percentage change in the number of reported assaults, from 4 weeks before the earthquake to 20 weeks after the earthquake.

What can we say about these data? And more important, what can we *not* say? We can say that after the earthquake there was an increase in the number of assaults reported to the police. However, we can say nothing about which factors actually produced the increase. Moreover, we do not know whether the increase in assaults was produced by a small percentage of the population or represented a larger phenomenon throughout the population.

Dr. Pennebaker designed a second study to find out whether people reported more arguments with their co-workers or families after the earthquake than before. To answer the question, Dr. Pennebaker used a device that randomly telephoned people within the community. He found that by the third week after the quake, the percentage of people who reported having arguments with family or co-workers had increased from 40% to 60%. Could this increase have been a chance occurrence? To help rule out the possibility that the results were not related to the earthquake, Dr. Pennebaker at the same time addressed the same question to people from three other cities, two in California and one in Texas. The results are presented in Figure 11.2.

**Figure 11.1**

Number of assaults reported in San Francisco before and after the 1989 Loma Prieta earthquake

*SOURCE:* Pennebaker (1991).

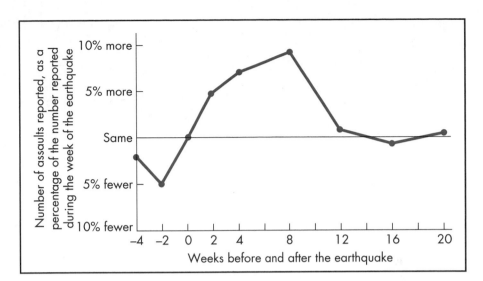

**Figure 11.2**

Percentage of individuals reporting conflict after the 1989 Loma Prieta earthquake

*SOURCE:* Pennebaker (1991).

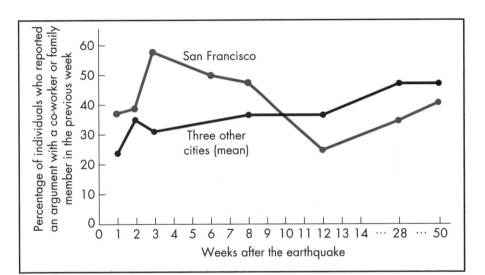

In a third study, people in San Francisco were asked whether they had dreamed about the earthquake during the previous week. These dream data were compared with dreams in response to another significant event: the Persian Gulf War. The results are presented in Figure 11.3. As a footnote, we can point out that Dr. Pennebaker had previously been conducting research in the San Francisco Bay Area on questions related to health and social psychology. Thus, his ability to conduct these three studies was in place when the earthquake took place. He just needed to act quickly and shift his focus to study this chance event.

Whenever we attempt to study real-life events or to increase the external validity of our inquiries by studying phenomena in real-life situations, we run a strong risk of decreasing the internal validity of our experiments. In most cases the internal validity of our research is jeopardized or even decreased as we move from the laboratory to more natural settings.

Figure 11.3

Percentage of individuals reporting dreams about the 1989 Loma Prieta earthquake and the 1991 Persian Gulf War

*SOURCE:* Pennebaker (1991).

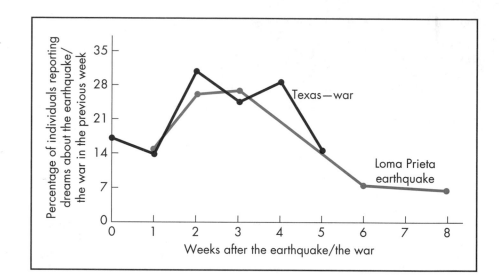

Yet the overall applicability and relevance of our research may be increased greatly, and this may enhance the value of our work. Thus, we are always faced with a trade-off between (1) precision and direct control over the experimental design and (2) generalizability and relevance to real-life situations. The process of conducting sound and relevant research requires a balance between our concerns for internal and external validity.

One solution to the difficulties faced when studying real-life events, although somewhat ambitious, is to combine naturalistic observation with more experimentlike procedures in a real-life situation. We present one set of such studies that took place over a number of years, beginning in the late 1940s. The initial study in the series was designed to explain the development and nature of prejudice. Later studies refined the procedure and may be familiar to you from introductory psychology books as the Robbers' Cave Experiment (see Sherif, Harvey, White, Hood, & Sherif, 1961). A portion of our discussion is based on an interview we had with one of the researchers, Carolyn Wood Sherif.

The impetus for performing the research was the experimenters' dissatisfaction with the theoretical notions of that time relating to the development of prejudice. The example of prejudice that many people were attempting to understand during that period was that of some German people against Jewish people. Some of the writers of the day tried to explain the behavior of Nazis during World War II by suggesting that the German people involved were somehow different from other people. The researchers of this study were not satisfied with that answer. The questions remained: What is the nature of prejudice and how does it develop? How might you go about studying prejudice?

The initial hypothesis was that normal, healthy people would develop all of the earmarks of prejudice when (1) they found themselves in situations of strong group identification and (2) their group was placed in such circumstances that it had to destroy the aspirations of another group in order to reach its most cherished goals. To test such an hypothesis, it was necessary to set up a situation involving groups in which only one group could win. Many alternatives might come to mind (a college sports event or a business competition between companies, for example). Because these researchers wanted as much control as possible over the experiment and were interested in the formation of group prejudice, they chose a summer camp. To better understand what naturally happens in a summer camp, one of the researchers, Muzafer Sherif, spent the summer of 1948 visiting camps and watching daily activities. Unlike such other group environments as businesses or universities, a summer camp offered the potential for few outside influences except letters from home or visits from parents, and thus extended to the researchers the possibility of a high degree of control in a naturalistic setting.

Once a camp was chosen for the experiment, the staff of the camp were trained in observational techniques, some of which we discuss later in this chapter. To allow for access and observation, some of the researchers became part of the staff. For example, one became a handyman and thus was able to wander around camp without being noticed. The counselors recorded observations twice a day. For ethical purposes, the parents were told of the experiment before they chose that particular camp.

To ensure reliability, additional measures were taken by independent raters; that is, when a counselor observed a boy behaving in a certain way over a period of time (he became a leader or a clown, for example), an independent observer was asked to observe that boy. To further validate the observations, miniexperiments were designed. For example, the researchers at one time created a baseball practice in which each camper threw a baseball at a target and the other campers rated the accuracy of his throw. Because it was difficult to judge exactly where the ball hit, the researchers wanted to know whether there was a systematic error related to status in the group; that is, were the most popular campers in the groups seen as being better at throwing? By using these miniexperiments and additional observations, the researchers could base their conclusions not just on a single set of data but on a combination of measures obtained in different situations.

In the third of the series of camp experiments, which has come to be called the Robbers' Cave Experiment (Sherif et al., 1961), the researchers observed the formation of group leadership structures. As the researchers had postulated, a group culture formed even when participants had no idea of the existence of another group. After about a week, each group learned of the existence of another group of campers, and the staff arranged a sports competition between the two groups. What the researchers were most interested in was whether prejudice would develop between the groups and, if so, how it would develop. Carolyn Wood Sherif describes this development:

> When they found out there was another group in camp, they said they would like to compete with them. So the camp staff arranged this event so that they could compete. They set up a tournament in which there were a series of events and points to be gained cumulatively. Great prizes offered—loving cup, Swiss Army knife for each boy on a winning team, and so on—lots of motivational things. The tournament went on for three or four days. The boys . . . would say "we will beat you," but in a very friendly way. They greeted one another, and after the first events they would give the cheer "Two, four, six, eight, who do we appreciate?" name the other team, and all of these good-sportsman sort of things.

> But this started to evaporate very quickly. The extent of the rivalry—the concern that the other group was doing them in, that they weren't playing fair, that things were being stacked against them, and so on—began to appear very quickly. So when those things would happen, they would then start to behave more aggressively toward the other group. These sorts of aggressive actions, in turn, would feed the fuel, if you will, of the images that they had of the other boys. So that very shortly, rather clear-cut stereotype views of the other group developed. They were cheats, stinkers, you know. And we, of course, are brave, honorable, and true. [After the tournament, each group said] they would just as soon never see those guys again.

At this point, the researchers sought to intervene and reduce the conflict that had developed. In the first study, they arranged for a sporting event with another camp nearby, thus requiring that the two teams work together. This intervention was effective, and it represents a case in which outside competition reduced group conflict. This result permitted a clearer hypothesis for two later studies. To quote Dr. Sherif, "So the hypothesis stated that in order to reduce intergroup conflict and prejudice once it was generated, it would be necessary to have conditions in which there were goals strongly desired by members of both groups, but absolutely not obtainable without the resources and efforts of both groups together." Those were called superordinate goals. In the first study, the researchers used a sporting event with another camp to bring the two groups together; in the third study, they used a water shortage for the same purpose.

The researchers describe a complex series of interactions in the development and reduction of group prejudice. The findings supported the notion that given the right situation, prejudice can be found in any person, not just in those with psychological problems. Such a conclusion offers us the possibility of generalizing these findings to the present-day situation and the prejudice one ethnic group faces from another. For our purposes, this series of studies presents one approach to using naturalistic settings in answering psychological questions. We have only touched on the surface of the studies, and we recommend reading them for an interesting account of conducting psychological research in the field.

We hope to encourage you to see the potential of psychological research for asking important theoretical and practical questions when tight experimental control is not possible. To this end, we introduce research designs in this chapter that offer alternatives to the designs presented previously in this book. With the first group of designs, we lack sufficient experimental control over the variable under study and over potentially confounding variables to make logical statements about the relationship between the independent and dependent variables. We rely instead on logically discounting alternative interpretations of the data. To emphasize that these designs are less rigorous, many researchers call them *quasi-experimental designs.* Because these designs often are used to evaluate the impact of some variable on an ongoing process, they are also called *evaluation research designs.*

Although there are many ways in which *quasi-experimental designs* approximate true experimental designs, when using them we still cannot be as confident about the relationship between the independent and dependent variables as with true experimental designs. Nevertheless, they are extremely useful in uncovering potential relationships in complex psychological phenomena in a variety of settings. Consequently, because of our growing interest in studying complex psychological processes, these designs can play an important role. In a similar fashion, these designs are useful in showing where a relationship does not exist, thus reducing the need to perform more highly controlled designs. For example, if a new form of psychotherapy is shown not to work in quasi-experimental situations in which a variety of placebo and suggestibility factors would help its effectiveness, it would be difficult to argue that the therapy would work better in highly controlled situations.

Another type of procedure we consider is that of **correlational designs**. Correlational designs attempt to describe the relationship between two variables. Although a researcher may use these designs for confirming predictions, they do not allow one to infer causation. However, they are useful for disconfirming potential causal relationships. For example, if smoking cannot be shown to be correlated with cancer, then it would be impossible to infer that smoking causes cancer.

The final class of designs we examine is *naturalistic observation techniques*. These techniques provide an important tool for describing an ongoing process in its natural setting. In this chapter we describe some of the traditional ways in which these approaches have been used. We can point out that many researchers also use modified observational techniques in such areas as emotional expression (facial expression, for example), content analysis of conversations, and bodily reactions. Our overall purpose in this chapter is to point out that not only does one generate data in an experimental situation, but one also finds data in everyday situations, and there are techniques for studying these found data.

| CONCEPT CHECK 11.1 | Professor Rigid taught his class that if you could not randomly assign participants to groups, then you could never do science. How might you respond to such a position? |

# QUASI-EXPERIMENTAL DESIGNS

## ■ Time Series Design

A **time series design** is a within-subjects design; that is, the performance of a single group of participants is measured both before and after the experimental treatment. Before we continue, it should be noted that although it is similar to this design, we describe the single-case example of this procedure in Chapter 12. Overall, this design is useful when we are interested in the effects of an event that has happened to all members of the population we are studying.

For example, suppose you decide to become a college guidance counselor and, after obtaining your Ph.D., you take a job at a small college. One day you are talking to your friend, the gymnastics coach, and she mentions that her gymnasts perform very well in practice and during warm-ups but seem to fall apart during actual competition. As a psychologist you know that certain relaxation training and simple imagery concentration exercises have been shown to improve performance in other test situations. You mention this to the coach, and she immediately asks you to try these relaxation exercises with the team. You agree, and for the next week you spend time working with each athlete during daily practice. The entire team enjoys the exercises and feels that they are helpful. To evaluate the effectiveness of these relaxation procedures more objectively, you decide to compare the team's total score at the next meet with its total score at their previous meet. This particular design, which involves comparing a single pretest measure (total score at the first meet) with a single posttest measure (total score at the second meet), is called a *single-group pretest-posttest design*.

During their next meet, the gymnasts' composure is much improved and their total score is better than in the previous meet. Because the coach kept a record of each athlete's apparent composure during each performance, it is also possible to rate each gymnast's composure at each of these two meets. Hypothetical results for these two variables—performance and composure—are shown in Figure 11.4. Both the total score and the coach's estimate of composure increased markedly following the relaxation and concentration exercises. Before concluding that the exercises caused these changes, however, we should keep in mind that we have used only a single pretest and posttest measure; we have no idea how much fluctuation would normally occur between any two meets. Perhaps the sharp increase in the score and the shift in composure ratings are independent of the relaxation exercises. Not knowing the normal amount of fluctuation between any two measures is a serious weakness of the single-group pretest-posttest design.

## ■ Interrupted Time Series Design

One way to overcome the weakness of the single-group pretest-posttest design is to use an *interrupted time series design* that is discussed under the topic of single-case designs in Chapter 12. This design involves making several pretest and several posttest measurements. The basic idea behind this type of design is that the additional pretest and posttest scores give us a better estimate of the normal fluctuation from test to test. Once we know the amount of normal fluctuation, we can better interpret the impact of the phenomenon we are studying. Figure 11.5 is a schematic representation of an interrupted time series design.

As an example of a time series design, let us again consider the hypothetical experiment dealing with the effect of relaxation procedures on the performance of gymnasts. In this case, a time series design could incorporate the scores for several meets before and after the introduction of the relaxation and concentration exercises. Consider for a moment the three possible outcomes depicted in Figure 11.6. In Figure 11.6a, the pretest and posttest scores are fairly constant; it would be reasonable to assume that the

**Figure 11.4**

Hypothetical results of a single-group pretest-posttest design studying the effects of relaxation exercises on (a) the total points scored by a gymnastics team and (b) the coach's estimate of the gymnasts' composure

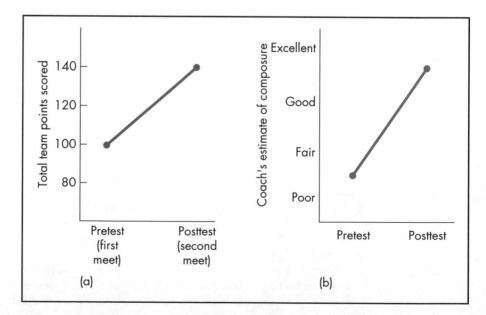

apparent change in performance reflected a real shift. In Figure 11.6b, there is considerable fluctuation in the pretest and posttest scores, so our best bet is to assume that the sharp increase in performance after introducing the relaxation procedures was simply chance fluctuation that would have occurred anyway. In each case we interpret the effect of the phenomenon under study by comparing its impact with the normally occurring fluctuations of weekly meet scores. An interrupted time series design can also provide some estimate of how long-lasting the influence of the phenomenon is. For example, Figure 11.6a shows a hypothetical outcome that would lead us to suspect a fairly long-lasting impact of the relaxation procedures. Figure 11.6c shows a hypothetical outcome consistent with the idea that the gymnasts' performance was improved only temporarily.

In the research literature, the interrupted time series design has been used to study changes before and after major changes in legislation (e.g., increasing speed limits). Carrington and Moyer (1994) examined suicide rates before and after the 1977 changes in the Canadian federal gun control law to better understand whether availability of guns was related to suicide rates, which it was. A number of studies have examined the introduction of various drunk-driving laws using interrupted time series designs. For example, Hilton (1984) found little effect of such laws on fatal accidents in California. West, Hepworth, McCall, and Reich (1989) found that after a reduction in vehicular fatalities following the introduction of driving while intoxicated (DWI) laws in Arizona and California, the fatality rate returned to prelaw levels. Likewise, Ross and White (1987) found that publishing names in the newspaper of people convicted of crimes had no effect on drunk driving but did reduce the incidence of shoplifting. This type of design is also used for examining health psychology interventions in a community by examining changes prior to and after an intervention (Biglan, Ary, & Wagenaar, 2000).

Although the interrupted time series design is a great improvement over the simple pretest-posttest design, it still leaves us far short of a clear statement of how one variable influenced the other. For example, if the results were those shown in Figure 11.6a, you could certainly feel confident that a real shift in team performance occurred at about the time you introduced your relaxation procedures. However, any number of other events might be contributing to this unusually abrupt shift in team performance. Perhaps the increased care and attention given to each athlete were responsible, not the exercises themselves, maybe some campus event that occurred about that time caused the shift, or perhaps there was a television special on gymnasts bound for the Olympics.

| Pretests | Phenomenon under study | Posttests |
|---|---|---|
| $O_1, O_2, O_3, O_4$ | X | $O_5, O_6, O_7, O_8$ |

Figure 11.5

Interrupted time series design. In this figure, $O$ represents each observation or test score and $X$ represents the occurrence of the phenomenon under study. Note that the phenomenon under study, $X$, interrupts the periodic measurement of our group of subjects (after Campbell & Stanley, 1963).

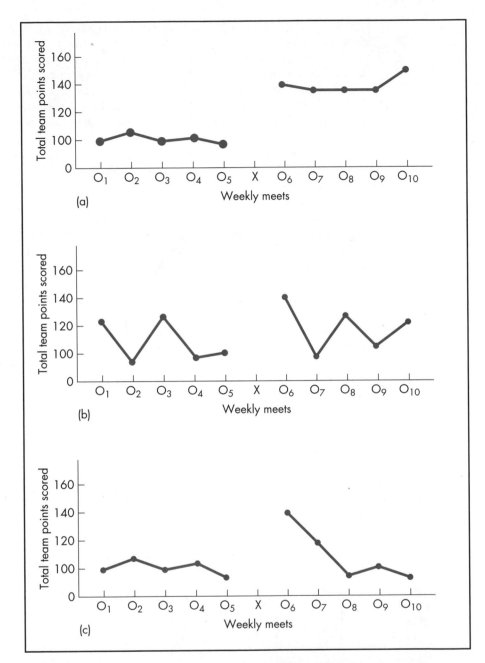

**Figure 11.6**

Hypothetical outcomes of an interrupted time series design examining the effects of relaxation exercises on the total points scored by a gymnastics team in 10 weekly meets. X marks the point at which the exercises were introduced. (a) Outcome in which the pretest and posttest scores are fairly consistent. (b) Outcome characterized by much variability in the pretest and posttest scores. (c) Outcome in which what might be a transient effect is superimposed on a more constant background.

In an ideal situation, we could control for many of these alternative interpretations by including a control group of some sort. However, because *all* members of the population under study have been exposed to the relaxation procedure, it is impossible to select a control group. This is an important limitation of the interrupted time series design, and it must be kept in mind when we are interpreting the outcome. As it turns out, it is sometimes possible to redefine the population we are studying to make use of control participants who were not directly exposed to whatever phenomenon is being studied. In this case we might see whether there was a shift in the performance of gymnasts from a nearby college. This expanded form of the interrupted time series design is called a *multiple time series design*.

## ■ Multiple Time Series Design

A multiple time series design attempts to rule out some alternative interpretations by including a control group that does not receive the experimental treatment. Because it uses a second group of participants, the multiple time series design is not a within-subjects design like the interrupted time series design; rather, it is a between-subjects design. A multiple time series design is schematically represented in Figure 11.7.

In our study of the effectiveness of relaxation procedures on the performance of gymnasts, it might be helpful to use a control group of gymnasts from a neighboring college. We could use their total weekly team scores as control data. To the extent that these participants are similar to our original participants in any relevant individual difference variable and are living under similar social and environmental influences, we can assume that the two groups are equal for factors other than the experience of the relaxation training itself. Figure 11.8 shows two sets of hypothetical data for each team.

Figure 11.8a shows the hypothetical scores from Figure 11.6c for the gymnasts who received the relaxation exercises, along with the total team scores for the gymnasts from the neighboring college who did not receive the special training. The difference between the scores of the two teams in the two meets following the special training is certainly consistent with the idea that the relaxation procedures had a definite but transient influence on

| Pretests | Phenomenon under study | Posttests |
|---|---|---|
| **Experimental group** | | |
| $O_1, O_2, O_3, O_4, O_5$ | X | $O_6, O_7, O_8, O_9, O_{10}$ |
| **Control group** | | |
| $O_1, O_2, O_3, O_4, O_5$ | | $O_6, O_7, O_8, O_9, O_{10}$ |

**Figure 11.7**

Multiple time series design. In the figure, *O* represents each periodic observation or test score; *X* represents the occurrence of the phenomenon under study. Note that the phenomenon under study, *X*, interrupts the periodic measurements of the experimental group but not of the control group (after Campbell & Stanley, 1963).

the overall performance of the gymnasts. Before accepting this conclusion, however, keep in mind that we may have overlooked some social or environmental influence that affected our experimental group and not our control group. For example, it is quite possible that some local campus event or even some independent event among the team members at about the same time influenced their team spirit and consequently their performance. This latter interpretation is *always* a real possibility when using the multiple time series design to study complex phenomena in their natural settings.

In Figure 11.8b, the hypothetical weekly scores for both teams show a sharp increase following the relaxation training. Because the gymnasts from the neighboring college did not receive the relaxation training, it is likely that some factor other than the relaxation

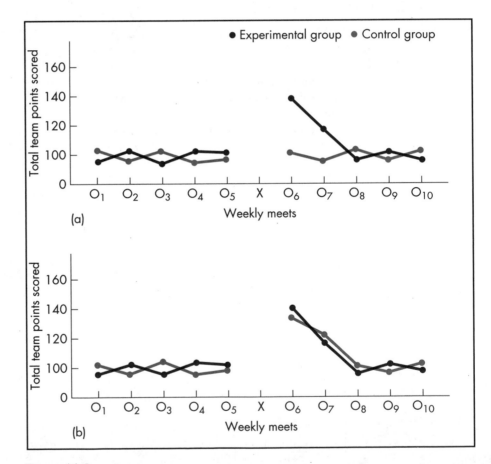

Figure 11.8

Hypothetical outcomes of a multiple time series design examining the effects of relaxation exercises on the total points scored by a gymnastics team in 10 weekly meets. *X* marks the point at which the exercises were introduced to the experimental group. (a) Outcome in which the experimental group's performance improved and the control group's did not. (b) Outcome in which both groups' performance temporarily improved.

training is responsible for this improvement. One possibility is that both teams were affected by some common event. Can you think of any common events that could account for this parallel performance? It should be increasingly evident that the interpretation of quasi-experimental designs is a tricky business and that there is always a danger that unknown variables may be contributing to the performance differences between our experimental and control groups. This adds to the difficulty of deciding which of several possible interpretations of our final outcome best reflects the true causal factor. In many cases, we will never know which interpretation is correct.

On September 12, 1983, New York State put into effect a bill that required a 5¢ deposit on bottles and cans. In order to test the effectiveness of this law, Levitt and Leventhal (1986) noted the number of bottles and cans found along a highway exit in New York and in a similar site in New Jersey, which did not have a returnable law. These researchers made seven observations 2 weeks apart before the enactment of the law and seven times after the enactment of the law. These researchers reported a decrease from 260 items of litter in New York before the enactment of the law to 145 items after the enactment. The litter in New Jersey showed a much less drastic change (221 items before and 214 after the New York law). These authors made their multiple time series design stronger by measuring nonreturnable litter at both sites, which showed no changes in relation to the law, and by doing a follow-up at both sites 1 year later that showed a continuing decrease in litter for the New York site but not for the New Jersey site. These results are presented in Figure 11.9.

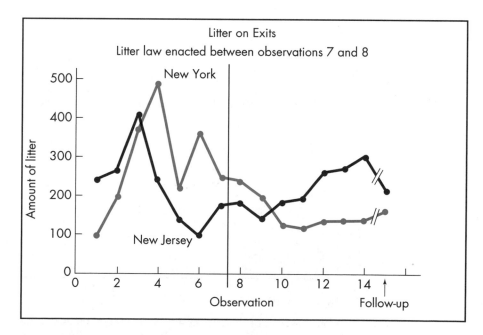

Figure 11.9

Amount of litter before and after the passage of New York's bottle and can deposit law.

*SOURCE:* Adapted from Levitt and Leventhal (1986).

## ■ Nonequivalent Before-After Design

A *nonequivalent before-after design* is used when we want to make comparisons between two groups that we strongly suspect may differ in important ways even before the experiment begins. Because the two groups in this design are initially unequal, there is an unusually high risk of ultimately confusing the initial differences with the effects of the independent variable. Consequently, in this design we avoid simply comparing both groups on a single dependent measure. Instead, each group is given a pretest and a posttest, and we compare the amount of change in the test scores for the experimental and control groups. By comparing the differences in scores rather than single dependent measures, we attempt to control more directly for the fact that we are dealing with initially unequal groups. Each group's pretest score serves as a baseline from which we estimate the amount of change from pretest to posttest. Then we compare the magnitude of the change for each group by comparing the difference in that group's scores. This design is represented schematically in Figure 11.10.

The nonequivalent before-after design is widely used in educational research, in which we often are interested in comparing different schools, classes, or programs. As an example, let us assume you have just completed your Ph.D. and have taken a job teaching psychology at the college level. One day your department head asks whether you would be willing to develop a new course in human sexuality and, if so, whether you could teach a morning and afternoon section next fall. Having never taught a course on sexuality before, you would like to know whether a lecture or discussion format would be more effective in influencing student attitudes concerning human sexuality. Because you will teach two sections, you could begin to answer this question by teaching the morning session with a discussion format and the afternoon session with a lecture format. Then at the end of the term, you could give an attitude questionnaire to each section and directly compare their scores.

Because teaching is still a new experience for you, you decide to ask one of the senior professors what she thinks about your idea. To your surprise, she points out that students who voluntarily schedule 8:00 A.M. classes are very different from those who take 4:00 P.M. classes. She warns that a direct comparison of attitudes at the end of the term

| | Pretreatment measure | Treatment | Posttreatment measure | Difference |
|---|---|---|---|---|
| Experimental group | $O_1$ | X | $O_2$ | $O_1 - O_2$ |
| Control group | $O_1$ | | $O_2$ | $O_1 - O_2$ |

**Figure 11.10**

Nonequivalent before-after design. In this figure, $O_1$ and $O_2$, respectively, represent the pretreatment and posttreatment dependent measures for each group; *X* represents the treatment or independent variable. Note that for this design, group comparisons are made between the differences in the scores for each group rather than directly between posttreatment scores (after Campbell & Stanley, 1963).

may reflect these initial participant differences as well as the effects of your discussion and lecture formats. Impressed by her comments, your initial impulse might be simply to assign students randomly to each class, as you would do in an experiment you were conducting in the laboratory. In this case, however, you are not in the laboratory, and because your students voluntarily select which section of your course they will enroll in, you have no control over the assignment of participants. Consequently, you cannot control for these potentially confounding individual differences by randomly assigning participants to each group.

At this point, while on the verge of abandoning the whole idea, you recall that quasi-experimental designs often can be used in real-life situations where experimental designs cannot. In this particular case, your major problem is that you strongly suspect that the two groups will be different at the onset of the experiment. Therefore, you decide to use the nonequivalent before-after design, which was developed for situations in which we cannot randomly assign participants to groups and are faced with having to compare groups that may differ at the onset of the experiment. The final design you might arrive at is depicted in Figure 11.11.

The nonequivalent before-after design often is used in such areas as evaluation research (see Mark, Cook, & Cook, 1984, for more detail). Many of the threats to internal validity, such as history, are ruled out by this design, but there are problems, such as the threat of selection-maturation. The selection-maturation threat occurs when one group changes at a different rate from the other. For example, suppose a television program to help learning is shown to disadvantaged children, and their progress scores are compared to those of children from higher socioeconomic levels who are not shown the television program. It might be difficult to show a treatment effect for the disadvantaged children because it is common for children from a higher socioeconomic level to progress faster during a given time period. Thus, we might conclude that the treatment did not have an effect when in fact it did. One of the best ways of ruling out alternative explanations when using this type of design is to have a thorough knowledge of the groups being used and of each group's expected rate of change on the variables being measured.

## ■ Retrospective and Ex Post Facto Designs

In the designs we have discussed thus far, the experimenter planned a study that would take place in the future. The **retrospective designs** and **ex post facto designs** attempt to use empirical procedures for suggesting meaningful relationships between events that have occurred in the past. Some researchers see this procedure as important for suggesting how a significant event in the past (for example, growing up under Hitler or watching television) might have influenced people. Schnelle and Lee (1974) used an ex post facto time series

**Figure 11.11**

Example of a nonequivalent before-after design

| | Pretreatment | Treatment | Posttreatment | Difference |
|---|---|---|---|---|
| Experimental group | Attitude questionnaire | Discussion | Attitude questionnaire | Pretest score − posttest score |
| Control group | Attitude questionnaire | Lecture | Attitude questionnaire | Pretest score − posttest score |

analysis when they studied the manner in which transferring problem prisoners to another prison affected the number of offenses committed by the prisoners who were not transferred. From prison records, these authors created an ex post facto ABA design, with *B* being the transfer of problem prisoners and *A* being the measurement of offenses by the prisoners not transferred. As with other quasi-experimental designs, such studies as this can say *whether* a change took place, but it is impossible to state *why* the change took place.

The use of the term *ex post facto design* historically has referred to a particular type of quasi-experimental design in which a relationship is identified between an earlier event (such as being on a school sports team or not) and some later event (such as being successful in business). However, today we see the term used in a broad manner to include a variety of retrospective approaches, such as attempts to determine which of many previous factors (e.g., anger, depression, eating certain types of foods) are associated with a given condition (e.g., cardiovascular problems). Consistent with this change in terminology, the studies in this section are referred to by the general term *retrospective,* and traditional *ex post facto designs* are included within this term.

The most common use of retrospective designs is in studies of educational techniques, disease, and psychopathology. For example, Barthell and Holmes (1968) studied the number of listed activities of students in a high school yearbook to determine whether there were differential rates of high school activity between people identified later in life as schizophrenic and nonschizophrenic. Because the study took place after the fact, these researchers had to determine a possible control group after the fact. For their control group they chose the students whose pictures appeared next to those of the schizophrenic students in the yearbooks. In one sense, you are working backward in the ex post facto procedure; you know the outcome and want to determine the antecedents of this outcome. Thus, one of the important questions is, "Did you select the correct measure (e.g., high school activities) to compare the two groups?" Of course, this question is unanswerable, and for this reason the procedure produces only a weak form of inference.

Let us consider another example of retrospective research, one that points out some additional interpretation problems. You might be interested in people who have a particular disease. If you have a theory that nutrition is important, you might study what healthy and diseased people ate for breakfast. You then might find that the people with the disease did not eat breakfast. Eating may or may not have been the important factor in the disease; you cannot know from a retrospective design. The same results may have been brought about because the people with the disease did not feel good when they woke up in the morning and hence chose not to eat breakfast. Thus, participants may have been self-selected on the treatment variable, and in this way invalidate your conclusion that the treatment variable affected the groups. In a true experiment, this objection would have been avoided because you would have selected the participants and assigned them to groups.

Although retrospective and ex post facto designs are weak forms of inference, Kerlinger (1973, 1986) suggested that these designs can be used to good advantage in one type of case: the testing of alternative hypotheses. His ideas are based on those of Chamberlin (1890/1965) and Platt (1964; see Chapter 3). Using retrospective procedures, one can examine *alternative dependent variables.* For example, retrospectively, cigarette smoking might be shown to be associated with lung cancer more than with brain tumors. Although the research still cannot make causal statements, testing alternatives can lead to a greater understanding of the phenomenon under study. Many retrospective designs also may be considered types of correlational studies, and we now turn to this topic.

> ☑ **CONCEPT CHECK 11.2**   The governor of a large state pointed to the results of an interrupted time series design in which, following an increase in the legal age at which one could buy alcohol (the treatment), the number of highway accidents was lower in the next 5 years than in the year before the drinking age was increased. How might you comment on such a conclusion?

# CORRELATIONAL PROCEDURES

Sometimes we have a process, be it trauma, AIDS, or intelligence, that we as scientists believe is important to study and understand. However, because of lack of knowledge or level of analysis, it is impossible or impractical to design a highly controlled experiment. In such a situation, there are a number of alternative solutions. One of the most common is identifying a situation in which the variables of interest occur and passively observing their occurrence. For example, if someone were interested in the relationship between how often a baby was held and how often it cried, a first step might be to collect data about these variables for a number of babies. Once data were collected for the two variables—amount of time crying and amount of holding—the correlational statistic (discussed in Chapter 4) would be one means of defining the degree of relationship between them. However, in this book we use the term *correlational designs* in a generic manner that does not imply that a particular statistical procedure is required or was used in the analysis.

It should be noted that there are a number of more advanced procedures built on describing the association between two variables and our ability to predict one variable based on another. These advanced procedures include regression, path analysis, and causal modeling; the interested reader should consult one of the general introductions to this area (Bentler, 1980; Connell & Tanaka, 1987).

Research studies developed with the goal of describing a relationship between two variables but not attempting to show how one variable influences the other are called *correlational studies* in psychology. This is because the statistic commonly used for establishing a degree of association is that of the correlation coefficient, which we presented in Chapter 4. In correlational studies, as with correlational statistics, the researcher is interested in asking whether there is a relationship between two variables. For example, a psychophysiologist might be interested in asking whether there is a relationship between electroencephalogram (EEG) activity and age. Assume that you discover that the frequency of EEG activity slows down in a fairly regular fashion as one ages from 30 to 70 years old. You cannot conclude that a decrease in EEG activity causes one to grow older because a number of processes remain unmeasured and uncontrolled in such a study.

Given a more bizarre relationship—such as the famous correlation between stock market prices and the length of women's skirts—one quickly realizes the importance of seeking unknown factors that influence both variables and thus produce the relationship. As you consider these for yourself, the meaning of the often-quoted statement "Correlation does not imply causality" becomes clearer.

Correlational procedures are an efficient alternative and an important initial step in the inferential process. For example, Bremner and Narayan (1998) were interested in the manner in which stress influences brain development and memory. The particular area of the brain of interest was the hippocampus, which is related to memory processes. As an initial step, they reviewed the literature and found that veterans with combat-related posttraumatic stress disorder (PTSD) showed a significant correlation between levels of combat exposure and hippocampal volume, as shown by brain imaging techniques as well as lower recall scores on a memory task. Although you might want to conclude that combat stress reduces the size of the hippocampus, these researchers point out that it could be the opposite situation: People who from birth have a smaller hippocampus may experience stressful situations as more traumatic and be at greater risk for PTSD. These researchers were able to strengthen their case that trauma influences hippocampal changes by using matched controls in additional studies of PTSD and examining survivors of childhood abuse and through animal studies that show that positive handling (the opposite of trauma) is protective.

However, before any statement of causation could be established, it was first necessary to establish that an association existed.

As pointed out in Chapter 2, one of the traditional requirements for establishing causation is a degree of association. Establishing such an association was one of the first tasks biomedical researchers attempted when they sought to show a causal link between smoking and cancer. If they could not have demonstrated a degree of association between the two variables, then it would have been impossible to conclude that one variable affected the other. With correlational designs, no variables are manipulated, and thus there are no independent and dependent variables. However, some researchers have attempted to portray a correlational design as if it were of an experimental nature.

To illustrate, assume that a researcher was interested in the question of how depression and study habits are related. Some people might try to answer this question by dividing participants at the median into high- and low-depression groups (based on some measure of depression, such as the Beck Depression Inventory) and then treating depression as an independent variable and the amount of study time as the dependent variable. Skinner (1984) suggested that there are a number of problems with this approach. First, following such a procedure, information is lost because one has created an artificial categorization—high- and low-depression groups—that was not present in the selection device and may not exist in the underlying population. Second, from a statistical standpoint, an analysis of variance or *t*-test procedure would be less sensitive than a correlational one in such a design. Third, the results, which should be interpreted in correlational terms, may be interpreted as if one variable (depression) had caused the changes in the other variable (study habits).

Let us discuss this third problem in more detail. In the example of depression and study time, no variable was manipulated; it is therefore not possible to infer that depression affected the amount of study time. In fact, one might just as well draw the opposite inference: that the amount of time spent studying influences how depressed a person feels. There is also another alternative, called the *third-variable problem*, in which a third, unmeasured variable influences the other two.

Consider the correlation between the number of schools in a city and the amount of alcohol consumed in that city. This correlation is a high positive one. However, there is no causal relationship between the amount of drinking and the number of schools. A third variable, that of population, influences both: Where there are more people, there are both more schools and more drinking.

As another example, consider the correlation between outdoor swimming and depression. Suppose such a correlation were highly negative; how would you interpret this result? You might conclude either that depression kept people away from swimming or that swimming cured depression. Either or both of these hypotheses might be true, but the correlation does not justify any causal representation. It is possible that swimming and depression are related, but it is also possible that there is a third variable. For example, more people swim in the summer, and there is a lower incidence of depression in the summer. Research suggests that some types of depression (e.g., seasonal affective disorder) are related to lack of sunshine; therefore, sunshine could be the third variable.

In conclusion, correlational research does not demonstrate that there is any causal relationship between two variables, however intuitively appealing such a relationship might be. However, a lack of correlation does rule out any possibility of causality.

> ☑ CONCEPT
> CHECK 11.3    A newspaper article suggested that drinking fine wine was associated with health. If you wanted to study this possibility in more detail, what possible hypotheses might you entertain?

# NATURALISTIC OBSERVATIONS

In the first two chapters we stressed that our basic scientific methods are direct extensions of ways we normally learn about and interact with the world. In many ways the method of naturalistic observation derives from what may be our most primitive way of learning about the world: simply paying attention and observing what happens. One elegant example of this approach sought to determine how men and women carry objects, which was part of a larger theoretical question about gender differences (Jenni & Jenni, 1976). These researchers simply observed male and female college students as they carried books around campus. In this study, which was published in *Science*, it was found that 92% of the women carried books in front of their bodies, with one or both arms wrapped around the books, whereas 95% of the men carried the books at their sides using one hand.

In addition to offering a method to study a focused question such as gender and posture, the method of naturalistic observation can also be useful in extremely complex situations, such as studying animals in the wild or the early stages of investigating a phenomenon. If little is known about the phenomenon, we can benefit tremendously from a detailed description of it. Natural scientists have used this technique for many years. They initially focused on simply classifying and describing a wide variety of plant and animal life on our planet. More recently, they have used a similar technique to study animal behavior.

Perhaps the greatest single application of the technique of naturalistic observation was Darwin's 5-year voyage on HMS *Beagle,* during which he compiled many detailed descriptions of plant and animal life over a large part of the world. As he observed and recorded his observations, ideas came to him about how this great abundance of plant and animal life developed. He later synthesized these ideas to form the foundation of the modern theory of organic evolution. Darwin's early work demonstrates two functions of naturalistic observation. First, it allows us to amass descriptive knowledge about a phenomenon. Second, as we become more familiar with it, we may gain insight about general patterns or lawful relationships in the phenomenon.

Researchers continue to rely on naturalistic methods today. The initial research may consist of recording descriptions of the behaviors that are observed. From these initial observations, new hypotheses and theories may be developed and further explored through observation. In one such study, Tinbergen (Lehner, 1979) observed young herring gulls obtaining food from their parents' bills. He was impressed particularly by how fast the young chicks could learn to peck the parents' bills, and he wondered how the chicks could distinguish them from other objects in their environment.

Tinbergen returned to the literature and discovered two conditions that would bring forth the pecking. The first was that a red object must be placed in front of the young bird; the second was that the red object must be kept low to the ground. By means of simple quasi-experimental designs, it was shown that the young bird would peck at many objects that were both red and low to the ground, including cherries and the red soles of bathing shoes. This understanding led Tinbergen into more experimental studies, using carved birds as stimuli. It also led to some beginning hypotheses concerning the sensory apparatus of herring gulls.

In this work, Tinbergen moved from naturalistic observation to experimental studies. This refinement of ideas is a natural process; scientists often begin with a broad perspective and then focus on a more narrow experimental question. However, it is important to return to the broad perspective of naturalistic observation to add validity to the experimental findings. Both Tinbergen (1972) and Lorenz (1973) argue that in the study of animal behavior it is necessary to create a balance between naturalistic and experimental methods.

As we begin to use naturalistic methods to study human beings, we are faced with greater complexity both in subject matter and in the scientist's own role in what is being observed. In some cases, the observer may choose to remain undetected or can just blend into the background. Krantz (1979) used this approach when he observed obese and nonobese people eating with others in a university cafeteria. In a study of family interactions during a child's second year of life, or the "terrible twos," Belsky, Woodworth, and Crnic (1996) made observations in the family's home during dinner time. By choosing this time, these researchers sought to blend into the background as the parents were preoccupied with preparing dinner and feeding their 2-year-olds.

In other cases, the scientist may find it more useful to become a participant in the situation under study. In an early study of doomsday cults, Festinger, Riecken, and Schachter (1956) became members of a cult whose leader, Marion Keech, claimed to hear messages from outer space that predicted the end of the world the following December 21. These researchers were able to observe not only the behavior of the members as they prepared for the end of the world but also their reactions and relationship with their leader as nothing happened on December 21.

Another classic and controversial example of scientists acting as participants in a naturalistic study is Rosenhan's 1973 study, titled "On Being Sane in Insane Places." Rosenhan's research focused on the manner in which mental hospital staff distinguish sane people from insane ones and on the types of experiences that patients in these hospitals face. In this study, eight sane people gained admission to 12 different hospitals across the country. Each of these "pseudopatients" called a hospital and reported that he or she heard voices. Initial interviews were established for admission. Except for the initial complaint of voices and the false names and occupations that were given, all the information given at these interviews was correct. Once admitted to the hospital, the pseudopatients ceased to simulate any symptoms, and they followed all instructions from the staff.

Surprising as it may seem, in none of the hospitals were the researchers treated in any way other than as insane patients, and their true identities were never realized. This was true even though most of the researchers openly took notes and attempted to have normal conversations with the staff. In the published report, Rosenhan discussed his observations and the subjective experiences of powerlessness and depersonalization that the researchers felt. Although there are a variety of criticisms about the methods and conclusions of this report, it is extremely interesting reading and often-debated research that points out the role of the scientist as investigative reporter using the methods of naturalistic observation.

## ■ Concerns While Making Naturalistic Observations

Although naturalistic methods do not tell us how one variable influences another, questions of validity are still important. In these designs we want to know whether our observations are valid and what factors might account for their not being accurate. In this subsection we consider possible problems in both steps in naturalistic observation: data collection and data analysis.

Data Collection    One problem any observer faces is that if the participants realize they are being observed, they may behave differently. When a participant's behavior is influenced by the mere presence of the observer, it is called **reactive behavior.** Reactive behaviors tell us what people are like when they know they are being observed; they tell us nothing about behavior under normal circumstances. To keep our observations free from reactive behaviors, we attempt, by concealing our identity as researchers, to avoid interfering in any way with the process we are studying. These undetected observations, which are called *unobtrusive observations,* greatly facilitate the task of interpreting observations (see Webb, Campbell, Schwartz, & Sechrest, 1966, for an excellent discussion of unobtrusive measures).

Researchers attempt to make unobtrusive observations in a variety of ways. In some cases they attempt to conduct their observations without being seen by the participant. Some use one-way mirrors; some use hidden, closed-circuit television cameras. In some cases ethologists and comparative psychologists have surgically implanted tiny radio-transmitters in wandering animals such as wild wolves to study their natural migratory patterns. This procedure obviously would not provoke any reactive behaviors on the part of the wolves, as would occur if they were tracked across the Arctic by a howling dogsled or a noisy helicopter.

As we mentioned in Chapter 2, simply observing can be difficult. Part of the difficulty is that we do not usually observe for prolonged periods of time without somehow interfering with the process because our natural tendency is to jump in and participate in some way. For example, try simply listening to a friend with no interference other than an occasional supportive statement. Another reason it is difficult to observe accurately is that we are influenced by *selective perception;* that is, the observations of untrained observers are markedly influenced by what they expect to see. The extent to which our observations are restricted by our selective perceptions has a great impact on the accuracy of our observations.

Fortunately, it is possible to teach observers to observe more accurately. One common first step is simply to emphasize the dangers of selective perception. Once we realize that what we expect to see acts as a filtering device, we have come a long way toward seeing things as they really are. The use of additional observers can also be a good way to increase the accuracy of observations, particularly if their expectations or selective perceptions are different from our own.

Another common problem, especially for new observers, is boredom. When you feel bored, you are observing boredom, not the phenomenon you are supposed to be observing. Use boredom as a warning sign that you are not focusing. A useful technique for minimizing selective perceptions and boredom is to pretend every few seconds that you have never before witnessed the setting you are observing. In this way, you are constantly looking at the scene with a fresh perspective or with a beginner's mind. With this attitude, you are constantly reopening yourself to any subtle changes or surprises.

The process of recording observations is crucial. Careful, immediately recorded, legible notes are of great value. If you cannot record your observations as they occur, then take sketchy notes and, after the observation session is over, use these highlights to assist you in recalling as much detail as you can. Mechanical devices such as videocassette and audiocassette recorders can be useful aids. Remember that these devices are limited; they capture only a portion of what is going on. Even miles of tape will never have a single theoretical insight.

Data Analysis   The task of processing and analyzing field study data may initially seem monumental. Many data are redundant, so the task of analyzing them usually is not as involved as it initially appears. A good way to begin is to review all your data several times so you get the whole picture of what happened. Next, it may be helpful to describe the major patterns of behavior. This initial emphasis on common or invariant behavior is helpful because it provides a baseline of the relevant behavior. Once these primary behavior patterns are outlined, it may be profitable to examine instances of atypical behavior. For example, if you are observing the play behavior of a group of children, ask, "Do a small number prefer not to play? What do they do instead?" Sometimes you will find situations in which no clear patterns of behavior emerge. In such cases it is useful to develop a complete behavioral taxonomy: an organized list of the behaviors observed and the relative frequency of each behavior.

Once the major results become apparent, you will have an excellent basis for evaluating any theoretical ideas you may have recorded while observing your participants. You may find that ideas that initially seemed fruitful do not reflect the major patterns of your overall empirical observations. Any incorrect notions can be disregarded easily and replaced by your empirical findings. As you process and analyze your data, you may get insights about what causal factors underlie the natural behaviors you are observing. These can be added to any factors you thought of while observing the participants in your study and can be evaluated later for possible study with formal experimental designs.

In some cases you may decide that a simple intervention in a future field setting may provide useful clues to how one variable influences another. If you decide to explore these issues in your field setting, keep in mind that you will no longer be using the method of naturalistic observation. Instead, you probably will be using one of the quasi-experimental designs discussed in the early part of this chapter. This is precisely what quasi-experimental designs were developed to do.

*"OUR REPUTATION FOR LONGEVITY IS BASED ON SEVERAL FACTORS: HARD WORK, SIMPLE FOOD, LACK OF STRESS AND THE INABILITY TO COUNT CORRECTLY."*

## ■ To Conceal or Not to Conceal; To Participate or Not to Participate

There are two issues every observer must face. Both stem from the fact that in actual practice the basic method we just outlined sometimes must be modified to fit the realities of the situation we are attempting to study. The first issue is whether to conceal our identities as researchers; the second is whether to participate in the social process we are observing.

In the previous subsection, we emphasized the importance of unobtrusive observation techniques as a means of minimizing the likelihood of reactive behaviors contaminating our observations. Sometimes, however, the phenomenon we are studying dictates that there is simply no reasonable way to collect data without being seen. In these cases we can best observe the process we are studying by concealing our identities as researchers and becoming actively involved in the process. For example, Alfred (1976) posed as a member of the Church of Satan for several years while he studied the sociology and psychology of its members. No one knew he was conducting research until he revealed his true purpose to their leader and requested permission to publish a summary of what he had learned.

Other researchers make no attempt to conceal themselves while collecting data. For example, anthropologists living among and observing people from other cultures typically do not attempt to conceal themselves. In her study of adolescents in Samoa, Margaret Mead (1928) made no attempt to conceal her identity from the people she studied. Mead found that Samoan adolescents do not experience psychological problems to the extent seen among adolescents in the United States. She suggested that their more open attitudes toward sexual behavior may underlie this difference; however, other researchers disagree with this suggestion.

The decision about whether to be an active participant in the process we are observing also depends on the phenomenon we are studying. In the cases of ethologists (such as Lorenz and Tinbergen) and anthropologists (such as Mead), data usually are collected without the researcher's becoming part of the process under study. In contrast, Alfred's valuable contribution was based on his active participation in the process he was observing. There is always a danger that the researcher's participation may unintentionally alter the process being observed. On the positive side, participation enables the researcher to experience the process personally. These introspective data can provide a fruitful source of new ideas about psychological processes.

Deciding whether to remain concealed or to reveal your identity depends to a large extent on whether you are observing highly reactive behaviors. If you suspect that the behavior of your participants will be different if they know they are being observed, then use some sort of concealed observation strategy. If you suspect that there is much to be gained by personally experiencing the process you are studying, and if you feel the overall process would not be significantly influenced by your participation, then you might consider participating.

## ■ Strengths and Weaknesses of Naturalistic Observation

It may be helpful to mention briefly some strengths and weaknesses of the method of naturalistic observation. One advantage is that it attempts to describe behavior as it naturally occurs in real-life settings. This emphasis on observing how things naturally occur enables us to begin our study of a new process with an accurate description of naturally occurring behaviors. As our observations unfold, new ideas about possible relationships or the possible survival value of the behavior we are observing may occur to us. Another advantage to naturalistic observation is that it studies behavioral processes as they unfold over a period of time. This emphasis on observing sequences of behavior provides an important temporal dimension to studying human behavior. This consideration of the flow of ongoing behavior is a valuable complement to experimental and quasi-experimental designs, which tend to focus on discovering the factors that may be influencing behavior at a given time.

One of the disadvantages of naturalistic observation is that it tends to be qualitative and to rely more on the subjective judgment of the observer than do other research methods. Consequently, selective perception can pose a serious threat to the validity of our data. Another disadvantage is that if we study a single instance of a process extensively, the representativeness of our sample may be compromised. Unless we also examine other instances of the same phenomenon, we run the risk of making inappropriate generalizations, and this is a serious threat to the external validity of our observations. Finally, naturalistic observations do not provide information about how one variable influences another. Of course, this is not really a weakness, any more than Beethoven is weak compared with Bach. Instead, it reminds us that no single technique answers all our questions. We return to this point later; in the meantime, keep in mind that science is a fluid yet pragmatic process that makes use of a variety of techniques and approaches to answer our questions about reality.

# KEY TERMS AND CONCEPTS

1. **Field research**
   A. External validity
   B. Voevodsky taxi study
   C. Sherif et al. camp study
2. **Quasi-experimental designs**
   A. Time series design
   B. Interrupted time series design
   C. Multiple time series design
   D. Nonequivalent before-after design
   E. Retrospective and ex post facto designs

3. **Correlational procedures**
4. **Naturalistic observation**
   A. Tinbergen
   B. Rosenhan
   C. Problems of data collection and analysis
   D. The role of the scientist (to observe, to participate, to do both)
   E. Strengths and weaknesses

# SUMMARY

1. Some distinctions have been made between various types of research. One of these distinctions reflects whether research is run in a laboratory or out in the field. Another distinction refers to whether the design of the study is a true experimental design or a quasi-experimental design. Although these are separate dimensions, it is often more difficult to conduct true experiments in the field. Thus, quasi-experimental designs often are used in field research.

2. Quasi-experimental designs are a set of designs that do not have the necessary controls to rule out important threats to internal validity, as true experimental designs do. Lacking strong experimental control, researchers in quasi-experimental designs attempt to discount alternative explanations logically.

3. Some types of quasi-experimental designs are time series designs, interrupted time series designs, multiple time series designs, and nonequivalent before-after designs.

4. An ex post facto design, or retrospective design, attempts to use empirical procedures for suggesting meaningful relationships between events that occurred in the past.

5. Correlational designs focus on describing a relationship between two variables. Although such designs cannot establish that causation does exist, they can be an important means of demonstrating that it does not.

6. Naturalistic observation is the process of observing organisms, usually in their natural environment. It is a descriptive procedure and is illustrated by the work of Tinbergen.

# REVIEW QUESTIONS

1. What is gained and what is lost when an experiment is conducted outside the laboratory?
2. What does it mean to say that there is a trade-off between external and internal validity in any experiment?
3. What are some of the problems and threats to internal validity with a simple time series design?

4. What is ex post facto research, and what are the problems associated with it?
5. How are data collected and how are analyses performed in a naturalistic observation study?
6. What are the strengths and weaknesses of naturalistic observation methods?

# DISCUSSION QUESTIONS AND PROJECTS

1. Discuss the advantages and disadvantages of time series designs.
2. Design a naturalistic observation study in which you would observe a child at play. What different roles might you take in relation to the child, and how might they affect your results?
3. Discuss medical research that uses an ex post facto design and give examples reported in the newspaper.

4. How are the explorations of Tinbergen and Rosenhan similar and how are they different? How could experimenter bias have influenced these studies?
5. What are some of the problems of interpretation in a multiple time series design?

# InfoTrac College Edition: Exercises

At times, we want to determine whether results found in a more experimental situation would also be similar in a more real-world situation. Thomas Dingus and his colleagues were interested in which factors influence driving using a navigational display. After conducting two studies in which drivers were required to drive a predetermined route, a third naturalistic study was performed using rental car drivers without an experimenter present. You can read this study, entitled "Effects of age, system experience and navigation technique on driving with an Advanced Traveler Information System," in the journal *Human Factors* (June 1997).

In the chapter, we discussed the robber's cave study as an example of a quasi-experimental design that exam-ined the manner in which prejudice could be induced in normal individuals. In the fifty years since this study was conducted, a variety of studies have contributed to an understanding of intergroup process. You can find a review of this work in the 1998 *Annual Review of Psychology* in an article entitled "Intergroup contact theory" by Thomas Pettigrew. You may also want to read the 1999 issue of the *Annual Review of Psychology* in which S. Mark Kopta and his colleagues discuss how to evaluate psychotherapy ("Individual psychotherapy outcome and process research: Challenges leading to greater turmoil or a positive transition"). In this discussion, they consider questions of research design, which we have discussed in the last three chapters.

# ☑ Answers to Concept Checks

**11.1** You might begin by saying that it is accurate that if you cannot randomly assign participants to groups, then the study may not be called a *true experiment*. However, you might also want to point out that with Professor Rigid's definition, a number of important topics, such as the reaction of people to earthquakes, to power plant meltdowns, and to war, would be beyond the methods of science. You might also point out that it is possible to use a different type of design—quasi-experimental design—that relies on logic to rule out alternative explanations to the hypotheses.

**11.2** Although you could not argue with the actual data, you could question the interpretation that the results were due to changing the drinking age. For example, in the same year that the drinking age was increased, the speed limit may have been reduced, which could contribute to a lower accident rate.

**11.3** One might research the possibility that fine wine is associated with good health in several ways; three possibilities follow. One possibility is that the newspaper stressed only one side of the correlation in inferring that wine was associated with health. The correlation may have resulted from a situation in which more people who are healthy drink wine. Perhaps unhealthy people do not like or want wine. Another possibility is that because a higher standard of living is required to buy fine wines, a third variable—the ability to afford better health care—could be the causal factor. That is, people with a higher standard of living may also take better care of themselves and use health care facilities in a more preventive manner. Finally, one could always look for particular causal factors (e.g., a biochemical substance found in wine) that might be associated with health.

# SINGLE-SUBJECT DESIGNS

Single-subject designs in their various forms are an important tradition in the history of science that is experiencing a resurgence in interest (Jones, 1993). In discussing single-subject designs we use a broad definition that extends from the more naturalistic single-subject designs to the more experimental single-subject designs. These designs historically have been used to study such areas as perception, learning, memory, and psychophysics. Examples of research directed at understanding a particular characteristic of an individual (such as a particular psychological or neuropsychological impairment) typically have been called case studies, although this distinction has lost its meaning over the years.

It should also be understood that single-subject designs may involve more than one participant in the research. Thus, you might see the term *small-N designs* being used in a manner similar to how we use the term *single-subject designs*. The general characteristic of these approaches is that the individual's data are not averaged with those of other participants. Thus, single-subject experimental research uses a somewhat different underlying philosophy from that of the designs previously discussed, which use the calculus of probability and inferential statistics to help make decisions. The emphases with these previous designs have been on such topics as the sampling of individuals and the averaging of experimental results to arrive at group means. Single-subject approaches do not require that emphasis.

The underlying philosophy of single-subject designs assumes that the process under study is found within that single subject and can be controlled appropriately. Thus, a sampling of research participants is not necessary. However, this is not to suggest that the ability to control variables or to specify operational definitions is no longer important. Quite the contrary, these factors are still critical in establishing a relationship between an independent variable and a dependent variable. Although somewhat different in single-subject designs, the issues of internal and external validity also must be considered (Mace & Kratochwill, 1986). To better understand single-subject research, let us consider briefly the history of these designs.

If you think about it, you will realize that most of the physics and chemistry experiments you performed in high school were single-subject in nature. You may have measured physical quantities—mass or acceleration, for example—using the same subject (e.g., a ball rolling down an inclined plane) a number of times. Or you may have done experiments to determine the chemical characteristics of a particular element. In doing this research, you never considered randomly choosing the particular sample of the element from all possible samples but simply used whatever sample of the element was available.

In the traditional physical science approach, one is not concerned with sampling of participants, nor does one expect large variations in the data. For example, to measure speed and acceleration in classic physics, a person simply rolls a steel ball down a measured incline and makes the necessary measurements. The scientist may repeat this procedure a number of times, but in the end he or she is able to make a precise or *point prediction* (within certain limits) about the speed and acceleration of a steel ball rolling down the inclined plane. Likewise, to determine the properties of a particular chemical element, one simply takes a sample and makes the measurement. It is assumed that every sample of the element—gold, for example—will have the same chemical properties. Because each sample is the same, there is no advantage to performing the same experiment on more than one sample of the element.

Psychology and the behavioral sciences have borrowed broadly from the approach and philosophy of the physical sciences, especially the approach associated with Sir Isaac Newton's classic physics. For example, Sigmund Freud, in his *Project for a Scientific Psychology* (1895/1966), set forth the task of making psychology scientific in a like manner to the physics and chemistry of his day. Wilhelm Wundt—who, along with William James, is credited with being the founder of modern psychology—used the experimental study of a few participants in depth as the appropriate method for psychological investigation.

In the late 19th century, Hermann Ebbinghaus conducted some of the most often described single-subject experiments in which he learned nonsense syllables and began the systematic study of memory processes (Ebbinghaus, 1885). Ebbinghaus was able to show that memory is influenced by such factors as the number of words on a list and the time between learning the list and being asked to recall the syllables—factors still studied today in memory research. Lest you think this is a dead tradition, you should know that for 6 years beginning in 1972, Marigold Linton recorded at least two events from her life each day. Every month she tested her ability to remember, order, and date a sample of the events she had recorded previously (Linton, 1982).

To continue the history of single-subject research, Thorndike (1898) studied intelligence by examining the ability of individual cats to solve problems. The psychophysical tradition of Ernst Weber and Gustav Fechner, whose physical measures were shown to represent a different scale from those of psychological experience, is another example of using single-subject research designs. In Russia, Ivan Pavlov conditioned single dogs in his classic conditioning studies. During the 1930s, B. F. Skinner began a series of conditioning experiments that emphasized the virtues of single-subject designs. Skinner's work used a method that came to be called *experimental analysis of behavior*. This approach often used a single pigeon, rat, or other organism as both the experimental and the control participant. Additional animals were used to replicate the previous research. One hallmark of these approaches was that the data from a single participant remained separate and were not statistically averaged with those of other participants.

As we have seen, the idea of single-subject designs has existed since the beginning of modern psychology at the end of the 19th century. In fact, it was not until the 1920s and the statistical work of R. A. Fisher with farming plots that psychology began to shift to larger sample sizes with statistical evaluation between groups. However, even Fisher included single-subject research in his original book. Based on the methods of Fisher, the idea of a control and an experimental group with generalizable results became the hallmark of psychology.

One problem with the Fisher approach was that individual differences became error variance and generally were ignored and averaged out. In the Fisher approach, as we have discussed in previous chapters, stability is achieved by averaging data from a number of participants. Based on this tradition, a negative view arose toward single-subject approaches, that to study an individual participant was somehow unscientific and that real science was performed only with groups of individuals. But even during this period, a minority of researchers emphasized the importance of knowing well the behavior of single individuals. Because the minority was largely influenced by the operant conditioning approach of Skinner, for years the term *single-subject design* was almost synonymous with the study of operant conditioning. Today, this is no longer the case, and we use a much broader definition of *single-subject design* in this chapter.

Although the philosophy of science concerning the experimental designs underlying these different approaches is extremely important, it is beyond the scope of our present discussion. For an important and informative discussion of the underlying philosophy of science traditions in psychological research, especially the tradition of Fisher as opposed to that of Karl Popper, the interested reader should consult Meehl (1978). Also, a comparison of single-subject analysis and inferential statistical analysis and a discussion of Type I and Type II errors are included in Parsonson and Baer (1978).

In the past few decades, a number of researchers have again sought to understand the individual participant within scientific psychology (e.g., Franklin, Allison, & Gorman, 1997; Hersen & Barlow, 1976; Kazdin, 1982; Kratochwill, 1978; Sidman, 1960; Valsiner, 1986). The task is not so much to ask which are better—single-subject or group designs—but to ask what kinds of questions each type of design is uniquely able to answer. Sanderson and Barlow (1991), for example, point out the value of single-case as well as other designs in answering particular questions in clinical psychology. Furthermore, the *Journal of Consulting and Clinical Psychology* devoted a special section to single-case methodologies in psychotherapy process and outcome research (Jones, 1993). One such use of the single-case design is quite practical. If it were your task to work with an autistic child over the next year, you might try a variety of means to maintain the child's attention and additional means to influence his or her behavior. Single-case designs offer a powerful method for determining which techniques work best with a given individual.

# TYPES OF SINGLE-SUBJECT DESIGNS

In general, we can discuss two different purposes of single-subject designs. The first purpose is primarily descriptive and is represented by the case study method, which has been used throughout the history of psychology. Such a descriptive approach could be either a single-subject naturalistic observation approach or an approach in which a single variable is observed after the application of a particular treatment. On the other end of the continuum are single-subject designs that are more experimental in their intent. These designs represent the second purpose of single-subject designs. That is, when our primary goal is to focus on how the introduction of a particular factor influences a particular aspect of an individual's behavior, then single-subject experimental designs such as the reversal design and multiple-baseline design may be used.

Often, descriptive and experimental intents may be combined. A classic study from the history of health psychology illustrates early attempts to achieve experimental control. In 1895, a 9-year-old boy named Tom swallowed some scalding hot clam chowder. This led to his esophagus being closed by scar tissue. An operation was performed to create an opening in the abdomen that allowed food to be placed directly into the stomach. Some 46 years later, in 1941, Wolf and Wolff (1943) began to study directly the effects of Tom's emotional reactions on his stomach. In general, they found that negative experiences, such as frustration, resulted in increased stomach motility and secretion. During the next 17 years, they combined both the descriptive and the experimental single-subject approaches to understand stomach function and its relation to emotionality.

Such intense study of one person offers insight into the manner in which emotions influence physiological processes and has led to a variety of experimental studies. Thus, at times we describe a person's behaviors or psychological processes in detail with the purpose of scientifically modeling these behaviors or cognitive processes, which in turn can be used to direct experimental procedures. As with all the designs we discuss in this book, the goal is to be able to understand a phenomenon, support our conclusions, and eliminate rival hypotheses. As we shall see, there are times when single-subject designs are essential in this quest.

# CASE STUDY DESIGNS

## ■ Naturalistic Case Studies

The *case study* is one of the most widely used methods for studying individual participants. It is based on the logic of describing, analyzing, interpreting, and evaluating a set of events and relationships within a framework or theory (Bromley, 1986). The typical descriptive case study focuses on either problematic or exceptional behaviors. Indeed, for years the case study approach has been the primary method for studying phenomena in clinical medicine, clinical psychology, and the neurosciences. Its advantage has been its ability to present the clinical implications of a particular disorder. One classic example that Freud discussed was the case study of Anna O. Another example is described in Morton Prince's book *The Dissociation of a Personality* (1913). Prince described a case of multiple personality (now called dissociative identity disorder) at a time when the existence of that diagnostic category was in question.

An advantage of such extended discussions is the ability to describe processes not easily reduced to a single variable. For example, Luria (1972) describes in great detail the attempt of one man to overcome a neuropsychological deficit that left him with "a shattered world." This is a story about a brilliant young Russian scientist, Zasetsky, who became a soldier in World War II and was shot in the head. Zasetsky's wound was such that areas of the brain that help us move in space or understand complex language were damaged, whereas areas that allow one to reflect on one's condition were not. Luria's intriguing work describes both his and the patient's own experiences over a 25-year period.

Likewise, Oliver Sacks has used the case study approach to give insight into the world experienced by people with particular clinical disorders. Two of the most famous of these became part of the popular culture with the movie based on Sacks's book *Awakenings* (1973) and his book *The Man Who Mistook His Wife for a Hat* (1985).

Ramachandran (1998) summarized his case study work on phantom limb pain, the situation in which a person continues to experience the existence of a limb that has been lost. Because there is evidence of the remapping of brain areas that were associated with sensation in the arm that differ from person to person, the case study approach accounts for individual differences in an important way.

Case studies are used not only for studies of disorders but also for studies of potential. For example, Maslow (1970) used the case study technique to study exceptional people whom he considered to be self-actualizing. Likewise, since the 19th century, developmental psychologists have kept records of the development of their own children (Bolgar, 1965). In the case of Jean Piaget, these observations led to his later theories.

A case study is a narrative description of an individual or some aspect of an individual that brings together relevant aspects of the person's history and present situation. The value of such an approach is that it is possible to describe the individual case in its actual context. The information that makes up the case study may come from a variety of sources, including the patient's recollection of events, information from friends or relatives, and public records.

In one sense, we all use case study techniques when we go to a professional complaining of a pain. The professional then diagnoses the problem and prescribes some form of therapy. After some time, we return and give the professional feedback on whether the pain decreased. Neither physical pain (such as headaches) nor psychological distress (such as feeling lost or without purpose) can be seen from behavior alone.

The case study is one of the oldest techniques of medical and psychological description. Case studies based solely on the reports of participants or patients are open to all the problems of self-report (such as selective forgetting, the desire to show ourselves in a positive light, and outright deception) but there are times when the case study can be a useful technique.

## ■ One-Shot Case Studies

In addition to the use of the case study method to provide a general description, there is a somewhat more specific use of the case study design. The case study is a narrative that summarizes an experimenter's direct observations of a participant's behavior after some sort of treatment has been performed. This design, sometimes called the *one-shot case study,* is represented in Figure 12.1. Gottmann (1973) suggests that systematic case study observation offers therapists a means of obtaining information about specific interventions in therapy during an ongoing series of sessions.

One could also use the one-shot case study, although less powerfully, in a retrospective manner to study the effects of an event that took place in the past. The study of reactions to various forms of trauma is one such retrospective study. For example, Scoville and Milner (1957) published a case study describing the effect of surgical removal of the hippocampal region of the brain from a man; that study has become a classic in the field (see Box 12.1). As a result of the surgery, this man, although able to remember events from his past, had no memory of the present. He would read the same newspaper over and over without retaining the information he had read.

From this tragic case study, a wealth of information has been obtained about memory. This information has been discussed, and more recent case studies of naturally occurring memory problems such as amnesia have been reviewed (Squire & Zola-Morgan, 1991). In instances such as that described by Scoville and Milner, the case study can be a useful tool in research. The observations may suggest new hypotheses, demonstrate rare phenomena, or even show exceptions to established facts.

Thus, the case study design can provide valuable initial descriptions of new phenomena, which can then be studied carefully with more rigorous experimental methods. Likewise, the case study approach can lead to important models and perspectives not available with traditional experimental methods. However, as an experimental design, the case study does not give us the ability to make strong inferences. As with the single-group, pretest-posttest design, we have no assurance that the observations would not be exactly the same without the treatment. Because of the lack of control procedures, we can say nothing about causal factors and

| | Treatment | Response |
|---|---|---|
| Single subject | X | O |

Figure 12.1

One-shot case study design. In the figure, *X* represents the treatment given to a single subject; *O* refers to the experimenter's observations.

## Box 12.1

# A Patient with Bilateral Temporal Lobe Damage

In 1957, Scoville and Milner first described a male patient (H. M.) who underwent bilateral temporal lobe surgery in 1953. The surgery consisted of the removal of tissue on the medial surface of both temporal lobes, including large portions of the hippocampi. The purpose of the operation was to relieve very frequent and severe epileptic seizures, which were unrelieved by anticonvulsant medication. (Dr. Scoville was encouraged to attempt this procedure because he had strong reason to believe that some abnormality of this region was responsible for the seizures and because evidence from nonhuman primates indicated no behavioral abnormalities following removal of this area.) Although the surgical procedure strikingly reduced the number of epileptic seizures, the operation had an unanticipated and awful consequence: The patient was unable to either learn or remember any new material!

Before the surgery, H. M. was a motorwinder who was unable to work because of his epileptic seizures. After the surgery he was pleasant and easygoing, as he had been before surgery. His measured IQ actually rose from 104 to 119 (presumably it was depressed before the surgery by the epileptic abnormality). However, H. M. exhibited striking memory deficits for events both before and after the surgery. For example, except for Dr. Scoville, whom he had known for many years before the surgery, he was completely unable to recognize members of the hospital staff; he could not even learn his way to the bathroom. He was unable to remember the death of a close uncle, even though he was reminded repeatedly and became genuinely upset every time he was informed.

As the years passed, his ability to remember events remained severely impaired. H. M. was unable to remember his new house address, even after living there for 6 years. He could not recognize neighbors and, when left alone, would invite strangers into his house, thinking they were friends whom he had forgotten. He was able to perform simple jobs such as mowing the lawn, but he could not remember where to find the lawnmower or that he had used it the previous day. He read newspapers over and over, forgetting that he had already read them. He spent many hours re-solving the same jigsaw puzzle without any sign of learning it. His memory deficit was paralleled by a total lack of appreciation of the passage of time. His deficit in registering new material remained severe many years later (Milner, 1966).

Over the years H. M. and his mother faithfully cooperated with a number of psychologists in the United States and Canada, who carefully examined the nature of his unfortunate deficit. Taken together, their findings provide a wealth of information about human temporal lobe function. Yet this case obviously raises moral issues, as Dr. Scoville (1968) stressed:

> This one case, so carefully studied, has demonstrated to many the grave danger of bilateral resection of the medial parts of the temporal lobes when the hippocampus is included in the removal. Even at this late date, however, scientific publications continue to propose the removal of the hippocampus bilaterally for relief of behavioral disorders, intractable pain, and other reasons; such proposals no longer seem justifiable in view of the profound anterograde amnesia which results.

Later case studies with naturally occurring memory problems such as amnesia have also led to a greater understanding of the role of the hippocampus in human memory. This information has been reviewed by Squire and Zola-Morgan (1991), and the interested student should consult this paper.

may risk confusing any number of confounding variables with our treatment. In order to strengthen our conclusions, we look to more experimentally based single-case designs.

Kazdin (1982) suggests not only that the single-subject design is misnamed, but that it is also misunderstood. Kazdin believes it is misnamed because at times a single-subject design may be used with a large number of participants. He believes the single-subject design is misunderstood because some people believe that it is not a *true experiment* and thus cannot reveal *causal relationships* between variables or generalize beyond the few participants under study. Kazdin considers that view to be a misunderstanding of the design.

Campbell has also discussed this point by suggesting that the subject-study design "should not be demeaned by identification with the one-group posttest-only design" (Cook & Campbell, 1979, p. 96). Although the descriptive subject-study approach has this problem, the more experimental single-subject designs do not. Of course, there are limitations to single-subject experimental designs, as there are with any designs. However, there are situations in which single-subject designs offer an important alternative to traditional experimental design.

---

☑ CONCEPT CHECK 12.1    After reading the first section of this chapter, one student decides that single-subject designs are important to use in situations in which there are too few participants for real experimental control to be achieved and statistics to be used. How might you respond to this conclusion?

---

# EXPERIMENTAL SINGLE-SUBJECT DESIGNS

With experimental single-subject designs, we want to determine the manner in which one variable influences another. Because single-subject designs are not based on the same methodological considerations as traditional experimental methods, the task of controlling for extraneous variables requires a different type of method. We have pointed out that even when more traditional means of experimental control are not used, we can reject some alternative hypotheses on logical grounds. One main way in which single-subject experimental designs accomplish this goal is through the use of a time series approach (see Kratochwill, 1978).

The logic of a *time series approach*, as we discussed in Chapter 11, is to establish a series of measurements over time. This series of measurements forms a basis of comparison with another series of measurements after the independent variable—a treatment, for example—is introduced. As you can imagine, the more stable the baseline measurement sequence, the easier it is to establish that the independent variable has influenced the dependent variable. Thus, establishing a baseline is extremely important; it serves as a reference point with which to compare changes associated with the introduction of the independent variable. Furthermore, the baseline gives us some sense of how stable or labile the dependent variable is when the independent variable is not present. Thus, if we can show a different pattern of responding when the independent variable is present from when it is not, we have some evidence to conclude that the independent variable influenced the dependent variable.

If the pattern is established with respect to a series of baseline and treatment conditions over time, then it is called **intrasubject replication** (i.e., the pattern is repeated within a single participant). As with the research methods discussed previously, it is important that the dependent variable be clearly described through *operational definitions*. Also, the data are dealt with differently in single-subject research. Unlike traditional designs, in which the data from a number of participants are averaged together, when more than one participant is used in it, single-subject research asks whether the data from each participant replicate the same pattern as the data of the other participants. This is sometimes called **intersubject replication** (i.e., the pattern is repeated between participants).

The case study may offer the best type of information when the goal is to note the change in a single individual. In that case, the average change in all patients or participants would give an incorrect picture of change. To illustrate this point, consider a treatment that produced a beneficial change in half the patients and a negative change in the other half. If group means or averages were calculated, one might erroneously conclude that the treatment had no effect on patients. Thus, in some cases it is more accurate to record a number of systematic, single-case studies than to record group data. Moras, Telfer, and Barlow (1993) illustrate the use of a single-case design for the treatment of a person with both generalized anxiety disorder and depression. They offer this design also as a means of showing efficacy of new treatment approaches that would lend support for the possibility of large-scale investigations.

In another example of a single-subject design, Osborne, Rudrud, and Zezoney (1990) sought to determine whether adding an orange stripe to a baseball could help members of the baseball team learn to hit a curveball better. The direction of spin on a baseball tells the batter whether the pitcher pitched a curveball (downward spin), a fastball (backward spin), or a knuckleball (no spin). However, the batter has only a little more than one-tenth of a second to decide whether to swing. These authors reasoned that if you could see the seams on the baseball better, then it would be possible to know more quickly the type of pitch.

To test this possibility, the authors designed a single-subject study. To add control to the study, a pitching machine was used. The marked baseballs had either 1/4-inch or 1/8-inch orange stripes marking the seams of the baseball. The dependent variable was the number of *well-hit balls* as operationally defined by seven criteria, including the distance the ball traveled after being hit. Graphs were constructed for each player, charting the number of balls hit from each of the three types (no marking, 1/8-inch orange stripe, or 1/4-inch orange stripe). The authors concluded that adding a marking to the ball improved the batters' performance. Let us now examine some particular types of single-subject designs.

## ■ Reversal Design

One common type of single-subject design is the *reversal design*. The term *reversal* comes from the shifting in this design of the baseline and treatment conditions. The rationale behind the reversal design is simple: If a participant behaves one way before a given treatment is presented, then behaves quite differently when it is presented, then returns to the original state when the treatment is removed, and finally changes again when the treatment is presented a second time, it is reasonable to suspect that this fluctuation in the participant's behavior is due to the treatment. It is hard to imagine how an extraneous variable might vary in a manner parallel with the treatment to produce a similar fluctuation in the participant's behavior; however, this possibility can never be ruled out completely.

Reversal designs may use any number of reversals. For example, a design that measures a participant's behavior before, during, and after a treatment is called an ABA design. The *before* and *after* conditions are designated the *A conditions,* and the treatment is designated the *B condition.* During the A conditions, baseline behavior is monitored in the absence of the treatment. (You should note that the single letter A or B generally represents numerous observations across time.) The purpose of the baseline period is to allow the aspect of interest to be monitored over a period of time without any type of intervention. During the B phase of the design, the participant's behavior is monitored during the intervention or treatment. As in any experimental design, it is necessary to clearly define and state the treatment. By recording observations made over time periods in which a treatment is and is not introduced, one is able to determine the effect of introducing that treatment. An ABAB reversal design, briefly described in the previous paragraph, is depicted in Figure 12.2. In Figure 12.3, we have diagrammed the same design in two different ways. You will discover that some areas of research prefer one method of diagramming over the other, but they both represent exactly the same design.

A variant of the general ABAB design is to compare two treatment conditions against each other rather than against a baseline. Dyer, Dunlap, and Winterling (1990) used such a reversal design with students from three schools for students with autism or mental retardation in order to study the participants' problem behaviors. In particular, these authors wanted to determine whether giving the students a choice of tasks and reinforcers would reduce problem behaviors, such as aggression, self-injury, and tantrums. The dependent variable in the study was the percentage of intervals that included instances of problem behaviors that were specified individually for each child. Because it is important that the measurement of the dependent variable show *reliability,* these authors had observers rate a videotape of the sessions. They found that the agreement among the raters was 92% for noting problem behaviors. Figure 12.4 shows the results for the three stu-

| | A<br>Baseline | B<br>Treatment | A<br>Baseline | B<br>Treatment |
|---|---|---|---|---|
| | | X | | X |
| Single subject | $O_1$ | $O_2$ | $O_3$ | $O_4$ |

Figure 12.2

This figure represents an ABAB single-subject reversal design. *X* represents the administration of the independent variable; O represents the behavioral observations made on the subject. Note that $O_1$ and $O_3$ represent the observations of the dependent variable in the absence of the treatment condition, and $O_2$ and $O_4$ represent the observations of the dependent variable in the presence of the treatment condition.

dents. This design would be described as an ABA design for the first student, a BABA for the second, and an ABABA for the third (where A = student has choice; B = teacher has choice, student has no choice).

It is also possible to treat a group as if it were a single participant and use a reversal design. For example, in Iceland, Ragnarsson and Björgvinsson (1991) studied the effects of placing signs along a highway on reducing drivers' speeds. These authors used an ABCA reversal design, with A being the baseline, B being the placement of a single sign along the highway, and C being the placement of two signs. The first sign read "YES-TERDAY _____% DROVE THROUGH HERE AT THE RIGHT SPEED," and the second sign read, "BEST RECORD SO FAR _____%." The percentages were selected randomly from numbers between 85 and 95 and were not based on actual observations. The de-pendent variable was the speed of the cars passing the signs. To ensure accuracy, the cars' speeds were measured by a radar device. In this study, the initial baseline (A) lasted for 10 sessions over 5 days. The single-sign condition (B) lasted for 8 sessions over 4 days, and the double-sign condition (C) lasted for 24 sessions over 12 days. Following the sign conditions, both signs were removed and speeds were measured for 10 sessions over 5 days. The results indicated that posting the signs reduced the percentage of drivers ex-ceeding 70 km/hr from 41% during baseline to around 20%. The percentage of speeders again increased during the second baseline.

In considering the reversal design, it is important to keep in mind that we are using the phenomenon of reversibility of some behavior in the presence or absence of the treatment condition to study the way that this behavior may be influenced by our treatment condition.

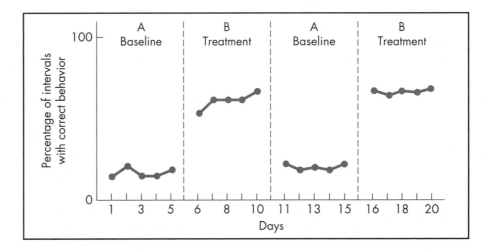

Figure 12.3

This figure represents an alternative method of diagramming an ABAB single-subject reversal design. Depending on the dependent variable, the change from baseline to treatment may be seen either as an increase (e.g., percentage of inter-vals with correct behavior) or as a decrease (e.g., percentage of intervals with prob-lem behavior).

*SOURCE:* Dyer, Dunlap, and Winterling (1990).

**Figure 12.4**

**Results of an ABA study of three students**

*SOURCE:* Dyer, Dunlap, and Winterling (1990).

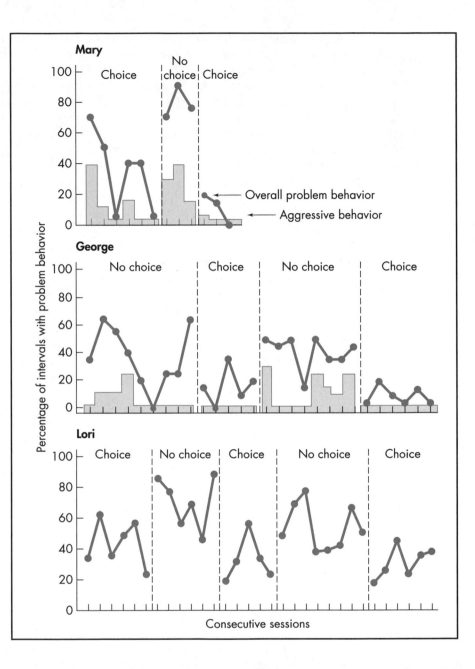

One limitation of the reversal design is that it will work only when we are studying the effect of treatment conditions on behaviors that return quickly to baseline levels once the treatment is over. The influence of all treatments is not this transient. When we are dealing with treatments that result in more permanent shifts in behavior, this particular design cannot be used. When we are interested in studying the long-lasting effects of various independent variables on single participants, one solution is to use a multiple-baseline design, which we discuss next.

> ☑ **CONCEPT CHECK 12.2**  Jim decides that he is going to perform an experiment using a single-subject design on his roommate, John. Jim wants to know whether playing music by Rusted Root or Beethoven piano sonatas influences John's decision to study at the library. How might Jim perform this experiment?

### ■ Multiple-Baseline Design

Like the reversal designs just discussed, the *multiple-baseline, single-subject design* relies primarily on logic to gain its degree of experimental control. With the multiple-baseline design, we monitor several behaviors of a single subject simultaneously. Once baseline levels are established for each behavior, we apply our treatment to one of these behaviors. The likelihood of a causal relation is inferred from the fact that, of the several monitored behaviors, *only* the behavior exposed to the experimental treatment changes, whereas all nontreated behaviors remain unchanged. Once this first behavioral shift is noted, the treatment is applied to the next behavior, and so on. The idea behind this design is that the baseline behaviors would be unlikely to shift by chance alone as each behavior received the treatment. To use the terminology of the first half of this book, each participant serves as his or her own control.

Consequently, in the multiple-baseline design the successive shifting of baseline levels as the treatment is applied gives us reason to suspect a relationship with the treatment. Unlike the reversal designs, which work only for behaviors that are readily reversible, multiple-baseline designs can be used for behaviors that are permanently changed by the experimental treatment. A schematic representation of a multiple-baseline, single-subject design is depicted in Figure 12.5.

Hersen and Bellack (1976) used a multiple-baseline design to demonstrate the effects of a treatment program for a schizophrenic patient. The patient made little contact with others, rarely engaged in conversation, and was compliant even to unreasonable requests. The treatment consisted of training in the development of assertiveness skills and skills for making contact with others. The measures taken over the baseline and treatment sessions were the amount of eye contact while talking, the amount of speaking without prolonged pauses, the number of requests made of another person,

| Several | A | Baseline | *Treatment* | Baseline | Baseline | Baseline |
| behaviors | B | Baseline | Baseline | *Treatment* | Baseline | Baseline |
| of a single | C | Baseline | Baseline | Baseline | *Treatment* | Baseline |
| subject | D | Baseline | Baseline | Baseline | Baseline | *Treatment* |

**Figure 12.5**

Multiple-baseline design. In this design, several behaviors (A, B, C, and D) are monitored simultaneously. The treatment is applied successively to each of these behaviors. The continuation of baseline measures after treatment sometimes is omitted. Note that evidence suggestive of a causal relationship would consist of a successive shift in baseline activity as each successive behavior receives the treatment condition.

and the number of unreasonable requests not complied with. This design requires that baselines be taken for the four measures and that treatments be introduced at different sessions for each of the behaviors to be changed, while measurements of all behaviors are continued. This type of design helps us to determine whether the treatment was specific to a particular behavior (see Figure 12.6).

Concerning the limitations of the multiple-baseline design, it is important to keep in mind that each behavior being monitored must be *independent* of the others. The behaviors we are monitoring must not be so highly interrelated that a change in one behavior results in parallel changes in other behaviors even though the participants did not receive the treatment conditions. If the behaviors under investigation were interdependent, then the successive unfolding of baseline shifts due to the successive application of our treatment condition would be destroyed, and this design would lose much of its usefulness. For example, Kazdin (1973) notes that this design may be of limited value in studying inappropriate classroom behaviors because many of these behaviors are interrelated and any treatment that is effective for one behavior is likely to influence other behaviors as well. Although the interrelatedness of these behaviors may eventually facilitate whatever intervention program is implemented, the fact that several of the behaviors may be altered simultaneously by the treatment of any one makes the multiple-baseline design of little use in studying interrelated classroom behaviors.

**Figure 12.6**

Multiple-baseline design. This type of representation is an alternative to the one presented in Figure 12.5. In this case the baseline measures were not continued after the treatment condition was introduced. The letters A, B, C, and D could represent either different behaviors of a given participant, the same behavior of one participant in different situations, or the same behavior of different participants.

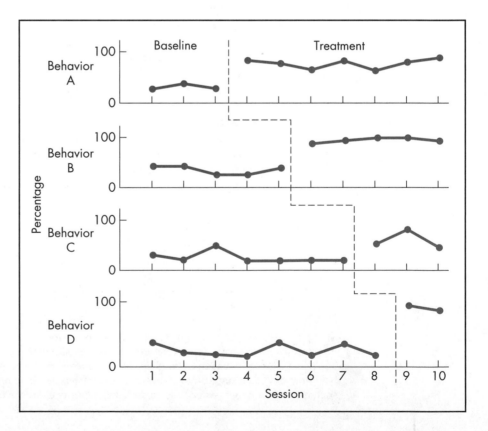

# Multielement Design

In a *multielement design,* one is comparing different levels of a given variable (e.g., treatment versus no treatment) or different treatments. This design is also called the *alternating treatment design* or *simultaneous treatment design* because it tests alternative treatments (Hains & Baer, 1989). For example, a teacher could ask, "What is the best procedure for helping a child with learning disabilities to pay attention?" Each procedure would form a different treatment, and these could be studied on alternate days or at different periods within the same day. Likewise, a researcher could study the effects of three different drugs on memory in an elderly participant, each on a different day. If we were studying two treatments, then the design would be similar to the ABAB *reversal* designs we discussed previously. However, the key element of the multielement design is that it incorporates *many reversals,* which may be fast paced.

Hains and Baer (1989) suggest that there are a number of advantages to this design. One advantage is that by having frequent reversals of the treatments, one is able to examine the changes within the context of background variables that are difficult or impossible to change. In a school setting, such background variables might include the weather, the cycle of extracurricular activities, and changes in class composition. Another advantage of this design is that any differences in the effects of different treatments seem to emerge quickly.

The limitation of such a design is that it is best suited to changes that are short-lived. For example, a study of the effects of different drugs on memory would be possible only if none of the drugs had a lasting effect on the participant. Thus, both the treatment and its effect cannot be long-lasting for this design to be useful. If there were long-lasting effects, then there would be a carryover problem similar to that discussed in Chapter 9. A similar problem, which we discussed in other chapters in terms of sequence or order effects, appears when one has multiple treatments (e.g., Drug A, Drug B, Drug C) such that one treatment is influenced by the treatment that precedes it. Thus, it is possible that our measurement of the effects of Drug B is influenced by the fact that Drug A preceded it. One answer to this problem is to counterbalance the treatments.

As we said previously, counterbalancing does not eliminate an order effect. However, with a single-subject design, any order effect would be visible across the time series. For example, if we were to perform the memory study using three drugs over a period of time, we would have an initial baseline condition followed by the drugs' being compared to each other followed by a final baseline condition, in a counterbalanced order. That is, on each day an experimenter could give a single participant either one of the drugs or a baseline condition in a counterbalanced order over a period of time. From such a time series we could observe not only which drug increased memory but also whether one particular counterbalanced order gave a different effect. That is, we might discover that Drug B produced an overall increase in words remembered when given after Drug C or no drug (i.e., the baseline condition) but not when given after Drug A.

# Making Sense of Single-Subject Experimental Results

Once you have conducted your single-subject experiment you must make a decision concerning what you have found. One of the first steps is to present the data visually in a graphic form, as illustrated throughout this chapter. Carr and Burkholder (1998) explain how to present single-subject design graphs using currently available spreadsheets. To aid in the interpretation of such graphic presentations, a number of guidelines have been suggested to ensure consistency of presentation and interpretation (Franklin, Gorman, Beasley, & Allison, 1998).

How do you know that the particular pattern of results you collected is meaningful? The main tool you have is logic. As we said previously, if the dependent variable changes when the treatment is added, then we have evidence that our treatment influenced our dependent variable. A further tool we use is that of replication. The ability to reproduce the same relationship a number of times suggests that the relationship is stable. In fact, researchers who use single-subject designs suggest that they obtain more stable relationships by performing the same experiment on one participant (or a few participants) 100 times than by using 100 participants, with each receiving the experimental procedure once.

As we suggested, a reversal type of design works only in areas (e.g., vision or operant conditioning) in which the experiment does not permanently modify the organism under study. Unlike traditional experimental procedures based on inferential procedures, traditional experimental single-subject designs do not offer a cutoff level such as the .05 probability level, so the researcher must determine the meaning of the pattern observed. For this reason, single-subject researchers often specify the criterion of change sought before the experiment begins and continue the treatment section until this degree of change is found.

> ☑ **CONCEPT CHECK 12.3**    A clinical psychologist was working with a psychotic patient in a state hospital. It was her desire to develop experimental conditions that would make permanent changes in a number of harmful behaviors. However, she read that reversal designs would not work in this situation because the behavior changes were to be permanent. What should she do?

# ALTERNATIVE TYPES OF SINGLE-SUBJECT RESEARCH

We have focused in this chapter on the more traditional single-subject designs, which do not rely on inferential statistics; however, one recent trend is to use inferential procedures in single-subject studies (Gorman & Allison, 1998). Many researchers have reported using single-subject approaches with group designs. For example, Ericsson and Polson (1988a, 1988b) combined a variety of research traditions to better understand everyday memory processes. They wanted to study the memorizing ability of a particular waiter who was able to remember dinner orders from more than 20 people sitting at different tables without writing them down. To gain greater experimental control, Ericsson and Polson reconstructed a restaurant-like situation in the laboratory. There they studied in greater detail the manner in which the waiter (J.C.) memorized orders, and they compared J.C.'s results with those of untrained control participants.

The research addressed three issues. First, by having J.C. verbally describe his thoughts while memorizing orders in the restaurant, the researchers began to develop a scientific model of his skills, which they intended to model on a computer. Second, to help determine the nature of J.C.'s memory ability, the researchers compared his performance with that of college students who had no experience waiting on tables. And third, the researchers sought to determine whether J.C.'s memory skills could be compared with theoretical models in the field of cognitive psychology. This work is an example of how research with a single participant may be combined with group studies to approach basic psychological questions.

Another trend is to use single-subject approaches conceptually as an aid in describing theoretical cognitive models. For example, Chi and Koeske (1983) studied for more than a year the knowledge structure and memory of a 4-year-old boy. This boy was very interested in dinosaurs, and the researchers used that interest to understand how he processed cognitive information. They constructed a map of how items of dinosaur information (e.g., types of dinosaurs and the foods they ate) were related in this child's mind and how these relationships influenced his memory for dinosaur names.

Likewise, Landau, Gleitman, and Spelke (1981) sought to determine which types of spatial and geometric information a 2-year-old child processed. The intriguing aspect of this study was that the child was blind from birth, so the manner in which vision played a role in spatial development could also be considered. Through a series of experiments, the researchers studied this child's spatial knowledge and geometric representation. They concluded that sight was not required for developing such skills as moving around and navigating through one's environment.

## KEY TERMS AND CONCEPTS

1. **History of single-subject research**
2. **Case study designs**
   A. Naturalistic case studies
   B. One-shot case studies
3. **Experimental single-subject designs**
   A. Types of replication
      - Intrasubject replication
      - Intersubject replication

B. Reversal design
C. Multiple-baseline design
D. Multielement design
4. **Alternative types of single-subject research**

## SUMMARY

1. This chapter briefly describes the history of single-subject research and its importance in psychology. A distinction is made between the descriptive case study approach and the experimental single-subject design.
2. The naturalistic case study has been a traditional means of describing an individual, especially in areas such as clinical psychology, medicine, and neuropsychology. Although important in its descriptive abilities, the naturalistic case study is weak in its ability to draw causal relationships or to make sound inferences.

3. Experimental single-subject designs use a series of measurements over time to establish stability. Within this context, stability is shown either within the same participant (intrasubject replication) or among different participants (intersubject replication).
4. Types of experimental single-subject designs include the reversal design, the multiple-baseline design, and the multielement design.
5. Some alternative types of single-subject designs use traditional inferential statistics.

## REVIEW QUESTIONS

1. Name some important points in the history of single-subject research.
2. How is the descriptive single-case approach different from the more experimental types of single-subject designs?
3. Describe a naturalistic case study.
4. What is the logic of experimental single-subject research that seeks to establish a relationship between the independent and the dependent variables?

5. What is the difference between intrasubject replication and intersubject replication?
6. Describe some of the most popular experimental single-subject designs and give an example of when each might be used.
7. What are some strengths and weaknesses of single-subject approaches?

# DISCUSSION QUESTIONS AND PROJECTS

1. Discuss how you might design a single-subject experiment to determine whether eating breakfast influences alertness during the day.
2. Diagram an ABABA single-subject design and discuss some types of dependent variables that could be used in such a design. Name some dependent variables that could *not* be used in such a design.
3. A student is interested in determining whether people become more tired when using a color or a monochrome computer screen. How might she design such a study using the single-subject method?
4. In the study referred to in Question 3, how might the experimenter control for such factors as beginning and end of term?

## InfoTrac College Edition: Exercises

We pointed to the case study approach as important in understanding particular disorders. In an article in the *Journal of Cognitive Neuroscience* (May 1998) Price et al. used brain imaging techniques to study individuals with deep dyslexia, a disorder in which individuals make semantic errors in reading single words aloud. In terms of single-subject designs, we pointed out that these designs were often used in studies of conditioning. For example, Chris Ninness and colleagues use four single-subject ABA designs to study which computer voices individuals preferred. Using InfoTrac, you can find this article in the Fall 2001 issue of *The Psychological Record*. In this same journal you can read a discussion concerning how single-subject experiments are described in experimental texts and a general discussion of these designs.

## ✓ Answers to Concept Checks

12.1 You would send the student back to reread the first section of this chapter. Although descriptive case studies lack experimental rigor, there are experimental single-subject designs that are valid experimental tools. The main theme of single-subject designs is the ability to study a single participant or group of participants in depth rather than making limited observations with more participants. With the more experimental types of single-subject designs, conclusions are based more on logically demonstrating a relationship between the independent and dependent variables through repeated observations.

12.2 A reversal design (e.g., ABAB) would be one possibility. However, one would still need to be careful that one particular condition did not always appear during special times (e.g., midterms and finals) when John would normally be going to the library. It should be noted that each condition (A or B) in the ABAB design represents a number of individual presentations over time.

12.3 Because she is working with a single patient, a single-subject design would be most appropriate. It is also true that if the behavior change were permanent, the reversal design would not work. However, a multiple-baseline design that monitored a variety of behaviors would be useful. The most common procedure would be to establish a baseline for each behavior under study and then apply the treatment condition to each of these, one at a time. The logic of this would be that we would expect only the behaviors exposed to the independent variable to change.

# QUESTIONNAIRES, SURVEY RESEARCH, AND SAMPLING

A psychotherapist might notice that more of the clients coming to see her with problems of depression are women. Puzzled by this observation, she could conduct a research project to help her understand the relationship between gender and depression. That is, she might want to know whether being depressed is statistically related to gender. One beginning approach would be to gather data from a variety of sources, such as hospitals, counseling centers and private practitioners, concerning the problems that people initially describe when they seek treatment. In fact, there are a number of sources detailing trends in the treatment of psychological disorders including depression (e.g., Olfson, Marcus, Druss, Elinson, Tanielian, & Pincus, 2002). The therapist could then single out depression and simply note the number of men and women who seek help.

Let us assume that the psychotherapist is interested in the question of whether more women are depressed than men, using the standard psychiatric definition of depression as the operational definition. One potential problem is that such a study might not tell us whether there are more women than men who are depressed, but rather whether more women than men seek psychological help for any problem in general and depression in particular. The observation that our therapist made might reflect not that there are more depressed women than depressed men but that more women than men seek help for their depression. To rule out this alternative, and to learn something about the incidence of depression in the general population, types of research techniques would be required that are different from those we have presented so far. One alternative would be to use survey research techniques. This chapter presents the main considerations in performing survey research. Survey research methods can help us to understand the characteristics of some particular group of people, which we call a *population*.

A number of Web sites are available for learning about survey research. For example, the survey research center at the University of Michigan (http://www.isr.umich.edu/src/index.html) offers a variety of details including data from surveys related to such topics as health, life development, and aging. One can also see a survey designed to study midlife development supported by the MacArthur Foundation at http://midmac.med.harvard.edu. This site goes through not only the rationale for performing the study but also the specifics of sampling and data collection.

Other sites such as that of the Gallup Organization (http://www.gallup.com), the American Statistical Association (http://www.stat.ncsu.edu/info/srms/srms.html), and the U.S. Census Bureau (http://www.census.gov) offer additional information on performing survey research as well as current surveys. For example, at these sites you can see our attitudes about drafting women for the military, which by the way have not changed in the last ten years, read about the history of sampling as used in surveys or view the latest census data for the United States. Other sites such as the Murray Research Center (http://www.radcliffe.edu/murray/data/index.htm) at Radcliffe contain the data from both survey and longitudinal research including Mary Ainsworth's study of attachment, Lewis Terman's study of gifted children, Jack Block's study of personality over the life span as well as a variety of other studies. Let's look at one of these classic survey studies related to well-being and life satisfaction.

This large-scale survey research project focused on the well-being and life satisfaction of people in the United States at two points in time: 1957 and 1976 (Veroff, Douvan, & Kulka, 1981). The 1957 survey and its replicate in 1976 were designed to answer questions about average men and women. These questions included how well or how badly adjusted people consider themselves to be; how happy (or unhappy), worried (or not), and optimistic (or pessimistic) people are in their outlook; what troubles people in the United States and what they do about their problems; and to whom they turn for help and how effective that help is. Such information would help the researcher in our previous example to understand the relationship between help-seeking and gender, as well as the specific issue of depression as it relates to differences between women and men. In this chapter we discuss the survey related to well-being as an exemplar of the types of questions to be considered and the particular steps to be accomplished in performing survey research.

As with any type of research, one of the first questions in designing a survey concerns the general purpose of the research (see Box 13.1). Veroff et al. (1981, p. 6) report two distinct purposes for conducting their surveys. The first purpose was "to assess the subject mental health, the life experiences of American adults," and the second was "to determine in some detail how American people cope with problems of adjustment which arise in their lives." The second question was of practical concern to the U.S. Congress, which, through the National Institute of Mental Health, helped to fund this study. Congress was interested in determining whether Americans would use mental health facilities if the government helped to provide them. Thus, in economic terms alone, the results of this survey would have far-reaching implications.

To fulfill the broad aims of the survey, the researchers addressed specific questions, such as how willing people are to seek psychological help and whether going to a mental health professional carries a stigma in people's minds. They also addressed more practical questions, such as how one decides whom to go to and how people decide whether the help they were given was good or bad. In relation to the broad aim of describing the life experiences of American adults, the researchers chose to examine feelings and sources of well-being, self-perceptions, marriage, parenthood, and work, as well as patterns of reported problems. The survey researchers also decided to differentiate the responses given by men and those given by women concerning the way in which people experience and report distress and satisfaction. Once the more specific aims have been determined, one is then faced with the task of developing the actual questions that will be used in the survey and deciding how to administer them.

The section that follows deals with the content of the survey: the actual questions asked and their construction. A later section focuses on the process of administering the survey: the manner in which questions are presented to a person, including both the manner of administration (e.g., face-to-face interview versus mail survey) and the relationship between the interviewer and the respondent. These two aspects are highly interrelated; the manner of administration often influences the format of the questions being asked.

CONCEPT CHECK 13.1    A number of studies have shown that women go to psychotherapists for depression more often than men. Does this mean that more women than men suffer from depression? What types of research methods would be useful to answer this question?

## Box 13.1

## Steps for Designing a Survey Research Project

Approximately 50 years ago, Campbell and Katona (1953) set up a simple nine-step flow chart describing the steps required for conducting a survey. These steps offer a review and checklist for any surveys you are designing.

1. *General objectives:* The first step is to state why the survey is necessary. What is the broad objective one is seeking to accomplish? For example, using the case of the psychotherapist presented at the beginning of this chapter, we would say that her overall objective was to describe the relationship between gender and depression.

2. *Specific objectives:* The second step is to be more specific—to state exactly what types of data will be collected and specify the particular hypotheses to be explored. Again using the example of depression, the specific objectives would include a statement of indicators of depression, such as feeling state (reporting that one feels blue, difficulty sleeping, and so on). The particular hypotheses

could be (1) that women report depression or symptoms of depression more often than men, and (2) that women report seeking help for these symptoms more often than men.

3. *Sample:* Two main decisions are needed at this point. The first decision requires that you state which population you are addressing; that is, to which group do you wish to generalize your results? The population that one designates is related to the original question. For example, in a political survey, the population might be all the registered voters in a particular state. Once the population is established, the second decision is required. This decision relates to how large a sample one is to use, as well as how the sample is to be chosen. Particular techniques for sample selection are discussed in this chapter.

4. *Questionnaire:* This step requires a decision about how the sample is to be surveyed (in person, by telephone, or by mail) as well as

# QUESTION CONSTRUCTION AND FORMATS

Constructing a survey seems at first an incredibly complicated process, with each decision affecting every other decision. Should you ask people general questions, or should you have them compare one viewpoint with another? How should you word a question so that respondents will give you an honest response rather than one that they think is socially acceptable? This section offers guidance.

## ■ Types of Questions

Many types of questions may be used in a survey. One of the more common types is called an *open-ended question*. An open-ended question, as the name implies, has no

the particular questions to be asked. The researcher at this point must decide on the types of questions and responses that will be included. Will the questions use an open-ended or fixed-alternative format or some combination of both? Once the actual questions are developed, it is important to pretest them to ensure clarity. With fixed-alternative questions, the pretest will help to determine whether adequate responses have been provided.

5. *Fieldwork:* This step is related to the people who will actually conduct the survey. The interviewers must be trained and thoroughly practiced. Other considerations such as the interrelationship between the sex, race, and socioeconomic level of the interviewer and the respondent also must be taken into account.

6. *Content analysis:* Some surveys return data in a qualitative form, and they must be transformed into a quantitative form. The information must be coded to ensure reliability across subjects—there must be a system of coding open-ended questions. Even if the data are presented in a numerical fashion, as on a Likert scale, there must be a systematic manner of grouping data for future analysis.

7. *Analysis plan:* Most surveys contain a large number of questions, each of which could be compared to every other, either singularly or in combination. Before the actual data are collected, it is important to specify a plan of analysis that will answer the research hypotheses. This does not preclude later reanalysis of the data for different purposes, but it is important to have an initial plan for data analysis.

8. *Tabulation:* This step is required in a large survey. The researcher must decide how the data are to be entered into the computer and in what form the data should be stored.

9. *Analysis and reporting:* The final stage is the preparation of a report, which would include not only how the data are related to the specific objectives but also such considerations as the reliability of the data from this study.

As Campbell and Katona point out, these nine steps may be interrelated: Decisions affecting one step may also have important implications for another step. With this qualification, these steps offer guidelines for the design of survey research.

fixed answer but allows the respondent to answer in any manner. For example, "What do you like best about college?" is an open-ended question. You could respond by naming a particular course or a good friend, by talking about being on your own, or by telling what you do on Saturday night. An open-ended question is flexible, and this flexibility carries a number of advantages. One advantage is that an open-ended question does not impose the researcher's point of view on the respondent. Another is that the person being interviewed may give you information that you had not considered previously, and this information may show you a new way of understanding the issue being investigated. Open-ended questions also offer an important way to begin a survey. For example, the survey of life satisfaction and well-being, discussed previously, used a number of open-ended questions. One of these asked about leisure and was worded as follows (Veroff et al., 1981, p. 552):

> One of the things we'd like to know is how people spend their time. For instance—how do you usually spend your time when your work is done—what kind of things do you do, both at home and away from home?

However, open-ended questions can pose a problem when you analyze the data and try to establish meaningful patterns of responding. It is sometimes difficult to know how to translate the responses to an open-ended question into categories that fit the original research hypothesis. Of course, it is possible for researchers to impose their own points of view and thus defeat one of the advantages of open-ended questions. Therefore, it is important to select scoring categories carefully. The life satisfaction and well-being survey conducted by Veroff et al. made 55 distinctions in order to score responses to the item "What are some of the things you feel pretty happy about these days?"

Another type of question is called a *fixed-alternative question,* which limits the number of responses a participant can make. This type of question is also called a *closed-ended question.* An example would be a question that asked

*Do you believe that Puerto Rico should become a state?*

Yes [   ]        No [   ]

With the fixed-alternative question, respondents are limited in their responses. Respondents cannot give a reason for their responses, as they could with the open-ended question. However, in constructing fixed-alternative questions you are not limited to *yes* or *no.* For example, a town might ask whether college students should be allowed to vote in local elections. The question could be

*Should students be allowed to vote?*

1. Yes, under any circumstances.
2. Yes, but only if they pay local taxes.
3. No.

Qualified answers such as "Yes, but . . ." or "No, but . . ." permit the answering of additional questions that the researchers might be interested in while retaining an easy-to-score survey question. It is also possible to combine open- and closed-ended questions in a single item. For example, someone might ask what your favorite TV show is, listing specific choices and then "Other" followed by a blank for you to write in a choice of your own. Such an item would appear as

*What is your favorite TV show?*

[   ] *Friends*

[   ] *X-Files*

[   ] *The Simpsons*

[   ] Other: Please specify

It is not uncommon for open-ended and closed-ended questions to be used in the same questionnaire. One technique is to use open-ended questions followed by fixed alternatives to achieve more specific responses. For example, in the survey on American life satisfaction, the question concerning leisure time was later followed by this closed-ended question:

*Next, how much of your free time do you spend doing things that challenge you? Would you say that you spend most, a lot, some, a little, or none of your free time doing such things?*

1. Most    2. A lot    3. Some    4. A little    5. None

When a researcher begins a line of questioning with an open-ended question and then follows this with more specific items, as in the previous example, the process is called *funneling*. Like a funnel, the questions initially are very broad and then become more and more narrow. However, it is important to begin with open-ended questions; otherwise, the closed-ended questions will limit the information the respondent gives.

It is important to choose responses that fit with the category of the question being asked. If the question has to do with frequency, such as "How often do you . . .," then the appropriate alternative answers might be *never, rarely, sometimes, often,* and *very often.* If the question asked how true you believe a certain statement to be, the alternatives might be *very true, somewhat true, not very true,* and *not at all true.* Although the responses offered for each question usually are balanced, it is also possible to present an unbalanced response set. That is, in response to the question, "Have you ever been dishonest on an exam?" the answers *always* and *almost always* would receive few if any checks. It would be appropriate to offer respondents some alternatives that suggest that they almost never are dishonest or look at anyone else's paper. The responses might be *sometimes, almost never, once or twice,* and *never.* Another important point is that if the response categories ask for specific information, then the categories must not overlap. Consider the following question:

*How many children do you have?*

**a.** 0–1 child
**b.** 1–2 children
**c.** 2 or more children

Which answer would you check if you had two children? Because the categories overlap, it is difficult to know how to respond. Although the problem may seem obvious in this example, it is sometimes seen in other surveys, such as those requesting salary information.

The types of items we have discussed only begin to touch on the number of possible alternatives that can be used. In the concluding part of this subsection, we want to introduce briefly a variety of other response formats. We present them for illustration only and suggest that you consult more in-depth presentations if you design a survey using these formats (e.g., Babbie, 2001; Edwards, Thomas, Rosenfeld, & Booth-Kewley, 1997; Fink & Kosecoff, 1998).

One alternative format is to use a nonverbal mode for describing preference. With special populations, such as children, it could be more appropriate to use graphic rather than verbal alternatives. For example, children might be asked to point to happy or sad faces to convey how much they like or dislike a certain game. Some other types of formats have been developed for particular purposes, such as analysis and scaling. We include them in this section because you may hear researchers describe their questionnaires as using *Likert-type items,* for example.

Likert (1932) published a technique for measuring attitudes. The general format is the same as that of the fixed-alternative items that we have presented. One item might be stated as

*If I heard someone calling for help in a large city, I would help him or her.*

| Strongly agree | Agree | Uncertain | Disagree | Strongly disagree |
|---|---|---|---|---|
| (5) | (4) | (3) | (2) | (1) |

As you can see, the format of the response is the same as that of items we have discussed. However, Likert developed a method of scaling items. Each item is given a certain weight, represented by the number in parentheses. A number of scale items are then added together to form an index, such as an index of helping behavior. The original procedure was to perform an item analysis to determine which items contributed to the index consistently across participants. Items that did not contribute consistently could be eliminated from the final version of the questionnaire.

Another type of response format is called the *semantic differential.* The semantic differential uses bipolar adjectives (such as *good* and *bad, soft* and *hard, modern* and *old-fashioned, interesting* and *boring, hot* and *cold, slow* and *fast*) in relation to a particular concept or idea. These adjectives usually are placed at each end of a seven-point scale. The instructions ask the respondent to check an appropriate place between each pair of adjectives to rate a concept or thing. For example, you could be asked to rate a course you were taking:

*Please rate your course in introductory psychology along the following dimensions.*

easy _____:_____:_____:_____:_____:_____:_____ hard
fun _____:_____:_____:_____:_____:_____:_____ dull
sexy _____:_____:_____:_____:_____:_____:_____ not sexy
fast _____:_____:_____:_____:_____:_____:_____ slow

For clarity you could list categories such as *very much, a lot, somewhat,* and so on, at the top of the semantic differential. Because the semantic differential was originally developed for measuring the meaning of objects, or what is called *semantic space of experience,* it is possible to use adjectives that may be related experientially to a concept. Thus, we can ask whether a musical recording is *hot* or a course *sexy* using this technique. When analysis is performed using a number of semantic response lines related to a single concept, it is possible to arrive at an overall profile (see Osgood, Suci, & Tannenbaum, 1957, for more information about the semantic differential).

## ■ General Considerations

Developing questions for a survey may be more difficult than you think at first, for a variety of reasons. One reason is the ambiguity of language. For example, we often say such things as, "I always eat with my friends," when we are trying to emphasize how close we are to our friends. However, if someone were to ask you the question, "Do you always eat with your friends?" on a survey, you would probably consider the question to be asking for specific information, and you might have some difficulty knowing exactly how to answer the question. In fact, in one poll in which respondents reported that the questions were clearly stated, the understanding of the phrase *over the last few years* was interpreted to mean less than 2 years by some of the respondents and more than 10 years by others. Thus, it is important in developing questions to be as clear as possible and to avoid unwanted ambiguity. Sometimes, the particular question you are asking may be difficult to phrase in a simple sentence, especially if you are asking about how someone feels or thinks about more global concepts, such as freedom, love, religion, his or her country, or family.

Sometimes, you may be asking for information that people do not want to give. How you phrase your question may determine whether the person is willing to answer. For example, many people will say whether their income is between $10,000 and $29,999, between $30,000 and $59,999, or above $60,000, but they will not tell you the exact figure. If you do not need to know the exact figure, do not ask. One of the first rules for developing questions is to ask only what you need to know.

Another important consideration is the order in which the questions are asked. For example, the life satisfaction and well-being survey discussed previously would probe for positive responses before negative ones. That is, on open-ended questions, such as general questions on marriage, the interviewer would ask about the *nicest things* in marriage before asking about things that are *not quite as nice as you would like them to be.* Some researchers who have studied order effects suggest that a person's response to one question has an effect on his or her response to the next question (Schuman & Presser, 1981). These effects seem to be strongest when the questions are of a general or summary type.

Another important guideline is to consider what you are asking not only from your own perspective but also from the perspective of those responding to the survey. Questions that seem perfectly clear when we are developing a questionnaire may not appear as clear when asked in a survey. The respondent may have a different frame of reference. For example, if I asked you about your worth, you would not know whether I wanted to know how much money you had in the bank or how you valued yourself psychologically. Again, it is important to reduce any unwanted ambiguity. One way of doing this is to establish a context in which the question is presented. As you may have noticed, in the life satisfaction and well-being survey, the researchers began by saying that they wanted to know how people spend their leisure time. This is a better approach than just asking, "What do you do when you are not working?"

Context is also important when we ask people to give us information that may be at odds with either what is accepted in society or their public image. For example, a question designed to learn about parents' anger toward their small children might begin with the statement, "All parents become angry with their children from time to time. What do you do when you become angry?" The established context—that all parents become angry at times—enables the respondent to feel freer to disclose information in relation to his or her own angry feelings and actions. By creating a context in which the person can answer the question, we gain more accurate information. However, it is also important not to go to the extreme and create an introduction to your questions that leads the person to answer in a manner that does not reflect his or her real attitude.

You should also avoid *leading* in developing questions. To avoid potential bias based on their own perceptions, some researchers develop fixed-alternative responses based on the initial administration of an open-ended question. To ensure that you do not have leading questions in the survey, you might begin by asking the question in an open-ended fashion to a group of people. You would tabulate their responses and use these as a basis for fixed-alternative items.

At this point, it is time to consider one of the most important guidelines for survey research: *Pretest the survey!* It is imperative that you give the questions you have developed to people and that you note any unwanted ambiguity in their responses or any misunderstanding of the items. One technique for understanding how those who take your survey understand the questions is to have them think out loud as they answer the survey. In this way you can determine that their understanding of the survey is the same as you intended. In the ideal situation, the survey should be pretested on the population to which it will be given. This is particularly important to help determine the adequacy of fixed-choice responses. Pretesting helps us to easily perceive that we have worded an item correctly (or incorrectly) and whether the alternatives offered actually represent the manner in which our target group would respond. It is not uncommon to pretest a survey more than once and to use the feedback from each testing to develop a better survey for answering the original research question.

---

✓ CONCEPT CHECK 13.2

A music professor wanted to know what type of music undergraduates like to listen to. To answer this question, he conducted a survey in which he asked a number of students the following three questions:

**1.** Do you like classical music?   Yes _____   No _____
**2.** Do you like acid rock?   Yes _____   No _____
**3.** Do you like polka music?   Yes _____   No _____

The professor was surprised to find that after the survey he still did not know what type of music undergraduates like to listen to. How might he have conducted this study to better answer his question?

---

## Special Techniques for Reactive Questions

What if you were to ask someone a question about his or her sexual fantasies or whether he or she had ever broken the law? How honestly do you think the person would respond? These are difficult questions to answer. Some people would answer honestly and some would not. Because it is not possible to know when someone is not answering a survey honestly, techniques have been developed to ask potentially reactive or embarrassing questions. These procedures have been shown to have a more valid response rate than asking the question directly.

One such technique is the *random response method* (Warner, 1965). We describe the most simple version of the technique using a coin, but you could also use dice or other methods that give equally randomized results. Using the coin, the person answering the survey is told to flip a coin for each question. If the coin is heads, she or he is to answer "yes." However, if the coin is tails, the participant is to answer the question truthfully. Because the researcher in this situation has no idea which questions the person answered honestly and which questions he or she answered in terms of the coin flip, it is assumed that the participant is more willing to tell the truth. Shotland and Yankowski (1982) tested this assumption by having people *overhear* answers to a test. These researchers compared the random response method to direct questioning of the participants. They found that the participants told the truth 64 to 80% of the time using the random response method but only 10 to 27% of the time using direct questioning.

How does the random response method work? It is simple: Assume you gave each of a large group of people a survey and a coin and told them to answer *yes* when the coin landed on heads and *no* when the coin landed on tails. What would you expect to find? The answer, of course, is that each question would have an equal number of *yes* responses and an equal number of *no* responses. Now change the situation slightly; suppose they are told to respond *yes* to heads but honestly to tails. What would the results be this time? The answer is that any result different from 50% can be considered not the result of chance but based on an *honest response*. Thus, if 80% of the responses to a hypothetical question ("Do you like watching soap operas on TV?") were *yes*, we would assume that if everyone were being honest when they were supposed to be, 60% of all respondents would have responded *yes* to this question.

How do we determine the honest response when the responses we recorded were composed of both honest responses and coin flips? We determine this by subtracting 50% (the expected probability) from 80% (the percentage of *yes* responses) and dividing by 50% (the expected probability). In conclusion, when you have questions that produce reactive or embarrassing responses, such as asking one about sexual practices, the random response method offers a valid alternative to direct questioning or even anonymous questionnaires.

## METHODS OF ADMINISTERING A SURVEY

### ■ Face-to-Face Interviews

When someone mentions the word *survey,* we may think of census takers coming to our house or of the exit polls that we see on television during political elections. In both of these cases, the interviewer presents the person with a series of questions face-to-face and records his or her answers. There are a number of advantages to this approach. One of the main advantages of face-to-face interviews, especially if the survey is somewhat complex, is that you are able to achieve a better idea of the psychological set from which the person is answering the questions. For example, you can determine how motivated the person may be to give you answers. You can also judge the respondent's comprehension and clear up any ambiguity or misunderstanding. With open-ended questions, it is possible to probe for additional information if the initial response is brief or incomplete. For example, in the survey question concerning what people do with their free time, if the person says only, "Have fun," it would be possible to follow up with a probe such as, "Tell me more," or "Can you name some particular activities?" and thus produce a more specific answer. The interviewer can also make and record observations related to race, gender, socioeconomic level, and so forth, without having to ask these questions directly. Compared with other forms of survey administration, such as sending questionnaires through the mail, face-to-face interviews generally give higher completion rates and more complete information.

There are also disadvantages to face-to-face interviews. First, face-to-face interviews are expensive in terms of time and personnel, thus limiting the number of interviews that can be conducted compared with other methods, such as mail or telephone surveys. Second, although the interviewer may help the respondents to understand the questions and may clarify the responses, the interviewer can also bias the results, either consciously or unconsciously. For example, some interviewers may probe more with men than with women, or they may probe less with older than with younger respondents, and thus systematically bias the results.

It may also happen that the respondent would give different answers face-to-face than with a written questionnaire. As you can imagine, some people find it difficult to discuss sensitive issues (such as sexuality, drug or alcohol use, or behaviors that might be considered deviant) in person, whereas they might answer an anonymous questionnaire quite easily. It is also possible that the respondent will not like the interviewer's looks, clothing, race, or sex, and may give biased information. For example, one interviewer reported that, after a productive interview session, the respondent said that the interviewer was really a civil rights worker

Box 13.2

## Verbal Report as Data: Can We Tell More Than We Know?

It is often said that if you want to know something, you should ask. In psychological research this simple suggestion has led to a great deal of debate. The debate centers on a number of themes, one of which asks whether there really is a relationship between attitudes and behaviors. Another asks whether a person can really know about himself or herself. For example, do you really know your attitude concerning the opposite sex? Can you really predict whether you will help someone in distress if you happen into such a situation walking through the streets of New York? Do you actually know how you think as you go about solving a problem, and can you report this to an experimenter? Although our tendency is to say that we know a great deal about ourselves, research has demonstrated that these questions represent complex considerations that cut across most of psychological research. They are particularly important to survey researchers because survey research relies heavily on self-report data.

Survey researchers have adopted two main approaches concerning self-report data. The first approach is to seek situations in which it can be assumed that survey responses will give a useful description of a person's attitudes, views, and behaviors. For example, it is assumed that people can report what they do in their leisure time, or whether they would vote for a particular person in an election. The second approach disconnects the attitude from behavior and places an emphasis on attitudes in themselves. For example, it is possible to ask people about their optimism for the future or their views of capital punishment or

what they think about free trade, all without involving references to a particular behavior.

With regard to the second approach, it has been suggested that verbal data are important in their own right and do not have to be related to nonverbal data (cf. Galtung, 1967). This theoretical position suggests that it is not necessary to validate a questionnaire related to behavior by actually observing behavior. To expand on this position, it is important to understand that social and psychological relationships are complex and that all modes of behavior—cognitive, emotional, and physiological, as well as self-report—are not expected to show identical patterns in every situation. This complexity makes psychological research interesting, and it is often amazing to discover how widely particular aspects of behavior vary.

For example, in one study the task was to listen to a tape recording of different voices and to report after each voice whether the voice was one's own or that of another person. It was shown that individuals would give a psychophysiological response (electrodermal) to hearing their own voices even though they reported that it was not their voice (Gur & Sackeim, 1979). This type of research suggests that people have multiple response systems and that self-report data cannot be expected to give a single, consistent picture across all of these. The research also suggests that when you tap the right channel, it is possible for people to tell you more than they know they know.

Whether people can tell you more than they know they know has been the topic of much debate. Nisbett and Wilson (1977), in a *Psychological Review* article, suggest that people may not be able to use introspection to describe their cognitive processes accurately. People may not actually know why they like someone or why they took a particular course or why they like one color of clothes as opposed to another. According to Nisbett and Wilson, people also may not have access to how they go about making decisions. In particular, these authors suggest that research participants may be unaware of stimuli that importantly influence a response, may be unaware of the response itself, and may be unaware that a particular stimulus has actually influenced a particular response. If Nisbett and Wilson are correct, then researchers would need to rethink survey research that addresses itself to asking people why they do what they do or research that asks people how they go about solving certain problems.

In a later article, Ericsson and Simon (1980) suggest that psychology has always used verbal behavior as data even in nonsense syllable experiments in which the participants report remembering which syllable was paired with which other syllable. That is, even in studies that claimed to measure only observable responses, self-report information was still considered valuable. Bcause Simon and his colleagues often use self-report data to study how people go about solving problems, it would be important to them if participants could not report how they went about solving problems. In Chapter 1 we discussed one of these studies using novice and expert chess players. Using an information-processing model, Ericsson and Simon suggest that situations do exist in which verbal reports may not be consistent with behavior, as suggested by Nisbett and Wilson, particular situations that do not require memory processes.

If you were asked how you would solve a particular problem had you been given the problem in a different manner, the self-report and the actual behavior—how you really would have solved the problem—might differ. You would have no actual behavior on which to base your self-report and thus would have to create a hypothetical situation and imagine hypothetical behavior. However, Ericsson and Simon would predict that if you had just solved the problem, then you would have this information in memory and self-report would be valid. Self-report may be consistent with behavior when the self-report describes an actual set of behaviors that have occurred in the recent past. However, there may be less consistency if the event has not occurred. This is only a statement of the idea that, whether it be solving a problem or responding to cries of help from a person on the streets of New York, we may not be able to predict our own future behavior.

With regard to survey research, the question ultimately becomes, "How will the data be used and why do we want the data in the first place?" If we are interested in attitudes, then self-report offers an historically important way of tapping into how people feel or think about a certain topic. Likewise, if we are interested in past behavior, self-report also offers a means of obtaining this information as perceived by the person giving it. However, if we want to know about future behavior, self-report may offer a good guess but not certainty. In addition, not everyone wants to give you the information you are seeking. Thus it may be important to include some type of question that assesses how readily that particular person has given out certain information in the past and to judge your results accordingly.

trying to integrate the neighborhood and that the respondent was not being fooled (Converse & Schuman, 1974). It is possible that this respondent's answers were biased by his or her perception of the interviewer. If you conduct interviews, you should consider the possibility that college students will be perceived as having values different from those of the surrounding communities. All of these possibilities must be considered when using face-to-face interviews. As with any piece of research, it is important to walk through each step and determine to the best of your ability whether there could be a potential problem or confound.

## ■ Telephone Interviews

One alternative to face-to-face interviews is the telephone interview. Often, surveys that we read about in the newspaper are the result of telephone interviews. For example, in 1983 the *New York Times* interviewed by telephone 1309 men and women, asking them about their attitudes toward work (Dowd, 1983). One of the questions asked was, "If you were free to do either, would you prefer to have a job outside the home, or would you prefer to stay home and take care of your house and family?" In this survey, 72% of the men and 45% of the women said they would prefer to have a job outside the home.

Surveys also help us to measure changing attitudes in response to particular events. For example, In May of 1999, 1000 individuals were telephoned and asked about reinstating the military draft in America, 22% were in favor at this time. However, after the attack on the World Trade Center on September 11, 2001, similar polls found 66% (Time/CNN), 77% (Gallup) and 76% (Fox Broadcasting) in favor of reinstating the draft. These and other telephone polls can be found in a polling database call "Polling the Nation," which may be available in your library.

A telephone interviewer can establish rapport, determine motivation, and clarify questions and responses while still being more cost-effective than a face-to-face interview. That is, it is possible in a given amount of time to conduct a larger number of telephone interviews than face-to-face interviews because face-to-face interviewing also requires time for traveling and finding a particular house or apartment. Also, in a telephone survey, if someone chooses not to participate, all one needs to do is to call the next number; in a face-to-face survey, one must walk away and look for the next participant.

At one time, survey researchers avoided telephone interviews because telephones were associated with higher socioeconomic levels; this is no longer the case. Today there are other problems. For example, some individuals use an answering machine and never answer their phone; others have unlisted numbers and many others use cell phones. These types of situations make finding a random sample a more difficult process. To avoid the potential bias of leaving out unlisted numbers for example, some surveys use telephone numbers obtained by randomly choosing four digits and adding these to the three-digit code for the area. This avoids the problem of unlisted numbers, but it creates another problem: It includes business numbers and disconnected numbers.

Telephone interviews also have a general time limitation. It is commonly known that interviews lasting more than 15 minutes make some people feel uncomfortable, and these people may actually end the interview by hanging up the telephone, whether or not you are finished. However, the MacArthur Foundation study on midlife development was able to use a 30-minute phone interview after an initial contact was established.

As with all areas of research, computers have created new possibilities in telephone interviews. It is now possible to have the computer randomly dial phone numbers from a preselected list; in addition, a computer can tell the interviewer what questions to ask and can record the responses. New technologies, such as voice mail, that automatically ask questions and direct calls in many large organizations, also may be used for telephone surveys.

## ■ Mail Questionnaires

A different type of survey procedure uses self-administered questionnaires delivered through the mail. One of the major advantages of mail questionnaires is that they can be sent almost anywhere in the world for the cost of postage. As you can imagine, however, one of the disadvantages is that they may not always be returned. In fact, the return rate of mail surveys is typically very low in comparison to the completion rate of face-to-face interviews. If you obtain a return rate above 75%, you can consider yourself fortunate. A return rate of 50% should be considered acceptable. The typical mail survey has a return rate of below 50%. With a return rate below 50% you need to reconsider the type of sample that is required, the purpose of the survey, and the manner in which the survey is to be used, and evaluate your data accordingly.

The problem with low response rates is that the sample may not represent the desired population. However, there are times that a low response rate may exactly reflect the desired population. For example, Visser et al. (1996) compared mail surveys and telephone surveys over a 15-year period in their ability to predict Ohio elections. Although the telephone surveys had a 60% response rate and the mail surveys only a 20% return rate, the mail surveys were better able to predict the outcome of the elections. How can this be? It appears that the people who took the time to fill out the survey were also people who would take the time to vote. Thus, the low response rate actually made the sample more representative. Overall, you must consider the response rate in the context of the research in order to evaluate your findings. (See Krosnick, 1999, for a review.)

Because you want people to respond to a mail survey, it is important that you do everything you can to ensure that they read, complete, and return your questionnaire. Although it is more expensive, the survey should be sent by first-class mail; some people open only their first-class mail and throw away the rest. Most survey researchers supply postage-paid return envelopes; you would not want your survey to be lost for lack of a stamp. It is also important that the questionnaire look professional. The first impression should be that the questionnaire will be easy to complete and return. It is also important that the respondent understand the importance of the survey; to this end you should include a carefully prepared cover letter explaining the survey and placing it in an appropriate context. One means of increasing the response rate is to use follow-up letters reminding the respondent of the survey and to enclose another copy of the questionnaire.

Some researchers have also increased response rates by including a shortened version of the original questionnaire in additional follow-up letters. They may lose some information with the less detailed version, but they are able to obtain the most important information. They are also able to obtain information on the type of respondent who did not initially fill out the questionnaire. Mail surveys lack some advantages of face-to-face interviews, such as personal contact and the ability to request additional information, but sometimes people are more open and honest with their answers in a mail survey. This is especially true if they believe themselves to be responding anonymously and are reporting areas of personal behavior, such as medical problems, sexuality, or attitudes not in keeping with currently held viewpoints.

### ■ Computer and Internet Questionnaires

Computers can be used for administering surveys in a variety of ways. For example, as previously mentioned, computers can be used in face-to-face interviews to aid in the data collection process. Computers also can be used with mail surveys such that individuals are mailed a Web address at which they can complete the survey. Given that many corporations, educational institutions and individuals are connected to the Web, it also possible to perform Web surveys.

Although Internet surveys have some of the same problems as mail surveys, they also have some advantages. For example, you might not initially think that taking the same survey on paper or via a computer would make a difference, but research suggests that people find a computer format both more enjoyable and faster than a paper survey (see Edwards et al., 1997). Computer administration of surveys also allows for easier branching or asking different questions depending on the answer to a specific question. For example, rather than saying "skip the next two questions if you answered no to the present question" on a paper format, the computer can simply present the appropriate question. In this same manner, the survey could restrict the survey to questions that were relevant to that particular respondent. Since not everyone has access to a computer, your Internet survey could be biased by excluding those individuals. We will discuss this issue in more depth when we discuss sampling procedures in the next section of this chapter.

### ■ Surveys: Conclusion

In conclusion, there are a variety of methods for administering surveys. The four most popular methods are face-to-face, telephone, mail, and Internet surveys. There are advantages and disadvantages to each, as we have discussed. Typically, one is faced with a trade-off between response rate and cost. In deciding which form of administration you should use, you will need to determine what is important in your survey research. If it is important for you to have a high rate of return on your surveys, then face-to-face or telephone interviews would be good choices. As you will learn in the next section, the ability to have a representative sample is extremely important in some situations; in such situations, mail surveys are ruled out. Time may also be a factor, as in political surveys taken the day before an election. When cost is an important factor and you need a large number of responses, a mail or Internet survey may be more appropriate. As with any research, you need to consider why you are doing the research in the first place, as well as what type of information will best answer your research question. (See Babbie, 2001; Edwards et al., 1997; Fink & Kosecoff, 1998, for more information on types of surveys.)

## SAMPLING

In discussions of research throughout this book, we have raised the question of generalizability and considered how the results from a particular experiment could be applied to a larger group. The question of generalizability or representativeness is also important for survey research. How can we ensure that the results obtained in giving our questionnaire or interview to a group of people will apply to some larger population? If we were developing a questionnaire for only one group—such as all senior psychology majors in your college—and if we gave it to every senior psychology major, then generalizability would not be an issue because our sample would represent the entire population. This type of survey is called a *census*. Like descriptive statistics, a census is aimed at obtaining descriptive information about a particular group of people and nothing more.

However, if we want to apply the results obtained beyond the specific group from which they were obtained, then we need to be concerned about generalizability. In laboratory experiments, one of the ways to accomplish this is through careful experimental controls and the selection of participants, as discussed in previous chapters. In survey research, for generalizability we place much of the emphasis on the selection of participants through sampling procedures. In this section, we want to introduce you to sampling techniques. For additional information, you can consult textbooks that specifically discuss sampling techniques (e.g., Scheaffer, Mendenhall, & Ott, 1979).

You probably are familiar with the general idea of sampling in relation to television ratings or attempts to predict who will win a political race. You may have wondered how raters can say that a television show is highly rated when fewer than 2000 people are sampled out of millions. You may also wonder what is meant by a statement such as, "Seventy-eight percent of the population really wants to take a course in methodology, with a sampling error of 4 percent" (besides wondering what weird population would have given that response). These types of sampling are covered in this section.

In 1936, asking over 2 million people for whom they would vote in the next presidential election led one magazine, *Literary Digest,* to conclude that Alfred Landon would beat Franklin Roosevelt (Gallup, 1972). To be precise, *Literary Digest* predicted that Landon would carry 32 states and 57% of the vote compared to Roosevelt's 43%. In fact, the results were very different with Landon carrying only 2 states and receiving 37% of the vote in comparison to Roosevelt's 61%.

George Gallup conducted a much smaller survey of 5000 voters, however, and correctly predicted the winner. Gallup's prediction was that Roosevelt would win 40 states with 56% of the popular vote. What was the secret of his success? How did he do more with less? The answer was in the sampling procedures. Although the magazine *Literary Digest* sampled 2,376,523 people, their names were drawn from automobile registration lists and telephone directories.

Realizing that this survey took place during the Depression, you can understand what the bias was in this sampling technique. During the Depression many people did not have money for cars or telephones and thus would not have been included in the survey. Those who did have telephones and cars tended to be wealthy and also to be Republicans. Thus, wealthy Republicans completed the survey, saying they would vote for Landon and against Roosevelt and the New Deal. Gallup used a sampling procedure that did not exclude the poor, who were mainly Democrats and more likely to vote for Roosevelt. Gallup thus had the more accurate representation, and his prediction was right.

Other election predictions seem even more amazing. For example, using a sample size of fewer than 2000 people, a *New York Times*-CBS poll in 1976 correctly predicted that of almost 80 million voters, 51.1% would vote for Jimmy Carter and 48.9% for Gerald Ford; the actual vote was 51.1% for Jimmy Carter and 48.9% for Gerald Ford—the same numbers as the prediction.

Of course, not every prediction is that good. In 1948, the Gallup Poll predicted that Dewey would beat President Truman, which was not the case. However, this may have had less to do with sampling than the decision to stop the polling ten days before the election in a race that had a late swing of support for Truman and a misinterpretation of what undecided voters would do, which turned out to be giving their votes to Truman.

In the 1984 election, in which Ronald Reagan won 59% of the popular vote and almost all the electoral college votes, there were discrepant estimates of the victory margin even when different polls were taken simultaneously (Converse & Traugott, 1986). Thus, sampling is only one part of the survey picture albeit a critical one. Let us examine sampling in some depth.

The basic idea behind sampling is that we would like to learn about the characteristics of a large group of people (called a *population*) by studying a smaller group (called a *sample*). If all people were equal in every way, then it would not matter which people we chose to study out of a large group. We could use any procedure we wanted for selecting a sample. No matter how respondents were grouped, the results would always be the same. However, people are not the same in every way, and thus we try to find ways of choosing people from the larger group in such a way that the characteristics found in the smaller group reflect those of the larger group.

One of the first tasks is to define the population in which we are interested, and this is usually related to the research questions being asked. If we are interested in memory and learning across the life span, then we would want to define our population so that people of all ages are included. If we are interested in the drinking habits of female college students, then we would have a more narrowly defined population. Once the population is defined, a question arises about the appropriate sample that is needed. Because our goal is to perform research—to examine a particular sample and from this sample make inferences about the larger population—it is important that our sample reflect the larger population. The more the sample reflects the larger population, the more confidence we have in any inference we make from our smaller sample to the larger population. A variety of sampling techniques are available, and we present some of the more popular ones, along with the major advantages and disadvantages of each. There are two main types of sampling: probability sampling and nonprobability sampling.

> ✓ CONCEPT CHECK 13.3
>
> The *Happy Valley News* ran a front-page story proclaiming that residents were opposed to adding more forms of mass transit in the city. These results came from a call-in poll to a local radio station one morning. Based on this information, what could you conclude about the views of the citizens of this town?

## ■ Probability Sampling

In *probability sampling,* the term *probability* refers to the predetermined chance of any individual's being selected for the study, given the particular constraints under study. There are several forms of probability sampling.

Simple Random Sampling    The main characteristic of a randomized procedure is that every member of the population has a known chance of being selected. In *simple random sampling,* each member has an equal chance of being selected. This is like putting the names of everyone in the population into a hat and drawing out a certain number of names. For example, if you were interested in how your campus radio station was rated, you might consider all students in your university as the population and then choose a sample from this population using a random number table (see Box 7.1). You could then conduct a survey on this sample.

Systematic Sampling    A variation on the random sampling procedure is to list the total population and then choose every *n*th person listed. For example, you might include every fifth person in your sample. This procedure, called *systematic sampling,* has the advantage of being more efficient than simple random sampling. However, it is important that the list you use contain the entire population in an unbiased order. Most alphabetical lists of a population would not introduce bias into a survey, but it is important to consider possible bias from a variety of sources. For example, if you sampled every fifth person in a classroom with 10 seats in each row, you might produce a biased sample without realizing it. In some classrooms the first seat in each row has a desk designed for someone who writes left-handed; thus, if you happened to sample every fifth person, beginning with the person sitting in the first seat, you might have 50% right-handed people and 50% left-handed people—probably not a representative sample of the population of students in that class. Of course, this is an extreme case of bias, but we include it to emphasize that there are types of bias that you might not anticipate but that can cause problems in the sample.

Stratified Random Sampling    At times, we may realize that in order to answer the research question in which we are interested, we need to ensure that certain people are represented systematically in our sample, especially if we expect that differences exist in certain groups. For example, we might want to make sure that certain age groups are included or that both male and female participants are represented. To accomplish this, we would use a *stratified random sampling* procedure. For example, if it were important to us that both male and female participants were included in our sample in a certain proportion, then we could divide the population according to this category and then take a separate random sample from each of the resulting divisions. Although stratification by sex is an easy example to understand, it is more common to stratify when a group of people is likely to be underrepresented because the actual numbers of that group are small. For example, if you conduct a survey requiring that the respondents include all minority groups, then stratification would be a useful procedure.

Cluster Sampling    There are situations in which the physical constraints, both in time and money, make it difficult to use a random sampling technique. For example, if you wanted to study language before the introduction of television, you would need geographic areas in which television had not yet been introduced. In areas that did not have television, it might be impractical to create a random sample from the entire area. It would be more economical to select a few villages and study them in some depth. Likewise, researchers interested in how people feel about the chance of their being the victims of crimes may choose to study the inhabitants of particular blocks in a large city. The general procedure in *cluster sampling* is to randomly select a certain number of population units (such as villages or city blocks) and then enlist the participation of the people who live in those units.

**Multistage Sampling**    A *multistage sampling procedure,* as the name implies, relies on sampling at different stages in the process. At times, we may use the same sampling technique but with different populations. For example, if we wanted to study U.S. college students, we might first randomly sample colleges throughout the country. Then we could randomly sample students in each selected college. Likewise, we might randomly sample cities in the country and then randomly sample people within these cities.

We might also change the type of sampling procedure from one stage to the next. For example, the study of life satisfaction and well-being discussed previously used a multistage sampling procedure. Before sampling, the researchers decided that the sample would be limited to private households, thus excluding prisons, hospitals, colleges, and other forms of group housing. In the first stage of the sampling procedure, standard metropolitan areas, single counties, and certain county groups within each region of the country were listed. Initial samplings were made proportional to population. That is, the sampling procedure was set up so that areas with larger populations would have a greater chance of being selected. This was changed to an equal probability in the final selection for location. Once specific addresses were selected, a single person at this address was chosen randomly to be interviewed.

## ◼ Nonprobability Sampling

One common example of nonprobability sampling is the use of introductory psychology students for research. Because most students do not randomly take a course in introductory psychology unless it is a required course (that is, they self-select and in this way form a special group), the question of generalizability arises; that is, to what populations can research performed with introductory psychology students be generalized? This is an important question that should be considered whenever one is using this or any other convenient group for research.

**Convenience Sampling**    In *convenience sampling,* we use the people who are available to us. Sometimes simple surveys use a convenience sampling procedure, as when people on the street or in shopping malls are interviewed as they happen to walk by the interviewer. Some students, for example, might choose their sample by picking every tenth person who comes into a snack bar over a 2-day period. Although this sample might be useful if the total population is snack bar users, it would not be useful if the survey is to be generalized to all college students. A sample selected in this manner would exclude students who never come to the snack bar and would also overinclude those who come in more than once a day.

**Quota Sampling**    Another type of nonprobability sampling is *quota sampling.* A quota sample sets up a quota or number of specific types of people. For example, we might decide to include in our survey three biology majors, three psychology majors, and three faculty members.

**Snowball Sampling**    Another type of nonprobability sampling is called *snowball sampling.* This sampling procedure is used most often when no list of the population exists. For example, if a medical researcher were interested in health issues related to prostitution, it would be impossible to obtain a list of prostitutes on which to base the sample. A common procedure is to find one prostitute who would agree to be part of the research, and then ask that person to help locate others, and these people would help locate others, in a snowball fashion.

# SAMPLE SIZE

In this chapter we have said little about one very important matter: sample size. Sample size in survey research is based on the types of considerations we discussed in Chapter 5 in our presentation of inferential statistics. We want to be able to choose a sample of people who have the same characteristics as the overall population. If we succeed with this goal, then we can generalize successfully from our sample to the overall population. Because research is expensive in terms of time and money, we want our sample to be as small as possible. But how do we go about deciding the actual size we need?

In simple terms, we determine the size of the sample we need by asking two questions. The first question concerns the characteristics of the population to which we want to generalize. How many people are available to be used in the survey, and how homogeneous are these people? As you can imagine, if the population is homogeneous on the characteristic we want to study, then fewer people would be needed for the sample to approximate the population. If there is a wide range of variation, then more participants would be needed. The second question asks how accurate an answer we need to the question we are asking. That is, how much difference can we tolerate between the characteristics found in the sample and those of the overall population? These two questions together determine sample size. In general, the larger the population to which we want to generalize—or the greater the variability and the more exact we want the results to be—the larger the sample size that is required.

Because we have little control over the size of the population in which we are interested, our main concern is with the second question—that of acceptable variations in the estimate of the population parameters. We establish an upper and lower bound within which we want the results to fall with some established probability; in other words, we make a statement of how much error we will tolerate. For example, if we were to conduct a survey as to how many students would want an outdoor café built onto the student union, we might decide that we would accept an error of 5%. Suppose the results of the survey indicated that 67% of the students were in favor of the outdoor café. We could then assume that if the entire student body had been questioned, the exact percentage in favor of the café would be in the range between 62% (the lower bound) and 72% (the upper bound). This range is called a *confidence interval*. In this example, we would say there was a *sampling error* of plus or minus 5%.

The amount of sampling error that is acceptable is related to the original purpose of the survey. In the beginning of a political campaign, for example, you might be interested only in survey results that give ballpark figures on which candidate is leading. However, as the election draws nearer, it might become important to have more exact estimates of how the vote is expected to go. Thus, in an initial survey, you might be willing for your survey to report that 40% of the voters favored a particular candidate with a sampling error of plus or minus 5%. This means that if the election were held that day, up to 45% would have voted for that candidate. In a survey nearer the time of the election, it might be less acceptable to risk being off by as much as 5%.

Once we have some idea of the size of our population, how variable it is, and the amount of error that we are willing to tolerate, we can determine the sample size we will need. The actual formula we use requires that we establish confidence levels. The 95% level is used traditionally. At this level, the probability of the results happening by chance is 5 out of 100. The general formula is

$$\text{sample size} = \left( \frac{\text{confidence level} \times \text{variation in population}}{\text{desired precision}} \right)^2$$

Assume we wanted to know how much the average college student pays for books. How many students would we need to survey? Using the formula, we could determine the appropriate number. The variation in the population that we use is the *standard deviation* (see Chapter 4). The standard deviation for a particular population is often known from previous surveys. (It also can be estimated from the sample standard deviation, although not before the survey is performed; for this figure, see advanced survey textbooks.)

Let us assume in this case that we know the standard deviation to be $20. The confidence level traditionally used is the 95% level, which is expressed in the formula as a standard score (*z* score) of $1.96. For the desired precision, assume that we want the error to be less than $2. Substituting these numbers in the formula, we would determine that we need 384.16 participants to satisfy our conditions:

$$\text{sample size} = \left( 1.96 \times \frac{20}{2} \right)^2 = 384.16 \text{ people}$$

We might also solve this equation using different levels of precision. For example, we would need 1537 participants if we wanted the error to be less than $1, but only 96 participants if we accepted an error of $4.

There are tables to aid researchers in determining the sample size for survey research (Yamane, 1967). These tables generally assume a large standard deviation and present the desired precision in terms of percentage error. From such a table, we would learn that if we were to perform a survey in a national election, we would need 10,000 respondents for a 1% error, 2500 for a 2% error, 1111 for a 3% error, 400 for a 5% error, and only 100 respondents for an error of 10% (Yamane, 1967).

# RELIABILITY AND VALIDITY

As with other types of research we have discussed, questions of reliability and validity are also important for survey research. A survey is reliable if it can be given a number of times and produce the same results. Many of the issues we discussed in this chapter, such as carefully considering the wording of questions and pretesting the survey, help to increase the reliability. However, there is little doubt that if the 1936 *Literary Digest* survey we discussed previously were to be given to the same or similar individuals, we would again obtain the same results that Roosevelt would lose the election. Thus, we not only want our surveys to be reliable but also valid. That is, the survey should accurately reflect what is being examined. Validity can be increased through sampling procedures as well as techniques to ensure increased response rates.

---

☑ **CONCEPT CHECK 13.4**    A group of students from Moosesylvania State University wants to know whether the library should be open longer during final exam week. Would it be better to randomly sample 2000 students from around the country or to take a census of the 500 students at the university?

---

# KEY TERMS AND CONCEPTS

1. **Survey research**
2. **Question construction and formats**
   A. Open-ended questions
   B. Closed-ended questions
   C. Funneling
   D. Likert scale
   E. Semantic differential
3. **Special techniques for reactive questions**
4. **Methods of administration**
   A. Face-to-face interviews
   B. Telephone interviews
   C. Mail questionnaires
5. **Probability sampling**
   A. Simple random sampling
   B. Systematic sampling

    C. Stratified random sampling
    D. Cluster sampling
    E. Multistage sampling
6. **Nonprobability sampling**
   A. Convenience sampling
   B. Quota sampling
   C. Snowball sampling
7. **Sample size**
   A. Confidence interval
   B. Sampling error
8. **Reliability and Validity**

# SUMMARY

1. Survey research is gaining popularity in the social sciences. Such research allows experimenters to ask broad questions, such as "How do Americans view their mental health?"
2. An open-ended question is one in which respondents can respond in any way they wish. An example would be to ask someone, "What do you like best about college?"
3. A closed-ended question is one in which respondents are limited in their responses. A multiple-choice question is an example of a closed-ended question.
4. In developing questions for a survey it is important to be clear, avoid unwanted ambiguity, and ask questions in such a manner that the respondent is able to give the information that you need. It is especially important that you pretest the survey.
5. There are a number of methods for administering a survey. Four of the most common ways are

face-to-face interviews, mail surveys, telephone interviews, and Internet surveys.
6. The problem of generalizability is especially critical for survey research. To ensure that the results from a single group can be applied to other groups, sampling techniques are used. A broad distinction is made between probability sampling and nonprobability sampling. The more common forms of probability sampling are simple random sampling, systematic sampling, stratified random sampling, cluster sampling, and combining methods in a multistage format. Nonprobability sampling techniques include convenience sampling, quota sampling, and snowball sampling.
7. The sample size required is related to three factors: confidence level, variation in the population, and the desired precision (amount of error).

# REVIEW QUESTIONS

1. What is the purpose of survey research? Give an example.
2. What is the value of an open-ended question?
3. How might open-ended and closed-ended questions be combined?
4. Give an example of a semantic differential.
5. Why must surveys always be pretested?

6. What are the major ways of presenting questionnaires to respondents? What are the advantages of each?
7. Why is sampling important?
8. Describe the major forms of probability sampling.
9. When would nonprobability sampling be appropriate?
10. What are the three major factors in determining sample size?

# DISCUSSION QUESTIONS AND PROJECTS

1. Many students in experimental psychology classes are interested in how music affects their moods. Discuss how you might determine whether this is an interest mainly of people taking experimental psychology or of all college students.
2. Outline a way to determine how people believe music affects their moods.
3. What could you conclude about how music actually does influence mood from the research conducted in Question 2?
4. Why is sampling so important for surveys? Observe how political candidates or others use surveys and what types of sampling procedures they use.

5. How is it possible to know how millions of people will vote in a national election from speaking with only a few thousand? Why would it be no better to ask as many people as you could?
6. A university wants to know whether the student union should sell beer. How might you help them answer this question? What are some of the issues that would have to be considered from the standpoints of both the university and the students?

## InfoTrac College Edition: Exercises

*The Annual Review of Psychology* 1999 reviews the empirical literature concerning survey research ("Survey research" by Jon Kosnick). Reading this article in InfoTrac College Edition will give you great insights into the factors that influence how people respond to surveys. For example, research suggests that individuals would rather answer "yes" than "no" to an item in a survey.

## ☑ Answers to Concept Checks

13.1 Although it is possible that more women than men are depressed, it may also be the case that the numbers are the same. The actual finding was that more women than men seek help for depression, and thus it may be that the difference between men and women is in their help-seeking behavior rather than depression *per se*. One possible approach to answering the original question would be through the use of survey research that examined both help-seeking behavior and the incidence of depression in the population of interest.

13.2 A number of approaches could answer the question better. One of these would be to reword the questions to allow for a greater variety of responses. Rather than just *yes* or *no*, the person could answer *not at all, a little, some,* or *very much.* The question could also be asked in terms of a behavior, such as

1. Compared with other music you listen to, how much time do you listen to classical music?

| Never | A little | Some | A lot | All the time |
|:---:|:---:|:---:|:---:|:---:|
| (1) | (2) | (3) | (4) | (5) |

**13.3** Nothing can be concluded from this poll, other than that the people who called were opposed to the idea. Although many radio stations and newspapers use these types of polls, they are highly biased and not representative. Ask yourself which people in a town would be listening to this particular radio station, have access to a telephone during the time of the survey, and make the effort to call. At the least, you would probably be excluding most working people and most students from such polls.

**13.4** If the question is when this particular library should be open, then the data from all 500 students of the university is the right choice. If one wanted to generalize these results to all college students in the country, then a random sample would be required.

# ETHICS

In Chapter 10, we discussed the ecology of an experiment. We assumed the viewpoint of the witness and focused on two issues: the relevance of our research and research participant-scientist interactions. We pointed out that participant-scientist interactions are complex and that these interactions can influence our results in unexpected and sometimes even biased ways. Our concern with participant-scientist interactions focused on the validity of our scientific findings. We examined the participant-scientist psychological interaction, hoping that with a more complete understanding of this interaction, we could better understand some limitations of the process of experimentation when studying human behavior and experience. With a clearer understanding of this interaction, we hoped to point out potential confounds and ways to eliminate them so that we could eventually increase both the internal and the external validity of our conclusions.

In this chapter, we shift our focus. We again examine the participant-scientist relationship from the viewpoint of the witness, yet we do so from a new perspective. As we said previously, it is the task of the witness to observe and evaluate the nature of the interaction between the scientist and participant in the research. We shift our concern from how that relationship influences the scientific validity of our research to the important issue of human ethics. Remember, an experiment is just another form of human interaction. Consequently, the witness must also view participant-scientist interactions as if they were interactions between any two people. In making this shift of perspective, we move from the world of observation and theory to the world of human values; thus, we can no longer use the same criteria for making decisions as we did in the world of science. The new criteria are based on human values. Yet how do we make value judgments? On what criteria do we base our ethical behavior? The study of ethics offers us one answer to these questions.

*Ethics* is the study of proper action. Ethics examines relationships between human beings and provides principles regarding how we should treat each other. The ultimate decision in ethical questions resides in judgments of value. Most people have either explicitly or implicitly formulated principles that reflect their values and give direction to their actions. Some of these principles may be based on a religious tradition. One example of such a principle is the Golden Rule, which states that you should do unto others as you would have them do unto you. Other principles may have a philosophical basis, such as *Kant's imperative.* Immanuel Kant, an 18th-century philosopher, suggested that one should "act so as to treat humanity, either yourself or others, always as an end also and never as a means only." Although rules of action may be useful in the abstract, problems often arise when one begins to apply these principles to concrete situations. In this chapter we want to look at one particular concrete situation—the scientific experiment—and attempt to determine some guidelines for making ethical decisions within this context.

Before we begin, there are four points we need to make clear. First, we want to point out that the scientist has responsibilities to the world at large, which relies on the accuracy of the findings. Thus, the fraud cases we discussed in Chapter 10 would clearly be unethical. However, our emphasis in this chapter is on the experimental situation itself. Second, although most research scientists are concerned about ethics, actual ethical problems are minimal in most psychological experimentation. As we point out, there are exceptions to this, and it is the exceptions that require careful consideration. Third, ethical decisions are regulated somewhat in our society by the federal government and by professional societies, such as the American Psychological Association (APA). In this chapter we present some of their recommended

"WE'LL ONLY DO 72% OF IT, SINCE IT'S BEEN REPORTED THAT 28% OF ALL SURGERY IS UNNECESSARY."

guidelines and procedures. Fourth, although there are guidelines, there are no hard-and-fast rules for every situation. *Whether in the role of scientist or research participant, you as a human being ultimately must decide how you will act and then assume responsibility for that action.*

## ETHICAL CONSIDERATIONS OF PSYCHOLOGICAL EXPERIMENTATION

Ethical considerations of psychological experimentation have at their heart the idea that people participating in research should not be harmed or affected in a way that would result in a lower level of any aspect of human functioning. In addition, ethical considerations must point out the scientist's right to know and to seek answers to questions; that is, it would also be considered unethical to prevent a scientist from seeking knowledge without considering his or her rights. Thus, we begin with the rights of the scientist to know and to pursue knowledge and the rights of the participants to be protected from undue harm.

In most cases, the scientist has a question that he or she wants to ask and that the participant is willing to help answer. In some cases, the participants learn something about themselves or about psychology from the experience, and they are glad to have participated. In psychophysiological experiments, for example, participants often report that they enjoy seeing their brain activity (e.g., fMRI, EEG), heart activity (electrocardiogram, EKG) displayed, and they are willing to participate in research in exchange for these types of experiences. Other participants, like some travelers to a foreign country, enter the world of experimentation and leave it again without ever realizing the underlying structure of the place they have been. Although ignorant of the underlying structure, they still leave with the experience of the event and may be changed by it.

If these experiences were always pleasant and any changes in the participant always positive, participants would participate gladly in experiments and scientists would face few ethical questions. However, at times the scientist may want to answer a question that requires that the participant experience psychological or physiological discomfort. These situations raise a number of questions: What are the responsibilities of the scientist toward the participant? What are the rights of the participant? Are there guidelines for reconciling conflicts between the rights of the participants to pursue happiness and the rights of the scientist to pursue knowledge? What type of relationship or dialogue would be most productive for helping the scientist and participant to fulfill their needs and desires? These are the questions we approach in this chapter.

Before concluding this introductory discussion, we want to point out that if we are not careful, how we view those involved in research can depersonalize the human qualities of those involved in the scientific enterprise—both the participants and the scientists. Although both the participant and the scientist have particular roles to play in science, they are first and foremost human beings. In performing psychological research, it is imperative that we value this fact.

# THE RIGHTS OF THE SCIENTIST AND THE RESEARCH PARTICIPANT

In our society, people have the right to search for the things that are important to them. The Declaration of Independence includes a reference to the individual's right to "life, liberty, and the pursuit of happiness." We begin with the idea that people, whether they are scientists or participants, have the right to pursue the activities that are important to them. However, some activities may infringe on the rights of others. Such activities range from the extreme case of murder, which violates the victim's right to life, to less harmful types of activities, such as someone's creating noise outside your bedroom window or throwing a cream pie at you across the cafeteria. When a conflict develops between my rights and your rights, we are forced to find a means of arriving at a solution to the problem. The traditional solutions are those of ethics and law; that is, people seek to establish ethical principles to guide their behavior, and society may adopt these ethical guidelines in the form of legal sanctions.

What does all this have to do with psychological experimentation? This is exactly the problem. We do not understand completely the relationship between ethics and experimentation, nor do we agree on the manner in which involvement in a scientific experiment infringes on someone's personal rights. For example, one researcher collected data online (e.g., through Internet groups) by viewing habits of college students, faculty, and staff, especially in relation to pornographic material, without their knowledge (reported in the American Association for the Advancement of Science Professional Ethics Report, http://www.aaas.org/spp/dspp/sfrl/per/per.htm; look in archives for Summer, 1995, and the article by Fowler). Is this acceptable research? Is it ethical to gather information about another person without his or her knowledge?

Science itself can give us few answers to the question of ethical relationships because science has focused on observation and theory. Thus, we are forced to look outside science. In this book, we use the concept of the witness to help us gain this broad perspective. In this chapter, we imagine ourselves to be the witnesses and examine in more detail the ethical relationship between the scientist and the participant. To accomplish this goal, let us now examine some specific experimental situations and bring forth some of the possible ethical considerations that must be examined.

## THE EXPERIMENT AS AN ETHICAL PROBLEM

Let us begin with an extreme case of conflictual experimentation: the Nazi medical experiments during World War II. In several concentration camps, such as Ravensbrueck, Dachau, and Buchenwald, prisoners were injected with a virus or bacterium and then received drugs to determine the drugs' effectiveness against the injections. Although medical knowledge was gained from these experiments, the world as a witness judged the experiments to be unethical and criminal. During the trials of these scientist-physicians, held at Nuremberg, it was determined that they were guilty of war crimes; seven of them were later hanged, and eight received long prison sentences. As a result of these trials, a code of ethics for medical experimentation with human participants (called the Nuremberg Code) was adopted as a guideline for future research.

What was unethical about the experiments at the Nazi concentration camps was not that human beings were given a virus. Almost all of our current procedures of preventive medicine (the polio vaccine, for example) require that the procedure eventually be tested on human beings. These physicians were convicted of conducting experiments *without the consent of their participants.* One of the first principles of research is that the participants must consent to being part of an experiment. Furthermore, they must also be informed of the experiment's purpose and its potential risks. Thus, major ingredients that the witness looks for in the dialogue between the scientist and the research participant are *voluntary participation* and *informed consent.*

## INGREDIENTS OF THE INITIAL SCIENTIST-PARTICIPANT DIALOGUE

### ■ Voluntary Participation

In the initial dialogue between the scientist and the prospective participant, the scientist must ask the participant to be a part of the experiment. This is the principle of *voluntary participation.* Information released in 1995 by the U.S. Department of Energy suggested that this principle was not followed in this country in about four decades of radiation studies with approximately 1600 people, including mental patients and prisoners. One of the major questions raised was whether the people involved were aware of and consented to being part of an experiment rather than believing they were receiving medical treatment. Did these people agree to participation in the radiation research, and did they know they could leave the study at any time? In essence, the voluntary participation principle suggests that a person should participate in an experiment only by her or his own free choice. In addition, this principle states that a participant should be free to leave an experiment at any time, whether or not the experiment has been completed.

The concept of voluntary participation involves a number of issues. One issue has to do with what is meant by the term *voluntary.* For example, is it ethical to use prisoners in an experiment? That is, is it really possible for a captive audience to say *no* without fear of reprisal? One answer to this problem has been to reduce the participants' sentences as a reward for participation in the research. Yet it has been argued that if a prisoner agrees to be in an experiment because he or she is seeking a reduced sentence, then this agreement is made not with free will but rather under a form of duress. In the same vein, it has been argued that giving a college student extra credit (points toward the final grade) for participation in psychological experimentation is unethical.

As you think about this issue, you will become entangled in the question of whether anyone can ever make a free decision and, if so, under what circumstances. As you might have realized already, this question becomes even more complicated for someone interested in developmental psychology, which requires research with children, or for someone interested in psychopathology, which requires research with patients who are mentally impaired.

## ■ Informed Consent

Assuming for a moment that someone can agree freely to participate in research, the scientist in the initial dialogue should inform the prospective participant about what will be required of him or her during the study. The scientist must also inform the prospective participant about any potential harm that may come from participation. Thus, the prospective participant must be given complete information on which to base a decision. This is the principle of *informed consent.* As you can imagine, the principle of informed consent raises the issue of how much information about an experiment is enough.

Can you ever tell prospective participants enough so that they could fully understand the study? It has been suggested that *informed* consent may not be the same as *educated* consent and that participants can never really be given enough information. Additional problems are raised when the research involves some form of deception, as when a new drug is being tested against a placebo to determine its effectiveness. Although there are many problems being debated in relation to informed consent, the working procedure at this time is for the scientist to tell prospective participants, as fully as possible without jeopardizing the value of the experiment, what will be required of them and to inform them of any possible risks they might be taking by participating in the experiment.

From the principles of voluntary participation and informed consent, one can see that it is the initial task of the scientist to fully discuss the experimental procedure with prospective participants and to remind them that they are human beings who do not give away their rights just because they are taking part in a psychological experiment.

## The Rights of the Research Participant and the Responsibilities of the Experimenter

In our society, research participants have the same rights during an experiment that they have outside the experimental situation. One major one is the *right to privacy*. Most of us at first think of the right to privacy as the right to spend time by oneself or with others of one's choosing, without being disturbed. This is the external manifestation of the right to privacy. But there is also an internal or intrapersonal manifestation of this right (see Raebhausen & Brim, 1967). This is the right to have private thoughts or, as it is sometimes called, a *private personality*. This means that the thoughts and feelings of a participant should not be made public without the participant's consent. It also means that a conversation between a participant and a scientist should be considered a private event, not a public one.

But how can the scientist ever report her or his findings? There are two considerations that are part of the scientist's responsibility to the participant: *confidentiality* and *anonymity*. The principle of confidentiality requires that the scientist not release data of a personal nature to other scientists or groups without the participant's consent. The principle of anonymity requires that the personal identity of a given participant be kept separate from his or her data. The easiest way to accomplish this is to avoid requesting names in the first place; however, there are times when this may be impossible. Another alternative is to use code numbers that protect the identity of the participant and to destroy the list of participants' names once the data analysis has been completed.

## What Is Harmful to a Research Participant?

As stated earlier in this chapter, it is the right of a participant not to be harmed. In most psychological research, physical pain and harm present no problems, either because they are absent completely or because the participant is fully informed of the particular procedure that will be used, such as making a loud noise or placing the participant's hand in cold water to measure physiological responsiveness. However, the question of psychological harm presents a much larger issue, one that will continue to be debated for years to come. Is it harmful to show a participant something true but negative about himself? Is it harmful to create situations in which a participant feels negative emotions such as fear or anger? Is it harmful to make a participant feel like a failure in order to determine how this affects his or her performance? These are the types of questions that are being debated currently.

As a scientist, where do you go for help? There are two major sources: the American Psychological Association's guidelines on ethics and the institutional review board (IRB, also known as the human subjects committee or office of research compliance) in the institution in which you study or work. In addition, many specialty organizations have adopted guidelines for specific populations. For example, the Society for Research in Child Development has established ethical standards for research with children.

✓ **CONCEPT CHECK 14.1**    Professor Doolittle was running an experiment in which she examined undergraduates' attitudes toward drinking on campus. She very carefully designed the experiment so that her control and experimental groups were randomly selected and assigned. However, on the last day one of her participants said, "I don't feel comfortable in this situation. You are asking me to tell you the names of all my friends who drink. I wish to leave." Dr. Doolittle said, "You are my last participant and school is over tomorrow. Please don't leave until you finish the experiment; you only have a few more questions to go. And besides, you need the experimental credit for your grade." Is there an ethical problem with this response?

# ETHICAL GUIDELINES OF THE AMERICAN PSYCHOLOGICAL ASSOCIATION

Because it may be difficult to determine how to resolve conflicts between the scientist's right to know and the participant's right not to be harmed from participating in an experiment, the APA first developed in 1953 a set of guidelines to help scientists determine their responsibilities toward participants and the manner in which the scientist-participant dialogue should be conducted. These have been updated and are part of a larger set of ethical principles that were published in the December 1992 issue of the *American Psychologist*. The guidelines were developed by the APA after much consideration and many revisions by the members of the association. The detailed ethical guidelines, titled *Ethical Principles of Psychologists and Codes of Conduct*, may be ordered from the APA (750 First Street N.E., Washington, DC 20002-4242) or can be found on their Web site (http://www.apa.org/ethics/) along with other related information on ethics. Since new ethical guidelines are scheduled to appear in 2002 or 2003, you may wish to consult the APA Web site. We now present the ethical guidelines directly related to research.

**6.06 Planning Research**

    **A.** Psychologists design, conduct, and report research in accordance with recognized standards of scientific competence and ethical research.

    **B.** Psychologists plan their research so as to minimize the possibility that results will be misleading.

    **C.** In planning research, psychologists consider its ethical acceptability under the Ethics Code. If an ethical issue is unclear, psychologists seek to resolve the issue through consultation with institutional review boards, animal care and use committees, peer consultations, or other proper mechanisms.

    **D.** Psychologists take reasonable steps to implement appropriate protections for the rights and welfare of human participants, other persons affected by the research, and the welfare of animal subjects.

**6.07 Responsibility**

    **A.** Psychologists conduct research competently and with due concern for the dignity and welfare of the participants.

    **B.** Psychologists are responsible for the ethical conduct of research conducted by them or by others under their supervision or control.

    **C.** Researchers and assistants are permitted to perform only those tasks for which they are appropriately trained and prepared.

    **D.** As part of the process of development and implementation of research projects, psychologists consult those with expertise concerning any special population under investigation or most likely to be affected.

**6.08  Compliance with Law and Standards**

Psychologists plan and conduct research in a manner consistent with federal and state law and regulations, as well as professional standards governing the conduct of research, and particularly those standards governing research with human participants and animal subjects.

**6.09  Institutional Approval**

Psychologists obtain from host institutions or organizations appropriate approval prior to conducting research, and they provide accurate information about their research proposals. They conduct the research in accordance with the approved research protocol.

**6.10  Research Responsibilities**

Prior to conducting research (except research involving only anonymous surveys, naturalistic observations, or similar research), psychologists enter into an agreement with participants that clarifies the nature of the research and the responsibilities of each party.

**6.11  Informed Consent to Research**

A. Psychologists use language that is reasonably understandable to research participants in obtaining their appropriate informed consent (except as provided in Standard 6.12, Dispensing with Informed Consent). Such informed consent is appropriately documented.

B. Using language that is reasonably understandable to participants, psychologists inform participants of the nature of the research; they inform participants that they are free to participate or to decline to participate or to withdraw from the research; they explain the foreseeable consequences of declining or withdrawing; they inform participants of significant factors that may be expected to influence their willingness to participate (such as risks, discomfort, adverse effects, or limitations on confidentiality, except as provided in Standard 6.15, Deception in Research); and they explain other aspects about which the prospective participants inquire.

C. When psychologists conduct research with individuals such as students or subordinates, psychologists take special care to protect the prospective participants from adverse consequences of declining or withdrawing from participation.

D. When research participation is a course requirement or opportunity for extra credit, the prospective participant is given the choice of equitable alternative activities.

E. For persons who are legally incapable of giving informed consent, psychologists nevertheless (1) provide an appropriate explanation, (2) obtain the participant's assent, and (3) obtain appropriate permission from a legally authorized person, if such substitute consent is permitted by law.

**6.12  Dispensing with Informed Consent**

Before determining that planned research (such as research involving only anonymous questionnaires, naturalistic observations, or certain kinds of archival research) does not require the informed consent of research participants, psychologists consider applicable regulations and institutional review board requirements, and they consult with colleagues as appropriate.

**6.13  Informed Consent in Research Filming or Recording**

Psychologists obtain informed consent from research participants prior to filming or recording them in any form, unless the research involves simply naturalistic observations in public places and it is not anticipated that the recording will be used in a manner that could cause personal identification or harm.

**6.14  Offering Inducements for Research Participants**

A. In offering professional services as an inducement to obtain research participants, psychologists make clear the nature of the services, as well as the risks, obligations, and limitations. (See also Standard 1.18, Barter [With Patients or Clients].)

B. Psychologists do not offer excessive or inappropriate financial or other inducements to obtain research participants, particularly when it might tend to coerce participation.

**6.15  Deception in Research**

A. Psychologists do not conduct a study involving deception unless they have determined that the use of deceptive techniques is justified by the study's prospective scientific, educational, or applied value and that equally effective alternative procedures that do not use deception are not feasible.

B. Psychologists never deceive research participants about significant aspects that would affect their willingness to participate, such as physical risks, discomfort, or unpleasant emotional experiences.

C. Any other deception that is an integral feature of the design and conduct of an experiment must be explained to participants as early as is feasible, preferably at the conclusion of their participation, but no later than at the conclusion of the research. (See also Standard 6.18, Providing Participants with Information about the Study.)

**6.16  Sharing and Utilizing Data**
Psychologists inform research participants of their anticipated sharing or further use of personally identifiable research data and of the possibility of unanticipated future use.

**6.17  Minimizing Invasiveness**
In conducting research, psychologists interfere with the participants or milieu from which data are collected only in a manner that is warranted by an appropriate research design and that is consistent with psychologists' roles as scientific investigators.

**6.18  Providing Participants with Information about the Study**
A. Psychologists provide a prompt opportunity for participants to obtain appropriate information about the nature, results, and conclusions of the research, and psychologists attempt to correct any misconceptions that participants may have.

**6.19  Honoring Commitments**
Psychologists take reasonable measures to honor all commitments they have made to research participants.

As stated, these principles should not be considered laws that a scientist follows, thereby handing over the problems of ethics to the group that makes the laws. Rather, these principles may be considered *guidelines that should direct one's thinking when ethical matters are considered.* In fact, the principles (e.g., 6.07) emphasize that the responsibility of research is always with the individual scientist, and it is the scientist who must make decisions about how to respond to the ethical considerations of an experiment.

# INSTITUTIONAL REVIEW BOARD

The U.S. Department of Health and Human Services requires that each scientist whose institution receives federal funds must seek a review of the ethical considerations of research with human participants, whether or not there is a deviation from the APA guidelines. This type of review is required not only of psychological research but of any type of research with human participants. The committee that reviews the research is to be made up of people who work at the same university, hospital, school, or other institution with the scientist, and also members of the community where the institution is located.

The main task of the IRB is to determine whether the participants are adequately protected in terms of both welfare and rights. Box 14.1 illustrates the types of questions required by a typical IRB report. One major question that the committee asks is, "Are there any risks—physical, psychological, or social—associated with participating in a given piece of research?" Almost everything we do each day involves varying degrees of risk, so the committee attempts to determine when a risk is unreasonable.

## Box 14.1

# Typical Format for Institutional Review Boards

1. Provide a brief description of the proposed study (e.g., purpose, problem to be investigated).
2. What are the qualifications of the investigator(s) for conducting the study? (If students, who will be supervising the research?)
3. What are the requirements for and characteristics of the participants (e.g., gender, age range, health, medical or psychological status, prisoners, institutionalized, etc.)?
4. How will the participants in the research be sampled or recruited?
5. Describe the method of the study.
6. Describe the personnel, materials, equipment, or other resource requirements for your study.
7. Describe the procedure for obtaining informed consent from the participants (e.g., how and when the study will be explained to participants). How will participants indicate their consent?
8. What are the potential risks to the participants, and what is the likelihood and

seriousness of these risks? (Risks can be physical, psychological, social, etc. Risks may result from experimental procedures or methods of obtaining, handling, or reporting data.)
9. Will deception be used in the research? Why is it necessary?
10. Describe any alternative methods that would reduce or eliminate risks, and discuss why these were not used. If applicable, how and by whom was the electrical or mechanical equipment checked for safety?
11. What procedures are used to protect the confidentiality of a participant and his or her data?
12. How is the participant to be debriefed?
13. What are the potential benefits to the research participants or society of the proposed research?
14. List names and addresses of experts in the field with whom the IRB could discuss the risks involved in this research if necessary.

The committee also considers the potential long-term effects of a particular treatment on a person. For example, asking a participant to run a mile, to give a small sample of blood, to have his or her heart rate measured, or to discuss his or her sexual preference or childhood involves some risks in the way the term is used by most internal review committees. However, the committee may decide that, in light of the information that would be gained, these risks are not sufficient to prevent the study from being performed. Thus, a second major question that a review committee asks is, "Are the risks to the participants outweighed by the potential benefits to them or by the estimated importance to society of the knowledge to be gained?" If the committee determines that the answer to this question is *yes,* a third question is asked: "Has the experimenter allowed the prospective participants to determine freely whether they will participate in the experiment?" And finally, "Has the experimenter obtained the participants' informed consent?"

Although everyone agrees that it is imperative that the scientists involved protect research participants, it should be pointed out that a complete description of a study may actually eliminate the very phenomenon being studied. For example, in one study using a traditional verbal conditioning paradigm, Resnick and Schwartz (1973) found that giving the participants a complete description of the experiment resulted in the participants not demonstrating conditioning. These authors also reported that although the informed participants took part in the study, they did so in a more uncooperative manner. Another argument against fully informed consent is that of Loftus and Fries (1979), who argue that fully informed consent may be more harmful than helpful (Box 14.2).

One consequence of adopting a strict definition of informed consent is that it becomes almost impossible to perform research that involves deception (that is, research in which the participant is not told the complete purpose of an experiment). Let us now examine deception studies and some of the ethical questions involved.

# DECEPTION STUDIES

**Deception research** is any study in which the participant is deceived about the true purpose of the experiment or the experimental procedures. For example, if an experimenter wanted to examine the effects of anxiety on performance in college students, he or she might create an anxiety-provoking situation followed by a performance measure. One method used to create anxiety in college students is to administer a so-called IQ test that cannot be completed in the allotted time and to state that most college students who later go to graduate school have no trouble finishing this test.

Another type of deception often used in medical research is the placebo treatment. For example, participants are given a pill made up of sugar or other inactive ingredients and told that it will cause certain physiological changes such as reducing the number of headaches they have been experiencing. It should be noted that as participants have become more sophisticated concerning medical research, the current trend is to acknowledge the existence of a placebo control.

Because it is impossible to obtain informed consent in deception research, is it unethical to perform this research? This is not an easy question to answer, and the professionals in the field currently fall into two camps. The first group suggests that any deception is unethical, and thus no deception research is possible; the second group argues that certain types of deception research are necessary. The second group further argues that given appropriate safeguards, deception research is the only way to answer certain questions. We do not attempt to determine which group is ethically correct here, but we present some important questions raised by deception research and discuss the ways in which some of these questions have been answered. To do this, we present three deception studies in further detail.

## ■ Obedience-to-Authority Research

One of the classic deception research studies is Milgram's (1963, 1977) obedience-to-authority study. Using as a background such authority situations as the Old Testament story of God (the authority) commanding Abraham to kill his son and the situation of war, where one person (the authority) tells another to go out and kill the enemy, Milgram asked

## Box 14.2

# Informed Consent May Be Hazardous to Your Health

The following was an editorial in *Science,* the journal of the American Association for the Advancement of Science. In this editorial, the authors suggest that informed consent may actually harm the subject in some cases (Loftus & Fries, 1979). Read the editorial and see what you think.

Before human subjects are enrolled in experimental studies, a variety of preliminary rituals are now required. These include an explanation of the nature of the experimental procedure and a specific elaboration of possible adverse reactions. The subjects, in turn, can either withdraw from the experiment or give their "informed consent." These rituals are said to increase the subjects' understanding of the procedures but, perhaps more important, they came into existence because of a strong belief in the fundamental principle that human beings have the right to determine what will be done to their minds and bodies.

Some, on the other hand, consider that the purpose of informed consent is not protection of sub-

jects, but rather protection of investigators and sponsoring institutions from lawsuits based on the charge of subject deception should a misadventure result. But lawsuits arise in any case; subjects simply claim that they did not understand the rituals. It is reasonable, then, to ask whether the putative beneficiary, the subject, might be harmed rather than helped by the current informed consent procedure.

A considerable body of psychological evidence indicates that humans are highly suggestible. Information has been found to change people's attitudes, to change their moods and feelings, and even to make them believe they have experienced events that never in fact occurred. This alone would lead one to suspect that adverse reactions might result from information given during an informed consent discussion.

An examination of the medical evidence demonstrates that there is also a dark side to the placebo effect. Not only can positive therapeutic effects be achieved by suggestion, but

the question, "Under what conditions would one person (who is not the authority) obey an instruction to harm another, and how is this related to authority?"

To examine this question in a concrete situation, Milgram chose the setting of a psychological experiment. Milgram had argued in an earlier study that there was a difference in conformity between people from Norway and those from France. In his next study, he wanted to compare participants from Germany and the United States. He sought to determine whether participants would be willing to harm other participants on the authority of the experimenter. However, as you will see, Milgram stopped the study after running only the initial American studies.

The participants in this experiment were people who varied in age and occupation. The general procedure was to have a participant come into the laboratory for a *learning experiment.* The participant met the experimenter and another participant, who was really an associate of the experimenter. It was explained to the participant that little is known about the effects of punishment on memory and that in the experiment one participant would be the learner and one would be the teacher. A rigged drawing was held in which the associ-

negative side effects and complications can similarly result. For example, among those subjects who participated in a drug study after the usual informed consent procedure, many of those given an injection of a placebo reported physiologically unlikely symptoms such as dizziness, nausea, vomiting and even mental depression. One subject given the placebo reported that these effects were so strong that they caused an automobile accident. Many other studies provide similar data indicating that to a variable but often scarifying degree, explicit suggestion of possible adverse effects causes subjects to experience these effects. Recent hypotheses that heart attack may follow coronary spasms indicate physiological mechanisms by which explicit suggestions, and the stress that may be produced by them, might prove fatal. Thus, the possible consequences of suggested symptoms range from minor annoyance to, in extreme cases, death.

If protection of the subject is the reason for obtaining informed consent, the possibility of iatrogenic harm [harm brought on by diagnosis or suggestion] to the subject as a direct result of the consent ritual must be considered. This clear cost

must be weighed against the potential benefit of giving some people an increased sense of freedom of choice about the use of their bodies. The current legalistic devices, which are designed in part to limit subject recourse, intensify rather than solve a dilemma.

The features of informed consent procedures that do protect subjects should be retained. Experimental procedures should be reviewed by peers and public representatives. A statement to the subject describing the procedure and the general level of risk is reasonable. But detailed information should be reserved for those who request it. Specific slight risks, particularly those resulting from common procedures, should not be routinely disclosed to all subjects. And when a specific risk is disclosed, it should be discussed in the context of placebo effects in general, why they occur and how to guard against them. A growing literature indicates that just as knowledge of possible symptoms can cause those symptoms, so can knowledge of placebo effects be used to defend against those effects. A move in this direction may ensure that a subject will not be at greater risk from self-appointed guardians than from the experiment itself.

ate of the experimenter drew the role of learner and the participant drew the role of teacher. Following this, the learner was taken to another room and strapped into a chair with what appeared to be shock electrodes. The participant did not know that the electrodes were not connected.

The participant was told that it was his or her job to teach the learner a series of words and to administer a shock as punishment whenever the learner made a mistake. The participant was further instructed to increase the shock with each error made by moving a switch on the control box. Voltage levels were marked on the control box, and at the higher voltage levels there were labels such as "Danger: Severe Shock."

Once the experiment began, the learner started making mistakes. The participant, following the instructions of the experimenter, administered shocks. As the voltage levels were increased, the participant began to hear moans coming from the learner. With more increases in voltage, the learner cried out in pain and later refused to answer any more questions. The experimenter told the participant to treat any nonresponse as a wrong answer and to administer additional shocks. When the participant refused to administer additional shocks, the experiment was concluded. The voltage level reached on the shock machine was used as a measure of the participant's willingness to obey authority even in the face of pressure from the learner not to inflict pain.

As you might imagine, objections have been raised to this research. One of the first objections to Milgram's work concerned whether the participants were protected in the experiment. In particular, Baumrind (1964) refers to the Milgram study as a case in which the participants were not treated with respect but rather were manipulated and made to experience the discomfort of emotional disturbance. Milgram responded that he did not foresee the emotional distress experienced by the participants. He stated that colleagues and psychiatrists with whom he discussed the proposed experiment all expected that most participants would terminate the experiment at an early stage by refusing to give shocks once the learner began to complain. Milgram agreed that once a number of participants had been run he could have terminated the experiment; however, he decided that "momentary excitement is not the same as harm." Thus, Milgram chose to continue the experiment.

Once the experiment had been concluded, it would have been unethical to allow a participant to leave the experimental situation without a true understanding of what had taken place. The process of explaining the true purpose of the experiment afterward is called **debriefing.** In the debriefing procedure, the experimenter, in accord with the APA principles 6.15 and 6.18, removes any misconceptions and offers a full discussion of the experiment. Although the APA's ethical principles had not been fully developed when Milgram first ran his experiment, he appears to have followed its principles. First, the participants all were told the nature of the hoax and that the learner never received any electric shock. Second, each participant had a friendly reconciliation with the learner and an opportunity to discuss the experiment. Third, participants were assured that their behavior was normal and that the tension or emotion they felt was also felt by other participants.

After the entire study was completed, all the participants received a report of the experiment. According to Milgram, in this follow-up report the participants' behavior was treated in a dignified manner. As suggested by the APA principles, Milgram also conducted follow-up evaluations. Together with the report, all participants received a questionnaire that allowed them to express their thoughts and feelings about their participation in the experiment. In response to these questions, Milgram reports that 84 percent of the participants were glad to have participated in the experiment, 15 percent were neutral, and 1.3 percent expressed negative feelings about their participation. In addition, 80 percent of the participants believed that this type of research should be carried out, and 74 percent said they had learned something of personal importance from their participation. A psychiatrist interviewed selected participants to check for any negative long-term effects of the experiment; he found none.

Although some people have been critical of Milgram's work, it is important to note that people who knew Milgram speak of his deep concern for people and his integrity as a human being and scientist. In fact, some of his follow-up procedures were not required in his day. In many ways, his procedures have helped us to consider in some detail the ethical treatment of participants and to establish appropriate guidelines. Today, it is not easy to follow the APA principles when it comes to deception research because it requires as much, if not more, work to follow up the participants as it does to run the original experiment. However, when there is a possibility of psychological or physiological long-term harm, it is necessary that this type of follow-up be performed.

## ■ It's Not a Crime the Way I See It

When reading newspaper reports of the break-in at the Watergate building as told by the press and by the Nixon administration, some people felt they were hearing reports of two different events. West, Gunn, and Chernicky (1975) pointed out the manner in which the differing reports fit into current theory in social psychology. As suggested by the theory of Jones and Nisbett (1971), those involved in Watergate tended to focus on environmental determinants of behavior; for example, they claimed that the break-in was necessary because of the violent nature of the radical left. Members of the press were observers and tended to explain the break-in in terms of the characteristics of the participants.

Other events in history have also given rise to such conflicting interpretations, according to West and colleagues (1975). For example, those involved in Nazi war crimes claimed that they had to follow orders or they would have been shot. They emphasized situational factors, whereas those who judged these people for war crimes saw the problem in terms of the characteristics of the people involved. Likewise, in reading about the case of Kitty Genovese in Chapter 3, you may have thought to yourself, "Why didn't anyone help?" or "What was wrong with those people?" You, as an outside observer, were reacting to the characteristics of the people involved, whereas the people involved seem to have been reacting to the situational characteristics.

Although the three cases of Watergate, Nazi soldiers, and Kitty Genovese lend support to the theory of Jones and Nisbett, a scientist would still like to see the theory tested in a laboratory situation. West, Gunn, and Chernicky (1975) decided to do this. They reasoned that if situational factors were important variables in the Watergate crime, then a significant percentage of people would agree to break the law if the situational pressure were high. Likewise, others, when being told of the crime, would attribute the event to the person involved and not to the situation. These authors designed the following experiment.

In a field study, participants were invited to participate in an illegal burglary. To determine the role of situational variables, rationales for the burglary varied across groups. The first rationale stated that the crime was being sponsored by a government agency. The second rationale offered the participants in that group a large amount of money for committing the crime. The third rationale offered immunity from prosecution for committing the crime. The fourth rationale, which served as a control for compliance, offered no money or immunity from prosecution. This last group was used to give the researchers some indication of how often participants would agree to be part of a crime without any particular inducement. Thus, it was used to assess the *demand characteristics* of the experiment.

A second experiment was performed with another group of participants. Each participant was given a booklet describing in detail one of the four conditions from the field experiment. These participants were asked to estimate how many people out of 100 would agree to participate in the burglary as described in the booklet. They were also asked whether they would participate and were given the opportunity to describe some characteristics of a person who would or would not participate. Based on the theory of Jones and Nisbett (1971), it was predicted that those who participated in the field experiment would attribute their actions to the situational cues, whereas those in the second experiment would focus on the characteristics of the person who agreed or refused to take part in the crime.

Imagine yourself in the field study. You do not know you are part of a study. As you go about your business, you are approached by someone you believe to be a local private investigator. He says to you that he has a project you might be interested in and suggests that you meet him at his home or a local restaurant. When you meet the private investigator, he has another person with him. They discuss a plan to burglarize a local advertising firm. The break-in is explained to you in terms of one of the four rationales just presented.

Some professionals believed this study violated the APA ethical principles; Cook (1975) suggested that the ethical principles were violated in two major ways. First, the study had a potential for negative effects on participants who went beyond their personal moral standards. Second, because the study paralleled the Watergate scandal, it would receive wide publicity.

The authors of the study responded to these concerns. Cook pointed out, and the authors agreed, that the participants should leave the experiment feeling that they had helped to gain new knowledge and that the experimenters were concerned for the welfare of the participants at all times. The authors described the procedures they included to protect the participants. First, the field study was carried out so that the participants could not leave the experiment feeling that they had become involved in an illegal activity. The participants in the study were debriefed about the real nature of the meeting and the concerns of the experimenters over having used deception. Second, the experimental meeting was not forced on any participant but took place only after an initial agreement to meet at another location. Third, alternative experimental procedures that did not involve deception were considered and rejected. For example, a study in which people role-played the situation might have been used. However, because the study was to determine the difference between observing and actually participating in the situation, such alternative designs were considered unsuitable. Fourth, a lawyer-psychologist served as a consultant during the planning and implementing of the field study to protect the rights of the participants and the experimenters. Also, the state attorney's office found the procedure to be legally acceptable. If you are interested in the actual results, you may look up Cook's article in the library (Cook, 1975).

## ■ Bypassing the Bypass

Let us examine one other study that required deception. It raised a number of interesting issues, particularly the question of when the information gained is important enough to violate normal ethical standards. This particular study deals with medical research to determine the effectiveness of a heart operation for the treatment of angina (Cobb, Thomas, Dillard, Merendino, & Bruce, 1959). However, the same questions raised by this study are also applicable to studies dealing with evaluating new techniques in psychotherapy, biofeedback, behavioral medicine, and other fields. This study was reported in 1959; with the adoption of human participant review committees, such a study probably would not be permitted today. However, you must decide for yourself whether this is an important study.

In the study, 17 patients with angina pectoris (pains in the chest) attributed to coronary artery disease were invited to participate in an experimental evaluation of an operation to relieve the angina. The patients knew that they were part of an experimental evaluation of the operation, but they did not know the nature of the evaluation. Furthermore, most patients knew from the popular press that the operation was considered to be a new and exciting treatment for angina. It should also be pointed out that the angina was severe enough to limit the activities of the patients, with the majority of them reported to be unable to work.

Once the patient was in the operating room and the anesthesia had been given, the surgeon opened an envelope that told him to which experimental group the patient belonged. For half the patients, the operation was carried out as usual; that is, there was a ligation of the internal mammary artery. For the other half of the patients, the chest was cut open and the artery of the heart was found, as in the normal procedure, but the artery was not cut and tied in the usual manner. Rather, the cardiac system was left untouched and the patient's chest closed. Both groups of patients were cared for normally, without the attending physician knowing to which group each belonged. Would you consider this experiment a violation of ethics?

Most people would consider it unethical to operate on another human being without his or her consent about the nature of the operation. Before you decide, let us look at the results of the study. During the first 6 months following the operation, the same number of patients in both the experimental (ligation) and the control (incision only) groups showed "significant participative improvement." Just opening and closing the chest was shown to be associated with the same improvement rate as actually performing the operation. Positive changes were also noted in EKG evaluations. For example, one patient, who before the operation showed irregular heart wave patterns on an EKG during exercise, showed no irregularities after the operation. Surprising as it may seem, this patient was in the control group.

We are now faced with some difficult questions. For example, how can we go about testing the value of new therapeutic procedures, whether they be surgical or psychotherapeutic, without violating the rights of the participant? Are there times when we might consider it ethical to deceive a participant so that knowledge about a procedure might be gained? That is, are there times in which the savings in patient distress and economic resources justify less than full disclosure? Should the patients in the control group have been debriefed if they were reporting a significant improvement in their symptoms?

A current debate centers around placebo treatments. One side suggests it is unethical to give a person a placebo when that means withholding active treatments for his or her disorder. The other side suggests that placebos offer an important method for testing new treatments. This debate and its ethical implications has been covered in such journals as *Science* (cf., Enserink, 1999, 2000). What complicates this debate even more are the reports that placebos result in psychological and physiological changes as measured by objective methods such as brain imaging and psychopharmacological assays and may be reversed once the participant is told that they were part of the placebo group. What do you think about this type of research in general?

## DEBRIEFING: WHEN IS ENOUGH ENOUGH?

Whether or not deception is used in an experiment, the experiment does not end without completing the dialogue between the scientist and the participant begun at the start of the experiment. Some researchers call this concluding dialogue *debriefing*. It is the goal of this dialogue to ensure that participants leave the laboratory with at least as much self-esteem and as little anxiety as when they came to the experiment (Kelman, 1968). The debriefing process consists of two major aspects. First, the debriefing is an opportunity for the participants to tell the experimenter how they felt about being part of the experiment. This not only is good feedback for the experimenter but also allows the participants to express any self-doubt about their performance and deal with thoughts and feelings that arose during the experiment. Second, the debriefing is an opportunity for the experimenter to explain the study to the participants in greater detail.

It often is difficult for the experimenter to determine how much information should be conveyed to the participants. For example, the design of the study might be too complex to describe in detail. When children are used as participants, it might be difficult to convey to the child what was being asked, and the experimenter might rely on the parents to help with this task. In the case of deception research, Carlsmith, Ellsworth, and Aronson (1976) suggest that just telling the truth is not enough and may even be more harmful than no explanation at all. These authors suggest that the experimenter include a discussion of why the deception was necessary and that the experimenter express regret for using deception. Furthermore, they suggest that the experimenter explain that the experiment was designed to deceive anyone and that it is normal to feel foolish or silly after being taken in by a deception. These authors also suggest that the participants be given the opportunity to develop and express their own reactions to deception research in general and to the present experiment in particular.

# THE PARTICIPANT AS COLLEAGUE

Throughout our discussion of ethics we have suggested that the experimenter value the participants and respect their rights. A useful metaphor is to consider the participant as a colleague, as someone who helps with the experiment. As with any colleague, you as a scientist would discuss with the participant what you were interested in doing and the manner in which you would go about doing it. Once the experiment was completed, you would discuss with your colleague-participant the results of the study. This not only would allow the participant to learn more about the experimentation but would also allow you as a scientist to understand the participant's *experience* of the experiment and thus aid in your interpretation of the results.

This model could also be used in performing deception research, although with more difficulty. For example, if one were using college students in a deception study, Campbell suggests that the students might be told at the beginning of the term that some of the research being performed that term involved some deception. The general nature of the whys and hows of deception studies could be discussed at this time, and the potential participant could be allowed to see the importance of this type of research, whether it be of the placebo type or more direct deception. Those who did not want to participate in a deception study could ask to be excluded from studies of that type.

In summary, participants should be treated as one treats a colleague, as someone who is valued and respected for the information he or she can offer. If you use this approach, many ethical questions of psychological research will remain in the background and arise only in rare and special circumstances.

| ✓ | CONCEPT CHECK 14.2 | A student was conducting an EEG study in which he noticed that the participant's brain activity on one side looked different from that on the other. At the end of the experiment, he said to the participant, "I think you should see a physician because your EEG looks funny to me." Are there any problems with this experimenter's attempt to help the participant? |

# ANIMALS AS SUBJECTS

One of the more difficult issues on which to achieve consensus is the use of animals in experimental research. Much of what you learned in your introductory psychology course, especially in the areas of physiology and health, stress, and coping, may have come from animal research (cf. Domjan & Purdy, 1995). Of course, human beings are also by definition animals, but in this section we use the word *animal* to refer to nonhuman animals. The debate over animal experimentation is broad-based and requires that we examine our fundamental assumptions about the nature of animal life. There are many extreme positions in this debate. Some people question whether it is ever ethical for us to use animals for experiments.

It has been argued that the ethical issues go beyond pain and suffering to that of control. This position has led some to suggest that animals should be able to run wild and that leash laws are a form of slavery. Do you consider it ethical to have a pet? As you think about this question, you might think of the strongest cases for using animals. For example, do we want to use dogs as aids for blind people?

Concerning the use of animals in research, it is clear that there are a number of emotional and polarized positions. The February 1997 issue of *Scientific American* offers a series of articles relating to animal research that illustrate well the opposing positions. For example, one position suggests that information learned from animal research is often redundant and unnecessary and may be misleading (Barnard & Kaufman, 1997; see the  paper at http://www.sciam.com/0297issue/0297barnard.html). On the other hand, other researchers suggest that at least since the time of Pasteur, animal research has offered important breakthroughs in the treatment of disease for both humans and animals (Botting & Morrison, 1997; see the paper at http://www.sciam.com/0297issue/0297botting.html).

In psychological research, one position suggests that our goal should be to eliminate all animal research because animals are exposed to pain and suffering in the form of shock, stress, heat, cold, withdrawal of food, and even mutilation. Of course, it is not routine to subject animals to pain and suffering in research. Those who support it point out that animal research is crucial to meet the goals of society and, if anything, we should be increasing, not decreasing, animal research. One propaganda poster points out that animal research has added 20 years (through medical research) to the lives of the people who protest against it. This debate reminds us of the role of values in shaping our position on this topic.

Of course, there is no one right answer for all situations. We seek to present you with some of the basic questions and considerations that must be pondered with regard to animal research. In this way we hope to help you become an informed consumer, able to consider and evaluate the extreme positions you hear, both pro and con, concerning the question of animal experimentation.

Various fields of the behavioral sciences perform research with animals. These include learning, psychopathology, behavioral genetics, neurosciences, and health psychology. It is partly our concern for animals that has led us to perform animal research, so that we can understand other species, and in turn ourselves. We have gained valuable information on the manner in which bats navigate through dark spaces with echolocation, the manner in which animals communicate with one another, and the social systems within given species. We have used animals to understand how patterns of infant development lead to later emotional or addictive patterns and how diets rich in fats lead to atherosclerosis in animals who live in unstable environments.

Although it has been estimated that animal research represents less than 10 percent of total psychological research, some areas such as biological psychology have a larger percentage. Kalat (1992) suggests there are five reasons for studying animals in biological psychology. First, we are interested in animals for their own sake. For example, the naturalistic observation studies of Lorenz, as well as many bird and insect ethological studies, were designed to learn about a particular species of animal for its own sake. Veterinary research, like human medical research, has benefited pets, farm animals, and wildlife. Second, what we learn about animals sheds light on human evolution. Recent fieldwork with finches in the Galápagos Islands has helped to clarify Darwin's original theories of evolution (Weiner, 1994). Third, a certain process may be highlighted or exaggerated in animals and therefore easier to notice than it is in humans. For example, pigs have a cardiovascular system similar to that of humans and have been used in health psychology research. Thus, animal models of disease processes have led to real progress in such areas as the development and treatment of heart disease. Also, many insects have a short reproductive cycle that allows the study of genetics. Fourth, the underlying mechanisms of behavior are similar across species and sometimes are easier to study in a nonhuman species. For example, mechanisms such as nerve cell membranes, synapses in insects, and operant conditioning processes are similar in humans and various animals. And fifth, certain experiments are impossible with humans because of legal or ethical restrictions. One of the major reasons for conducting such research is the ability to gain experimental control over the situation. For example, with animals it is possible to regulate exactly such factors as diet, sleep patterns, housing situations, and exercise, which would be difficult or impossible with humans. Also, certain types of animals are more susceptible to diseases such as cancer or hypertension and thus offer a way of determining which factors slow down or speed up the onset of the disorder.

Overall, it is this last category that brings forth the real concerns with animal research. The question asks whether it is acceptable to use animals in research that would not be acceptable using humans. Gray (1990) maintains that one answer to this question is to distinguish between ethical and moral issues. If it is an ethical principle not to inflict pain unnecessarily, then it is unethical to inflict pain unnecessarily regardless of the species. It would not matter ethically whether it is a human being, a cat, or a cockroach. However, the moral choice may place us in opposition to the ethical principle.

For example, if there were two children in a burning house, their mother might discover that she could save only one at a time and thus risk pain to and loss of the second. She would be forced to make a moral decision. Gray likens this example to the situation of animal research: If certain experiments are not carried out, then people who might have benefited from the knowledge gained through those experiments may be forced to endure suffering or pain that could have been avoided. Although the clearest examples are in medical research, examples in psychological research also exist.

Gray argued that in the end we, like the mother who saves her own son or daughter, will perform research that saves our own species. However, at some point the amount of suffering inflicted on animals may not represent a reasonable balance with the avoidance of human pain and suffering, and thus it may not be morally defensible. The extreme cases are easy, but the real conflict arises when one is unsure whether an experiment will indeed lead to a cure and thus less suffering. These are difficult situations for scientists and for internal review committees.

The bond between humans and animals is of long standing. Historical records suggest animals have been kept as pets and used for herding sheep, plowing fields, and transportation for thousands of years. To protect their welfare, various organizations have been formed over the years, including the Society for the Prevention of Cruelty to Animals (SPCA), formed in England in 1824 and in the United States in 1866. (Child abuse cases in the 19th century were brought to court under the laws against cruelty to animals because there were no similar laws for children.)

Greek physician Galen, who lived in the second century A.D., is credited with the first documented use of living animals for research. Galen was able to demonstrate that arteries contain blood and not air. Until the 18th century, there was little if any ethical concern about animal research. However, by the 19th century, groups were formed in England to abolish painful animal research. Near the end of the 19th century, a committee of the British Association for the Advancement of Science presented a set of guidelines that contained four major points. First, medical experiments should be performed under anesthesia when appropriate. Second, a painful experiment is not justified if it merely demonstrates a fact already known. Third, if pain is involved, the research should be performed by skilled researchers with sufficient instrumentation in a properly regulated laboratory. Fourth, veterinary operations should not be performed only for the purpose of becoming more proficient at the operation.

Presented in 1871, these four principles formed the basis of many of the ethical considerations that were to be debated throughout Europe during the latter part of the 19th century and into the 20th century. In a paradox of history, it was under Hitler's government that federal laws pertaining to the protection of animals, especially as related to tormenting or rude treatment, were established in Germany in 1934. This history, along with a contemporary discussion of ethical approaches to animal research worldwide, has been published by Phillips and Sechzer (1989). We have drawn on this scholarly presentation for part of our discussion.

In the United States, contemporary regulation began with the publication of the *Guide for Laboratory Facility and Care* by the federal government in 1962. In 1966, the Animal Welfare Act was enacted. The Public Health Service issued regulations in 1985, which were revised in 1986 and again in 1996 (see Box 14.3). Phillips and Sechzer maintain that, as a nation, our view of animal research changed during the two decades between the 1966 regulations and the 1985/1986 regulations, with both scientists and laypeople becoming more concerned about animal experimentation. For a discussion of how one large research institution, Harvard, balances the tension between animal research and animal care, see Lauerman (1999).

An important consideration has been the use of research to help us scientifically understand animals and thus make more informed ethical decisions about them. For example, Dawkins (1990), in the journal *Behavioral and Brain Sciences,* asks how we can study animal welfare empirically. She suggests that in order to answer this question, we need an objective basis for deciding when an animal is suffering. To answer this question, Dawkins suggests that we need to direct our attention to the inner experience of animals. This is an important challenge for behavioral scientists because at present the only good way we have to gain access into the experiential world of animals is through behavioral research. For example, animals can be trained to respond differentially according to their subjective experience of a drug. Because an animal can make choices, we can begin such a dialogue, albeit in a limited way. Although we are far from having a simple answer to this question, the empirical approach of Dawkins and others offers an important start.

The ethical guidelines of the APA described earlier include a section on the care and use of animals. This version was published in the December 1992 issue of the *American Psychologist* and is presented here. An expanded version can also be found on APA Web site (http://www.apa.org/science/anguide.html).

## Box 14.3

## Public Health Service Principles for the Care and Use of Animals

The issue of animal research has raised a number of questions over the past couple of decades. A 1997 essay in *Scientific American* suggests that concern for animals has greatly changed the manner in which animals are treated in research and has resulted in an overall drop in animal research over the past 20 years (Mukerjee, 1997; see the complete article at http://www.sciam.com/0297issue/0297 trends.html). In order to protect animals from undue suffering or harm, a number of professional organizations have issued guidelines concerning the care and use of laboratory animals, which are described in the text. In this box we describe the federal guidelines issued by the Public Health Service in 1985 and updated in 1996. In this policy statement, the Public Health Service describes the manner in which animals are to be used and cared for. Further information about the policy can be obtained from the Office for Protection from Research Risks, National Institutes of Health, 6100 Executive Boulevard, MSC 7507, Rockville, MD 20892-7507.

### Principles for the Care and Use of Animals Used in Testing, Research, and Training

The principles below were prepared by the Interagency Research Animal Committee. This committee, which was established in 1983, serves as a focal point for federal agencies' discussions of issues involving all animal species needed for biomedical research and testing. The committee's principal concerns are the conservation, use, care, and welfare of research animals. Its responsibilities include information exchange, program coordination, and contributions to policy development.

### U.S. Government Principles for the Utilization and Care of Vertebrate Animals Used in Testing, Research, and Training

The development of knowledge necessary for the improvement of the health and well-being of humans as well as other animals requires in vivo experimentation with a wide variety of animal species. Whenever U.S. Government agencies develop requirements for testing, research, or training procedures involving the use of vertebrate animals, the following principles shall be considered; and whenever these agencies actually perform or sponsor such procedures, the responsible Institutional Official shall ensure that these principles are adhered to:

**I.** The transportation, care, and use of animals should be in accordance with the Animal Welfare Act (7 U.S.C. 2131 et seq.) and other applicable Federal laws, guidelines, and policies.[1]

6.21 **Care and Use of Animals in Research**

A. Psychologists who conduct research involving animals treat them humanely.

B. Psychologists acquire, care for, use, and dispose of animals in compliance with current federal, state, and local laws and regulations, and with professional standards.

C. Psychologists trained in research methods and experienced in the care of laboratory animals supervise all procedures involving animals and are responsible for ensuring appropriate consideration of their comfort, health, and humane treatment.

D. Psychologists ensure that all individuals using animals under their super-

**II.** Procedures involving animals should be designed and performed with due consideration of their relevance to human or animal health, the advancement of knowledge, or the good of society.

**III.** The animals selected for a procedure should be of an appropriate species and quality and the minimum number required to obtain valid results. Methods such as mathematical models, computer simulation, and in vitro biological systems should be considered.

**IV.** Proper use of animals, including the avoidance or minimization of discomfort, distress, and pain when consistent with sound scientific practices, is imperative. Unless the contrary is established, investigators should consider that procedures that cause pain or distress in human beings may cause pain or distress in other animals.

**V.** Procedures with animals that may cause more than momentary or slight pain or distress should be performed with appropriate sedation, analgesia, or anesthesia. Surgical or other painful procedures should not be performed on unanesthetized animals paralyzed by chemical agents.

**VI.** Animals that would otherwise suffer severe or chronic pain or distress that cannot be relieved should be painlessly killed at the end of the procedure or, if appropriate, during the procedure.

**VII.** The living conditions of animals should be appropriate for their species and contribute to their health and comfort. Normally, the housing, feeding, and care of all animals used for biomedical purposes must be directed by a veterinarian or other scientist trained and experienced in the proper care, handling, and use of the species being maintained or studied. In any case, veterinary care shall be provided as indicated.

**VIII.** Investigators and other personnel shall be appropriately qualified and experienced for conducting procedures on living animals. Adequate arrangements shall be made for their in-service training, including the proper and humane care and use of laboratory animals.

**IX.** Where exceptions are required in relation to the provisions of these Principles, the decisions should not rest with the investigators directly concerned but should be made, with due regard to Principle II, by an appropriate review group such as an institutional animal care and use committee. Such exceptions should not be made solely for the purposes of teaching or demonstration.

---

[1]For guidance throughout these principles, the reader is referred to the *Guide for the Care and Use of Laboratory Animals* prepared by the Institute of Laboratory Animal Resources, National Academy of Sciences.

vision have received instruction in research methods and in the care, maintenance, and handling of the species being used, to the extent appropriate to their role.

**E.** Responsibilities and activities of individuals assisting in a research project are consistent with their respective competencies.

**F.** Psychologists make reasonable efforts to minimize the discomfort, infection, illness, and pain of animal subjects.

**G.** A procedure subjecting animals to pain, stress, or privation is used only when an alternative procedure is unavailable and the goal is justified by its prospective scientific, educational, or applied value.

**H.** Surgical procedures are performed under appropriate anesthesia; techniques to avoid infection and minimize pain are followed during and after surgery.

**I.** When it is appropriate that the animal's life be terminated, it is done rapidly, with an effort to minimize pain, and in accordance with accepted procedures.

The APA has further described the manner in which they consider animal research essential for its contribution to psychological science. This overview can be found at their Web site (http://www.apa.org/science/animal2.html). The American Association for the Advancement of Science (AAAS), which publishes the journal *Science,* has also considered the question of animal research, which they considered "to be essential not only in applied and clinical research, but also in research that furthers the understanding of biological processes." Further discussions by the AAAS on the use of animals in research, testing, and education can be accessed on the AAAS Web page (http://www.aaas.org) in the section "Scientific Freedom, Responsibility, and Law." Finally, just as there are IRBs for human participants in research, there are also institutional animal care and use committees (IACUC) for examining the care and use of animals in research.

As we conclude our considerations, let us remind ourselves that ethical questions have at their base issues of relationships and traditions. As scientists, we ask what *is* and what *ought to be* our relationship with our participants and our society with regard to research. To answer this question, we stress that part of our ethical responsibility is to consult with others about our research. In this context, we described the manner in which the ethics of research is evaluated by internal review committees and the guidelines (e.g., those of the APA and the federal government) used to direct our evaluations. With both humans and animals, we are only beginning to develop methods for the study of inner experience that can help inform our ethical considerations.

---

**☑ CONCEPT CHECK 14.3**    Jim does not believe that animals should be used in experiments. To make his point, he goes into one of the animal labs and modifies the equipment to make the experiment give false results. If he really believes in his values, is what he did unethical?

---

# KEY TERMS AND CONCEPTS

1. **Ethical considerations in research**
2. **Participants' rights**
   **A.** Voluntary participation
   **B.** Informed consent
   **C.** Right to privacy
      ▪ Confidentiality
      ▪ Anonymity
3. **Scientists' rights**
4. **Guidelines of the American Psychological Association**

5. **Use of deception in research**
   **A.** Milgram
   **B.** West et al.
   **C.** Cobb et al.
6. **Debriefing**
7. **The participant as colleague**
8. **Animals as subjects**
   **A.** APA ethical principles
   **B.** Ethical versus moral questions

# SUMMARY

1. Although the purpose of research is to gain understanding and knowledge, the search for knowledge takes place in the context of an interaction between the scientist and the participant. This being the case, it is necessary to ask what the obligations of the scientist and the participant are toward each other. This leads to a study of proper action and values: the study of ethics.

2. Three important points were presented. First, although actual ethical problems are minimal in most psychological experiments, there are exceptions that require careful consideration. Second, ethical considerations are partly regulated both by federal agencies and by professional societies such as the APA. Third, whether you are a participant or a scientist, you must decide how you will act and assume responsibility for that action.

3. Ethical consideration of psychological experimentation has at its heart the idea that a person participating in psychological research should not be harmed or negatively affected in a way that would result in a lower level of any aspect of human functioning.

4. Two ways in which participants' rights are ensured are through the principles of voluntary participation and informed consent. The principle of voluntary participation requires that the participant not be coerced into taking part in an experiment and that the participant be able to leave at any time during the experi-

ment. The principle of informed consent requires that the participant be informed about what is to take place in an experiment and about any potential harm, either physical or psychological, that may result from participation in the research.

5. The principle of privacy requires the scientist to maintain the participant's anonymity and to not release any personal information about a particular participant without that person's consent.

6. Questions of an ethical nature arise mainly from research that involves deception. Examples of these studies, such as the Milgram obedience study, point out the problems and promises of such research.

7. In all research except certain deception research, debriefing is a necessary component. In a debriefing session, participants are told about any deception that occurred as well as the importance of their participation in the research.

8. A recommended attitude to adopt as a researcher is to treat participants as colleagues who are there to help give valuable information about important psychological processes.

9. The use of nonhuman animals in research requires similar considerations as with human participants. To help with these considerations, the federal government and the APA have developed guidelines for the care and use of animals in research.

# REVIEW QUESTIONS

1. What are the rights of the scientist and the participant in an experiment?

2. Why are the medical experiments conducted by the Nazis during World War II considered unethical?

3. What do you see as the difference between informed and educated consent?

4. What are the main themes of the APA guidelines on ethics?

5. What is an internal review committee?

6. What are the pros and cons of deception research?

7. What is debriefing, and why is it important?

8. In the final analysis, who is responsible for ethical concerns in an experiment?

# DISCUSSION QUESTIONS AND PROJECTS

1. Discuss the participant's rights and the scientist's rights in performing research.

2. In performing an experiment that uses heart rate as a measure, you notice that the record of one of the participants looks different from every other one you have seen. Although the person told you at the beginning of

the experiment that his heart was normal, you think there might be a medical problem. What should you do about your concern?

3. Discuss the ethics of the heart surgery study presented in this chapter. What are the benefits and problems with such research? You could also look

*(continued)*

## DISCUSSION QUESTIONS AND PROJECTS *(continued)*

in your library for the research published in 1992 and 1993 on the effectiveness of the heart bypass operation. Does knowing the effectiveness of the operation 25 years later make the earlier research more or less ethical?

4. One study not discussed in this chapter that has raised some ethical questions is the prison experiment conducted by Zimbardo in the 1970s (Zimbardo, Haney, Banks, & Jaffe, 1975). In this study, students were assigned the role either of guard or of prisoner for a week. Before the experiment could be completed, it was stopped because the guards were beginning to treat the prisoners in a cruel manner and prisoners began to obey the guards in what has been called a demeaning manner. Before the experiment began, it is unlikely that any of the students would have predicted they would act as they did. Discuss the ethics of conducting this research and what safeguards should be required. In what ways could it be considered unethical to show someone something true but unpleasant about himself or herself? What harm could have been done by this study?

5. Are there times when deception research might be useful, or should it be banned altogether?

6. What ethical considerations would one need to consider in using children as research participants?

7. How might you design a study to allow animals to choose the type of housing (e.g., individual versus group) that they preferred? What ethical objections might there be to performing this research?

### InfoTrac College Edition: Exercises

InfoTrac College Edition can be used to learn more about research ethics. If you enter "research ethics" into the search, you will see a variety of articles in both the popular press and in scientific journals. One advantage of such an approach is that you can learn about how ethical concerns are being addressed in other fields and in other countries. For example, you can read about the problems faced by the Institution Review Boards in Britain in an article entitled "Meeting the challenges facing research ethics committees: Some practical suggestions," which was published in the January 1998 issue of the *British Medical Journal.*

### ☑ Answers to Concept Checks

**14.1** There are ethical problems with both the response and the situation. One aspect of an experiment is that participants have the right to object to or withdraw from any procedure in which they do not want to engage. Voluntary participation requires that a participant be able to leave at any time during an experiment. Many people would consider it unethical to require that a person's participation in an experiment be a required part of the grade for a course. That is, the participant must have an alternative to the experimental situation for participation to be voluntary.

**14.2** Yes, there are a number of problems with the student's sharing his reaction with the participant. Because the student was not a neurologist or someone trained to diagnose abnormal brain activity, his conclusion that the EEG was abnormal may have been false. Thus, he may have created undue concern in the participant without just cause. In fact, the problem may have come from bad equipment or laboratory procedure and be unrelated to the participant. If it were determined that the record was accurate, a better procedure would be to take the record anonymously to a qualified specialist, who in turn could make an informed decision. Because many participants accept an experiment's conclusions as true, it is necessary to be especially careful not to make evaluations of participants' responses that are unrelated to the experiment.

**14.3** Of course it is unethical (and in some cases illegal) to falsify data. Science requires that experiments be run honestly and data collected accurately. If one does not believe in using animals in experiments, there are a number of places for making this point, including the review board of one's institution.

# SHARING THE RESULTS

In the preceding chapters, we traced the unfolding of an experiment from its initial conception through the analysis of the results. Once the final outcome is known, we can integrate these new facts into our understanding of the phenomenon we are studying, and in this way we slowly expand our understanding of the world. One important responsibility of the scientist in this process is to communicate new facts to other scientists and, equally important, to nonscientists. In this way, we not only expand our own understanding but also share our findings with others so that they, too, may integrate our new findings into their understanding of the world. The idea that science is a shared activity is by no means new. More than 2000 years ago, Aristotle emphasized that science has two parts: *inquiry* and *argument. Inquiry* for us includes the actual experiments or observations that generate the new facts. *Argument* includes our responsibility to communicate our findings in oral or written form.

The particular manner in which we choose to communicate our findings is directed by the audience with whom we want to communicate. In psychology, there are generally two types of audiences to whom we direct our communication. In the majority of instances, we are addressing other scientists who are studying related phenomena and might be interested in our findings. The availability of our findings to other scientists helps them to consider new questions and replicate our results in their own labs. As scientists from around the world experience similar findings, the pervasiveness of a phenomenon becomes apparent. With such an understanding, scientists can move on to studying a new aspect of the phenomenon.

In addition to making our findings available to other researchers, we have a responsibility to convey to nonscientists the essential direction of our findings and their ethical and moral implications. This second responsibility is particularly relevant to psychologists, whose findings may have direct bearing on how we relate to one another, interact with our children, and understand ourselves. In this chapter, we describe how scientists communicate with each other by describing how a formal scientific paper is written.

## COMMUNICATION WITH OTHER SCIENTISTS: THE SCIENTIFIC ARTICLE

There are many ways we can share our findings with other scientists. In some cases, new facts are shared in informal conversations with colleagues over a drink at the local coffee house or bar. In other cases, new material is presented orally at scientific meetings, or perhaps an entire book is written describing a lengthy series of experiments. In most cases, however, formal communication between scientists takes the form of published journal articles. We now describe the process of writing a scientific article and the steps by which an article is accepted for publication and published.

## PREPARING YOUR ARTICLE

In simple terms, a scientific article is the story of an experiment. It begins with a description of what is already known about the particular phenomenon being studied and a clear statement of the purpose of the experiment. Thus, your research article begins with what is already known in terms of research about the particular phenomenon you are studying. You then describe the question you want to ask based on this knowledge. It is important that you explain your rationale for doing the experiment at this point and the results you expect to find. Next, you are ready to describe the manner in which the experiment was performed in enough detail so that others wanting to replicate your study can do so. You then describe the results of the experiment. Finally, you interpret the results in relation to themselves (are there any confounds or interpretation problems?) and then in relation to what we already know about the phenomenon under study. That is, how do your results fit into the established body of knowledge in the area? Your conclusion draws the reader back to the rationale for doing the experiment you established in the beginning of your paper. You may also discuss how the results of your experiment might be related to other experiments in the area under study.

To facilitate this communication process, a specific format or outline for scientific papers has been developed. Scientific articles are divided into five parts: (1) abstract, (2) introduction, (3) method, (4) results, and (5) discussion. Detailed descriptions of what should be covered in each section and other guides to writing style are presented in the APA's *Publication Manual* (2001; available from APA, 750 First Street N.E., Washington, DC 20002). There are also Web sites that offer additional information on APA style. For example, Georgia Southern University has an overview of APA style (http://www.psychwww.com/resource/apacrib.htm) with reference to a variety of specifics. In addition, APA has a Web site devoted to information concerning APA style (http://www.apastyle.org) that also includes information on how to cite electronic resources (http://www.apastyle.org/elecref.html), and a frequently asked questions page (http://www.apastyle.org/faqs.html). A number of books also describe how to write papers in psychology (e.g., Rosnow & Rosnow, 2001; Sternberg, 1993).

The current publication manual also includes three major guidelines for referring to individuals and groups. The first guideline is to describe at the appropriate level of specificity. This guideline suggests that scientific writing requires precision and thus there is more clarity if you say individuals in the study were 65 to 85 years of age rather than the study involved older individuals. Likewise, if your study used Mexican Americans or Chinese Americans, it would be more precise to say this rather than Hispanic Americans or Asian Americans. If you are referring to both men and women, your writing should reflect that (i.e., not just "man" or "men"). The current *Publication Manual* also suggests that the term "gender" is cultural and should be used when referring to men and women as social groups. The term "sex," on the other hand, is biological and should be used when a biological distinction is predominant.

The second guideline found in the *Publication Manual* is to be sensitive to labels. Rather than labeling individuals as "schizophrenic" or "gays," it is suggested that you use phases such as "individuals diagnosed with schizophrenia" or "gay men" as a way to retain a person's individuality. Also, it is suggested that parallel forms be used when describing different groups of individuals. For example, rather than saying "man and wife" it would be more parallel to say "husband and wife" or "man and woman."

The third guideline is to acknowledge participation. This change, which began with the 1994 *Publication Manual,* directs researchers to refer to those who participate in research as *participants* and other more specific terms (e.g., *children, patients, clients, respondents,* and so on) rather than the older term *subjects.* The idea is that individuals actively participate in research and our language should reflect this. Thus, it would also be more accurate to use the active voice and say "students completed the survey" rather than the passive "students were given the survey." Additional suggestions for referring to gender, sexual orientation, racial and ethnic identity, age, disabilities, and other descriptors of people are included in the *Publication Manual* and reproduced in Appendix A in this book.

According to the APA, one purpose of this change was to allow researchers to be more specific. It is important that you become familiar with both the APA format and the APA style because these are used by many scientific journals around the world. Once you are familiar with them, you will find it easier to read articles and locate information quickly in those you are just skimming. Furthermore, you will undoubtedly use the APA format as a model in preparing your own proposals or papers. We now briefly describe each of the five parts of a scientific article.

## ■ Abstract

Most scientific papers open with a brief 100- to 120-word *abstract,* or summary of the entire article. The purpose of the abstract is to give an overall description of the experiment. By reading the abstract, we can quickly decide whether we want to take the time to read the entire paper. In this way, we avoid reading halfway through an article before we realize it is not the sort of experiment we thought it was simply from reading the title. The typical abstract provides a brief, clear statement of the purpose, method, and results of the experiment. It is written in a concise manner and describes the essential features of the article.

With the use of electronic databases, the abstract has taken on an even more important role. Because scientists around the world use electronic databases (such as PsycINFO, which includes the abstract), it is important that the abstract be written carefully. It is also important that the abstract include the key words that will allow for efficient computer searching of such databases. Because abstracts are being included in databases, abstracts currently are limited to 960 characters, including spaces. To give you an idea of how an abstract is written, an example follows. This abstract comes from an article published in the *Journal of Experimental Psychology: General* (Fox, Russo, Bowles, & Dutton, 2001).

> Biases in information processing undoubtedly play an important role in the maintenance of emotion and emotional disorders. In an attentional cueing paradigm, threat words and angry faces had no advantage over positive or neutral words (or faces) in attracting attention to their own location, even for people who were highly state-anxious. In contrast, the presence of threatening cues (words and faces) had a strong impact on the disengagement of attention. When a threat cue was presented and a target subsequently presented in another location, high state-anxious individuals took longer to detect the target relative to when either a positive or a neutral cue was presented. It is concluded that threat-related stimuli affect attentional dwell time and the disengage component of attention, leaving the question of whether threat stimuli affect the shift component of attention open to debate.

Another abstract is taken from an article published in the *Journal of Consulting and Clinical Psychology* (Hanson, Kilpatrick, Freedy, & Saunders, 1995).

> The impact of the 1992 Los Angeles (L.A.) civil disturbances on psychosocial functioning was assessed as part of a larger project investigating the views and attitudes of residents in L.A. County. Random digit dialing methodology identified a household probability sample of 1,200 adults (age 18 or older) from L.A. County. Respondents completed a telephone interview 6 to 8 months after the disturbances. Respondents' degree of exposure to the disturbances, mental health impact of the disturbances, and mental health effects of chronic versus acute exposure to violence were assessed. Consistent with hypotheses, the impact of the disturbances was the worst in the South Central communities. Higher rates of posttraumatic

stress disorder (PTSD; both diagnostic level and subclinical symptomatology) were found among respondents who reported disturbance-related experiences. Exposure to an acute event (i.e., the disturbances) was predictive of current PTSD symptomatology after controlling for demographics, lifetime trauma, and other types of stressful events.

A third example of an abstract is from the work of Cooper, Frone, Russell, and Mudar (1995), which appeared in the *Journal of Personality and Social Psychology.* This research tested a particular model of alcohol use that suggests that people use alcohol in two separate ways: One is an attempt to reduce negative emotions, and the second is an attempt to enhance positive emotional experiences. These authors tested this model in a sample of adults and adolescents using the advanced statistical techniques of moderated regression and path analysis.

> The present study proposed and tested a motivational model of alcohol use in which people are hypothesized to use alcohol to regulate both positive and negative emotions. Two central premises underpin this model: (a) that enhancement and coping motives for alcohol use are proximal determinants of alcohol use and abuse through which the influence of expectancies, emotions, and other individual differences are mediated and (b) that enhancement and coping motives represent phenomenologically distinct behaviors having both unique antecedents and consequences. This model was tested in random samples (1 of adults, 1 of adolescents) using a combination of moderated regression and path analysis corrected for measurement error. Results revealed strong support for the hypothesized model in both samples and indicate the importance of distinguishing psychological motives for alcohol use.

The next example describes a dolphin's use of echolocation (the emitting of a click in order to perceive its reflection from an object) in a study by Helweg, Roitblat, Nachtigall, and Hautus (1996) in the *Journal of Experimental Psychology: Animal Behavior Processes.*

> We examined the ability of a bottlenose dolphin *(Tursiops truncatus)* to recognize aspect-dependent objects using echolocation. An aspect-dependent object such as a cube produces acoustically different echoes at different angles relative to the echolocation signal. The dolphin recognized the objects even though the objects were free to rotate and sway. A linear discriminant analysis and nearest centroid classifier could classify the objects using average amplitude, center frequency, and bandwidth of object echoes. The results show that dolphins can use varying acoustic properties to recognize constant objects and suggest that aspect-independent representations may be formed by combining information gleaned from multiple echoes.

The final example comes from a study published in the *Journal of Abnormal Psychology* (Watkins & Teasdale, 2001) that examines what is referred to as overgeneral memory. Overgeneral memory is seen in depression and posttraumatic stress disorder that reflect a summary of repeated occasions rather than a single autobiographical event.

> Previous research has shown that, compared with a rumination induction, a brief distraction procedure reduces overgeneral autobiographical memory in depression. The authors investigated whether this effect depends on reduction in analytic thinking or reductions in self-focus. Focus of attention (high vs. low self-focus) and thinking style (high vs. low analytical thinking) were independently manipulated in depressed patients in a $2 \times 2$ design. Autobiographical recall was measured pre- and postmanipulation. Thinking style significantly affected overgeneral memory, whereas focus of attention significantly affected despondent mood. Reducing analytical self-focus reduced overgeneral memory, suggesting that high levels of naturally occurring ruminative analytic thinking may be important in the maintenance of overgeneral memory. Overgeneral memory in depression may be associated with chronic ruminative attempts to make sense of current or past difficulties.

# ■ Introduction

The *introduction* of a scientific paper is designed to provide background information about the phenomenon you are studying and to help the reader understand how you arrived at your hypothesis and the experiment you eventually performed. The key to writing a good introduction is to be clear in your own mind about the reasons you are performing the research before you begin. It is your task in the introduction to lay out the logic of the research you conducted. A typical introduction begins with a simple sentence or two explaining the nature of the research problem in broad terms. It then describes what we already know about the phenomenon being studied. As this narrative unfolds, relevant facts and theoretical speculations are described.

Once this background information has been presented and the reader knows the present status of the research area, the introduction concludes with a clear statement of purpose, which may include the particular hypothesis being evaluated. For example, in the Watkins and Teasdale (2001) article just described, the introduction begins with the sentence:

> When asked to recall memories of specific autobiographical events, depressed patients are more likely than control to retrieve overgeneral, categoric memories that are summaries of repeated occasions—for instance, waiting at bus stops or making mistakes.

Wood and Cowan (1995) studied aspects of the *cocktail party phenomenon,* in which one is able to pay attention to a single conversation in the midst of a number of other conversations. Although the task in such a situation is to pay attention to a single conversation, these authors were interested in how much information is processed and recalled from the other conversations, which they refer to as task-irrelevant. They begin their introduction with the following sentence:

> A basic, yet unanswered, question in selective attention research is the extent to which task-irrelevant information is processed and recalled.

Likewise, DeSchepper and Treisman (1996), in a study of visual memory for novel shapes, begin the introduction as follows:

> When people attend to a familiar object, like a coffeepot or a camel, they automatically see it as an instance of its category. They identify it as part of seeing it, by matching the new instance to their stored models for coffeepots or camels.

When Shotland and Straw (1976) wrote an article describing their research on bystander behavior (discussed in Chapter 3), they began their article like this:

> From time to time newspapers report that bystanders have witnessed an attack by a man on a woman without adequately helping the victim.

Shotland and Straw continue by describing some current theories that attempt to explain why bystanders do not help. Because the theories were derived from the reports of actual events and after-the-fact reports of witnesses, the authors sought to test empirically certain aspects of these theories. They conclude their introduction section with a statement of purpose and an hypothesis. Notice the clear statement of logical consequences in the following statement:

> The set of experiments we describe explores the implications and effects of a perceived relationship between a victim and her attacker on helping behavior. Specifically, the hypothesis for Experiment 1 was: If bystanders perceive a relationship between a woman and her attacker, they will be less likely to intervene than if the victim and attacker are perceived as strangers.

Likewise, Newcombe and Arnkoff (1979) begin the report on their research on speech styles and the sex of the speaker (also described in Chapter 3) with the following sentence:

> Our impressions of other people are derived from many sources: what they say, what they do, what others think of them, and so on.

The authors continue the introduction by discussing some important research that has been performed in this area, and they help the reader to understand why they performed this particular study. The introduction concludes with a statement of why the study was performed. In this particular study the purpose is stated as follows:

> In these initial experiments, the concern was to evaluate the effects, if any, of a variable over which people have some control (speech style) as compared to the effects of a set of variables over many of which they have less or no control (the pitch of their voice, their sex).

Thus, the general form of an introduction is to begin with a broad conception of the problem, followed by a discussion of previous research related to the topic, and then to end with a specific statement of the hypothesis or purpose of the study. Notice that as an introduction unfolds there is a progression from a general topic to a specific purpose. You might think of an introduction as the simple story of relevant published experiments, which leads us from our general topic of interest to our specific purpose or rationale underlying the hypothesis.

Introductions may be brief, as we shall see. The following is the introduction from a study on eating rate and obesity (Gaul, Craighead, & Mahoney, 1975). Note again how the last part of the introduction presents the purpose or hypothesis of the study.

> In their recent review Stunkard and Mahoney (in press) concluded that behavior modification techniques have demonstrated considerable effectiveness in the treatment of obesity. Many of these techniques were based in part on the behavioral analysis of eating patterns first presented by Ferster, Nurnberger, and Levitt (1962).
>
> An implicit assumption of many behavior modification programs has been that eating patterns differ for obese and nonobese people. Specifically, it has been presumed that overweight individuals eat faster and take fewer bites (cf. Stuart & Davis, 1972). However, virtually no empirical data regarding that assumption have been presented. The purpose of the present study was to determine if obese people consume their food more rapidly than nonobese people, and if consummatory behaviors (chewing and drinking) differ for two groups.

The next example of an introduction is from an exploratory study by Ravizza (1977) examining the subjective experiences of athletes during sporting events. Again, you will see how the author first describes the focus of his study in relation to previous research. He helps the reader to understand how this specific research is both different from and similar to other studies, and then concludes with a statement of purpose. Because the research is an exploratory study into an unknown area, the purpose is presented not in the form of an hypothesis but in the form of the goals of the study.

> The traditional emphasis of research on sports has been to develop techniques to improve physical performance. One result of this emphasis is that the major focus in sport research has been on motor performance. In contrast, the subjective experience of the athlete has been minimized (Kleinman, 1973; Park, 1973). One explanation for this emphasis on motor performance is that athletes' subjective experiences are difficult to measure and to study scientifically. Some progress has been made in studying nonpathological, yet extraordinary, psychological experience (Laski, 1961; Maslow, 1968). The limited research dealing with this

aspect of sport reveals that participation provides the athlete with a wide domain of subjective experiences (Leonard, 1975; Metheny, 1968; Slusher, 1967; Thomas, 1972). Some of these studies have focused on specific aspects of the subjective experience of the athlete (Beisser, 1967; Csikszentmihalyi, 1975; Gallwey, 1974; Murphy, 1972, 1973; Ravizza, 1973).

The purpose of the present investigation is twofold: first, to use the interview technique to ascertain the personal experiences of athletes; and second, to achieve a general characterization of at least one subjective aspect in sport, those experiences involved in an athlete's "greatest moment" while participating in sport.

Of course, not all studies have a brief introduction. At times, you must describe in some detail theoretical aspects of a model you are testing as well as how the model can be tested. For example, Bolger and Zuckerman (1995) seek to provide a framework for understanding the role of personality in terms of reactivity to stress. They begin their introduction with the following paragraph.

Personality is an important determinant of health and psychological outcomes (Contrada, Leventhal, & O'Leary, 1990; Friedman, 1990). Although researchers do not fully understand how personality leads to these outcomes, it has become clear that stressful experiences and how people cope with them play an important explanatory role (Bolger & Schilling, 1991). In this article, we propose a framework that delineates this explanatory role, a framework that combines trait and process approaches to the study of personality (see Mischel & Shoda, 1994). Our framework specifies that personality may affect exposure to stressful events, reactivity to those events, or both, and that these processes can help explain how personality affects outcomes. Our framework also specifies that personality differences in reactivity to stressors can be due to differential choice of coping strategies, differential effectiveness of the strategies chosen, or both. Below, we elaborate on this framework and provide an empirical test of the alternative models it implies.

In summary, the introduction section can be viewed as being composed of five tasks. The first task is to tell the reader what the research is about—that is, to describe the particular topic you will be studying. The second task is to describe the relevant background, to inform the reader about what is already known about a topic. Once the reader has the relevant background, then it is possible to move to the third task, to tell the reader why further research is necessary. In essence, at this point you justify your study to the reader, including how the study logically follows from the information you have previously presented in the introduction. Following this, the fourth task is to state the purpose of the study. The fifth task is to make predictions or state hypotheses.

The manner in which each of these five tasks is accomplished has been illustrated in the previous examples. One thing you may notice is that the first time a reference is presented in the text it is always presented in its entirety, with all of the authors included. After the first presentation, publications with more than three authors may be referenced by the first author and the Latin phase *et al.,* which is an abbreviation for "and others." For example, you might see (Ruiz, Pincus, & Ray, 1999) presented in any of the sections of the text initially but only (Ruiz et al., 1999) after this initial presentation.

## ■ Method

The third section of a scientific paper is called the *method* section and consists of a detailed description of how the experiment was conducted. The goal of this section is to provide enough detail for another researcher to conduct an exact replication of your experiment. In

"I THINK YOU SHOULD BE MORE EXPLICIT HERE IN STEP TWO."

addition, the procedural details provided in the method section allow the reader to visualize exactly how you conducted your experiment. In this way a careful reader may spot design problems that escaped your attention. The APA *Publication Manual* suggests that the method section be divided into three parts: participants, apparatus (or materials), and procedure.

The method section typically begins with a description of the participants in the study—that is, whether they were males or females, college students or patients in a hospital, and so forth. It is important to include the number of participants who took part in the experiment as well as the manner in which they were recruited. The selection of the control group, if any, should be described as well. Two examples of how participants might be described follow. The first is from Stadler (1995).

### Participants

One hundred students from introductory psychology courses at the University of Missouri–Columbia participated in return for course credit. Twenty students were randomly assigned to each of the five conditions by order of entry into the laboratory. All participants reported normal or corrected-to-normal vision and hearing.

The next example of a participants section comes from the clinical literature and was published in the *Journal of Abnormal Psychology* (March, Cienfuegos, Goldbloom, Ritter, Cowan, & Javitt, 1999). Notice that this description not only tells how participants were selected but also gives the important characteristics of the groups.

### Participants

Informed consent was obtained from 14 chronic schizophrenic inpatients and 16 nonpsychiatric comparison participants of similar age (patients = 39.6 ± 8.9 years; controls = 39.2 ± 7.0 years). All of the participants were of normal hearing by self-report. Participants with significant musical training were excluded. Schizophrenic participants were recruited from the inpatient units of the Bronx Psychiatric Center, a New York State inpatient treatment setting, and diagnosed according to criteria from the Diagnostic and Statistical Manual of Mental Disorders (3rd ed., rev.: DSM-III-R; American Psychiatric Association, 1987) by a board-certified attending research psychiatrist using semistructured clinical interview (DSM-III-R checklist) and other clinical materials as required. Participants with DSM-III-R Axis I disorders other than schizophrenia, including alcoholism or substance abuse, were excluded from the study. All but one patient were on antipsychotic medication at the time of testing (this patient had been prescribed haloperidol but was noncompliant with medication at the time of test). Of these, 5 were receiving typical antipsychotics and 8 were receiving atypical antipsychotics (2 clozapine, 2 risperidone, 3 sertindole, and 1 seroquel); 4 participants were receiving additional treatment with anticholinergics, 2 were receiving valproate, 1 was receiving lithium, and 1 was receiving fluoxetine. Control participants were recruited by personal contact from faculty, trainees, and staff of the Bronx Psychiatric Center. The schizophrenic and control groups differed significantly in sex distribution, with more women included among the controls (6 men, 10 women) than among the patients (12 men, 2 women). Control participants were also significantly higher than patients in the Quick Test (Ammons & Ammons, 1962; IQ: patients = 96.9 ± 10.2, controls = 110.7 ± 14.4). t(26) = 2.9, p < .01. All of the participants received a small honorarium for their participation.

Following the description of the participants in the experiment, there is a statement of the experimental situation and any equipment or apparatus that was used, including their brand names and model numbers. In physiological, psychophysiological, and other such studies, this would include a statement of the instrumentation settings (such as amplification and filters) that were used in the study.

For example, in an electroencephalogram (EEG) study reported in the *Journal of Experimental Psychology: Human Perception and Performance,* Bernstein, Scheffers, and Coles (1995) describe their psychophysiological procedures:

### Psychophysiological Recording

The electroencephalogram (EEG) was recorded from midline and lateral scalp electrode sites: frontal midline (Fz), central midline (Cz), parietal midline (Pz), C3′ (4 cm left of Cz), and C4′ (4 cm right of Cz) according to the 10/20 system (Jasper, 1958), referenced to linked mastoids. Signals were amplified using Grass Model 7P122 (Quincy, MA) amplifiers set to a high-frequency cut-off of 35 Hz (3dB/Octave roll-off) and a time constant of 8 s. Horizontal and vertical eye movements were recorded from stand locations (see Gratton, Coles, Sirevaag, Eriksen, & Donchin, 1988) and extended by Miller, Gratton, and Yee (1988). Additional filtering was accomplished off-line using a digital low-pass filter (of a type described by Farwell, Martinerie, Bashore, Rapp, & Goddard, 1993) with a passband of 8 Hz, a stop band of 10 Hz, and a width of 39 points.

The final part of the method section is a statement of the procedure used in the study. In describing the manner in which the study was conducted, it is important to include everything that the participants were told or were led to believe. Because every experiment is a social situation, it is also important to include some statement of the manner in which the experimenters treated the participants, as well as the important social characteristics of each of the experimenters.

When your design calls for dividing participants into various groups, it is necessary to describe how group assignment was determined (random, matching, and so on). It is also necessary to describe how you operationally defined your independent and dependent variables and how your various groups were tested. For example, if you used an individual difference variable such as anxiety, you would want to include the mean scores and standard deviations on whatever anxiety scale you used in assigning participants to either low- or high-anxiety conditions. You also should state whether the experimenter who tested the participants knew to which group a given participant belonged and, if there was a scoring procedure, whether it was performed blind. For example, in a study that examined the content of dreams of anxious and nonanxious participants, it is important to know whether the dream coder knew whether a given dream belonged to a high- or low-anxiety participant.

In some psychology experiments, it is necessary to have an extended method section so that other scientists understand exactly what happened to a participant during the experiment and how particular behaviors were measured. This is particularly true in social psychology experiments in which any type of deception is used. The method section in a deception study should include not only the method but also the safeguards—such as debriefing and follow-up measures—that were used in the study. The following example of a method section is taken from the Shotland and Straw (1976) study on bystander behavior.

### Method

The first procedure attempted was similar to the one used by Borofsky et al. (1971) in which a male attacked a female during a psychodrama. The fight was actually videotaped and played for each subject, who was told he or she had been arbitrarily selected to act in the next psychodrama pairing of the three subjects and was asked to leave the other two subjects (the confederates) so as not to inhibit them and to watch their psychodrama on television in the next room. This procedure proved unworkable as approximately 40% of the subjects thought the fight was staged.

A second procedure was needed that was more believable. The local police department was made aware of the impending experiment and their advice was sought. Three of the first author's colleagues in the Department of Psychology were asked to review the procedure for ethical considerations.

#### Subjects

The subjects were 51 male and female students who participated in order to receive course credit for either an introductory psychology or Man–Environment Relations course during the summer of 1974 at The Pennsylvania State University.

#### Procedure

Two couples with theatrical training were recruited through the cooperation of a faculty member in the Drama Department. One couple (Team 1) consisted of a man who was 1.70 m, 63.50 kg (5 feet 7 inches, 140 pounds) with brown hair conventionally cut, paired with a woman who was 1.57 m, 49.90 kg (5 feet 2 inches, 110 pounds) with shoulder-length black hair. The second couple (Team 2) consisted of a man who was 1.85 m, 90.72 kg (6 feet 1 inch, 200 pounds) with light brown hair conventionally cut, paired with a 1.70 m, 54.43 kg (5 feet 7 inches, 120 pounds) woman with long blonde hair. All of the college-age actors wore the usual jeans and shirts.

Each couple worked on alternate nights with subjects' being randomly assigned to conditions, the only provision being that the conditions contained an equal number of male and female subjects. The student came to take part in a study of attitudes in which he or she expected to answer a questionnaire and be interviewed. The student arrived at the appointed room and found a note explaining that the experimenter would arrive later to interview him or her and asking that the subject begin filling out the questionnaire. On the table with the questionnaires were what appeared to be a university phone with a standard sticker giving emergency telephone numbers, including the police. The telephone was not functioning and was rigged to provide a dial tone when it was appropriate, and to record any telephone number that the subject might try to call.

Other rooms on the floor had apparent activity in them. From the room across the hall emanated the sound of a computer printer, and in the room next to the experimental room a radio played.

After the subject entered the room 5 minutes passed, during which time the subject proceeded to fill out the questionnaire. The confederates, on a different floor of the building, received a signal by walkie-talkie and took the elevator to the proper floor. Before the doors opened, a loud verbal argument could be heard. The woman was accused by the man of picking up a dollar he claimed to have dropped. After approximately 15 sec of heated discussion, the man physically attacked the woman, violently shaking her while she struggled, resisting and screaming. The screams were loud piercing shrieks, interspersed with pleas to "get away from me." Along with the shrieks one of two conditions was introduced and then repeated several times. In the stranger condition the woman screamed, "I don't know you," and in the married condition, "I don't know why I ever married you." From the first designation of the condition the physical fight lasted a maximum of 45 sec, with the entire incident not lasting more than a minute.

The fight was immediately terminated with the attacker fleeing at any attempt by the subject to intervene. If no one intervened, the fight was terminated by a third confederate (male), who came out of a nearby room and demanded in a loud voice that the attacker stop beating up the woman. The attacker then ran away while the false intervener consoled the woman. Every effort was made to keep a direct intervener away from the actors to insure their safety. Two confederates were placed in concealed locations between the actors and the subject, one to falsely intervene, the other to inform the subject it was an experiment, if necessary.

A subject was considered an intervener if he or she called the police on our phone, asked a person in the computer room to help stop the fight, shouted at the attacker to stop, or acted to intervene directly. The fight was staged 15.85–16.15 m (52–53 feet) away from the room containing the subject. If the subject came down the hall toward the fight some 9.14 m (30 feet) and did not turn into an intersecting hallway, he or she was counted as intervening.

The subjects were interviewed immediately following the experiment and fully debriefed by the first author, who spent up to 45 minutes with each subject. The interviews were unstructured except for several standard questions. First, the subjects were asked to describe what they had seen. If they did not adequately describe the experimental condition to which they were assigned, they were asked: (a) What was the relationship between the two people fighting? (b) How do you know? Subjects were asked (c) What caused the fight? and (d) Did you think it was a rape? They were then asked to describe their thoughts and behavior in the sequence in which they had occurred while witnessing the fight. After the debriefing each subject was specifically asked: (e) Do you think we have done any harm to you by having you go through that experience? and (f) Do you think that the potential results and implications of the research are worth the experience you went through? Each subject was urged to call the first author if he or she wished to discuss any aspect of the experiment in the future.

# Results

The fourth part of a research article is the results section. The chief purpose of this section is simply to state the outcome of the experiment and then indicate whether the outcome was statistically significant. For example, a results section might begin with the statement that the experimental and control groups did or did not differ significantly in terms of whatever dependent variable was measured. Following this general statement, the actual group scores may be presented, and then the manner in which the results were analyzed is briefly described. Quite often the results section also contains figures or tables that aid the reader in visualizing the outcome of the experiment (see Appendix B for examples).

Any hypothesis presented in the introduction should have the corresponding results presented in the results section. Although there are no hard-and-fast rules concerning discussion of or references to other studies in the results section, these usually are saved for the discussion section. Granholm, Asarnow, and Marder (1996) examined an attentional task with schizophrenic outpatients and a matched nonpsychiatric control group. The beginning of their results section follows.

> A 2 (group) × 2 (array sizes) × 2 (visual angles) × 4 (target quadrant locations) mixed model analysis of variance (ANOVA) was carried out on the percentage of correct detections. This ANOVA yielded significant main effects for group, $F(1, 48) = 21.54, p < .001$, array size, $F(1, 48) = 190.40, p < .001$, and target location, $F(3, 144) = 60.74, p < .001$, but not for visual angle, $F(1, 48) = 0.97$. Significant interactions were found between group and array size, $F(1, 48) = 7.06, p < .01$, group and visual angle, $F(1, 48) = 4.62, p < .05$, array size and visual angle, $F(1, 48) = 4.20, p < .05$, and array size and target location, $F(3, 144) = 29.09, p < .001$. No other two-way or higher order interaction was statistically significant.

Following the initial statement of the statistical results, Granholm et al. described the manner in which each group performed the task.

In Chapter 5, we discussed the concept of effect size and power and its relation to the number of individuals necessary to adequately test our hypotheses. Because of its importance, a number of publications including the latest edition of the APA *Publication Manual* are suggesting that these measures be included in the results section (Wilkinson and Task Force on  Statistical Inference, 1999; available at http://www.apa.org/journals/amp/amp548594.html). The measure of effect size or strength of relationship is generally placed after the probability level.

For example, Chang and Lenzenweger (2001) used a signal detection procedure to compare biological relatives of individuals with schizophrenia and control individuals. In such a task, if an individual reports the presence of a stimuli that is not present, it is called a false alarm. Note that in describing the false alarm rates, these authors present the mean and the standard deviation of their data and then the *t*-test results with the exact probability measure and then effect size (Cohen's *d*).

> The false-alarm rates for the two-point task are derived from the 60 one-point stimulation trials. The schizophrenia relatives false alarm rate ($M = .028, SD = .019$) did not differ from that of the control subjects ($M = .027, SD = .021$), $t(67) = 0.115, p < .91$, Cohen's $d = .05$.

Öhman, Flykt and Esteves (2001) sought to determine if individuals would be quicker to detect a fear relevant stimulus (e.g., spider or snake) surrounded by more neutral pictures (e.g., flower or mushroom) or the other way around. Nine of these pictures were presented in a matrix (3 rows and 3 columns) for 1 second and could include either nine pictures of the same objects or different objects. In this reaction time (RT) study, the participant was asked to respond as quickly as possible as to whether the pictures were of the same object (spider, snake, flower, or mushroom) or contained different objects (some combination). They began their results section as follows:

### Results

The mean RTs to fear-relevant and fear-irrelevant targets for all positions in the matrix are displayed in Figure 1. In agreement with the main hypothesis of the study, the analysis showed that the participants were clearly faster in detecting fear-relevant than fear-irrelevant targets, $F(1, 24) = 22.29$, $p < .0001$.

As mentioned, authors often present tables or figures to exhibit the results of a study. For example, McKenna and Sharma (1995) performed a series of experiments to explore the Stroop effect with emotional and neutral words. The traditional Stroop effect is produced when words for colors (e.g., *red, green, blue*) are presented in different-color inks and the individual is asked to indicate the color of the ink. This produces an interference because the individual finds it difficult not to read the word itself. McKenna and Sharma asked whether emotional words (e.g., *fail, fear, grief, death*) would also produce an interference effect. The dependent variable in this study was the reaction time (RT) required to indicate the color. The results section follows.

### Results

An analysis of errors showed no significant differences. The mean number of errors were 4.33% and 4.34% for neutral and emotional words, respectively.

*Analysis of emotional Stroop.* The mean correct RT across blocks is presented in Figure 3. The RT scores were analyzed in a three-way ANOVA, with order as a between-subjects variable and emotional class and block as within-subject variables.

The analysis revealed that the color identification took longer for emotional words (931 ms) than for neutral words (901 ms), $F(1, 38) = 7.16$, $MSE = 9,511$, $p < .01$. As in the previous experiments, there was no main effect of order, and order did not interact with any other variable. There was a main effect of block, $F(3, 114) = 21.17$, $MSE = 8,297$, $p < .001$. Tukey multiple comparison tests showed that this was due to the first block showing significantly faster RTs than any of the other three blocks.

In graphing the results, the dependent variable is placed on the $y$-axis (vertical axis) and the independent variable is placed on the $x$-axis (horizontal axis) of the graph. In this study there are two independent variables: blocks and the nature of words (emotional versus neutral). If one of the independent variables involved time (order of presentation), then this is the variable that typically is plotted on the $x$-axis. The graph depicting the results of this aspect of the experiment is illustrated in Figure 15.1.

## ■ Discussion

The final section is called the *discussion* section. In general, the discussion is in three parts. In the first part, you report the chief finding of the present experiment. In doing so, you draw the reader back to the rationale you established in the introduction section of your article and conclude the manner in which your results support or refute the theoretical rationale you developed previously. In the second part, you point out any limitations or potential confounds

Figure 15.1

Mean reaction time
(RT) to color name
category—neutral
and emotional
words for the
four blocks in
Experiment 3

*SOURCE:* McKenna
and Sharma (1995).

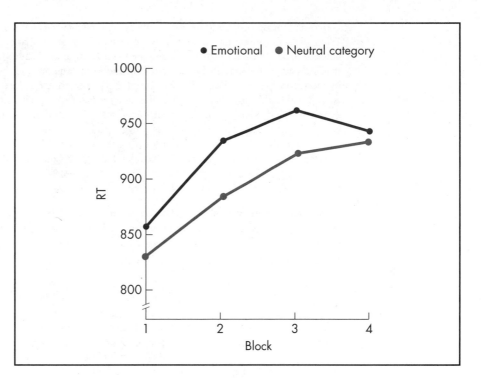

that might affect your interpretation of the results and restate them in light of these limitations. We believe this is an essential step in any discussion, and we encourage you to make it
a part of your scientific papers. In the third part of the discussion, you directly relate the results of your experiment to other published experiments on the same topic and describe how
the present experiment expands our understanding of the phenomenon under study. For example, Graffin, Ray, and Lundy (1995) examined patterns of EEG activity with high and low
hypnotically susceptible individuals. Their discussion of the baseline results follows.

**Baseline Individual Differences**

The present study presents a consistent picture of state-independent patterns of EEG activity
which differentiated subjects carefully selected according to hypnotic susceptibility. Overall, high
susceptible subjects in comparison to low susceptible subjects demonstrated more theta activity in
the frontal areas (frontal and temporal cortex) as compared to the more posterior areas of the
brain (parietal and occipital cortex). This finding is consistent with previous hypnosis research
(e.g., Tebecis et al., 1975; Sabourin & Cutcomb, 1980; Sabourin et al., 1990). The current finding
of individual differences in theta activity can be seen to bring together a variety of parallel
research tracks and suggest future research. In psychophysiological research greater frontal
midline theta has been associated with attentional readiness or the continuous concentration of
attention (Ishihara & Yoshii, 1972; Mizuki et al., 1980; Bruneau et al., 1993). Considering these
findings in the light of our current research suggests that high susceptible subjects either possess,
or can manifest, a heightened state of attentional readiness and concentration of attention. This
might also be related to the finding that absorption remains one of the most consistent correlates
of hypnotizability (cf. Tellegen & Atkinson, 1974; Nadon et al., 1991; Glisky et al., 1991).
Considering these independent lines of research may also move us closer to determining the
physiological and biochemical mechanisms involved in the hypnotic experience. For example, the
amount of frontal midline theta has been shown to be negatively correlated with MAO activity

and lower DA (dopaminergic) metabolism as measured by platelet MAO (Hashimoto et al., 1988). Since dopaminergic pathways play a role in the regulation of attentional processes and anterior theta is related to attentional readiness (see Bruneau et al., 1993 for an overview), we might expect both differential DA metabolism and frontal midline theta activity in high vs. low hypnotic susceptible subjects. The study could also be performed in the opposite direction. That is, we could test the presence of frontal theta as a predictor of hypnotic suggestibility. In such an experiment, individuals would be screened in terms of EEG and divided into high and low theta groups. The hypothesis to be tested would suggest that those who displayed higher frontal theta would score higher on traditional measures of hypnotizability (e.g., SHSS) than those displaying less frontal theta. Given the reported difficulty (cf. Kirsch & Council, 1992) of finding a stable psychometric indicator of hypnotic susceptibility, a psychophysiological marker (i.e., anterior theta activity) might offer a more stable individual difference measure.

In the discussion section, it is also important to discuss the way in which your results either do or do not support your hypotheses. For example, in the Hanson, Kilpatrick, Freedy, and Saunders (1995) study of the effects of the 1992 civil disturbances in Los Angeles on mental health, they include the following:

> In support of Hypothesis 2, higher rates of current PTSD, posttraumatic stress sequelae (i.e., reexperiencing, avoidance, and arousal criteria), and subthreshold symptoms of PTSD were found among respondents who reported that they had experienced disturbance-related violence or destruction, compared with those who did not. These findings are consistent with previous research that has examined rates of PTSD among victims of other types of traumatic events (Breslau et al., 1991; Kilpatrick et al., 1989; Resnick et al., 1993; Ullman, 1995). The results of this study indicated that exposure to the disturbances did negatively impact mental health.

At times, you may present more than one experiment in a single paper. The basic procedure is to have a single introduction section, then a method, results, and discussion section for each experiment followed by a general discussion section that interprets the results of all of the studies in relation to your hypotheses. For example, the Öhman et al. (2001) article that examined reaction time to fear related stimuli describes three different experiments. The general discussion section begins as follows:

> The results from the experiments reported in this article can be summarized in a number of broad generalizations. First, participants were consistently faster to find a fear-relevant stimulus (snake or spider) than a fear-irrelevant stimulus (flower or mushroom) against backgrounds of fear-irrelevant and fear-relevant stimuli, respectively. This finding suggests that humans share a predisposition to preferentially direct attention toward potentially threatening animal stimuli. Second, the latency of finding a fear-relevant target stimulus was independent of where in the matrix it was located.

Let us look at another example. Klein and Boals (2001) performed two experiments to determine the effects of emotional disclosure through expressive writing on working memory (WM). The final section of their paper was a general discussion that brought together the results of both studies.

**General Discussion**

> The findings from these two experiments shed new light on available WM capacity and markedly expand the benefits of expressive writing to this widely studied cognitive process. We have show that usable WM is not a static variable but can change as a function of a psychosocial manipulation, with such changes reflecting variations in intrusive and avoidant thoughts about offtask topics. . . .

To help you grasp the fundamental differences among the sections of an article, we suggest that the method and results sections be written in an exact manner. The method section must be detailed enough to permit another scientist to perform an exact replication of your experiment; the results section must be an accurate statement of what actually happened in your experiment. In a sense, because these sections are a statement of how you performed your experiment and what your results were, they are a record of your experiment and can be expected to be an accurate description of what happened. In contrast, the discussion is a statement of what you think your finding means for our understanding of the phenomenon you are studying. Although your finding will last forever, your interpretation of your data may vary considerably as your understanding of the phenomenon grows with each successive experiment.

Once you have finished writing the five major sections of the article, the remaining steps are to find a title for your paper and to list your references. The title of your paper is important because, like the abstract, it describes the nature of your experiment. Consequently, many titles are written so that they describe the nature of the independent and dependent variables. For example, in 1958 Silverstein and Klee published an article in the *American Medical Association Archives of Neurology and Psychiatry* titled "Effects of Lysergic Acid Diethylamide (LSD-25) on intellectual functions." The title of this paper tells us the independent variable (lysergic acid diethylamide) and the dependent variables (some measure of intellectual function).

## ■ References

The author, title, and reference information for every study you cite in your paper are listed in a *references* section at the end of the paper. The references section is important for the valuable information it gives to other scientists. There are no hard-and-fast rules for referring to other studies, but general guidelines suggest that you do so for one of three purposes. The first purpose is to acknowledge a scientific fact, assumption, or working hypothesis. For example, a study by Castonguay et al. (1996) begins with the statement, "Despite support for the effectiveness of cognitive therapy for depression, researchers are still confronted with a high degree of uncertainty about its underlying processes of change." Following this sentence, the authors can give one or more references directing the reader to theoretical or research articles that have examined this question. A second purpose of the references section is to direct the reader to a more detailed discussion of a theoretical concept or a specific experimental or statistical procedure. Because a research report is by its nature short, it is important to direct others to extended discussions of the concept under study, as might be found in *Psychological Bulletin* or *Psychological Review*. The third purpose is to give credit to other scientists for developing an idea, technique, or line of research.

The latest version of the *Publication Manual* suggests that references be presented in the same manner as they would appear in a printed journal article with each reference using a hanging indent (first line of reference is at the left margin and all lines below that are indented), and that titles of journals and books are in italic. However, the *Publication Manual* also allows for variations to this format if it cannot be accomplished by your word processing system. In either case, the chosen format should be consistent throughout the references.

The following is an example of the APA style of citing books and journals, including Internet references.

References

American Psychological Association. (1995, September 15). *APA public policy action alert: Legislation would affect grant recipients* [Announcement posted on the World Wide Web]. Washington, DC: Author. Retrieved January 25, 1996 from the World Wide Web: http://www.apa.org/ppo/istook.html.

Bianchi, L. (1895). The function of the frontal lobes. *Brain, 18,* 497–522.

Darwin, C. R. (1965). *The expression of the emotions in man and animals.* Chicago: University of Chicago Press. (Original work published 1872)

Flynn, J. R. (1984). The mean IQ of Americans: Massive gains 1932 to 1978. *Psychological Bulletin, 95,* 3–28.

Leventhal, H. (1980). Toward a comprehensive theory of emotions. In L. Berkowitz (Ed.), *Advances in experimental psychology* (Vol. 13, pp. 139–207). New York: Academic Press.

Surman, O. S., Gottlieb, S. K., Hackett, T. P., & Silverberg, E. (1973). Hypnosis in the treatment of warts. *Archives of General Psychiatry, 28,* 439–441.

A journal article as it was published is presented in Appendix B. For additional help with preparing papers in APA format, we have reproduced in Appendix C the typed copy of selected parts of this article showing the proper spacing, headings, and so forth. This shows both the format a student might use to submit a research paper to a class and the manner in which it *must* be submitted for publication in an APA journal or other journals. As you may have noticed, the five major parts of this study—the abstract, introduction, method, results, and discussion—along with the title and references are presented in Appendix B in their entirety. Also, if you look at the conclusion of the references section, you can see the date on which the journal received the article.

Now that you know the sections required in an article, we can turn to the next step: submitting the article for publication. Before we do this we want to remind you that proposals for research may also follow the APA format. In a proposal, of course, you would not have actual data. Your results section would describe how your data would be quantified and which specific statistical tests you would use. Likewise, the discussion section could discuss possible outcomes and what these might mean scientifically. To aid you in preparing proposals, in Box 15.1 we have reproduced a checklist for preparing a research proposal.

| ✓ | CONCEPT CHECK 15.1 | Describe the basic sections of a research paper. |

| ✓ | CONCEPT CHECK 15.2 | In which section would you find a statement of the hypothesis? |

| ✓ | CONCEPT CHECK 15.3 | Lauren read an article about an experiment that related one's musical preference to IQ. She thought this would be a good study to replicate for her experimental psychology class. Although the ideas and data in the article were well presented, she could not determine how the original study was conducted. Which section of the original paper must be improved? |

## Box 15.1

# Preparing a Research Proposal

For some students, there is less emphasis on the writing of formal research papers for publication and more emphasis on the development of sound research proposals. In developing proposals, many conceptual and procedural questions must be considered. In this process a checklist is helpful. The following checklist was developed by Robert Holt. Students who have particular problems with developing a research project will find Dr. Holt's clear-cut advice helpful and should consult his original article (Holt, 1965).

## Checklist of Questions to Be Asked About a Research Proposal

1. What is the problem?
   **a.** Is it clearly stated?
   **b.** Is it focused enough to facilitate efficient work (i.e., are hypotheses directly testable)?
2. What are the underlying objectives?
   **a.** Is the problem clearly related to the objectives?
3. What is the significance of the proposed research?
   **a.** How does it tie in with theory?
   **b.** What are its implications for application?
4. Has the relevant literature been surveyed adequately?
   **a.** Is the research adequately related to other people's work on the same or similar topics?
5. Are the concepts and variables adequately defined (theoretically and operationally)?
6. Is the design adequate?
   **a.** Does it meet formal standards for consistency, power, and efficiency?
   **b.** Is it appropriate to the problem and the objectives?
   **c.** Will negative results be meaningful?
   **d.** Are possibly misleading and confounding variables controlled?

   **e.** How are the independent and dependent variables measured or specified?
7. What instruments or techniques will be used to gather data?
   **a.** Are the reliabilities and validities of these techniques well established?
8. Is the sampling of subjects adequately planned for?
   **a.** Is the population (to which generalizations are to be aimed) specified?
   **b.** Is there a specific and acceptable method of drawing a sample from this population?
9. Is the sampling of objects (or situations) adequately planned for?
   **a.** To what population of objects (situations) will generalizations be aimed?
   **b.** Is there a specific and acceptable method of drawing a sample from this population?
10. What is the setting in which data will be gathered?
    **a.** Is it feasible and practical to carry out the research plan in this setting?
    **b.** Is the cooperation of the necessary persons obtainable?
11. How are the data to be analyzed?
    **a.** What techniques of data reduction are contemplated?
    **b.** Are methods specified for analyzing data qualitatively?
    **c.** Are methods specified for analyzing data quantitatively?
12. In the light of available resources, how feasible is the design?
    **a.** What compromises must be made in translating an idealized research design into a practical research design?
    **b.** What limitations or generalizations will result?
    **c.** What will be needed in terms of time, money, personnel, and facilities?

# Publishing Your Article

Now that we have discussed the basic form of a research article, let us talk about the process of submitting an article for publication. One of the first questions a scientist asks is, "Who, or what portion of the scientific community, do I want to read my article?" For example, suppose someone has performed a study that examines the EEG changes in humans over a period of years and how these changes correlate with the participants' education and psychological development. Depending on the particular hypothesis of the study and its focus, the final article might be sent to a journal that reports physiological research, such as *Psychophysiology* or *Neuropsychologia,* to a journal emphasizing developmental processes, such as *Developmental Psychology,* or even to a journal that discusses educational development. Each of these journals is read by a different group of scientists, so publishing an article in one journal will give you a different audience from publishing in another.

To help the potential author, most journals include a statement at the beginning about the types of articles they publish. If your study is a replication and continuation of some of the articles cited in your introduction, probably the same journal that published the other studies would be interested in your work. Once you have decided on an audience and a journal, it is a good procedure to look through recent issues of the journal to see whether the particular style that is used deviates from the APA recommendation. For example, journals may differ in the references and results sections. Thus, the particular form of reference citation must be checked carefully, as well as the manner in which statistical significance is reported.

Another issue is the question of placing your work on the Web. Sometimes, researchers may want to place their newly found results on their Web pages. However, there are some precautions that should be considered. First, if it is placed on the Web it should be clearly noted as an unpublished paper. The American Psychological Association  (www.apa.org/journals/posting.html) suggests that the following be placed on such a paper "Draft version 4, 5/3/2002. This paper has not been peer reviewed. Please do not copy or cite without author's permission." It should also be noted that some journals will not consider publishing a paper if it has been placed on the Web because they consider this prior publication, although this is not the case with most psychological journals. Of course, you should check with the journal to which you plan to submit your paper before you place it on the Web.

Once your paper is published, the requirements vary by journal. APA journals allow you to post a copy of the final manuscript with three limitations: (1) the posted article must carry an APA copyright notice and include a link to the APA Journal home page; (2) it cannot be archived with any other non-APA repositories; and (3) APA will not provide electronic copies of the APA published version for this purpose, and authors are not permitted to scan in the APA published version. Most journals allow authors to place abstracts on their Web pages and to electronically send the full article to others.

Once you have written the article following the guidelines in the front of the journal, you send the number of copies requested to the editor of the journal and wait. Some journals give information about publication decisions quickly and others take months. To understand why there is a delay before your article is accepted or rejected, let us examine what happens when an article is received by the editor of a journal. In most cases the editor is a scientist employed by a university or research laboratory who has agreed to be editor for a few years. The editor thus has another job on which he or she spends considerable time. The day-to-day processes of the journal generally are performed by a paid assistant. Once the manuscript is received by the editor, the editor usually chooses two scientists who are studying phenomena similar to yours and asks them to recommend whether the article should be accepted for publication. The process of review by other scientists is called the peer review system.

Each reviewer reads your article and evaluates it in terms of the clarity of presentation, the logic of the experiment, the appropriateness of the data analysis used, and the meaningfulness of the discussion section. This is similar to the type of feedback your professors give you about your research reports and proposals. In the next section we present in more detail some criteria that are used for research evaluation.

After a reviewer has read and evaluated an article, she or he writes a review, which is sent to the editor. Usually these reviews are a couple of pages long and are designed to give feedback to the author. In some cases the reviewers point out limitations of the experiment itself or critiques of the way the article is written. Specific suggestions often are made to improve your paper. And in each case a general recommendation is made about whether the article should be published. The editor reads these reviews, makes a final decision about whether to publish the paper, and then informs the author of the decision. Sometimes the reviewers differ over the quality of the article, and the editor must decide between the views of the reviewers. Other times the reviewers suggest publication only if the author will agree to rewrite or reanalyze part of the study. Thus, after some wait, you receive the reviews and the editor's disposition regarding publication of your article.

If the editor agrees to publish your article as it stands, there is still another wait for the article to be printed. This delay is called the publication lag. It is generally brought about because a journal accepts many good articles and is able to publish only a few of them in any given issue. The publication lag may range from a month or two to more than a year.

## WHAT MAKES A GOOD ARTICLE?

One question students ask is, "What criteria do editors and reviewers keep in mind as they are reviewing papers for publication?" Obviously, the answer is important; it should give you an idea of what senior scientists consider both good research and a well-written experiment. Brendan Maher, editor of the *Journal of Consulting and Clinical Psychology,* reports that four out of every five articles submitted to the journal are rejected. Because most of these are rejected for methodological reasons, Maher produced a set of guidelines for publishing articles  (Maher, 1978a). These guidelines have been reconsidered by Kazdin (1995), who poses a series of questions for authors and reviewers to consider. These questions, which Kazdin designed to guide the preparation of journal articles, are reproduced in Box 15.2.

## Box 15.2

# Major Questions to Guide Journal Article Preparation

### Abstract

What were the main purposes of the study?
Who was studied (sample, sample size, special characteristics)?
How were participants selected?
To what conditions, if any, were participants exposed?
What type of design was used?
What were the main findings and conclusions?

### Introduction

What is the background and context for the study?
What in current theory, research, or clinical work makes this study useful, important, or of interest? What is different or special about the study in focus, methods, or design to address a need in the area? Is the rationale clear regarding the constructs to be assessed?
What specifically were the purposes, predictions, or hypotheses?

### Method

*Participants*

Who were the participants and how many of them were there in this study? Why was this sample selected in light of the research goals?
How was this sample obtained, recruited, and selected?
What are the participant and demographic characteristics of the sample (e.g., gender, age, ethnicity, race, socioeconomic status)?
What inclusion and exclusion criteria were invoked (i.e., selection rules to obtain participants)?

How many of the participants eligible or recruited actually were selected and participated in the study?
Was informed consent solicited? How and from whom, if special populations were used?

*Design*

What is the design (e.g., longitudinal, cross-sectional) and how does the design relate to the goals of the study?
How were participants assigned to groups or conditions?
How many groups were included in the design?
How were the groups similar and different in how they were treated in the study?
Why were these groups critical to address the questions of interest?

*Assessment*

What were the constructs of interest and how were they measured?
What are the relevant reliability and validity data from previous research (and from the present study) that support the use of these measures for the present purposes? Were multiple measures and methods used to assess the constructs?
Are response sets or styles relevant to the use and interpretation of the measures?
How was the assessment conducted? By whom (as assessors or observers)? In what order were the measures administered?
If judges (raters) were used in any facet of assessment, what is the reliability (inter- or intrajudge consistency) in rendering their judgments or ratings?

### Procedures

Where was the study conducted (setting)?

What materials, equipment, or apparatuses were used in the study?

What was the chronological sequence of events to which participants were exposed? What intervals elapsed between different aspects of the study (e.g., assessment occasions)?

What procedural checks were completed to avert potential sources of bias in implementation of the manipulation and assessments?

What checks were made to ensure that the conditions were carried out as intended?

What other information does the reader need to know to understand how participants were treated and what conditions were provided?

## Results

What were the primary measures and data on which the predictions depend?

What are the scores on the measures of interest for the different groups and sample as a whole (e.g., measures of central tendency and variability)?

How do the scores compare with those of other study, normative, or standardization samples?

Are groups of interest within the study similar on measures and variables that could interfere with interpretation of the hypotheses?

What analyses were used and how specifically did these address the original hypotheses and purposes?

Were the assumptions of the data analyses met?

If multiple tests were used, what means were provided to control error rates?

If more than one group was delineated, were they similar on variables that might otherwise explain the results (e.g., diagnosis, age)?

Were data missing due to incomplete measures (not filled out completely by the participants) or due to loss of participants? If so, how were these handled in the data analyses?

Are there ancillary analyses that might further inform the primary analyses or exploratory analyses that might stimulate further work?

## Discussion

What were the major findings of the study?

How do these findings add to research and how do they support, refute, or inform current theory?

What alternative interpretations can be placed on the data?

What limitations or qualifiers must be placed on the study given method and design issues?

What research follows from the study to move the field forward?

*Note:* Further discussion of questions that guide the preparation of journal articles can be obtained in additional sources (Kazdin, 1992; Maher, 1978a). Concrete guidelines on the format for preparing articles are provided by the American Psychological Association (2001).

*Source:* From "Preparing and Evaluating a Research Report" by Alan Kazdin in *Journal of Psychological Assessment*, 1995, 7, p. 232. Copyright © 1995 by the American Psychological Association. Reprinted with permission.

## Key Terms and Concepts

1. **Parts of an article**
   A. Abstract
   B. Introduction
   C. Method

   D. Results
   E. Discussion
   F. References
2. **What makes a good proposal or article?**

## Summary

1. An important part of research is communicating the results to others, and for this purpose a particular format has evolved. This format includes five parts: (1) abstract, (2) introduction, (3) method, (4) results, and (5) discussion. Also included are references, tables, and figures as required.
2. The abstract is a 100- to 120-word summary of the article. The typical abstract provides a clear statement of purposes, method, and results.
3. The introduction of a paper is designed to review what is already known about the topic being studied, to explain the reason for the present study, and to outline the hypothesis.
4. The method section consists of a detailed description of what was done so that another scientist can pre-

cisely replicate the experiment. This description covers which participants were used and how they were selected, what the experimental situation was, any equipment that was used, and the procedures, including what the participants were told or led to believe.
5. The results section describes the outcome of an experiment and states what statistical procedures were used and the results of the analyses.
6. The discussion section describes the results of the study as they relate to previous research and theoretical interpretation as well as any potential limitations of the experiment.
7. An excellent set of guidelines for assessing research reports is reproduced in Box 15.2.

## Review Questions

1. What are the major parts of a research article?
2. What is an abstract and where is it located in a paper?
3. How do you determine which references to include in a paper?
4. Where would the research hypothesis be located in a paper?
5. Statistical tests would be reported in which section of a paper?

6. What is the purpose of the discussion section?
7. Why are many articles rejected for publication in the *Journal of Consulting and Clinical Psychology*?
8. How are a proposal and a published article the same, and how are they different?

## Discussion Questions and Projects

1. Pick an article published in one of the APA journals (e.g., *Journal of Experimental Psychology, Journal of Personality and Social Psychology, Journal of Abnormal Psychology*). Place a piece of paper over the abstract and read the article. Now write an abstract of your own. How did your abstract differ from the existing one?
2. Pick an article of interest to you (it should not be one published this year). Read the article and write a sum-

mary of it. Look up this same article in the appropriate issue of *Psychological Abstracts* or PsycINFO and compare your summary with the existing one. What are the differences between your summary and the one in *Psychological Abstracts* or PsycINFO?
3. Discuss the function of the discussion section.
4. Why do people use references? What are the reasons for including or excluding a reference to a particular article?

5. Take a simple task such as balancing a ruler on the end of your finger in two conditions: (1) singing a song to yourself and (2) saying the alphabet backwards. Measure the amount of time you can balance the ruler in each condition. Assume that you have used the appropriate control procedures, such as counterbalancing the order of conditions. Write the procedure section of a research article describing such a task with the various conditions.

## InfoTrac College Edition: Exercises

In this chapter we discussed the necessary parts of a research article. Using InfoTrac College Edition, look up the article entitled "If you changed your name and appearance to those of Elvis Presley, who would you be? Historical features in categorization," by Robert Sternberg and his colleagues, which was published in the *American Journal of Psychology* (Fall 1998). As you go through the article, note what type of information is contained in each of the sections—Abstract, Introduction, Method, Results, Discussion, and References. This article is different than the ones discussed in the chapter in that more than one experiment is presented in the report. How was this accomplished? By clicking on PowerTrac and then journal name under "Select an Index," you can enter a journal that is included, such as the *American Journal of Psychology.* By viewing the search results, you can then scan recently published articles to see what information was included in each of the sections. If you choose a journal such as the *Journal of Cognitive Neuroscience,* you will notice that these journals do not organize their presentation in the same manner as we discussed in the chapter. These journals are organized like other journals in physics, chemistry, biology, and the neurosciences. How does this organization differ from that presented in the chapter?

## ☑ Answers to Concept Checks

15.1 The basic sections of a research paper are (1) abstract, (2) introduction, (3) method, (4) results, and (5) discussion, followed by a references section.

15.2 A statement of the hypothesis traditionally is found at the end of the introduction section.

15.3 The method section. It is one purpose of the method section to describe the original study in enough detail so that another experimenter could conduct a similar study. Most method sections describe the participants in the experiment, the types of equipment or test materials used, if any, and the procedures that were followed.

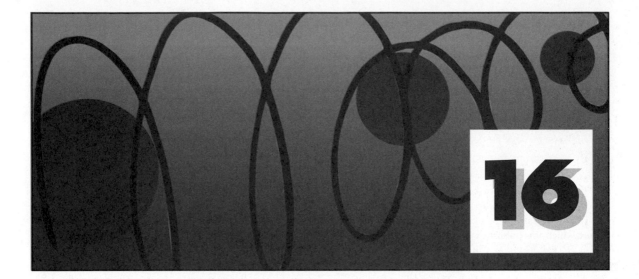

# BEYOND METHOD

Throughout this book, we have considered more than just methods because we believe that the process of science is *more* than simply applying the scientific method to the study of human behavior and experience. In this chapter, we intend to move beyond the specific application of particular designs, as important as these approaches are, and focus on some of the broad themes we have presented throughout this book. The title of this final chapter, "Beyond Method," emphasizes this intention. Let us first review schematically the approaches to research we have presented thus far.

## DIMENSIONS OF RESEARCH

In the preceding chapters, we discussed the contemporary research methods used to study human behavior and experience. Now we attempt to bring them together in a single schematic representation. To facilitate viewing them together, let us consider three dimensions of research approaches (Figure 16.1). Although we discuss the end points of these dimensions, it should be noted that each of these dimensions represents a continuum. The first dimension is the extent to which we intervene directly in the phenomenon we are studying. At one extreme is the true experiment. This is an active method that makes it possible to study relationships between variables by directly manipulating an independent variable and observing its effect on the dependent variable. Experimenters typically are interested in how one factor affects another at a given time. At the other extreme is the method of naturalistic observation. This typically is a passive method that makes it possible for researchers to attempt to describe a process as it unfolds.

It is important to realize that something is gained and something is lost whenever we adopt either of these methods. When we use naturalistic observation, we find ourselves

Figure 16.1

Schematic representation of the three-dimensional nature of research approaches

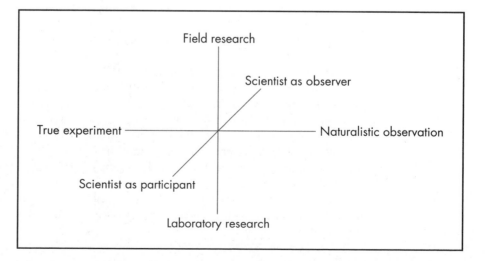

unable to test important relationships. Likewise, it is impossible to produce changes in the people who participate in our research; we must wait until new behaviors and experiences appear spontaneously. The experimental method gives us the advantage of increased control and thus the ability to infer important relationships between events. However, we have to know what we are looking for to use this method successfully. As soon as we choose a dependent variable, certain information is excluded. In general, the information that is excluded is *what we do not know to begin with.* For example, how many of us consider the weather (temperature, pressure, humidity) when we design experiments? We assume that weather is not an important factor. But some migraine sufferers, for example, report an increase of episodes before storms.

For these reasons, we suggest using the experimental method and naturalistic observation simultaneously. When conducting a true experiment, we are interested not only in the dependent variable that is being collected but also in watching the total experiment. Likewise, when observing people in naturalistic research, we consider what variables might be related and what variables might affect others. Thus, as one is developing ideas concerning a topic, there is a continuous interplay between naturalistic and experimental methods. This is true both for research and for developing ideas.

The second dimension is the research setting: laboratory versus field research. Laboratory research creates an experimental situation that includes all the important variables that affect the phenomenon we are studying. By moving our research into the laboratory, we obtain greater control over environmental factors. Field research gives us less control over environmental factors and allows for more ecologically valid behavior on the part of the person we are studying. By performing research in the field, many researchers believe the responses of the participants are more natural and thus less controlled by the demand characteristics of the experiment.

There is also a third dimension of research approach: the scientist's participation in the experiment. At one extreme is the scientist as observer; in this case it is assumed that the scientist is in no way involved in the experiment and only records data passively. At the other extreme is the scientist as participant; in this case the scientist is actually part of the study. There is no hard-and-fast determination about whether scientist-as-observer or scientist-as-participant gives the greater objectivity; it depends on the questions being asked. If you were studying the social psychology of a motorcycle gang, then more accurate information might be obtained by being part of the group rather than observing the group as an outsider. However, if you wanted to see how other people react to a motorcycle gang driving through their town, then it might be better to be an observer so that you could see the reaction of the town both during and after the event.

As you look at the dimensions of research approaches in Figure 16.1, you can see that you as a scientist have available a variety of methods and approaches to understand the questions you are studying. No one approach or method is superior. Methods are useful only in relation to a particular question being asked. To help illustrate this point, let us now divide the three-dimensional illustration in Figure 16.1 into two two-dimensional ones (Figure 16.2). As an exercise, try to determine in which quadrant the various research studies discussed in this book should be placed. Depending on the particular topic you want to study and the particular questions you ask, you will choose one of the research methods. This brings us to the next aspect of science that we want to address: the questions we study.

Field research                              Field research
            |                                           |
            |                                           |
Scientist as        Scientist as    True        _____|_____  Naturalistic
                ____|____                                |
participant         observer        experiment          |          observation
            |                                           |
            |                                           |
   Laboratory research                       Laboratory research

Figure 16.2

Two-dimensional diagrams for representing research approaches

# BEGINNING WITH A QUESTION

As we have stressed throughout our discussion, the process of science is more than the mere application of method. In fact, much of the important work of learning to be a scientist lies in the realm of remembering how to ask questions. We said *remembering* rather than *learning* because performing science is not some special activity that sets us apart from the rest of humanity; it is an activity that stems from it. To emphasize this point, in the beginning of this book, we described the scientist as being like a child out to discover the world. Part of your task as a scientist is to recapture that childlike perspective—to remember how to find the wonder and excitement of asking questions. Once you become fascinated with a process or phenomenon, then you naturally consider it, explore it, and begin to ask questions about it.

Excitement and wonder are not enough, however. Just as the child grows up and matures, the scientist moves beyond the initial excitement of a question and begins to formulate a systematic approach about how to answer the question. This usually means not just one experiment but a series of directed research studies called a *research program* (Box 16.1). In formulating such an approach, the scientist draws on both the work of others and his or her own independent ideas. We discuss the scientist's reliance on others and himself or herself in greater detail later in this chapter. For now we only want to emphasize that being excited about an idea or research question is an important beginning, but it is only a beginning. The hard work comes next.

# Philosophy of Science: Imre Lakatos

Imre Lakatos suggests that the important advances in science are made through adherence to research programs. By saying this, Lakatos means that science is more than following trial-and-error hypotheses. A research program is the examination of a number of major and minor hypotheses about a topic. Some examples Lakatos gives of research programs are Newton's theory of gravity, Einstein's relativity theory, and the theories of Freud.

An important point is whether the research program is progressive or degenerating. How do you tell the difference? The main characteristic of a progressive research program is that it predicts novel facts. Thus a progressive program leads to the discovery of new facts, whereas a degenerating program only reinterprets known facts in light of that theory. By this, Lakatos means that a degenerating research program only explains the results of already existing experiments, whereas a progressive research program leads in new directions and predicts new facts. In this way, Lakatos proposes that science changes not by sudden revolutions, as Kuhn suggested, but through the replacement of degenerating research programs with progressive ones.

For more information, see Lakatos (1978) and Eysenck (1976).

# LIMITATIONS TO FINDING ANSWERS

The scientist encounters many obstacles within the hard work of research that may limit the types of questions that can be asked. Three of the most important limitations are the tools we have available to us, our shared view of the world, and our personal psychological limitations, such as fear of making mistakes or of being rejected by our colleagues and friends.

## ■ Our Tools

Many of the questions we want to ask in science may be limited by the particular techniques available to us in the period in which we live. This is true of physical tools and technologies as well as methodological sophistication. In the same way that the telescope and the microscope allowed scientists to see worlds that were unknown, electronic developments such as the computer, the physiological amplifier, and various brain imaging devices allow us to study worlds of human behavior and experience that were previously beyond our limits. With new tools come new methodological advances. However, it is a trap to fall in love with a particular tool or research technique, be it methodological, statistical, or me-

INSTITUTE for ADVANCED HINDSIGHT

RESEARCH INTO WHAT SHOULD HAVE BEEN

S. Harris

chanical. In such a situation, a scientist is apt to try to make all human behavior and experience conform to measurement by the favored tool. There is an old saying that if you give a child *only* a hammer, he or she will treat everything as if it were a nail. This is not the fault of the hammer but of the child's view of how a hammer should be used. The same is true for the scientist's view of the purpose of research tools, which leads us to our next point.

## ■ Our Shared View of the World

In science, a number of approaches are available, yet what we study is largely a personal decision shaped by our shared conceptions and personal perceptions. At times these conceptions can be culture-bound, leading us to believe that what we do is what people throughout the world do. For example, research in social psychology suggests that some traditional social psychology phenomena such as cognitive dissonance or the often-cited attribution error may not apply in non-Western cultures (Gilbert, Fiske, & Lindzey, 1998). At other times, our personal views or desires may influence our approach or conclusions. Research on reasoning shows that we are better at being critical of others' inferences than of our own and that we are more likely to construct models that support our own views rather than refute them (Johnson-Laird, 1999). Although we all think and act in accordance with our representations of reality, scientists are just beginning to study when children first come to realize that it is the representation of reality rather than reality itself that guides much of behavior and experience (Flavell, 1999).

One of the greatest problems for a scientist interested in discovering new truths is related to our views of the world. Some writers call these views *tacit* or *metaphysical,* as well as *unconscious.* We all have assumptions that guide and direct our behavior, such as "People are evil," "Humankind is an aggressive species," "All behavior is learned," or "All behavior is innate." Even the law of parsimony (which states that the best explanation in science is the least complicated) is itself an untested metaphysical assumption. Having assumptions is not the problem; the real problem, as biologist David Bohm suggests, occurs when a person confuses the assumptions with directly observed facts (Bohm, 1969). Take a common example of this problem: In the morning we *see* the sunrise and in the evening we *see* the sunset. But the sun neither rises nor sets; it is we who are turning in space and move into sight of the sun and out of sight of the sun. Once this discrepancy is pointed out to you, you will agree, and you even may see the next sunrise or sunset differently.

A scientific example of the problem is that people once believed heavy objects would reach the ground faster than lighter ones. Two more recent examples are the belief that organs innervated by the autonomic nervous system (the heart, the stomach, and certain glands) are beyond self-regulation and the belief that our immune system is not influenced by psychological processes such as grief. These beliefs have been called into question, and we have come to recognize that our thoughts, feelings, and actions have a profound influence on our bodies. For example, experimental demonstrations show clearly the importance of psychological interventions in cancer survival (Baum & Posluszny, 1999; Cohen & Herbert, 1996; Spiegel, Bloom, Kraemer, & Gotthel, 1989).

From the discovery of the manner in which our emotions influence our biochemistry to the finding that jogging reduces depression, we are coming to discover important interactions between our behaviors and the physiological and biochemical processes of the brain. In fact, we are learning that experience is a major contributor to the manner in which the brain develops (Kolb & Whishaw, 1998, Pantev, Engelien, Candia, & Elbert, 2001).

Psychology is also gaining a new appreciation of genetics, a field largely ignored during a time when learning was thought to account for all behavior (McGuffin, Riley, & Plomin, 2001), as well as for what can be learned from ethology and evolutionary biology. For example, the New York Academy of Sciences published a volume (April 2000) on evolutionary psychology with an emphasis on human reproductive behavior. Traditional psychological journals such as *Child Development* (Bjorklund & Pellegrini, 2000) and *Journal of Abnormal Psychology* (August 1999 series of articles on "Evolutionary versus prototype analysis on the concept of disorder") have devoted recent issues to understanding their fields from an evolutionary perspective.

As we reconsider the questions that our organism is designed to answer, especially from the perspective of evolution, we find ourselves rethinking the nature of emotion, language, and even consciousness itself. This and other shifts in our views highlight the importance of new approaches to studying human functioning. Much traditional scientific research and thought have been directed at "normal behavior" and the pathological exception exemplified by neuroses and psychoses.

One area yet to be explored systematically is that of human potential—although there are suggestions for how this field could appear (Seligman & Csikszentmihalyi, 2000). Questions of potential ask what a person can do in the *best of cases*. In relation to this question, researchers are exploring creativity, musical and artistic abilities, genius, and even what makes excellent scientists.

Scientists recently have begun to shift in their view of the world, from seeing processes as stable to asking how instability and fluctuations are a part of nature. Included in this shift is a renewed interest in patterns of behavior, complexity, and the manner in which processes evolve. One example of such an approach uses models based on nonlinear system analysis or chaos (Elbert et al., 1994; Gleick, 1987; Ruelle, 1991). This approach has been applied to a variety of systems, including meteorology, physiology, and physical systems. The chaos approach suggests that small changes in initial conditions may produce

"I HOPE WE GET TO COMMUNICATE WITH THEM. I'D JUST LIKE TO TELL THEM WE HAVE NO INTEREST IN COMMUNICATING WITH THEM."

large deviations in expected trajectories later. In developmental psychology, clinical psychology, and health psychology, it is easy to imagine situations in which initial brief exposures (e.g., to a second language, abuse, health, or illness) would greatly influence one's later trajectory through life.

In a different context, Bandura (1982) argues that many of what we consider significant events in our lives (whom we marry, where we go to college, where we work, etc.) are often the results of brief chance encounters. Such thinking makes us reconsider what the "normal" trajectory is in terms of behavior, which in turn may give way to the possibility that our simple *view of regularity* may not offer the best alternative. For example, in Chapter 1 we brought to your attention the paper by Goldberger and Rigney (1991), in which the authors suggest that the normal heart pattern is chaotic and that a regular pattern may be a sign of pathology. Such work requires that we rethink our shared view of the world. The chaos approach has been applied to a variety of other processes, including psychology in general (Abraham, 1990) and cognitive and sensory processes within the brain (Ray, Wells, Elbert, Lutzenberger, & Birbaumer, 1991) in particular.

## ■ Our Psychological Limitations

Emotional learning blocks have been of great interest to cognitive psychologists (Bransford, 1979). Such blocks may result from a fear of performing poorly, looking stupid in the eyes of others, or feeling foolish. Some authors (Horner, 1972; Maslow, 1971) suggest that some of us fear success. In all fairness, if the people in our learning experiments and other studies display these fears, then we must entertain the possibility that we as scientists possess the same fears. Thus, one major limitation to new discovery is our own fear of what the discovery might mean for us personally.

Some scientists have begun to record their psychological processing as they perform the work of science, giving us valuable insight into some of our psychological limitations.

One famous example is Watson's *The Double Helix* (1968). This book records not only the scientific search for the structure of DNA but also the psychological jealousies and ego motivation that surrounded this search, as well as something of the manner in which they influenced science. In a formal study, Mitroff studied scientists and their psychological reactions to science. In particular, he examined how scientists who studied the composition of the moon reacted when rock specimens were brought back initially, especially when these rock formations were in conflict with the scientists' own theories. Mitroff also examined how scientists relate psychologically to their families and their work and how they express their emotions (Mitroff, 1974; Mitroff & Fitzgerald, 1977). Mitroff and Fitzgerald end their report by agreeing with Maslow's conclusion that science can serve as a defense and a way of avoiding life, or it can serve as a means of increasing psychological health (Maslow, 1966). Likewise, Mahoney (1976) attempted to examine our myths of the scientist and replace them with a more accurate picture of science as performed by real people who, like everyone else, have real emotions and limitations.

---

✓ **CONCEPT CHECK 16.1**   Professor Finn taught his class that in science, "Data speak for themselves," and that in research, "We leave our human problems behind." How might you respond?

---

# SCIENCE AS A COMPLEX HUMAN PROCESS

In this section, we want to make more explicit some of the themes we have presented throughout this book. With many of these themes we have emphasized that science is a complex human process involving a deep commitment to experiencing the world as it is, regardless of our preconceived notions or hypotheses about its nature; a strong concern for both the scientist and the research participant, involving both ethical and moral issues; and a profound desire to better understand the many issues and problems that confront us in our world. Thus, we are saying that science concerns itself with truth, value, and relevance.

In 1890, T. C. Chamberlin, a scientist and president of the University of Wisconsin, published a paper in the journal *Science* (Chamberlin, 1890/1965) in which he addresses many of the issues we have been indirectly concerned with in this book. In particular, he discusses the means for transcending our own preconceptions and pet theories to arrive at a more accurate picture of reality. Chamberlin begins his article by suggesting that there are two fundamental approaches to learning about the world. The first consists of "attempting to follow by close imitation the processes of previous thinkers, or to acquire by memorizing the results of their investigations." By this, Chamberlin means that you learn science by copying the experiments of previously successful scientists, and you come to learn the methods that they used. This type of study has constituted the majority of the material in this book. As a student of science, it is your first task to be able to replicate the successful procedures of others, and to do this you must know the accepted methods of study. We refer to many of these procedures in Figures 16.1 and 16.2.

The second approach Chamberlin calls *primary* or *creative study:*

In it the effort is to think independently, or at least individually, in the endeavor to discover new truth, or to make new combinations of truth, or at least to develop an individualized aggregation of truth. The endeavor is to think for one's self, whether the thinking lies wholly in the fields of previous thought or not. It is not necessary to this habit of study that the subject-material be new; but the process of thought and its results must be individual and independent, not the mere following of previous lines of thought ending in predetermined results. (Chamberlin, 1890/1965, p. 754)

One clear example of this approach is presented by Einstein. In the early 1900s, physicists relied on either Newton's theory or Maxwell's equations to help them understand the world. Einstein chose neither approach but began with what he considered a *thought experiment.* He imagined a person riding on a streetcar moving away from a town clock. What would happen, Einstein wondered, if the car traveled at the speed of light? Because the light reflected from the clock would be traveling at the speed of light and the person in the car was also traveling at the speed of light, the light reflecting from the clock would be traveling at the same speed as the person perceiving the clock. Thus the person would always be *seeing* the same time on the clock; time would have stopped. If one imagines the person in the car going faster than the speed of light, he would actually be going faster than the light reflected from the clock, and thus he would see the clock going backward.

These thought experiments helped Einstein see the world in a new and independent way, of which he himself was unsure. Because these thought experiments made predictions that Einstein did not believe initially, he turned to philosophy to consider his predictions. The result was that Einstein realized that our concept of time comes out of the unconscious. That is to say, our concept of time is not something absolute but rather an unconscious conclusion of our mind based on the input of sensory information. We had always *assumed* time to be an absolute. The real absolute, as Einstein soon suggested, was not time but the speed of light. Later experimentation supported this conclusion.

Not only does the example of Einstein help us to understand Chamberlin's second, or creative, approach to science, but it is also a good illustration of the scientist's willingness to work through a problem logically and consider surprising outcomes, even when the outcomes go against personal or traditional conceptions of the world.

Chamberlin suggests that a scientist's desire to see the world from a particular perspective can be transcended through a method he called *multiple working hypotheses.* This method is one that considers a family of hypotheses, each leading to different conclusions or interpretations. For Chamberlin this method could be applied both to one's thinking and to one's research. (In Chapter 3 we presented Platt's interpretation of this method in relation to research.) By considering two or more alternative hypotheses, we often are able to advance to more sophisticated questions. For example, in the early history of psychology, some scientists argued that all behavior was innate, and they were able to find support for this theory. Other scientists suggested that all behavior was environmentally determined, and they found support for this theory. Today, by considering both theories, it has been possible to move beyond either and to study how environmental *and* innate factors interact.

Here again, we do not want to consider just one hypothesis but rather a family of hypotheses that compete with each other and offer alternative views of reality. Chamberlin suggests that the method of multiple working hypotheses can be applied not only to hypotheses but also to methods themselves. We demonstrate this application later in the chapter. Chamberlin suggests that by adopting the method of multiple working hypotheses, one will not accidentally place one's motivation in the demonstration that a pet theory is true but rather will search for truth.

# VALUE IN SCIENCE

The second theme we have emphasized in this book is the role of value in science. As we have suggested, the domain of value is separate from the domain of science. However, this is not to say that there is no overlap between domains. Consider Figure 16.3. In this diagram, the domain of science represents the world in which we test hypotheses and create theory. The domain of value cuts across the domain of science and thus influences science. The question of ethical research and moral concern for the scientist and the research participant is one clear example of the manner in which the world of value influences science. We should remember that although we are influenced in science by value, we in no way test the validity of our ethical and moral values; that is, every scientist brings with him or her specific values that remain unexamined in the process of science. However, based on our common heritage and collective statements of guidance, such as the APA's ethical principles, we hope that there is little actual difference between scientists in terms of ethical values.

As important as ethics are, there are other values that people bring to the scientific enterprise. Like ethics, these values are untestable from the standpoint of science, but they often enter into the choice of research questions as well as the interpretation of information. For example, many atomic scientists have been committed to the peaceful use of atomic energy, and some of these scientists have refused to work on projects that could lead to weapons of

**Figure 16.3**

Intersection of the planes of science and value

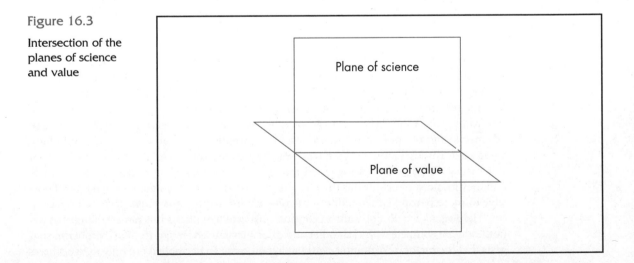

Plane of science

Plane of value

war. However, other scientists have felt that a strong defense system is necessary for maintaining their values, and they have engaged in scientific searches that could lead to better weapons of war. Likewise, in the behavioral sciences, some scientists suggest that behavior modification or particular drugs—or even hormone changes—offer important means of rehabilitating prisoners, whereas others see these techniques as a denial of freedom and refuse to support such efforts. In health care, we also have seen a recent emphasis on the necessity of not just prolonging life but also evaluating the psychological quality of a prolonged life.

Beyond the question of applying scientific knowledge to technological advances, individual scientists also hold personal values not directly connected with their scientific work. For example, Jonas Salk, the developer of the Salk polio vaccine, concerned himself with humanity and worked to understand how we shape our own evolution (Salk, 1973). In particular, he stressed how our own ego gives human beings the possibility to destroy our species unless we are willing to become actively involved in trying to understand the value judgments facing us. Other scientists have stressed the importance of universal love or the nonviolent teachings of Gandhi. Einstein, for example, stressed the importance of opposing war. Still others have pursued music or poetry on a personal level. Newton spent much of his time reading the Book of Revelation in the Bible, trying to understand its meaning and relevance for the future.

The important point is that the scientist has never been without values; there is no such person as a completely dispassionate scientist. *Science cannot be performed in a value-free way.* Science historian Jacob Bronowski (1965) argues "that the practice of science compels the practitioner to form for himself a fundamental set of universal values." An example of a scientist's attempt to describe his values in relation to science and the study of consciousness is Roger Sperry's 1983 book *Science and Moral Priority.*

# RELEVANCE

The third theme we want to discuss is that scientists possess a desire to better understand the world in which we live, as well as the organisms (including ourselves) that live in it. For many scientists, this desire has manifested itself in a cry for relevance. Some scientists have directed their research toward broad ecological concerns. Others have focused their explorations on understanding physical and mental disorders. Still others have attempted to explore new areas that hold promise for the future development of humans as a species.

In recent years, increasing efforts have been made not only to understand psychological disorders but also to develop and evaluate new methods of treatment. One example of such work is Skinner's early attempts, through applying learning theory techniques, to help neurotic and psychotic people. Another is Neal Miller's attempt to apply learning principles to modify physiological disorders.

Other psychologists have attempted to move beyond normal and pathological processing and ask, "What is a person's potential?" Maslow (1970) has tried to study people who are living up to their abilities. He calls these people *self-actualized* and has begun initial descriptive explorations into their behaviors and experiences.

Other researchers point out that because we study lessened states of awareness such as sleep and coma, we should also study hyperaware states or altered states of consciousness. In an article in *Science,* Tart (1972) suggests that we need to develop a state-specific science. By this, he means that scientific methods and approaches that are appropriate to the study of one state of consciousness (such as sleep) may not be appropriate to the study of other states of consciousness (such as drug experiences or states of ecstasy). Thus, each state of consciousness may require different scientific approaches.

Not only does the question of relevance address broad concerns, but it also leads us to evaluate specific research efforts. One case in point is the need to distinguish *scientifically significant* results from results that are *statistically significant.* When researchers compare experimental and control groups in an experiment, it is possible to find statistically significant differences, suggesting that the variations were not the result of chance. *However, the differences themselves, even if statistically significant, may be so small as to have no significant scientific meaning.*

Let us look at a simple example. Assume you developed a new technique for decreasing blood pressure through relaxation. After months of testing, you might find that your technique did result in statistically significant differences between experimental and control groups. However, on close examination, you might discover that members of the experimental group reduced their blood pressure by only 2 to 4 mm Hg and still showed blood pressures in the hypertensive range. Your results, although statistically significant, would not be clinically significant and thus could not be presented as a treatment for high blood pressure. Thus, it is possible to achieve statistically significant differences in science that are of such small magnitude as to be considered scientifically insignificant.

 CONCEPT CHECK 16.2   "The way to get ahead is to work all the time, read every piece of literature, and perform study after study." Do you think this is good advice if you want to make a contribution to science?

# SCIENCE AS A MEANS OF TRANSCENDENCE

In the previous sections, we suggested that scientists are influenced by considerations of truth, value, and relevance. Thus, science is and always has been something beyond mere methods. We approached these considerations from the standpoint of the scientist. However, science can serve another function besides expanding knowledge. It can aid us in our own growth and development both as individuals and as a society. We suggest that one value of science is its ability to aid us in transcending our personal and collective limitations. In the process of science we commit ourselves to the search for truth over and above our personal beliefs. To begin a search for understanding carries with it the commitment to accept the answers that we find and to share these answers with others (Box 16.2).

In this manner, scientific knowledge represents a superior knowledge—a knowledge that remains constantly open to question and revision. Scientific knowledge represents

Box 16.2

## Lewis Thomas on the Nature of Science

It is hard to predict how science is going to turn out, and if it is really good science it is impossible to predict. This is the nature of the enterprise. If the things to be found are actually new, they are by definition unknown in advance, and there is no way of telling in advance where a really new line of inquiry will lead. You cannot make choices in this matter, selecting things you think you're going to like and shutting off the lines that make for discomfort. You either have science or you don't, and if you have it you are obliged to accept the surprising and disturbing pieces of information, even the overwhelming and upheaving ones, along with the neat and promptly useful bits. It is like that.

The only solid piece of scientific truth about which I feel totally confident is that we are profoundly ignorant about nature. Indeed, I regard this as the major discovery of the past hundred years of biology. It is, in its way, an illuminating piece of news. It would have amazed the brightest minds of the eighteenth-century Enlightenment to be told by any of us how little we know, and how bewildering seems the way ahead. It is this sudden confrontation with the depth and scope of ignorance that represents the most significant contribution of twentieth-century science to the human intellect. We are, at last, facing up to it. In earlier times, we either pretended to understand how things worked or ignored the problem, or simply made up stories to fill the gaps. Now that we have begun exploring in earnest, doing serious science, we are getting glimpses of how huge the questions are, and how far from being answered. Because of this, these are hard times for the human intellect, and it is no wonder that we are depressed. It is not so bad being ignorant if you are totally ignorant; the hard thing is knowing in some detail the reality of ignorance, the worst spots and here and there the not-so-bad spots, but no true light at the end of any tunnel nor even any tunnels that can yet be trusted. Hard times, indeed.

But we are making a beginning, and there ought to be some satisfaction, even exhilaration, in that. The method works. There are probably no questions we can think up that can't be answered, sooner or later, including even the matter of consciousness. To be sure, there may well be questions we can't think up, ever, and therefore limits to the reach of human intellect which we will never know about, but that is another matter. Within our limits, we should be able to work our way through to all our answers, if we keep at it long enough, and pay attention.

*Source:* From Thomas (1979, pp. 73–74)

superior knowledge not in the sense that it is correct but in the sense that it is open to question, rebuttal, and change. Without the willingness to reconsider, reexamine, and reevaluate knowledge, that knowledge—however valuable at the moment in which it is presented—becomes dogma and lacks the life to lead us to an increasing understanding of the world in which we live.

As Karl Popper (1959, 1972), G. Spencer-Brown (1979), Thomas Kuhn (1970), and others have shown us, we must consider that every theory is inadequate and will one day be refuted. This should cause not despair but hope—the hope that through science we can reduce the amount of ignorance we collectively hold. With each new theory we advance, we give ourselves the opportunity to understand the world in a new way. Each new approach and theory is somewhat like a pair of glasses that shapes our perspective and gives a certain focus to what we view. With a particular pair of glasses we are able to view our world and to draw a map of what we see. As useful as this process is for science, it is equally important that we remember there is a difference between the map and the reality that the map represents. Herein lie both the hope and the limitation of science. The hope is that through science we can produce maps useful for our times. The limitation is that we may forget that there is a difference and confuse the map we have drawn with the reality with which we live.

To point out that there is a distinction between the world in which we live and the manner in which we describe it scientifically, we have introduced three separate perspectives in this book: the perspectives of the scientist, the research participant, and the witness. At this time we can reunite these perspectives and remind ourselves that they are not separate but actually highly interrelated. As single beings incorporating these perspectives, we can begin to understand our world from a multifaceted perspective. It is through the interplay of these three aspects that science comes alive. Just as we suggested at the beginning of this book that to understand life we must experience it, we suggest now that to know science we must fully perceive these three aspects—the scientist, the research participant, and the witness—within ourselves.

It is also important that we reexamine the domains of exploration as presented in Chapter 1. Consider the matrix in Figure 16.4, which represents one way of studying ourselves and others. On one side of the matrix are the categories *I* and *You* and across the top the categories *Experience* and *Behavior*. Throughout the brief history of scientific psychology we have focused our energy on the fourth cell—the study of external behavior—although originally psychology also emphasized the first cell, personal experience. As the science of psychology developed, the early work directed at the first cell was ignored or discarded, often in the name of being *scientific*. Psychology became almost a battleground between those who were interested in behavior and those who were interested in experience.

Today this has begun to change, and we are seeing a new group of scientists emerging who are interested in the study of both behavior *and* experience, not only in others but also in themselves. Whereas psychology had been attempting to reduce the specific cells in the matrix we were studying, the field is beginning to include topics and approaches from all the cells.

**Figure 16.4**

**Four fields of knowing**

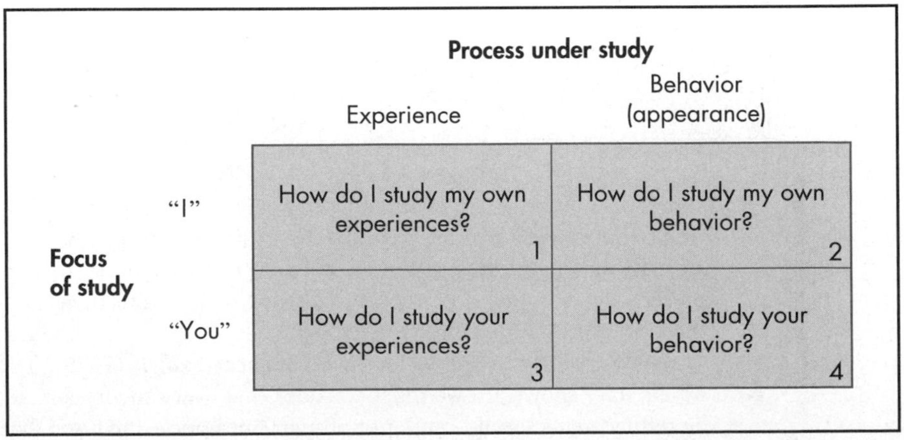

| | | Process under study | |
|---|---|---|---|
| | | Experience | Behavior (appearance) |
| Focus of study | "I" | How do I study my own experiences? 1 | How do I study my own behavior? 2 |
| | "You" | How do I study your experiences? 3 | How do I study your behavior? 4 |

We are just beginning to explore the behavior and experience available to us, and there are many gaps in our knowledge that need to be filled. We hope that you have come to see that the topics we study in psychology are complex and defy single-minded approaches. It should be clear that the study of any cell of the matrix we discussed in this section, although an important and useful beginning, can never give us a complete picture of psychological functioning. It is your job to understand the traditional methods and approaches and be able to replicate important work. However, it is also your job to look to a fuller understanding of behavior and experience in the future.

> ☑ CONCEPT CHECK 16.3    Throughout the history of psychology, we have gone through periods that emphasized either the experience of the individual or the behavior of the individual. How might behavior and experience be considered together in any future science of psychology?

# KEY TERMS AND CONCEPTS

1. **Types of research and the relationship of the scientist and the research participant**
   A. Field research
   B. Laboratory research
   C. True experiment
   D. Naturalistic observation
   E. Scientist as observer
   F. Scientist as participant
2. **Limitations to knowing**
   A. Available tools
   B. Shared view of the world
   C. Personal psychological limitations

3. **Lakatos: Research programs**
4. **Science as a complex human process**
5. **Chamberlin**
   A. Two types of science
      ▪ Imitations
      ▪ Primary or creative study
   B. Method of multiple working hypotheses
6. **Value in science**
7. **Relevance in science**
8. **Science as a means of transcendence**

# SUMMARY

1. Research is a multifaceted process that can be divided along three dimensions. The first dimension relates to the research setting (laboratory versus field). The second dimension relates to the type of method used (naturalistic observation versus true experiment). The third dimension relates to the role of the experimenter (observer or participant). A given piece of research may lie anywhere along these three dimensions.
2. The process of science is more than merely applying methods. It is an important part of being human and as such requires that we consider both human limitations and human values.
3. Three important limitations are the tools available to us, our shared view of the world, and our personal psychological limitations.

4. In 1890, Chamberlin suggested two fundamental approaches to learning about the world. The first approach consists of learning by imitating other scientists. The second approach involves making an effort to think independently in the endeavor to discover new truth. Einstein and his use of thought experiments presents an example of this second approach.
5. Science cannot be viewed as value free. All scientists have values, and these values influence how they perform science and what topics they research.
6. The desire for relevance has directed some scientists to attempt a better understanding of our human condition. For example, many scientists have turned their attention toward the question of aging because more people are living longer. Other researchers are looking

(continued)

## SUMMARY *(continued)*

not only to questions of psychopathology but also to those of human potential.

7. A distinction can be drawn between results that are statistically significant and results that are scientifically significant.

8. We are only beginning to understand ourselves as humans. Many questions have yet to be answered, such as those related to consciousness and self-awareness. Many of these questions are complex and defy single-minded approaches.

9. Behavior and experience are two important aspects that must be included in any attempt to describe and understand human processes.

## REVIEW QUESTIONS

1. Why do we have to know what we are looking for in order to use the experimental method?

2. Give an example of when it would be more useful for a scientist to be a participant in an experiment and when it would be more useful to be an observer.

3. What is a research program?

4. What does this chapter suggest are the major limitations to our learning about the world? Give examples of each type of limitation.

5. Describe the two approaches to knowing discussed by Chamberlin.

6. What is the difference between statistical significance and scientific significance?

7. According to Lewis Thomas, how has science changed since the 18th century?

8. In what way can it be said that science has the potential to be a superior knowledge?

9. Discuss the four fields of knowing (Figure 16.4).

## DISCUSSION QUESTIONS AND PROJECTS

1. Give some examples of how untested assumptions have shaped what we study in psychology.

2. What is meant by the statement, "If you give a child only a hammer, he or she will treat everything like a nail"? How does this idea apply to research?

3. How are emotional blocks to learning, such as fear of failure or even fear of success, related to performing research?

4. Some people say that science is value free. Discuss this statement and describe ways in which values enter science.

5. What does Lakatos mean by the term *novel fact*?

6. What is similar about Lakatos's and Thomas's views of science?

7. What might the study of experience offer psychology?

## InfoTrac College Edition: Exercises

This chapter sought to move beyond questions of methodology *per se* and ask broader questions concerning human behavior and experience. Using InfoTrac College Edition, you can begin such a quest in the *Annual Reviews of Psychology*. For example, in the chapter, we referred to the Kolb & Whishaw (1998) article on brain plasticity ("Brain plasticity and behavior"), which describes the manner in which experience is able to shape the brain's development. We also discussed a psychology of potential and ask what a person can do in the best of cases. The *Annual Review* (1998) article "Giftedness: An exceptionality examined" discusses the question of being exceptional. Another view of potential is to examine the question of well-being which can be seen in the 2001 *Annual Review of Psychology* article "On happiness and human potentials." Also the 1999 *Annual Review* has an article entitled

"Trust and distrust in organizations: Emerging perspectives, enduring questions" discusses the question of trust and cooperation in organizations.

We also introduced you to questions of animal cognition. Also in the 1999 *Annual Review* is an article reviewing the current theory and research in this area by S. Boysen and G. Himes. In this last chapter, we also return to our theme of better understanding the individuals who do science. Fortunately, the *Journal of Cognitive Neuroscience* has published interviews with well-known neuroscientists such as Michael Posner, Larry Squire, Jon Kaas, and others. These can be found by searching for the *Journal of Cognitive Neuroscience* and looking for articles beginning with the word *Interview*.

## ☑ Answers to Concept Checks

**16.1** Although some data do seem to make a point very clearly, these data are always interpreted within the context of a particular theoretical approach to the world. Thus, data are always interpreted within the context of a shared world and never in isolation. In addition, numerous studies have shown that our humanness enters into the process of science. Although we seek through the scientific enterprise to transcend our limitations, on a very real level we always carry our humanness—and therefore our frailty—with us, even in science.

**16.2** Actually, it is bad advice. Of course, it is important to understand the literature and to work hard. However, as Chamberlin suggested more than 100 years ago, it is equally important to think. That is, it is important to reconsider the question that one is asking from a variety of perspectives and not to accept the interpretations of others. A colleague of ours suggests that his graduate students take a notepad, go out into the woods, and just think about the questions they want to answer in their research.

**16.3** Although we can tell you how it is being accomplished today, it becomes your job to tell us how you will accomplish this feat as you begin to direct psychological research that is relevant and accurate and reflects both the behavior and experiences of the people you study.

# GUIDELINES TO REDUCE BIASED LANGUAGE IN SCIENTIFIC WRITING

Over the years, the issue of biased language in writing about individuals and groups has become an important consideration. Over the past 30 years, the *Publication Manual* of the American Psychological Association has emphasized nonsexist language. Other task forces of the APA have developed guidelines in relation to sexual orientation, racial and ethnic identity, disability and age. These can be viewed at the APA Web site (www.apa.org).

With the 7th edition of the *Publication Manual of the American Psychological Association*, work of the various task forces has been brought together in a single set of guidelines. These guidelines are designed to reduce ambiguity and bias in language in terms of gender, sexual orientation, racial and ethnic identity, disabilities and age.

## APA GUIDELINES TO REDUCE BIAS IN LANGUAGE

As a publisher, APA accepts authors' word choices unless those choices are inaccurate, unclear, or ungrammatical. As an organization, APA is committed both to science and to the fair treatment of individuals and groups, and this policy requires authors of APA publications to avoid perpetuating demeaning attitudes and biased assumptions about people in their writing. Constructions that might imply bias against persons on the basis of gender, sexual orientation, racial or ethnic group, disability, or age should be avoided. Scientific writing should be free of implied or irrelevant evaluation of the group or groups being studied.

Long-standing cultural practice can exert a powerful influence over even the most conscientious author. Just as you have learned to check what you write for spelling, grammar, and wordiness, practice reading over your work for bias. You can test your writing for implied evaluation by reading it while (a) substituting your own group for the group or groups you are discussing or (b) imagining you are a member of the group you are discussing (Maggio, 1991). If you feel excluded or offended, your material needs further revision. Another suggestion is to ask people from that group to read your material and give you candid feedback.

What follows is a set of guidelines, followed in turn by discussions of specific issues that affect particular groups. These are not rigid rules. You may find that some attempts to follow the guidelines result in wordiness or clumsy prose. As always, good judgment is required. If your writing reflects respect for your participants and your readers, and if you write with appropriate specificity and precision, you will be contributing to the goal of accurate, unbiased communication. Specific examples for each guideline are given in Table 2.1 on p. 381 at the end of this appendix.

## ■ Guideline 1: Describe at the Appropriate Level of Specificity

Precision is a necessity in scientific writing; when you refer to a person or persons, choose words that are accurate, clear, and free from bias. The appropriate degree of specificity depends on the research question and the present state of knowledge in the field of study. When in doubt, it is better to be more specific rather than less, because it is easier to aggregate published data than to diaggregate them. For example, using *man* to refer to all human beings is simply not as accurate as the phrase *men and women*. To describe age groups, it is better to give a specific age range ("ages 65–83") instead of a broad category ("over 65"; see Schaie, 1993). When describing racial and ethnic groups, be appropriately specific and sensitive to issues of labeling. For example, instead of describing participants as Asian American or Hispanic American, it may be helpful to describe them by their nation or region of origin (e.g., Chinese Americans, Mexican Americans). If you are discussing sexual orientation, realize that some people interpret *gay* as referring to men and women, whereas others interpret the term as including only men (for clarity, *gay men* and *lesbians* currently are preferred).

Broad clinical terms such as *borderline* and people at *risk* are loaded with innuendo unless properly explained. Specify the diagnosis that is borderline (e.g., "people with borderline personality disorder"). Identify the risk and the people it involves (e.g., "children at risk for early school dropout").

*Gender* is cultural and is the term to use when referring to men and women as social groups. *Sex* is biological; use it when the biological distinction is predominant. Note that the word *sex* can be confused with *sexual behavior*. *Gender* helps keep meaning unambiguous, as in the following example: "In accounting for attitudes toward the bill, sexual orientation rather than gender accounted for most of the variance. Most gay men and lesbians were for the proposal; most heterosexual men and women were against it."

Part of writing without bias is recognizing that differences should be mentioned only when relevant. Marital status, sexual orientation, racial and ethnic identity, or the fact that a person has a disability should not be mentioned gratuitously.

## ■ Guideline 2: Be Sensitive to Labels

Respect people's preferences; call people what they prefer to be called (Maggio, 1991). Accept that preferences will change with time and that individuals within groups often disagree about the designations they prefer (see Raspberry, 1989). Make an effort to determine what is appropriate for your situation; you may need to ask your participants which designations they prefer, particularly when preferred designations are being debated within groups.

Avoid labeling people when possible. A common occurrence in scientific writing is that participants in a study tend to lose their individuality; they are broadly categorized as objects (noun forms such as *the gays* and *the elderly*) or, particularly in descriptions of people with disabilities, are equated with their conditions—*the amnesiacs, the depressives, the schizophrenics, the LDs,* for example. One solution is to use adjectival forms (e.g., "gay *men,*" "elderly *people,*" "amnesic *patients*"). Another is to "put the person first," followed by a descriptive phrase (e.g., "people diagnosed with schizophrenia"). Note that the latter solution currently is preferred when describing people with disabilities.

When you need to mention several groups in a sentence or paragraph, such as when reporting results, do your best to balance sensitivity, clarity, and parsimony. For example, it may be cumbersome to repeat phrases such as "person with _____." If you provide operational definitions of groups early in your paper (e.g., "Participants scoring a minimum

of X on the X scale constituted the high verbal group, and those scoring below X constituted the low verbal group"), it is scientifically informative and concise to describe participants thereafter in terms of the measures used to classify them (e.g., ". . . was significant:
high verbal group, $p < .05$"), *provided the terms are inoffensive.* A label should not be used
in any form that is perceived as pejorative; if such a perception is possible, you need to find
more neutral terms. For example, *the demented* is not repaired by changing it to *demented
group,* but *dementia group* would be acceptable. Abbreviations or series labels for groups
usually sacrifice clarity and may offend: *LDs* or *LD group* to describe people with specific
learning difficulties is offensive; *HVAs* for "high verbal ability group" is difficult to decipher.
*Group A* is not offensive, but neither is it descriptive.

Recognize the difference between *case,* which is an occurrence of a disorder or illness,
and *patient,* which is a person affected by the disorder or illness and receiving a doctor's
care (Huth, 1987). "Manic-depressive cases were treated" is problematic; revise to "The patients with bipolar disorders were treated."

Bias may be promoted when the writer uses one group (usually the writer's own
group) as the standard against which others are judged. In some contexts, the term *culturally deprived* may imply that one culture is the universally accepted standard. The unparallel nouns in the phrase *man and wife* may inappropriately prompt the reader to evaluate
the roles of the individuals (i.e., the woman is defined only in terms of her relationship to
the man) and the motives of the author. The phrase *husband and wife* or *man and woman*
is parallel and undistracting. Usage of *normal* may prompt the reader to make the comparison of *abnormal,* thus stigmatizing individuals with differences. For example, contrast-
ing lesbians with "the general public" or with "normal women" portrays lesbians as marginal to society. More appropriate comparison groups might be "heterosexual women,"
"heterosexual women and men," or "gay men."

## ■ Guideline 3: Acknowledge Participation

Write about the people in your study in a way that acknowledges their participation. Replace
the impersonal term *subjects* with a more descriptive term when possible and appropriate—
*participants, individuals, college students, children,* or *respondents,* for example. *Subjects* and
*sample* are appropriate when discussing statistics, and *subjects* may also be appropriate when
there has been no direct consent by the individual involved in the study (e.g., infants or some
individuals with severe brain damage or dementia). The passive voice suggests individuals
are *acted on* instead of being actors ("the students *completed* the survey" is preferable to "the
students *were given* the survey" or "the survey was *administered* to the students").
"Participants completed the trial" or "we collected data from the participants" is preferable
to "the participants *were run.*" Although not grammatically passive, "presented with symptoms" suggests passiveness; "reported symptoms" or "described symptoms" is preferred
(Knatterud, 1991). Similarly, consider avoiding terms such as *patient management* and *patient placement* when appropriate. In most cases, it is treatment, not patients, that is managed; some alternatives are "coordination of care," "supportive services," and "assistance." If
patients are able to discuss their living arrangements, describe them as such. *Failed,* as in "8
participants failed to complete the Rorschach and the MMPI," can imply a personal short-
coming instead of a research result; *did not* is a more neutral choice (Knatterud, 1991).

As you read the rest of this appendix, consult Table 2.1 on p. 381 for examples of
problematic and preferred language. Section 9.03 lists references for further information

about nondiscriminatory language and for the guidelines that the APA Publications and Communications Board received as working papers for the additions to this section; the full texts of these papers are available in updated form on an ongoing basis.

**2.13 Gender**    Avoid ambiguity in sex identity or sex role by choosing nouns, pronouns, and adjectives that specifically describe your participants. Sexist bias can occur when pronouns are used carelessly, as when the masculine pronoun *he* is used to refer to both sexes or when the masculine or feminine pronoun is used exclusively to define roles by sex (e.g., "the nurse . . . *she*"). The use of *man* as a generic noun or as an ending for an occupational title (e.g., *policeman*) can be ambiguous and may imply incorrectly that all persons in the group are male. Be clear about whether you mean one sex or both sexes.

To avoid stereotypes, use caution when providing examples:

> To illustrate this idea, **an American boy's** potential for becoming a football player might be an aggregate of strength, running speed, balance, fearlessness, and resistance to injury. [The manuscript was revised to *a child's.*]

There are many alternatives to the generic *he* (see Table 2.1), including rephrasing (e.g., from "When an individual conducts this kind of self-appraisal, *he* is a much stronger person" to "When an individual conducts this kind of self-appraisal, that person is much stronger" or "This kind of self-appraisal makes an individual much stronger"), using plural nouns or plural pronouns (e.g., from "A therapist who is too much like his client can lose *his* objectivity" to "Therapists who are too much like their clients can lose *their* objectivity"), replacing the pronoun with an article (e.g., from "A researcher must apply for *his* grant by September 1" to "A researcher must apply for *the* grant by September 1"), and dropping the pronoun (e.g., from "The researcher must avoid letting *his* own biases and expectations. . ." to "The researcher must avoid letting biases and expectations. . ."). Replacing *he* with *he or she* or *she or he* should be done sparingly because the repetition can become tiresome. Combination forms such as *he/she* or *(s)he* are awkward and distracting. Alternating between *he* and *she* also may be distracting and is not ideal; doing so implies that *he* or *she* can in fact be generic, which is not the case. Use of either pronoun unavoidably suggests that specific gender to the reader.

**2.14 Sexual Orientation**    *Sexual orientation* is not the same as *sexual preference.* In keeping with Guideline 2, *sexual orientation* currently is the preferred term and is to be used unless the implication of choice is intentional.

The terms *lesbians* and *gay men* are preferable to *homosexual* when referring to specific groups. *Lesbian* and *gay* refer primarily to identities and to the culture and communities that have developed among people who share those identities. Furthermore, *homosexuality* has been associated in the past with negative stereotypes. Also, the term *homosexual* is ambiguous because some believe it refers only to men. *Gay* can be interpreted broadly, to include men and women, or more narrowly, to include only men. Therefore, if the meaning is not clear in the context of your usage, specify gender when using this term (e.g., *gay men*). The clearest way to refer inclusively to people whose orientation is not heterosexual is to write *lesbians, gay men,* and *bisexual women or men*—although somewhat long, the phrase is accurate.

Sexual behavior should be distinguished from sexual orientation; some men and women engage in sexual activities with others of their own sex but do not consider themselves to be gay or lesbian. In contrast, the terms *heterosexual* and *bisexual* currently are used to describe both identity and behavior; adjectives are preferred to nouns. *Same-gender, male-male, female-female,* and *male-female sexual behavior* are appropriate terms for specific instances of sexual behavior in which people engage, regardless of their sexual orientation (e.g., a married heterosexual man who once had a same-gender sexual encounter).

**2.15 Racial and Ethnic Identity**    Preferences for terms referring to racial and ethnic groups change often. One reason for this is simply personal preference; preferred designations are as varied as the people they name. Another reason is that over time, designations can become dated and sometimes negative (see Raspberry, 1989). Authors are reminded of the two basic guidelines of specificity and sensitivity. In keeping with Guideline 2, authors are encouraged to ask their participants about preferred designations and are expected to avoid terms perceived as negative. For example, some people of African ancestry prefer *Black* and others prefer *African American;* both terms currently are acceptable. One the other hand, *Negro* and *Afro-American* have become dated; therefore, usage generally is inappropriate. In keeping with Guideline 1, precision is important in the description of your sample (see section 1.09); in general, use the more specific rather than the less specific term.

Racial and ethnic groups are designated by proper nouns and are capitalized. Therefore, use *Black* and *White* instead of *black* and *white* (colors to refer to other human groups currently are considered pejorative and should not be used). For modifiers, do not use hyphens in multiword names, even if the names act as unit modifiers (e.g., *Asian American* participants).

Designations for some ethnic groups are described next. These groups frequently are included in studies published in APA journals. The list is far from exhaustive but serves to illustrate some of the complexities of naming (see Table 2.1).

Depending on where a person is from, individuals may prefer to be called *Hispanic, Latino, Chicano,* or some other designation; *Hispanic* is not necessarily an all-encompassing term, and authors should consult with their participants. In general, naming a nation or region of origin is generally helpful (e.g., *Cuban* or *Central American* is more specific than *Hispanic*).

*American Indian* and *Native American* are both accepted terms for referring to indigenous peoples of North America, although *Native Americans* is a broader designation because the U.S. government includes Hawaiians and Samoans in this category. There are close to 450 Native groups, and authors are encouraged to name the participants' specific groups.

The term *Asian* or *Asian American* is preferred to the older term *Oriental.* It is generally useful to specify the name of the Asian subgroup: Chinese, Vietnamese, Korean, Pakistani, and so on.

**2.16 Disabilities**    The guiding principle for "nonhandicapping" language is to maintain the integrity of individuals as human beings. Avoid language that equates persons with their condition (e.g., *neurotics, the disabled*); that has superfluous, negative overtones (e.g., stroke *victim*); or that is regarded as a slur (e.g., *cripple*).

Use *disability* to refer to an attribute of a person and *handicap* to refer to the source of limitations, which may include attitudinal, legal, and architectural barriers as well as the disability itself (e.g., steps and curbs handicap people who require the use of a ramp).

*Challenged* and *special* are often considered euphemistic and should be used only if the people in your study prefer those terms (Boston, 1992). As a general rule, "person with _____," "person living with _____," and "person who has _____" are neutral and preferred forms of description (see Table 2.1).

2.17 Age    Age should be defined in the description of participants in the Method section (see section 1.09). Be specific in providing age ranges; avoid open-ended definitions such as "under 18" or "over 65" (Schaie, 1993). *Boy* and *girl* are correct terms for referring to people of high school age and younger. *Young man* and *young woman* and *male adolescent* and *female adolescent* may be used as appropriate. For persons 18 and older (or of college age and older), use *men* and *women*. *Elderly* is not acceptable as a noun and is considered pejorative by some as an adjective. *Older person* is preferred. Age groups may also be described with adjectives; gerontologists may prefer to use combination terms for older age groups (*young-old, old-old, very old,* and *oldest old*), which should be used only as adjectives. *Dementia* is preferred to *senility; senile dementia of the Alzheimer's type* is an accepted term.

Table 2.1

| Guidelines for Unbiased Language | |
| --- | --- |
| Problematic | Preferred |

### Guideline 1: Use an appropriate level of specificity

| | |
| --- | --- |
| The client's behavior was typically female. | The client's behavior was [specify] |

*Comment:* Being specific avoids stereotypic bias.

### Guideline 2: Be sensitive to labels

| | |
| --- | --- |
| Participants were 300 Orientals. | There were 300 Asian participants [perhaps adding "150 from Southeast Asia (Thailand, Laos, and Vietnam) and 150 from east Asia (North and South Korea)"]. |

*Comment: Orientals* is considered pejorative; use *Asian,* or be more specific.

| | |
| --- | --- |
| the elderly | older people |

*Comment:* Use adjectives as adjectives instead of as nouns.

| | |
| --- | --- |
| girls and men | women and men |

*Comment:* Use parallel terms; *girls* is correct if females of high school age or younger are meant.

### Guideline 3: Acknowledge participation

| | |
| --- | --- |
| Our study included 60 subjects. | Sixty people participated in our study. |

*Comment: Participants* is preferred to *subjects.*

### Gender

| | |
| --- | --- |
| 1. The client is usually the best judge of the value of his counseling. | The client is usually the best judge of the value of counseling. |
| | The client is usually the best judge of his or her counseling. |
| | Clients are usually the best judges of the value of the counseling they receive. |
| | The best judge of the value of counseling is usually the client. |
| 2. man, mankind | people, humanity, human beings, humankind, human species |
| man a project | staff a project, hire personnel, employ staff |
| man-machine interface | user-system interface, person-system interface, human-computer interface |

Table 2.1
(continued)

| Guidelines for Unbiased Language | |
|---|---|
| Problematic | Preferred |
| manpower | workforce, personnel, workers, human resources |
| man's search for knowledge | the search for knowledge |
| 3. males, females | men, women, boys, girls, adults, children, adolescents |

*Comment:* Specific nouns reduce the possibility of stereotypic bias and often clarify discussion. Use *male* and *female* as adjectives where appropriate and relevant (*female experimenter, male participant*). *Males* and *females* may be appropriate when the age range is quite broad or ambiguous. Avoid unparallel usage such as 10 *men* and 16 *females.*

| | |
|---|---|
| 4. Research scientists often neglect their wives and children. | Research scientists often neglect their spouses and children. |

*Comment:* Alternative wording acknowledges that women as well as men are research scientists.

| | |
|---|---|
| 5. woman doctor, lady lawyer, male nurse, woman driver | doctor or physician, lawyer, nurse, driver |

*Comment:* Specify sex only if it is a variable or if sex designation is necessary to the discussion ("13 female doctors and 22 male doctors"). *Woman* and *lady* are nouns; *female* is the adjective counterpart to *male.*

| | |
|---|---|
| 6. mothering | parenting, nurturing [or specify exact behavior] |
| 7. chairman (of an academic department) | chairperson, chair [use *chairman* only if it is known that the institution has established that form as an official title] |

*Comment: Department head* may be appropriate; however, the term is not synonymous with *chair* and *chairperson* at all institutions.

| | |
|---|---|
| chairman (presiding officer of a committee or meeting) | chairperson, chair, moderator, discussion leader |

*Comment:* In parliamentary usage, *chairman* is the official term and should not be changed. Alternatives are acceptable in most writing.

| | |
|---|---|
| 8. foreman, mailman, salesmanship | supervisor or superintendent, postal worker or letter carrier, selling ability |

Table 2.1
(continued)

| Guidelines for Unbiased Language | |
|---|---|
| Problematic | Preferred |

*Comment:* Substitute preferred noun.

| | |
|---|---|
| 9. The authors acknowledge the assistance of Mrs. John Smith. | The authors acknowledge the assistance of Jane Smith. |

*Comment:* Use given names.

| | |
|---|---|
| 10. cautious men and timid women | cautious women and men, cautious people |
| | timid men and women, timid people |

*Comment:* Some adjectives, depending on whether the person described is a man or a woman, connote bias. The examples illustrate some common usages that may not always convey exact meaning, especially when paired, as in the first column.

| | |
|---|---|
| 11. Participants were 16 men and 4 women. The women were housewives. | The men were [specify], and the women were [specify]. |

*Comment:* Describe women and men in parallel terms, or omit description of both. Do not use *housewife* to identify occupation, a term that indicates sex and marital status and excludes men. Use *homemaker,* which can denote a man.

### *Sexual orientation*

| | |
|---|---|
| 1. The sample consisted of 200 adolescent homosexuals. | The sample consisted of 200 gay male adolescents. |
| | The sample consisted of 100 gay male and 100 lesbian adolescents. |

*Comment:* Avoid use of *homosexual,* and specify gender of participants.

| | |
|---|---|
| 2. Manuscript title: "Gay Relationships in the 1990s" | "Gay Male Relationships in the 1990s" |
| | "Lesbian and Gay Male Relationships in the 1990s" |

*Comment:* Specify gender equitably.

| | |
|---|---|
| 3. Participants were asked about their homosexuality. | Participants were asked about the experience of being a lesbian or a gay man. |

*Comment:* Avoid the label *homosexuality.*

**Table 2.1**
(continued)

| Guidelines for Unbiased Language | |
| --- | --- |
| Problematic | Preferred |
| 4. The women reported lesbian sexual fantasies. | The women reported female-female sexual fantasies. |

*Comment:* Avoid confusing lesbian orientation with specific sexual behaviors.

| | |
| --- | --- |
| 5. It was the participants' sex, not their sexual orientation, that affected number of friendships. | It was the participants' gender, not their sexual orientation, that affected number of friendships. |

*Comment:* Avoid confusing gender with sexual activity.

| | |
| --- | --- |
| 6. participants who had engaged in sexual intercourse | participants who had engaged in penile-vaginal intercourse |
| | participants who had engaged in sexual intercourse or had sex with another person |

*Comment:* The first preferred example specifies kind of sexual activity, if penile-vaginal intercourse is what is meant. The second avoids the assumption of heterosexual orientation if sexual experiences with others is what is meant.

| | |
| --- | --- |
| 7. Ten participants were married, and 5 were single. | Ten participants were married, 4 were unmarried and living with partners, and 1 was unmarried and living alone. |

*Comment:* The preferred example increases specificity and acknowledges that legal marriage is only one form of committed relationship. Marital status is sometimes not a reliable indicator of cohabitation (e.g., married couples may be separated), sexual activity, or sexual orientation.

### Racial and ethnic identity

| | |
| --- | --- |
| 1. The sample included 400 undergraduate participants. | The sample of 400 undergraduates included 250 White students (125 men and 125 women) and 150 Black students (75 men and 75 women). |

*Comment:* Human samples should be fully described with respect to gender, age, and, when relevant to the study, race or ethnicity. Where appropriate, additional information should be presented (generation, linguistic background, socioeconomic status, national origin, sexual orientation, special interest group membership, etc.). Note that *African American* currently may be preferred.

**Table 2.1**
(continued)

| Guidelines for Unbiased Language | |
|---|---|
| Problematic | Preferred |

2. The 50 American Indians represented. . . .

The 50 American Indians (25 Choctaw, 15 Hopi, and 10 Seminole) represented. . . .

*Comment:* When appropriate, authors should identify American Indian groups by specific group or nation; when the broader designation is appropriate, note that *Native American* may be preferred to *American Indian.* In general, American Indian, African, and other groups prefer *people* or *nation* to *tribe.*

3. We studied Eskimos

We studied Inuit from Canada and Aleuts

*Comment:* Native peoples of northern Canada, Alaska, eastern Siberia, and Greenland may prefer *Inuk (Inuit* for plural) to *Eskimo.* Alaska Natives include many groups in addition to Eskimos.

4. Table entries:

| Race | | | Race | | |
|---|---|---|---|---|---|
| White | 21 | 15 | White | 21 | 15 |
| Non-White | 15 | 4 | African American | 10 | 1 |
| | | | Asian | 5 | 3 |

*Comment: Non-White* implies a standard of comparison and is imprecise.

5. the articulate Mexican American professor

the Mexican American professor

*Comment:* Qualifying adjectives may imply that the "articulate" Mexican American professor is an exception to the norm (for Mexican American professors). Depending on the context of the sentence, ethnic identity may not be relevant and therefore should not be mentioned.

### *Disabilities*

1. *Put people first, not their disability*

| | |
|---|---|
| disabled person | person with (who has) a disability |
| defective child | child with a congenital disability |
| | child with a birth impairment |
| mentally ill person | person with mental illness |

*Comment:* Preferred expressions avoid the implication that the person as a whole is disabled.

Table 2.1
(continued)

| Guidelines for Unbiased Language | |
|---|---|
| Problematic | Preferred |

2. *Do not label people by their disability or overextend its severity*

| | |
|---|---|
| depressives | people who are depressed |
| epileptics | individuals with epilepsy |
| borderlines | people diagnosed with borderline personality disorder |
| neurotic patients | patients with a neurosis (or neuroses) |
| the learning disabled | children with [specify the learning characteristics] |
| retarded adult | adult with mental retardation |

*Comment:* Because the person is *not* the disability, the two concepts should be separate.

3. *Use emotionally neutral expressions*

| | |
|---|---|
| stroke victim | individual who had a stroke |
| person afflicted with cerebral palsy | person with cerebral palsy |
| population suffering from multiple sclerosis | people who have multiple sclerosis |
| individual confined to a wheelchair | individual who uses a wheelchair |

*Comment:* Problematic expressions have excessive, negative overtones and suggest continued helplessness.

# PRINTED ARTICLE

Journal of Experimental Psychology: General
2001, Vol. 130, No. 3, 520–533

# Expressive Writing Can Increase Working Memory Capacity

Kitty Klein and Adriel Boals
North Carolina State University

The effect of emotional disclosure through expressive writing on available working memory (WM) capacity was examined in 2 semester-long experiments. In the first study, 35 freshmen assigned to write about their thoughts and feelings about coming to college demonstrated larger working memory gains 7 weeks later compared with 36 writers assigned to a trivial topic. Increased use of cause and insight words was associated with greater WM improvements. In the second study, students ($n = 34$) who wrote about a negative personal experience enjoyed greater WM improvements and declines in intrusive thinking compared with students who wrote about a positive experience ($n = 33$) or a trivial topic ($n = 34$). The results are discussed in terms of a model grounded in cognitive and social psychological theory in which expressive writing reduces intrusive and avoidant thinking about a stressful experience, thus freeing WM resources.

The beneficial effects of emotional disclosure through expressive writing about traumatic or stressful experiences have been widely reported (Smythe, 1998). Compared with individuals assigned to write about trivial topics, experimental participants who wrote about their deepest thoughts and feelings showed reductions in physician visits (Pennebaker & Francis, 1996), improvements in immune function (Pennebaker, Kiecolt-Glaser, & Glaser, 1988), increased antibody production (Petrie, Booth, Pennebaker, Davison, & Thomas, 1995), and increases in psychological well-being (Lepore, 1997; Murray & Segal, 1994) for several months after the expressive writing intervention. There is considerable speculation about how writing might achieve such benefits. In contrast to earlier theorizing, which emphasized the cathartic release of thoughts and feelings associated with stressful experiences (e.g., Pennebaker, 1989), current explanations focus on the cognitive changes produced by expressive writing (Pennebaker, 1997). Although there is a long tradition of examining self-reported cognitive activity in the wake of stressful events (e.g., Horowitz, 1975), the cognitive changes associated with expressive writing are inferred from analysis of the linguistic characteristics of writers' essays. Across writing episodes, participants whose essays contained increases in words reflecting causality and insight (Pennebaker & Francis, 1996; Pennebaker, Mayne, & Francis, 1997) experienced the greatest health and behavioral benefits. Pennebaker et al. (1997) believe these linguistic changes reflect the cognitive processes associated with encoding and storing features

of the experience "in a more organized, coherent, and simplified manner . . . that reduces the associated emotional arousal" (p. 864). The purpose of our experiments was to investigate directly how expressive writing might affect cognitive processing, and in particular whether working memory capacity is affected by expressive writing.

Working memory (WM) is a fundamental cognitive process, often conceived as a limited capacity system (Pennington, 1994). The central executive function of WM (Baddeley & Hitch, 1974) is responsible for the controlled processing and attention (Engle, Tuholski, Laughlin, & Conway, 1999) needed for higher order processes such as comprehension, reasoning, planning, and problem solving (Wickelgren, 1997). Measures of controlled processing, often called WM capacity tests, require the simultaneous storage and processing of information. Compared with simple short-term memory tasks, controlled attention tasks elicit different patterns of prefrontal cortex activation (Jonides et al., 1997). There are substantial and reliable correlations between controlled processing measures and higher order cognitive tasks, such as general fluid intelligence (Engle, Tuholski, et al., 1999). These relationships stand in sharp contrast to the weaker associations between higher order cognitive tasks and traditional short-term memory tasks (Engle, Kane, & Tuholski, 1999). Not surprisingly, WM capacity measures are also strongly related to performance tasks used to assess frontal lobe damage and dysfunction (Lehto, 1996; Welsh, Satterlee-Cartmell, & Stine, 1999).

To the extent that people can direct attention to task-relevant materials and operations, they will perform well on tasks requiring executive functions (Roberts & Pennington, 1996). However, in a limited capacity system, irrelevant distractors compete with task-relevant demands for attentional resources. Inhibiting responses to off-task demands leaves fewer resources for the task at hand (Stoltzfus, Hasher, & Zacks, 1996). The rationale for our research is that among the irrelevant demands that compete for resources are cognitions about ongoing stressful events and that expressive writing about these experiences reduces their draw on resources. Support for these assumptions comes from a diverse literature, including the laboratory writing paradigm (Pennebaker, 1997),

Kitty Klein and Adriel Boals, Department of Psychology, North Carolina State University.

Parts of this research and writing were supported by National Science Foundation Grant SBR 9890947. We thank James W. Pennebaker and Martha E. Francis for the use of their Second Linguistic Inquiry and Word Count program. We thank Tori Branch, Marielle Chamas, Amy Powell, Sara Snyder, and Melanie Wegener, who assisted with the data collection.

Correspondence concerning this article should be addressed to Kitty Klein, Department of Psychology, Box 7801, North Carolina State University, Raleigh, North Carolina 27695. Electronic mail may be sent to kitty_klein@ncsu.edu.

Wegner's (1994) theory of mental control, and theories about individual differences in WM capacity (Engle, Kane, & Tuholski, 1999), particularly the importance of inhibitory processes in accounting for these differences (Stoltzfus et al., 1996).

The idea that attentional resources must be shared between task-relevant and -irrelevant cognitions has received empirical support (Antrobus, 1968; Rapee, 1993; Teasdale et al., 1995; Teasdale, Proctor, Lloyd, & Baddeley, 1993). There is also experimental evidence (Darke, 1988; Sorg & Whitney, 1992) that ego-threatening manipulations impair performance on traditional WM tasks, and correlational evidence that people experiencing larger numbers of stressful life events, as well as people who report more intrusive and avoidant thinking about stressful events, are disadvantaged on WM tasks (Klein & Boals, in press). These WM impairments presumably arise because thoughts associated with the stressful experimental or life situations compete with ongoing task requirements for attentional resources.

Wegner and others (Petrie, Booth, & Pennebaker, 1998; Wegner, 1988, 1992) have proposed that people want to inhibit thoughts involving negative emotion, losses, and stressful events. Wegner's (1994) ironic processing model holds that the detection of such unwanted thoughts is an automatic process, but attempts to inhibit these cognitions require attentional resources. When there is competition for resources, inhibition is less successful. Studying under cognitive load leads to better memory for items participants are told not to remember compared with studying without a cognitive load (Wegner & Erber, 1992). Compared with no-load conditions, reaction times are longer on a modified Stroop task under load when the target words are related to events people were told to inhibit (Wegner, Erber, & Zanakos, 1993).

Wegner has also addressed the effects of directed suppression on the cognitive representation of events. Wegner, Quillian, and Houston (1996) found that people told not to think about a brief videotape subsequently were less able to remember the order of the taped events compared with people told to rehearse the tape mentally. These findings led Wegner et al. to conclude that not thinking about longer episodes causes a loss of coherence in the memory representation for the events involved, making them even more difficult to suppress. Clinicians have often noted a similar loss of coherence in accounts of trauma survivors (Foa & Kozak, 1986; Foa, Steketee, & Rothbaum, 1989). Creating a narrative about these events is associated with improved outcomes (Foa, Molnar, & Cashman, 1995). We argue here that narrative creation also frees the claims of stressful events on attentional processes.

On the basis of the cognitive and social psychological theories outlined above, our first experiment was designed to test the hypothesis that the production of a coherent narrative about a stressful experience would lead to improvements on a WM task. People experiencing similar stressful situations who write about a nonstressful topic should not experience equivalent WM benefits, because memory representations of nonstressful events are presumed to exert only minimal draws on cognitive resources.

We further hypothesized that WM improvements would be associated with the linguistic changes Pennebaker et al. (1997) noted as evidence of coherence in expressive writers' essays. Specifically, increases in the use of cause and insight words were predicted to be associated with increases in WM scores. If writing leads people to represent a stressful situation with propositions that have causal or temporal relatedness, a cohesive mental model can

be built that contains all the information initially stored as separate events (Radvansky & Zacks, 1991). The result of moving from many representations to a single mental model of the event will be that fewer resources are required for its inhibition, with the consequence that more resources will be available for other WM requirements (Cantor & Engle, 1993).

The WM task we used in these studies is a widely used dual-task span measure (Turner & Engle, 1989) consisting of a series of information-processing and storage operations that vary in their WM requirements. The task measures "the capacity for controlled, sustained attention in the face of interference or distraction" (Engle, Kane, & Tuholski, 1999, p. 104). Performance on such complex span tasks reflects individual differences in currently available WM resources (Chiappe, Hasher, & Siegel, 2000). In other words, the task is sensitive not only to relatively stable individual differences in WM resources but also to competition for these resources from off-task demands. At any point in time, these off-task demands will vary between people. They will also vary within a person across time as external and internal conditions change. There are at least two experiments that have sought to demonstrate within-person changes on WM tasks in response to an experimental manipulation. Blackwood, MacHale, Power, Goodwin, and Lawrie (1998) reported that patients with chronic fatigue syndrome showed greater WM decreases following exercise than did matched healthy controls. Lane (1997) found some support for similar effects of brief caffeine deprivation on habitual coffee drinkers. In the present experiment, we measured WM three times in an attempt to link changes in attentional processes to the expressive writing manipulation.

In addition to investigating the effects of writing on available WM, these experiments examined the effects of such disclosure on our participants' grade point averages (GPAs). At present the only evidence that expressive writing directly affects any sort of cognitive processing comes from studies in which writing about coming to college produced marginal but consistent GPA improvements (Pennebaker, Colder, & Sharp, 1990; Pennebaker & Francis, 1996). GPA is related to WM span (Turner & Engle, 1989), and WM is further related to processes that can affect GPA, such as following directions and vocabulary acquisition (Engle, Carullo, & Collins, 1991). Although far from conclusive, the relationships between writing and GPA, and between WM and GPA, suggest that if the manipulation improves WM there should be a concomitant increase in GPA.

Finally, there is some evidence that expressive writing has more beneficial effects on health for men than for women (Smythe, 1998). Although not a primary question in the present study, the data were examined to determine whether such gender differences appear on WM processes.

## Experiment 1

### Method

*Participants.* Thirty male and 47 female first semester college freshmen, ages 18–19 years, participated for partial course credit. Participants were assigned randomly to one of two conditions: an experimental group asked to write about a stressful event, in this case, their deepest thoughts and feelings about coming to college ($n = 39$), or a control group asked to write about a nonstressful event, time management ($n = 38$).

KLEIN AND BOALS

*Materials.* Turner and Engle's (1989) arithmetic operation-word memory span task (OSPAN) and procedure was used to assess participants' WM. The OSPAN task has high internal consistency (.75) and reliability (.88) and is stable across time (Klein & Fiss, 1999). Following Engle's method, we had participants read a simple arithmetic equation (e.g., $(9 \times 1) - 9 = 1$) on the computer followed by a one-syllable word (e.g., *back*). Participants indicated verbally whether the answer given to the problem was true or false and read the word aloud. The experimenter then advanced the program to the next operation. After sets of two to seven problems, participants were prompted to write down as many of these words as possible from the previous set. In all, three sequences containing one set of each size were presented, for a total of 81 operations. The operations and words were selected from the pools developed by Cantor and Engle (1993). Additional one-syllable words matched for frequency were also generated for use in subsequent administrations of the task. Different equations and words were used in each sequence and each time the test was administered. WM scores were the total number of words recalled that were associated with correctly solved equations.

To assess college freshmen's levels of anxieties about coming to college, we used the College Adjustment Test (CAT; Pennebaker et al., 1990). The CAT is a 19-question survey designed specifically to assess college freshmen's levels of homesickness, loneliness, and college-related difficulties.

*Procedure.* The participants were tested individually in six separate experimental sessions during the fall semester of their freshman year. The first session was scheduled 3–4 weeks after classes began. The next four sessions were scheduled during the 5th, 6th, and 7th weeks of the semester. The final session was held during the 13th and 14th weeks of the 15-week term. A timeline displaying the experimental sessions is presented in the upper panel of Figure 1. There were two experimenters, one man and one woman. All the writing sessions were supervised by the male experimenter; both experimenters ran the WM test sessions. Experimenters were unaware of the condition to which a participant was assigned.

At the first session, all participants gave informed consent and took the first WM test followed by the CAT. Three writing periods lasting 20 min each were scheduled during the following 2-week period. Before each writing period, the participant received an envelope containing a printed copy of standard instructions (Pennebaker et al., 1990; Pennebaker & Francis, 1996). In the expressive writing condition the instructions asked students to write about their deepest thoughts and feelings about coming to college and do their best to "tie it all together" at the end of their essays. The control condition instructions asked students to write about everything they had done that day and describe how they might have done a better job, concluding with a plea that their description be as objective as possible. When students had completed their essays, they placed them in the envelope. All writers were told they did not have to turn in their essays if they did not wish, but none refused.

At the fifth session, scheduled 1 week after the third writing period, participants took a second WM test. Six weeks after this test, all participants completed a third version of the WM task, took the CAT, and completed a questionnaire asking them about their essays and their reactions to writing. All participants received an explanation of the study at the final session.

Near the middle of the subsequent spring semester, we made four attempts to reach each participant by telephone. We asked them to send us written permission to obtain their GPAs directly from university records. We also asked them three questions adapted from the Perceived Stress Scale (Cohen, Kamarck, & Mermelstein, 1983). These items asked how often the participant had felt nervous, calm, or stressed during the past week, rated on a 4-item response scale ranging from *never* to *very often*.

## Results

Altogether, 71 (92%) of the participants completed all six experimental sessions. Data from 6 participants (3 from each condition) who did not attend one or more of the experimental sessions were not analyzed. The final sample sizes for the experimental group and the control group were 36 (23 women and 13 men) and 35 (20 women and 15 men), respectively.

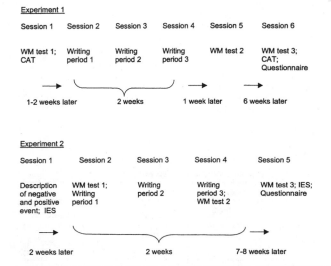

*Figure 1.* Timelines for Experiments 1 and 2. WM = working memory; CAT = College Adjustment Test; IES = Impact of Events Scale.

We were able to establish telephone contact with 30 experimental group participants and 29 control group participants, giving us self-reports of stress from 83% of the writers. One of the experimental group participants refused to give permission to access his grades, and 3 of the control group participants failed to send written permission. Three students who gave permission to access their grades withdrew from the university or had late grade reports for the spring semester, preventing their inclusion in the GPA analyses. The GPA analyses were thus performed on data from 27 experimental group members and 25 control group participants.

*Effects of expressive writing on WM.* Raw WM scores are presented in Table 1. Prior to condition assignment, there were no differences in WM scores (mean number of words correctly recalled = 54.5) as a function of gender or writing topic. In line with the analyses used by Pennebaker et al. (1990) and King and Miner (2000), we used the prewriting WM scores as predictors to calculate residual WM scores for the WM tests administered 1 week and 6 weeks after writing. To the extent that the postwriting scores are completely predicted by the prewriting scores, residual scores will be 0. Residuals in excess of 0 indicate better performance than what would have been predicted from the prewriting score; residuals less than 0 indicate poorer than predicted performance. We subjected the two residual scores to a 2 (writing condition) × 2 (gender) × 2 (time) repeated measures multivariate analysis of variance (MANOVA). The only significant multivariate effect was the interaction between condition and time, $F(1, 63) = 7.49$, $p < .01$. The interaction indicated that the groups displayed differential changes in residual WM scores from the test administered 1 week postwriting to that administered 6 weeks later. The residual WM scores are presented in Figure 2. One week after writing, the expressive writers' WM scores were lower than would have been expected on the basis of their initial WM test results, and the control group's WM scores were higher than predicted, but this difference was not significant. Six weeks later, residual WM scores for the experimental group increased to a level greater than predicted, whereas the control group's residual scores decreased.

In the analysis of the residual scores, the only other effect to approach significance was the interaction between condition, time, and gender, $F(1, 63) = 3.26$, $p < .08$. Examination of the raw change scores indicated that men assigned to the control group showed the least improvement ($M = 0.93$ words) from the second to the third WM tests, and men assigned to the experimental group showed the greatest improvement ($M = 5.4$ words). There was less difference in the change scores between women assigned to the control group ($M = 3.4$ words) and women assigned to the experimental group ($M = 4.4$ words).

*Analysis of essay content.* We assessed linguistic characteristics using a text analysis program, the Linguistic Inquiry and Word Count (LIWC; Pennebaker & Francis, 1999). As shown in the first panel of Table 2, there were significant differences (all $ps < .0001$) in the use of word categories of particular interest for this study. Similar to the data reported by Pennebaker and Francis (1996), the expressive writers used a greater percentage of negative, positive, cause, and insight words than did the control group writers.

*The relationship of cognitive word changes to WM changes.* To test the prediction that increased use of cause and insight words would be associated with subsequent increases in WM, we added the percentages of cause and insight words used in the first and third essays and computed the difference. Differences greater than 0 indicated an increase in the use of causal words; differences less than or equal to 0 indicated a decline. The mean differences for the expressive writing group ($M = 0.37$, $SD = 1.57$) and for the writing control group ($M = 0.23$, $SD = 0.97$) did not differ significantly, and there was no difference in the percentage of individuals in the expressive writing condition who increased their use of cognitive words (60%) compared with the writing control group (56%). A 2 (direction of cognitive change) × 2 (writing condition) analysis of variance on the raw WM change scores from the second to the third administrations of the task indicated main effects of direction of cognitive change, $F(1, 67) = 3.92$, $p < .05$, and condition, $F(1, 67) = 4.25$, $p < .04$, but not their interaction. In the control group, writers who decreased their use of cognitive words from Essay 1 to Essay 3 showed smaller WM gains ($M = 1.3$ operations) compared with writers who increased their cognitive word use ($M = 3.5$ operations). Similar differences occurred in the experimental group. Experimental group participants who decreased their use of cognitive words showed smaller WM gains ($M = 3.7$ operations) than did experimental writers who increased their cognitive word use ($M = 5.2$ operations) from Essay 1 to Essay 3. Essay 1 to Essay 2 difference scores were unrelated to WM changes.

In contrast to the association between changes in cognitive word usage and WM gains, there was no relationship between WM changes and changes in the use of emotion words from Essay 1 to Essay 3 or from Essay 1 to Essay 2.

*Self-reports of writing and reactions to the experiment.* We analyzed responses to the questionnaire administered during the last session to examine how participants perceived their essays and their reactions to the experiment. Participants in the writing conditions did not differ in the frequency with which they made phone calls or sent e-mail to family and friends about their feelings and

Table 1

*Mean Unadjusted Working Memory Scores at Each Test Time: Experiments 1 and 2*

| Topic | Experiment 1[a] | | | Experiment 2[b] | | |
|---|---|---|---|---|---|---|
| | Test 1 | Test 2 | Test 3 | Test 1 | Test 2 | Test 3 |
| Time management | 54.6 (6.8) | 59.0 (6.30) | 61.2 (7.6) | 43.4 (7.9) | 43.6 (9.3) | 44.2 (8.2) |
| Coming to college | 54.4 (8.4) | 57.8 (8.2) | 62.7 (8.8) | | | |
| Negative experience | | | | 42.5 (8.5) | 46.2 (8.3) | 47.6 (8.3) |
| Positive experience | | | | 41.7 (7.1) | 43.8 (6.5) | 44.0 (6.3) |

*Note.* Standard deviations are in parentheses.
[a] Maximum possible correct = 81.    [b] Maximum possible correct = 75.

KLEIN AND BOALS

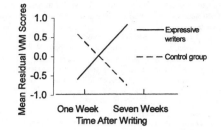

*Figure 2.* Mean residual working memory (WM) scores as a function of writing topic and time: Experiment 1.

experiences, or in their judgments of the value of the experiment, or how well organized they thought their essays were. As Table 2 shows, the experimental group indicated they had disclosed more personal information and revealed their emotions more than control group participants. Students assigned to write about their deepest thoughts and feelings also reported they had thought more and talked more about the topic before the experiment and had wanted to talk about the topic more since the experiment.

We next examined the correlations between self-reports of disclosure and WM scores. The only variable related to pretest WM scores was how extensively students said they had talked about the topic prior to the experiment, $r(68) = .31$, $p < .01$. Students who had talked more about the topic had higher WM scores at the beginning of the experiment. The only self-rating related to working memory measured one week after completing the final essay

was how much personal information the writer claimed to have disclosed, $r(69) = .28$, $p < .02$. Final session working memory scores obtained 7 weeks after writing were higher for participants who said they had disclosed more personal information, $r(69) = .24$, $p < .05$, revealed more emotions, $r(69) = .36$, $p < .01$, and believed their essays were more well-organized, $r(69) = .27$, $p < .03$.

Finally, consistent with the findings of Pennebaker et al. (1990), the groups did not differ in their initial or final CAT scores, nor was there any relationship between either adjustment score and any of the WM measures. Adjustment scores did predict the degree to which students said they had felt stressed, calm, or nervous when queried 4 months later during the telephone interview, $r(53) = .56$, $p < .0001$. The self-reports of stress were not related to experimental condition, WM, or either GPA index.

*Relationship of WM changes and GPA.* We conducted a repeated measures ANOVA using condition and WM changes from the second to the third time of testing on participants' GPAs for the fall and spring semesters. Overall there was a nonsignificant decline in GPAs from the fall semester during which the experiment was conducted ($M = 3.18$, $SD = 0.70$) to the following spring semester ($M = 2.97$, $SD = 0.88$). This decline did not differ as a function of condition. Using condition and WM changes as predictors in a MANOVA on the fall and spring GPAs produced only a significant multivariate main effect of WM, $F(1, 48) = 4.95$, $p < .03$. Students showing greater improvement in WM scores between the second and third WM tests earned higher GPAs for both the experimental semester, $r(53) = .23$, $p < .10$, and the following spring, $r(50) = .29$, $p < .04$. The same MANOVA using the final WM score as the predictor produced no significant findings.

Table 2
*Mean Number and Percentage of Words in Each Linguistic Category and Mean Ratings of Essay Characteristics: Experiments 1 and 2*

| | Experiment 1 | | Experiment 2 | | |
|---|---|---|---|---|---|
| Essay topic | Time management ($n = 36$) | Coming to college ($n = 35$) | Time management ($n = 34$) | Negative personal event ($n = 34$) | Positive personal event ($n = 33$) |
| LIWC categories | | | | | |
| Mean number of words | 296.4$_b$ (89.6) | 356.2$_a$ (89.3) | 352.6 (118.1) | 345.0 (102.6) | 357.3 (119.4) |
| Emotion processes | | | | | |
| Negative emotion (%) | 0.34$_a$ (0.65) | 2.00$_b$ (0.71) | 0.36$_a$ (0.40) | 2.30$_b$ (0.67) | 1.00$_c$ (0.59) |
| Positive emotion (%) | 1.3$_a$ (0.59) | 3.0$_b$ (0.65) | 0.84$_a$ (0.34) | 2.6$_b$ (0.85) | 3.8$_c$ (1.1) |
| Cognitive processes | | | | | |
| Causal terms (%) | 0.53$_a$ (0.35) | 1.10$_b$ (0.35) | 0.30$_a$ (0.27) | 1.30$_b$ (0.47) | 1.20$_b$ (0.50) |
| Insight terms (%) | 0.74$_a$ (0.41) | 2.40$_b$ (0.65) | 0.56$_a$ (0.30) | 2.70$_b$ (0.86) | 2.60$_b$ (0.93) |
| Self-ratings of essay[a] | | | | | |
| Disclosing information | 4.2$_a$ (1.5) | 5.2$_b$ (1.0) | 5.0$_a$ (1.4) | 5.7$_b$ (1.0) | 5.5$_b$ (1.0) |
| Revealing emotions | 3.4$_a$ (1.4) | 5.5$_b$ (1.0) | 3.5$_a$ (1.7) | 5.7$_b$ (1.0) | 5.4$_b$ (0.9) |
| How well organized | 3.4$_a$ (1.4) | 3.4$_a$ (1.5) | 3.7$_a$ (1.6) | 3.4$_a$ (1.4) | 3.6$_a$ (1.0) |
| Experiment's benefits | 3.7$_a$ (1.4) | 4.4$_b$ (1.4) | 3.4$_a$ (1.5) | 4.1$_b$ (1.5) | 4.1$_b$ (1.3) |
| How upsetting to write | | | 2.2$_a$ (1.6) | 3.6$_b$ (2.0) | 2.0$_a$ (1.2) |

*Note.* Within each experiment, means with different subscripts differ significantly, $p < .05$. Standard deviations are in parentheses. LIWC = Linguistic Inquiry and Word Count.
[a] Response scales ranged from 1 (*not at all*) to 7 (*a great deal*).

*Discussion*

Our results supported both hypotheses: Expressive writing improves available WM, and the linguistic changes associated with increased narrative coherence are also related to WM improvements. Seven weeks after the writing sessions, participants assigned to write about their deepest thoughts and feelings about coming to college exhibited WM improvements compared with the control group who wrote about time management. There was a trend in the data suggesting that men may have profited more from the manipulation than women, although this difference did not reach conventional levels of statistical significance. WM increases were related to higher GPAs earned during the semester of the experiment as well as the subsequent semester.

As was expected, students who wrote about coming to college used more cognitive insight words as well as more emotion words. Our hypothesis that increases in the use of the cognitive words from Essay 1 to Essay 3 would predict increases in WM was supported. Changes in the percentage of cognitive words from Essay 1 to Essay 2 were not related to WM change, echoing Pennebaker and Francis's (1996) finding that only the Essay 1 to Essay 3 cognitive word differences were related to health outcomes. Changes in the percentages of emotion words across essays were unrelated to increases in the delayed posttest WM scores. The latter findings are congruent with previous work (Pennebaker et al., 1997) in which cognitive rather than emotional changes were the best predictors of improved general functioning. The data also support Smythe's (1998) contention that if writing influences health by evoking changes in cognitive processes, changes in measures of cognitive functioning should be closely tied to writing and to the cognitive effects of writing.

Analysis of self-reports of essay characteristics lends further support to the rationale underlying the experiment. Individuals who said they had talked about the essay topic before the experiment had higher initial WM scores, and writers who reported high levels of disclosure of personal information and emotions in their essays had higher WM scores at the final session.

As reported by Pennebaker and others, the effects of the experimental manipulations are surprisingly long lasting. For the students assigned to write about their deepest thoughts and feelings, WM capacity increased across the 7 weeks of the experiment. Just how long the effects of writing persist should be explored in further research.

The results of the experiment have implications for both cognitive approaches to WM processes and social psychological perspectives on emotional disclosure. With the exception of caffeine deprivation (Lane, 1997) and exercise (Blackwood, MacHale, Power, Goodwin, & Lawrie, 1998), there has been little effort devoted to the question of whether measured WM can increase or decrease as a consequence of other variables. The data we report is perhaps the first to show that a psychosocial manipulation can alter available WM capacity and that these changes persist and have consequences for other important outcomes, such as academic performance.

The relevance of our results for social psychological theory is that they point to a possible mediator of the disclosure–health relationship reported in so many previous studies. To the extent that production of a coherent narrative about a stressful experience frees WM resources for more effective coping, the increased availability of these resources can be marshaled to help cope with life stressors that otherwise manifest themselves in various health problems.

The data showing that WM increases are related to academic performance have practical implications. Although WM itself has been related to academic achievement (Turner & Engle, 1989), our findings suggest that it is not necessarily the absolute level of WM that predicts better performance, but the improvement in the ability to store and transform information. There is, however, an alternative to this interpretation. It may be that students who best followed the writing prompts, as indexed by their own reports and by the linguistic analyses of their essays, are more likely to follow directions generally. There are, in fact, data supporting a link between WM and following directions (Engle et al., 1991). Thus, the effectiveness of expressive writing may not be tied to a freeing of attentional resources but may reflect the ability or motivation to follow instructions.

Despite significant differences in the rates of WM improvement as a function of writing topic, the groups did not differ on the final measure of WM. Such a pattern of results provides only modest support for the thesis that expressive writing can affect available WM capacity. One reason for these results may have been the instructions for the control group, which asked writers to describe how they had spent the day and then to decide how they might better have spent their time. Although there were significant differences in the use of cognitive insight words, the linguistic categories Pennebaker et al. (1997) used as markers of narrative cohesion, our instructions may have inadvertently encouraged the formation of more cohesive cognitive representations in the control group writers. Further evidence for this suspicion is the finding that participants in both writing groups showed similar increases in cognitive insight words across essays.

Another factor that may have contributed to the equivalence of the groups' final WM scores was the choice of experimental topic. In Experiment 1 all participants in the experimental condition wrote on the same topic, "coming to college." The topic has been a standard in expressive writing research (Pennebaker, Colder, & Sharpe, 1990; Pennebaker & Francis, 1996), allowing us the luxury of direct comparisons of our data with those reported elsewhere. However, college is not equally stressful for all freshmen, and it is possible that our manipulations were more effective for some writers than for others.

## Experiment 2

Given these theoretical and methodological concerns, we conducted a second experiment focusing on these and other issues. The first issue we address is whether the WM improvements demonstrated by expressive writers in Experiment 1 can be attributed to a decline in thoughts about the stressful experience. Although first-semester freshmen writing about coming to college did evidence greater increases in available WM than did freshmen writing about how they spent their time, the assumption that these benefits are the consequence of reduced resource competition from stressful thoughts was not addressed directly. We have suggested that thoughts about stressful events compete for attentional resources, either through their intrusiveness or through people's effortful attempts to avoid them. We also proposed that expressive writing reduces this competition for WM resources through a decline in intrusive and avoidant thinking. Thus, our first hypothesis was that expressive writing produces less intrusive and avoidant thinking, which in turn leads to WM improvements.

The cognitive and social psychological explanations for how irrelevant and unwanted thoughts disrupt cognitive activities have a direct counterpart in the clinical literature (Horowitz, Field, & Classen, 1993; Janoff-Bulman, 1992). Horowitz demonstrated that stressful events produce intrusive thoughts and that people often attempt to avoid such thoughts. Horowitz claimed that unwanted thoughts occur both effortfully and automatically until the stressful event has been effectively integrated into an individual's schema. While clinicians disagree (Greenberg, 1995) on whether intrusive thoughts indicate ineffective coping, or whether their presence is necessary for an individual to make a satisfactory poststressor adjustment, their ubiquity following stressful events is well documented. Directly relevant to our hypothesis is the evidence that intrusive thoughts are related to poorer performance on cognitive tasks such as proofreading (Baum, Cohen, & Hall, 1993).

Not surprisingly, a number of investigators have hypothesized that expressive writing should reduce reports of unwanted thoughts. In some experiments, emotional disclosure through expressive writing or talking has produced declines in such cognitive activities (Segal, Bogaards, & Chatman, 1998; Segal & Murray, 1994). In other research, disclosure has had no effect on intrusive or avoidant thinking, but the level of these thoughts has moderated the effects of disclosure on physical or psychological symptoms (Lepore, 1997; Lepore & Greenberg, in press) and on immune system function (Lutgendorf, Antoni, Kumar, & Schneiderman, 1994). If emotional disclosure improves WM through a reduction in intrusive and avoidant thinking, expressive writers should report fewer intrusive and avoidant thoughts after writing, and participants reporting fewer unwanted thoughts should experience greater WM gains.

The second question we address is whether the creation of a coherent narrative about a positive life-changing experience has similar effects on WM and intrusive thinking as does writing about a negative experience. Typically, general or specific negative emotional events are studied in the expressive writing paradigm, although two recent experiments have examined the effects of potentially positive events and the positive aspects of negative events. Páez, Velasco, and González (1999) assigned one group to write expressively about a social event. Compared with writers about disclosed and undisclosed traumatic events, this group showed less avoidant, but not less intrusive, thinking about the event before writing. They did not differ in intrusive or avoidant thinking after writing, and writing had no effect on changes in intrusive and avoidant thinking for any group. King and Miner (2000) compared mood, essay content, and physical health of students instructed to write about a traumatic experience, about the perceived benefits of a traumatic experience, about both the trauma and its benefits, or about a control topic. Overall, there were few differences between the experimental conditions. Compared with the control group, individuals in all three expressive writing conditions were lower in positive affect after writing, used more negative emotion words and words referring to cognitive mechanisms in their essays, and had fewer health center visits 3 months after writing. Compared with the other expressive writers, students assigned to write only about perceived benefits used more words referring to cognitive mechanisms in their essays.

Whereas researchers investigating the effects of expressive writing generally focus on adverse events, the cognitive and social psychological theories on which our research was based focus on less emotional topics. Cognitive psychologists interested in inhibitory processes in WM have rarely addressed the valence of the experience responsible for off-task cognitions. For example, Stoltzfus et al. (1996) provide "what to have for dinner" as an example of task-irrelevant cognitions that must be inhibited to do well on WM tasks. Rosen and Engle (1998) examined people's ability to suppress previously learned paired associates as a function of their WM capacity. Likewise, much of Wegner's work with directed suppression requires participants to inhibit thoughts about nonemotional stimuli such as white bears (Wegner, Schneider, Carter, & White, 1987) and fictitious cities (Wegner, 1992). In one experiment in which Wegner did require the suppression of emotional experiences, both positive memories (of personal success) and negative memories (of personal failures) had equal slowing effects on a modified Stroop task in which the words to be ignored were related to the target memory. Similarly, Roemer and Borkovec (1994) report no differences in subsequent thought occurrence about negative, positive, or neutral topics following a period of directed suppression.

It would appear that neither the cognitive nor social psychological accounts of the inhibition of unwanted thoughts require such thoughts to involve negative emotions, although prevailing theories about emotional disclosure (e.g., Páez et al., 1999) emphasize its ability to reduce negative emotions. Thus our second question is whether expressive writing about positive topics produces equivalent changes in WM and thought intrusion, as does writing about negative topics.

A third feature of Experiment 2 is the inclusion of participants' reports of how much they reveal in their essays as a predictor of WM and intrusive thinking. In Experiment 1, self-reports of disclosure correlated with postwriting WM scores. Individual differences in disclosure have been assessed in a number of writing studies and appear to moderate the effects of the manipulated variable. Lutgendorf et al. (1994) reported marked variability in the intensity of the disclosure in their study and found that the more participants said they revealed their feelings, the greater their improvement in immune function following disclosure. Similarly, Pennebaker et al. (1988) found that experimental writers who reported that they had written about topics they had previously held back enjoyed greater immune benefits than low disclosers. According to Kelley, Lumley, and Leisen (1997), the greatest benefits occur in participants "who access their most affectively charged memories (especially memories inhibited from prior processing); experience fully the negative affect and accompanying physiological arousal . . . actively attempt to reconstruct, make sense of, or alter the meaning of the experience" (p. 337). In Experiment 2, we predicted that participants with the highest self-disclosure ratings would experience the greatest declines in intrusive thinking and the greatest increases in WM capacity.

Finally, in Experiment 2 we attempted to redress concerns about the topics and instructions used in Experiment 1. Although rates of improvement differed significantly between expressive writers and the control group, the groups did not differ significantly on the final test of WM. As noted earlier, one reason for these results may have been the prompt for the control group, which asked writers to describe how they might better have spent their time. In Experi-

EXPRESSIVE WRITING AND WORKING MEMORY

ment 2, the control group's instructions warned against any disclosure of emotions and did not ask for any evaluation of the day's schedule. As a further precaution against the development of a coherent narrative, we asked the control group to describe different days each time they wrote.

We were also concerned that the stressfulness of the topic used in Experiment 1, "coming to college," could vary widely among participants. In Experiment 2 participants in the two experimental conditions themselves nominated the topic of their essays: an experience that has had an extremely negative or extremely positive impact on their lives.

Finally, as in Experiment 1, we examined the WM results to determine whether men and women benefit equally from the manipulations.

## Method

*Participants.* One hundred twenty-one college students completed the first session in exchange for partial course credit in their introductory psychology course. Of these, 10 did not wish to continue in the study because they had already completed the course research requirement and 5 declined to continue for other reasons. Altogether, 106 students (60 women and 45 men) participated in the first writing session.

Thirty-five students were randomly assigned to write about time management, 36 to write about the negative event they had described at the first session, and 35 to write about the positive event they had described at the first session. Subsequently we eliminated data from 5 participants (1 assigned to the control group, 2 from the group assigned to write about a negative event, and 2 from the group assigned to write about a positive event) who did not keep all their appointments. Thus, after assignment to writing condition, 95% ($n = 101$) of the participants participated in all sessions: 34 (19 women and 15 men) in the control group, 34 (20 women and 14 men) in the negative topic group, and 33 (20 women and 13 men) in the positive topic group.

*Materials.* We used Horowitz's Impact of Events Scale (IES; Horowitz, Wilner, & Alvarez, 1979) to measure reactions to the memories associated with both the positive and the negative stressful life events participants described at the first session. The IES consists of 15 items and asks how often during the past 7 days participants had the reactions listed. The response scale ranges from 0 (*not at all*) to 5 (*often*). Seven of these items ask about the frequency of undesired memory intrusions, and 8 items ask about the frequency of avoiding thoughts of these experiences. The Intrusive and Avoidance subscales are highly correlated (Creamer, 1995; Weiss & Marmar, 1997). The developers report test–retest reliabilities of .89, with internal reliability estimates ranging from .79 to .92. Depending on the analysis, we used two different scores from the IES. Following Horowitz et al. (1979) and Lepore and Greenberg (in press), we added the scores from the Intrusive and Avoidant subscales to compute the IES scores for each event participants described. We also computed the IES total impact score by summing the IES scores for the two events.

To measure WM we used Turner and Engle's (1989) OSPAN task as described in Experiment 1 with the exception that we used three repetitions of the five operations of set sizes three to seven for a total of 75 operations. The 2-operation sets were eliminated because in Experiment 1, all participants successfully recalled both words from these easy-to-remember small sets.

*Procedure.* Participants were tested in five sessions during the spring semester. The first session was scheduled 3 to 5 weeks after classes began; the next three sessions occurred during the 5th through 8th weeks. The final session was scheduled during the 13th and 14th weeks of the semester. There were three experimenters, one man and two women, who ran both the writing sessions and WM test sessions. Experimenters were unaware of the condition to which a participant was assigned.

At the first session, attended by groups of 2 to 15 people, we asked for brief written descriptions of two major events from their lives, one that had had a very positive impact and one that had had a very negative impact; when each event began; and when (if) it had ended. A copy of the IES followed these instructions for both the positive and negative event requests. Half of the participants were asked to describe a positive event first; half were asked first about a negative event.

Approximately 2 weeks later, we administered the OSPAN test in individual sessions. Participants were then randomly assigned to one of three writing topics: the positive experience they had described at the first session, the negative experience, or how they spent their time. Participants in the two experimental groups were given an envelope containing a verbatim typed copy of the positive or negative experience they had described and written instructions for their essay. Instructions for the expressive writers emphasized that they should "dig down to your very deepest thoughts and feelings about the positive [negative] event . . . and try to 'tie it all together' at the end of the writing."

The control group received an envelope containing instructions that asked them to describe how they had spent the previous day, how they had spent the current day, or what they planned to do the following day. Each control group member wrote about a different day for each essay. The instructions emphasized that the essays should describe how they spent their time as factually and unemotionally as possible. When students had completed their essays, they placed them in the envelope.

Two additional writing sessions of 20 min each were scheduled within the next 2 weeks. As in Experiment 1, writers were told they did not have to turn in their essays if they did not wish, but none refused. At the end of the last writing session, we again administered the WM task.

At the last experimental session, scheduled 7 to 8 weeks after the last writing session, each participant took a third WM test and then completed the IES for both the positive and the negative event they had described at the first session. A final questionnaire asked students about their essays and their reactions to the experiment. After asking for written permission to access their semester grades directly from university records, we debriefed participants and thanked them for their participation. The second panel of Figure 1 presents the timeline for this experiment.

## Results

*Effects of expressive writing on WM.* There were no differences in WM scores at the first testing session as a function of writing assignment, gender, or self-ratings of disclosure ($M = 42.4$ words). As in Experiment 1, we used these prewriting WM scores to predict the WM posttest scores and then calculated residual WM scores for the two posttests. We used these residual scores in a 3 (writing condition) $\times$ 2 (gender) $\times$ 2 (time) repeated measures MANOVA with self-disclosure ratings as a fourth, quantitative, independent variable. None of the multivariate statistics were significant. There were no significant differences in residual scores on the WM test administered immediately after writing. On the WM test given 7–8 weeks later, there was a main effect of condition, $F(2, 90) = 3.30$, $p < .04$. Figure 3 presents the residual scores from this analysis. Participants who wrote about a negative event had higher than predicted final session scores, and these residual scores were greater than those of participants who wrote about a positive event, $p < .02$, or about time management, $p < .11$, who did not differ from each other. For these latter two groups, the final WM scores were lower than would have been predicted on the basis of their prewriting scores.

We next assessed the comparability of the OSPAN scores obtained in Experiment 2 and those obtained in Experiment 1. Because the two-operation sets were not used in Experiment 2, and

KLEIN AND BOALS

because performance was at ceiling on these sets in Experiment 1, we added 6 points to the initial WM score of each participant in the present study. A *t* test indicated that the Experiment 1 mean (54.6 words) and the adjusted Experiment 2 mean (48.4 words) on the first WM test did not differ significantly.

*Effect of expressive writing on intrusive and avoidant thinking.* Analysis of the first session IES scores indicated that prior to assignment to condition, the groups did not differ in intrusive and avoidant thinking about either negative, $F(2, 98) = 0.82, p < .44$, or positive events, $F(2, 98) = 0.95, p < .38$.[1] To examine the question of whether writing about negative or positive topics would have similar effects on intrusive and avoidant thinking, we first computed simple difference scores between pre- and postwriting IES scores for the negative events and for the positive events. We subjected these difference scores to a repeated measures MANOVA using writing condition and disclosure as between-subjects variables and valence (positive vs. negative) of the event being described as the repeated measures variable. The analysis produced a three-way interaction between writing condition, valence (positive vs. negative) of the event being described, and disclosure, $F(2, 93) = 3.93, p < .02$. Examination of the univariate tests indicated no differences in IES difference scores for positive events as a function of condition or disclosure. For the IES difference scores for negative events, there were significant effects of experimental condition, $F(2, 93) = 5.00, p < .01$; of self-ratings of disclosure, $F(1, 93) = 9.79, p < .003$; and of the Condition $\times$ Disclosure interaction, $F(2, 93) = 5.28, p < .005$. As shown in Figure 4, IES scores for the negative event declined in all groups, and this decline was significantly greater in the group assigned to write about the negative event.

To explore the interaction, we examined the correlation between the IES difference scores for the negative event and emotional disclosure ratings separately for each writing condition. Self-ratings of emotional disclosure were related to changes in IES scores only for individuals assigned to write about a negative

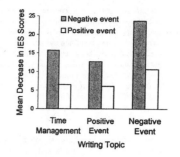

*Figure 4.* Mean decreases in intrusive and avoidant thoughts for positive and negative events as a function of writing topic. IES = Impact of Events Scale.

event. For these participants, disclosure ratings and the decline in intrusive and avoidant thoughts were correlated for both the negative event, $r(31) = .62, p < .0001$, and the positive event, $r(31) = .36, p < .05$. The more that the negative event writers reported they had revealed in their essays, the greater the decline in their IES scores.

*The relationship of intrusive thinking and WM.* Given the effects of writing condition on both IES scores and WM, our next analysis examined the relationship between IES and WM. IES scores for positive and negative events were highly correlated at both pretest, $r(99) = .35$, and posttest, $r(99) = .49$, both $p$s < .001. Because our model predicts that intrusive and avoidant thinking from any source, either positive or negative, can impair working memory, we summed the IES scores for the positive and negative events obtained at the final session to produce a single combined index of the impact of these events.

To test the prediction that expressive writing increases WM function through the reduction of off-task cognitions related to stressful events, we conducted a series of analyses as recommended by Baron and Kenny (1986). The first ANOVA indicated that both condition, $F(2, 93) = 2.99, p < .05$, and self-rated disclosure, $F(1, 93) = 4.21, p < .04$, affected the IES total impact scores observed in the final experimental session. The IES total impact index did not differ between the control group ($M = 36.9$, $SD = 18.3$) and the writers assigned to a positive topic ($M = 39.5$, $SD = 26.6$). Both groups reported significantly more intrusive and avoidant thinking ($p < .03$) compared with participants who had written about a negative topic ($M = 24.2, SD = 26.3$). Higher self-disclosure ratings were associated with higher IES impact scores reported at the final session, $r(99) = .23, p < .02$.

The next step in the test of mediation requires the demonstration that levels of intrusive and avoidant thoughts are related to WM. An analysis of covariance (ANCOVA) using the IES total impact scores as a quantitative independent variable and covarying initial WM scores indicated that lower IES impact scores were associated with higher scores on the final WM test, $F(1, 93) = 9.46, p < .003$.

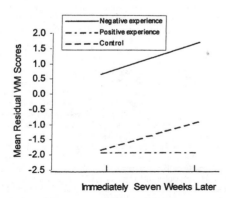

*Figure 3.* Mean residual working memory (WM) scores as a function of writing topic and time: Experiment 2.

---

[1] A more complete report of the IES data for positive and negative events is available from Kitty Klein.

The final step in the test that intrusive thinking is a mediator of the effects of expressive writing on WM requires the demonstration that when intrusive/avoidant thinking is entered as a predictor of WM, the effects of writing condition and self-ratings of disclosure are reduced. Initial WM scores were covaried. The ANCOVA on the posttest measure of WM using the impact scores, experimental condition, and disclosure ratings as predictors indicated that the condition effect found previously was no longer present. The only significant effect was that of the IES total impact scores, $F(1, 93) = 6.95$, $p < .009$, thus supporting the hypothesis that intrusive thinking mediates the effects of expressive writing on WM.

*Analysis of essay content.* An informal reading of the essays revealed a wide variety of topics for both the positive and the negative prompts. Among the negative experiences were death of a parent, sibling, or grandparent; wrecking an automobile; loneliness; and a parent's drinking problem. The positive experiences included events such as winning an athletic contest, a trip to Europe, living in one's first apartment, and having an adult mentor.

As in Experiment 1, we analyzed the essays using Pennebaker and Francis's (1999) LIWC text analysis program. We then conducted a MANOVA repeated measures analysis of the LIWC variables of interest across the three essays, using writing condition and self-rated disclosure as independent variables. The variables analyzed were the percentages of positive emotion words, negative emotion words, words denoting cause, and words denoting insight. Overall means are presented in the second panel of Table 2. In contrast to Experiment 1, there were no differences in the length of the essays as a function of writing condition. Not surprisingly, participants who wrote about a positive topic used a greater percentage of positive emotional words than did writers of negative events or control condition writers, $F(2, 93) = 5.17$, $p < .007$. The converse was true for negative emotion words, $F(2, 93) = 10.98$, $p < .001$. Writers about both negative events and positive events used more causal words compared with the control group writers, $F(2, 93) = 7.93$, $p < .001$. Control group writers also used a smaller percentage of insight words than the negative event group or the positive event group, $F(2, 93) = 9.42$, $p < .001$, who did not differ from each other.

The only linguistic category directly sensitive to self-rated disclosure was causal word use, $F(1, 93) = 5.55$, $p < .02$. Writers who said they had revealed more personal information used a greater percentage of causal words.

*The relationship of cognitive word changes and WM changes.* As in Experiment 1 we categorized individuals into two categories on the basis of whether the percentage of cause and insight words increased or decreased from Essay 1 to Essay 3. The average increase in the use of these words from Essay 1 to Essay 3 was very small and did not vary as a function of essay topic ($M = 0.07\%$). The percentage of individuals showing an increase in the use of cognitive words across essays was equivalent in the groups assigned to write about time management (41%), a negative event (56%), or a positive event (49%). A 2 (direction of cognitive word change) × 3 (writing condition) repeated measures analysis of the Time 2 and Time 3 WM scores produced no significant effects. In a similar analysis, we examined the relationship of positive and negative emotion words to changes in WM and found that WM did not differ as a function of whether writers increased their use of emotion words.

In a further test of the relationship of word use to WM, we considered each of the linguistic variables separately. We conducted a series of four repeated measures MANOVAs on the raw WM scores with experimental condition and linguistic category change from Essay 1 to Essay 3 as the predictor variables. Two of the categories, negative emotion word increases, $F(4, 184) = 2.63$, $p < .04$, and causal word increases, $F(4, 184) = 3.40$, $p < .03$, interacted with time of the WM tests and condition. These interactions indicated that the relationship of changes in the linguistic variables to changes in WM differed between the three conditions. To dissect these interactions we looked at the correlations between word use changes and WM changes from the immediate posttest to the final session 7 to 8 weeks later. The pattern of correlations indicated that increased use of causal words was positively related to WM increases for the negative experience writers, $r(32) = .30$, $p < .08$, but negatively related to WM increases for the control group, $r(32) = -.29$, $p < .10$. For writers about positive topics, causal word increases were unrelated to WM differences, $r(31) = .04$, $p > .8$.

Correlations between increases in negative emotion word use and WM change also differed between the groups. For the control group and for writers about negative events, there was no relationship between changes in the use of negative emotion words and WM change, $r(32) = .05$ and $r(32) = .02$, respectively. For writers about positive topics, a decline in the use of negative emotion words predicted WM increases, $r(31) = -.23$, $p < .19$.

Given the support for the earlier hypothesis that the reduction of intrusive and avoidant thinking mediates the relationship between writing and WM, we looked at the relationship between IES scores and writers' use of cognitive words. None of the correlations between the final session's combined IES index and changes in the use of cognitive words approached significance.

*Self-reports of writing and reactions to the experiment.* As shown in Table 1, at the end of Experiment 2, writers assigned to positive or negative events reported they had disclosed more personal information, revealed their emotions more, and believed the experiment to have been more beneficial than did writers assigned to the control condition. Writing about a negative event was more upsetting than writing about either a positive event or time management. Furthermore, the more upsetting the writing was, the lower were the WM scores at all three administrations of the WM task, $F(1, 95) = 8.34$, $p < .004$.

None of the three items assessing participants' judgments of their writing was related to their IES scores at the beginning of the experiment. However, individuals reporting more intrusive and avoidant thinking at the end of the experiment said they disclosed more personal information, $r(99) = .20$, claimed to have revealed more emotional information, $r(99) = .22$, and found it more upsetting to write, $r(99) = .27$, all $ps < .05$.

None of the self-reports were associated with the linguistic categories of interest in this study.

*Relationship of WM changes and intrusive thinking to GPA.* Ninety-four participants (93%) gave us permission to retrieve their grades from the previous (fall) and current (spring) semesters. Six students were new transfers or had not been in school the previous fall, leaving 88 participants with grades available for both spring and fall. GPAs increased from the fall ($M = 2.86$, $SD = 0.87$) to the spring ($M = 2.91$, $SD = 0.79$). There was no relationship between WM improvements from the second to the third WM test and GPAs for the previous semester or the experimental semesters. There was, however, a positive relationship between WM improvements and improvements in GPA, $F(1, 86) = 4.95$, $p < .03$. Students showing the greatest improvements in WM capacity showed the largest increases in GPA, $r(86) = .22$. This relationship did not differ as a function of condition.

Consistent with the correlations between WM and intrusive thinking, students reporting more intrusive and avoidant cognitions about negative events at the last session of the experiment earned significantly lower spring grades, $r(91) = -.32$, $p < .002$. Reported thoughts about positive events were unrelated to GPAs.

*Discussion*

The results of Experiment 2 lend further support to the proposal that expressive writing can produce sizable and lasting improvements in available WM resources. These benefits were limited to people who wrote about a negative experience; writing about a positive life-changing event or about daily routines had very little effect, or even negative effects, on WM scores. Expressive writing produced its largest effects 8 weeks after writing. In contrast to Experiment 1, there were significant differences in final WM scores, with people assigned to the control group and the positive event group performing more poorly than people who wrote about their negative experiences. Unlike in Experiment 1, there was no evidence of any gender effects on WM capacity.

Expressive writing did affect reports of intrusive and avoidant thinking about negative events. Individuals assigned to write about a negative experience showed the greatest decline in intrusive and avoidant thinking about the negative event they described at the first session. They were also the only group in which reported self-disclosure was linked to declines in intrusive and avoidant thinking. Decreases in unwanted thoughts about positive experiences did not vary as a function of experimental condition.

Our analysis further indicated that the WM improvements enjoyed by expressive writers may be mediated by a decline in intrusive and avoidant thinking about negative stressful experiences. Participants who reported lower levels of unwanted cognitions at the final session had higher final WM scores and also showed the greatest improvement in WM scores. When we examined WM scores as a function of both intrusive/avoidant thinking and experimental condition, the effects of the manipulation were substantially reduced.

The results from both the WM measures and reports of unwanted thoughts coincide to suggest that writing about a positive experience has little effect on either variable. The ineffectiveness of writing about a positive experience can be contrasted with King and Miner's (2000) data. In their study, writing about the positive aspects of a negative experience produced health benefits similar to those achieved by writing only about the negative experience. At least in regard to cognitive processing, writing about positive events is ineffective. It would be interesting to know whether writing about positive experiences would have similar null effects on health.

In Experiment 2, writers about positive and negative experiences used equivalent amounts of cause and insight words that have been used to define narrative coherence. Although the essays were equally coherent, writing about a positive event had effects equivalent to unemotional writing about daily events. The finding

that intrusive thoughts about the positive event showed small and equivalent declines regardless of essay topic lends further support to the inefficacy of writing about positive experiences.

Results for the linguistic analyses were not as straightforward as those obtained in Experiment 1. Compared with Experiment 1, participants showed smaller increases in the use of cause and insight words across essays. For the negative event writers, WM improvements were linked to increases in the use of causal words; the opposite was true for the control group, whose WM scores declined as their use of causal words increased. This interaction mirrors one Pennebaker and Francis (1996) obtained for the relationship between causal word change and illness. Pennebaker and Francis explained the positive relationship between causal word increases and illness in their control group as an instance of trying to find too much meaning in meaningless events. Perhaps a similar explanation applies to the effects observed on WM in Experiment 2.

As in Experiment 1, WM improvements were associated with academic performance. Students who showed the largest increases in WM showed the greatest GPA improvements, regardless of what they wrote about. The level of intrusive and avoidant thinking about negative events reported at the last experimental session was strongly predictive of the GPAs obtained; there was no relationship between unwanted thoughts about positive experiences and GPA.

Consideration of participants' reports of how much they revealed in their essays did improve the predictability of some measures, although generally there were condition main effects qualified by Condition × Self-Disclosure interactions. In the case of WM, self-disclosure ratings obtained at the end of the experiment did not predict final WM scores or improvements in WM. In regard to intrusive thinking, self-disclosure interacted with experimental condition. Self-reported disclosure of writers assigned to the negative event condition was related to declines in unwanted thoughts about both the negative topic of their essays and about positive event described at the first session.

Several of the methodological and theoretical concerns raised in Experiment 1 are addressed by the present findings. Eliminating the request for control group writers to "see how they might have done a better job of time management" was apparently effective in that the control group in Experiment 2 showed no improvement in WM. Furthermore, the differences between the groups on the final measure of WM were significant.

A second question left unanswered in the first experiment was whether the GPA benefits of expressive writing are simply the consequence of adhering to instructions as opposed to a reduction in intrusive thinking about stressful events. In Experiment 2, the similar percentages of cause and insight words in both positive and negative topic essays suggests that both groups of writers followed the prompt's directions to "tie it all together." Nonetheless, writing about a positive experience had no effect on WM, suggesting that simply following directions is not a viable alternative explanation for the link between WM increases and GPA.

The failure to find any WM or intrusive thinking effects from writing about a positive event poses some difficulty for the theoretical rationale underlying this research. We have assumed that the more coherent the mental model representing a stressful experience is, the less it will compete with primary task demands for WM resources. We also assumed that the linguistic markers we have used to identify increases in narrative coherence across essays index the coherence of the cognitive representations of the stressful events described. The present data suggest that this model, with its emphasis on the cognitive features of event representation, is not entirely adequate. Specifically, the data supported the model only for people who wrote about negative experiences in their lives. People assigned to write about a positive event, whose essays showed linguistic coherence equivalent to those who wrote about a negative event, did not experience a concomitant increase in WM scores. Apparently, constructing a coherent account of a negative event frees WM resources to a greater extent than constructing an account of a positive event. Whether this difference is the consequence of positive events' having less cognitive impact or whether there is something unique about writing about negative experiences requires further investigation.

## General Discussion

The findings from these two experiments shed new light on available WM capacity and markedly expand the benefits of expressive writing to this widely studied cognitive process. We have shown that usable WM is not a static variable but can change as a function of a psychosocial manipulation, with such changes reflecting variations in intrusive and avoidant thoughts about off-task topics. We drew on theories of WM processes, control of unwanted thoughts and emotional disclosure to develop our hypotheses. According to many cognitive psychologists, WM is a limited capacity system in which resources must be used to inhibit off-task cognitions in order to do well on the task at hand (Engle, 1996; Roberts & Pennington, 1996). Clinical reports (e.g., Foa et al., 1989; Horowitz et al., 1993) suggest that unwanted thoughts about stressful experiences are particularly difficult to inhibit, a viewpoint echoed in the theory of ironic processes (Wegner, 1994). Although the data support our proposal that creating a narrative "packages" stressful experiences into manageable mental models that make fewer demands on cognitive resources than do the original fragmented representations, this explanation requires further research.

First, our standard for narrative coherence relies on Pennebaker's (1997) definition of narrative: an increase in cognitive word use. Other researchers have offered various criteria for what constitutes a "good" narrative in the context of how people tell stories about their experiences (e.g., Barclay, 1996; Meichenbaum & Fitzpatrick, 1993; Wong & Watt, 1991). It would be interesting to apply other narrative coding schemes to our students' essays to learn whether writing similarly affected these measures.

A second limitation of the present findings is our use of a single measure of WM capacity, Turner and Engle's (1989) OSPAN task. The task has good psychometric properties (Klein & Fiss, 1999) and correlates highly with other complex dual-span measures of controlled processing (Engle, Tuholski, et al., 1999). A drawback of the OSPAN, as well as other WM tasks designed to assess individual differences, is that they must be administered by highly trained experimenters in close physical proximity to the participant. In the first study reported here, two experimenters were used; three experimenters were used in the second study. Variability in a single experimenter's behavior as well as between-experimenter differences can easily produce error variance in WM scores. Thus,

our data might have been even stronger had we been able to use a mechanized controlled attention task.

There are also challenges to our assumption that narrative development is responsible for the decline in intrusive and avoidant thinking that leads to increased WM. One strong contender for how writing might affect WM is that writing about stressful experiences may make attitudes toward these experiences more accessible. Highly accessible attitudes are automatically activated from memory whereas, less accessible attitudes require effortful processing (Fazio, Roskos-Ewoldson, & Powell, 1994). It is possible that less accessible attitudes are heavy consumers of cognitive resources. If emotional disclosure increases attitude accessibility, resources would be freed for other tasks, such as the WM task used in our experiments. This line of reasoning meshes with the results from Fazio and Powell (1997). These investigators demonstrated that given equivalent levels of self-reported stress, college freshmen with more accessible attitudes toward college subsequently report better physical and psychological health. Fazio and Powell make essentially the same argument for accessibility that we make here for WM, namely that attitude accessibility frees cognitive resources to cope more effectively with other stressors. In further research, accessibility and WM could be contrasted as the most likely potential mediators of the writing–health relationship.

An important extension of our work is the possibility that changes in available WM are at least in part responsible for the widely documented writing–health relationship. Resources claimed by unwanted thoughts could impair problem solving to the extent that proactive coping and appropriate responses to subsequent stressors become unlikely. As a consequence, more stress is produced, and this continued stress produces decrements in psychological and physical health. Writing about a stressful experience might attenuate the stress–illness cycle by means of its effects on WM. Obviously, in the absence of health data, the present results cannot be interpreted as evidence for such mediation. However, our findings that writing affects available WM capacity and that the linguistic variables associated with health outcomes have similar relationships with WM suggest such a possibility. Whether the WM increases we observed are of sufficient magnitude or duration to support more effective problem solving and possible attendant improvements in health outcomes requires further study.

## References

Antrobus, J. S. (1968). Information theory and stimulus-independent thought. *British Journal of Psychology, 59,* 423–430.

Baddeley, A. D., & Hitch, G. (1974). Working memory. In G. A. Bower (Ed.), *The psychology of learning and motivation* (Vol. 8, pp. 47–89). New York: Academic Press.

Barclay, C. R. (1996). Autobiographical remembering: Narrative constraints on objectified selves. In D. Rubin (Ed.), *Remembering our past* (pp. 94–128). Cambridge, England: Cambridge University Press.

Baron, R. M., & Kenny, D. A. (1986). The moderator–mediator variable distinction in social psychological research: Conceptual, strategic, and statistical considerations. *Journal of Personality and Social Psychology, 51,* 1173–1182.

Baum, A., Cohen, L., & Hall, M. (1993). Control and intrusive memories as possible determinants of chronic stress. *Psychosomatic Medicine, 55,* 274–286.

KLEIN AND BOALS

Blackwood, S. K., MacHale, S. M., Power, M. J., Goodwin, G. M., & Lawrie, S. M. (1998). Effects of exercise on cognitive and motor function in chronic fatigue syndrome and depression. *Journal of Neurology, Neurosurgery and Psychiatry, 65,* 541–546.

Cantor, J., & Engle, R. W. (1993). Working memory capacity as long-term memory activation: An individual differences approach. *Journal of Experimental Psychology: Learning, Memory, and Cognition, 19,* 1101–1114.

Chiappe, P., Hasher, L., & Siegel, L. S. (2000). Working memory, inhibitory control and reading disability. *Memory & Cognition, 28,* 8–17.

Cohen, S., Kamarck, T., & Mermelstein, R. (1983). A global measure of perceived stress. *Journal of Health and Social Behavior, 24,* 385–396.

Creamer, M. (1995). A cognitive processing formulation of posttrauma reactions. In R. J. Kleber, C. R. Figley, & B. P. R. Gersons (Eds.), *Beyond trauma: Cultural and societal dynamics* (pp. 55–74). New York: Plenum Press.

Darke, S. (1988). Anxiety and working memory capacity. *Cognition and Emotion, 2,* 145–154.

Engle, R. W. (1996). Working memory and retrieval: An inhibition-resource approach. In J. T. E. Richardson, R. W. Engle, L. Hasher, R. H. Logie, E. R. Stoltzfus, & R. T. Zacks (Eds.), *Working memory and human cognition* (pp. 89–117). New York: Oxford University Press.

Engle, R. W., Carullo, J. W., & Collins, K. W. (1991). Individual differences in working memory for comprehension and following directions. *Journal of Educational Research, 84,* 253–262.

Engle, R. W., Kane, M. J., & Tuholski, S. W. (1999). Individual differences in working memory capacity and what they tell us about controlled attention, general fluid intelligence and functions of the prefrontal cortex. In A. Miyake & P. Shah (Eds.), *Models of working memory: Mechanisms of active maintenance and executive control* (pp. 102–131). Cambridge, England: Cambridge University Press.

Engle, R. W., Tuholski, S. W., Laughlin, J. E., & Conway, R. A. (1999). Working memory, short-term memory, and general fluid intelligence: A latent-variable approach. *Journal of Experimental Psychology: General, 128,* 309–331.

Fazio, R. H., & Powell, M. C. (1997). On the value of knowing one's likes and dislikes: Attitude accessibility, stress and health in college. *Psychological Science, 8,* 430–436.

Fazio, R. H., Roskos-Ewoldson, D. R., & Powell, M. C. (1994). Attitudes, perception and attention. In P. M. Niedenthal & S. Kitayama (Eds.), *The heart's eye: Emotional influences in perception and attention* (pp. 197–216). San Diego, CA: Academic Press.

Foa, E. B., & Kozak, M. J. (1986). Emotional processing of fear: Exposure to corrective information. *Psychological Bulletin, 99,* 20–35.

Foa, E., Molnar, C., & Cashman, L. (1995). Change in rape narratives during exposure therapy for posttraumatic stress disorder. *Journal of Traumatic Stress, 8,* 675–690.

Foa, E. B., Steketee, G., & Rothbaum, B. O. (1989). Behavioral/cognitive conceptualizations of post-traumatic stress disorder. *Behavior Therapy, 20,* 155–176.

Greenberg, M. A. (1995). Cognitive processing of traumas: The role of intrusive thoughts and reappraisals. *Journal of Applied Social Psychology, 25,* 1262–1296.

Horowitz, M. J. (1975). Intrusive and repetitive thoughts after experimental stress: A summary. *Archives of General Psychiatry, 32,* 1457–1463.

Horowitz, M. J., Field, N. P., & Classen, C. C. (1993). Stress response syndromes and their treatment. In L. Goldberger & S. Breznitz (Eds.), *Handbook of stress: Theoretical and clinical aspects* (2nd ed., pp. 757–773). New York: Free Press.

Horowitz, M. J., Wilner, N., & Alvarez, W. (1979). Impact of Event Scale: A measure of subjective stress. *Psychosomatic Medicine, 41,* 209–218.

Janoff-Bulman, R. (1992). *Shattered assumptions.* New York: Free Press.

Jonides, J., Schumacher, E. H., Smith, E. E., Lauber, E. J., Awh, E., Minoshima, S., & Koeppe, R. A. (1997). Verbal working memory load affects regional brain activation as measured by PET. *Journal of Cognitive Neuroscience, 9,* 462–473.

Kelley, J. E., Lumley, M. A., & Leisen, J. C. C. (1997). Health effects of emotional disclosure in rheumatoid arthritis patients. *Health Psychology, 16,* 331–340.

King, L. A., & Miner, K. N. (2000). Writing about the perceived benefits of traumatic events: Implications for physical health. *Personality and Social Psychology Bulletin, 26,* 220–230.

Klein, K., & Boals, A. (in press). The relationship of life event stress and working memory capacity. *Applied Cognitive Psychology.*

Klein, K., & Fiss, W. H. (1999). The reliability and stability of the Turner and Engle working memory task. *Behavior Research Methods, Instruments and Computers, 31,* 429–432.

Lane, J. D. (1997). Effects of brief caffeinated-beverage deprivation on mood, symptoms and psychomotor performance. *Pharmacology, Biochemistry and Behavior, 58,* 203–298.

Lehto, J. (1996). Are executive function tests dependent on working memory capacity? *The Quarterly Journal of Experimental Psychology, 49A(1),* 29–50.

Lepore, S. J. (1997). Expressive writing moderates the relation between intrusive thoughts and depressive symptoms. *Journal of Personality and Social Psychology, 73,* 1030–1037.

Lepore, S. J., & Greenberg, M. A. (in press). Mending broken hearts: Effects of expressive writing on mood, cognitive processing, social adjustment and health following a relationship breakup. *Psychology and Health.*

Lutgendorf, S. K., Antoni, M. H., Kumar, M., & Schneiderman, N. (1994). Changes in cognitive coping strategies predict EBV-antibody titre change following a stressor disclosure induction. *Journal of Psychosomatic Research, 38,* 63–78.

Meichenbaum, D., & Fitzpatrick, D. (1993). A constructivist narrative perspective on stress and coping: Stress inoculation applications. In L. Goldberger & S. Breznitz (Eds.), *Handbook of stress: Theoretical and clinical aspects* (2nd ed., pp. 706–723). New York: Free Press.

Murray, E. J., & Segal, D. L. (1994). Emotional processing in vocal and written expression of feelings about traumatic experiences. *Journal of Traumatic Stress, 7,* 391–405.

Páez, D., Velasco, C., & González, J. L. (1999). Expressive writing and the role of alexythimia as a dispositional deficit in self-disclosure and psychological health. *Journal of Personality and Social Psychology, 77,* 630–641.

Pennebaker, J. W. (1989). Confession, inhibition and disease. In L. Berkowitz (Ed.), *Advances in experimental social psychology* (Vol. 22, pp. 211–244). Orlando, FL: Academic Press.

Pennebaker, J. W. (1997). Writing about emotional experiences as a therapeutic process. *Psychological Science, 8,* 162–166.

Pennebaker, J. W., Colder, M., & Sharp, L. K. (1990). Accelerating the coping process. *Journal of Personality and Social Psychology, 58,* 528–537.

Pennebaker, J. W., & Francis, M. E. (1996). Cognitive, emotional and language processes in disclosure. *Cognition and Emotion, 10,* 621–626.

Pennebaker, J. W., & Francis, M. (1999). *Linguistic Inquiry and Word Count: LIWC.* Mahwah, NJ: Erlbaum.

Pennebaker, J. W., Kiecolt-Glaser, J., & Glaser, R. (1988). Disclosure of traumas and immune function: Health implications for psychotherapy. *Journal of Consulting and Clinical Psychology, 56,* 239–245.

Pennebaker, J. W., Mayne, T. J., & Francis, M. E. (1997). Linguistic predictors of adaptive bereavement. *Journal of Personality and Social Psychology, 72,* 863–871.

Pennington, B. F. (1994). The working memory function of the prefrontal cortices. In M. M. Haith, J. B. Benson, R. J. Robert, Jr., & B. F. Pennington (Eds.), *The development of future-oriented processes* (pp. 243–289). Chicago, IL: University of Chicago Press.

Petrie, K. J., Booth, R. J., & Pennebaker, J. W. (1998). The immunological

EXPRESSIVE WRITING AND WORKING MEMORY

effects of thought suppression. *Journal of Personality and Social Psychology, 75,* 1264–1272.

Petrie, K. J., Booth, R. J., Pennebaker, J. W., Davison, K. P., & Thomas, M. G. (1995). Disclosure of trauma and immune response to a hepatitis B vaccination program. *Journal of Consulting and Clinical Psychology, 63,* 787–792.

Radvansky, G. A., & Zacks, R. T. (1991). Mental models and the fan effect. *Journal of Experimental Psychology: Learning, Memory, and Cognition, 17,* 940–953.

Rapee, R. M. (1993). The utilization of working memory by worry. *Behaviour Research and Therapy, 31,* 617–620.

Roberts, R. J., & Pennington, B. F. (1996). An interactive framework for examining prefrontal cognitive processes. *Developmental Neuropsychology, 12,* 105–126.

Roemer, L., & Borkovec, T. D. (1994). Effects of suppressing thoughts about emotional material. *Journal of Abnormal Psychology, 103,* 467–474.

Rosen, V. M., & Engle, R. W. (1998). Working memory capacity and suppression. *Journal of Memory and Language, 39,* 418–436.

Segal, D. L., Bogaards, J. A., & Chatman, C. (1998, August). Emotional expression improves adjustment to spousal loss in the elderly. Poster session presented at the 106th Annual Convention of the American Psychological Association, San Francisco, CA.

Segal, D. L., & Murray, E. J. (1994). Emotional processing in cognitive therapy and vocal expression of feeling. *Journal of Social and Clinical Psychology, 13,* 189–206.

Smythe, J. M. (1998). Written emotional expression: Effect sizes, outcome types, and moderating variables. *Journal of Consulting and Clinical Psychology, 66,* 174–184.

Sorg, B. A., & Whitney, P. (1992). The effect of trait anxiety and situational stress on working memory capacity. *Journal of Research in Personality, 26,* 235–241.

Stoltzfus, E. R., Hasher, L., & Zacks, R. T. (1996). Working memory and aging: Current status of the inhibitory view. In J. T. E. Richardson, R. W. Engle, L. Hasher, & R. H. Logie (Eds.), *Working memory and human cognition* (pp. 66–88). New York: Oxford University Press.

Teasdale, J. D., Dritschel, M. J. T., Proctor, L., Lloyd, C. A., Nimmo-Smith, I., & Baddeley, A. D. (1995). Stimulus-independent thought depends on central executive resources. *Memory and Cognition, 23,* 551–559.

Teasdale, J. D., Proctor, L., Lloyd, C. A., & Baddeley, A. D. (1993). Working memory and stimulus-independent thought: Effects of memory load and presentation rate. *European Journal of Cognitive Psychology, 5,* 417–433.

Turner, M. L., & Engle, R. W. (1989). Is working memory capacity task dependent? *Journal of Memory and Language, 28,* 127–154.

Wegner, D. M. (1988). Stress and mental control. In S. Fisher & J. Reason (Eds.), *Handbook of stress, cognition and health* (pp. 685–699). Chichester, England: Wiley.

Wegner, D. M. (1992). You can't always think what you want: Problems in the suppression of unwanted thoughts. *Advances in Experimental Social Psychology, 25,* 193–225.

Wegner, D. M. (1994). Ironic processes of mental control. *Psychological Review, 101,* 34–52.

Wegner, D. M., & Erber, R. (1992). The hyperaccessibility of suppressed thoughts. *Journal of Personality and Social Psychology, 63,* 903–912.

Wegner, D. M., Erber, R., & Zanakos, S. (1993). Ironic processes in the mental control of mood and mood related thought. *Journal of Personality and Social Psychology, 65,* 1093–1105.

Wegner, D. M., Quillian, F., & Houston, C. E. (1996). Memories out of order: Thought suppression and the disturbance of sequence memory. *Journal of Personality and Social Psychology, 71,* 680–691.

Wegner, D. M., Schneider, D. J., Carter, S. R., & White, T. L. (1987). Paradoxical effects of thought suppression. *Journal of Personality and Social Psychology, 53,* 5–13.

Weiss, D. S., & Marmar, C. R. (1997). The Impact of Event Scale—revised. In J. P. Wilson & T. M. Keane (Eds.), *Assessing psychological trauma* (pp. 399–411). New York: Guilford Press.

Welsh, M. C., Satterlee-Cartmell, T., & Stine, M. (1999). Towers of Hanoi and London: Contribution of working memory and inhibition to performance. *Brain and Cognition, 41,* 231–242.

Wickelgren, I. (1997, March 14). Getting a grasp on working memory. *Science, 275,* 1580–1582.

Wong, P. T. P., & Watt, L. M. (1991). What types of reminiscence are associated with successful aging? *Psychology and Aging, 6,* 272–279.

Received January 21, 2000
Revision received August 1, 2000
Accepted September 28, 2000 ■

# ARTICLE MANUSCRIPT (SELECTED PAGES)

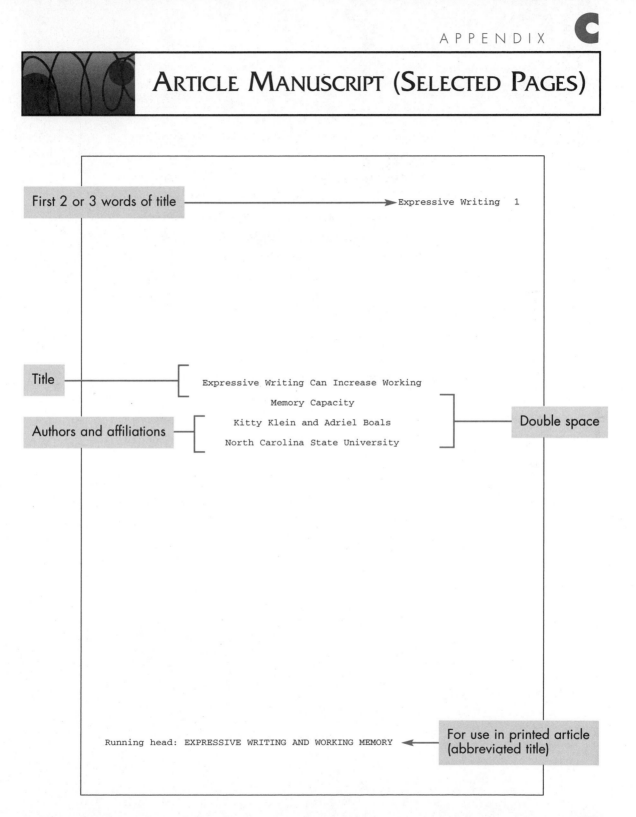

First 2 or 3 words of title → Expressive Writing    1

Title — Expressive Writing Can Increase Working

Memory Capacity

Authors and affiliations — Kitty Klein and Adriel Boals

North Carolina State University

Double space

Running head: EXPRESSIVE WRITING AND WORKING MEMORY ← For use in printed article (abbreviated title)

Abstract begins on new page

Abstract

Not indented

The effect of emotional disclosure through expressive writing on available working memory (WM) capacity was examined in two semester-long experiments. In the first study, 35 freshmen assigned to write about their
thoughts and feelings about coming to college demonstrated larger working
memory gains seven weeks later compared to 36 writers assigned to a
trivial topic. Increased use of cause and insight words was associated
with greater WM improvements. In the second study, students ($n = 34$) who
wrote about a negative personal experience enjoyed greater WM improvements and declines in intrusive thinking compared to students who wrote
about a positive experience ($n = 33$) or a trivial topic ($n = 34$). The results are discussed in terms of a model grounded in cognitive and social
psychological theory in which expressive writing reduces
intrusive/avoidant thinking about a stressful experience, thus freeing WM
resources.

Statistical symbols and abbreviations are in italics

Single paragraph

First page of text

Title

Expressive Writing Can Increase Working

Memory Capacity

Indent and begin text

The beneficial effects of emotional disclosure through expressive writing about traumatic or stressful experiences have been widely reported (Smythe, 1998). Compared to individuals assigned to write about trivial topics, experimental participants who write about their deepest thoughts and feelings show reductions in physician visits (Pennebaker & Francis, 1996), improvements in immune function (Pennebaker, Kiecolt-Glaser & Glaser, 1988), increased antibody production (Petrie, Booth, Pennebaker, Davison & Thomas, 1995), and increases in psychological well-being (Lepore, 1997; Murray & Segal, 1994) for several months after the expressive writing intervention. There is considerable speculation about how writing might achieve such benefits. In contrast to earlier theorizing which emphasized the cathartic release of thoughts and feelings associated with stressful experiences (e.g., Pennebaker, 1989), current explanations focus on the cognitive changes produced by expressive writing (Pennebaker, 1997). While there is a long tradition of examining self-reported cognitive activity in the wake of stressful events (e.g., Horowitz, 1975), the cognitive changes associated with expressive writing are inferred from analysis of the linguistic characteristics of writers' essays. Across writing episodes, participants whose essays contain increases in words reflecting causality and insight (Pennebaker & Francis, 1996; Pennebaker, Mayne & Francis, 1997) experience the greatest health and behavioral benefits. Pennebaker, Mayne and Francis believe these linguistic changes reflect the cognitive processes associated with encoding and storing features of the experience "in a more organized, coherent, and simplified manner . . . that reduces the associated emotional arousal" (p. 864). The purpose of our experiments is to investigate directly how expressive writing might affect cognitive processing, and in particular whether working memory capacity is affected by expressive writing.

Refer to articles and books by authors and year

Include page reference for quotes

If this report contained only one experiment the format would be as below. Method would be centered. *Participants* would be flush to left margin and in italics.

Finally, there is some evidence that expressive writing has more beneficial effects on health for men than for women (Smythe, 1998). Although not a primary question in the present study, the data will be examined to determine if such gender differences appear on WM processes.

## Method

### Participants

Thirty male and 47 female first semester college freshmen, ages 18-19 years, participated for partial course credit. Participants were assigned randomly to one of two conditions: an experimental group asked to write about a stressful event, in this case, their deepest thoughts and feelings about coming to college ($n = 39$), or a control group asked to write about a nonstressful event, time management ($n = 38$).

### Materials

Turner & Engle's (1989) arithmetic operation-word memory span task (OSPAN) and procedure was used to assess participants' working memory. The OSPAN task has high internal consistency (.75), reliability (.88), and is stable across time (Klein & Fiss, 1999). Following Engle's method, participants read a simple arithmetic equation, e.g. "$(9 \times 1) - 9 = 1$" on the computer followed by a one-syllable word, e.g. "back". Participants indicated verbally whether the answer given to the problem was true or false and read the word aloud. The experimenter then advanced the program to the next operation. After sets of 2 to 7 problems, participants were prompted to write down as many of these words as possible from the previous set. In all, three sequences containing one set of each size were presented, for a total of 81 operations. The operations and words were selected from the pools developed by Cantor & Engle (1993). Additional one-syllable words matched for frequency were also generated for use in subsequent administrations of the task. Different equations and words were used in each sequence and each time the test was administered. WM scores were the total number of words recalled that were associated with correctly solved equations.

To assess college freshmen's levels of anxieties about coming to college we used the College Adjustment Test (CAT; Pennebaker, Colder & Sharp, 1990). The CAT is a 19-question survey designed specifically to assess college freshmen's levels of homesickness, loneliness and college-related difficulties.

### Procedure

The participants were tested individually in six separate experimental sessions during the fall semester of their freshman year. The fist session was scheduled

In single experiment report, results is centered.

Results

Altogether, 71 (92%) of the participants completed all six experimental sessions. Data from six participants (three from each condition) who
did not attend one or more of the experimental sessions were not analyzed.
The final sample sizes for the experimental group and the control group were
36 (23 women and 13 men) and 35 (20 women and 15 men), respectively.

We were able to establish telephone contact with 30 experimental
group participants and 29 control group participants, giving us self-
reports of stress from 83% of the writers. One of the experimental group
participants refused to give permission to access his grades and three of
the control group participants failed to send written permission. Three
students who gave permission to access their grades withdrew from the university or had late grade reports for the spring semester, preventing their
inclusion in the GPA analyses. The GPS analyses were thus performed on data
from 27 experimental group members and 25 control group participants.

*Effects of expressive writing on working memory.* Raw WM scores are
presented in Table 1. Prior to condition assignment, there were no differences in WM scores, $M$ words correctly recalled $= 54.5$, as a function of gender or writing topic. In line with the analyses employed by Pennebaker,
Colder and Sharp (1990) and King and Miner (2000), we used the pre-writing
WM scores as predictors to calculate residual WM scores for the WM tests
administered one week and six weeks after writing. To the extent that the
post-writing scores are completely predicted by the pre-writing scores,
residual scores will be 0. Residuals in excess of 0 indicate better performance than what would have been predicted from the pre-writing score;
residuals less than 0 indicate poorer than predicted performance. We subjected the two residual scores to a 2 (writing condition) $\times 2$

● ● ●

Expressive Writing  22

A 2 (direction of cognitive change) × 2 (writing condition) ANOVA on the raw WM change scores from the second to the third administrations of the task indicated main effects of direction of cognitive change, $F(1, 67) = 3.92$, $p < .05$ and condition, $F(1, 67) = 4.25$, $p < .04$, but not their interaction. In the control group, writers who decreased their use of cognitive words from Essay 1 to Essay 3 showed smaller WM gains ($M = 1.3$ operations) compared to writers who increased their cognitive word use ($M = 3.5$ operations). Similar differences occurred in the experimental group. Experimental group participants who decreased their use of cognitive words showed smaller WM gains ($M = 3.7$ operations) than did experimental writers who increased their cognitive word use ($M = 5.2$ operations) from Essay 1 to Essay 3. Essay 1 to Essay 2 difference scores were unrelated to WM changes.

In contrast to the association between changes in cognitive word usage and working memory gains, there was no relationship between working memory changes and changes in the use of emotion words from Essay 1 to Essay 3 or from Essay 1 to Essay 2.

*Self-reports of writing and reactions to the experiment.* We analyzed responses to the questionnaire administered during the last session to examine how participants perceived their essays and their reactions to the experiment. Participants in the writing conditions did not differ in the frequency with which they made phone calls or sent e-mail to family and friends about their feelings and experiences, or in their judgments of the value of the experiment, or how well organized they thought their essays were. As Table 2 shows, the experimental group indicated they had disclosed more personal information and revealed their emotions more than control group participants. Students assigned to write about their deepest thoughts and feelings also reported they had thought more and talked more about the topic before the experiment and had wanted to talk about the topic more since the experiment.

We next examined the correlations between self-reports of disclosure and working memeory scores. The only variable related to pretest working memory scores was how extensively students said they had talked

Include degrees of freedom

Include probability level

Expressive Writing  26

Students showing greater improvement in WM scores between the second and third WM tests earned higher GPAs for both the experimental semester, $r(53) = .23$, $p < .10$ and the following spring, $r(50) = .29$, $p < .04$. The same MANOVA using the final WM score as the predictor produced no significant findings.

Discussion  ←——— In a single experiment report, discussion is centered

Our results supported both hypotheses: expressive writing improves available working memory, and the linguistic changes associated with increased narrative coherence are also related to working memory improvements. Seven weeks after the writing sessions, participants assigned to write about their deepest thoughts and feelings about coming to college exhibited working memory improvements compared to the control group who wrote about time management. There was a trend in the data suggesting that men may have profited more from the manipulation than women, although this difference did not reach conventional levels of statistical significance. WM increases were related to higher GPAs earned during the semester of the experiment as well as the subsequent semester.

As was expected, students who wrote about coming to college used more cognitive insight words as well as more emotion words. Our hypothesis that increases in the use of the cognitive words from Essay 1 to Essay 3 would predict increases in working memory was supported. Changes in the percentage of cognitive words from Essay 1 to Essay 2 were not related to WM change, echoing Pennebaker & Francis's (1996) finding that only the Essay 1-Essay 3 cognitive word differences were related to health outcomes. Changes in the percentages of emotion words across essays were unrelated to increases in the delayed posttest WM scores. The latter findings are

●   ●   ●

**References are placed on separate page**

References

Antrobus, J. S. (1968). Information theory and stimulus-independent thought. *British Journal of Psychology*, *59*, 423–430.

Baddeley, A. D. & Hitch, G. (1974). Working memory. In G. A. Bower (Ed.), *The psychology of learning and motivation* (Vol. 8, pp. 47–89). New York: Academic Press.

**Chapter in a book Include page numbers of chapter**

Barclay, C. R. (1996). Autobiographical remembering: Narrative constraints on objectified selves. In D. Rubin (Ed.), *Remembering our past*. (pp. 94–128). Cambridge: Cambridge University Press.

Baron, R. M. & Kenny, D. A. (1986). The moderator-mediator variable distinction in social psychological research: Conceptual, strategic, and statistical considerations. *Journal of Personality and Social Psychology*, *51*, 1173–1182.

Baum, A., Cohen, L. & Hall, M. (1993). Control and intrusive memories as possible determinants of chronic stress. *Psychosomatic Medicine*, *55*, 274–286.

**Journal article**

Blackwood, S. K., MacHale, S. M., Power, M. J., Goodwin, G. M. & Lawrie, S. M. (1998). Effects of exercise on cognitive and motor function in chronic fatigue syndrome and depression. *Journal of Neurology, Neurosurgery and Psychiatry*, *65*, 541–546.

Cantor, J. & Engle, R. W. (1993). Working memory capacity as long-term memory activation: An individual differences approach. *Journal of Experimental Psychology: Learning Memory and Cognition*, *19*, 1101–1114.

Chiappe, P., Hasher, L. & Siegel, L. S. (2000). Working memory, inhibitory control and reading disability. *Memory and Cognition*, *28*, 8–17.

Cohen, S., Kamarck, T. & Mermelstein, R. (1983). A global measure of perceived stress. *Journal of Health and Social Behavior*, *24*, 385–396.

**Following the reference section, in order, are appendixes, author notes, footnotes, tables, figure captions, and figures. Each starts on a separate page.**

Expressive Writing  51

Table I

*Mean unadjusted WM scores at each test time, Experiments 1 and 2*

| Topic | Experiment 1[a] | | | Experiment 2[b] | | |
|---|---|---|---|---|---|---|
| | Test 1 | Test 2 | Test 3 | Test 1 | Test 2 | Test 3 |
| Time management | 54.6 | 59.0 | 61.2 | 43.4 | 43.6 | 44.2 |
| | (6.8) | (6.30) | (7.6) | (7.9) | (9.3) | (8.2) |
| Coming to college | 54.4 | 57.8 | 62.7 | | | |
| | (8.4) | (8.2) | (8.8) | | | |
| Negative experience | | | | 42.5 | 46.2 | 47.6 |
| | | | | (8.5) | (8.3) | (8.3) |
| Positive experience | | | | 41.7 | 43.8 | 44.0 |
| | | | | (7.1) | (6.5) | (6.3) |

Note. Standard deviations are in parentheses.

[a] Maximum possible correct = 81

[b] Maximum possible correct = 75

Place each table including caption on a separate page.

Figure Captions

Figure 1. Timelines for Experiments 1 and 2.

Figure 2. Mean residual WM scores as a function of writing topic and time, Experiment 1.

Figure 3. Mean residual WM scores as a function of writing topic and time, Experiment 2.

Figure 4. Mean decreases in intrusive/avoidant thoughts for positive and negative events as a function of writing topic.

Place captions for all figures on a separate page.
Each figure is placed on a separate page following this.

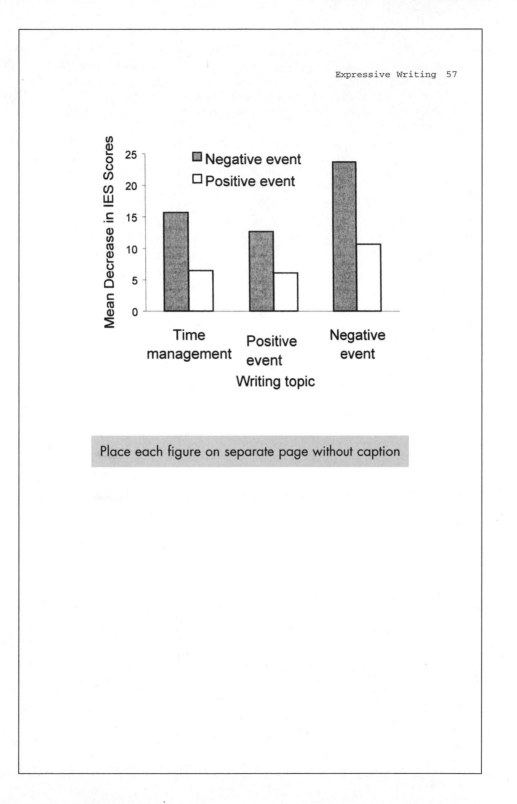

Multi-experiment Reports
A multi-experiment report has a single introduction section followed by a method, results, and discussion section for each experiment. A general discussion section follows. The presentation of references, tables and figures are the same as with single experiment reports.

In a report of more than one experiment center "Experiment 1" as below. *Method* is flush left and in italics. *Participants* is indented and in italics.

Finally, there is some evidence that expressive writing has more beneficial effects on health for men than for women (Smythe, 1998). Although not a primary question in the present study, the data will be examined to determine if such gender differences appear on WM processes.

Experiment 1

*Method*

*Participants.* Thirty male and 47 female first semester college freshmen, ages 18-19 years, participated for partial course credit. Participants were assigned randomly to one of two conditions: an experimental group asked to write about a stressful event, in this case, their deepest thoughts and feelings about coming to college ($n = 39$), or a control group asked to write about a nonstressful event, time management ($n = 38$).

*Materials.* Turner & Engle's (1989) arithmetic operation-word memory span task (OSPAN) and procedure was used to assess participants' working memory. The OSPAN task has high internal consistency (.75), reliability (.88), and is stable across time (Klein

● ● ●

> When presenting results from two or more experiments in the same paper, the headings "Results" and "Discussion" are flush left and in italics.

often the participant had felt nervous, calm or stressed during the last week with a 4-item response scale ranging from "never" to "very often."

*Results*

Altogether, 71 (92%) of the participants completed all six experimental sessions. Data from six participants (three from each condition) who did not attend one or more

of Spring, $r(50) = .29$, $p < .04$. The same MANOVA using the final WM score as the predictor produced no significant findings.

*Discussion*

   Our results supported both hypotheses: expressive writing improves available working memory, and the linguistic changes associated with increased

> Additional experiments using the same format (methods, results, discussion) follow experiment 1.

narrative coherence are cognitive impact, or whether there is something unique about writing about negative experiences requires further investigation.

General Discussion

   The findings from these two experiments shed new light on available working memory capacity and markedly expand the benefits of expressive writing to this widely studied cognitive

> A general discussion follows the presentation of two or more experiments. Heading is centered.

> The general discussion section is followed by the same sequence (references, author notes, footnotes, tables, and figure captions) as with single experiment reports.

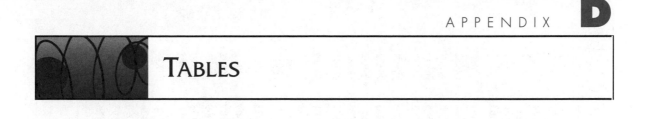

# TABLES

## Table D.1   Random Numbers

| | | | | | | | | | | | | | |
|---|---|---|---|---|---|---|---|---|---|---|---|---|---|
| 10480 | 15011 | 01536 | 02011 | 81647 | 91646 | 69179 | 14194 | 62590 | 6207 | 20969 | 99570 | 91291 | 90700 |
| 22368 | 46573 | 25595 | 85393 | 30995 | 89198 | 27982 | 53402 | 93965 | 34095 | 52666 | 19174 | 39615 | 99505 |
| 24130 | 48360 | 22527 | 97265 | 76393 | 64809 | 15179 | 24830 | 49340 | 32081 | 30680 | 19655 | 63348 | 58629 |
| 42167 | 93093 | 06243 | 616580 | 07856 | 16376 | 39440 | 53537 | 71341 | 57004 | 00849 | 74917 | 97758 | 16379 |
| 37570 | 39975 | 81837 | 16656 | 06121 | 91782 | 60468 | 81305 | 49684 | 60672 | 14110 | 06927 | 01263 | 54613 |
| 77921 | 06907 | 11008 | 42751 | 27756 | 53498 | 18602 | 70659 | 90655 | 15053 | 21916 | 81825 | 44394 | 42880 |
| 99562 | 72095 | 56420 | 69994 | 98872 | 31016 | 71194 | 18738 | 44013 | 44840 | 63213 | 21069 | 10634 | 12952 |
| 96301 | 91977 | 05463 | 07972 | 18876 | 20922 | 94595 | 56869 | 69014 | 60045 | 18425 | 84903 | 42508 | 32307 |
| 89579 | 14342 | 63661 | 10281 | 17453 | 18103 | 57740 | 84378 | 25331 | 12566 | 58768 | 44947 | 05585 | 56941 |
| 85475 | 36857 | 53342 | 53988 | 53060 | 59533 | 38867 | 62300 | 08158 | 17983 | 16439 | 11458 | 18593 | 64952 |
| 29818 | 69589 | 88231 | 33276 | 70997 | 79936 | 56865 | 05859 | 90106 | 31595 | 01547 | 85590 | 91610 | 78188 |
| 63553 | 40961 | 48235 | 03427 | 49626 | 69445 | 18663 | 72695 | 52180 | 20847 | 12234 | 90511 | 33703 | 90322 |
| 09429 | 93969 | 52636 | 92737 | 88974 | 33488 | 36320 | 17617 | 30015 | 08272 | 84115 | 27156 | 30613 | 74952 |
| 10365 | 61129 | 87529 | 85689 | 48237 | 52267 | 67689 | 93394 | 01511 | 26358 | 85104 | 20285 | 29975 | 89868 |
| 07119 | 97336 | 71048 | 08178 | 77233 | 13916 | 47564 | 81056 | 97735 | 85977 | 29372 | 74461 | 28551 | 90707 |
| 51085 | 12765 | 51821 | 51259 | 77452 | 16308 | 60756 | 92144 | 49442 | 53900 | 70960 | 63990 | 75601 | 40719 |
| 02368 | 21382 | 52404 | 60268 | 89368 | 19885 | 55322 | 44819 | 01188 | 65255 | 64835 | 44919 | 05944 | 55157 |
| 01011 | 54092 | 33362 | 94904 | 31273 | 04146 | 18594 | 29852 | 71585 | 85030 | 51132 | 01915 | 92747 | 64951 |
| 52162 | 53916 | 46369 | 58586 | 23216 | 14513 | 83149 | 98736 | 23495 | 64350 | 94738 | 17752 | 35156 | 35749 |
| 07056 | 97628 | 33787 | 09998 | 42698 | 06691 | 76988 | 13602 | 51851 | 46104 | 88916 | 19509 | 25625 | 58104 |
| 48663 | 91245 | 85828 | 14346 | 09172 | 30168 | 90229 | 04734 | 59193 | 22178 | 30421 | 61666 | 99904 | 32812 |
| 54164 | 58492 | 22421 | 74103 | 47070 | 25306 | 76468 | 26384 | 58151 | 06646 | 21524 | 15227 | 96909 | 44592 |
| 32639 | 32363 | 05597 | 24200 | 13363 | 38005 | 94342 | 26384 | 58151 | 06646 | 21524 | 15227 | 96909 | 44592 |
| 29334 | 27001 | 87637 | 87308 | 58731 | 00256 | 45834 | 15398 | 46557 | 41135 | 10367 | 07684 | 36188 | 18510 |
| 02488 | 33062 | 28834 | 07351 | 19731 | 92420 | 60952 | 61280 | 50001 | 67658 | 32586 | 86679 | 50720 | 94953 |
| 81525 | 72295 | 04839 | 96423 | 24878 | 82651 | 66566 | 14778 | 76797 | 14780 | 13300 | 87074 | 79666 | 95725 |
| 29676 | 20591 | 68086 | 26432 | 46901 | 20849 | 89768 | 81536 | 86645 | 12659 | 92259 | 57102 | 80428 | 25280 |
| 00742 | 57392 | 39064 | 66432 | 84673 | 40027 | 32832 | 61362 | 98947 | 96067 | 64760 | 64584 | 96096 | 98253 |
| 05366 | 04213 | 25669 | 26422 | 44407 | 44048 | 37937 | 63904 | 45766 | 66134 | 75740 | 66520 | 34693 | 90449 |
| 91921 | 26418 | 64117 | 94305 | 26766 | 25940 | 39972 | 22209 | 71500 | 64568 | 91402 | 42416 | 07844 | 69618 |

SOURCE: Beyer (1960).

## Table D.1    Random Numbers

| | | | | | | | | | | | | | |
|---|---|---|---|---|---|---|---|---|---|---|---|---|---|
| 00582 | 04711 | 87917 | 77341 | 42206 | 35126 | 74087 | 99547 | 81817 | 42607 | 43808 | 76655 | 62028 | 76630 |
| 00725 | 69884 | 62797 | 56170 | 86324 | 88072 | 76222 | 36086 | 84637 | 93161 | 76038 | 65855 | 77919 | 88006 |
| 69011 | 65795 | 95876 | 55293 | 18988 | 27354 | 26575 | 08625 | 40801 | 59920 | 29841 | 80150 | 12777 | 48501 |
| 25976 | 57948 | 29888 | 88604 | 67917 | 48708 | 18912 | 62274 | 65424 | 69774 | 33611 | 54262 | 85963 | 03547 |
| 09763 | 83473 | 73577 | 12908 | 30883 | 18317 | 28290 | 35797 | 05998 | 41688 | 34952 | 37888 | 38917 | 88050 |
| 91567 | 42595 | 27958 | 30134 | 04024 | 86385 | 29880 | 99730 | 55536 | 84855 | 29080 | 09250 | 79656 | 73211 |
| 17955 | 56439 | 90999 | 49127 | 20044 | 59931 | 06115 | 20542 | 18059 | 02008 | 73708 | 83517 | 36103 | 42791 |
| 46503 | 18584 | 18845 | 49618 | 02304 | 51038 | 20655 | 58727 | 28168 | 15475 | 56942 | 53389 | 20562 | 87338 |
| 92157 | 89634 | 94824 | 78171 | 84610 | 82834 | 09922 | 25417 | 44137 | 48413 | 25555 | 21246 | 35509 | 20468 |
| 14577 | 62765 | 35605 | 81263 | 39667 | 47358 | 56873 | 56307 | 61607 | 49518 | 89656 | 20103 | 77490 | 18062 |
| 98427 | 07523 | 33362 | 64270 | 01638 | 92477 | 66969 | 98420 | 04800 | 45585 | 46565 | 04102 | 46880 | 45709 |
| 34914 | 63976 | 88720 | 82765 | 34476 | 17032 | 87589 | 40836 | 32427 | 70002 | 70663 | 88863 | 77775 | 69348 |
| 70060 | 28277 | 39475 | 46473 | 23219 | 53416 | 94970 | 25382 | 69975 | 94884 | 19661 | 72828 | 00102 | 66794 |
| 53976 | 54914 | 06990 | 67425 | 68350 | 82948 | 11398 | 42878 | 80287 | 88267 | 47363 | 46634 | 06541 | 97809 |
| 76072 | 29515 | 40980 | 07391 | 58745 | 25774 | 22987 | 80059 | 39911 | 96189 | 41151 | 14222 | 60697 | 59583 |
| 90725 | 52210 | 83974 | 29992 | 65831 | 38857 | 50490 | 83765 | 55657 | 14361 | 31720 | 57375 | 56228 | 41546 |
| 64364 | 67412 | 33339 | 31926 | 14883 | 24413 | 59744 | 92351 | 97473 | 89286 | 35931 | 04110 | 23726 | 51900 |
| 08962 | 00358 | 31662 | 2538 | 61642 | 34072 | 81249 | 35648 | 56891 | 69352 | 48373 | 45578 | 78547 | 81788 |
| 95012 | 68379 | 93526 | 70765 | 10592 | 04542 | 76463 | 54328 | 02349 | 17247 | 28865 | 14777 | 62730 | 92277 |
| 15664 | 10493 | 20492 | 38391 | 91132 | 21999 | 59516 | 81652 | 27195 | 48223 | 46751 | 22923 | 32261 | 85653 |
| 16408 | 81899 | 04153 | 53381 | 79401 | 21438 | 83035 | 92350 | 36693 | 31238 | 59649 | 91754 | 72772 | 02338 |
| 18629 | 81953 | 05520 | 91962 | 04739 | 13092 | 97662 | 24822 | 94730 | 06496 | 35090 | 04822 | 86774 | 98289 |
| 73115 | 35101 | 47498 | 97637 | 99016 | 71060 | 88824 | 71013 | 18735 | 20286 | 23153 | 72924 | 35165 | 43040 |
| 57491 | 16703 | 23167 | 49323 | 45021 | 33132 | 12544 | 41035 | 80780 | 45393 | 44812 | 12515 | 98931 | 91202 |
| 30405 | 83946 | 23792 | 14422 | 15059 | 45799 | 22716 | 19792 | 09983 | 74353 | 68668 | 30429 | 20735 | 25499 |
| 16631 | 35006 | 85900 | 98275 | 32388 | 52390 | 16815 | 69298 | 82732 | 38480 | 73817 | 32523 | 41961 | 44437 |
| 96773 | 20206 | 42559 | 78985 | 05300 | 22164 | 24369 | 54224 | 35083 | 19687 | 11052 | 91491 | 60383 | 19746 |
| 38935 | 64202 | 14349 | 82674 | 66523 | 44133 | 00697 | 35552 | 35970 | 19124 | 63318 | 29686 | 03387 | 59846 |
| 31624 | 76384 | 17403 | 53363 | 44167 | 64486 | 64758 | 75366 | 76554 | 31601 | 12614 | 33072 | 60332 | 92325 |
| 78919 | 19474 | 23632 | 27889 | 47914 | 02584 | 37680 | 20801 | 72152 | 39339 | 34806 | 08930 | 85001 | 87820 |

*(continued)*

## Table D.1  Random Numbers (continued)

| | | | | | | | | | | | | | |
|---|---|---|---|---|---|---|---|---|---|---|---|---|---|
| 03931 | 33309 | 57047 | 74211 | 63445 | 17361 | 62825 | 30908 | 05607 | 91284 | 68833 | 25570 | 38818 | 46920 |
| 74426 | 33278 | 43972 | 10119 | 89917 | 15665 | 52872 | 73823 | 73144 | 88662 | 88970 | 74492 | 51805 | 99378 |
| 09066 | 00903 | 20795 | 95452 | 92648 | 45454 | 09552 | 88815 | 16553 | 51125 | 79375 | 97596 | 16296 | 66092 |
| 42238 | 12526 | 87025 | 14267 | 20979 | 04508 | 64535 | 31355 | 86064 | 29472 | 47689 | 05974 | 52468 | 16834 |
| 16153 | 08002 | 26504 | 41744 | 81959 | 65642 | 74240 | 56302 | 00033 | 67107 | 77510 | 70625 | 28725 | 34191 |
| 21457 | 40742 | 29820 | 96873 | 29400 | 21840 | 15035 | 34537 | 33310 | 06116 | 95240 | 15957 | 16572 | 06004 |
| 21581 | 57802 | 02050 | 89728 | 17937 | 37621 | 47075 | 42080 | 97403 | 48626 | 68995 | 43805 | 33386 | 21597 |
| 55612 | 78095 | 83197 | 33732 | 05810 | 24813 | 86902 | 60397 | 16489 | 03264 | 88525 | 42786 | 05269 | 92532 |
| 44657 | 66999 | 99324 | 51281 | 84463 | 60563 | 79312 | 93454 | 68876 | 25471 | 93911 | 25650 | 12682 | 73572 |
| 91340 | 84979 | 46949 | 81973 | 37949 | 61023 | 43997 | 15263 | 80644 | 43942 | 89203 | 71795 | 99533 | 50501 |
| 91227 | 21199 | 31935 | 27022 | 84067 | 05462 | 35216 | 14486 | 29891 | 68607 | 41867 | 14951 | 91696 | 85064 |
| 50001 | 38140 | 66321 | 19924 | 72163 | 09538 | 12151 | 06878 | 91903 | 18749 | 34405 | 56087 | 82790 | 70925 |
| 65390 | 05224 | 72958 | 28609 | 81406 | 39147 | 25549 | 48542 | 42627 | 45233 | 57202 | 94617 | 23772 | 07896 |
| 27504 | 96131 | 83944 | 41575 | 10573 | 08619 | 64482 | 73923 | 36152 | 05184 | 94142 | 25299 | 84387 | 34925 |
| 37169 | 94851 | 39117 | 89632 | 00959 | 16487 | 65536 | 49071 | 39782 | 17095 | 02330 | 74301 | 00275 | 48280 |
| 11508 | 70225 | 51111 | 38351 | 19444 | 66499 | 71945 | 05422 | 13442 | 78675 | 84081 | 66938 | 93654 | 59894 |
| 37449 | 30362 | 06694 | 54690 | 04052 | 53115 | 62757 | 95348 | 78662 | 11163 | 81651 | 50245 | 34971 | 52924 |
| 46515 | 70331 | 85922 | 38320 | 57015 | 15765 | 97161 | 17869 | 45349 | 61796 | 66345 | 81073 | 49106 | 79860 |
| 30986 | 81223 | 42416 | 58353 | 21532 | 30502 | 32305 | 86482 | 05174 | 07901 | 54339 | 58861 | 74818 | 46942 |
| 63798 | 64995 | 46583 | 09785 | 44160 | 78128 | 83991 | 42865 | 92520 | 83531 | 80377 | 35909 | 81250 | 54238 |
| 82486 | 84846 | 99254 | 67632 | 43218 | 50076 | 21361 | 64816 | 51202 | 88124 | 41870 | 52689 | 51275 | 83556 |
| 21885 | 32906 | 92431 | 09060 | 64297 | 51674 | 64126 | 62570 | 26123 | 05155 | 59194 | 52799 | 28225 | 85762 |
| 60336 | 98782 | 07408 | 53458 | 13564 | 59089 | 26445 | 29789 | 85205 | 41001 | 12535 | 12133 | 14645 | 23541 |
| 43937 | 46891 | 24010 | 25560 | 86355 | 33941 | 25786 | 54990 | 71899 | 15475 | 95434 | 98227 | 21824 | 19585 |
| 97656 | 63175 | 89303 | 16275 | 07100 | 92063 | 21942 | 18611 | 47348 | 20203 | 18534 | 03862 | 78095 | 50136 |
| 03299 | 01221 | 05418 | 38982 | 55758 | 92237 | 26759 | 86367 | 21216 | 98442 | 08303 | 56613 | 91511 | 75928 |
| 79626 | 06486 | 03574 | 17668 | 07785 | 76020 | 79924 | 25651 | 83325 | 88428 | 85076 | 72811 | 22717 | 50585 |
| 85636 | 68335 | 47539 | 03129 | 65651 | 11977 | 02510 | 26113 | 99447 | 68645 | 34327 | 15152 | 55230 | 93448 |
| 18039 | 14367 | 61337 | 06177 | 12143 | 46609 | 32989 | 74014 | 64708 | 00533 | 35398 | 58408 | 13261 | 47908 |
| 08362 | 15656 | 60627 | 36478 | 64648 | 16764 | 53412 | 09013 | 07832 | 41574 | 17639 | 82163 | 60859 | 75567 |

## Table D.1  Random Numbers

| | | | | | | | | | | | | | |
|---|---|---|---|---|---|---|---|---|---|---|---|---|---|
| 79556 | 29068 | 04142 | 16268 | 15387 | 12856 | 66227 | 38358 | 22478 | 73373 | 88732 | 09443 | 82558 | 05250 |
| 92608 | 82674 | 27072 | 32534 | 17075 | 27698 | 98204 | 63863 | 11951 | 34648 | 88022 | 56148 | 34925 | 57031 |
| 23982 | 25835 | 40055 | 67006 | 12293 | 02753 | 14827 | 23235 | 35071 | 99704 | 37543 | 11601 | 35503 | 85171 |
| 09915 | 96306 | 05908 | 97901 | 28395 | 14186 | 00821 | 80703 | 70426 | 75647 | 76310 | 88717 | 37890 | 40129 |
| 59037 | 33300 | 26695 | 62247 | 69927 | 76123 | 50842 | 43834 | 86654 | 70959 | 79725 | 93872 | 28117 | 12933 |
| 42488 | 78077 | 69882 | 61657 | 34136 | 79180 | 97526 | 43092 | 04098 | 73571 | 80799 | 76536 | 71255 | 64239 |
| 46764 | 86273 | 63003 | 93017 | 31204 | 36692 | 40202 | 35275 | 57306 | 5543 | 53203 | 18098 | 47625 | 88684 |
| 03237 | 45430 | 65417 | 63282 | 90816 | 17349 | 88298 | 90183 | 36600 | 78406 | 06216 | 95787 | 42579 | 90730 |
| 86591 | 81482 | 52667 | 61582 | 14972 | 90053 | 89534 | 76036 | 49199 | 43716 | 97548 | 04379 | 46370 | 28672 |
| 38534 | 01715 | 94964 | 87288 | 65680 | 43772 | 39560 | 12918 | 86537 | 62738 | 19636 | 51132 | 56947 | |

| Table D.2 | Distribution of $t$ | | | |
|---|---|---|---|---|
| $n$ | .05 | .02 | .01 | .001 |
| 1 | 12.706 | 31.821 | 63.657 | 636.619 |
| 2 | 4.303 | 6.965 | 9.925 | 31.598 |
| 3 | 3.182 | 4.541 | 5.841 | 12.924 |
| 4 | 2.776 | 3.747 | 4.604 | 8.610 |
| 5 | 2.571 | 3.365 | 4.032 | 6.869 |
| 6 | 2.447 | 3.143 | 3.707 | 5.959 |
| 7 | 2.365 | 2.998 | 3.499 | 5.408 |
| 8 | 2.306 | 2.896 | 3.355 | 5.041 |
| 9 | 2.262 | 2.821 | 3.250 | 4.781 |
| 10 | 2.228 | 2.764 | 3.169 | 4.587 |
| 11 | 2.201 | 2.718 | 3.106 | 4.437 |
| 12 | 2.179 | 2.681 | 3.055 | 4.318 |
| 13 | 2.160 | 2.650 | 3.012 | 4.221 |
| 14 | 2.145 | 2.624 | 2.977 | 4.140 |
| 15 | 2.131 | 2.602 | 2.947 | 4.073 |
| 16 | 2.120 | 2.583 | 2.921 | 4.015 |
| 17 | 2.110 | 2.567 | 2.898 | 3.965 |
| 18 | 2.101 | 2.552 | 2.878 | 3.922 |
| 19 | 2.093 | 2.539 | 2.861 | 3.883 |
| 20 | 2.086 | 2.528 | 2.845 | 3.850 |
| 21 | 2.080 | 2.518 | 2.831 | 3.819 |
| 22 | 2.074 | 2.508 | 2.819 | 3.792 |
| 23 | 2.069 | 2.500 | 2.807 | 3.767 |
| 24 | 2.064 | 2.492 | 2.797 | 3.745 |
| 25 | 2.060 | 2.485 | 2.787 | 3.725 |
| 26 | 2.056 | 2.479 | 2.779 | 3.707 |
| 27 | 2.052 | 2.473 | 2.771 | 3.690 |
| 28 | 2.048 | 2.467 | 2.763 | 3.674 |
| 29 | 2.045 | 2.462 | 2.756 | 3.659 |
| 30 | 2.042 | 2.457 | 2.750 | 3.646 |
| 40 | 2.021 | 2.423 | 2.704 | 3.551 |
| 60 | 2.000 | 2.390 | 2.660 | 3.460 |
| 120 | 1.980 | 2.358 | 2.617 | 3.373 |
| $\infty$ | 1.960 | 2.326 | 2.576 | 3.291 |

SOURCE: Fisher and Yates (1974).

## Table D.3 The F Distribution (Values of $F_{.05}$)

| | Degrees of Freedom for Numerator | | | | | | | | | | | | | | | | | | |
|---|---|---|---|---|---|---|---|---|---|---|---|---|---|---|---|---|---|---|---|
| | 1 | 2 | 3 | 4 | 5 | 6 | 7 | 8 | 9 | 10 | 12 | 15 | 20 | 24 | 30 | 40 | 60 | 120 | ∞ |
| 1 | 161 | 200 | 216 | 225 | 230 | 234 | 237 | 239 | 241 | 242 | 244 | 246 | 248 | 249 | 250 | 251 | 252 | 253 | 254 |
| 2 | 18.5 | 19.0 | 19.2 | 19.2 | 19.3 | 19.3 | 19.4 | 19.4 | 19.4 | 19.4 | 19.4 | 19.4 | 19.4 | 19.5 | 19.5 | 19.5 | 19.5 | 19.5 | 19.5 |
| 3 | 10.1 | 9.55 | 9.28 | 9.12 | 9.01 | 8.94 | 8.89 | 8.85 | 8.81 | 8.79 | 8.74 | 8.70 | 8.66 | 8.64 | 8.62 | 8.59 | 8.57 | 8.55 | 8.53 |
| 4 | 7.71 | 6.94 | 6.59 | 6.39 | 6.26 | 6.16 | 6.09 | 6.04 | 6.00 | 5.96 | 5.91 | 5.86 | 5.80 | 5.77 | 5.75 | 5.72 | 5.69 | 5.66 | 5.63 |
| 5 | 6.61 | 5.79 | 5.41 | 5.19 | 5.05 | 4.95 | 4.88 | 4.82 | 4.77 | 4.74 | 4.68 | 4.62 | 4.56 | 4.53 | 4.50 | 4.46 | 4.43 | 4.40 | 4.37 |
| 6 | 5.99 | 5.14 | 4.76 | 4.53 | 4.39 | 4.28 | 4.21 | 4.15 | 4.10 | 4.06 | 4.00 | 3.94 | 3.87 | 3.84 | 3.81 | 3.77 | 3.74 | 3.70 | 3.67 |
| 7 | 5.59 | 4.74 | 4.35 | 4.12 | 3.97 | 3.87 | 3.79 | 3.73 | 3.68 | 3.64 | 3.57 | 3.51 | 3.44 | 3.41 | 3.38 | 3.34 | 3.30 | 3.27 | 3.23 |
| 8 | 5.32 | 4.46 | 4.07 | 3.84 | 3.69 | 3.58 | 3.50 | 3.44 | 3.39 | 3.35 | 3.28 | 3.22 | 3.15 | 3.12 | 3.08 | 3.04 | 3.01 | 2.97 | 2.93 |
| 9 | 5.12 | 4.26 | 3.86 | 3.63 | 3.48 | 3.37 | 3.29 | 3.23 | 3.18 | 3.14 | 3.07 | 3.01 | 2.94 | 2.90 | 2.86 | 2.83 | 2.79 | 2.75 | 2.71 |
| 10 | 4.96 | 4.10 | 3.71 | 3.48 | 3.33 | 3.22 | 3.14 | 3.07 | 3.02 | 2.98 | 2.91 | 2.85 | 2.77 | 2.74 | 2.70 | 2.66 | 2.62 | 2.58 | 2.54 |
| 11 | 4.84 | 3.98 | 3.59 | 3.36 | 3.20 | 3.09 | 3.01 | 2.95 | 2.90 | 2.85 | 2.79 | 2.72 | 2.65 | 2.61 | 2.57 | 2.53 | 2.49 | 2.45 | 2.40 |
| 12 | 4.75 | 3.89 | 3.49 | 3.26 | 3.11 | 3.00 | 2.91 | 2.85 | 2.80 | 2.75 | 2.69 | 2.62 | 2.54 | 2.51 | 2.47 | 2.43 | 2.38 | 2.34 | 2.30 |
| 13 | 4.67 | 3.81 | 3.41 | 3.18 | 3.03 | 2.92 | 2.83 | 2.77 | 2.71 | 2.67 | 2.60 | 2.53 | 2.46 | 2.42 | 2.38 | 2.34 | 2.30 | 2.25 | 2.21 |
| 14 | 4.60 | 3.74 | 3.34 | 3.11 | 2.96 | 2.85 | 2.76 | 2.70 | 2.65 | 2.60 | 2.53 | 2.46 | 2.39 | 2.35 | 2.31 | 2.27 | 2.22 | 2.18 | 2.13 |
| 15 | 4.54 | 3.68 | 3.29 | 3.06 | 2.90 | 2.79 | 2.71 | 2.64 | 2.59 | 2.54 | 2.48 | 2.40 | 2.33 | 2.29 | 2.25 | 2.20 | 2.16 | 2.11 | 2.07 |
| 16 | 4.49 | 3.63 | 3.24 | 3.01 | 2.85 | 2.74 | 2.66 | 2.59 | 2.54 | 2.49 | 2.42 | 2.35 | 2.28 | 2.24 | 2.19 | 2.15 | 2.11 | 2.06 | 2.01 |
| 17 | 4.45 | 3.59 | 3.20 | 2.96 | 2.81 | 2.70 | 2.61 | 2.55 | 2.49 | 2.45 | 2.38 | 2.31 | 2.23 | 2.19 | 2.15 | 2.10 | 2.06 | 2.01 | 1.96 |
| 18 | 4.41 | 3.55 | 3.16 | 2.93 | 2.77 | 2.66 | 2.58 | 2.51 | 2.46 | 2.41 | 2.34 | 2.27 | 2.19 | 2.15 | 2.11 | 2.06 | 2.02 | 1.97 | 1.92 |
| 19 | 4.38 | 3.52 | 3.13 | 2.90 | 2.74 | 2.63 | 2.54 | 2.48 | 2.42 | 2.38 | 2.31 | 2.23 | 2.16 | 2.11 | 2.07 | 2.03 | 1.98 | 1.93 | 1.88 |
| 20 | 4.35 | 3.49 | 3.10 | 2.87 | 2.71 | 2.60 | 2.51 | 2.45 | 2.39 | 2.35 | 2.28 | 2.20 | 2.12 | 2.08 | 2.04 | 1.99 | 1.95 | 1.90 | 1.84 |
| 21 | 4.32 | 3.47 | 3.07 | 2.84 | 2.68 | 2.57 | 2.49 | 2.42 | 2.37 | 2.32 | 2.25 | 2.18 | 2.10 | 2.05 | 2.01 | 1.96 | 1.92 | 1.87 | 1.81 |
| 22 | 4.30 | 3.44 | 3.05 | 2.82 | 2.66 | 2.55 | 2.46 | 2.40 | 2.34 | 2.30 | 2.23 | 2.15 | 2.07 | 2.03 | 1.98 | 1.94 | 1.89 | 1.84 | 1.78 |
| 23 | 4.28 | 3.42 | 3.03 | 2.80 | 2.64 | 2.53 | 2.44 | 2.37 | 2.32 | 2.27 | 2.20 | 2.13 | 2.05 | 2.01 | 1.96 | 1.91 | 1.86 | 1.81 | 1.76 |
| 24 | 4.26 | 3.40 | 3.01 | 2.78 | 2.62 | 2.51 | 2.42 | 2.36 | 2.30 | 2.25 | 2.18 | 2.11 | 2.03 | 1.98 | 1.94 | 1.89 | 1.84 | 1.79 | 1.73 |
| 25 | 4.24 | 3.39 | 2.99 | 2.76 | 2.60 | 2.49 | 2.40 | 2.34 | 2.28 | 2.24 | 2.16 | 2.09 | 2.01 | 1.96 | 1.92 | 1.87 | 1.82 | 1.77 | 1.71 |
| 30 | 4.17 | 3.32 | 2.92 | 2.69 | 2.53 | 2.42 | 2.33 | 2.27 | 2.21 | 2.16 | 2.09 | 2.01 | 1.93 | 1.89 | 1.84 | 1.79 | 1.74 | 1.68 | 1.62 |
| 40 | 4.08 | 3.23 | 2.84 | 2.61 | 2.45 | 2.34 | 2.25 | 2.18 | 2.12 | 2.08 | 2.00 | 1.92 | 1.84 | 1.79 | 1.74 | 1.69 | 1.64 | 1.58 | 1.51 |
| 60 | 4.00 | 3.15 | 2.76 | 2.53 | 2.37 | 2.25 | 2.17 | 2.10 | 2.04 | 1.99 | 1.92 | 1.84 | 1.75 | 1.70 | 1.65 | 1.59 | 1.53 | 1.47 | 1.39 |
| 120 | 3.92 | 3.07 | 2.68 | 2.45 | 2.29 | 2.18 | 2.09 | 2.02 | 1.96 | 1.91 | 1.83 | 1.75 | 1.66 | 1.61 | 1.55 | 1.50 | 1.43 | 1.35 | 1.25 |
| ∞ | 3.84 | 3.00 | 2.60 | 2.37 | 2.21 | 2.10 | 2.01 | 1.94 | 1.88 | 1.83 | 1.75 | 1.67 | 1.57 | 1.52 | 1.46 | 1.39 | 1.32 | 1.22 | 1.00 |

SOURCE: Merrington and Thompson (1943).

## Table D.4  The $F$ Distribution (Values of $F_{.01}$)

Degrees of Freedom for Numerator

| | 1 | 2 | 3 | 4 | 5 | 6 | 7 | 8 | 9 | 10 | 12 | 15 | 20 | 24 | 30 | 40 | 60 | 120 | ∞ |
|---|---|---|---|---|---|---|---|---|---|---|---|---|---|---|---|---|---|---|---|
| 1 | 4,052 | 5,000 | 5,403 | 5,625 | 5,764 | 5,859 | 5,928 | 5,982 | 6,023 | 6,056 | 6,106 | 6,157 | 6,209 | 6,235 | 6,261 | 6,287 | 6,313 | 6,339 | 6,366 |
| 2 | 98.5 | 99.0 | 99.2 | 99.2 | 99.3 | 99.3 | 99.4 | 99.4 | 99.4 | 99.4 | 99.4 | 99.4 | 99.4 | 99.5 | 99.5 | 99.5 | 99.5 | 99.5 | 99.5 |
| 3 | 34.1 | 30.8 | 29.5 | 28.7 | 28.2 | 27.9 | 27.7 | 27.5 | 27.3 | 27.2 | 27.1 | 26.9 | 26.7 | 26.6 | 26.5 | 26.4 | 26.3 | 26.2 | 26.1 |
| 4 | 21.2 | 18.0 | 16.7 | 16.0 | 15.5 | 15.2 | 15.0 | 14.8 | 14.7 | 14.5 | 14.4 | 14.2 | 14.0 | 13.9 | 13.8 | 13.7 | 13.7 | 13.6 | 13.5 |
| 5 | 16.3 | 13.3 | 12.1 | 11.4 | 11.0 | 10.7 | 10.5 | 10.3 | 10.2 | 10.1 | 9.89 | 9.72 | 9.55 | 9.47 | 9.38 | 9.29 | 9.20 | 9.11 | 9.02 |
| 6 | 13.7 | 10.9 | 9.78 | 9.15 | 8.75 | 8.47 | 8.26 | 8.10 | 7.98 | 7.87 | 7.72 | 7.56 | 7.40 | 7.31 | 7.23 | 7.14 | 7.06 | 6.97 | 6.88 |
| 7 | 12.2 | 9.55 | 8.45 | 7.85 | 7.46 | 7.19 | 6.99 | 6.84 | 6.72 | 6.62 | 6.47 | 6.31 | 6.16 | 6.07 | 5.99 | 5.91 | 5.82 | 5.74 | 5.65 |
| 8 | 11.3 | 8.65 | 7.59 | 7.01 | 6.63 | 6.37 | 6.18 | 6.03 | 5.91 | 5.81 | 5.67 | 5.52 | 5.36 | 5.28 | 5.20 | 5.12 | 5.03 | 4.95 | 4.86 |
| 9 | 10.6 | 8.02 | 6.99 | 6.42 | 6.06 | 5.80 | 5.61 | 5.47 | 5.35 | 5.26 | 5.11 | 4.96 | 4.81 | 4.73 | 4.65 | 4.57 | 4.48 | 4.40 | 4.31 |
| 10 | 10.0 | 7.56 | 6.55 | 5.99 | 5.64 | 5.39 | 5.20 | 5.06 | 4.94 | 4.85 | 4.71 | 4.56 | 4.41 | 4.33 | 4.25 | 4.17 | 4.08 | 4.00 | 3.91 |
| 11 | 9.65 | 7.21 | 6.22 | 5.67 | 5.32 | 5.07 | 4.89 | 4.74 | 4.63 | 4.54 | 4.40 | 4.25 | 4.10 | 4.02 | 3.94 | 3.86 | 3.78 | 3.69 | 3.60 |
| 12 | 9.33 | 6.93 | 5.95 | 5.41 | 5.06 | 4.82 | 4.64 | 4.50 | 4.39 | 4.30 | 4.16 | 4.01 | 3.86 | 3.78 | 3.70 | 3.62 | 3.54 | 3.45 | 3.36 |
| 13 | 9.07 | 6.70 | 5.74 | 5.21 | 4.86 | 4.62 | 4.44 | 4.30 | 4.19 | 4.10 | 3.96 | 3.82 | 3.66 | 3.59 | 3.51 | 3.43 | 3.34 | 3.25 | 3.17 |
| 14 | 8.86 | 6.51 | 5.56 | 5.04 | 4.70 | 4.46 | 4.28 | 4.14 | 4.03 | 3.94 | 3.80 | 3.66 | 3.51 | 3.43 | 3.35 | 3.27 | 3.18 | 3.09 | 3.00 |
| 15 | 8.68 | 6.36 | 5.42 | 4.89 | 4.56 | 4.32 | 4.14 | 4.00 | 3.89 | 3.80 | 3.67 | 3.52 | 3.37 | 3.29 | 3.21 | 3.13 | 3.05 | 2.96 | 2.87 |
| 16 | 8.53 | 6.23 | 5.29 | 4.77 | 4.44 | 4.20 | 4.03 | 3.89 | 3.78 | 3.69 | 3.55 | 3.41 | 3.26 | 3.18 | 3.10 | 3.02 | 2.93 | 2.84 | 2.75 |
| 17 | 8.40 | 6.11 | 5.19 | 4.67 | 4.34 | 4.10 | 3.93 | 3.79 | 3.68 | 3.59 | 3.46 | 3.31 | 3.16 | 3.08 | 3.00 | 2.92 | 2.83 | 2.75 | 2.65 |
| 18 | 8.29 | 6.01 | 5.09 | 4.58 | 4.25 | 4.01 | 3.84 | 3.71 | 3.60 | 3.51 | 3.37 | 3.23 | 3.08 | 3.00 | 2.92 | 2.84 | 2.75 | 2.66 | 2.57 |
| 19 | 8.19 | 5.93 | 5.01 | 4.50 | 4.17 | 3.94 | 3.77 | 3.63 | 3.52 | 3.43 | 3.30 | 3.15 | 3.00 | 2.92 | 2.84 | 2.76 | 2.67 | 2.58 | 2.49 |
| 20 | 8.10 | 5.85 | 4.94 | 4.43 | 4.10 | 3.87 | 3.70 | 3.56 | 3.46 | 3.37 | 3.25 | 3.09 | 2.94 | 2.86 | 2.78 | 2.69 | 2.61 | 2.52 | 2.42 |
| 21 | 8.02 | 5.78 | 4.87 | 4.37 | 4.04 | 3.81 | 3.64 | 3.51 | 3.40 | 3.31 | 3.17 | 3.03 | 2.88 | 2.80 | 2.72 | 2.64 | 2.55 | 2.46 | 2.36 |
| 22 | 7.95 | 5.72 | 4.82 | 4.31 | 3.99 | 3.76 | 3.59 | 3.45 | 3.35 | 3.26 | 3.12 | 2.98 | 2.83 | 2.75 | 2.67 | 2.58 | 2.50 | 2.40 | 2.31 |
| 23 | 7.88 | 5.66 | 4.76 | 4.26 | 3.94 | 3.71 | 3.54 | 3.41 | 3.30 | 3.21 | 3.07 | 2.93 | 2.78 | 2.70 | 2.62 | 2.54 | 2.45 | 2.35 | 2.26 |
| 24 | 7.82 | 5.61 | 4.72 | 4.22 | 3.90 | 3.67 | 3.50 | 3.36 | 3.26 | 3.17 | 3.03 | 2.89 | 2.74 | 2.66 | 2.58 | 2.49 | 2.40 | 2.31 | 2.21 |
| 25 | 7.77 | 5.57 | 4.68 | 4.18 | 3.86 | 3.63 | 3.46 | 3.32 | 3.22 | 3.13 | 2.99 | 2.85 | 2.70 | 2.62 | 2.53 | 2.45 | 2.36 | 2.27 | 2.17 |
| 30 | 7.56 | 5.39 | 4.51 | 4.02 | 3.70 | 3.47 | 3.30 | 3.17 | 3.07 | 2.98 | 2.84 | 2.70 | 2.55 | 2.47 | 2.39 | 2.30 | 2.21 | 2.11 | 2.01 |
| 40 | 7.31 | 5.18 | 4.31 | 3.83 | 3.51 | 3.29 | 3.12 | 2.99 | 2.89 | 2.80 | 2.66 | 2.52 | 2.37 | 2.29 | 2.20 | 2.11 | 2.02 | 1.92 | 1.80 |
| 60 | 7.08 | 4.98 | 4.13 | 3.65 | 3.34 | 3.12 | 2.95 | 2.82 | 2.72 | 2.63 | 2.50 | 2.35 | 2.20 | 2.12 | 2.03 | 1.94 | 1.84 | 1.73 | 1.60 |
| 120 | 6.85 | 4.79 | 3.95 | 3.48 | 3.17 | 2.96 | 2.79 | 2.66 | 2.56 | 2.47 | 2.34 | 2.19 | 2.03 | 1.95 | 1.86 | 1.76 | 1.66 | 1.53 | 1.38 |
| ∞ | 6.63 | 4.61 | 3.78 | 3.32 | 3.02 | 2.80 | 2.64 | 2.51 | 2.41 | 2.32 | 2.18 | 2.04 | 1.88 | 1.79 | 1.70 | 1.59 | 1.47 | 1.32 | 1.00 |

SOURCE: Merrington and Thompson (1943).

# GLOSSARY

**Abstract** Summary (of approximately 100 words) at the beginning of a research article; describes purpose, methods, and results of the research.

**Affirming the consequent** Form of reverse confirmatory reasoning in which one case is used to draw the illogical conclusion relating to all similar cases.

**Alpha level** The probability of making a Type I error.

**Analysis of variance (ANOVA)** Inferential statistical technique used to compare differences between two or more groups with the purpose of making a decision that the independent variable influenced the dependent variable.

**Antecedent** The first of two propositions in a logical argument of the form *If antecedent is true, then consequent follows.*

**A priori tests** Statistical tests that are planned before the experiment is performed and therefore are part of the design of the experiment. These are contrasted with *post hoc tests*, which are decided upon after the data have been examined.

**Archival research** Research using previously collected records that were not gathered for the purpose of the present study.

**Baseline** Measure of a particular behavior or process taken before the introduction of the independent variable or treatment.

**Beta level** The probability of making a Type II error.

**Between-subjects design** Design in which comparisons are made between one group and another. Participants in a given group do not receive the same level of the independent variable or treatment as those in another group.

**Bias** Prejudice in the design, performance, analysis, or presentation of a research project.

**Bimodal distribution** Refers to the situation in which the scores of a distribution form two separate nodes or peaks, one at each end of the distribution (e.g., the distribution of scores from a class exam in which most students made either an A or an F).

**Blind controls** Participants in a research project who are not informed of the important factors in the procedure.

**Blocking** Matching of groups before the beginning of the experiment according to some important variable the participants possess (e.g., placing an equal number of males and females in each group). Grass and Stanley (1970) suggest the term *blocking* be used with nominal scale variables.

**Chance variation** Occurrence of events without any known antecedent as seen from the standpoint of the experiment.

**Completely randomized design** Also referred to as the *simple randomized design;* this is a design in which participants are randomly assigned to each of the possible groups in an experiment.

**Confound** Factor that systematically biases the research but was not purposely introduced by the experimenter.

**Confounding variables** A variable that systematically varies with the independent variable that could provide an alternative explanation for the influence of the independent variable on the dependent variable.

**Consequent** The second of two propositions in a logical argument of the form *If antecedent is true, then consequent follows.*

**Construct** Generalized concept, such as anxiety or gravity, that is constructed in a theoretical manner.

**Control** Techniques used to reduce the effects of extraneous variables on results and to ensure greater certainty that the changes in the dependent variable result from the independent variable.

**Control group** Traditionally, the group that receives a zero level of the independent variable and that is used to assess the effects of the independent variable or treatment.

**Correlation** A statistical technique for determining the degree of association between two or more variables.

**Correlational approach** See Correlational design.

**Correlational design** Design that is used to establish the relationship between two variables without the ability to infer causal relationships.

**Debriefing** Process of informing a participant after the experiment about the nature of the experiment, clarifying any misunderstanding, and answering any questions that the participant may have concerning the experiment; a necessary and important aspect of deception experiments.

**Deception research** Research in which participants are led to believe that the purpose of the study or their performance in the experiment is something different from the actual case.

**Deduction** Reasoning from the general to the particular, as in the case of creating an expected hypothesis for a particular experiment from a general theoretical statement. Opposite of *induction.*

**Demand characteristics** Overall effects of the situation on a participant's behavior; generally used to denote aspects of an experiment that bias the results and prevent adequate influence of the independent variable.

**Denying the antecedent** Form of reasoning in which a false premise is illogically concluded to result in a false consequent.

**Dependent variable** In an experiment, the variable that is said to depend on the action of another variable (i.e., the independent variable).

**Double blind** Situation in which both the participant and the experimenter or agent of the experimenter are blind to certain key aspects of the experiment. Double-blind studies are

**Double blind** *(continued)* often used in drug research in which neither the participant nor the person who administers the drug knows whether it contains the active ingredients or a placebo.

**Effect size** The statistical magnitude of change that the independent variable has on the dependent variable.

**Empiricism** An emphasis on using direct observation as a means of gaining information.

**Experimental group** The group that receives the independent variable in an experiment.

**Experimental method** A method based on strict control in experimentation, for making valid inferences concerning the relationships between one variable and another.

**Experimenter effects** Effects upon participants in an experiment that can be traced to the behavior of the experimenter but are not designed to be part of the experimental manipulation.

**Ex post facto design** Design in which the experimenter attempts to reconstruct the important factors in a situation after the fact.

**External validity** Generalizability of an experimental outcome to other groups, settings, treatment variables, and measurement variables.

**Extraneous variables** Variables that are not directly related to the hypothesis under study and that the experimenter does not actively attempt to control (e.g., time of day and color of room are assumed to affect both groups equally and do not reduce the internal validity of the experiment).

**Factorial design** A design in which there is more than one independent variable and each independent variable is present at every level of the other independent variable.

**Falsificationism** Philosophical position that the goal of science is to falsify hypotheses. A major proponent of this position is Karl Popper. It is further suggested that, to be scientific, a hypothesis must be stated so that it can be falsified through research.

**F-ratio** Statistic for comparing the variance attributed to chance with that attributed to treatment effects, calculated in an analysis of variance.

**Frequency distribution** Set of scores organized according to frequency of occurrence.

**Generalizability** Ability to extend a set of findings observed in one piece of research to other situations and groups.

**Hawthorne effect** Situation in which the participants' knowledge that they are part of an experiment influences the results differentially.

**Hypothesis** A statement or expectation developed in relation to an explicit or implicit theory concerning potential outcomes of an experiment (i.e., the relationship between the independent and dependent variable).

**Independent variable** The variable that is defined by the experimenter and thus is outside the experimental situation (and therefore is independent).

**Induction** Process of reasoning from a part to a whole, as might be performed when data from a particular study are used to develop a general theory.

**Inferential statistics** Used to infer from a given sample of scores parameters related to the set of all possible scores from which that sample was drawn.

**Interaction effect** The situation in a factorial design whereby one variable influences another variable differently at different levels.

**Internal validity** Refers to one's ability to make valid inferences concerning the relationship between a dependent and an independent variable in an experimental situation.

**Interrater reliability** Correlation between ratings of two or more raters in a research study.

**Intersubject replication** The case in single-subject research in which a pattern of results is replicated between participants.

**Intragroup counterbalancing** A procedure ensuring that every possible sequence appears at each presentation of the treatment.

**Intrasubject counterbalancing** A procedure in which all participants receive the tasks in the same counterbalanced order.

**Intrasubject replication** The procedure in single subject designs in which the independent variable is introduced and removed in a manner to observe its influence within a single individual.

**Main effects (treatment effect)** Changes in the dependent variable that are

seen to have resulted from changes in the independent variable.

**Marker variables** A variable that occurs with the construct under study and thus can index or indicate its presence.

**Matched-subjects design** A procedure for equating groups in an experiment and reducing within-groups variance by using participants who are similar.

**Mean** Average of a set of scores.

**Measurement** The process of determining a dimensional or quantitative representation of a construct.

**Median** Middle score in a distribution.

**Mixed designs** Designs that include both within-subjects and between-subjects components.

**Mode** Score that occurs with the greatest frequency.

**Modeling** A procedure using either a conceptual or a mathematical model to generate data.

**Modus ponens (confirmatory reasoning)** Reasoning that a true premise leads to a true consequent.

**Modus tollens (disconfirmatory reasoning)** Reasoning that a false consequent leads to a false premise.

**Naturalistic observation** A scientific approach that focuses on observation and description; it is generally used with naturally occurring and ongoing phenomena, with little experimenter intervention.

**Null hypothesis** Hypothesis that the differences between two or more population parameters are zero. Used nontechnically to refer to the condition that no differences exist between groups in an experiment.

**Operational definition** A definition that presents a construct in terms of observable operations that can be measured and utilized in research.

**Order effects** Effects in which participation in one condition of the experiment influences results in a later condition.

**Paradigm** Worldview and set of assumptions that direct what a scientist examines, what measurements are made, and how these are to be understood.

**Personal equation** Constant factor related to a person's psychology and physiology that results in individual differences in the measurement of variables.

**Placebo** (Latin: I shall please) Although the term is used in a variety of ways,

**Placebo** *(continued)*
it is common to speak of a placebo control, which controls for the effects of suggestibility (e.g., in drug study, one group [the placebo control] receives an inert pill but is treated in every other way like the group that receives the pill with active ingredients).

**Post hoc tests**  Statistical tests that are conceived and performed after an experiment has been run.

**Posttest**  A measurement occasion that occurs at the conclusion of the presentation of the treatment or independent variable.

**Power**  The inverse $(1-\beta)$ of the probability of making a Type II error; related to the number of individual results required to show a significant difference given a particular effect size.

**Practice effects**  Effects brought about by the continued repetition of a task.

**Pretest**  A measurement occasion that occurs prior to the introduction of the independent variable.

*Psychological Abstracts*  Cumulative index that includes summaries and listings of past and current research of a psychological nature.

*PsycInfo*  Computerized searching system available on CD or the Internet that includes summaries and listings of past and current research of a psychological nature.

**Qualitative methods**  Methods that emphasize verbal descriptions and narratives rather than traditional statistical methods.

**Quantitative methods**  Methods that emphasize measures using numbers and traditional statistical techniques.

**Quasi-experimental design**  Design used when sufficient control over the variables under study and potentially confounding variables is lacking. Because of this lack of control, definite statements cannot be made about cause and effect.

**Random assignment**  Occurs when participants' chances of being assigned to each group in an experiment are equal.

**Random number table**  Table of numbers created so that their occurrence cannot be predicted from a mathematical formula.

**Random sampling**  The selection of participants in an unbiased manner so that each potential participant has an equal possibility of being selected for the experiment.

**Range**  Measure of dispersion reflecting the difference between the largest and smallest scores in a set of data.

**Reactive behavior**  Change in the participant's behavior due to the mere presence of an observer.

**Reliability**  Requirement that a measure be consistent and reproducible.

**Replication**  Repeating a procedure under a similar set of conditions to check the outcome, thereby decreasing the likelihood that the results may have occurred by chance.

**Retrospective designs**  See Retrospective methods.

**Retrospective methods** or **post hoc methods**  A procedure by which a researcher examines data available prior to the beginning of the study (e.g., medical records from the past 20 years) to answer the research question.

**Scales of measurement**  Refers to the type of information a number conveys. Several basic types of scales include nominal, ordinal, interval, and ratio.

*Science Citation Index*  Cumulative listing of articles published in the physical sciences (chemistry, biology, and physics) and in the social sciences (psychology and sociology).

**Secondary variance**  Variation in an outcome of an experiment that is due to variables other than the planned independent variables.

**Single-subject designs**  Designs based on a limited number of participants, usually one.

*Social Science Citation Index*  Cumulative index of articles published in the social sciences.

**Standard deviation**  Measure of variability calculated by taking the square root of the variance.

**Subject factors**  Characteristics of the participants' behavior that cause them to behave in unexpected ways in the experimental setting.

**Subject variable**  A variable that refers to an existing attribute of an individual (e.g., gender) that an experimenter selects rather than manipulates.

**Sum of squares**  Number used in the determination of the variance; calculated by summing the squared values for the deviation of each data point from the mean of that data set.

**Systematic variation**  Variation due to systematic factors.

**Test-retest reliability**  A measure of consistency (usually the correlation coefficient) in which a measurement is conducted at two separate times and their similarity determined.

**Time series design**  Within-subjects design requiring the measurement of data both before and after an experimental treatment.

**Treatment effect**  The effect produced by the treatment or independent variable on the dependent variable.

**Type I error**  Error of rejecting the null hypothesis when it is true.

**Type II error**  Error of accepting the null hypothesis when it is false.

**Validity**  Accuracy of our ideas and our research; degree to which these are true and capable of support.

**Variability**  The manner in which measurements vary within an experimental condition. The statistical measurement of variability are those of standard deviation and variance.

**Within-subjects design**  Design in which the participants receive more than one level of the independent variable.

**x-axis**  The horizontal axis of a graph also referred to as the abscissa. The independent variable is typically placed on the x-axis.

**x-axis (abscissa)**  Horizontal axis on a graph.

**y-axis**  The vertical axis of a graph also referred to as the ordinate. The dependent variable is typically placed on the y-axis.

# BIBLIOGRAPHY

Abraham, F. (1990). *A visual introduction to dynamical systems theory for psychology.* Santa Cruz, CA: Aerial Press.

Alfred, R. (1976). The Church of Satan. In C. Glock & R. Bellah (Eds.), *The new religious consciousness* (pp. 180–202). Berkeley: University of California Press.

American Psychological Association. (2001). *Publication manual* (5th ed.). Washington, DC: Author.

Aserinsky, E., & Kleitman, N. (1953). Regularly occurring periods of eye motility and concomitant phenomena during sleep. *Science, 118,* 273–274.

Babbie, E. R. (2001). *The practice of social research* (9th ed.). Belmont, CA: Wadsworth.

Bakeman, R., & Gottman, J. (1989). *Observing interaction: An introduction to sequential analysis.* Cambridge, UK: Cambridge University Press.

Bandura, A. (1982). The psychology of chance encounters and life paths. *American Psychologist, 37,* 747–755.

Barber, T. X. (1976). *Pitfalls in human research.* New York: Pergamon.

Barefoot, J., Dahlstrom, G., & Williams, R. (1983). Hostility, CHD incidence, and total mortality: A 25-year follow-up study of 255 physicians. *Psychosomatic Medicine, 45,* 59–63.

Barnard, N., & Kaufman, S. (1997). Animal research is wasteful and misleading. *Scientific American, 276,* 80–82.

Barthell, C. N., & Holmes, D. S. (1968). High school yearbooks: A nonreactive measure of social isolation in graduates who later become schizophrenic. *Journal of Abnormal Psychology, 73,* 313–316.

Baum, A., & Posluszny, D. (1999). Health psychology: Mapping biobehavioral contributions to health and illness. *Annual Review of Psychology, 50,* 137–163.

Baumrind, D. (1964). Some thoughts on ethics of research: After reading Milgram's "Behavioral study of obedience." *American Psychologist, 19,* 421–423.

Bechara, A., Tranel, D., Damasio, H., Adolphs, R., Rockland, C., & Damasio, A. (1995). Double dissociation of conditioning and declarative knowledge relative to the amygdala and hippocampus in humans. *Science, 269,* 1115–1118.

Beilock, S., & Carr, T. (2001). On the fragility of skilled performance: What governs choking under pressure? *Journal of Experimental Psychology: General, 130,* 701–725.

Belsky, J., Woodworth, S., & Crnic, K. (1996). Trouble in the second year: Three questions about family interaction. *Child Development, 67,* 556–578.

Bentler, P. (1980). Multivariate analysis with latent variables: Causal modeling. *Annual Review of Psychology, 31,* 419–456.

Berkowitz, L. (1970). The contagion of violence: An S-R mediational analysis of some effects of observed aggression. *Nebraska Symposium on Motivation, 18,* 95–136.

Bernstein, P., Scheffers, M., & Coles, M. (1995). "Where did I go wrong?" A psychophysiological analysis of error detection. *Journal of Experimental Psychology: Human Perception and Performance, 21,* 1312–1322.

Beyer, W. H. (1960). *Handbook of Tables for Probability and Statistics,* 2nd. Ed. Cleveland: The Chemical Rubber Company.

Biglan, A., Ary, D., & Wagenaar, A. (2000). The value of interrupted time-series experiments for community intervention research. *Prevention Science, 1,* 31–49.

Bjorklund, D., & Pellegrini, A. (2000). Child development and evolutionary psychology. *Child Development, 71,* 1687–1708.

Bohm, D. (1969). Further remarks on order. In C. H. Waddington (Ed.), *Towards a theoretical biology* (Vol. 2). Edinburgh: Edinburgh University Press.

Bolgar, H. (1965). The case study method. In B. B. Wolman (Ed.), *Handbook of clinical psychology* (pp. 28–39). New York: McGraw-Hill.

Bolger, N., & Zuckerman, A. (1995). A framework for studying personality in the stress process. *Journal of Personality and Social Psychology, 69,* 890–902.

Boring, E. G. (1950). *A history of experimental psychology* (2nd ed.). New York: Appleton-Century-Crofts.

Botella, P., Bosch, F., Romero, F., & Parra, A. (2001). Sex differences in estimation of time intervals and in reaction time are removed by moderate but not high doses of caffeine in coffee. *Human Psychopharmacology Clinical and Experimental, 16,* 533–540.

Botting, J., & Morrison, A. (1997). Animal research is vital to medicine. *Scientific American, 276,* 83–85.

Bower, G. H. (1981). Mood and memory. *American Psychologist, 36,* 129–148.

Bower, G. H., & Gilligan, S. G. (1979). Remembering information related to one's self. *Journal of Research in Personality, 13,* 420–432.

Bower, G. H., Monteiro, K. P., & Gilligan, S. G. (1978). Emotional mood as a context of learning and recall. *Journal of Verbal Learning and Verbal Behavior, 17,* 573–585.

Bransford, J. D. (1979). *Human cognition.* Belmont, CA: Wadsworth.

Bransford, J. D., & Johnson, M. K. (1972). Contextual prerequisites for understanding: Some investigations of comprehension and recall. *Journal of Verbal Learning and Verbal Behavior, 11,* 717–726.

Bremner, J., & Narayan, M. (1998). The effects of stress on memory and the hippocampus throughout the life cycle: Implications for childhood development and aging. *Development and Psychopathology, 10,* 871–885.

Bridgman, P. W. (1927). *The logic of modern physics.* New York: Macmillan.

Broad, W. J. (1980). Imbroglio at Yale (I): Emergence of a fraud. *Science, 210,* 38–41.

Bromley, D. (1986). *The case-study design in psychology and related disciplines.* New York: Wiley.

Bronfenbrenner, U. (1979). *The ecology of human development.* Cambridge, MA: Harvard University Press.

Bronowski, J. (1965). *Science and human values.* New York: Harper & Row.

Bruning, J. L., & Kintz, B. L. (1968). *Computational handbook of statistics.* Glenview, IL: Scott, Foresman.

Brunswik, E. (1947). *Systematic and representative design of psychological experiments.* Berkeley: University of California Press.

Budianski, S. (1998). *If a lion could talk: Animal intelligence and the evolution of consciousness.* New York: The Free Press.

Campbell, A. A., & Katona, G. (1953). The sample survey: A technique for social science research. In L. Festinger & D. Katz (Eds.), *Research methods in the behavioral sciences.* New York: Dryden.

Campbell, D. T., & Stanley, J. C. (1963). *Experimental and quasi-experimental designs for research.* Chicago: Rand McNally.

Carlsmith, J. M., Ellsworth, P. C., & Aronson, E. (1976). *Methods of research in social psychology.* Reading, MA: Addison-Wesley.

Carr, J., & Burkholder, E. (1998). Creating single-subject design graphs with Microsoft Excel™. *Journal of Applied Behavioral Analysis, 31,* 245–251.

Carrington, P., & Moyer, S. (1994). Gun availability and suicide in Canada: Testing the displacement hypothesis. *Studies on Crime and Crime Prevention, 3,* 168–178.

Castonguay, L. G., Goldfried, M. R., Wiser, S. L., Raue, P. J., & Hayes, A. M. (1996). Predicting the effect of cognitive therapy for depression: A study of unique and common factors. *Journal of Consulting and Clinical Psychology, 64,* 497–504.

Chamberlin, T. C. (1965). The method of multiple working hypotheses. *Science, 148,* 754–759. (Original work published in 1890)

Chang, B., & Lenzenweger, M. (2001). Somatosensory processing in the biological relatives of schizophrenia patients: A signal detection analysis of two-point discrimination. *Journal of Abnormal Psychology, 110,* 433–442.

Chi, M., & Koeske, R. (1983). Network representation of a child's dinosaur knowledge. *Developmental Psychology, 19,* 29–39.

Cobb, L. A., Thomas, G. I., Dillard, D. H., Merendino, K. A., & Bruce, R. A. (1959). An evaluation of internal-mammary-artery ligation by a double-blind technique. *New England Journal of Medicine, 260,* 1115–1118.

Cohen, J. (1990). Things I have learned (so far). *American Psychologist, 45,* 1304–1312.

Cohen, J., Dunbar, K., & McClelland, J. (1990). On the control of automatic processes: A parallel distributed processing account of the Stroop effect. *Psychological Review, 97,* 332–361.

Cohen, L., & Holliday, M. (1982). *Statistics for social scientists.* London: Harper & Row.

Cohen, M., & Nagel, E. (1934). *An introduction to logic and scientific method.* New York: Harcourt.

Cohen, S., & Herbert, T. (1996). Health psychology: Psychological factors and physical disease from the perspective of human psychoneuroimmunology. *Annual Review of Psychology, 47,* 113–142.

Cole, P. (1986). Children's spontaneous control of facial expression. *Child Development, 57,* 1309–1321.

Connell, J. P., & Tanaka, J. S. (Eds.). (1987). Special section on structural equation modeling. *Child Development, 58,* 1–175.

Converse, J. M., & Schuman, H. (1974). *Conversations at random: Survey research as interviewers see it.* New York: Wiley.

Converse, P., & Traugott, M. (1986). Assessing the accuracy of polls and surveys. *Science, 234,* 1094–1098.

Cook, S. W. (1975). A comment on the ethical issues involved in West, Gunn, and Chernicky's "Ubiquitous Watergate: An attributional analysis." *Journal of Personality and Social Psychology, 32,* 66–68.

Cook, T. D., & Campbell, D. T. (1979). *Quasi-experimentation: Design and analysis issues for field settings.* Chicago: Rand McNally.

Coombs, C. H., Raiffa, H., & Thrall, R. M. (1954). Some views on mathematical models and measurement theory. *Psychological Review, 61,* 132–144.

Copi, I. (1986). *Introduction to logic.* New York: Macmillan.

Cowles, M., & Davis, C. (1982). On the origins of the .05 level of statistical significance. *American Psychologist, 37,* 553–558.

Cronbach, L. J., & Meehl, P. (1955). Construct validity in psychological tests. *Psychological Bulletin, 52,* 281–302.

Cunningham, M. R. (1979). Weather, mood, and helping behavior: Quasi-experiments with the sunshine samaritan. *Journal of Personality and Social Psychology, 37,* 1947–1956.

Cytowic, R. (1989). *Synesthesia.* New York: Springer-Verlag.

Danziger, K. (1985). The origins of the psychological experiment as a social institution. *American Psychologist, 40,* 133–140.

Dawkins, M. (1990). From an animal's point of view: Motivation, fitness, and animal welfare. *Behavioral and Brain Sciences, 13,* 1–61.

DeSchepper, B., & Treisman, A. (1996). Visual memory for novel shapes: Implicit coding without attention. *Journal of Experimental Psychology: Learning, Memory, and Cognition, 22,* 27–47.

Deutsch, F., & Saxon, S. (1998). The double standard of praise and criticism for mothers and fathers. *Psychology of Women Quarterly, 22,* 665–683.

De Waal, F. (2000). Primates—A natural heritage of conflict resolution. *Science, 289,* 586–590.

Domjan, M., & Purdy, J. (1995). Animal research in psychology: More than meets the eye of the general psychology student. *American Psychologist, 50,* 496–503.

Dowd, M. (1983, Dec. 4). Many women in poll equate values of job and family life. *The New York Times.*

Dyer, K., Dunlap, G., & Winterling, V. (1990). Effects of choice making on the serious problem behaviors of students with severe handicaps. *Journal of Applied Behavior Analysis, 23,* 515–524.

Ebbinghaus, H. (1885). *Memory.* New York: Teacher's College.

Edgington, E. S. (1974). A new tabulation of statistical procedures used in APA journals. *American Psychologist, 29,* 25–26.

Edwards, A. L. (1962). *Experimental design in psychological research.* New York: Holt, Rinehart & Winston.

Edwards, J., Thomas, M., Rosenfeld, P., & Booth-Kewley, S. (1997). *How to conduct organizational surveys.* Thousand Oaks, CA: Sage.

Elbert, T., Ray, W., Kowalik, Z., Skinner, S., Graf, K., & Birbaumer, N. (1994). Chaos and physiology: Deterministic chaos in excitable cell assemblies. *Physiological Reviews, 74,* 1–47.

Enserink, M. (2000). Are placebo-controlled drug trials ethical? *Science, 288,* 416.

Ericsson, K. A., & Polson, P. (1988a). A cognitive analysis of exceptional memory for restaurant orders. In M. Chi, R. Glaser, & M. Farr (Eds.), *The nature of expertise.* Hillsdale, NJ: Erlbaum.

Ericsson, K. A., & Polson, P. (1988b). An experimental analysis of the mechanisms of a memory skill. *Journal of Experimental Psychology: Learning, Memory, and Cognition, 14,* 305–316.

Ericsson, K. A., & Simon, H. A. (1980). Verbal report as data. *Psychological Review, 87,* 215–251.

Eysenck, H. J. (1976). Behavior therapy: dogma or applied science. In M. P. Feldman & A. Broadhurst (Eds.), *Theoretical and experimental bases of the behavior therapies.* London: Wiley.

Festinger, L., Riecken, H., & Schachter, S. (1956). *When prophecy fails.* Minneapolis: University of Minnesota Press.

Fink, A., & Kosecoff, J. (1998). *How to conduct surveys* (2nd ed.). Thousand Oaks, CA: Sage.

Fisher, R., (1935). *The design of experiments.* Edinburgh: Oliver & Boyd.

Fisher, R., & Yates, F. (1948). *Statistical tables for biological, agricultural and medical research* (3rd ed.). Edinburgh: Oliver & Boyd.

Fisher, R., & Yates, F. (1974). *Statistical Tables for Biological, Agricultural, and Medical Research* (6th ed.). London: Longman Group Ltd.

Flavell, J. (1999). Cognitive development: Children's knowledge about the mind. *Annual Review of Psychology, 50,* 21–45.

Fox, E., Russo, R., Bowles, R., & Dutton, K. (2001). Do threatening stimuli draw or hold visual attention in subclinical anxiety? *Journal of Experimental Psychology: General, 130,* 681–700.

Franklin, R., Allison, D., & Gorman, B. (1997). *Design and analysis of single-case research.* Hillsdale, NJ: Erlbaum.

Franklin, R., Gorman, B., Beasley, T., & Allison, D. (1998). Graphical display and visual analysis. In R. Franklin, D. Allison, & B. Gorman (Eds.), *Design and analysis of single-case research* (pp. 119–158). Hillsdale, NJ: Erlbaum.

Freeman, W. (1991). The physiology of perception. *Scientific American, 264,* 78–85.

Freeman, W. (1999). *How brains make up their minds.* London: Weidenfeld & Nicolson.

Freud, S. (1966). Project for a scientific psychology. In J. Strachey (Ed. and Trans.), *The standard edition of the complete psychological works of Sigmund Freud* (Vol. 1, pp. 281–397). London: Hogarth. (Original work published 1895)

Fry, L. W., & Greenfield, S. (1980). Examination of attitudinal differences between policemen and policewomen. *Journal of Applied Psychology, 65,* 123–126.

Furumoto, L. (1992). Joining separate spheres: Christine Ladd-Franklin, woman-scientist (1847–1930). *American Psychologist, 47,* 175–182.

Furumoto, L., & Scarborough, E. (1986). Placing women in the history of psychology: The first American women psychologists. *American Psychologist, 41,* 35–42.

Gaito, J. (1980). Measurement scales and statistics: Resurgence of an old misconception. *Psychological Bulletin, 87,* 564–567.

Galen. (1827). De praenotione. In D. C. G. Kuhn (Ed.), *Opera omnia,* cap. vi (Vol. 9, pp. 630–635). Lipsiae: Officina Libraria Car. Cnoblochii.

Gallup, G. (1972). Opinion polling in a democracy. In J. Tanur (Ed.), *Statistics: A guide to the unknown.* San Francisco: Holden-Day.

Galtung, J. (1967). *Theory and methods of social research.* New York: Columbia University Press.

Gaul, D. J., Craighead, W. E., & Mahoney, M. J. (1975). Relationship between eating rates and obesity. *Journal of Consulting and Clinical Psychology, 43,* 123–125.

Gilbert, D., Fiske, S., & Lindzey, G. (1998). *The handbook of social psychology.* New York: McGraw-Hill.

Glass, G. V., & Stanley, J. C. (1970). *Statistical methods in education and psychology.* Englewood Cliffs, NJ: Prentice Hall.

Glasser, R. J. (1976). *The body is the hero.* New York: Random House.

Gleick, J. (1987). *Chaos.* New York: Penguin.

Goldberger, A., & Rigney, D. (1991). Nonlinear dynamics at the bedside. In L. Glass, P. Hunter, & A. McCulloch (Eds.), *Theory of heart.* New York: Springer-Verlag.

Gorman, B., & Allison, D. (1998). Statistical alternatives for single-case designs. In R. Franklin, D. Allison, & B. Gorman (Eds.), *Design and analysis of single-case research* (pp. 159–214). Hillsdale, NJ: Erlbaum.

Gottman, J. M. (1973). N-of-1 and N-of-2 research in psychotherapy. *Psychological Bulletin, 80,* 93–105.

Gould, S. J. (1978). The finagle factor. *Human Nature, 1,* 80–87.

Graffin, N., Ray, W., & Lundy, R. (1995). EEG concomitants of hypnosis and hypnotic susceptibility. *Journal of Abnormal Psychology, 104,* 123–131.

Granholm, E., Asarnow, R., & Marder, S. (1996). Display visual angle and attentional scanpaths on the span of apprehension task in schizophrenia. *Journal of Abnormal Psychology, 105,* 17–24.

Gray, J. A. (1990). In defense of speciesism. *Behavioral and Brain Sciences, 13,* 22–23.

Gur, R. C., & Sackeim, H. (1979). Self-deception: A concept in search of a phenomenon. *Journal of Personality and Social Psychology, 37,* 147–169.

Hains, A., & Baer, D. (1989). Interaction effects in multi-element designs: Inevitable, desirable, and ignorable. *Journal of Applied Behavioral Analysis, 22,* 57–69.

Hanson, R., Kilpatrick, D., Freedy, J., & Saunders, B. (1995). Los Angeles County after the 1992 civil disturbances: Degree of exposure and impact on mental health. *Journal of Consulting and Clinical Psychology, 63,* 987–996.

Hass, H., Fink, H., & Hartfelder, G. (1963). The placebo problem. *Psychopharmacology Service Center Bulletin, 2,* 1–65.

Hearnshaw, L. S. (1979). *Cyril Burt, psychologist.* Ithaca, NY: Cornell University Press.

Helweg, D., Roitblat, H., Nachtigall, P., & Hautus, M. (1996). Recognition of aspect-dependent three-dimensional objects by an echolocating Atlantic bottlenose dolphin. *Journal of Experimental Psychology: Animal Behavior Processes, 22,* 19–31.

Herodotus. (1942). In F. R. B. Godolphin (Ed.), *The Greek historians.* New York: Random House.

Hersen, M., & Barlow, D. (1976). *Single case experimental designs.* New York: Pergamon.

Hersen, M., & Bellack, A. (1976). A multiple baseline analysis of social skills training in chronic schizophrenics. *Journal of Applied Behavior Analysis, 9,* 239–245.

Hilton, M. (1984). The impact of recent changes in California drinking-driving laws on fatal accident levels during the first postintervention year: An interrupted time series analysis. *Law and Society Review, 18,* 605–627.

Holt, R. R. (1965). Experimental methods in clinical psychology. In B. B. Wolman (Ed.), *Handbook of clinical psychology.* New York: McGraw-Hill.

Holton, G. (1952). *Introduction to concepts and theories in physical science.* Reading, MA: Addison-Wesley.

Horner, M. S. (1972). Toward an understanding of achievement related conflicts in women. *Journal of Social Issues, 28,* 157–176.

Irwin, J., & Whitehead, P. (1991). Toward an objective psychophysics of pain. *Psychological Science, 2*, 230–235.

Jaccard, J., & Becker, M. (1990). *Statistics for the behavioral sciences* (2nd ed.). Belmont, CA: Wadsworth.

Jenni, D., & Jenni, M. (1976). Carrying behaviour in humans: Analysis of sex differences. *Science, 194*, 859–860.

Johnson-Laird, P. (1999). Deductive reasoning. *Annual Review of Psychology, 50*, 109–135.

Jones, E. (1993). Introduction to special section: Single case research in psychotherapy. *Journal of Consulting and Clinical Psychology, 61*, 371–372.

Jones, E. E., & Nisbett, R. E. (1971). *The actor and the observer: Divergent perceptions of the causes of behavior.* Morristown, NJ: General Learning Press.

Kalat, J. (1992). *Biological psychology* (4th ed.). Belmont, CA: Wadsworth.

Kardas, E. (1999). *Psychology resources on the World Wide Web.* Pacific Grove, CA: Brooks/Cole.

Kazdin, A. E. (1973). Methodological and assessment considerations in evaluating reinforcement programs in applied settings. *Journal of Applied Behavioral Analysis, 6*, 517–531.

Kazdin, A. E. (1982). *Single-case research designs.* New York: Oxford University Press.

Kazdin, A. E. (1995). Preparing and evaluating research reports. *Psychological Assessment, 7*, 228–237.

Kazdin, A. (1998). *Research design in clinical psychology.* Needham Heights, MA: Allyn & Bacon.

Kelman, H. C. (1968). *A time to speak.* San Francisco: Jossey-Bass.

Keppel, G., & Saufley, W. H. (1980). *Introduction to design and analysis: A student's handbook.* San Francisco: W. H. Freeman.

Kerlinger, F. N. (1973). *Foundations of behavioral research* (2nd ed.). New York: Holt, Rinehart & Winston.

Kerlinger, F. N. (1986). *Foundations of behavioral research* (3rd ed.). New York: Holt, Rinehart & Winston.

Klein, K., & Boals, A. (2001). Expressive writing can increase working memory capacity. *Journal of Experimental Psychology: General, 130*, 520–533.

Koestler, A. (1964). *The act of creation.* New York: Macmillan.

Kolb, B., & Whishaw, I. (1998). Brain plasticity and behavior. *Annual Review of Psychology, 49*, 43–64.

Kolb, F., & Braum, J. (1995). Blindsight in normal observers. *Nature, 377*, 336–338.

Kourany, J. (1987). *Scientific knowledge.* Belmont, CA: Wadsworth.

Kraft, C. L. (1978). A psychophysical contribution to air safety: Simulator studies of visual illusions in night visual approaches. In H. L. Pick, H. W. Leibowitz, J. E. Singer, A. Steinschneider, & H. W. Stevenson (Eds.), *Psychology: From research to practice.* New York: Plenum.

Krantz, D. H., Luce, R. D., Suppes, P., & Tversky, A. (1971). *Foundations of measurement* (Vol. 1). New York: Academic Press.

Krantz, D. S. (1979). Naturalistic study of social influences on meal size among moderately obese and nonobese subjects. *Psychosomatic Medicine, 41*, 19–27.

Kratochwill, T. (Ed.). (1978). *Single subject research.* New York: Academic Press.

Krosnick, J. (1999). Survey research. *Annual Review of Psychology, 50*, 537–567.

Kuhn, T. (1970). *The structure of scientific revolutions* (2nd ed.). Chicago: University of Chicago Press.

Lakatos, I. (1978). *The methodology of scientific research programs.* Cambridge, UK: Cambridge University Press.

Landau, B., Gleitman, H., & Spelke, E. (1981). Spatial knowledge and geometric representation in a child blind from birth. *Science, 213*, 1275–1278.

Landers, D. M., Obermier, G. E., & Patterson, A. H. (1976). Iris pigmentation and reactive motor performance. *Journal of Motor Behavior, 8*, 171–179.

Lauerman, J. (1999). Animal research. *Harvard Magazine, 101*, 49–57.

Lehner, P. N. (1979). *Handbook of ethological methods.* New York: Garland STPM Press.

Leong, F., & Austin, J. (Eds.). (1996). *The psychology research handbook: A guide for graduate students and research assistants.* Newbury Park, CA: Sage.

Levitt, L., & Leventhal, G. (1986). Litter reduction: How effective is the New York State bill? *Environment and Behavior, 18*, 467–479.

Likert, R. (1932). A technique for the measurement of attitudes. *Archives of Psychology, 19*, 44–53.

Linton, M. (1982). Transformations of memory in everyday life. In U. Neisser (Ed.), *Memory observed.* San Francisco: W. H. Freeman.

Linton, M., & Gallo, P. S. (1975). *The practical statistician.* Pacific Grove, CA: Brooks/Cole.

Loftus, E. F., & Fries, J. F. (1979). Informed consent may be hazardous to your health. *Science, 204*, 11.

Lord, F. M. (1953). On the statistical treatment of football numbers. *American Psychologist, 8*, 750–751.

Lorenz, K. (1952). *King Solomon's ring.* New York: Thomas Y. Crowell.

Lorenz, K. (1973). The fashionable fallacy of dispensing with description. *Naturwissenschaften, 60*, 1–9.

Luce, D., & Narens, L. (1987). Measurement of scales on the continuum. *Science, 236*, 1527–1532.

Luria, A. R. (1972). *The man with a shattered world.* New York: Basic Books.

Lyons, E., & Chryssochoou, X. (2000). Cross-cultural research methods. In B. Breakwell & S. Hammond (Eds.), *Research methods in psychology* (2nd ed.) (pp. 134–146). London: Sage.

Mace, C., & Kratochwill, T. (1986). The individual subject in behavioral analysis research. In J. Valsiner (Ed.), *The individual subject and scientific psychology.* New York: Plenum.

MacLeod, C., Mathews, A., & Tata, P. (1986). Perceptual bias with emotional stimuli in normal and abnormal populations. *Journal of Abnormal Psychology, 95,* 15–20.

Maher, B. A. (1978a). A reader's, writer's and reviewer's guide to assessing research reports in clinical psychology. *Journal of Consulting and Clinical Psychology, 46,* 835–838.

Maher, B. A. (1978b). Stimulus sampling in clinical research: Representative design reviewed. *Journal of Consulting and Clinical Psychology, 46,* 643–647.

Mahoney, M. J. (1976). *Scientist as subject.* Cambridge, MA: Ballinger.

March, L., Cienfuegos, A., Goldbloom, L., Ritter, W., Cowan, N., & Javitt, D. (1999). Normal time course of auditory recognition in schizophrenia, despite impaired precision of the auditory sensory ("echoic") memory code. *Journal of Abnormal Psychology, 108,* 69–75.

Mark, M., Cook, T. D., & Cook, F. (1984). Randomized and quasi-experimental designs in evaluation research. In L. Rutman (Ed.), *Evaluation research methods: A basic guide* (2nd ed.). Beverly Hills, CA: Sage.

Maslow, A. H. (1966). *The psychology of science.* New York: Harper & Row.

Maslow, A. H. (1970). *Motivation and personality* (2nd ed.). New York: Harper & Row.

Maslow, A. H. (1971). *The farthest reaches of human nature.* New York: Viking.

McCall, R. B. (1980). *Fundamental statistics for psychology* (2nd ed.). New York: Harcourt Brace Jovanovich.

McGuffin, P., Riley, B., & Plomin, R. (2001). Genomics and behavior: Toward behavioral genomics. *Science, 291,* 1232–1249.

McKenna, F., & Sharma, D. (1995). Intrusive cognitions: An investigation of the emotional Stroop task. *Journal of Experimental Psychology: Learning, Memory, and Cognition, 21,* 1595–1607.

Mead, M. (1928). *Coming of age in Samoa.* New York: Morrow.

Meehl, P. (1978). Theoretical risks and tabular asterisks: Sir Karl, Sir Ronald, and the slow progress of soft psychology. *Journal of Consulting and Clinical Psychology, 46,* 806–834.

Mesulam, M., & Perry, J. (1972). The diagnosis of lovesickness: Experimental psychophysiology without the polygraph. *Psychophysiology, 9,* 546–551.

Milgram, S. (1963). Behavioral study of obedience. *Journal of Abnormal and Social Psychology, 67,* 371–378.

Milgram, S. (1977). *The individual in a social world: Essays and experiments.* Reading, MA: Addison-Wesley.

Miller, G. T. (1988). *Living in the environment: An introduction to environmental science* (5th ed.). Belmont, CA: Wadsworth.

Milner, B. (1966). Amnesia following operation on the temporal lobes. In C. W. M. Whitty & O. L. Zangwill (Eds.), *Amnesia.* London: Butterworths.

Mitchell, J. (1986). Measurement scales and statistics: A clash of paradigms. *Psychological Bulletin, 100,* 398–407.

Mitroff, I. I. (1974). Norms and counter-norms in a select group of the Apollo moon scientists: A case study of the ambivalence of scientists. *American Sociological Review, 39,* 579–595.

Mitroff, I. I., & Fitzgerald, I. (1977). On the psychology of the Apollo moon scientists: A chapter in the psychology of science. *Human Relations, 30,* 657–674.

Moras, K., Telfer, L., & Barlow, D. (1993). Efficacy and specific effects data on new treatments: A case study strategy with mixed anxiety-depression. *Journal of Clinical and Consulting Psychology, 61,* 412–420.

Morell, V. (1996). Life at the top: Animals pay the high price of dominance. *Science, 271,* 292.

Mukerjee, M. (1997). Trends in animal research. *Scientific American, 276,* 86–93.

Murphy, K. & Myors, B. (1998). *Statistical power analysis.* Mahwah, NJ: Erlbaum.

Nelson, R., Badura, L., & Goldman, B. (1990). Mechanisms of seasonal cycles of behavior. *Annual Review of Psychology, 41,* 81–108.

Newcombe, N., & Arnkoff, D. (1979). Effects of speech style and sex of speaker on person perception. *Journal of Personality and Social Psychology, 37,* 1293–1303.

Newton, I. (1969). *Mathematical principles* (F. Cajori, Trans.). New York: Greenwood. (Translation first published 1729)

Nisbett, R. E., & Wilson, T. D. (1977). Telling more than we can know: Verbal reports on mental processes. *Psychological Review, 84,* 231–259.

Öhman, A., Flykt, A., & Esteves, F. (2001). Emotion drives attention: Detecting the snake in the grass. *Journal of Experimental Psychology: General, 130,* 466–478.

Okazaki, S. (1997). Sources of ethnic differences between Asian American and White American college students on measures of depression and social anxiety. *Journal of Abnormal Psychology, 106,* 52–60.

Olfson, M., Marcus, S., Druss, B., Elinson, L., Tanielian, T., & Pincus, H. (2002). National trends in the outpatient treatment of depression. *JAMA, 287,* 203–209.

Orne, M. (1969). Demand characteristics and the concept of quasi-controls. In R. Rosenthal & R. L. Rosnow (Eds.), *Artifact in behavioral research.* New York: Academic Press.

Orne, M. T., & Evans, F. J. (1966). Inadvertent termination of hypnosis on hypnotized and simulating subjects. *International Journal of Clinical and Experimental Hypnosis, 14,* 61–78.

Orne, M. T., & Scheibe, K. (1964). The contribution of nondeprivation factors in the production of sensory deprivation effects: The psychology of the "panic button." *Journal of Abnormal and Social Psychology, 68,* 3–12.

Osborne, K., Rudrud, E., & Zezoney, F. (1990). Improved curveball hitting through the enhancement of visual cues. *Journal of Applied Behavioral Analysis, 23,* 371–377.

Osgood, C., Suci, G., & Tannenbaum, P. (1957). *The measurement of meaning.* Urbana: University of Illinois Press.

Pantev, C., Engelien, A., Candia, V., & Elbert, T. (2001). Representational cortex in musicians: Plastic alternations in response to musical practice. *Annals of the New York Academy of Science, 930,* 300–314.

Parsonson, B., & Baer, D. (1978). The analysis and presentation of graphic data. In T. Kratochwill (Ed.), *Single subject research.* New York: Academic Press.

Pennebaker, J. (1991). Personal communication.

Petrinovich, L. (1979). Probabilistic functionalism: A conception of research methods. *American Psychologist, 34,* 373–390.

Petty, R., Fabrigar, L., Wegener, D., & Priester, J. (1996). Understanding data when interactions are present or hypothesized. *Psychological Science, 7,* 247–252.

Phillips, M., & Sechzer, J. (1989). *Animal research and ethical conflict.* New York: Springer-Verlag.

Piattelli-Palmarini, M. (1994). *Inevitable illusions.* New York: Wiley.

Platt, J. R. (1964). Strong inference. *Science, 146,* 347–353.

Plomin, R., Corley, R., DeFries, J., & Fulker, D. (1990). Individual differences in television viewing in early childhood. *Psychological Science, 1,* 371–377.

Popper, K. R. (1959). *The logic of scientific discovery.* New York: Basic Books.

Popper, K. R. (1972). *Objective knowledge.* Oxford, UK: Oxford University Press.

Press, W., Teukolsky, S., Vetterling, W., & Flannery, B. (1992). *Numerical recipes.* New York: Cambridge University Press.

Prince, M. (1913). *The dissociation of a personality.* New York: Longmans, Green.

Raebhausen, O. M., & Brim, O. G. (1967). Privacy and behavioral research. *American Psychologist, 22,* 423–437.

Ragnarsson, R., & Björgvinsson, T. (1991). Effects of public posting on driving speed on Icelandic traffic. *Journal of Applied Behavior Analysis, 24,* 53–58.

Ramachandran, V. (1998). *Phantoms in the brain.* New York: William Morrow.

Rammsayer, T., & Rammstedt, B. (2000). Sex-related differences in time estimation: The role of personality. *Personality and Individual Differences, 29,* 301–312.

Ramsey, F., & Schafer, D. (2002). *The statistical sleuth,* 2nd ed., Pacific Grove, CA: Duxbury.

Ravizza, K. (1977). Peak experiences in sports. *Journal of Humanistic Psychology, 17,* 35–40.

Ray, W. J. (1989). Research designs in behavioral cardiovascular research. In N. Schneiderman, S. Weiss, & P. Kaufmann (Eds.), *Handbook of research methods in cardiovascular medicine* (pp. 573–588). New York: Plenum.

Ray, W. J., Katahn, M., & Snyder, C. R. (1971). Effects of test anxiety on acquisition, retention, and generalization of a complex verbal task in a classroom situation. *Journal of Personality and Social Psychology, 20,* 147–154.

Ray, W. J., Newcombe, N., Semon, J., & Cole, P. (1981). Spatial abilities, sex differences and EEG functioning. *Neuropsychologia, 19,* 719–722.

Ray, W. J., Wells, R., Elbert, T., Lutzenberger, W., & Birbaumer, N. (1991). EEG and chaos: Dimensional estimation of sensory and hypnotic processes. In D. Duke & W. Pritchard (Eds.), *Measuring chaos in the human brain* (pp. 199–215). New York: World Scientific.

Resnick, J. H., & Schwartz, T. (1973). Ethical standards as an independent variable in psychological research. *American Psychologist, 28,* 134–139.

Ristau, C. (Ed.). (1991). *Cognitive ethology: The minds of other animals.* Hillsdale, NJ: Erlbaum.

Roberts, F. S. (1979). *Measurement theory with applications to decision making utility and the social sciences.* Reading, MA: Addison-Wesley.

Roechelein, J. E. (1972). Sex differences in time estimation. *Perceptual and Motor Skills, 35,* 859–862.

Rogoff, B. (1990). *Apprenticeship in thinking: Cognitive development in social context.* New York: Oxford University Press.

Rosenhan, D. L. (1973). On being sane in insane places. *Science, 179,* 250–258.

Rosenthal, R. (1979). How often are our numbers wrong? *American Psychologist, 33,* 1005–1008.

Rosenthal, R. (1990). How are we doing in soft psychology? *American Psychologist, 45,* 775–777.

Rosenthal, R., & Fode, K. L. (1963). The effects of experimenter bias on the performance of the albino rat. *Behavioral Science, 8,* 183–189.

Rosenthal, R., & Lawson, R. (1964). A longitudinal study of the effects of experimenter bias on the operant learning of rats. *Journal of Psychiatric Research, 2,* 61–72.

Rosenthal, R., & Rubin, D. B. (1978). Interpersonal expectancy effects: The first 345 studies. *Behavioral and Brain Sciences, 1,* 377–386.

Rosnow, R., & Rosenthal, R. (1995). "So things you learned aren't so." *Psychological Science, 6,* 3–9.

Rosnow, R., & Rosenthal, R. (1996). Contrasts and interactions redux: Five easy pieces. *Psychological Science, 7,* 253–257.

Rosnow, R., & Rosnow, M. (2003). *Writing papers in psychology: A student guide* (6th ed.). Belmont, CA: Wadsworth.

Ross, A., & White, S. (1987). Shoplifting, impaired driving, and refusing the breathalyzer: On seeing one's name in public places. *Evaluation Review, 11,* 254–260.

Rowsemitt, C. (1986). Seasonal variations in activity rhythms of male voles: Mediation by gonadal hormones. *Physiology and Behavior, 37,* 797–803.

Rubin, Z. (1974). Lovers and other strangers: The development of intimacy in encounters and relationships. *American Scientist, 62,* 182–190.

Ruelle, D. (1991). *Chance and chaos.* Princeton, NJ: Princeton University Press.

Rumelhart, D., & McClelland, J. (1986). *Parallel distributed processing* (Vols. 1 & 2). Cambridge, MA: MIT Press.

Rush, C., Higgins, S., Hughes, J., & Bickel, W. (1994). Acute behavioral effects of triazolam and caffeine, alone and in combination, in humans. *Experimental and Clinical Psychopharmacology, 2,* 211–222.

Russell, B. (1984). *A history of Western philosophy.* New York: Simon & Schuster.

Sacks, O. (1974). *Awakenings.* Garden City, NY: Doubleday.

Sacks, O. (1985). *The man who mistook his wife for a hat and other clinical tales.* New York: Summit Books.

Salk, J. (1973). *The survival of the wisest.* New York: Harper & Row.

Sanderson, W., & Barlow, D. (1991). Research strategies in clinical psychology. In E. Walker (Ed.), *Clinical psychology: Historical and research foundations.* New York: Plenum.

Scarborough, E., & Furumoto, L. (1987). *Untold lives: The first generation of American women psychologists.* New York: Columbia University Press.

Scheaffer, R. L., Mendenhall, W., & Ott, L. (1979). *Elementary survey sampling* (2nd ed.). North Scituate, MA: Duxbury.

Schnelle, J. F., & Lee, J. F. (1974). Quasi-experimental retrospective evaluation of a prison policy change. *Journal of Applied Behavior Analysis, 7,* 483–496.

Schumacher, E. F. (1977). *A guide for the perplexed.* New York: Harper & Row.

Schuman, H., & Presser, S. (1981). *Questions and answers in attitude surveys.* New York: Academic Press.

Scoville, W. B. (1968). Amnesia after bilateral medial temporal-lobe excision: Introduction to case H. M. *Neuropsychologia, 6,* 211–213.

Scoville, W. B., & Milner, B. (1957). Loss of recent memory after bilateral hippocampal lesions. *Journal of Neurology, Neurosurgery, and Psychiatry, 20,* 11–21.

Seligman, M., & Csikszentmihalyi, M. (2000). Positive psychology: An introduction. *American Psychologist, 55,* 5–14.

Shapiro, A. (1997). *The powerful placebo: From ancient priest to modern physician.* Baltimore: Johns Hopkins University Press.

Shepard, R. N. (1983). Perceptual and analogical bases of cognition. In D. Genter & A. L. Stevens (Eds.), *Mental models.* Hillsdale, NJ: Erlbaum.

Sherif, M., Harvey, O. J., White, B., Hood, W., & Sherif, C. W. (1961). *Intergroup conflict and cooperation: The robber's cave experiment.* Norman, OK: University Book Exchange.

Shotland, R. L. (1992). *Sexual precedence, compliant sexual behavior, and token resistance to sex.* Paper presented at the 6th International Conference on Personal Relationships, Orono, ME.

Shotland, R. L., & Goodstein, L. (1983). Just because she doesn't want to doesn't mean it's rape: An experimentally based causal model of the perception of rape in a dating situation. *Social Psychology Quarterly, 46,* 220–232.

Shotland, R. L., & Stebbins, C. (1980). Bystander response to rape: Can a victim attract help? *Journal of Applied Social Psychology, 10,* 510–527.

Shotland, R. L., & Straw, M. K. (1976). Bystander response to an assault: When a man attacks a woman. *Journal of Personality and Social Psychology, 34,* 990–999.

Shotland, R. L., & Yankowski, L. (1982). The random response method: A valid and ethical indicator of the "truth" in reactive situations. *Personality and Social Psychology Bulletin, 8,* 174–179.

Sidman, M. (1960). *Tactics of scientific research.* New York: Basic Books.

Silverstein, A., & Klee, G. (1958). Effects of lysergic acid diethylamide (LSD-25) on intellectual functions. *American Medical Association Archives of Neurology and Psychiatry, 80,* 477–480.

Simon, J. L. (1978). *Basic research methods in social sciences* (2nd ed.). New York: Random House.

Skinner, H. (1984). Correlational methods in clinical research. In A. Bellack & M. Hersen, *Research methods in clinical psychology.* New York: Pergamon.

Solomon, R. L. (1949). An extension of control group design. *Psychological Bulletin, 46,* 137–150.

Spencer-Brown, G. (1979). *Laws of form.* New York: Dutton.

Sperry, R. (1983). *Science and moral priority.* New York: Columbia University Press.

Spiegel, D., Bloom, J., Kraemer, H., & Gotthel, E. (1989). Effect of psychosocial treatment on survival of patients with metastatic breast cancer. *Lancet, 2,* 901.

Squire, L., & Zola-Morgan, S. (1991). The medial temporal lobe memory system. *Science, 253,* 1380–1386.

Stadler, M. (1995). Role of attention in implicit learning. *Journal of Experimental Psychology: Learning, Memory, and Cognition, 21,* 674–685.

Sternberg, R. (1993). *The psychologist's companion: A guide to scientific writing for students and researchers.* New York: Cambridge University Press.

Stevens, S. S. (1946). On the theory of scales of measurement. *Science, 103,* 677–680.

Stevens, S. S. (1951). Mathematics, measurement, and psychophysics. In S. S. Stevens (Ed.), *Handbook of experimental psychology.* New York: Wiley.

Stevens, S. S. (1957). On the psychophysical law. *Psychological Review, 64,* 153–181.

Stewart, H., & McAllister, H. (2001). One-at-a-time versus grouped presentation of mug book pictures: Some surprising results. *Journal of Applied Psychology, 86,* 1300–1305.

Strupp, H. H., & Hadley, S. W. (1979). Specific vs. nonspecific factors in psychotherapy. *Archives of General Psychiatry, 36,* 1125–1136.

Student [W. S. Gossett]. (1908). The probable error of a mean. *Biometrika, 6,* 1–25.

Sue, S., Fujino, D., Hu, L., Takeuchi, D., & Zane, N. (1991). Community mental health services for ethnic minority groups: A test of the cultural responsiveness hypothesis. *Journal of Consulting and Clinical Psychology, 59,* 533–540.

Suppe, F. (1977). *The structure of scientific theories* (2nd ed.). Urbana: University of Illinois Press.

Tart, C. T. (1972). States of consciousness and state specific sciences. *Science, 176,* 1203–1210.

Taylor, S., & Bogdan, R. (1998). *Introduction to qualitative research methods.* New York: Wiley.

Thomas, L. (1979). *The medusa and the snail.* New York: Viking.

Thorndike, E. (1898). *Animal intelligence.* New York: Macmillan.

Tinbergen, E. A., & Tinbergen, N. (1972). *Early childhood autism: An ethological approach.* Berlin: Paul Parey.

Tinbergen, N. (1972). *The animal in its world.* Cambridge, MA: Harvard University Press.

Tukey, J. (1962). The future of data analysis. *Annals of Mathematical Statistics, 33,* 1–67.

Valsiner, J. (1986). *The individual subject and scientific psychology.* New York: Plenum.

Veroff, J., Douvan, E., & Kulka, R. A. (1981). *The inner American.* New York: Basic Books.

Visser, P. S., Krosnick, J. A., Marquette, J., Curtain, M. (1996). Mail surveys for election forecasting? An evaluation of the Columbus Dispatch poll. *Public Opinion Quarterly, 60,* 181–227.

Voevodsky, J. (1974). Evaluation of deceleration warning light for reducing rear-end automobile collisions. *Journal of Applied Psychology, 59,* 270–273.

Wallas, G. (1926). *The art of thought.* New York: Harcourt, Brace.

Warner, S. (1965). Randomized response: A survey technique for eliminating evasive answer bias. *Journal of the American Statistical Association, 60,* 63–69.

Warren, J. M., Zerweck, C., & Anthony, A. (1982). Effects of environmental enrichment on old mice. *Developmental Psychobiology, 15,* 13–18.

Wason, P. C. (1977). Self-contradictions. In P. N. Johnson-Laird & P. C. Wason (Eds.), *Thinking.* Cambridge, UK: Cambridge University Press.

Watkins, E., & Teasdale, J. (2001). Rumination and overgeneral memory in depression: Effects of self-focus and analytic thinking. *Journal of Abnormal Psychology, 110,* 353–357.

Watson, J. D. (1968). *The double helix.* New York: Atheneum.

Webb, E. J., Campbell, D. T., Schwartz, R. D., & Sechrest, L. (1966). *Unobtrusive measures.* Chicago: Rand McNally.

Webster-Stratton, C., & Spitzer, A. (1996). Parenting of a young child with conduct problems: New insights using qualitative methods. In T. Ollendick & R. Prinz (Eds.), *Advances in clinical child psychology* (Vol. 18, pp. 1–62). New York: Plenum.

Weiner, J. (1994). *The beak of the finch.* New York: Knopf.

West, S., Hepworth, J., McCall, M., & Reich, J. (1989). An evaluation of Arizona's July 1982 drunk driving law: Effects on the city of Phoenix. *Journal of Applied Social Psychology, 19,* 1212–1237.

West, S. G., Gunn, S. P., & Chernicky, P. (1975). Ubiquitous Watergate: An attributional analysis. *Journal of Personality and Social Psychology, 32,* 55–65.

White, L., Tursky, B., & Schwartz, G. (Eds.). (1985). *Placebo: Theory, research, and mechanism.* New York: Guilford.

Whitehead, A. N. (1925). *Science and the modern world.* New York: Macmillan.

Winer, B. J. (1971). *Statistical principles in experimental design.* New York: McGraw-Hill.

Wolf, S., & Wolff, H. G. (1943). *Human gastric functioning.* New York: Oxford University Press.

Wood, N., & Cowan, N. (1995). The cocktail party phenomenon revisited: Attention and memory in the classic selective listening procedure of Cherry (1953). *Journal of Experimental Psychology: General, 124,* 243–262.

Yamane, T. (1967). *Elementary sampling theory.* Englewood Cliffs, NJ: Prentice Hall.

Zimbardo, P. G., Haney, C., Banks, W. C., & Jaffe, D. (1975). The psychology of imprisonment: Privation, power and pathology. In D. Rosenhan & P. London (Eds.), *Theory and research in abnormal psychology* (2nd ed.). New York: Holt, Rinehart & Winston.

# CREDITS

This page constitutes an extension of the copyright page. We have made every effort to trace the ownership of all copyrighted material and to secure permission from copyright holders. In the event of any question arising as to the use of any material, we will be pleased to make the necessary corrections in future printings. Thanks are due to the following authors, publishers, and agents for permission to use the material indicated.

**Chapter 3: 61,** Excerpt used with permission of Jude Cassidy. **62,** Excerpt used with permission of Lance Shotland. **65,** Excerpt used with permission of Nora Newcombe. **74,** Sample screen capture and search results reprinted with permission of the American Psychological Association, publisher of the PsycINFO Database (Copyright 1887–present by the American Psychological Association.) All rights reserved. For more information contact *psycinfo@apa.org*. **77,** From *Social Science Citation Index,* copyright © Institute for Scientific Information, Philadelphia. Used with permission.

**Chapter 6: 130,** From "Contextual Prerequisites for Understanding," by J. D. Bransford and M. K. Johnson, 1972, *Journal of Verbal Learning and Verbal Behavior, 11,* 717–726. Copyright ©1972 Academic Press, Inc. Reprinted with permission. **131,** From "Contextual Prerequisites for Understanding," by J. D. Bransford and M. K. Johnson, 1972, *Journal of Verbal Learning and Verbal Behavior, 11,* 717–726. Copyright ©1972 Academic Press, Inc. Reprinted with permission.

**Chapter 7: 150,** From the *Handbook of Tables for Probability and Statistics,* Second Edition, by William Beyer (Ed.). Copyright ©1968 Chemical Rubber Co. (CRC Press, Inc.). Reprinted with permission.

**Chapter 8: 168,** From "Contextual Prerequisites for Understanding," by J. D. Bransford and M. K. Johnson, 1972, *Journal of Verbal Learning and Verbal Behavior, 11,* 717–726. Copyright ©1972 Academic Press, Inc. Reprinted with permission.

**Chapter 11: 237,** Reprinted by permission of Dr. James W. Pennebaker, Southern Methodist University, Dallas, Texas. **237,** Reprinted by permission of Dr. James W. Pennebaker, Southern Methodist University, Dallas, Texas. **238,** Reprinted by permission of Dr. James W. Pennebaker, Southern Methodist University, Dallas, Texas.

**Chapter 12: 272,** From "Effects of Choice Making on the Serious Problem Behaviors of Students with Severe Handicaps," by K. Dyer, G. Dunlap, and V. Winterling, 1990, *Journal of Applied Behavior Analysis, 23,* 515–524. Copyright ©1990 University of Kansas Press. Reprinted with permission.

**Chapter 14: 311–313,** From "Ethical Principles of Psychologists and Code of Conduct," 1992. Copyright © 1992 by the American Psychological Association. Reprinted with permission. (The 1992 APA Ethics Code is in revision for Fall 2002, please see *www.apa.org/ethics*.) **316,** From "Informed Consent May Be Hazardous to Your Health," by E. F. Loftus and J. F. Fries, 1979, *Science, 204,* p. 4388. Copyright ©American Association for the Advancement of Science. Reprinted by permission. **326–328,** From "Ethical Principles of Psychologists and Code of Conduct," 1992. Copyright © 1992 by the American Psychological Association. Reprinted with permission. (The 1992 APA Ethics Code is in revision for Fall 2002, please see *www.apa.org/ethics*.)

**Chapter 15: 341,** From "Bystander Response to an Assault: When a Man Attacks a Woman," by R. L. Shotland and M. K. Straw, 1976, *Journal of Personality and Social Psychology, 34,* 990–999. Copyright ©1976 American Psychological Association. Reprinted with permission. **345,** From "Intrusive Cognitions: An Investigation of the Emotional Stroop Task," by Frank P. McKenna and Dinkar Sharma, 1995, *Journal of Experimental Psychology, 21,* No. 6, 1600–1601. Copyright ©1995 American Psychological Association. Reprinted with permission. **349,** Checklist from "Experimental Methods in Clinical Psychology," by R. R. Holt. In B. B. Wolman (Ed.), *Handbook of Clinical Psychology.* Copyright ©1965 McGraw-Hill, Inc. Reprinted with permission. **352,** From "Preparing and Evaluating a Research Report," by A. Kazdin, 1995, *Journal of Psychological Assessment, 7,* 228–237. Copyright ©1995 American Psychological Association. Reprinted with permission.

**Chapter 16: 369,** From *The Medusa and the Snail,* by L. Thomas. Copyright ©1979 Viking Press. Reprinted with permission of the author.

**Appendix A: 375–380,** From *Publication Manual of the American Psychological Association,* 5th Edition. Copyright © 2001 by the American Psychological Association. Reprinted with permission.

**Appendix B: 387–400,** "Expressing Writing Can Increase Working Memory Capacity" by Kitty Klein and Adriel Boals from *Journal Of Experimental Psychology: General, 2001, 13,* 520–533. Copyright © 2001 by the American Psychological Association. Reprinted with permission.

**Appendix D: 416,** From *Handbook of Tables for Probability and Statistics,* Second Edition, by W. H. Beyer. Copyright ©1960 The Chemical Rubber Company. Reproduced by permission of the publishers, The Chemical Rubber Company. **420,** From R. A. Fisher and F. Yates, *Statistical Tables for Biological, Agricultural, and Medical Research,* Sixth Edition, published by Longman Group Ltd. London, 1974 (previously published by Oliver & Boyd Ltd. Edinburgh), is reprinted by permission of the authors and publisher. **421,** From Merrington & Thompson, *Biometrika,* 1943, 33. Reprinted by permission of the Biometrika Trustees, London.

# INDEX

## TO THE OWNER OF THIS BOOK:

I hope that you have found *Methods Toward a Science of Behavior and Experience,* 7th Edition, useful. So that this book can be improved in a future edition, would you take the time to complete this sheet and return it? Thank you.

School and address: _____

Department: _____ Instructor name: _____

The name of the course in which I used this book is: _____

1. What I liked most about this book is: _____

   _____

2. What I liked least about this book is: _____

   _____

3. Were all chapters assigned for you to read?   Yes _____   No _____

4. If not, which were omitted?_____

5. Did you receive a free subscription to InfoTrac College Edition with this text?  If yes, did you use it?

   Yes _____   No _____

6. Did you find InfoTrac College Edition to be a useful tool?   Yes _____   No _____

7. Was InfoTrac College Edition easy to use?_____

8. Did you utilize the website (see web address on the back of this book)?   Yes _____   No _____

9. In what ways did you utilize the website? Please explain: _____

   _____

10. Was this the only book you used in this course? If not, please explain: _____

11. In the space below, or on a separate sheet of paper, please write specific suggestions for improving this book and anything else you'd care to share about your experience in using the book. _____

    _____

    _____

    _____

12. What is your major course of study?_____

13. Do you plan to keep this text?   Yes_____   No _____

14. Do you own a computer?   Yes _____   No _____

15. Do you access the World Wide Web from your own computer or a computer at school? _____

OPTIONAL:

Your name: _____ Date: _____

May we quote you, either in promotion for *Methods Toward a Science of Behavior and Experience,* 7th Edition, or in future publishing ventures?

Yes: _____ No: _____

Sincerely yours,

*William J. Ray*

FOLD HERE

**BUSINESS REPLY MAIL**

FIRST CLASS        PERMIT NO. 34        BELMONT, CA

POSTAGE WILL BE PAID BY ADDRESSEE

ATTN:  *William J. Ray*

WADSWORTH/THOMSON LEARNING

10 DAVIS DRIVE

BELMONT, CA        94002-9801

FOLD HERE